Wonders

Mc Graw Hill

Also Available from McGraw Hill

studysync

TIME for KiDS

mheducation.com/prek-12

Send all inquiries to:
McGraw Hill
1325 Avenue of the Americas.
New York, NY 10019

ISBN: 978-1-26568814-1
MHID: 1-26-568814-1

Printed in the United States of America

3 4 5 6 7 8 9 LMN 26 25 24 23 22

Wonders

Welcome to *Wonders*

Designed to support teachers and empower students.

You want all your students to build knowledge while fostering exploration of our world through literacy. Literacy is the key to understanding — across time, across borders, across cultures — and will help students realize the role they play in the world they are creating.

The result: an evidence-based K–5 ELA program, aligned with standards and based on the Science of Reading, that empowers students to take an active role in learning and exploration. Your students will enjoy unparalleled opportunities for student-friendly self-assessments and self-expression through reading, writing, and speaking. By experiencing diverse perspectives and sharing their own, students will expand their learning. Best-in-class differentiation ensures that all your students have opportunities to become strong readers, writers, and critical thinkers.

We're excited for you to get to know *Wonders* and honored to join you and your students on your pathways to success!

Authors and Consultants

With unmatched expertise in English Language Arts, supporting English language learners, intervention, and more, the *Wonders* team of authors is composed of scholars, researchers, and teachers from across the country. From managing ELA research centers, to creating evidence-based classroom practices for teachers, this highly qualified team of professionals is fully invested in improving student and district outcomes.

Authors

Dr. Douglas Fisher
Close Reading and Writing,
Writing to Sources,
Text Complexity

Dr. Diane August
English Language Learners,
Dual Language

Kathy Bumgardner
Instructional Best Practices,
Multi-Sensory Teaching,
Student Engagement

Dr. Vicki Gibson
Small Group Instruction,
Social Emotional Learning,
Foundational Skills

Dr. Josefina V. Tinajero
English Language Learners,
Dual Language

Dr. Timothy Shanahan
Text Complexity,
Reading and Writing,
Oral Reading Fluency,
Close Reading,
Disciplinary Literacy

Dr. Donald Bear
Word Study, Vocabulary,
Foundational Skills

Dr. Jana Echevarria
English Language Learners,
Oral Language Development

Dr. Jan Hasbrouck
Oral Reading Fluency,
Foundational Skills,
Response to Intervention

"My hope for our students is that their teacher can help every student become a skillful reader and writer." - Dr. Jan Hasbrouck

Consultants

Dr. Doris Walker-Dalhouse
Multicultural Literature

Dr. David J. Francis
Assessment, English Language
Learners Research

Jay McTighe
Understanding by Design

Dr. Tracy Spinrad
Social Emotional Learning

Dinah Zike
Professional Development,
Multi-Sensory Teaching

"My hope for our students including English Learners, is that they will receive outstanding English language arts and reading instruction to allow them to reach their full academic potential and excel in school and in life." - Dr. Josefina V. Tinajero

Developing
Student Ownership
of Learning

Reflect on What You Know	Monitor Learning	Choose Learning Resources	Reflect on Progress	Set Learning Goals

The instructional routines in *Wonders* guide students to understand the importance of taking ownership of their own learning. The **Reading/Writing Companion** Welcome pages introduce students to routines they will be using throughout the year.

AUTHOR INSIGHT

Learning how to identify what they are learning, talk about what they know, figure out what they need more help with, and figure out next steps are all important aspects of taking ownership of learning that students develop in *Wonders*.

- Dr. Douglas Fisher

Reflect on What You Know

Text Set Goals

Students are introduced to three overarching goals for each text set. Students first evaluate what they know before instruction begins.

Reading and Writing

Students evaluate what they know about reading in a particular genre and writing in response to texts using text evidence.

Build Knowledge Goals

Each text set is focused on building knowledge through investigation of an Essential Question. After an introduction to the Essential Question, students self-evaluate how much they already know about the topic.

Extended Writing Goals

Students also think about their ability to write in a particular genre before instruction begins.

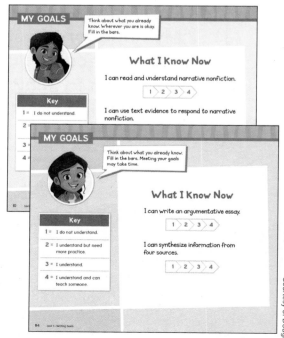

Monitor Learning

Lesson Learning Goals

The journey through a text set and extended writing is made up of a sequence of lessons. The learning goals of these lessons build toward achieving the overarching goals. At the start of each lesson, a targeted learning goal, presented as a "We Can" statement, is introduced to students.

The learning goals are shared with students and parents so that they can track their learning as they work through the lessons.

Check-In Routine

At the end of each lesson, students are asked to self-assess how well they understood the lesson learning goal.

At the end of the lesson, students conference with a partner. They review the lesson learning goal "We Can" statement.

Review

Students share their self-assessments with you by holding up their fingers and sharing the filled-in bars. This lets you know how students think they are doing.

Share

CHECK-IN ROUTINE

Review the lesson learning goal.
Reflect on the activity.
Self-Assess by
- filling in the bars in the Reading/Writing Companion
- holding up 1, 2, 3, or 4 fingers

Share with your teacher.

Reflect

Students take turns self-reflecting on how well they understood the learning goal.

TEACHING TIP
Valuing students' self-assessments is important to enabling students to take ownership of their learning. As students progress throughout the year, they become more adept at self-assessing what they know and what help they need moving forward.

TEACHING TIP
As students develop their ability to reflect on their work, provide sentence frames to support them.

Ask yourself:
Can I _____?
Respond:
I can almost _____.
I am having trouble_____.
I need to work on _____.

Self Assess

Students hold up 1, 2, 3 or 4 fingers to self-assess how well they understood the learning goal. When appropriate, they will fill in the bars in the Reading/Writing Companion as well. At the start of the year, review the ratings with students emphasizing that we all learn differently and at a different pace. It is okay to score a 1 or 2. Understanding what they do not know will help students figure out what to do next.

TEACHING TIP
1 I did not understand the learning goal.
2 I understood some things about the learning goal. I need more explanation.
3 I understood how to do the lesson, but I need more practice.
4 I understood the learning goal really well. I think I can teach someone how to do it.

Developing
Student Ownership
of Learning

Choose Learning Resources

Student-Teacher Conferencing

As students evaluate what they understand, the next step is to think about whether they need more teaching or more practice. The **Reading/Writing Companion** can serve as a powerful conferencing tool. Reviewing their filled-in bars while conferring with each student provides you the opportunity to guide students into identifying what they should do next to improve their understanding.

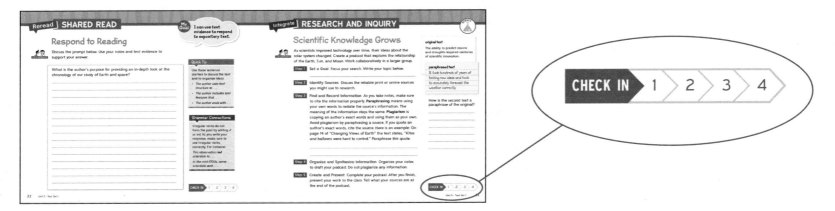

Small Group Teacher-Led Instruction

You and the student may decide that they need more teaching. Student Check-Ins and your observations at the end of each lesson provide timely data that informs the focus for teacher-led small group instruction. Teachers can choose from the small group differentiated lessons provided.

Small Group Independent/Collaborative Work

While meeting with small groups, other students can practice the skills and concepts they have determined they need practice with.

My Independent Work lists options for collaborative and independent practice. Based on student input and your informal observations, you identify "Must Do" activities to be completed. Students then choose activities focused on areas of need and interests they have identified—promoting student choice and voice.

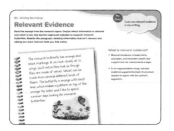

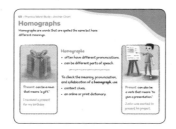

Reflect on Progress

After completing the lessons in the text set and extended writing, students reflect on their overall progress, taking notes to share with their peers and at teacher conferences. The focus of the conversations is on progress made and figuring out next steps to continued progress.

TEACHING TIP

As students discuss their progress, ask them to reflect on the following:

- In what areas did you feel that you made a lot of progress?
- What are some examples?
- What areas do you still need to work on?
- What things can you do to make more progress in these areas?

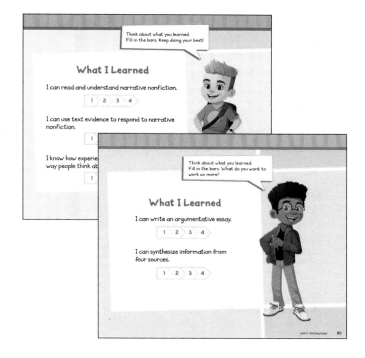

Set Learning Goals

At the end of the unit, students continue to reflect on their learning. They are also asked to set their own learning goals as they move into the next unit of instruction.

See additional guidance online for supporting students in evaluating work, working toward meeting learning goals, and reflecting on progress.

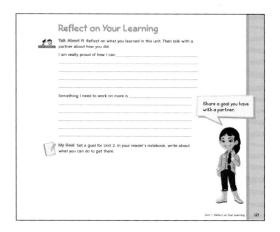

Equity and Access

Differentiated Resources

Every student deserves high-quality instruction. *Wonders* provides high-quality, rigorous instruction that supports access to grade-level content and ELA Skills through equitable, differentiated instruction and resources.

Scaffolded Instruction

Gradual Release Model of Instruction Explicit skills lessons start with teacher explanation and modeling, then move to guided and collaborative practice, then culminate with independent practice with the Your Turn activities.

A C T **Access Complex Text** The complex features of texts students are asked to read are highlighted. Point-of-use scaffolds are provided to help students to attend to those complex aspects of the text.

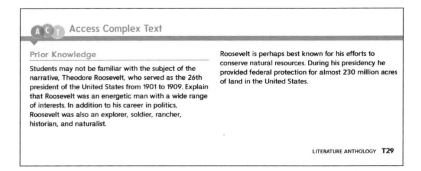

Data Informed Instruction *Wonders* offers frequent opportunities for informal and formative assessment. The student Check-Ins and teacher Check for Success features provide daily input allowing adjustments for instruction and student practice. The Data Dashboard collects data from online games and activities and the Progress Monitoring assessments.

Differentiated Small Group Time

Teacher-Led Instruction Key skills and concepts are supported with explicit differentiated lessons. The Differentiated Genre Passages and Leveled Readers provide a variety of differentiated texts. Literature Small group lessons guide teachers in scaffolding support so all students have access to the same text.

TIER 2 **Tier 2** instruction is incorporated into the Approaching level lessons. Additional Tier 2 instruction is available online.

GIFTED and TALENTED **Gifted and Talented** activities are also provided for those students who are ready to extend their learning.

Independent/Collaborative Work
A range of choices for practice and extension are provided to support the key skills and concepts taught. Students use this time to work on their independent reading and writing. Resources include the Center Activity Cards, online games, Practice Book, and Content Area Reading blackline masters.

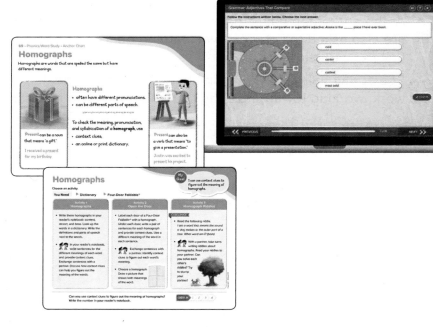

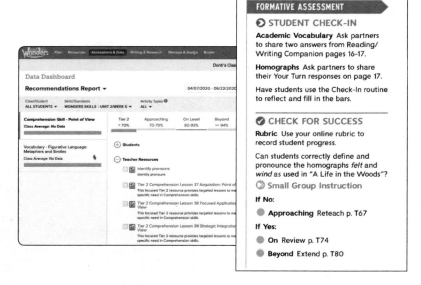

ELL English Language Learners

Access to Grade Level Lessons

English Language Proficiency Levels Targeted support addressing the different English Language Proficiency Levels allows all students to participate.

Spotlight on Language Point-of-use support that highlights English phrases and vocabulary that may be particularly difficult for English Language Learners.

Multilingual Resources

Home Language Support The following features are available in Spanish, Haitian-Creole, Portuguese, Vietnamese, French, Arabic, Chinese, Russian, Tagalog, and Urdu:

- Summaries of the Shared Read and Anchor Texts.
- School–to-Home Letters that help families support students in their learning goals.
- Multilingual Glossary of key content words with definitions from grade-level texts.
- Spanish and Haitian-Creole Leveled Readers available online.

English Language Learners

Use the following scaffolds with **Guided Practice**. For small group support, see the ELL Teacher's Guide.

Beginning
Review primary and secondary sources with students. Reread the third sentence in "Cabin Life" with students. Have students point to quotations marks. Remind them that quotation marks show that a person wrote or said this. Ask: *What did Thoreau write?* "I have a great deal of company in my house." *Is this quote from a primary source?* (yes)

Intermediate
Review primary and secondary sources with students. Have students reread the first three sentences of "Cabin Life" and point to the quotation marks. Ask: *What do the quotation marks show?* They show that a person wrote or said this. *Who wrote* "I have a great deal of company in my house"? (Thoreau) Help partners discuss if this quote is from a primary or secondary source using: The words "he wrote" tells me this quote is from a primary source.

Advanced/Advanced High
Have partners take turns reading "Cabin Life" on page 4. Have them identify the quote and tell if it's a primary source. Ask questions to guide them: *Who wrote or said this? How do you know? Why is the primary source unique?*

Strategic Support

A separate resource is available for small group instruction focused specifically on English Language Learners. The lessons are carefully designed to support the language development, grade level skills, and content. The instruction and resources are differentiated to address all levels of English Language Proficiency and carefully align with the instruction in Reading and Writing.

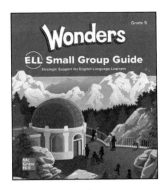

Additional Resources for Differentiation

Newcomer Kit Instructional cards and practice focused on access to basic, high-utility vocabulary.

Language Development Kit Differentiated instruction and practice for key English grammar concepts.

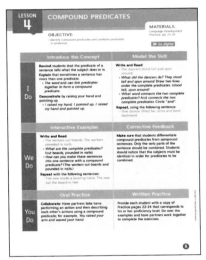

Collection of Diverse Literature

The literature in *Wonders* provides a diverse representation of various individuals and cultures. The texts give students the opportunity to see themselves and others within and outside of their communities. As students read, listen to, discuss, and write about texts, they are able to make real-life connections to themselves and the world around them.

Culturally Responsive Teaching

Drawing from the research, there are a number of factors that support classroom equity and enable the underpinnings of culturally responsive teaching: high academic expectations for all students; a socially and emotionally positive classroom; a safe school climate; authentic and rigorous tasks; inclusive, relevant, and meaningful content; open and accepting communication; drawing from students' strengths, knowledge, culture, and competence; critically and socially aware inquiry practices; strong teaching; and school staff professional support and learning about equity and inclusion (Aronson & Laughter, 2016; Gay, 2010; Krasnoff, 2016; Ladson-Billings, 2006; Morrison, Robbins, & Rose, 2008; NYSED, 2019; Saphier, 2017; Snyder, Trowery & McGrath, 2019; Waddell, 2014). It is important to note the emphasis on developing classrooms and instructional practices that support all students, rather than focusing solely on who the students are and what they bring to school.

Through the high-quality content and research-based best practices of the instructional routines embedded in the program, the *Wonders* curriculum supports all important aspects of culturally responsive teaching.

The Learning Community: providing avenues for the development of a classroom community grounded in collaboration, risk-taking, responsibility, perseverance, and communication. This allows all learners to find a pathway to deep learning and academic success.

Wonders promotes classroom practices that best support meaningful learning and collaboration among peers. Valuing students' voices on what they think about the world around them and what they know allows teachers to build on students' funds of knowledge and adapt instruction and application opportunities. Starting in Kindergarten and progressing through the grades, students develop their ability to engage in focused academic discussions, assisting each other in deep understanding of the texts they read and building knowledge on various topics.

Authentic and Rigorous Learning Tasks: providing multiple methods to learn new material, challenging content for all levels of learners, opportunities to discuss, grapple with, and critique ideas, and space to personally connect to the content. This allows all learners to develop enthusiasm and dedication in their academic endeavors.

In *Wonders*, many of the texts center on relevant issues, examples, and real-world problems, along with prompts and questions that encourage students to engage and think critically about how they would address a similar problem or issue. The Essential Question for each text set introduces the topic that will be explored, culminating in a Show Your Knowledge activity. This allows students to synthesize information they learned analyzing all the texts. Extended writing tasks allow additional opportunities for flexible connections, elaboration of student thinking, and original expression.

Differentiation Opportunities: providing instructional pathways to meet the individual needs of all learners, which creates a more equitable learning experience.

In *Wonders*, clarity around differentiation of instruction, flexibility, adaptability, and choice are some of the key guiding principles on which the resources have been built. In addition to providing a range of differentiated leveled texts, *Wonders* is designed to ensure all students have access to rich, authentic grade-level informational and literary texts. A variety of print and digital resources are provided as options for differentiating practice opportunities.

Evidence of Learning: providing continuous opportunities to gather information about each learner's academic progress through a variety of assessment methods. This allows for timely feedback to learners and supports differentiation for meeting the needs of all learners.

In *Wonders*, students' self-evaluation of their own learning and progress over time is integral to student success. Student Check-In Routines assist students in documenting how well they understand leaning goals and encourage them to reflect on what may have been difficult to understand. Resources such as the Learning Goals Blackline Masters and features in the Reading/Writing Companion assist students in monitoring their progress. Teachers use the results of the Student Check-Ins and their informal observations of students with the Check for Success features in the Teacher's Edition to inform decisions about small group differentiated instruction. A range of innovative tools equip the teacher for assessment-informed instructional decision making, and ensure students are equipped to fully participate in responsive, engaging instruction. This Data Dashboard uses student results from assessments and activities to provide instructional recommendations tailored to the individual needs.

Relevant, Respectful, and Meaningful Content: providing content that represents the lives and experiences of a range of individuals who belong to different racial, ethnic, religious, age, gender, linguistic, socio-economic, and ability groups in equitable, positive, and non-stereotypical ways. This allows all learners to see themselves reflected in the content they are learning.

In *Wonders*, resources have been created and curated to promote literacy and deepen understanding for every student. A commitment to multicultural education and our nation's diverse population is evident in the literature selections and themes found throughout every grade. *Wonders* depicts people from various ethnic backgrounds in all types of environments, avoiding stereotypes. Students of all backgrounds will be able to relate to the texts. The authors of the texts in *Wonders* are also diverse and represent a rich range of backgrounds and cultures, which they bring to their writing.

Supporting Family Communication: providing open communication avenues for families by developing regular and varied interactions about program content. This provides opportunities for all families to be involved in the academic progress of their learner.

In *Wonders*, the School to Home tab on the ConnectEd Student Workspace provides information to families about what students are learning. The letters introduce the Essential Questions that the students will be investigating in each text set, as well as the key skills and skills. Activities that families can complete with students at home are provided. Access to texts that students are reading is also available through the Student Workspace. Home-to-school letters and audio summaries of student texts are available in multiple languages, including English, Spanish, Haitian-Creole, Portuguese, Vietnamese, French, Arabic, Chinese (Cantonese and Mandarin), Russian, Tagalog, and Urdu.

Professional Learning: providing instructional guidance for administrators and teachers that supports enacting culturally responsive and sustaining pedagogical practices and focuses on asset-based approaches, bias surfacing, cultural awareness, and connections to learner communities, cultures, and resources.

In *Wonders*, a comprehensive set of resources assists administrators and teachers in a successful implementation of the program to ensure teacher and student success. Information embedded in the Teacher's Edition, and targeted components such as the Instructional Routines Handbook, as well as online Professional Learning Videos and resources, provide a wide range of support. Resources focused on helping teachers reflect on their understanding of the different cultures of their students, as well as assisting teachers in facilitating meaningful conversations about texts, are also provided.

Teaching the
Whole Child

Your students are learning so much more than reading from you. They're learning how to learn, how to master new content areas, and how to handle themselves in and out of the classroom. Research shows that this leads to increased academic success. *Wonders* resources have been developed to support you in teaching the whole child, for success this year and throughout your students' lives.

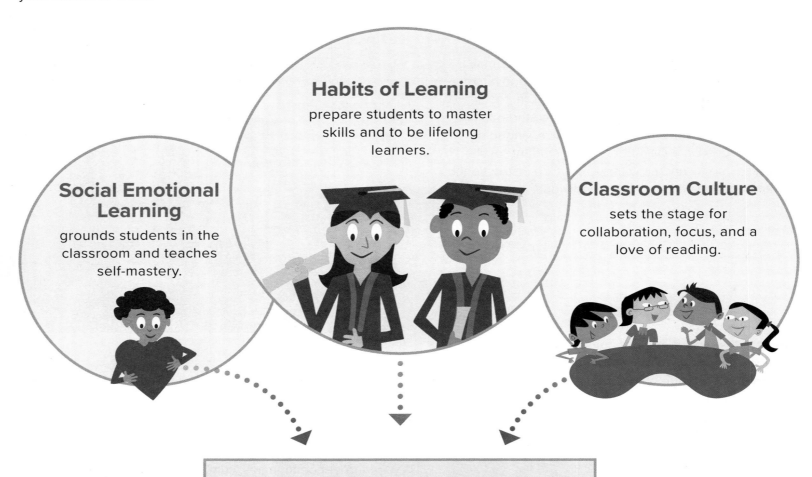

Social Emotional Learning

grounds students in the classroom and teaches self-mastery.

Habits of Learning

prepare students to master skills and to be lifelong learners.

Classroom Culture

sets the stage for collaboration, focus, and a love of reading.

DEVELOPING CRITICAL THINKERS

- Mastery of reading, writing, speaking, and listening
- Knowledge that spans content areas
- College and career readiness
- Strong results this year and beyond

Habits of Learning

I am part of a community of learners.

☐ I listen actively to others to learn new ideas.
☐ I build upon others' ideas in a conversation.
☐ I work with others to understand my learning goals.
☐ I stay on topic during discussion.
☐ I use words that will make my ideas clear.
☐ I share what I know.
☐ I gather information to support my thinking.

I use a variety of strategies when I read.

☐ I make predictions.
☐ I take notes.
☐ I think about how a text is organized.
☐ I visualize what I'm reading.
☐ I think about the author's purpose.

I think critically about what I read.

☐ I ask questions.
☐ I look for text evidence.
☐ I make inferences based on evidence.
☐ I connect new ideas to what I already know.

I write to communicate.

☐ I think about what I read as models for my writing.
☐ I talk with my peers to help make my writing better.
☐ I use rubrics to analyze my own writing.
☐ I use different tools when I write and present.

I believe I can succeed.

☐ I try different ways to learn things that are difficult for me.
☐ I ask for help when I need it.
☐ I challenge myself to do better.
☐ I work to complete my tasks.
☐ I read independently.

I am a problem solver.

☐ I analyze the problem.
☐ I try different ways.

Classroom Culture

We respect and value each other's experiences.

☐ We value what each of us brings from home.
☐ We work together to understand each other's perspectives.
☐ We work with our peers in pairs and in small groups.
☐ We use new academic vocabulary we learn when we speak and write.
☐ We share our work and learn from others.

We promote student ownership of learning.

☐ We understand what our learning goals are.
☐ We evaluate how well we understand each learning goal.
☐ We find different ways to learn what is difficult.

We learn through modeling and practice.

☐ We practice together to make sure we understand.
☐ We access many different resources to get information.
☐ We use many different tools when we share what we learn.

We foster a love of reading.

☐ We create inviting places to sit and read.
☐ We read for enjoyment.
☐ We read to understand ourselves and our world.

We build knowledge.

☐ We investigate what we want to know more about.
☐ We read many different types of texts to gain information.
☐ We build on what we know.

We inspire confident writers.

☐ We analyze the connection between reading and writing.
☐ We understand the purpose and audience for our writing.
☐ We revise our writing to make it stronger.

Social Emotional
Learning

 Social emotional learning is one of the most important factors in predicting school success. *Wonders* supports students in social emotional development in the following areas so that they can successfully engage in the instructional routines.

Relationships and Prosocial Behaviors

Engages in and maintains positive relationships and interactions with familiar adults and other students.

Social Problem Solving

Uses basic problem solving skills to resolve conflicts with other students.

Rules and Routines

Follows classroom rules and routines with increasing independence.

Working Memory

Maintains and manipulates distinct pieces of information over short periods of time.

Focus Attention

Maintains focus and sustains attention with minimal teacher supports.

Self Awareness

Recognizes self as a unique individual as well as belonging to a family, community, or other groups; expresses confidence in own skills and perspectives.

Creativity

Expresses creativity in thinking and communication.

Initiative

Demonstrates initiative and independence.

Task Persistence

Sets reasonable goals and persists to complete the task.

Logic and Reasoning

Thinks critically to effectively solve a problem or make a decision.

Planning and Problem Solving

Uses planning and problem solving strategies to achieve goals.

Flexible Thinking

Demonstrates flexibility in thinking and behavior to resolve conflicts with other students.

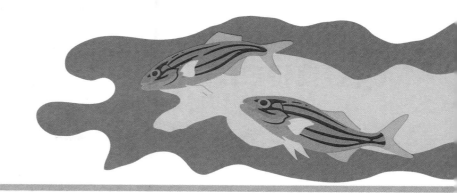

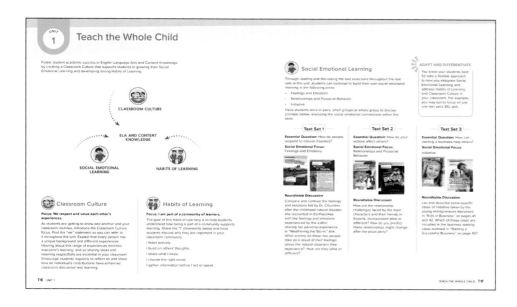

For each text set in a unit, a social emotional focus is identified and discussed in the context of the texts students read.

Weekly School-to-Home Communication

Weekly school-to-home family communication letters, ready to send in multiple languages, encourage parents to log on and share resources with their children, including listening to audio summaries of all main selections so they can ask questions. This deepens the connection between community and classroom, supporting social emotional development. This helps ensure that each and every child comes to school engaged, motivated, and eager to learn!

- English
- Spanish
- Chinese
- French
- Portuguese
- Tagalog
- Vietnamese
- Urdu
- Arabic
- Haitian-Creole
- Russian

E-books include audio summaries in the same languages.

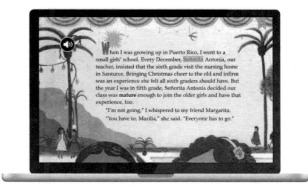

Wonders and the Science of Reading

Wonders supports the delivery of high-quality literacy instruction aligned to the science of reading. It provides a comprehensive, integrated plan for meeting the needs of all students. Carefully monitoring advances in literacy research, the program is developed to ensure that lessons focus on teaching the right content at the right time. The right content refers to teaching sufficient amounts of the content that has been proven to deliver learning advantages to students. The right time refers to a carefully structured scope and sequence within a grade and across grades. This ensures that teaching is presented in the most effective and efficient manner, with sound guidance to better support diverse learners.

Dr. Timothy Shanahan

Foundational Skills

English is an alphabetic language; developing readers must learn to translate letters and spelling patterns to sounds and pronunciations, and to read text accurately, automatically, and with proper expression. When students learn to manage these foundational skills with a minimum of conscious attention, they will have the cognitive resources available to comprehend what they read.

Research shows that the explicit teaching of phonemic awareness, phonics, and text reading fluency are the most successful ways to succeed in foundational skills. *Wonders* presents a sequence of research-aligned learning activities in its grade-level placements, sequences of instruction, and instructional guidance across the following areas:

- Phonemic Awareness
- Phonics/Decoding
- Text Reading Fluency

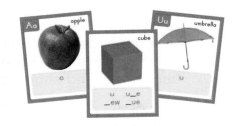

Reading Comprehension

Reading comprehension requires that students extract and construct meaning from text. To comprehend, students must learn to apply the prior knowledge they bring to the text to the information expressed through written language in the text. To accomplish this successfully, readers must do three things. They must:

- expand their knowledge through the reading of high-quality informative texts;
- learn to negotiate increasingly sophisticated and complex written language;
- develop the cognitive abilities to manage and monitor these processes.

Wonders provides lessons built around a high-quality collection of complex literary and informational texts, focused on both the natural and social worlds. Teachers using *Wonders* will find explicit, research-based lessons in vocabulary and other language skills, guidance for high-level, high-quality discussions, and well-designed lessons aimed at building the executive processes that can shift reading comprehension into high gear, including:

- Building Knowledge/Using Knowledge
- Vocabulary and other aspects of written language
- Text complexity
- Executive processes and comprehension strategies

Writing

In the 21st century, it is not enough to be able to read, understand, and learn from the writing of others. Being able to communicate one's own ideas logically and effectively is necessary, too. As with reading, writing includes foundational skills (like spelling and handwriting), as well as higher-order abilities (composition and communication) and the executive processes required to manage the accomplishment of successful writing. Research shows that reading and writing strengthen one another. Focusing writing instruction in the following areas will help students improve their reading:

- Writing foundations
- Quality writing for multiple purposes
- The writing processes
- Writing to enhance reading

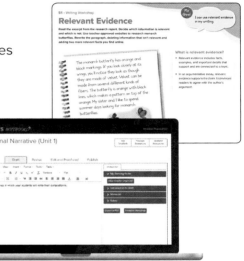

Quality of Instruction

The science of reading is dependent upon the sciences of teaching and learning, as well as on reading research. Reading research has identified specific best practices for teaching particular aspects of literacy. However, research has also revealed other important features of quality instruction that have implications for all learners and that may better support certain student populations. *Wonders* lessons reflect these quality issues in teaching:

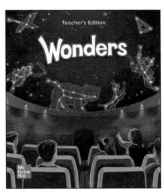

- Lessons with explicit and appropriate purposes
- High-challenge levels
- Appropriate opportunities for review
- Quality discussions promoted by high DOK-level questions
- Ongoing monitoring of learning
- Supports for English language learners
- Connections to social emotional learning

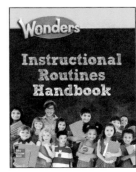

Build Critical Readers, Writers, Communicators, and Thinkers

LISTENING

SPEAKING

READING

Build Knowledge Through a Text Set

- **Investigate** an Essential Question.
- **Read** a variety of texts.
- **Closely read** texts for deeper meaning.
- **Respond** to texts using text evidence.
- **Conduct** research.
- **Share** your knowledge.
- **Inspire** action.

WRITING

Communicate Effectively Through Writing

- **Analyze** mentor texts and student models.
- **Understand** purpose and audience.
- **Plan** writing, using sources as needed.
- **Conference** with peers and teachers.
- **Evaluate** work against a rubric.
- **Improve** writing continuously.
- **Share** your writing.

SMALL GROUP

EXTEND   CONNECT

ASSESS

COLLABORATING

Instruction Aligned to the **Science of Reading**

Reading

Explicit instruction supports students in building knowledge.

- Foundational Reading Skills
  - Phonics/Word Analysis
  - Fluency
- Reading Literature
- Reading Informational Texts
- Comparing Texts
- Vocabulary
- Researching

Writing

Skills-based minilessons support students in developing their writing.

- Writing
  - Narrative
  - Argumentative
  - Expository
- Handwriting
- Speaking and Listening
- Conventions
- Creating and Collaborating

Differentiation

Differentiate resources, instruction, and level of scaffolds.

Small Group Teacher-Led Instruction

- Choose from small group skills lesson options to target instruction to meet students' needs.
- Read texts with scaffolded support.

Independent/Collaborative Work

- Students transfer knowledge of skills to independent reading and practice.
- Students transfer skills to their writing.

Extend, Connect, and Assess

At the end of the unit, students transfer and apply knowledge gained to new contexts.

Demonstrate Understanding

- Extend knowledge through online reading and Reader's Theater.
- Connect ELA skills to content area reading with science and social studies texts.
- Assess learning with program assessments.

Grade 5
Resources

The resources in *Wonders* support skills mastery, differentiated instruction, and the transfer and application of knowledge to new contexts. Teachers will find ways to enhance student learning and ownership through multimodal supports, a strong focus on foundational skills, opportunities to build knowledge, and fostering of expression through writing. All of your *Wonders*-created print resources are available digitally to support a variety of learning environments. The resources shown represent the key instructional elements of your *Wonders* classroom and are a portion of the supports available to you and your students. Login to your **Teacher Workspace** to explore multimedia resources, professional learning, and thousands of resources to meet your students where they are.

SMALL GROUP

EXTEND CONNECT
ASSESS

Component		Differentiate	Extend, Connect, Assess	Available Digitally
Teacher's Edition		●	●	●
Reading/Writing Companion			●	●
Literature Anthology			●	●
Classroom Library		●		
Classroom Library Lessons		●		●

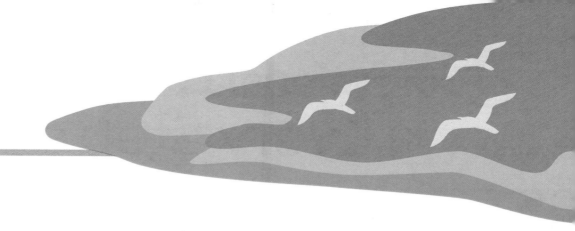

Component	Differentiate	Extend, Connect, Assess	Available Digitally
Leveled Readers & Lesson Cards	●	●	●
Center Activity Cards	●	●	●
ELL Small Group Guide	●		●
Data Dashboard	●	●	●
Progress Monitoring Assessment		●	●
Unit Assessment		●	●
Benchmark Assessments		●	●
Practice Book Blackline Masters		●	●
Inquiry Space		●	●
Online Writer's Notebook		●	●
Foundational Skills Resources: multimodal manipulatives, cards, activities, and games to build key skills	●	●	●
Skills-Based Online Games	●	●	●
Differentiated Genre Passages	●	●	●
Content Area Reading Blackline Masters		●	●

Professional Learning
Every Step of the Way

Get Started Using *Wonders*. Every day of instruction is based on evidence-based classroom best practices, which are embedded into the daily routines to strengthen your teaching and enhance students' learning. Throughout *Wonders*, you'll find support for employing these new routines and making the most of your literacy block.

Use this checklist to access support resources to help you get started with *Wonders* during the first weeks of school. Then refer to this list during the year for ongoing implementation support and to get the most from *Wonders*.

Beginning the Year

We encourage you to review these resources before the first day of school and then use them to support your first weeks of instruction.

In Your Teacher's Edition: Support pages for planning and teaching are embedded throughout your Teacher's Edition to support your big-picture understanding and help you teach effectively.

- ☐ **Start Smart:** In Unit 1 of your Teacher's Edition, Start Smart provides an overview of the instructional lessons and routines within *Wonders* by providing an explanation of the Unit 1 Text Set 1 Teacher's Edition lessons and select other lessons.

- ☐ **Text Set Support:** Each text set is accompanied by an introduction that supports your understanding of the content and simplifies instructional planning. These pages include a daily planner, differentiated learning support, guidance for developing student ownership and building knowledge, and more.

- ☐ **Progress Monitoring and Assessment:** Use data to track progress toward mastery of skills-based content, lesson objectives, and student goals.
  The **My Goals Routine** supports continuous self-monitoring and student feedback.

Online Resources: The digital Teacher Dashboard is your access point for key resources to get you up and running with *Wonders*. From the Teacher Dashboard, select *Resources > Professional Development > Overview*

- ☐ ***Wonders* Basics Module:** Set up your classroom, get to know your materials, learn about the structure of *Wonders*, and receive support for placement testing and grouping students for small group learning.
  - ▶ Select *Learn to Use Wonders*

- ☐ **Placement and Diagnostic Assessment:** Access assessments, testing instructions, and placement charts that can be used at the beginning of the year to assess and place students in small groups.
  - ▶ Select *Assessment & Data*

Ongoing Support

Your online **Teacher Workspace** also includes a wide range of additional resources. Use them throughout the year for ongoing support and professional learning. From the Teacher Dashboard, select *Resources > Professional Development*

☐ **Instructional Routines Handbook:** Reference this handbook throughout the year for support implementing the *Wonders* evidence-based routines and understanding the research behind them, and for guidance on what student success looks like.
- ▶ Select *Overview > Instructional Routines*

☐ **Small Group Differentiated Learning Guide:** Use the first few weeks of small group time to teach and model routines and establish small group rules and procedures.
- ▶ Select *Overview > Instructional Routines > Managing Small Groups: A How-to Guide PDF*

☐ **Suggested Lesson Plans and Pacing Guides:** Adjust your instruction to your literacy block and meet the needs of your classroom with flexible lesson plans and pacing.
- ▶ Select *Overview > Instructional Routines*

☐ **Classroom Videos:** Watch *Wonders* teachers model classroom lessons in reading, writing, collaboration, and teaching English language learners.
- ▶ Select *Classroom Videos*

☐ **Small Group Classroom Videos:** Watch *Wonders* teachers model small group instruction and share tips and strategies for effective differentiated lessons.
- ▶ Select *Classroom Videos > Small Group Instruction*

☐ **Author & Coach Videos:** Watch Dr. Douglas Fisher, Dr. Timothy Shanahan, and other *Wonders* authors as they provide short explanations of best practices and classroom coaching. Also provided are videos from Dr. Sheldon Eakins, founder of the Leading Equity Center, that focus on important aspects of educational equity and cultural responsive teaching.
- ▶ Select *Author & Coach Videos*

☐ **Assessment Handbook:** Review your assessment options and find support for managing multiple assessments, interpreting their results, and using data to inform your instructional planning.
- ▶ Select *Overview > Assessment & Data*

☐ **Assessment & Data Guides:** Review your assessment resources and get to know your reporting tools.
- ▶ Select *Overview > Assessment & Data*

☐ **Digital Help:** Access video tutorials and printable PDFs to support planning, assessment, writing and research, assignments, and connecting school to home.
- ▶ Select *Digital Help*

Explore the Professional Development section in your Teacher Workspace for more videos, resources, and printable guides. Select *Resources > Professional Development*

Notes

Contents

Unit Overview

English Language Arts is not a discrete set of skills. Skills work together to help students analyze the meaningful texts. In *Wonders*, skills are not taught in isolation. Rather they are purposefully combined to support student learning of texts they read.

Reading

Text Set 1

Essential Question: What do good problem solvers do?

Phonics and Word Analysis
Variant Vowel /ô/; Diphthongs /oi/, /ou/; Plurals

Fluency
Accuracy and Rate;
Accuracy and Expression

Reading Informational Text
✓ Text Features: Headings and Timelines
✓ Text Structure: Problem and Solution
✓ Text Features: Print and Graphic Features
Summarize

Compare Texts
Compare and contrast information

Vocabulary
Academic Vocabulary
✓ Context Clues
Dictionary and Glossary

Researching
Founders Solve Problems

Text Set 2

Essential Question: When has a plan helped you accomplish a task?

Phonics and Word Analysis
Inflectional Endings; Contractions

Fluency
Expression and Phrasing; Rate

Reading Literature
✓ Plot: Setting
✓ Theme
Summarize

Reading Information Text
✓ Text Structure: Sequence

Compare Texts
Compare and contrast information

Vocabulary
Academic Vocabulary
✓ Personification
Roots

Researching
Accomplishing a Task

Text Set 3

Essential Question: What motivates you to accomplish a goal?

Phonics and Word Analysis
Closed Syllables

Fluency
Expression and Phrasing

Reading Literature
✓ Poetic Elements: Repetition and Rhyme
✓ Theme
✓ Poetic Elements: Form and Line Breaks
Summarize

Compare Texts
Compare and contrast information

Vocabulary
Academic Vocabulary
✓ Homographs

Researching
Achieving Goals

Writing

Extended Writing 1

Writing
Handwriting
✓ Expository Writing: Write to Sources
Improving Writing: Writing Process

Speaking and Listening
Oral Presentation

Conventions
✓ Grammar: Kinds of Nouns; Singular and Plural Nouns; More Plural Nouns; Possessive Nouns
Spelling: Words with Variant Vowel /ô/; Diphthongs /oi/, /ou/; Plurals; Inflectional Endings; Contractions

Creating and Collaborating
Writer's Notebook

Extended Writing 2

Writing
Handwriting
✓ Expository Writing: Write to Sources
Improving Writing: Writing Process

Speaking and Listening
Oral Presentation

Key

Extend, Connect, and Assess

Extend previously taught skills and connect to new content.

Extend

Reading Informational Text
Reading Digitally
  Text Structure: Problem and Solution
  Conduct Research

Fluency
Reader's Theater
  Phrasing and Rate

Connect

Connect to Science
  Scientific Investigation and the Steps of the Scientific Method; Physical and Chemical Changes; Basic Forms of Energy

Connect to Social Studies
  Timelines of American History; Individuals Responsible for the Development of Colonies

Assess

✓ **Unit Assessment Test**

Fluency Assessment

Conventions
  ✓ Grammar: Prepositional Phrases
  Spelling: Words with Closed Syllables

Creating and Collaborating
  Writer's Notebook

Key Skills Trace

Reading Literature

Plot
Introduce: Unit 1 Text Set 2
Review: Unit 2 Text Set 2; Unit 3 Text Set 1; Unit 5 Text Set 2; Unit 6 Text Set 1
Assess: Unit 1, Unit 2, Unit 3, Unit 5, Unit 6

Theme
Introduce: Unit 2 Text Set 2
Review: Unit 2 Text Set 3; Unit 3 Text Set 1; Unit 4 Text Set 3; Unit 6 Text Set 1
Assess: Unit 2, Unit 3, Unit 4, Unit 6

Poetic and Story Elements
Introduce: Unit 2 Text Set 3
Review: Unit 4 Text Set 2, Text Set 3; Unit 6 Text Set 3
Assess: Unit 2, Unit 4, Unit 6

Reading Informational Text

Text Structure
Introduce: Unit 1 Text Set 1
Review: Unit 1 Text Set 2; Unit 2 Text Set 1, Text Set 2; Unit 3 Text Set 2, Text Set 3; Unit 4 Text Set 1; Unit 5 Text Set 2; Unit 6 Text Set 2
Assess: Unit 1, Unit 2, Unit 3, Unit 4, Unit 5, Unit 6

Text Features
Introduce: Unit 1 Text Set 3
Review: Unit 2 Text Set 1; Unit 4 Text Set 1; Unit 5 Text Set 1, Text Set 3; Unit 6 Text Set 1, Text Set 2
Assess: Unit 1, Unit 2, Unit 4, Unit 5, Unit 6

Vocabulary

Personification
Introduce: Unit 2 Text Set 2
Review: Unit 6 Text Set 3
Assess: Unit 2, Unit 6

Homographs and Homophones
Introduce: Unit 1 Text Set 1
Review: Unit 2 Text Set 3; Unit 6 Text Set 1
Assess: Unit 1, Unit 2, Unit 6

Context Clues
Introduce: Unit 1 Text Set 2
Review: Unit 2 Text Set 1; Unit 3 Text Set 1, Text Set 3; Unit 6 Text Set 2
Assess: Unit 1, Unit 2, Unit 3, Unit 6

Grammar

Nouns
Introduce: Unit 2
Review: Grammar Handbook and Extended Writing: Unit 2, Unit 3, Unit 4, Unit 5, Unit 6
Assess: Unit 2

Extended Writing

Unit 1: Argumentative Writing/Write to Sources

Unit 2: Expository Writing/Write to Sources

Unit 3: Argumentative Writing/Write to Sources

Unit 4: Expository Writing/Write to Sources

Unit 5: Expository Writing, Personal Narrative

Unit 6: Fictional Narrative, Poem

Self-Selected Reading Options

Classroom Library Titles

Students can choose from the following titles to read and further investigate text set Essential Questions.

Online Lessons Available

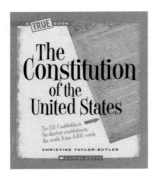

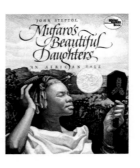

The Constitution of the United States
Christine Taylor-Butler
Expository Text
Lexile 650L

If You Lived at the Time of the American Revolution
Kay Moore
Expository Text
Lexile 860L

Mufaro's Beautiful Daughters
John Steptoe
Folktale
Lexile 790L

Where the Mountain Meets the Moon
Grace Lin
Fairy Tale
Lexile 810L

More Leveled Readers to Explore

Search the **Online Leveled Reader Library** and choose texts to provide students with additional texts at various levels to apply skills or read about various topics.

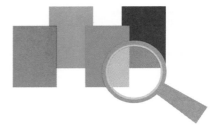

Unit Bibliography

Have students self-select independent reading texts related to the text set Essential Question. Titles in the same genre as the Anchor Text as well as titles in different genres are provided. See the online bibliography for more titles.

Text Set 1

Compare Texts

Lawson, Robert. *Ben and Me*. Little, Brown. Fantasy **Lexile** 1010L

Freedman, Russell. *Lafayette and the American Revolution*. Holiday House, 2010. Biography **Lexile** 1160L

More Expository Texts

Ransom, Candice. *What Was the Continental Congress?: And Other Questions About the Declaration of Independence*. Lerner, 2011. **Lexile** 780L

Cook, Peter. *You Wouldn't Want to Be at the Boston Tea Party!* Franklin Watts, 2013. **Lexile** 1020L

Text Set 2

Compare Texts

Clements, Andrew. *The School Story*. Atheneum, 2002. Realistic Fiction **Lexile** 760L

Riddles, Libby. *Storm Run: The Story of the First Woman to Win the Iditarod Sled Dog Race*. Sasquatch, 2002. Narrative Nonfiction **Lexile** 1010L

More Folktales

Charles, Veronika Martenova. *Maiden of the Mist: A Legend of Niagara Falls*. Fitzhenry and Whiteside, 2001. **Lexile** 710L

Bania, Michael. *Kumak's Fish: A Tall Tale from the Far North*. Alaska Northwest Books, 2004. **Lexile** 500L

Text Set 3

Compare Texts

Cooper, Floyd. *Jump! From the Life of Michael Jordan*. Penguin, 2004. Biography. **Lexile** 760L

Turnbull, Ann. *Maroo of the Winter Caves*. Harcourt, 2004. Historical Fiction **Lexile** 840L

More Poetry

Janeczko, Paul B. *That Sweet Diamond*. Atheneum, 1998. **Lexile** NP

Corcoran, Jill. *Dare to Dream . . . Change the World*. Kane/Miller Book Publishers, 2013. **Lexile** NP

Teach the Whole Child

Foster student academic success in English Language Arts and Content Knowledge by creating a Classroom Culture that supports students in growing their Social Emotional Learning and developing strong Habits of Learning.

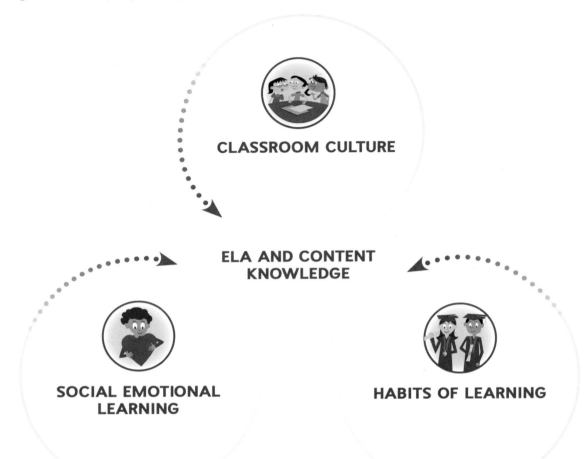

CLASSROOM CULTURE

ELA AND CONTENT KNOWLEDGE

SOCIAL EMOTIONAL LEARNING

HABITS OF LEARNING

 ## Classroom Culture

Focus: We foster a love of reading.

Introduce the unit's focus by explaining to students why you love reading and telling them about some of your favorite books. Have them share about their favorite books. Review the importance of your classroom library and the routines for using it. Read the "we" statements below. Have students discuss ways they are supported in your classroom.

We read for enjoyment.

We read to find out information.

We read to understand ourselves and our world.

We create inviting places to sit and read.

 ## Habits of Learning

Focus: I am a critical thinker and problem solver.

The goal of this Habit of Learning is for students to see themselves as critical thinkers who know how to solve problems. Share the "I" statements below. Have students discuss how each one helps them to evaluate information and solve problems.

I define the problem.

I ask questions.

I consider different viewpoints.

I look for evidence.

I look for logical relationships.

Social Emotional Learning

Through reading and discussing the text selections throughout the text sets in this unit, students can continue to build their own social emotional learning in the following areas:

- Initiative
- Planning and Social Problem-Solving
- Creativity

Have students work in pairs, small groups, or whole group to discuss prompts below, analyzing the social emotional connections within the texts.

⟍ **ADAPT AND DIFFERENTIATE**

You know your students best. So take a flexible approach to how you integrate Social Emotional Learning and address Habits of Learning and Classroom Culture in your classroom. For example, you may opt to focus on just one text set's SEL skill.

Text Set 1

Essential Question: What do good problem solvers do?

Social Emotional Focus: Initiative

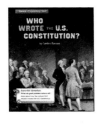 

Roundtable Discussion

In *Who Wrote the U.S. Constitution?*, how did Edmond Randolph take initiative to solve problems? How are these actions similar to or different from the problem-solving initiative and actions taken by Lucy Terry Prince or Phillis Wheatley in "Wordsmiths"?

Text Set 2

Essential Question: When has a plan helped you accomplish a task?

Social Emotional Focus: Planning and Social Problem-Solving

Roundtable Discussion

In each folktale read in the text set, the story presents a sequence of problems a character must navigate in order to solve a problem or to reach a goal. Ask: *How are some of the problems found in the settings alike or different?*

Text Set 3

Essential Question: What motivates you to accomplish a goal?

Social Emotional Focus: Creativity

Roundtable Discussion

One of the lines in "Stage Fright" by Lee Bennett Hopkins is "my mind simply snapped." How does it relate to the line "You have to be quick." in "Catching Quiet" by Marci Ridlon? In what ways were Lee and Marci creative as they crafted their poems?

Notes

Text Set 1

Essential Question: What do good problem solvers do?

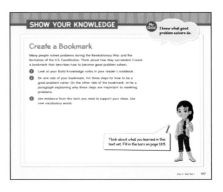

Text Set 2

Essential Question: When has a plan helped you accomplish a task?

Text Set 3

Essential Question: What motivates you to accomplish a goal?

Classroom Library Books

Student Outcomes

✓ Tested in *Wonders* Assessments

FOUNDATIONAL SKILLS

Phonics and Word Analysis

- Decode words with variant vowel /ô/ and diphthongs /oi/, /ou/
- Decode words using knowledge of plurals

Fluency

- Read grade-level texts with accuracy, appropriate rate, expression, and automaticity

READING

Reading Informational Text

- ✓ Explain how headings and timelines contribute to the understanding of a text
- ✓ Explain how a problem-and-solution text structure contributes to the overall meaning of a text
- ✓ Explain how print and graphic features contribute to the overall meaning of a text
- Read and comprehend texts in the grades 4–5 text complexity band
- Summarize a text to enhance comprehension
- Write in response to texts

Compare Texts

- ✓ Compare and contrast how authors present information on the same topic or theme

COMMUNICATION

Writing

Write to Sources

- ✓ Write an expository text about a topic using multiple sources and including an organizational structure with a clear central idea
- With guidance and support from peers and adults, develop and strengthen writing as needed by planning, revising, and editing

Speaking and Listening

- Report on a topic or text or present an opinion, sequencing ideas; speak clearly at an understandable pace

Conventions

Grammar

- ✓ Identify different kinds of nouns
- ✓ Capitalize proper nouns
- ✓ Identify singular and plural nouns
- ✓ Form plural nouns correctly

Spelling

- Spell words with variant vowel /ô/ and diphthongs /oi/, /ou/
- Spell words using knowledge of plurals

Researching

- Conduct short research projects that build knowledge through investigation of different aspects of the topic

Creating and Collaborating

- Add audio recordings and visual displays to presentations when appropriate
- With some guidance and support from adults, use technology to produce and publish writing

VOCABULARY

Academic Vocabulary

- Acquire and use grade-appropriate academic vocabulary

Vocabulary Strategy

- ✓ Use context to determine the meaning of multiple-meaning words

CONTENT AREA LEARNING

 Birth of a New Nation and Foundations of Government

- Identify the issues that led to the creation of the U.S. Constitution. **Social Studies**
- Identify the contributions of individuals who helped create the U.S. Constitution. **Social Studies**

 Cultural Contributions

- Explain how examples of art, music, and literature reflect the times during which they were created. **Social Studies**

ELL Scaffolded supports for English Language Learners are embedded throughout the lessons, enabling students to communicate information, ideas, and concepts in English Language Arts and for social and instructional purposes within the school setting.

See the **ELL Small Group Guide** for additional support of the skills for the text set.

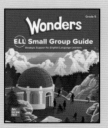

FORMATIVE ASSESSMENT

For assessment throughout the text set, use students' self-assessments and your observations.

Use the Data Dashboard to filter class, group, or individual student data to guide group placement decisions. It provides recommendations to enhance learning for gifted and talented students and offers extra support for students needing remediation.

DATA DASHBOARD

Develop Student Ownership

To build student ownership, students need to know what they are learning and why they are learning it, and to determine how well they understood it.

Students Discuss Their Goals

READING

TEXT SET GOALS

- I can read and understand expository text.
- I can use text evidence to respond to expository text.
- I know what good problem solvers do.

Have students think about what they know and fill in the bars on **Reading/Writing Companion** page 124.

WRITING

EXTENDED WRITING GOALS

Extended Writing 2:

- I can write an expository essay.
- I can synthesize information from three sources.

Have students think about what they know and fill in the bars on **Reading/Writing Companion** page 198.

Students Monitor Their Learning

LEARNING GOALS

Specific learning goals identified in every lesson make clear what students will be learning and why. These smaller goals provide stepping stones to help students reach their Text Set and Extended Writing Goals.

CHECK-IN ROUTINE

The Check-In Routine at the close of each lesson guides students to self-reflect on how well they understood each learning goal.

Review the lesson learning goal.
Reflect on the activity.
Self-Assess by
- filling in the bars in the **Reading/Writing Companion**
- holding up 1, 2, 3, or 4 fingers
Share with your teacher.

Students Reflect on Their Progress

READING

TEXT SET GOALS

After completing the Show Your Knowledge task for the text set, students reflect on their understanding of the Text Set Goals by filling in the bars on **Reading/Writing Companion** page 125.

WRITING

EXTENDED WRITING GOALS

After completing both extended writing projects for the unit, students reflect on their understanding of the Extended Writing Goals by filling in the bars on **Reading/Writing Companion** page 199.

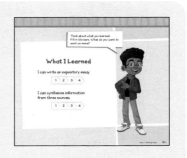

Build Knowledge

TEXT SET 1

Shared Read
Reading/Writing Companion p. 126

Anchor Text
Literature Anthology p. 96

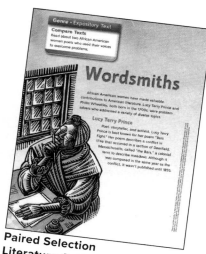

Paired Selection
Literature Anthology p. 114

Essential Question
What do good problem solvers do?

Video America became a country because its leaders were problem solvers who knew how to make compromises.

Study Sync Blast The Bill of Rights and additional amendments are created as ways to solve the problem of injustice—for example, the First Amendment allowed for a protest in 1963, calling for racial equality.

Interactive Read Aloud Elected delegates of the Haudenosaunee Confederacy—a representative democracy that governed six Native American tribes—work together to solve problems and make decisions on their tribes' behalf, which helps build peace and unity among them.

Shared Read American colonists try to solve the problems they have with Great Britain. From protests to a failed peace proposal, colonists have no choice but to go to war.

Anchor Text The nation's first leaders work together to create the U.S. Constitution and keep the nation united.

Paired Selection Lucy Terry Prince and Phillis Wheatley were African American poets born in the 1700s who addressed societal problems in their writing and actions.

Make Connections Most organizations have issues that need compromise, including schools.

Differentiated Sources

Leveled Readers
Delegates had to work together and decide how to form a new government, so that there was a balance of power.

Differentiated Genre Passages
American colonists receive financial help from both Spain and France during the American Revolution.

Build Knowledge Routine

After reading each text, ask students to document what facts and details they learned to help answer the Essential Question of the text set.

 Talk About the source.

 Write About the source.

 Add to the Class Anchor Chart.

- Add to your Vocabulary List.

Show Your Knowledge

Create a Bookmark

Have students show how they built knowledge across the text set by creating a bookmark. They should begin by thinking about the Essential Question: *What do good problem solvers do?* Students will create a bookmark with steps to becoming a problem solver and explain why these steps are important.

Social Emotional Learning

Initiative

Anchor Text: Initiative involves taking action after seeing that something needs to be done. Ask: *What provided initiative for the men who wrote the Constitution?*

Paired Selection: Initiative also involves taking the first step when faced with a task. When Lucy Terry Prince and Phillis Wheatley were faced with problems, they knew they would have to take a different path to get a solution. Ask: *What different things did Lucy Terry Prince and Phillis Wheatley need to do to solve their problems?*

Roundtable Discussion: Compare and contrast the problem-solving used by the men in *Who Wrote the U.S. Constitution* and "Wordsmiths." Ask: *How did Edmond Randolph take initiative to solve problems? How are these actions alike, or different from, the problem-solving initiative and actions taken by Lucy Terry Prince or Phillis Wheatley in "Wordsmiths"?*

Explore the Texts

Essential Question: What do good problem solvers do?

> Access Complex Text (ACT) boxes throughout the text set provide scaffolded instruction for seven different elements that may make a text complex.

A C T

The Constitution of the United States (Reprinted by permission of Children's Press and Franklin Watts, both imprints of Scholastic Library Publishing, Inc.); Cover illustration by Daniel O'Leary from ...IF YOU LIVED AT THE TIME OF THE AMERICAN REVOLUTION by Kay Moore. Illustrations copyright © 1997 by Scholastic, Inc. Used by permission.

Teacher's Edition	Reading/Writing Companion	Literature Anthology	
		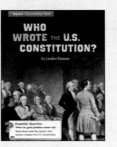	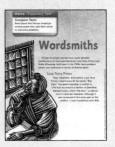
"The Haudenosaunee Confederacy" Interactive Read Aloud p. T7 Expository Text	**"Creating a Nation"** Shared Read pp. 126–129 Expository Text	***Who Wrote the U.S. Constitution?*** Anchor Text pp. 96–111 Expository Text	**"Wordsmiths"** Paired Selection pp. 114–117 Expository Text

Qualitative

Teacher's Edition	Reading/Writing Companion	Literature Anthology	
Meaning/Purpose Moderate Complexity **Structure** Low Complexity **Language** Moderate Complexity **Knowledge Demands** Moderate Complexity	**Meaning/Purpose** Moderate Complexity **Structure** Moderate Complexity **Language** Moderate Complexity **Knowledge Demands** Moderate Complexity	**Meaning/Purpose** High Complexity **Structure** Moderate Complexity **Language** High Complexity **Knowledge Demands** Moderate Complexity	**Meaning/Purpose** Moderate Complexity **Structure** Moderate Complexity **Language** High Complexity **Knowledge Demands** High Complexity

Quantitative

Lexile 910L	**Lexile** 690L	**Lexile** 760L	**Lexile** 970L

Reader and Task Considerations

Reader Students may need background knowledge of the Haudenosaunee Confederacy and its influence on American democracy.	**Reader** Students will need background knowledge on events predating those in the text, including the thirteen colonies, Revolutionary War, Articles of Confederation, and Bill of Rights.	**Reader** Students will need background knowledge on events predating those in the text, including the thirteen colonies, Revolutionary War, Articles of Confederation, and Bill of Rights.	**Reader** Students will not need background knowledge to understand the text.

Task The questions for the read aloud are supported by teacher modeling. The tasks provide a variety of ways for students to begin to build knowledge and vocabulary about the text set topic. The questions and tasks provided for the other texts are at various levels of complexity, ensuring that all students can interact with the text in meaningful ways.

Additional Texts

Classroom Library
The Constitution of the United States
Genre: Expository Text
Lexile: 650L
If You Lived at the Time of the American Revolution
Genre: Expository Text
Lexile: 860L
See **Classroom Library Lessons**

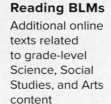

Content Area Reading BLMs
Additional online texts related to grade-level Science, Social Studies, and Arts content

Leveled Readers

(A) *The Bill of Rights*   **(O)** *The Bill of Rights*   **(B)** *The Bill of Rights*   **(ELL)** *The Bill of Rights*

Qualitative

Meaning/Purpose Moderate Complexity	**Meaning/Purpose** Moderate Complexity	**Meaning/Purpose** Moderate Complexity	**Meaning/Purpose** Moderate Complexity
Structure Low Complexity	**Structure** Moderate Complexity	**Structure** Moderate Complexity	**Structure** Low Complexity
Language Low Complexity	**Language** Moderate Complexity	**Language** High Complexity	**Language** Low Complexity
Knowledge Demands Moderate Complexity	**Knowledge Demands** Moderate Complexity	**Knowledge Demands** Moderate Complexity	**Knowledge Demands** Moderate Complexity

Quantitative

Lexile 820L   **Lexile** 920L   **Lexile** 1000L   **Lexile** 840L

Reader and Task Considerations

Reader Students will need background knowledge of the events that led to the Revolutionary War and the war itself.	**Reader** Students will need background knowledge of the events that led to the Revolutionary War and the war itself.	**Reader** Students will need background knowledge of the events that led to the Revolutionary War and the war itself.	**Reader** Students will need background knowledge of the events that led to the Revolutionary War and the war itself.

Task The questions and tasks provided for the Leveled Readers are at various levels of complexity, ensuring that all students can interact with the text in meaningful ways.

Differentiated Genre Passages

(A) "Secret Help from Spain"   **(O)** "Secret Help from Spain"   **(B)** "Secret Help from Spain"   **(ELL)** "Secret Help from Spain"

Qualitative

Meaning/Purpose Moderate Complexity	**Meaning/Purpose** Moderate Complexity	**Meaning/Purpose** Moderate Complexity	**Meaning/Purpose** Moderate Complexity
Structure Low Complexity	**Structure** Low Complexity	**Structure** Low Complexity	**Structure** Low Complexity
Language Low Complexity	**Language** Moderate Complexity	**Language** Moderate Complexity	**Language** Low Complexity
Knowledge Demands Moderate Complexity	**Knowledge Demands** Moderate Complexity	**Knowledge Demands** High Complexity	**Knowledge Demands** Low Complexity

Quantitative

Lexile 730L   **Lexile** 800L   **Lexile** 880L   **Lexile** 740L

Reader and Task Considerations

Reader Students will need background knowledge of the Revolutionary War and how other countries helped the colonies.	**Reader** Students will need background knowledge of the Revolutionary War and how other countries helped the colonies.	**Reader** Students will need background knowledge of the Revolutionary War and how other countries helped the colonies.	**Reader** Students will need background knowledge of the Revolutionary War and how other countries helped the colonies.

Task The questions and tasks provided for the Differentiated Genre Passages are at various levels of complexity, ensuring that all students can interact with the text in meaningful ways.

Week 1 Planner

Customize your own lesson plans at
my.mheducation.com

LESSON 1   **LESSON 2**

60+ mins Reading Suggested Daily Time

READING LESSON GOALS

- I can read and understand expository text
- I can use text evidence to respond to expository text
- I know what good problem solvers do.

SMALL GROUP OPTIONS
The designated lessons can be taught in small groups. To determine how to differentiate instruction for small groups, use Formative Assessment and Data Dashboard.

30+ mins Writing Suggested Daily Time

WRITING LESSON GOALS

I can write an expository essay.

Reading

LESSON 1

Introduce the Concept, T4–T5
Build Knowledge

Listening Comprehension, T6–T7
"The Haudenosaunee Confederacy"

Shared Read, T8–T11
Read "Creating a Nation"
Quick Write: Summarize

Vocabulary, T12–T13
Academic Vocabulary
Context Clues

Expand Vocabulary, T58

LESSON 2

Shared Read, T8–T11
Reread "Creating a Nation"

Minilessons, T14–T21
Reread
Text Features: Headings and Timelines
Text Structure: Problem and Solution
Craft and Structure

Respond to Reading, T22–T23

Phonics, T24–T25
Variant Vowel /ô/; Diphthongs /oi/, /ou/

Fluency, T25
Accuracy and Rate

Research and Inquiry, T26–T27

Expand Vocabulary, T58

Writing

Extended Writing 1: Expository Writing

Writing Lesson Bank: Craft Minilessons, T266–T269

Teacher and Peer Conferences

Grammar Lesson Bank, T270	Grammar Lesson Bank, T270
Kinds of Nouns	Kinds of Nouns
Talk About It	Talk About It
Spelling Lesson Bank, T280	**Spelling Lesson Bank, T280**
Variant Vowel /ô/; Diphthongs /oi/, /ou/	Variant Vowel /ô/; Diphthongs /oi/, /ou/

Teacher-Led Instruction

Differentiated Reading
Leveled Readers
- *The Bill of Rights*, T60–T61
- *The Bill of Rights*, T70–T71
- *The Bill of Rights*, T76–T77

Differentiated Skills Practice
Approaching Level
Phonics/Decoding, T64
- Decode Words with Variant Vowel /ô/ and Diphthongs /oi/, /ou/
- Practice Words with Variant Vowel /ô/ and Diphthongs /oi/, /ou/

Vocabulary, T66
- Review High-Frequency Words
- Review Academic Vocabulary
Fluency, T68
- Accuracy and Rate
Comprehension, T68–T69
- Text Structure: Problem and Solution
- Self-Selected Reading

SMALL GROUP

Independent/Collaborative Work   See pages T3I–T3J.

Reading
Comprehension
- Expository Text
- Text Structure: Problem and Solution
- Reread
Fluency
Independent Reading

Phonics/Word Study
Phonics/Decoding
- Variant Vowel /ô/; Diphthongs /oi/, /ou/
Vocabulary
- Context Clues

Writing
Extended Writing 1: Expository Writing
Self-Selected Writing
Grammar
- Kinds of Nouns
Spelling
- Variant Vowel /ô/; Diphthongs /oi/, /ou/
Handwriting

ACADEMIC VOCABULARY
committees, convention, debate, proposal, representatives, resolve, situation, union

SPELLING
joint, foul, coil, hoist, stout, dawdle, mouthful, counter, brought, bawl, fountain, sprawls, douse, clause, sprouts, cautious, turmoil, scrawny, foundation, turquoise

Review *work, thirst, squirm*
Challenge *buoyant, renown*
See pages T280–T281 for Differentiated Spelling Lists.

 LESSON 3   **LESSON 4**   **LESSON 5**

Reading

Anchor Text, T28–T45	**Anchor Text, T28–T45**	**Anchor Text, T28–T45**
Read *Who Wrote the U.S. Constitution?* Take Notes About Text	Read *Who Wrote the U.S. Constitution?* Take Notes About Text	Reread *Who Wrote the U.S. Constitution?*
Expand Vocabulary, T59	**Expand Vocabulary, T59**	**Expand Vocabulary, T59**

Writing

Extended Writing 1, T230–T231	**Extended Writing 1, T232–T233**	**Extended Writing 1, T234–T235**
Analyze the Rubric	Central Idea	Analyze the Student Model

Writing Lesson Bank: Craft Minilessons, T266–T269

Teacher and Peer Conferences

Grammar Lesson Bank, T271	**Grammar Lesson Bank, T271**	**Grammar Lesson Bank, T271**
Kinds of Nouns Talk About It	Kinds of Nouns Talk About It	Kinds of Nouns Talk About It
Spelling Lesson Bank, T281 Variant Vowel /ô/; Diphthongs /oi/, /ou/	**Spelling Lesson Bank, T281** Variant Vowel /ô/; Diphthongs /oi/, /ou/	**Spelling Lesson Bank, T281** Variant Vowel /ô/; Diphthongs /oi/, /ou/

● **On Level**
Vocabulary, T74
• Review Academic Vocabulary
• Context Clues
Comprehension, T75
• Review Problem and Solution
• Self-Selected Reading

● **Beyond Level**
Vocabulary, T80
• Review Domain-Specific Words
• Context Clues
Comprehension, T81
• Review Problem and Solution
• Self-Selected Reading ⭐ **GIFTED and TALENTED**

 ● **English Language Learners**
See ELL Small Group Guide, pp. 48–59

Content Area Connections

Content Area Reading
• Science, Social Studies, and the Arts
Research and Inquiry
• Founders Solve Problems
Inquiry Space
• Options for Project-Based Learning

 ● **English Language Learners**
See ELL Small Group Guide, pp. 48–59

Week 2 Planner

Customize your own lesson plans at
my.mheducation.com

LESSON 6

LESSON 7

**60+ mins** Reading **Suggested Daily Time**

Reading

READING LESSON GOALS

- I can read and understand expository text
- I can use text evidence to respond to expository text
- I know what good problem solvers do.

▶ **SMALL GROUP OPTIONS**
The designated lessons can be taught in small groups. To determine how to differentiate instruction for small groups, use Formative Assessment and Data Dashboard.

30+ mins Writing **Suggested Daily Time**

WRITING LESSON GOALS

I can write an expository essay.

Lesson 6	Lesson 7
Anchor Text, T28–T45 ▶ Reread *Who Wrote the U.S. Constitution?* ▶ **Respond to Reading, T46–T47** **Expand Vocabulary, T58**	**Paired Selection, T48–T51** Read "Wordsmiths" **Expand Vocabulary, T58**

Writing

Lesson 6	Lesson 7
Extended Writing 1, T236–T237 Analyze the Student Model	**Extended Writing 1, T236–T237** Analyze the Student Model
▶ **Writing Lesson Bank: Craft Minilessons, T266–T269**	
Teacher and Peer Conferences	
Grammar Lesson Bank, T272 Singular and Plural Nouns Talk About It	**Grammar Lesson Bank, T272** Singular and Plural Nouns Talk About It
Spelling Lesson Bank, T282 Plurals	▶ **Spelling Lesson Bank, T282** Plurals

Teacher-Led Instruction

Differentiated Reading
Differentiated Genre Passages
- ● "Secret Help from Spain," T62–T63
- ● "Secret Help from Spain," T72–T73
- ● "Secret Help from Spain," T78–T79

Differentiated Skills Practice
● **Approaching Level**
Phonics/Decoding, T65
- Decode Plurals 🔁2
- Practice Plurals

Vocabulary, T67
- Identify Related Words
- Context Clues

Fluency, T68
- Accuracy and Expression 🔁2

Comprehension, T69
- Review Problem and Solution
- Self-Selected Reading

SMALL GROUP

Independent/Collaborative Work See pages T3I–T3J.

Reading
Comprehension
- Expository text
- Text Structure: Problem and Solution
- Reread

Fluency
Independent Reading

Phonics/Word Study
Phonics/Decoding
- Plurals

Vocabulary
- Context Clues

Writing
Extended Writing 1: Expository Writing
Self-Selected Writing
Grammar
- Singular and Plural Nouns

Spelling
- Plurals

Handwriting

ACADEMIC VOCABULARY
committees, convention, debate, proposal, representatives, resolve, situation, union

SPELLING
rattlers, fangs, countries, liberties, potatoes, rodeos, taxes, reptiles, surroundings, beliefs, difficulties, batches, abilities, lashes, identities, losses, possibilities, notches, zeroes, eddies

Review *brought, counter, coil*
Challenge *mangoes, sinews*
See pages T282–T283 for Differentiated Spelling Lists.

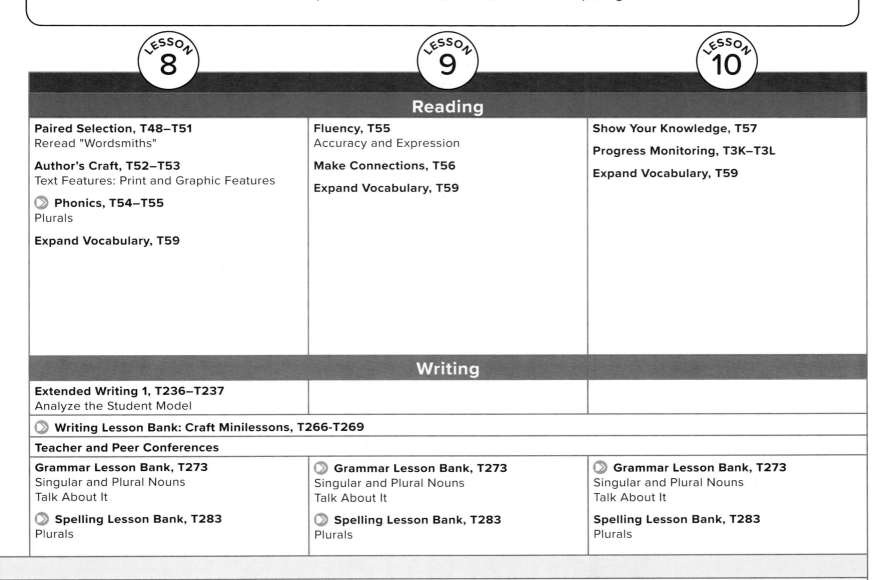

LESSON 8 / LESSON 9 / LESSON 10

Reading

LESSON 8

Paired Selection, T48–T51
Reread "Wordsmiths"

Author's Craft, T52–T53
Text Features: Print and Graphic Features

Phonics, T54–T55
Plurals

Expand Vocabulary, T59

LESSON 9

Fluency, T55
Accuracy and Expression

Make Connections, T56

Expand Vocabulary, T59

LESSON 10

Show Your Knowledge, T57

Progress Monitoring, T3K–T3L

Expand Vocabulary, T59

Writing

LESSON 8

Extended Writing 1, T236–T237
Analyze the Student Model

Writing Lesson Bank: Craft Minilessons, T266-T269

Teacher and Peer Conferences

Grammar Lesson Bank, T273
Singular and Plural Nouns
Talk About It

Spelling Lesson Bank, T283
Plurals

LESSON 9

Grammar Lesson Bank, T273
Singular and Plural Nouns
Talk About It

Spelling Lesson Bank, T283
Plurals

LESSON 10

Grammar Lesson Bank, T273
Singular and Plural Nouns
Talk About It

Spelling Lesson Bank, T283
Plurals

On Level
Vocabulary, T74
• Review Academic Vocabulary
• Context Clues
Comprehension, T75
• Review Problem and Solution
• Self-Selected Reading

Beyond Level
Vocabulary, T80
• Review Domain-Specific Words
• Context Clues
Comprehension, T81
• Review Problem and Solution
• Self-Selected Reading 🌟 GIFTED and TALENTED

 English Language Learners
See ELL Small Group Guide, pp. 48–59

Content Area Connections
Content Area Reading
• Science, Social Studies, and the Arts
Research and Inquiry
• Founders Solve Problems
Inquiry Space
• Options for Project-Based Learning

 English Language Learners
See ELL Small Group Guide, pp. 48–59

Independent and Collaborative Work

As you meet with small groups, the rest of the class completes activities and projects that allow them to practice and apply the skills they have been working on.

Student Choice and Student Voice

- Print the My Independent Work blackline master and review it with students. Identify the "Must Do" activities.
- Have students choose additional activities that provide the practice they need.
- Remind students to reflect on their learning each day.

My Independent Work BLM

Reading

Independent Reading Texts

Students can choose a Center Activity Card to use while they read independently.

B.E.S.T. Literature Library
Shh! We're Writing the Constitution
Genre: Narrative Nonfiction
Lexile: 950L
Support students' independent reading using the
B.E.S.T. Literature Library lesson.

Classroom Library
The Constitution of the United States
Genre: Expository Text
Lexile: 650L

If You Lived at the Time of the American Revolution
Genre: Expository Text
Lexile: 860L

Unit Bibliography
Have students self-select independent reading texts about the Revolutionary War era.

Leveled Texts Online
- Additional Leveled Readers in the **Leveled Reader Library Online** allow for flexibility.
- Six leveled sets of **Differentiated Genre Passages** in diverse genres are available.
- **Differentiated Texts** offer ELL students more passages at different proficiency levels.

Additional Literature
Literature Anthology
The Boy Who Drew Birds, pp. 144–154
Genre: Biography

"Daedalus and Icarus," pp. 158–161
Genre: Myth

Center Activity Cards

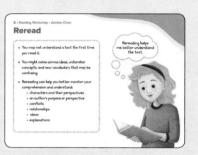

Reread Card 2

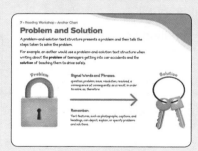

Problem and Solution Card 7

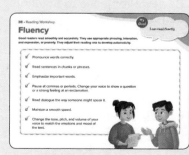

Fluency Card 38

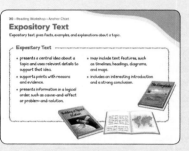

Expository Text Card 30

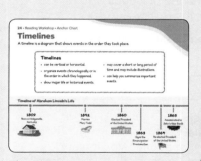

Timelines
Card 24

Digital Activities

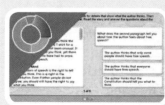

Comprehension

Phonics/Word Study

Center Activity Cards

Variant Vowels and Diphthongs
Card 93

Plurals Card 97

Context Clues Card 71

Practice Book BLMs

Phonics: pages 67–67B, 70, 79–79B, 82

Vocabulary: pages 71–72, 83–84

Digital Activities

Phonics

Vocabulary

Writing

Center Activity Cards

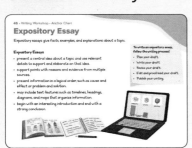

Expository Essay Card 45

Central Idea Card 54

Self-Selected Writing

Share the following prompts.
- What was living in the American colonies like? Write from a colonist's perspective.
- What new law would you like to see passed? Explain.
- Write about a problem in your community and suggest a solution.
- If you could speak with anyone from the past, whom would it be? What would you ask?
- Think about an object you lost. Why was it important to you?

Extended Writing

Have students continue developing their **expository essays**.

Practice Book BLMs

Grammar: pages 61–65, 73–77
Spelling: pages 66–70, 78–82
Handwriting: pages 361–396

Digital Activities

Grammar

Spelling

Content Area Connections

Content Area Reading Blackline Masters
- Additional texts related to Science, Social Studies, and the Arts

Research and Inquiry
- Founders Solve Problems

Inquiry Space
- Choose an activity

Progress Monitoring
Moving Toward Mastery

FORMATIVE ASSESSMENT

❯ STUDENT CHECK-IN

✓ CHECK FOR SUCCESS

For ongoing formative assessment, use students' self-assessments at the end of each lesson along with your own observations.

Assessing skills along the way . . .

SKILLS	HOW ASSESSED	
Comprehension Vocabulary	Digital Activities, Rubrics	
Text-Based Writing	Reading/Writing Companion: Respond to Reading	
Grammar, Mechanics, Phonics, Spelling	Practice Book, Digital Activities including word sorts	
Listening/Presenting/Research	Checklists	
Oral Reading Fluency (ORF) Fluency Goal: 111–131 words correct per minute (WCPM) Accuracy Rate Goal: 95% or higher	Fluency Assessment	

At the end of the text set . . .

SKILLS	HOW ASSESSED	
Text Features: Headings and Timelines **Text Structure: Problem and Solution** **Text Features: Print and Graphic Features**	Progress Monitoring	
Context Clues		

Making the Most of Assessment Results

Make data-based grouping decisions by using the following reports to verify assessment results. For additional student support options refer to the reteaching and enrichment opportunities.

ONLINE ASSESSMENT CENTER
- *Gradebook*

DATA DASHBOARD
- *Recommendations Report*
- *Activity Report*
- *Skills Report*
- *Progress Report*
- *Grade Card Report*

 Assign practice pages online for auto-grading.

Reteaching Opportunities with Intervention Online PDFs

TIER 2

IF STUDENTS SCORE . . .	THEN ASSIGN . . .
below 70% in **comprehension** . . .	lessons 140 and 141 on Headings and Timelines in **Comprehension PDF,** lessons 83–84 on Problem and Solution in **Comprehension PDF,** and/or lessons 138 and 139 on Headings and Subheadings and Print Features in **Comprehension PDF**
below 70% in **vocabulary** . . .	lesson 87 on Using Definition and Restatement Clues in **Vocabulary PDF**
102–110 WCPM in **fluency** . . .	lessons from Section 1 or 7–10 of **Fluency PDF**
0–101 WCPM in **fluency** . . .	lessons from Sections 2–6 of **Fluency PDF**

Use the **Phonics/Word Study PDF** *and* **Foundational Skills Kit** *for additional reteaching opportunities.*
Use the **Foundational Skills Kit** *for students who need support with phonemic awareness and other early literacy skills.*

Enrichment Opportunities

Beyond Level small group lessons and resources include suggestions for additional activities in these areas to extend learning opportunities for gifted and talented students:

- *Leveled Readers*
- *Genre Passages*
- *Vocabulary*

- *Comprehension*
- *Leveled Reader Library Online*
- *Center Activity Cards*

OBJECTIVES

Engage effectively in a range of collaborative discussions (one-on-one, in groups, and teacher-led) with diverse partners, building on others' ideas and expressing their own clearly.

Follow agreed-upon rules for discussions and carry out assigned roles.

Pose and respond to specific questions by making comments that contribute to the discussion and elaborate on the remarks of others.

Build background knowledge on solving a problem.

ELA ACADEMIC LANGUAGE

• *problem, solution, discussion*
• Cognates: *problema, solución, discusión*

DIGITAL TOOLS

Show the image during class discussion.

Discuss Concept

Watch Video

VOCABULARY

commander-in-chief (*el comandante en jefe*) person in charge of a country's armed forces

flag (*bandera*) patterned fabric representing a nation or state

seamstress (*costurera*) a woman who sews; tailor

solution (*solución*) a way to solve or fix a problem

design (*diseño*) pattern

 10 mins

Build Knowledge

 MULTIMODAL

 Essential Question

What do good problem solvers do?

Read the Essential Question on **Reading/Writing Companion** page 122. Tell students that they will read expository texts that focus on how people debate, or discuss, problems and build knowledge about what good problem solvers do. They will use words to read, write, and talk about how people resolve their problems.

Watch the Video Play the video without sound first. Have partners narrate what they see. Then replay the video with sound as students listen.

Talk About the Video Have partners discuss how people resolve differences.

Write About the Video Have students add their ideas to their Build Knowledge pages of their reader's notebook.

 Anchor Chart Begin a Build Knowledge anchor chart. Write the Essential Question at the top of the chart. Have volunteers share what they learned about what good problem solvers do and record their ideas. Students will add to the anchor chart after they read each text.

Build Knowledge

Discuss the illustration with students. Point out that George Washington and Betsy Ross are discussing the design of the first flag for the American colonies. Ask: *What solutions might they be discussing to represent the colonies with a flag?* Have students discuss in pairs or groups.

Build Vocabulary

Model using the graphic organizer to write new words related to problem solving. Have partners continue the discussion and add the organizer and new words to their reader's notebook. Students will add words to the Build Knowledge pages in their notebook throughout the text set.

 Collaborative Conversations

Take Turns Talking As students engage in partner, small-group, and whole-class discussions, encourage them to follow discussion rules by taking turns speaking. Remind students to

• wait for others to finish before they speak and to not speak over them.

• quietly raise a hand to let others know they would like a turn to speak.

• ask others in the group to share their opinions.

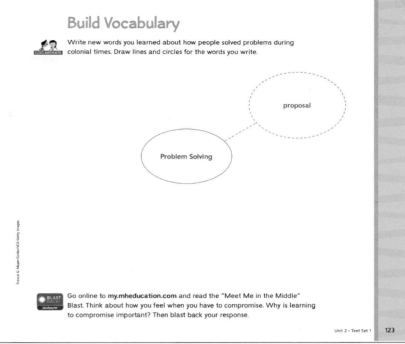

Build Knowledge

? Essential Question
What do good problem solvers do?

Build Vocabulary

Write new words you learned about how people solved problems during colonial times. Draw lines and circles for the words you write.

proposal

Problem Solving

Go online to **my.mheducation.com** and read the "Meet Me in the Middle" Blast. Think about how you feel when you have to compromise. Why is learning to compromise important? Then blast back your response.

122 Unit 2 · Text Set 1   Unit 2 · Text Set 1 123

Reading/Writing Companion, pp. 122–123

 Share the "Meet Me in the Middle" Blast assignment with students. Point out that you will discuss their responses about solutions in the Make Connections lesson at the end of this text set.

English Language Learners

Use the following scaffolds to build knowledge and vocabulary. Teach the ELL Vocabulary, as needed.

Beginning
Describe the picture with students. Say: *Washington and Ross are discussing the design of the flag. The problem is they want the design to represent the colonies. What solutions might they be discussing?* Guide them to the stars and stripes and help partners respond: One solution might be to use stars/stripes for the colonies.

Intermediate
Use the picture to point out that Washington and Ross are discussing the design of the first flag for the colonies. Say: *They want the design to represent the colonies. What solutions might they be discussing?* Guide them to the stars and stripes and have partners respond: One solution might be to use stars/stripes to represent the colonies.

Advanced/Advanced High
Describe what Washington and Ross are discussing in the picture with students. Then have partners discuss what solutions Washington and Ross might be discussing and complete the graphic organizer.

NEWCOMERS
To help students develop oral language and build vocabulary, use **Newcomer Cards 15–19** and the accompanying materials in the **Newcomer Teacher's Guide**. For thematic connection, use **Newcomer Cards 15 and 23** with the accompanying materials.

MY GOALS ROUTINE

What I Know Now

Read Goals Have students read the goals on Reading/Writing Companion page 124.

Reflect Review the key. Ask students to reflect on each goal and fill in the bars to show what they know now. Explain they will fill in the bars on page 125 at the end of the text set to show their progress.

LESSON 1

We can actively listen to learn how people solve problems.

OBJECTIVES

Explain the relationships or interactions between two or more individuals, events, ideas, or concepts in a historical, scientific, or technical text based on specific information in the text.

Summarize a written text read aloud or information presented in diverse media and formats, including visually, quantitatively, and orally.

Determine or clarify the meaning of unknown and multiple-meaning words and phrases based on grade 5 reading and content, choosing flexibly from a range of strategies.

Use context as a clue to the meaning of a word or phrase.

Listen for a purpose.

Identify characteristics of expository text.

ELA ACADEMIC LANGUAGE

• *expository text, comprehension*

• Cognates: *texto expositivo, comprensión*

DIGITAL TOOLS

Read or play the Interactive Read Aloud.

Interactive Read Aloud

 STUDENT CHECK-IN

Have partners discuss how the Haudenosaunee Confederacy helped resolve differences. Ask them to reflect using the Check-In routine.

---

 10 mins # Interactive Read Aloud

Connect to Concept: Reaching a Compromise

Tell students that people in challenging situations must often compromise to be successful or to get what they want or need. Let students know that you will be reading aloud an expository text passage that shows how Native American tribes worked together to develop a system of government called the Haudenosaunee Confederacy.

Preview Expository Text

Anchor Chart Explain that the text you will read aloud is expository text. Start an Expository Text anchor chart and ask students to add characteristics of the genre. Explain that students may want to add characteristics to the chart as they read more expository texts. Discuss the features of expository text:

- provides facts, examples, and explanations about a topic, unlike fiction where details are not real
- may include text features such as headings and timelines
- presents information in a logical order
- uses certain text structures to organize information

Ask students to think about other texts they have read aloud or they have read independently that were expository text.

Read and Respond

Read the text aloud to students. Then reread it using the Teacher Think Alouds and Student Think Alongs on page T7 to build knowledge and model comprehension and the vocabulary strategy, Context Clues.

Summarize Have students determine the central idea and relevant details in "The Haudenosaunee Confederacy." Then have them summarize the information in their own words to enhance their comprehension.

 ## Build Knowledge: Make Connections

Talk About the Text Have partners discuss one way the Haudenosaunee Confederacy resolved differences between Native American tribes.

Write About the Text Have students add their ideas to their Build Knowledge pages of their reader's notebook.

Anchor Chart Record any new ideas on the Build Knowledge anchor chart.

Add to the Vocabulary List Have students write down any words they learned about problem solving in their reader's notebook.

The Haudenosaunee Confederacy

A Native American Union

The Iroquois or Haudenosaunee (pronounced hoe-dee-no-SHOW-nee) Confederacy, also called the Iroquois League, Six Nations, is the 1722 union of six Native American tribes: the Mohawk, Seneca, Onondaga, Oneida, Cayuga, and Tuscarora. In 1722, the Tuscarora joined the league and the Five Nations became Six Nations. The history of the League dates further back than 1722, probably to the late 1500s or early 1600s. For millennia, these Native nations lived in their ancestral homelands, part of which is now upstate New York. The confederacy was created to establish peace among the tribes and to protect themselves from enemies. Members lived according to a constitution called the Great Law of Peace. ∘∘**1**

How Did It Work?

The Haudenosaunee Confederacy was a representative democracy. Each nation chose people to represent them in the confederacy. Clan mothers chose the chiefs and leaders. Each representative had one vote. The vote on any issue had to be agreed upon by every representative. If it wasn't, the representatives kept talking and voting until they reached a compromise. During the meetings, traditions and customs were strictly followed. For example, a wampum belt was a very important part of the meetings. A wampum is a shell bead used to make these woven belts. A representative usually held the belt to symbolize the importance of his words. At the meetings, laws and decisions that were agreed upon became a part of the Great Law of Peace, also called the Great Binding Law. ∘∘**2**

How Successful Was the Haudenosaunee Confederacy?

The confederacy was highly successful in governing the six tribes. There was peace and unity among the tribes. The American colonists became aware of this form of government and the Great Law of Peace, since they often traded with members of the six tribes. The Iroquois Confederacy still exists today. Its tradition of a representational democracy has influenced more than its own members. ∘∘**3**

1∘∘ **Teacher Think Aloud**

Rereading helps me figure out words I may not know. I'm not sure what a *confederacy* is. I will reread and look for context clues to help me. I see that the Haudenosaunee Confederacy is made up of many groups of Native Americans. This leads me to believe that a *confederacy* must be a group formed by several other groups.

Student Think Along

Which word(s) did you have a hard time understanding? Listen for context clues as I reread the first paragraph. Work with a partner to determine the word's meaning.

2∘∘ **Teacher Think Aloud**

Rereading helps me understand something I may have missed. I'm not sure what the Haudenosaunee Confederacy did to solve problems. As I reread, I see that the representatives had to keep talking and voting until they reached a compromise. The decisions they agreed upon became part of the Great Law of Peace.

Student Think Along

How is the Haudenosaunee Confederacy a representative democracy? Listen as I reread the paragraph. Nod when you hear the answer. Then share with a partner.

3∘∘ **Teacher Think Aloud**

I can reread the last section to review an example of how the Haudenosaunee Confederacy were good problem solvers. The confederacy promoted peace and unity amongst the six tribes. This had an impact on early American colonists who traded with them.

Student Think Along

Think about the impact of the Haudenosaunee Confederacy. What does the author mean by "its tradition of a representational democracy has influenced more than its own members"? Turn and discuss with a partner.

"Creating a Nation"

Lexile 690L

LEARNING GOALS

We can read and understand expository text.

OBJECTIVES

Quote accurately from a text when explaining what the text says explicitly and when drawing inferences from the text.

Compare and contrast the overall structure (e.g., chronology, comparison, cause/effect, problem/solution) of events, ideas, concepts, or information in two or more texts.

Use context to confirm or self-correct word recognition and understanding, rereading as necessary.

Determine or clarify the meaning of unknown and multiple-meaning words and phrases, choosing flexibly from a range of strategies.

Use context (e.g., cause/ effect relationships and comparisons in text) as a clue to the meaning of a word or phrase.

🌐 Identify the issues that led to the creation of the U.S. Constitution, including the weaknesses of the Articles of Confederation.

Close Reading Routine

Read DOK 1–2

- Identify important ideas and details.
- Take notes and summarize.
- Use **ACT** prompts as needed.

Reread DOK 2–3

- Analyze the text, craft, and structure.
- Use the **Reread minilessons** and **prompts**.

Integrate DOK 3–4

- Integrate knowledge and ideas.
- Make text-to-text connections.
- Use the Integrate lesson.
- Complete the Show Your Knowledge task.
- Inspire action.

Read

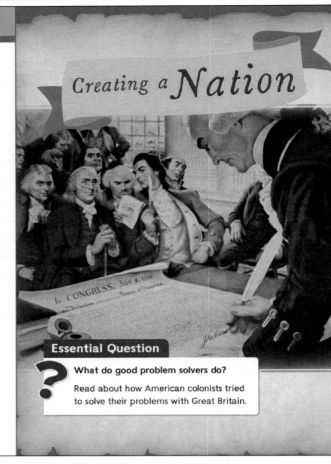

SHARED READ

My Goal: I can read and understand expository text.

Creating a Nation

TAKE NOTES

As you read, make note of interesting words and important information.

Essential Question

What do good problem solvers do?

Read about how American colonists tried to solve their problems with Great Britain.

126 Unit 2 · Text Set 1

Reading/Writing Companion, pp. 126–127

Set a Purpose Before they begin, have students think about the Essential Question, what they know about early American history, and then set a purpose for reading. As students read they should use the left column of page 126 to note their questions, list words they would like to learn, and identify key details from the text.

Focus on the **Read** prompts now. For additional support, use the extra prompts not included in the **Reading/Writing Companion**. Use the **Reread** prompts during the Craft and Structure lesson on pages T20–T21. Consider preteaching vocabulary to some students.

⟩ DIFFERENTIATED READING

Approaching Level Elicit note-taking techniques and interesting words. Complete all Read prompts with the group.

On Level Have partners do the Read prompts before you meet.

Beyond Level Discuss how partners responded to the Read prompts. Analyze how the timeline supports the prompts.

🎧 **English Language Learners** Preteach the vocabulary. Have Beginning and Early-Intermediate ELLs listen to the selection summary, available in multiple languages, and use the **Scaffolded Shared Read**. See also **ELL Small Group Guide**.

Taxes and Protests

In 1765, King George III of Great Britain needed money to rule his empire. How could he raise it? With taxes! Parliament, the law-making branch of the British government, passed a new tax called the Stamp Act. Every piece of paper sold in the American colonies had to carry a special stamp. Want to buy a newspaper? Stamp! Pay the tax.

To most colonists, the Stamp Act was unfair. The citizens of Great Britain had the right to choose **representatives** to speak for them in Parliament. Although British citizens, the colonists had no such right. How could Parliament tax them if they had no voice in government?

The colonists held protests against the Stamp Act. Consequently, it was repealed, or canceled. But more taxes followed. Women protested a tax on cloth imported from Britain. How? They wove their own cloth at home.

Boston Tea Party: Colonists throw tea into the harbor.

Before long, the **situation** grew worse. In 1770, British soldiers fired into a disorderly crowd in Boston. Five colonists died. This tragedy is known as the Boston Massacre.

By 1773, most taxes had been repealed, or canceled, except the one on tea. One night, colonists held a protest called the Boston Tea Party. Dressed in disguise, they slipped onto three British ships in Boston Harbor and then they tossed the ships' cargo—tea—overboard.

EXPOSITORY TEXT

FIND TEXT EVIDENCE 🔍

Read

Paragraphs 1–2
Problem and Solution
Underline the problem King George III faced. Write it here.

King George III needed money to rule

his empire.

Circle the king's solution to the problem. Discuss why the colonists thought the Stamp Act was unfair.

It was unfair because the colonists had

no voice in government.

Paragraphs 3–5
Reread
Draw a box around text evidence that tells how the colonists reacted to taxes imposed by the British.

Reread
Author's Craft
How does the author use text structure to demonstrate the relationship between the British and the colonists?

Unit 2 · Text Set 1   127

Check for Understanding DOK 2

Page 127: Monitor students' understanding of British Parliament, the importance of government representatives, and the act of repealing a law. Ask: *Why did the colonists believe that they had no voice in government? What did they do about it?* (The colonists felt voiceless because although they were British citizens, they could not choose anyone in government to speak for them against laws such as the Stamp Act. They fought to have the law overturned.) To show how far-reaching the Stamp Act's effects were, have students brainstorm a list of paper items that might have been taxed. (ships' papers, legal documents, licenses, and playing cards)

ELL Spotlight on Language

Page 127, Paragraph 2 Check students' understanding of the words *right* and *voice*. Point out that these words have more than one meaning. *A* right *is also something a person is allowed to do. People have rights because of a law or because having this right is fair.* Provide one example of a right students have at school. Then help pairs brainstorm other rights: We have the right to _____. Point to the last sentence in the paragraph. Say: Voice *can mean a person's right to vote* (cognate: *votar*). The colonists did not have the right to vote.

Text Structure: Problem and Solution DOK 1

Paragraphs 1–2: *Why did King George III raise taxes? Why did the colonists think the Stamp Act was unfair?*

Think Aloud I read that in 1765, Parliament passed a tax on paper because King George III needed money to rule his empire. This action must have upset the colonists. It seemed unfair because they were being taxed but had no representation in Parliament. Have students predict how the colonists might respond to being taxed.

Reread DOK 1

Paragraphs 3–5: *How did the colonists react to taxes imposed by the British?*

Think Aloud I will look for text evidence about this question. I read in the third paragraph that the colonists responded to this problem by holding protests and not buying items from Britain that were taxed, such as cloth. Later I read that in 1773, they staged a protest called the Boston Tea Party and dumped all of the recently imported tea into Boston Harbor. Have students confirm or revise the predictions they made after reading the first two paragraphs.

Text Structure: Problem and Solution DOK 1

Paragraph 1: Read the first five lines. Ask: *What were the "Intolerable Acts?"* (King George's harsh punishments on the colonists in response to the Boston Tea Party, such as closing down the port and banning town meetings) Discuss why these two acts would be particularly harmful to the citizens of Boston.

Check for Understanding DOK 2

Paragraphs 1–2: Finish reading the first paragraph. Ask: *How did the colonists differ in their response to the "Intolerable Acts"?* Help students use text evidence. (The text says some colonists wanted peace while others wanted to fight for independence. They disagreed on how to solve their problems with Great Britain.) Help students use this evidence and personal experience to make an inference about the mood in the colonies. (When people disagree, it creates tension. This idea suggests that the colonists were tense or worried.)

Context Clues DOK 2

Paragraph 2: Read the second paragraph. Ask: *Which words help us determine the meaning of* delegates? (The first sentence says that "representatives from each colony" were asked to attend the convention. This makes me think *delegates* are people who represent their colonies.) Have students generate other forms of the word *delegates*. (delegate, delegation, delegated)

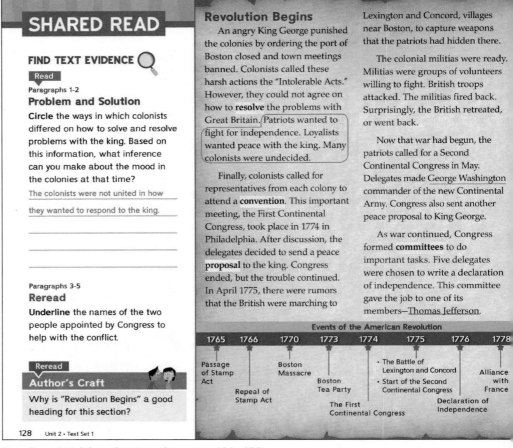

Reading/Writing Companion, pp. 128–129

Reread DOK 1

Paragraphs 3–5: Read the last three paragraphs. Ask: *What role did Congress assign to George Washington? Thomas Jefferson?* (Congress appointed, or made, George Washington commander of the Continental Army. Thomas Jefferson was appointed to write the Declaration of Independence.) Discuss with students what qualities they think these men possessed that would lead Congress to appoint them to such important roles.

 Access Complex Text

Prior Knowledge

Explain that prior to the Revolutionary War and just after it began, the American colonies did not have an official military. Most of the battles were fought by militia. These militia were often ordinary citizens who came from all kinds of backgrounds. It was not until after two months of fighting that the Continental Army was formed. The Continental Army became the first arm of the military.

Ask: *Why did the colonies officially form a military?* Help students make inferences to grasp that having an organized military made it easier to train, plan, and fight.

Independence Declared

Jefferson knew he had to convince many colonists of the need for independence. As a result, he combined a variety of ideas to make his case. Individuals, he explained, had certain rights. These included life, liberty, and the pursuit of happiness. Governments were created to protect those (rights). Instead, King George had taken away colonists' rights and (freedoms.) Therefore, the colonies had to separate from Britain.

Congress went on to **debate** Jefferson's points. As a result, his strong words against slavery were deleted. There were other compromises, too. But on July 4, 1776, Congress approved the Declaration of Independence. A nation was born. Washington's army fought on. Finally, in 1778, France joined the fight on America's side.

This was a turning point. In 1781, British troops surrendered in the war's last major battle. That year, Congress approved the Articles of Confederation. This document outlined a government for the former colonies. The United States was created as a confederation, or a **union**, of separate states. The Articles gave the states, rather than a central government, the power to make most decisions.

In 1783, King George finally recognized the nation's independence. By then, though, the United States government clearly wasn't working very well. The states often didn't agree with one another.

The revolution had ended. The work of shaping a government had just started. It would continue with a Constitutional Convention in 1787.

Summarize

Use your notes and the timeline to orally summarize important events and details in "Creating a Nation."

1781	1783
· Last major battle of the war	
· Approval of the Articles of Confederation	King George recognizes independence of United States

---

EXPOSITORY TEXT

FIND TEXT EVIDENCE 🔍

Read

Paragraphs 1–5
Context Clues

Circle context clues that help you determine the meaning of *liberty*.

Timeline

Look at the timeline. Did the Boston Tea Party take place before the repeal of the Stamp Act or after?

after the repeal of the Stamp Act

_____

_____

_____

_____

_____

Reread

Author's Craft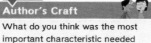

What do you think was the most important characteristic needed among the men responsible for creating the Declaration of Independence? Explain your answer.

Unit 2 · Text Set 1   129

Context Clues DOK 2

Paragraphs 1–4: Read the first paragraph. Point out the word *liberty*. Ask: *Which words can help us determine the meaning of* liberty? (Words such as *rights* and *freedom* are used in surrounding text. *Rights* is used three times, so it must be important.) **Discuss the meaning of the word** *liberty*. (*Liberty* must mean "freedom" because having the right to do something means a person is free.)

Organization

Explain that the author organized the text by presenting problems and solutions. Ask: *What do the headings in the text tell you about the problem the colonists had and how it was solved?* (The problem was taxes. The solution was revolution and declaring independence.)

Text Features: Timeline DOK 2

Timeline: Remind students that authors often use different types of text features in expository texts. Ask: *Why did the author include the timeline?* (The timeline helps readers see the order of events that led to American independence.) *How does the timeline support the problem-and-solution text structure?* (Problems and solutions are represented by events on the timeline such as the Stamp Act and its repeal.)

Summarize DOK 2

Analytical Writing **Quick Write** After their initial read, have partners summarize the selection orally using their notes. Then have them write a summary in their reader's notebook. Remind them only to include important events. Students may decide to digitally record presentations of summaries.

⟮ELL⟯ Spotlight on Language

Page 129, Paragraph 1 Help students understand how pronouns take the place of nouns. As you mention each noun and pronoun, point to its location in the text: *The writer mentions Jefferson in the first sentence. Which words does the writer use in the second sentence to refer back to Jefferson?* (he/his) Have students find a plural pronoun that replaces the word *rights* in the same paragraph: *Which word replaces* rights? (These)

FORMATIVE ASSESSMENT

⟩ STUDENT CHECK-IN

Have partners share their summaries from Reading/ Writing Companion page 129. Ask them to reflect using the Check-In routine.

LESSON **1**

- We can use new vocabulary words to read and understand expository text.
- We can use context clues to figure out the meaning of unknown words.

OBJECTIVES

Determine the meaning of general academic and domain-specific words and phrases in a text relevant to a grade 5 topic or subject area.

Use context (e.g., cause/effect relationships and comparisons in text) as a clue to the meaning of a word or phrase.

ELA ACADEMIC LANGUAGE

- *context, define, restatement*
- Cognates: *contexto, definir*

DIGITAL TOOLS

Visual Vocabulary Cards

TEACH IN SMALL GROUP

Academic Vocabulary

⬤ ⬤ **Approaching Level** and **ELL** Preteach the words before beginning the Shared Read.

⬤ **On Level** Have students look up each word in the online **Visual Glossary**.

⬤ **Beyond Level** Have pairs write a context sentence for each word.

Reread

 10 mins

Academic Vocabulary

 MULTIMODAL

Use the routine on the **Visual Vocabulary Cards** to introduce each word.

Committees are groups of people chosen to do certain work.
Cognate: *comités*

A **convention** is a meeting for a specific purpose.

Debate means "to argue or discuss."
Cognate: *debatir*

A **proposal** is a plan or suggestion.
Cognate: *propuesta*

Representatives are people chosen to speak or act for others.
Cognate: *representantes*

When you **resolve** something, you make a choice about how to solve a problem. **Cognate:** *resolver*

A **situation** is a condition or state of affairs.
Cognate: *situación*

A **union** is formed by joining two or more people or things together.
Cognate: *unión*

Encourage students to use their newly acquired vocabulary in their discussions and written responses about the texts in this text set.

 10 mins

Context Clues

1 **Explain**

 Writers sometimes **define** or **restate** the meaning of an unknown word by using commas and clue words, such as synonyms. They may put a definition in parentheses after a word or define it in a nearby sentence. Have volunteers add to the Context Clues anchor chart.

2 **Model**

In the third paragraph on **Reading/Writing Companion** page 127, model locating the word *repealed* and the comma that follows it. Then model using the restatement context clue, "or canceled," to find the meaning of *repealed*. Explain that *canceled* is a synonym of *repealed*.

 COLLABORATE

3 **Guided Practice**

Help student pairs determine the meanings of *Parliament* on page 127 and *retreated* on page 128. Guide them as they circle the context clues. Discuss how the clues help them determine meanings.

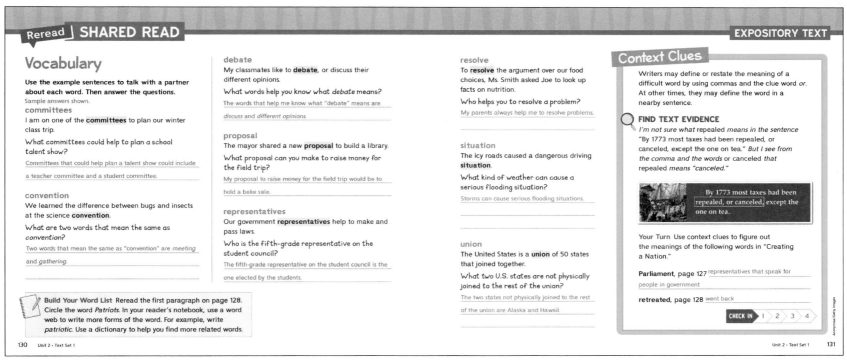

Reading/Writing Companion, pp. 130–131

 # English Language Learners

Use the following scaffolds with **Guided Practice**. For small group support, see the **ELL Small Group Guide**.

Beginning

Read the third paragraph on **Reading/Writing Companion** page 128 with students. Have them look at the comma after the word *retreated*. Explain that a comma and the word *or* sometimes introduce a definition. *What does* retreated *mean?* (went back) *How do you know?* The phrase "or went back" is a context clue. It tells what retreated means.

Intermediate

Have partners read the first paragraph on **Reading/Writing Companion** page 127. Explain that commas can signal a definition context clue. *What is Parliament?* Parliament is the law-making branch of the British government. Have pairs discuss how they found the meaning: I used context clues. The definition appears after the word Parliament. There are commas before and after the definition. Repeat for *retreated.*

Advanced/Advanced High

Have partners read the first paragraph on page 127 to find the meaning of *Parliament.* Then have them read the third paragraph on page 128 to find the meaning of *retreated.* Have partners discuss how the context clues helped them determine the meanings.

BUILD YOUR WORD LIST

Students might choose *patriots* from page 128. Have them use a dictionary to explore the meaning and find related word forms.

FORMATIVE ASSESSMENT

❯ STUDENT CHECK-IN

Academic Vocabulary Ask partners to share two answers from Reading/Writing Companion pages 130–131.

Context Clues Ask partners to share their Your Turn responses on page 131.

Have students use the Check-In routine to reflect and fill in the bars.

✓ CHECK FOR SUCCESS

Rubric Use your online rubric to record student progress.

Can students identify and use context clues to determine the meaning of *Parliament* and *retreated*?

❯ **Small Group Instruction**

If No:
● **Approaching** Reteach p. T67

If Yes:
● **On** Review p. T74
● **Beyond** Extend p. T80

LESSON 2

Reread

10 mins

LEARNING GOALS

We can reread to understand expository text.

OBJECTIVES

Quote accurately from a text when explaining what the text says explicitly and when drawing inferences from the text.

Explain different characters' perspectives in a literary text.

Determine two or more central, or main, ideas of a text and explain how they are supported by relevant, or key, details; summarize the text.

Read grade-level text with purpose and understanding.

Reread difficult sections of text to increase understanding.

ELA ACADEMIC LANGUAGE

• reread, expository text

• Cognate: *texto expositivo*

1 Explain

Tell students that expository texts often explore unfamiliar concepts and use new vocabulary. Remind students that they can reread difficult sentences or sections and ask and answer questions in order to monitor and adjust their comprehension.

- When they encounter a difficult section in the text, students should read more slowly and, if necessary, stop and reread that section. They may need to reread it multiple times before the meaning becomes clear.

- Students should pause occasionally to reread and determine what the central, or main, idea might be. Point out that the central idea is not always stated directly in the text; sometimes they will need to use relevant, or key, details to make an inference.

Point out that monitoring their comprehension can help students ensure they understand what they read.

 Anchor Chart Have a volunteer add any additional points about the strategy to the Reread anchor chart.

2 Model

Model how monitoring your comprehension by rereading can help you make an inference about why the British troops began marching on Lexington and Concord. Reread the second paragraph on **Reading/ Writing Companion** page 128 of "Creating a Nation." Explain that rereading the paragraph helps you understand that King George sent British troops after he disagreed with the delegates' proposal.

3 Guided Practice

Direct students to reread the third paragraph under "Revolution Begins" on page 128 to find out how colonists responded to the British troops. Then have them ask and answer questions to recall what the colonists did. Have students reread page 128 to verify their answers. Circulate to make sure that students remain on track. Discuss other sections of "Creating a Nation" that students might have questions about or want to reread.

Reread | SHARED READ

Reread

As you read, you should monitor, or check, your comprehension to make sure you understand the meaning of the text. When you read something that confuses you, you may have to go back and reread an earlier part of the selection. Rereading can help you check your understanding of facts and details in "Creating a Nation."

Quick Tip

The topic sentence in each paragraph can be used to help you monitor your comprehension. As you read, pay attention to how the details in the rest of the paragraph relate to the topic sentence.

🔍 **FIND TEXT EVIDENCE**

When you read the second paragraph of the section "Revolution Begins" on page 128, you may be confused about why the British troops began marching to Lexington and Concord.

Page 128

After discussion, the delegates decided to send a peace **proposal** to the king. Congress ended, but the trouble continued.

When I reread <u>the delegates decided to send a peace proposal to the king. Congress ended, but the trouble continued,</u> I ask myself, "Why did the trouble continue even though the delegates sent a peace plan?" I can make the inference that King George did not agree to the proposal.

Your Turn Reread page 128. Discuss and retell how the patriots responded to the British troops marching to Lexington and Concord. What happened after the British troops attacked? Reread to find the answer.

The patriots fired back after the British attacked. Then, the British retreated.

CHECK IN ⟩ 1 ⟩ 2 ⟩ 3 ⟩ 4 ⟩

132 Unit 2 • Text Set 1

Reading/Writing Companion, p. 132

ⒺⓁⓁ English Language Learners

Use the following scaffolds with **Guided Practice**. For small group support, see the **ELL Small Group Guide.**

Beginning

Review with students how to monitor their comprehension by rereading. Reread sentences 3–5 of paragraph 3 on page 128 with students. Explain to them that *troops* (cognate: *tropas*) means *soldiers* (cognate: *soldados*). Use gestures to clarify the actions such as "fired back" and "retreated." Ask: *What did the militia do?* The militia <u>fired back</u>. Then the British <u>retreated/left/went back</u>.

Intermediate

Review with students how to monitor their comprehension by rereading. Have partners reread paragraph 3 on page 128. Help them describe how the colonists responded to the British troops by asking: *What did the colonial militia do when the British attacked?* The colonial militia <u>fired back</u>. *Then what happened?* The British troops <u>retreated</u>.

Advanced/Advanced High

Have partners read paragraph 3 on page 128. Direct them to describe the colonists' response to the British. Provide guiding questions to help them monitor their comprehension: *What did the militia do? Were they prepared?* Have them cite text evidence to verify their answers.

HABITS OF LEARNING

I am a critical thinker and problem solver.

At times, students may need to reread parts of texts they find difficult. Support the development of this habit of learning by reminding them that rereading is an effective strategy to use when they are clarifying their understanding of complex text.

FORMATIVE ASSESSMENT

❯ **STUDENT CHECK-IN**

Ask partners to share their Your Turn responses on Reading/Writing Companion page 132. Have them use the Check-In routine to reflect and fill in the bars.

✓ **CHECK FOR SUCCESS**

Do students reread sections of expository text they do not understand? Do they monitor their comprehension as needed?

❯ **Small Group Instruction**

If No:

● **Approaching** Reteach p. T60

If Yes:

● **On** Review p. T70

● **Beyond** Extend p. T76

COMPREHENSION STRATEGY **T15**

LESSON 2

LEARNING GOALS

We can use headings and timelines to read and understand expository text.

OBJECTIVES

Explain the relationships or interactions between two or more individuals, events, ideas, or concepts in a historical, scientific, or technical text based on specific information in the text.

Compare and contrast the overall structure (e.g., chronology, comparison, cause/effect, problem/solution) of events, ideas, concepts, or information in two or more texts.

Read grade-level text with purpose and understanding.

Use text features and search tools (e.g. key words, sidebars, hyperlinks) to locate information relevant to a given topic efficiently.

ELA ACADEMIC LANGUAGE

- *expository text, text feature, heading, timeline*
- Cognate: *texto expositivo*

Reread

Text Features: Headings and Timelines

10 mins

1 Explain

Share with students the following key features of expository text.

- Expository text gives facts, examples, and explanations about a topic, such as an important period in history.

- Expository text often includes text features that help readers visualize information presented in the text or that provide additional information about the topic.

- Text features common to expository text include headings, charts, graphs, diagrams, and timelines.

2 Model

Model identifying and using one of the text features on **Reading/ Writing Companion** pages 128–129 of "Creating a Nation." Tell students that previewing text features can help them make predictions about what they will read.

Headings Remind students that headings tell what sections of text are mostly about. Point out that the heading "Revolution Begins" tells readers that the section of text below it will contain information about events in the early days of the American Revolution.

Timeline Point out the timeline that stretches across pages 128 and 129 and read the title. Explain that major events described in the text are included on this timeline. Remind students that timelines organize events chronologically, or in the order in which they happened. Ask: *How does the timeline help readers understand events described in the text?*

 Anchor Chart Have a volunteer add details about headings and timelines to the Expository Text anchor chart.

COLLABORATE

3 Guided Practice

Circulate as students work with partners to locate the first year on the timeline in which more than one event occurred. Partners should identify which important event happened the following year and discuss how it is connected to the events that happened earlier. Have pairs discuss how the timeline contributes to the overall meaning of the text.

Independent Practice Have students read the online **Differentiated Genre Passage**, "Secret Help from Spain."

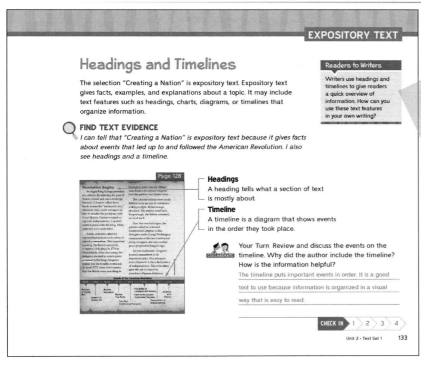

Reading/Writing Companion, p. 133

 # English Language Learners

Use the following scaffolds with **Guided Practice**. For small group support, see the **ELL Small Group Guide**.

Beginning

Review with students how timelines are organized. Have them point to the timeline on **Reading/Writing Companion** pages 128–129. Guide them to identify the events that happened in 1775 and 1776. Then help partners discuss the timeline by asking them: *Are the events in order?* (yes) *Why does the author include the timeline?* The author includes the <u>timeline</u> to show important <u>events</u> in order.

Intermediate

Have partners review the timeline on **Reading/Writing Companion** pages 128–129. Ask: *What happened in 1775?* (Battle of Lexington and Concord, start of the Second Continental Congress) *What happened a year later?* (Declaration of Independence) *How does the timeline organize events?* The timeline organizes events <u>in order</u>. *Why does the author include a timeline?* The author includes a timeline to show _____.

Advanced/Advanced High

Have partners review the timeline on pages 128–129 and answer the following questions: *What events occurred in 1775? What happened the next year? How are those events connected?* Then have them discuss why the author includes a timeline using the term *events*.

FORMATIVE ASSESSMENT

❯ STUDENT CHECK-IN

Ask partners to share their Your Turn responses on Reading/Writing Companion page 133. Have them use the Check-In routine to reflect and fill in the bars.

✓ CHECK FOR SUCCESS

Can students read expository text and identify specific dates and events on a timeline? Can they explain why headings and timelines are useful?

❯ Small Group Instruction

If No:
- **Approaching** Reteach p. T62

If Yes:
- **On** Review p. T72
- **Beyond** Extend p. T78

LESSON
2

We can read and understand expository text by identifying the problem and solution text structure.

OBJECTIVES

Explain the relationships or interactions between two or more individuals, events, ideas, or concepts in a historical, scientific, or technical text based on specific information in the text.

Compare and contrast the overall structure (e.g., chronology, comparison, cause/effect, problem/solution) of events, ideas, concepts, or information in two or more texts.

Link opinion and reasons using words, phrases, and clauses (e.g., *consequently, specifically*).

ELA ACADEMIC LANGUAGE

• *text structure, problem, solution*

• Cognates: *estructura del texto, problema, solución*

DIGITAL TOOLS

To differentiate instruction for key skills, use the results of the activity.

Reread

Text Structure: Problem and Solution

1 **Explain**

Remind students that a text's structure supports the way ideas within the text are organized. It is often used to support the author's purpose.

- Tell students that one way authors can structure expository texts is to present a **problem** and then explain the **solution**, or steps taken to solve the problem.

- Remind students to keep an eye out for signal words and phrases that indicate a problem-and-solution structure. Examples include *consequently, as a result, and so,* and *therefore.*

 Anchor Chart Begin a Text Structure: Problem and Solution anchor chart.

2 **Model**

Reread **Reading/Writing Companion** page 129. Point out the signal phrase *As a result* in the first paragraph, and identify the problem Thomas Jefferson faced and his solution. Then model listing this problem and solution in the graphic organizer to help students visualize and understand the text's overall structure.

3 **Guided Practice**

Have students work in pairs to list other problems and solutions they identify in "Creating a Nation." Remind them to look for signal words and phrases that indicate a problem-and-solution text structure. Have partners discuss how the text structure contributes to the overall meaning of the text as they complete the graphic organizers.

Analytical Writing **Write About Reading: Problem and Solution** Ask pairs to work together to summarize how the colonists solved another problem they faced. Select pairs of students to share their summaries.

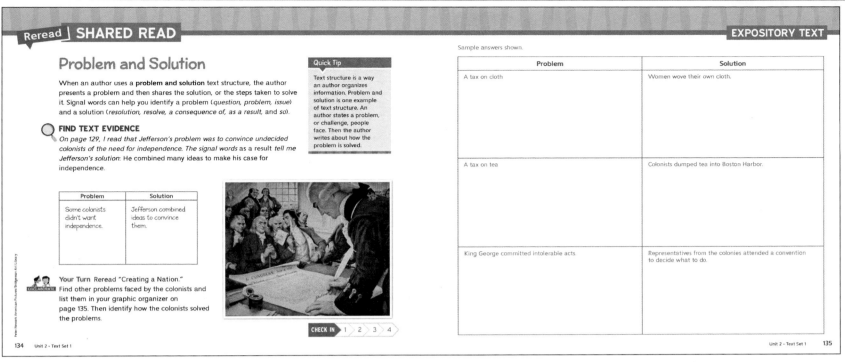

Reading/Writing Companion, pp. 134–135

English Language Learners

Use the following scaffolds with **Guided Practice**. For small group support, see the **ELL Small Group Guide**.

Beginning

Read with students the first paragraph on page 129 of "Creating a Nation." Restate sentences as needed. Help partners identify the problem by asking: *Who took away the colonists' rights?* (King George) Say: *The word* therefore *means as a result. It can signal a problem-and-solution structure.* Help pairs discuss the problem and solution using: The problem was that <u>King George</u> took away <u>rights</u>. Therefore, the colonists <u>separated</u> from Britain. This was the <u>solution</u>.

Intermediate

Have pairs reread the first paragraph on page 129 of "Creating a Nation" and point out the signal words *as a result* and *therefore*. Ask: *Do these words indicate a problem-solution structure?* (yes) Help pairs discuss the problem and solution and fill in their graphic organizer using: The problem was that King George <u>took away colonists' rights</u>. Therefore, the colonists separated <u>from Britain</u>. This was <u>the solution</u>.

Advanced/Advanced High

Have pairs read the first paragraph on page 129 to find other signal words. Guide them to write sentences in their graphic organizers explaining why the colonists separated from Britain using the terms: *problem, solution, as a result.*

FORMATIVE ASSESSMENT

◗ STUDENT CHECK-IN

Ask partners to share their graphic organizers on Reading/Writing Companion page 135. Have them use the Check-In routine to reflect and fill in the bars.

✔ CHECK FOR SUCCESS

Rubric Use your online rubric to record student progress.

Are students able to identify and list on the graphic organizer other problems and solutions in the text?

◖ Small Group Instruction

If No:

● **Approaching** Reteach p. T69

If Yes:

● **On** Review p. T75

● **Beyond** Extend p. T81

LESSON 2

LEARNING GOALS

We can reread to analyze craft and structure in expository text.

OBJECTIVES

Quote accurately from a text when explaining what the text says explicitly and when drawing inferences from the text.

Identify the author's purpose.

Explain the relationships or interactions between two or more individuals, events, ideas, or concepts in a historical, scientific, or technical text based on specific information in the text.

Compare and contrast the overall structure (e.g., chronology, comparison, cause/effect, problem/solution) of events, ideas, concepts, or information in two or more texts.

ELA ACADEMIC LANGUAGE

• techniques, author's craft

▷ TEACH IN SMALL GROUP

● **Approaching Level** Use the scaffolded questions to help students answer the Reread prompts.

● **On Level** Help partners complete the Reread prompts and share their answers.

● **Beyond Level** Allow pairs to work independently to answer the Reread prompts.

● **ELL** Have Beginning and Early-Intermediate ELLs first use the **Scaffolded Shared Read**.

Reread

Craft and Structure

Tell students that they will now reread parts of "Creating a Nation" and analyze the techniques the author used in writing the selection. When authors write expository text, they often use certain structures to present their information.

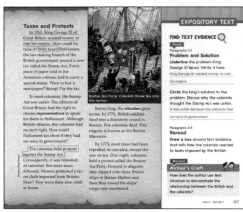

Reading/Writing Companion, p. 127

AUTHOR'S CRAFT DOK 2

Review text structure with students prior to rereading page 127. Ask: *What evidence shows that the author is using problem and solution on most of page 127?* (Throughout page 127, we read about the many problems that colonists have with Great Britain and the way they try to resolve these problems.)

ELL Have students refer to their Problem and Solution charts on page 127. Use prompts such as the following to reinforce the text structure: *What was the problem?* (King George needed money.) *What was the solution?* (Parliament raised taxes.) *There was another problem. What was the next problem?* Continue in this way to reinforce the text structure.

How does the author use text structure to demonstrate the relationship between the British and the colonists? (By using problem and solution as a text structure, the author makes it clear to the reader that there were many disagreements between the king and the colonists, and neither party was able to find a resolution they could agree on.)

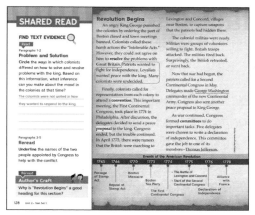

Reading/Writing Companion, p. 128

AUTHOR'S CRAFT DOK 2

Reread the first two paragraphs on page 128 with students. Ask: *What words and phrases does the author use to help you know that the situation between the colonists and the British is getting worse?* (The phrases "angry King George," "harsh actions," and "trouble continued" help me understand that something is going to happen. The relationship between the colonists and the British is getting worse.)

ELL Point to the first sentence in the second paragraph and read it with students. Ask: *What does the word* Finally *tell you?* (After a long period, something is changing.) *What is finally changing?* (A group of colonists is meeting to decide what to do next.)

Why is "Revolution Begins" a good heading for this section? (The author shows how things are changing and getting worse. The events are leading to war.)

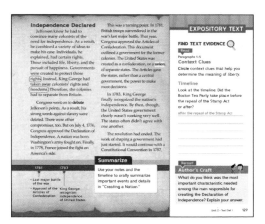

Reading/Writing Companion, p. 129

AUTHOR'S CRAFT DOK 2

Reread the first two paragraphs on page 129 with students. Ask: *What characteristics do you think made Thomas Jefferson a good choice to write the Declaration of Independence?* (Thomas Jefferson was a good writer whose words convinced the colonists that they needed to be free from British rule. He was respected by his peers and shared ideas that would protect the rights of individuals.)

ELL Rephrase the sentences 2-6 in the first paragraph with students to help them identify the ideas he used to convince the colonists. (Each person has rights, and it is the government's job to protect the rights. But King George took away the rights.)

What do you think was the most important characteristic needed among the men responsible for creating the Declaration of Independence? Explain your answer. (The ability to compromise was the most important characteristic. Without compromise among the colonies, the war may not have been won, and the Declaration of Independence never written.)

MAKE INFERENCES

Explain that when you make inferences, you use text evidence and what you already know to make decisions about details that the author does not state directly. Making inferences can help you to better understand each detail and how it relates to other details in the text.

Think Aloud On page 129, I read that when France joined the fight on America's side in 1778, it was a "turning point." Why was this event so important? British troops surrendered in 1781. I can infer that the French army was strong and helped the American army defeat the British.

Integrate

BUILD KNOWLEDGE: MAKE CONNECTIONS

Talk About the Text Have partners discuss how the founding fathers were good problem solvers.

Write About the Text Have students add ideas to the Build Knowledge pages of their reader's notebook.

Anchor Chart Record any new ideas on the Build Knowledge anchor chart.

Add to the Vocabulary List Have students write down any words they learned about solving problems in their reader's notebook.

FORMATIVE ASSESSMENT

❯ STUDENT CHECK-IN

Have partners share their responses to one of the Reread prompts on Reading/Writing Companion pages 127-129. Ask them to reflect using the Check-In routine.

Reread

Write About the Shared Read

10 mins

LEARNING GOALS

We can use text evidence to respond to expository text.

OBJECTIVES

Quote accurately from a text when explaining what the text says explicitly and when drawing inferences from the text.

Identify the author's purpose.

Explain the relationships or interactions between two or more individuals, events, ideas, or concepts in a historical, scientific, or technical text based on specific information in the text.

Compare and contrast the overall structure (e.g., chronology, comparison, cause/effect, problem/solution) of events, ideas, concepts, or information in two or more texts.

ELA ACADEMIC LANGUAGE

• *prompt, analyze, chronological*

• Cognate: *analizar*

▷ TEACH IN SMALL GROUP

● **Approaching Level** Have partners work together to plan and complete the response to the prompt.

●● **On Level** and **Beyond Level** Have students write their responses independently and then discuss them.

● **ELL** Group students of mixed proficiency levels to discuss and respond to the prompt.

Analyze the Prompt DOK 3

Read the prompt aloud: *Explain why the division between the colonists on whether or not to support the king was significant.* Ask: *What is the prompt asking?* (to explain the significance of whether or not colonists supported the king) Say: *Let's reread to see how the text uses a problem-and-solution text structure and chronological order to show the significance of the events facing the colonists. We can cite text evidence to explain and justify our reasoning and make inferences. Doing this will help you write your response.*

Analyze Text Evidence

Remind students that problem and solution text structures often present events in chronological order, or the order in which events happened. In the **Reading/Writing Companion**, have students skim "Creating a Nation" for important dates. Ask: *What actions led to the First Continental Congress?* (The King continued to tax the colonies and seemed unwilling to compromise.) *Why was the First Continental Congress so important?* (The convention brought forth representatives from each colony to agree on the best way to respond. They chose to fight for independence.) Have students scan for other significant events that influenced the colonies. Review the timeline with students and tell them they can use it to inform their responses.

Respond

COLLABORATE

Direct student pairs to the sentence starters on Reading/Writing Companion page 136. Ask: *How does the response of the colonists to the British help you figure out how the relationship between Britain and America changed?* As needed, model a response.

Think Aloud At the beginning of the selection, the author tells about the many disagreements between the king and the colonists and tells when they occurred. I read that they could not agree on a solution. Then the author lists why they went to war. By the end of the selection, the war has ended and King George recognizes the colonists' independence. The colonies are no longer under British rule. The colonists eventually came to an agreement which helped to end the war.

Analytical Writing Students should use the sequence words in the sentence starters to form their responses. Their first paragraph should state the central idea of their response. Relevant details should support the central idea. Students may continue their responses on a separate piece of paper.

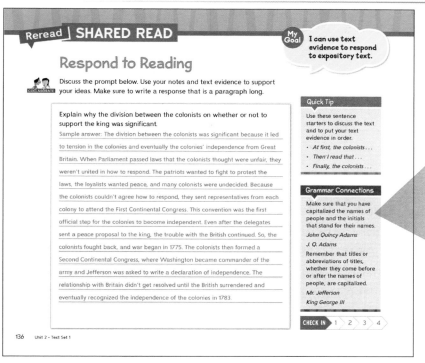

Reading/Writing Companion, p. 136

 # English Language Learners

Use the following scaffolds with **Respond**.

Beginning

Read the prompt with students and discuss what they will write about. Explain the meaning of *division* and *tension* to students. Ask: *Did the division cause tension in the colonies?* (yes) *Did the colonists come to an agreement in the end?* (yes) *Who did they get independence from?* (Great Britain) Help partners discuss why the division was significant, or important, and respond using: The division caused tension in the colonies. The colonists came to an agreement in the end. They got independence from Great Britain.

Intermediate

Read the prompt with students. Ask: *Did the division cause tension in the colonies?* (yes) *What happened in the end?* The colonists came to an agreement. They got independence from Great Britain. Have partners discuss their responses and write using: The division between the colonists was significant because _____. In the end, the colonists came to an _____, and they got _____.

Advanced/Advanced High

Review the prompt and sentence starters on page 136 with students. Have partners discuss what happened when there was a division between the colonists. Then have them write their responses using the sentence starters.

ELL NEWCOMERS

Have students listen to the summaries of the **Shared Read** in their native language and then in English to help them access the text and develop listening comprehension. Help students ask and answer questions with a partner. Use these sentence frames: What problem did the colonists have? The colonists ____. Then continue the lessons in the **Newcomer Teacher's Guide**.

FORMATIVE ASSESSMENT

❯ STUDENT CHECK-IN

Ask partners to share their response on Reading/Writing page 136. Have them use the Check-In routine to reflect and fill in the bars.

LEARNING GOALS

- We can decode words with variant vowels and diphthongs.
- We can identify and read multisyllabic words.
- We can read fluently with accuracy at an appropriate rate.

OBJECTIVES

Know and apply grade-level and word analysis skills in decoding words.

Use combined knowledge of all letter-sound correspondences, syllabication patterns, and morphology (e.g., roots and affixes) to read accurately unfamiliar multisyllabic words in context and out of context.

Read with sufficient accuracy and fluency to support comprehension.

Rate: 111–131 WCPM

ELA ACADEMIC LANGUAGE

- *rate, accuracy*
- Cognate: *ritmo*

▶ TEACH IN SMALL GROUP

Phonics

●● **Approaching Level** and **ELL** Use the Tier 2 activity on page T64 before teaching the lesson.

●● **On Level** and **Beyond Level** As needed, use the Read Multisyllabic Words section only.

● **ELL** See page 5 in the **Language Transfers Handbook** for guidance in identifying sounds and symbols that may not transfer for speakers of certain languages, and support in accommodating those students.

OPTION 10 mins

Variant Vowel /ô/; Diphthongs /oi/, /ou/

1 Explain

Show students the *Straw, Boy,* and *Cow* **Sound-Spelling Cards** for /ô/, /oi/, and /ou/. Remind students that /oi/ and /ou/ are diphthongs: gliding vowel sounds that combine two sounds into one syllable. Say the sounds as you point to each card and have students repeat the sounds. Tell students that each of these sounds can be spelled in different ways. List the sounds on the board and provide a sample word for each spelling.

- /ô/ as in <u>law</u>n, v<u>au</u>lt, br<u>ou</u>ght, w<u>a</u>lk
- /oi/ as in f<u>oi</u>l, t<u>oy</u>
- /ou/ as in h<u>ou</u>se, g<u>ow</u>n

2 Model

Write the following words on the board. Underline the variant vowel and diphthong spelling in each word and say the sound. Then model blending the word.

/ô/: dawn, thought, talk

/oi/: toil, boy

/ou/: mouse, town

Emphasize how the same sound is spelled differently in the words.

3 Guided Practice

Write these words on the board. Ask students to underline the letter or letters that spell the vowel sound. Then have students read the words chorally. Assist as needed.

straw	draw	enjoy	boil	growl
frown	shout	sour	launch	haunt
soy	shawl	coil	loin	round
bawl	gaunt	bought	joy	blouse

Finally, have students sort the words by their variant vowel and diphthong sounds. Write these heads on the board: /ô/, /oi/, and /ou/. Ask students to write each word in the appropriate column.

For practice with decoding and encoding, use **Practice Book** page 67 or online activities.

Read Multisyllabic Words

Transition to Longer Words Help students transition from reading one-syllable words to reading multisyllabic words with /ô/, /oi/, and /ou/. Have students read the one-syllable words. Then model how to read the longer words. Point out the added syllable(s) in each, including prefixes and suffixes, to help students gain awareness of these common word parts. Finally, have students read the word pairs chorally.

growl, growling	straw, strawberry	draw, redraw
launch, prelaunch	joy, joyfully	round, around
crowd, crowded	haunt, haunted	sour, sourness
thought, thoughtful	soy, soybean	coil, uncoil

Fluency

Accuracy and Rate

Explain/Model Tell students that accuracy improves with an appropriate reading rate. Reading rate refers to the rate at which students read a text. Explain that adjusting the reading rate can add excitement and drama to a section of text. Read aloud the first three paragraphs of "Creating a Nation" on **Reading/Writing Companion** page 127. Model varying the rate of your reading to create a sense of drama or excitement. Tell students to be mindful of their accuracy when they change their rate.

Practice/Apply Have groups choral read the same passage, modeling your accuracy and reading rate. Remind students that you will be listening for these qualities in their reading during the week. Explain that you will help them improve their reading by pointing out where they can adjust their reading rate and maintain accuracy.

Daily Fluency Practice

Automaticity Students can practice reading with accuracy and appropriate rate to develop automaticity using the online **Differentiated Genre Passage**, "Secret Help from Spain."

MULTIMODAL LEARNING

After Guided Practice, give each **Sound-Spelling Card** to a student. Say random words from the list and have students hold up their card when they hear a word with that sound. Say multisyllabic words with the variant vowel /ô/ and diphthongs /oi/ and /ou/ (*awful, royal, shouting*). Have students repeat each word, and then spell and write it.

FORMATIVE ASSESSMENT

◆ STUDENT CHECK-IN

Variant Vowels and Diphthongs Have partners share three words with variant vowels and diphthongs.

Multisyllabic Words Have partners read the following words: *prelaunch, strawberry,* and *soybean*.

Fluency Have partners read "Secret Help from Spain" fluently.

Have partners reflect using the Check-In routine.

✓ CHECK FOR SUCCESS

Rubric Use your online rubric to record student progress.

Can students decode multisyllabic words with variant vowels and diphthongs? Can students read words accurately at an appropriate rate?

◆ Small Group Instruction

If No:

● **Approaching** Reteach T64, T68

● **ELL** Develop p. T64

If Yes:

● **On** Apply p. T70

● **Beyond** Apply p. T76

- **We can use the research process to create a multimedia slideshow about the U.S. Constitution.**
- **We can compare and contrast primary and secondary sources on the same topic.**

OBJECTIVES

Analyze multiple accounts of the same event or topic, noting important similarities and differences in the point of view they represent.

Recall relevant information from experiences or gather relevant information from print and digital sources; summarize or paraphrase information in notes and finished work, and provide a list of sources.

Produce clear and coherent writing in which the development and organization are appropriate to task, purpose, and audience.

Come to discussions prepared, having read or studied required material; explicitly draw on that preparation and other information known about the topic to explore ideas under discussion.

🌐 Identify the contributions of individuals who helped create the U.S. Constitution.

🌐 Identify the issues that led to the creation of the U.S. Constitution.

ELA ACADEMIC LANGUAGE

- *primary, secondary, accounts, firsthand, secondhand*
- Cognates: *primaria, secundaria*

▶ **TEACH IN SMALL GROUP**

You may wish to teach the Research and Inquiry lesson during Small Group time. Have groups of mixed abilities complete the page and work on the culture square.

10 mins

Founders Solve Problems

Explain to students that for the next two weeks they will work collaboratively in large groups to create a multimedia slideshow.

Use Primary and Secondary Sources Tell students they will conduct research using primary and secondary sources to identify how and when delegates solved issues that led to the creation of the U.S. Constitution. Discuss examples of primary and secondary sources with students:

- Primary sources are firsthand accounts of an event. Examples of primary sources might include delegate's letters, diaries, journals, autobiographies, or speeches. It can also include official or historical documents, such as the U.S. Constitution.
- Secondary sources are secondhand accounts of an event. Encyclopedias and textbooks are examples of secondary sources.

Have students find the signatures on the Declaration of Independence on **Reading/Writing Companion** page 137. Point out that this is a primary source. Have students name primary and secondary sources that would help them conduct research. Support them as they go through each step in the Research Process as outlined on page 137 to create their slideshows.

STEP 1 **Set Research Goals** Remind students that delegates from 12 states met in Philadelphia in 1787 to create a new government. Guide students in thinking about the delegates, the issues of the time period, and the need for a document that would unify the young nation. Offer feedback as students generate questions about who the delegates were, when and where they met, how they compromised, and what the U.S. Constitution represents. Have students use a **Four-Door Foldable®**, available online, to help organize their information.

STEP 2 **Identify Sources** Discuss the kinds of digital and print resources groups can use for their research. Remind them to use credible primary and secondary sources. Model how to locate historical documents online.

STEP 3 **Find and Record Information** Review with students how to take notes and cite the sources they use to gather information for their slideshows. Have them compare and contrast the information they gathered from the primary and secondary sources they used.

STEP 4 **Organize and Synthesize Information** Show students how to organize the places and information that they want to add to their slideshows. Discuss which primary and secondary sources were most informative and interesting to include.

STEP 5 **Create and Present** Review with students the information they should include in their slideshows. Encourage them to add images, graphics, or music to emphasize or clarify important ideas they researched. Then have them share their slideshows with the class.

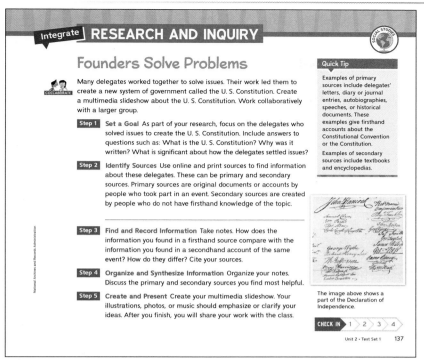

Reading/Writing Companion, p. 137

 # English Language Learners

Use the following scaffold with **Step 2**.

Beginning

Review examples of primary and secondary sources with students. Guide students to primary and secondary sources and help them identify the type of source. Help partners describe the information they gathered using: This a primary/secondary source. It gives a firsthand/secondhand account. Review the students' sources and provide feedback.

Intermediate

Review examples of primary and secondary sources with students. Have partners research primary and secondary sources and identify the type of source. Then have them describe the information they gathered using: This information is a primary/secondary source because it gives a firsthand/secondhand account. Review the students' sources and provide feedback.

Advanced/Advanced High

Have students review examples of primary and secondary sources. Allow partners to research information about how delegates solved issues that led to the creation of the U.S. Constitution. Then have them describe the type of source they found and discuss the information they gathered.

DIGITAL TOOLS

   Evaluate Sources for Reliability; Organizing Notes

FOLDABLES

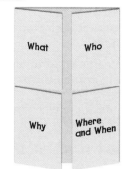

Four-Door Foldable®

FORMATIVE ASSESSMENT

❯ STUDENT CHECK-IN

Slideshow Ask students to share their U.S. Constitution slideshows.

Primary and Secondary Sources Have students share an example of how they used primary and secondary sources to create their slideshows.

Have them use the Check-In routine to reflect and fill in the bars on Reading/Writing Companion page 137.

LESSONS 3-6

Who Wrote the U.S. Constitution?

Lexile 760L

LEARNING GOALS

Read We can apply strategies and skills to read expository text

Reread We can reread to analyze text, craft, and structure and compare texts.

Have students apply what they learned as they read.

ACT *What makes this text complex?*
▶ **Prior Knowledge**
▶ **Specific Vocabulary**
▶ **Connection of Ideas**
▶ **Genre/Structure**

🌐 Identify the contributions of individuals, including James Madison, and others such as George Mason and Roger Sherman, who helped create the U.S. Constitution.

Close Reading Routine

Read DOK 1-2

• Identify important ideas and details.
• Take notes and summarize.
• Use **ACT** prompts as needed.

Reread DOK 2-3

• Analyze the text, craft, and structure.
• Use *Reading/Writing Companion*, pp. 138–140.

Integrate DOK 3-4

• Integrate knowledge and ideas.
• Make text-to-text connections.
• Use the Integrate lesson.
• Complete the Show Your Knowledge task.
• Inspire action.

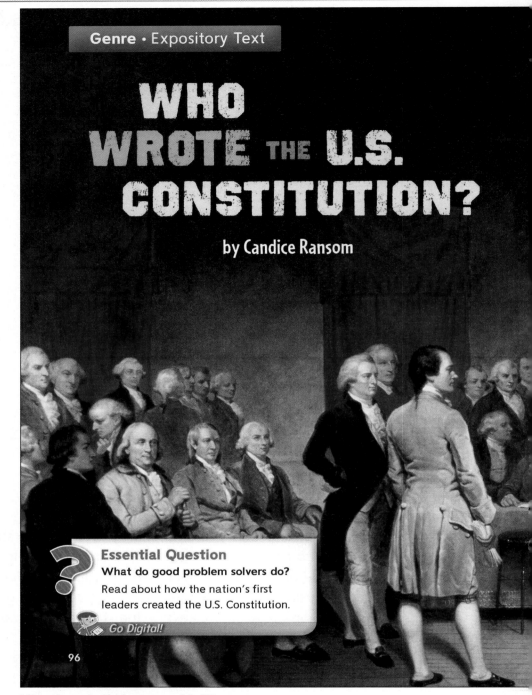

Genre • Expository Text

WHO WROTE THE U.S. CONSTITUTION?

by Candice Ransom

? Essential Question
What do good problem solvers do?
Read about how the nation's first leaders created the U.S. Constitution.

Go Digital!

96

Literature Anthology, pp. 96–97

⏩ DIFFERENTIATED READING

You may wish to read the full selection aloud once with minimal stopping before you begin using the Read prompts.

Approaching Level Have students listen to the selection summary. Use the Reread prompts during Small-Group time.

On Level and **Beyond Level** Pair students or have them independently complete the Reread prompts on **Reading/Writing Companion** pages 138–140.

🎧 **English Language Learners** Have ELLs listen to the summary of the selection, available in multiple languages. See also **ELL Small Group Guide**.

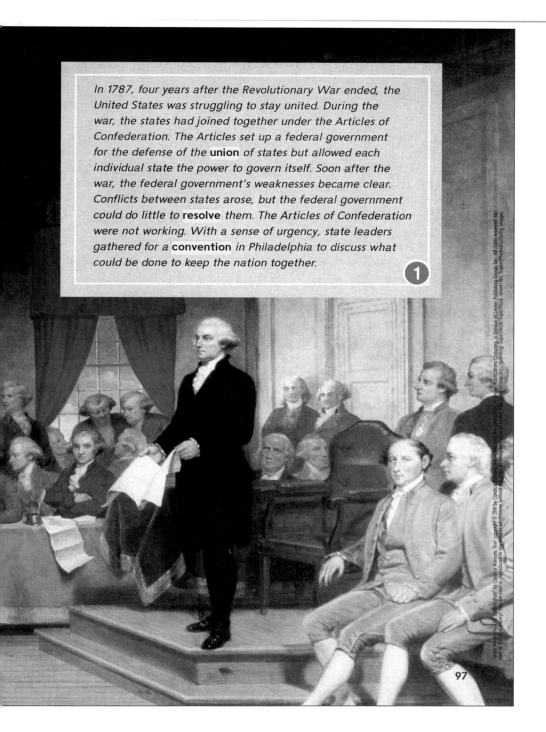

In 1787, four years after the Revolutionary War ended, the United States was struggling to stay united. During the war, the states had joined together under the Articles of Confederation. The Articles set up a federal government for the defense of the **union** of states but allowed each individual state the power to govern itself. Soon after the war, the federal government's weaknesses became clear. Conflicts between states arose, but the federal government could do little to **resolve** them. The Articles of Confederation were not working. With a sense of urgency, state leaders gathered for a **convention** in Philadelphia to discuss what could be done to keep the nation together.

1

97

Read

Set a Purpose Tell students to preview the text and set a purpose for reading. Remind them that setting a purpose can help them monitor comprehension.

Note Taking: Use the Graphic Organizer

Analytical Writing Remind the students to take notes as they read. Distribute copies of online Problem and Solution **Graphic Organizer 4**. Have students record the problems the delegates faced and their solutions. They can also note words they don't understand and questions they have.

1 **Text Features: Insets** DOK 2

Expository texts about historical events often include visual depictions of the event. How does the inset help you understand what this painting shows? (The inset describes why so many of our early leaders decided to meet.) Remind students to synthesize information to create a new understanding.

Build Vocabulary on page 97

Have students add the Build Vocabulary words to their reader's notebook.

arose: came into being

urgency: the state in which a problem demands immediate attention and quick action

A C T Access Complex Text

Prior Knowledge

Explain that the thirteen original colonies of the United States belonged to Great Britain. The Revolutionary War, also called the American Revolution, took place from 1775–1783. Patriots of the thirteen colonies fought and obtained their independence from Great Britain during this war.

The Articles of Confederation were created during the Revolutionary War, when states were focused on working as a union against a single enemy. The Articles served as the only plan for the new country's federal government as of 1787, when this selection begins.

Read

2 Text Structure: Problem and Solution DOK 2

On the previous page, you read that state leaders gathered for a convention to discuss how to keep the nation together. As described on page 98, what specific problems was the nation facing? Paraphrase your answer. (border disagreements; states had no money or had money that was worthless; some states wouldn't agree to pay taxes to cover debt; in states that did charge taxes, many people couldn't pay them) Add this information to your organizer.

Problem	Solution
Articles of Confederation weren't working:	State leaders decided to gather for a convention to discuss the problems.
States argued over borders.	
State governments either had no money or their money wasn't worth anything.	
Some states wouldn't agree to pay taxes to cover debt.	
In states that did charge taxes, many people couldn't pay them.	

Build Vocabulary on page 98

livestock: animals raised on a farm or a ranch

A NEW PLAN

Virginia governor Edmund Randolph spoke first on Tuesday, May 29, 1787. Randolph brought up the problems with the Articles of Confederation. Many states argued over borders shared with other states. People had trouble conducting business across state lines. State governments had no money. Some states printed money. But the money was not backed up by gold or silver. Much of it was worthless.

Randolph spoke about another serious problem—taxes. The cost of the Revolutionary War left the United States in debt. The government owed money to wealthy U.S. citizens and to foreign countries such as France and the Netherlands. To raise money to pay the debt, the U.S. government asked each state to tax its residents.

Not every state agreed to do so. But states such as Virginia and Massachusetts taxed their citizens. Taxes had to be paid in cash. And that was a problem for many people. Ordinary working people did not use much cash. They lived off what they owned and grew—their land, houses, tools, livestock, and crops. If they needed something—a new tool or a pair of boots—they traded for it. But they could not trade with the state to pay their taxes.

The **situation** was especially bad for farmers. States began taking to court farmers who could not pay their taxes and other debts. The courts took away farmers' land and livestock. Some farmers were even thrown in prison.

During the summer of 1786, hundreds of angry Massachusetts farmers formed a rebel force. One of the leaders was Daniel Shays, a Revolutionary War hero, politician, and farmer. From August 1786 to January 1787, the rebels stormed courthouses in Northhampton, Worcester, and other Massachusetts towns.

They forced the courts to close. Shays's Rebellion shocked the country.

With all these problems before them, what could the convention delegates do?

98

Literature Anthology, pp. 98–99

Access Complex Text

Prior Knowledge

Help students understand the economic concepts described on page 98.

- *An example of printed money is a dollar bill. Printed money that is "backed up" by gold or silver means that the paper itself represents a certain value of gold or silver. That gold or silver, which states did not have, is what gives the money its value.*

- *The government borrowed money to pay for the cost of the Revolutionary War. If you borrow money, you are in debt until you pay it back.*

- *A tax is a way for a government to collect money from citizens to pay for public services.*

- *What are some things we pay tax on today?* (items we buy at the store, homes, income)

This woodcut shows Daniel Shays (*left*) and fellow rebel leader Job Shattuck. The image was printed in *Bickerstaff's Boston Almanack* in 1787.

Why Was Shays's Rebellion Important?

In October 1786, the Confederation Congress decided to use federal troops to stop the rebels. But Congress could not convince state governments to help pay for the soldiers. Massachusetts leaders had to raise the money themselves. In January 1787, Shays and his rebels attacked an armory (a building used to store weapons) in Springfield, Massachusetts. Troops stopped the raid, and many rebels were arrested.

In the spring of 1787, Massachusetts passed laws to help farmers in debt. The rebellion began to fade. But for many people, Shays's Rebellion showed how weak the federal government was. For them, it proved that the Articles of Confederation were failing.

99

Read

3 Reread DOK 1

Teacher Think Aloud I want to make sure that I understand why Shays's Rebellion was important. As I reread and paraphrase pages 98–99, I see that the rebellion took place because farmers were angry that they lost their land and livestock and were thrown in prison over taxes they couldn't pay. The state of Massachusetts had to pay soldiers to stop the rebellion because the federal government couldn't get states to help pay. Shays's Rebellion showed that the federal government and the Articles of Confederation were not effective. I understand that money was a big problem for people and for the government.

Reread

Author's Purpose DOK 2

Reread page 98. Why does the author discuss Daniel Shays's past? Cite evidence from the text in your answer. (The author mentions Daniel Shays's past to emphasize that he was a patriot who had made sacrifices for his country. That someone with his status was so upset was something the new nation could not ignore.)

ELL Spotlight on Language

Page 98, Paragraphs 4 and 5 Clarify the concept of rebellion (cognate: *rebelión*). Read paragraph 4 aloud. *Why did the new taxes make farmers angry?* (lost land and livestock, thrown in prison because they could not pay taxes) *When you are angry about something, you may rebel, or refuse to do something.* Read paragraph 5 aloud. Explain that *storm* here means *attack*. Use gestures to clarify as needed. *What did the farmers do?* (formed rebel force, stormed courthouses)

ELL Newcomers

Use the **Newcomer Online Visuals** and their accompanying prompts to help students expand vocabulary and language about Community **(15–19)**. Use the Conversation Starters, Speech Balloons, and the Games in the **Newcomer Teacher's Guide** to continue building vocabulary and developing oral and written language.

Read

4 Text Structure: Problem and Solution DOK 2

What new plan was presented at the convention? (Madison presented the Virginia Plan.) What problem was the Virginia Plan meant to solve? (The federal government was too weak.) Add this information to your organizer. What new problem did the plan create? (The plan ignored the Articles of Confederation.)

Problem	Solution
The federal government was too weak.	Madison presented the Virginia Plan.

 STOP AND CHECK   **DOK 1**

Reread How would the Virginia Plan change the government?

Teacher Think Aloud I can **reread** to find that the Virginia Plan would make the federal government stronger and therefore protect the American people.

Build Vocabulary on page 100

overrule: decide that someone else's actions or decisions are wrong

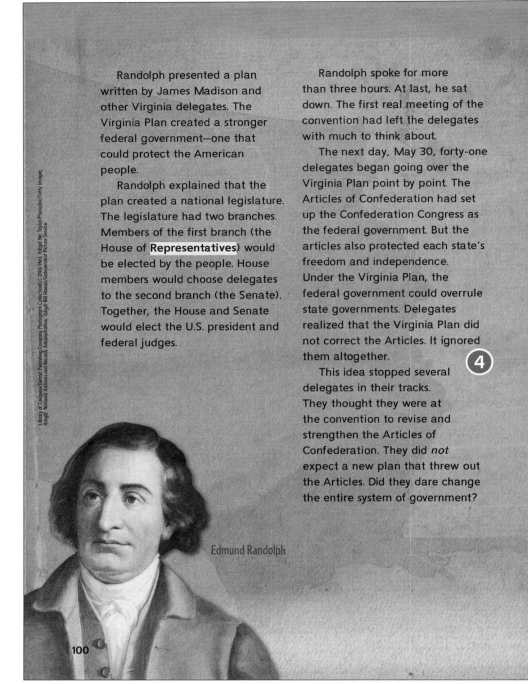

Randolph presented a plan written by James Madison and other Virginia delegates. The Virginia Plan created a stronger federal government—one that could protect the American people.

Randolph explained that the plan created a national legislature. The legislature had two branches. Members of the first branch (the House of **Representatives**) would be elected by the people. House members would choose delegates to the second branch (the Senate). Together, the House and Senate would elect the U.S. president and federal judges.

Randolph spoke for more than three hours. At last, he sat down. The first real meeting of the convention had left the delegates with much to think about.

The next day, May 30, forty-one delegates began going over the Virginia Plan point by point. The Articles of Confederation had set up the Confederation Congress as the federal government. But the articles also protected each state's freedom and independence. Under the Virginia Plan, the federal government could overrule state governments. Delegates realized that the Virginia Plan did not correct the Articles. It ignored them altogether.

This idea stopped several delegates in their tracks. They thought they were at the convention to revise and strengthen the Articles of Confederation. They did *not* expect a new plan that threw out the Articles. Did they dare change the entire system of government?

Edmund Randolph

100

Literature Anthology, pp. 100–101

A C T Access Complex Text

Specific Vocabulary

Explain that authors of informational texts use vocabulary specific to the topic. Point out that in this text, the words related to government are often terms that the writers of the Constitution used. Students may use context clues, word parts, or a dictionary to help them understand this vocabulary.

- *Read the first paragraph on page 100. Based on the context clues, what is a* delegate? (A *delegate* is a representative from a state.)

Discuss the term *proportional representation* at the end of page 101. *Paraphrase what this term means, using the last two paragraphs on page 101.* (*Proportional representation* is representation for a state that is based on a state's population.) Have students add this social studies term to their reader's notebook.

SEPARATION OF POWERS

On May 31, 1787, convention delegates voted to create a stronger national government. They decided that it should consist of three parts: the legislative, the executive, and the judicial. The legislative part, called Congress, would make the laws. The president would be the head of the executive part. He would carry out the laws. The national court system was the judicial part. It would decide the meaning of the laws and if they were being obeyed. With three parts, or branches, power would be shared. No one branch would have more control of the federal government than the other two.

Discussion swung to the one-vote-for-one-state system described in the Articles of Confederation. In 1787 a state's importance was measured by the number of its citizens. For example, Georgia had a lot of land. But it was still considered small because of its low population. The three biggest states—Virginia, Pennsylvania, and Massachusetts—

held nearly half the nation's population. But under the articles, each state had only one vote, no matter its size or population. Tiny Rhode Island's voice in Congress carried as much weight as mighty Massachusetts. This is called equal representation.

The Virginia Plan changed that. Under the plan, the House of Representatives would be elected by the people. And the number of representatives would be based on a state's population. The number of members in the Senate would also depend on population. This is known as proportional (an amount determined by size) representation.

Immediately, the convention broke into two camps: big states versus small states. The small states fought against the Virginia Plan. With proportional representation, they felt they would not have as strong a voice in the federal government. **(5)**

101

Read

(5) Text Structure: Problem and Solution DOK 2

How did proportional representation, proposed in the Virginia Plan, create a problem? (If the number of representatives became based on a state's population, then small states would not have as strong a voice in the federal government.) Add this problem to your organizer.

Build Vocabulary on page 101
versus: against

Reread

Author's Purpose DOK 2

Why does the author use headings to help you understand the text? (The headings "A New Plan" and "Separation of Powers" give readers a general idea of what each section will be about, so readers know what to focus on as they read. By breaking the text into smaller pieces, the author is helping readers better understand all of the information.)

 English Language Learners

Build Background: Page 101, Paragraph 1 Draw three boxes to show the branches of the federal government. *The government has three parts, or branches.* Say: *The heading "Separation of Powers" shows that the 3 branches have different tasks.* Then help pairs to describe each branch using these frames: The Legislative Branch makes laws. The Executive Branch carries out laws. The Judicial Branch decides the meaning of the law. Explain that the three branches share power so the president cannot become as powerful as a king.

LESSONS 3-6

Read

6 Context Clues DOK 2

Find the word *merchants* in the first paragraph on page 102. Which context clues within or beyond the sentence give the meaning of *merchants*? (The sentence that follows *merchants* defines it as "people who run businesses and stores.")

7 Make Inferences DOK 2

From the information on page 102, what inference can you make about the situation at the convention? (It was tedious and uncomfortable.) What evidence in the text supports your inference? ("Day after day," "The room grew hot. The hours grew long.") Reread the last two paragraphs on page 103. What inference can you make about the delegates? Cite evidence from the text. (The delegates were struggling to reach consensus on the plan; "members argued;" "never solved;" "tempers flared.") Think about high-pressure situations in uncomfortable surroundings that you may have been in. How does that experience help you understand how the delegates at the convention might have felt? (Answers may vary.)

The states had other differences beyond size. Southerners grew tobacco, sugar, and rice on large farms called plantations. Many people in the middle of the country—Pennsylvania, New Jersey, Delaware, and New York—were merchants. They ran businesses and stores. People in Massachusetts and Connecticut were shipbuilders and fishers.

Slavery was another big issue dividing the states. Southern plantation owners used African slaves to work the plantations. Slaves were treated as property. Slavery was against the law in most northern states. Some northerners wanted to make slavery illegal in every state. But southern states fiercely defended their right to own slaves.

At the 1787 convention, slavery became part of the **debate** over proportional representation. Should slaves be counted as part of a state's population? Thousands of slaves lived in states such as Georgia and South Carolina. Counting slaves would give southern states more representatives in the federal government. Northern delegates felt this was unfair. Southern states did not treat slaves like people in any other case. Why should they be allowed to use the slave population to gain more representation?

Day after day, the delegates chewed over parts of the representation issue. The room grew hot. The hours grew long.

The Virginians had taken control of the convention. Their delegates were good writers and speakers. But Virginia was not the entire nation. The small states needed to be heard.

William Paterson, a New Jersey lawyer, presented the New Jersey Plan. It was the small states' answer to the Virginia Plan.

Under the New Jersey Plan, Congress would have only one house. It would not have a House of Representatives and a Senate. The federal government would not have a president. And there would be no federal courts except the Supreme Court.

William Paterson

102

Literature Anthology, pp. 102–103

A C T Access Complex Text

Connection of Ideas

Point out that the process of forming the new government was complex. Some disagreements that the delegates had during the convention could not be resolved. The issue of slavery, for example, was to be debated for years and remained unresolved until the American Civil War, 1861–1865. *Why was the question of representation in the government such a problem?*

(Representation was to be based on state population. Thousands of slaves lived in southern states, such as Georgia and South Carolina, which would give those states more representation in the federal government than Northern states would have. The North said that was unfair.)

The New Jersey Plan proposed that all states—no matter how big or small—would have the same number of representatives. Most important, Paterson's plan did not create a new constitution. The plan was designed to become additional amendments, or formal changes, to the Articles of Confederation.

On June 19, James Madison jumped to his feet to speak first. He wanted to convince the delegates to vote for the Virginia Plan. He argued against the New Jersey Plan point by point. When he was finished, the delegates voted.

Seven states chose the Virginia Plan. Three states voted for the New Jersey Plan. (Maryland was divided and did not cast a vote). The big states had won. For the next several days, members argued. Two houses in Congress or one? The same issues were brought up but never solved. Tempers flared. The small states felt the big states were pushing them around again.

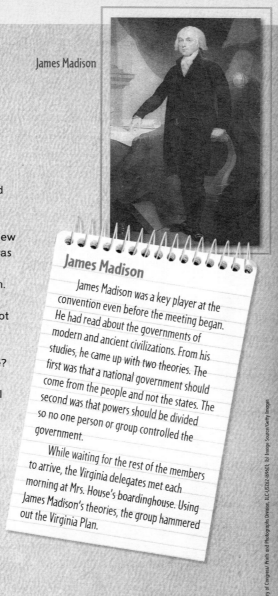

James Madison

James Madison

James Madison was a key player at the convention even before the meeting began. He had read about the governments of modern and ancient civilizations. From his studies, he came up with two theories. The first was that a national government should come from the people and not the states. The second was that powers should be divided so no one person or group controlled the government.

While waiting for the rest of the members to arrive, the Virginia delegates met each morning at Mrs. House's boardinghouse. Using James Madison's theories, the group hammered out the Virginia Plan.

(t) The Library of Congress/ Prints and Photographs Division, LLC-USZ62-69601; (b) Image Source/Getty Images

103

 Spotlight on Idioms

Page 103, Paragraph 3 Explain that *cast a vote* means to vote, or to pick someone or something. Clarify by having the class vote on something by show of hands. Then guide pairs as they share a time when they cast a vote for something, such as a talent show or a class leader: *We voted on _____.* Define the idiom *tempers flared. When something* flares, *it grows or gets brighter quickly, like a fire. What happens if someone's temper flares?* (gets angry) Gesture or act out to clarify. *Why did the small states feel angry?* (felt the bigger states were bullying them)

✔ STOP AND CHECK   DOK 1

Reread Why did state differences lead to a debate about state representation? (The Virginia Plan proposed that representation be based on population, which benefitted large states. Small states preferred the New Jersey Plan, which proposed that all states have the same number of representatives.)

Reread

Author's Craft: Figurative Language DOK 2
Reading/Writing Companion, p. 138
Reread the fourth paragraph on page 102. What effect does the idiom *chewed over* create? (It shows that the delegates went over the issue thoroughly, knowing their decisions would have long-lasting effects. They are not actually chewing on anything!)

Text Features: Sidebar DOK 2

Reread page 103. How does the sidebar give more insight into the role James Madison played in the Virginia Plan? (It explains James Madison's ideas about the structure of the government. Our current government is based on many of his ideas. Without his input, our government might be different.)

💡 Make Inferences   DOK 2

Explain The sidebar on page 103 gives background on James Madison.

Discuss *James Madison's knowledge of government was extensive.* Ask: *What details help you make this inference?* (The sidebar says that he had studied about ancient and modern governments.)

Apply As students read pages 104 and 105, have them point out the sidebars. Ask them to paraphrase each sidebar and discuss how it adds to their understanding.

Read

8 Ask and Answer Questions

DOK 1

COLLABORATE To monitor comprehension, generate a question about the events described in the first paragraph. Share it with a partner. To find the answer, reread the text. For example, you might ask, "How did delegates feel about equal representation?" To find the answer, you can reread the beginning of page 104. (States were divided about equal representation in government. Some states wanted it and some states didn't.)

9 Context Clues DOK 2

Find the word *compromise* on page 104. Which context clues in the surrounding words give the meaning of *compromise*? (The word *compromise* is preceded by the phrase "give up something in order for everyone to gain." This means that a *compromise* is a situation in which each party gives up something to get something it wants.)

Build Vocabulary on pages 104–105

brink: a crucial point of an important situation

proposed: suggested

THE GREAT COMPROMISE

8 July 2, 1787, was a Monday. By the time the delegates met in the morning, the East Room was already hot. Once again, delegates voted on whether states should have equal representation in the Senate. Five states said yes, five said no, and Georgia was divided. A tie. Everyone was discouraged.

9 Benjamin Franklin understood that each state had to give up something in order for everyone to gain. He suggested a compromise. The delegates could choose parts from the Virginia and New Jersey plans that would please both the big and small states.

The delegates took off the next two days for Independence Day. On July 4, bells rang and guns fired salutes. People celebrated the country's freedom from British rule. Few knew that the entire convention was on the brink of failure.

When the members met again on July 5, they took up the same argument.

A Good Compromiser

Benjamin Franklin urged delegates to settle convention issues by compromise. He often hosted dinner parties to make the delegates feel more at home in Philadelphia. The parties also gave the delegates a chance to get to know one another better. That made it easier for delegates to discuss and decide issues at the convention.

These life-size bronze statues of convention delegates are at the National Constitution Center in Philadelphia. Benjamin Franklin is shown seated, holding a cane.

104

Literature Anthology, pp.104–105

A C T Access Complex Text

Genre

Explain that this expository text includes a variety of text features to deliver information. On pages 104 and 105, point out the photo and caption, "notebook" sidebars, and the portrait with the quotation bubble. These are ways an author can break complex information into small pieces.

- *What do you learn in the sidebar on page 104?* (Benjamin Franklin played an important role in helping the parties compromise.)

- *What do you learn in the speech bubble on page 105?* (Roger Sherman spoke in favor of states having individual rights, using a Senate to represent them.)

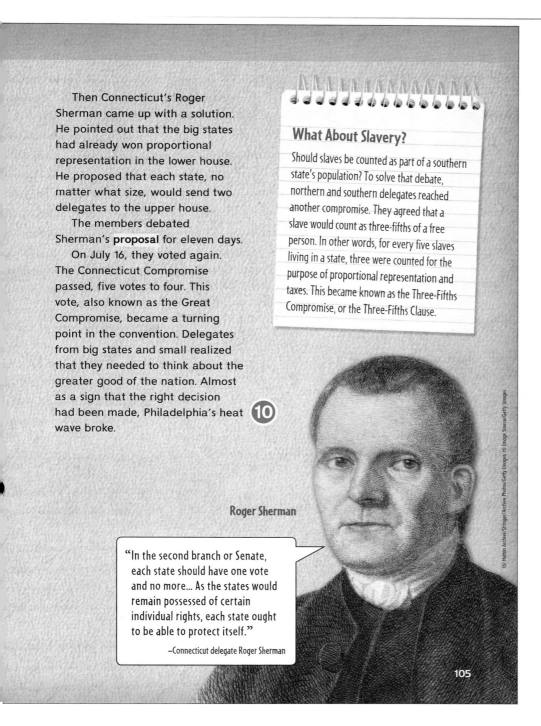

Then Connecticut's Roger Sherman came up with a solution. He pointed out that the big states had already won proportional representation in the lower house. He proposed that each state, no matter what size, would send two delegates to the upper house.

The members debated Sherman's **proposal** for eleven days.

On July 16, they voted again. The Connecticut Compromise passed, five votes to four. This vote, also known as the Great Compromise, became a turning point in the convention. Delegates from big states and small realized that they needed to think about the greater good of the nation. Almost as a sign that the right decision had been made, Philadelphia's heat wave broke. **10**

What About Slavery?

Should slaves be counted as part of a southern state's population? To solve that debate, northern and southern delegates reached another compromise. They agreed that a slave would count as three-fifths of a free person. In other words, for every five slaves living in a state, three were counted for the purpose of proportional representation and taxes. This became known as the Three-Fifths Compromise, or the Three-Fifths Clause.

"In the second branch or Senate, each state should have one vote and no more... As the states would remain possessed of certain individual rights, each state ought to be able to protect itself."

—Connecticut delegate Roger Sherman

Roger Sherman

105

ELL Spotlight on Language

Page 105, Speech Bubble Point to the speech bubble and then read the quote. *The words in the bubble are a quotation. Someone wrote or said these words. Who said or wrote this quote?* (Roger Sherman) *The phrase* possessed of *means "to own or be in control."* Use a prop to model being possessed of something. Say: Ought to *means "should."* Then read aloud the first paragraph on page 105 while students follow along. *Why would states feel more in control with this plan?* (gave all states two delegates to upper house, equal representation)

Read

10 Text Structure: Problem and Solution DOK 2

COLLABORATE What problem is presented at the beginning of the section titled "The Great Compromise"? (The delegates could not agree on representation in the upper house.) What solution is presented on page 105? Turn to a partner and discuss your answers. (The delegates created a plan that satisfied everyone.) Add these answers to your organizer.

Problem	Solution
The delegates could not agree on whether states would have equal representation in the upper house.	The delegates compromised. States would have proportional representation in the lower house as well as two delegates each in the upper house.

Reread

Author's Craft: Mood DOK 2

Reading/Writing Companion, p. 139

Reread page 104. How does the author build suspense in "The Great Compromise"? (The author contrasts the mood of the delegates with that of the people. While the delegates were on the brink of failure, the people celebrated the country's freedom.)

Synthesize Information DOK 2

Explain Meaning is created as readers synthesize information from the text with what they already know.

Model Point out suspenseful language.

"A tie" signals suspense. Also, the delegates were "discouraged." "Bells rang and guns fired salutes." "Few knew that the entire convention was on the brink of failure." Being close to failure is suspenseful.

Apply How is suspense created on page 106? (The image of Washington finding his camp in ruins is suspenseful.)

LESSONS 3-6

Read

11 Reread DOK 1

Teacher Think Aloud I hadn't **COLLABORATE** considered that the nation didn't have a system for electing presidents at this time. How was Washington chosen? We can **reread** to understand what the text says.

Prompt students to reread the information about Washington on page 106 and then turn to a partner to paraphrase why Washington was chosen.

Student Think Aloud As I reread, I see that Washington was a strong leader, and he fought in the Revolutionary War. His history and leadership made him a good choice to be president.

12 Make Inferences DOK 2

Why do you think George Washington returned to Valley Forge during the break? (He had spent a winter there during the war, freezing and hungry, so visiting likely reminded him that forming a new nation was not easy, but it was possible.)

Build Vocabulary on page 106

rural: having to do with the countryside

⑪ Convention members voted over and over. They sometimes voted again on issues they had already settled. Through it all, George Washington sat in the high-backed chair and listened. Most members believed that Washington would be the perfect first president. He had already proved to be a strong leader. And people liked him. But who would be president after Washington? The delegates knew they had to be careful about the way future presidents would be elected.

On July 26, the convention took a ten-day break. Delegates who lived close by went home. Others headed for cooler air in the mountains. Washington visited Valley Forge, a rural area northwest of Philadelphia. During the Revolutionary War, Washington and his troops had camped at Valley Forge. Freezing and hungry, they spent the winter of 1777 and 1778 in tiny log huts. The old camp was in ruins when Washington visited it that July.

Washington (*right*) and an army officer walk past troops at Valley Forge during the winter of 1777 and 1778. This image is a print made of a painting by Howard Pyle (1853-1911).

106

Literature Anthology, pp. 106–107

A C T Access Complex Text

Specific Vocabulary

Help students understand that the U.S. Constitution was a list of resolutions, or decisions, about how the government should work.

- *On page 107, how does the author define* constitution*?* (It is defined as "a new plan for the government.")

- Constitution *is lower-cased when it is used as a common noun to name any plan for a government. It is a proper noun and capitalized when it refers to our country's plan for government, the U.S. Constitution.*

Have students add this social studies word in their reader's notebook.

This document (*right*) is the first draft, or version, of the U.S. Constitution.

Not everyone went on vacation. Five delegates remained in Philadelphia. John Rutledge, Nathaniel Gorham, Oliver Ellsworth, Edmund Randolph, and James Wilson made up the Committee of Detail. They had the important job of copying down the resolutions that had been decided so far. It was hard work. But they finished a rough outline of a document. The document was a new plan for the government—a constitution. The draft was printed and ready to be handed out when the convention met again.

Botin Picture Library/The Bridgeman Art Library International

107

 Spotlight on Language

Page 107, Paragraph 1 Read the paragraph aloud. Point to the names. *These are names of delegates. They helped write the Constitution.* Clarify *resolution* (cognate: *resolución*) and *copying down.* Say: *A resolution is a decision. The delegates had to* copy down, *or write notes, about their resolutions.* Mime to clarify as needed. *Why did they copy down the resolutions?* (remember what they decided) *Why was the document important?* (plan for the new government, or Constitution) Ask students to point to the Constitution. Explain: *The notes became the Constitution.*

13 Primary Source DOK 2

What text feature is found on page 107? (photo of a primary source document with caption) **How does it help you understand the ideas in the selection?** (The primary source shows the first draft of the U.S. Constitution. This helps me better understand the process of how the Constitution was written.)

Reread

Author's Purpose DOK 3

Reread the first paragraph on page 106. **Why does the author point out that the delegates wanted to be careful about how future presidents were elected?** (The delegates were not just solving the problems that faced them at the time. They were planning for the future of the country. They wanted all future presidents to be strong leaders, as they knew Washington would be.) **Why is this information important?** (It helps the reader understand the magnitude of the work that was carried out in Philadelphia that summer.)

Connect to Content

Government and Rights

During the Revolutionary War, the states formed a unified government under the Articles of Confederation. After the war, the U.S. Constitution redefined the federal government in order to better unify the individual states. To limit the power of the federal government and to protect the individual rights of citizens, the Bill of Rights was added to the Constitution. It protected citizens' natural rights to liberty and property, as well as individual freedoms. Have students explain how and why the U.S. government was created and why certain delegates believed a Bill of Rights was important.

LESSONS 3-6

Read

14 Text Features: Headings DOK 2

How does the heading "Of and for the People" relate to this section? (This section shows how the U.S. Constitution was finalized to benefit the people of the United States.)

15 Reread DOK 1

Reread page 108 to check your understanding of the role of committees.

Student Think Aloud I'm not clear about the role of committees, so I'll reread page 108 and paraphrase the text. I see that there were twenty-three articles in the Constitution, and each article had sections. Since the delegates were going to debate every sentence, it was going to take a lot of time to get through it. Items were divided and assigned to committees to resolve so it wouldn't take as long.

Continue to generate questions about the text as you read to deepen your understanding and gain information.

OF AND FOR THE PEOPLE 14

On Monday, August 6, delegates received their copies of the Constitution—seven freshly inked pages. Starting the next day and all through hot, steamy August, they debated every sentence.

The Constitution had twenty-three articles. Each article was divided into sections. The delegates needed to speed up the process of discussing and voting on all the articles. To achieve this, many items were given to **committees** to settle. 15

108

Literature Anthology, pp. 108–109

 Access Complex Text

Connection of Ideas

Help students understand the role of the Committee of Postponed Parts on page 109. Explain that *postponed* means to place after, or put off to a later time. This committee, then, had to discuss many issues that had been put off and resolve them.

- *What were the two possible ways of choosing the president?* (One way was to let Congress or state legislatures choose the president, and the second, James Wilson's plan, was for the people to choose.)

The Committee of Postponed Parts had the most issues to work out. It had to decide where the new government would be located and how Congress would charge taxes. But the executive branch was its most pressing problem.

The Committee of Postponed Parts decided the president of the United States would serve a term of four years and could be reelected. He must be a U.S. citizen and at least thirty-five years old.

The committee added the office of vice president. The vice president would lead the Senate and take over if the president died or had to leave office. The members made sure the president and Congress had the power to get things done. But each branch would not have too much power **(16)** over the other.

A huge question remained. How would the country choose the president? Most delegates felt the president should be selected by Congress or state legislatures.

Back in June, James Wilson said the people should pick the president. No one had liked that idea. But members of the committee changed their minds. They agreed that Wilson's plan was a good one after all.

Wilson's plan included what came to be called the electoral college. The country would be divided into areas, or districts. People from each district would choose an elector. Those electors would decide who would be president.

The Committee of Style revised the final draft of the Constitution. Gouverneur Morris wrote the preamble with its stirring words: *"We, the People of the United States..."* The U.S. Constitution became a document of and for the people.

109

- *How was the issue of choosing the president resolved?* (At first no one liked the idea of the people choosing the president, but committee members changed their minds and agreed it was a good plan.)

Read

16 Text Structure: Problem and Solution DOK 2

The convention used committees to help solve many important problems. On page 109, what pressing problem did the committees face? (They had to define the executive branch.) **What was the solution?** (The president would serve a four-year term and could be reelected. He must be a citizen and be at least thirty-five years old. The vice president would take over if the president died or left office. The power of the president and Congress was balanced.) **Add this problem and solution to your organizer.**

STOP AND CHECK   **DOK 1**

Ask and Answer Questions
Why did delegates ask committees to settle problems? (There were twenty-three articles in the Constitution. The delegates needed to speed up the process of discussing and voting on them, so many items were given to committees to settle.)

ELL   Spotlight on Language

Page 109, Paragraph 1 Read the paragraph with students. Point out how the writer connects ideas. *The committee had many tasks. What did the committee have to decide?* (where government would be located, how to charge taxes) *Which word does the writer use to transition, or connect the last sentence to the rest of the paragraph?* (*But*) Explain that the word *but* can show a contrast between two ideas: But *shows that the author will talk about a different idea. What was the biggest problem?* (executive branch)

LESSONS 3-6

Read

17 Text Structure: Problem and Solution DOK 2

Look back at your organizer. Recall the problem that the Articles of Confederation were no longer able to keep the nation together. How did the convention finally solve the problem? (Delegates worked together to write the U.S. Constitution.)

Problem	Solution
The Articles of Confederation weren't working.	The delegates at the convention worked together to write the U.S. Constitution.

Build Vocabulary on page 110

guaranteed: promised

witnessed: saw something happen

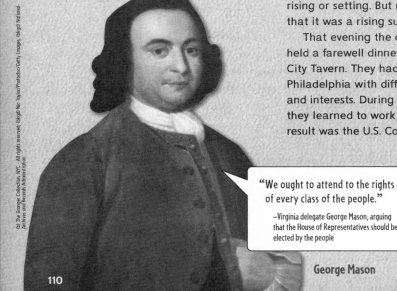

The final version was presented to the convention on September 12. George Mason felt that there should be a Bill of Rights—a list of important rights guaranteed to citizens. Elbridge Gerry agreed, but the other members did not. They believed people's rights were already protected by state constitutions.

On Monday, September 17, forty-two delegates were present. William Jackson, the convention secretary, read aloud the final version of the Constitution. Benjamin Franklin gave a speech to James Wilson to read for him.

Franklin did not like parts of the Constitution. But even with its faults, he doubted anyone could create a better system of government. He urged each man present to sign the Constitution.

George Washington signed first. Then state by state, thirty-nine delegates signed their names. Secretary Jackson witnessed their signatures. Three men refused to sign. Edmund Randolph, George Mason, and Elbridge Gerry would not sign without a Bill of Rights.

When the Constitution was signed, Franklin pointed to the half sun carved on the back of Washington's chair. He said he never could tell if the sun was rising or setting. But now he knew that it was a rising sun.

That evening the delegates held a farewell dinner at the City Tavern. They had come to Philadelphia with different ideas and interests. During the summer, they learned to work together. The result was the U.S. Constitution. **17**

"We ought to attend to the rights of every class of the people."

–Virginia delegate George Mason, arguing that the House of Representatives should be elected by the people

George Mason

110

Literature Anthology, pp. 110–111

A C T **Access Complex Text**

Prior Knowledge

Explain that the Bill of Rights was later added to the U.S. Constitution to help protect people's rights. It is a list of amendments that limits the power of the government.

• *What does this suggest about the U.S. Constitution?* (It is not perfect, and it can be changed if and when it is necessary.)

This is a copy of the U.S. Constitution. The original U.S. Constitution is kept in the National Archives Building in Washington, D.C.

National Archives and Records Administration

111

Return to Purpose Review students' purpose for reading. Then ask partners to share how setting a purpose helped them understand the text.

Reread

Author's Craft: Anecdote DOK 2

Reading/Writing Companion, p. 140

Reread page 110. How does the author use an anecdote to help you understand how Benjamin Franklin's outlook changes? Cite supporting text evidence. (The author uses an anecdote to demonstrate the positive change in Franklin's outlook. When looking at the half-sun carved on the back of Washington's chair, Franklin could never tell if the sun was rising or setting. He came to realize that it was rising. The decisions the delegates made symbolized the beginning of a new era in American history, much like the rising sun signals the start of a new day.)

 Make Inferences DOK 3

Explain Remind students that readers often make inferences to gain a better understanding of a person's motivations, or reasons, for taking action. Model citing supporting text evidence.

Model As I read page 110, I wondered why it was so important to Franklin that his mixed feelings toward the Constitution were made public to the delegates. Then I remembered reading that it was Franklin's idea to compromise in the first place. He must have known even then that it would be just about impossible to create a form of government that everyone would be happy with. He wanted the other delegates to know that they should be happy and proud of their work.

Apply Have students make additional inferences that help them understand Franklin's outlook toward the Constitution.

 ## Spotlight on Language

Page 110, Paragraph 3 Discuss that *witness* means "to see something." Point out that the verb is related to the noun *witness*, or a person who sees something. *When someone signs an important document, a witness watches him or her signing it. Why do you think Senator Jackson was asked to witness the delegates signing the Constitution?* (prevent a delegate from later saying that he did not sign it)

LESSONS 3-6

Read

Meet the Author DOK 2

Candice Ransom

Have students read the biography of the author. Ask:

- How do you think Candice Ransom feels about her home state of Virginia? Why do you think that?

- If Candice Ransom were to visit your school, what would you ask her about writing books for young people? What questions about the selection would you ask her?

- How do you feel about your home state? What do you like about it?

Author's Purpose DOK 2

To Inform: Remind students that authors use text features to provide information about a topic. Students may say the author uses portraits, biographies, and quotations to introduce key individuals at the convention. These text features also bring the text to life. Knowing more about the delegates helps readers understand their opinions and actions.

Reread

Author's Perspective DOK 2

Candice Ransom describes how many of the details of the U.S. Constitution were decided. Based on the description of the summer of 1787 in Philadelphia, how does the author feel about the men who shaped the country's future? (The author portrays these men as determined and mindful of the future. She thinks highly of their decision to take on the work and to carry it out as best as they could.)

ABOUT THE AUTHOR

CANDICE RANSOM

grew up in Virginia. In fact, her ancestors settled there even before the American Revolution. So her interest in our nation's founders isn't surprising. Today, Candice lives in the city of Fredericksburg, Virginia, a place where Thomas Jefferson and George Washington once lived.

Candice is the author of more than 100 books, from board books to chapter books. She has won many awards, and her work has been translated into about a dozen different languages.

In addition to writing, Candice teaches children's literature at a university. She helps her students learn all about writing children's books. She also visits schools to discuss some of her favorite subjects, including writing and American history.

AUTHOR'S PURPOSE

In this selection, the author includes portraits, short biographies, and even quotes from delegates. Why do you think the author includes this information?

112

Literature Anthology, pp. 112

 Spotlight on Language

Page 112, Paragraph 2 Say: *Words that describe are called adjectives.* Provide examples of simple adjective-noun combinations, such as *heavy book*, to clarify as needed. *In this paragraph* board *and* chapter *are adjectives. They describe the books the author writes.* Explain that *board books* refer to books with thick cardboard covers and text for younger readers and *chapter books* to books with longer stories broken into chapters. Show examples to clarify. Then ask students to name a board or chapter book they have read.

Read

Summarize

Tell students they will use the details from their Problem and Solution Chart to summarize. *As I read Who Wrote the U.S. Constitution?, I collected information from the text by taking notes about the problems and solutions early Americans faced. To summarize, I will paraphrase the most important details.*

Reread

Analyze the Text

 After students summarize the selection, have them reread to develop a deeper understanding of the text and to answer the questions on **Reading/Writing Companion** pages 138–140. For students who need support in citing text evidence, use the Reread prompts on pages T31–T44.

Integrate

Build Knowledge: Make Connections

Talk About the Text Have partners discuss the Essential Question: *What do good problem solvers do?*

Write About the Text Have students add their ideas to their Build Knowledge pages of their reader's notebooks.

Anchor Chart Record any new ideas on the Build Knowledge anchor chart.

Add to the Vocabulary List Have students write down any words they learned about problem solving in their reader's notebooks.

Compare Texts DOK 4

Have students compare how the authors present information on problem solving in "Creating a Nation" and *Who Wrote the U.S. Constitution?* Ask: *What was similar about the way delegates worked together to resolve differences while creating the Declaration of Independence and the U.S. Constitution? What was different?*

LEARNING GOALS

We can use text evidence to respond to expository text.

OBJECTIVES

Explain the relationships or interactions between two or more individuals, events, ideas, or concepts in a historical, scientific, or technical text based on specific information in the text.

Compare and contrast the overall structure of events, ideas, concepts, or information in two or more texts.

Draw on information from multiple print or digital sources, demonstrating the ability to locate an answer to a question quickly or to solve a problem efficiently.

Draw evidence from literary or informational texts to support analysis, reflection, and research.

Apply grade 5 Reading standards to informational texts.

ELA ACADEMIC LANGUAGE

• *expository text, chronological order, text structure*

• Cognates: *texto expositivo, estructura del texto*

▶ TEACH IN SMALL GROUP

●● **Approaching Level** and **On Level** Have partners work together to plan and complete the response to the prompt.

● **Beyond Level** Ask students to respond to the prompt independently.

● **ELL** Group students of mixed proficiency levels to discuss and respond to the prompt.

Reread

Write About the Anchor Text

10 mins

Analyze the Prompt DOK 3

Read the prompt aloud: *Why did the 1787 convention last for several months? What does this suggest about the men who wrote the U.S. Constitution? Cite text evidence in your answer.* Ask: *What is the prompt asking?* (to explain why the convention lasted as long as it did and what that says about the men involved) Say: *Let's reread to see how the text features, word choice, and text structure contribute to our understanding of the selection. This will help us make inferences to answer the prompt.*

Analyze Text Evidence

Remind students that problem and solution text structures require the reader to pay attention to the chronological order of events. These events present relevant, or key, details in a logical order and by order of importance. Have students look at Literature Anthology page 97, the introduction to *Who Wrote the U.S. Constitution?* Ask: *What kind of background information does the inset give?* (It describes problems caused by the weak government under the Articles of Confederation. It explains that the delegates came together to fix the government.) **Look at page 104.** Ask: *Why is "The Great Compromise" a good title for this section?* (The title tells me that the delegates found a way to satisfy both the big states and the small states.) *Why is this important?* (This compromise was a turning point. The delegates could move forward to draft a plan for the new government.) **Have partners discuss how the text features and text structure contributes to the overall meaning of the text.**

Respond

Review pages 138–140 of the **Reading/Writing Companion**. Have partners or small groups refer to and discuss their completed charts and writing responses from those pages. Then direct students' attention to the sentence starters on page 141 of the **Reading/Writing Companion**. Have them use sentence starters to guide their responses.

Analytical Writing Students should focus on two or three ways the delegates worked together to address and resolve problems. They should put events in order to show the delegates' step by step process that was done to write the U.S. Constitution. They should use this information to help them determine what this means about the men who created the U.S. Constitution. Remind students to vary sentence structure by combining short sentences and adding phrases and clauses to others. Students may use additional paper to complete the assignment if needed.

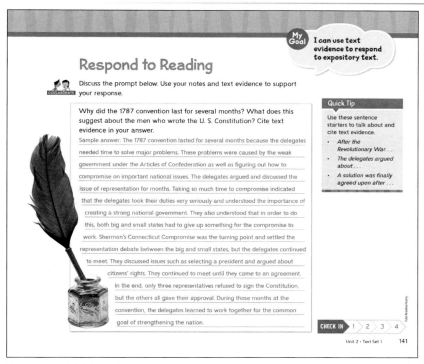

Reading/Writing Companion, p. 141

ELL English Language Learners

Use the following scaffolds with **Respond.**

Beginning

Read the prompt with students and explain what they will write about. Review the students' completed charts on **Reading/Writing Companion** pages 138-140. Clarify the meaning of *representation* with students. Ask: *Were the delegates divided on the issue of representation?* (yes) Help partners discuss why the 1787 convention lasted for several months and respond using: The delegates needed <u>time</u> to solve a <u>problem</u>. They discussed the issue of <u>representation</u>.

Intermediate

Read the prompt with students and discuss what they will write about. Have partners review their completed charts on **Reading/ Writing Companion** pages 138-140. Ask: *What issue were the delegates divided on?* The delegates were divided on the issue of <u>representation</u>. Then have partners discuss why the 1787 convention last for several months and respond using: The 1787 convention lasted for several months because the delegates needed _____.

Advanced/Advanced High

Review the prompt and sentence starters on page 141 with students. Have them discuss their completed charts on pages 138-140. Then have partners discuss what problem, or issue, the delegates needed to solve and respond using the sentence starters.

ELL NEWCOMERS

Have students listen to the summaries of the **Anchor Text** in their native language and then in English to help them access the text and develop listening comprehension. Help students ask and answer questions with a partner. Use these sentence frames: *What does this text explain? The text explains ___.* Then have them complete the online **Newcomer Activities** individually or in pairs.

FORMATIVE ASSESSMENT

STUDENT CHECK-IN

Ask partners to share their response on Reading/Writing Companion page 141. Have them reflect using the Check-In routine to fill in the bars.

LESSONS 7-8

"Wordsmiths"

Lexile 970L

LEARNING GOALS

Read We can apply strategies and skills to read expository text.

Reread We can reread to analyze text, craft, and structure and compare texts.

Have students apply what they learned as they read.

🌐 Explain how examples of art, music, and literature reflect the times during which they were created.

A C T **What makes this text complex?**
▶ **Connection of Ideas**
▶ **Genre**

Analytical Writing **Compare Texts** DOK 4

As students read and reread "Wordsmiths" encourage them to take notes about the Essential Question: *What do good problem solvers do?* Ask them how this text compares with what they learned about how our government was formed in *Who Wrote the U.S. Constitution?*

Read

❶ Text Structure: Problem and Solution DOK 2

How did Terry solve her problem with neighbors who tried to claim her land as their own? (Terry and her husband took the neighbors to court.) Why was this unusual? Make an inference using text evidence. (Terry and her husband lived during a period of history where African Americans did not have many rights. Many were afraid to stand up for justice, so it was exceptional that they did.)

Genre • Expository Text

Compare Texts
Read about two African American women poets who used their voices to overcome problems.

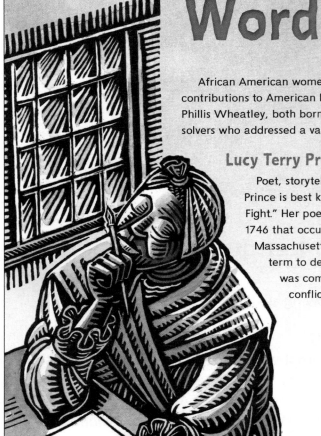

Wordsmiths

African American women have made valuable contributions to American literature. Lucy Terry Prince and Phillis Wheatley, both born in the 1700s, were problem solvers who addressed a variety of diverse topics.

Lucy Terry Prince

Poet, storyteller, and activist, Lucy Terry Prince is best known for her poem "Bars Fight." Her poem describes a conflict in 1746 that occurred in a section of Deerfield, Massachusetts, called "the Bars," a colonial term to describe meadows. Although it was composed in the same year as the conflict, it wasn't published until 1855.

Literature Anthology, pp. 114–115

A C T **Access Complex Text**

Connection of Ideas

Explain that Africans who lived in the Americas during colonial times were enslaved. Some enslaved Africans were eventually freed by their masters, and some were able to purchase their freedom. Lucy Terry's freedom was purchased by the man she eventually married. Lucy Terry was one of few freed slaves, but there were other remarkable things about her, too.

Terry was born in Africa in the early 1730s. As a young child, she was stolen from her homeland, enslaved, and brought to Bristol, Rhode Island. Terry later met Abijah Prince, a free man of color. He purchased her freedom, and they married in 1756. The couple eventually settled on their own land in present-day Vermont.

Terry regularly used her voice to **resolve** problems and fight for social equality. When white neighbors attempted to claim the Princes' land as their own, they took their neighbors to court to address the **situation**. "Bars Fight," her **1** only surviving poem, established Terry as the first African American female poet in the United States. Remembered as a woman who brought words to life, Terry died in 1821 in Sunderland, Vermont.

Terry's remarkable life was celebrated in *The Franklin Herald* of Greenfield, Massachusetts, with a lengthy obituary. The following excerpt was reprinted in *The Vermont Gazette*.

Words to Know
*volubility: ability to speak continuously
*destitute: lacking

In this remarkable woman there was an assemblage of qualities rarely to be found... Her volubility* was exceeded by none, and in general the fluency of her speech was not destitute* of instruction and education. She was much respected among her acquaintance, who treated her with a degree of deference. **2**

115

Read

2 Reread DOK 1

Reread the obituary. What aspect of Terry's character does it celebrate? (her great ability to speak) What details from the obituary support this trait? ("Her volubility was exceeded by none"; "her speech was not without instruction and education")

Build Vocabulary pages 114–115

activist: someone who works to create political or social change

obituary: a written piece in a newspaper that announces a person's death

deference: polite behavior that shows respect

Reread

Author's Craft: Print Features DOK 2

How does the obituary support what the author says about Terry? (It gives a firsthand account about how Terry was a powerful speaker and respected in her community.) Have students compare and contrast the primary and secondary sources on Lucy Terry Prince and discuss how including primary sources can support a writer's ideas and statements.

ELL Spotlight on Idioms

Page 115, Paragraph 2 Explain that *brought words to life* means to create a powerful image or feeling with words. *Lucy Terry brought words to life through her poems. What other ways can you* bring something to life? (possible answers: songs, stories, paintings)

- *What made Lucy Terry stand out amongst other people who lived during colonial times?* (Lucy Terry was a former slave who owned land, fought for her equal rights, and was the first African American female poet in the United States.)

- *Lucy Terry was a problem solver as well as a poet. She was respected by many people. What can you infer about Lucy Terry?* (Possible answer: She was educated and smart.)

Read

③ Text Structure: Problem and Solution DOK 2

What problem did Wheatley have? (No one would publish her poetry.) How did Wheatley solve her problem? (She traveled to London to offer a proposal to publishers. Eventually, a friend of the family helped her publish her first book of poetry.)

Build Vocabulary on page 116

native: original

plight: a bad situation

oppression: the state of being treated cruelly without any rights

deliverance: being saved from harm

Reread

Author's Purpose DOK 3

Reading/Writing Companion, p. 144

What is the author's purpose for writing about the two poets? (The author's purpose for writing about these two poets is to inform the reader about two female African American poets, and to show the power of their words and the problems they addressed at the time.)

Phillis Wheatley

Phillis Wheatley was born around 1753 in West Africa. As a young girl, she was captured from her native land, enslaved, and taken to Boston, Massachusetts. She was sold to John and Susanna Wheatley. They named her Phillis, after the ship that brought her to America. She learned to read and write at a young age. She quickly mastered English, Latin, and Greek.

When she was about 13, Wheatley wrote her first poem. It was published in the *Newport Mercury* newspaper in 1767. In the early 1770s, Wheatley had to take a test to prove that she had actually written her poems. Even though she passed the test, she was unable to find a Boston publisher. She traveled to London, England, to offer a **proposal** to publishers there. In 1773, a friend of the family helped Wheatley publish a book of her poetry, *Poems on Various Subjects, Religious and Moral.* ③

When she returned to colonial America, Wheatley gained her freedom. As a free woman, she continued to publish poetry. There is some **debate** that Wheatley allegedly ignored the plight of enslaved African Americans. However, John Shields, editor of *The Collected Works of Phillis Wheatley*, states that a letter by Wheatley written after her emancipation proves that she was concerned "for the fate of her Black brothers and sisters still suffering under slavery."

Words to Know
*pants: wants
*disposition: belief

> *Love of freedom; it is impatient of Oppression and pants* for Deliverance... How well the cry for Liberty, and the reverse Disposition* for the exercise of oppressive Power over others...*

This excerpt from Wheatley's letter condemning slavery was written to Reverend Samson Occom and published throughout Boston in 1774.

PHILLIS WHEATLEY
CA 1753-1784

BORN IN WEST AFRICA AND SOLD AS A SLAVE FROM THE SHIP *PHILLIS* IN COLONIAL BOSTON. SHE W...

This bronze statue of Phillis Wheatley was installed in Boston in 2003 as part of the "Boston Women's Memorial."

...AND MORE WAS THE FIRST BOOK PUBLISHED BY AN AFRICAN WRITER IN AMERICA.

116

Literature Anthology, pp. 116–117

A C T   Access Complex Text

Genre

On pages 116–117, the author includes two excerpts from letters—one written by Wheatley herself and one written about her by George Washington. Discuss the purpose behind including primary sources such as this.

- *What do you learn about Phillis Wheatley from her letter?* (It shows that she greatly disliked the unfair treatment of Africans living in America and wanted change.)

- *What do you learn about Phillis Wheatley from George Washington's letter?* (Washington's letter shows that Phillis Wheatley was highly respected.)

- *Why did the author include these letters?* (The author wanted to show how powerful Wheatley's words were and how much they affected those around her.)

In 1778, Wheatley married John Peters. She lived in poverty throughout the rest of her life and died at the birth of her third child on December 5, 1784.

Wheatley is remembered as the first African American to publish a collection of poetry. She also wrote and sent a poem to General George Washington in 1775 that praised him for his success during the American Revolution. His response to her shows how highly regarded Wheatley was. Below is part of Washington's letter.

> *Mrs Phillis,*
> *I thank you most sincerely for your polite notice of me, in the elegant Lines you enclosed; and however undeserving I may be...*
> *If you should ever come to Cambridge, or near Head Quarters, I shall be happy to see a person so favourd* by the Muses*...*
>
> *—G. Washington*

Words to Know
*favourd: well liked
*Muses: inspirational forces

Make Connections
Talk about how Lucy Terry Prince and Phillis Wheatley solved some of their problems.
ESSENTIAL QUESTION

How were the actions of other historical figures you've read about similar to the actions of Terry and Wheatley? TEXT TO TEXT

117

ELL Spotlight on Language

Page 116, Paragraph 2 Read aloud the paragraph. Point to the word *published* in the third sentence. Say: Publish *means "to print something for the public to read." When you publish something, you make it available to everyone. Was Wheatley's poem published in 1767?* (yes) *Who published Wheatley's poem?* The <u>Newport Mercury</u> newspaper published Wheatley's poem. Have students discuss what other things can be published. (articles, songs, essays, photographs)

Summarize

Guide students to summarize the selection.

Analyze the Text

After students summarize, have them reread to develop a deeper understanding of the text by annotating and answering questions on **Reading/Writing Companion** pages 142–144.

Build Knowledge: Make Connections

Talk About the Text Have partners discuss what good problem solvers do.

Write About the Text Have students add their ideas to their Build Knowledge pages of their reader's notebooks.

Anchor Chart Record any new ideas on the Build Knowledge anchor chart.

Add to the Vocabulary List Have students write down any words they learned about problem solving in their reader's notebooks.

Compare Texts DOK 4

Text to Text <u>Answer</u>: Like Terry and Wheatley, the delegates in *Who Wrote the Constitution?* used the power of their writing to solve problems and address injustice.
<u>Evidence</u>: On page 107, the delegates drafted a rough outline of a document that was to become the U.S. Constitution.

FORMATIVE ASSESSMENT

❯ STUDENT CHECK-IN

Read Ask partners to share their summaries. Then have them reflect using the Check-In routine.

Reread Ask partners to share their responses on Reading/Writing Companion pages 142-144. Then have them use the Check-In routine to reflect and fill in the bars.

LESSONS 7-8

LEARNING GOALS

We can identify print and graphic features to help us read and understand expository text.

OBJECTIVES

Draw on information from multiple print or digital sources, demonstrating the ability to locate an answer to a question quickly or to solve a problem efficiently.

Explain how an author uses reasons and evidence to support particular points in a text, including which reasons and evidence support which point(s).

Identify the author's purpose.

Come to discussions prepared, having read or studied required material; explicitly draw on that preparation and other information known about the topic to explore ideas under discussion.

ELA ACADEMIC LANGUAGE

- *features, evidence, primary sources, credibility*
- Cognates: *evidencia, credibilidad*

Reread

10 mins

Print and Graphic Features

1 Explain

Have students turn to **Reading/Writing Companion** page 145. Share with students the following key points of print and graphic features.

- Print features are pieces of information that are not included in the main text. Print features can help an author support information in the main text and make the text more interesting to readers.

- Primary sources are one kind of feature an author may include in text. A primary source is a firsthand account written or created during the time an event took place. For example, an obituary is an account of someone's life written at the time of his or her death. Graphic features like letters a person wrote, photographs, and art created at the time the person lived or died are also primary sources a writer might use to support information.

- Primary sources and other print and graphic features add credibility to an author's writing by helping readers understand what a person or place was like at a certain period of time.

2 Model

Model identifying and analyzing print features on page 142 of the **Reading/Writing Companion**. Have students read the excerpt from Terry's obituary. Discuss the ways in which the obituary both mourns and celebrates Terry's life, as well as how it helps the author convey a respectful tone and perspective. As a group, compare and contrast the obituary with the main text. Ask: *What does the primary source add to the main text?*

COLLABORATE

3 Guided Practice

Now have students turn to Reading/Writing Companion page 143. Have them identify ways in which the excerpt from Washington's letter to Wheatley and the photograph of the sculpture support the main text and add credibility to the author's writing. Ask: *How does Washington's letter help you understand how he felt about Wheatley?* (It shows he admired her.) *How does the photograph of the sculpture enhance the text?* (It shows what she looked like. Also, she is posed in a way that makes her look thoughtful.)

Have partners identify any additional relevant details in the print and graphic features and discuss how they support the main text before sharing their ideas with the class.

Allow students time to enter their responses on Reading/Writing Companion page 145.

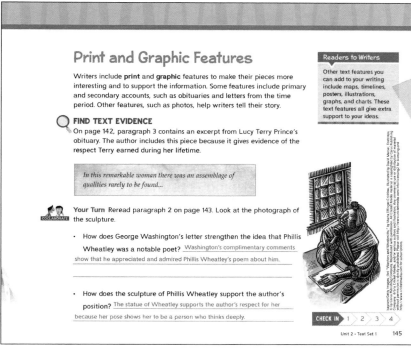

Reading/Writing Companion, p. 145

 # English Language Learners

Use the following scaffolds with **Guided Practice**.

Beginning

Restate Washington's letter in simpler language: *Dear Phillis, Thank you for the beautiful poem you wrote about me. I am not sure I have earned your praise. If you visit, I would be happy to meet you because you are so talented.* Ask: *What does George Washington do in the first line?* He thanks Phillis for her poem. *Do you think Washington liked Phillis's poem?* (yes) Washington thinks Phillis is a talented poet.

Intermediate

Read aloud the excerpt on page 143. Model restating using the definitions provided in the excerpt and explain that Lines *means "poem."* Ask: *What words show that Washington admired, or liked Wheatley's poem?* (thank you, polite, elegant) *What words tell that he admired Wheatley?* (happy, favoured/well liked) Have students discuss how Washington's letter helps them understand how he felt about Wheatley: George Washington says comments that show he admired Wheatley's poems. He thinks she is a talented/good poet.

Advanced/Advanced High

Have students read Washington's excerpt on page 143 and identify words and phrases that express his feelings about Phillis Wheatley's poem. Then have partners discuss how the photograph of the sculpture supports the author's position.

FORMATIVE ASSESSMENT

❯ STUDENT CHECK-IN

Ask partners to share their Your Turn responses on Reading/Writing Companion page 145. Then have them reflect using the Check-In routine to fill in the bars.

LESSONS 8-9

LEARNING GOALS

- We can identify and decode words with plurals.
- We can identify and read multisyllabic words.
- We can read fluently with accuracy and expression.

OBJECTIVES

Use combined knowledge of all letter-sound correspondences, syllabication patterns, and morphology (e.g., roots and affixes) to read accurately unfamiliar multisyllabic words in context and out of context.

Read with sufficient accuracy and fluency to support comprehension.

Read grade-level text with purpose and understanding.

Use context to confirm or self-correct word recognition and understanding, rereading as necessary.

- Rate: 111–131 WCPM

ELA ACADEMIC LANGUAGE

- *plurals, consonant, expression*
- Cognates: *consonante, expresión*

TEACH IN SMALL GROUP

Word Study

⬤ **Approaching Level** Use the Tier 2 activity on page T65 before teaching the lesson.

⬤⬤ **On Level** and **Beyond Level** As needed, use the Read Multisyllabic Words section only.

⬤ **ELL** See page 5 in the **Language Transfers Handbook** for guidance in identifying sounds and symbols that do not transfer for speakers of certain languages.

OPTION 10 mins

Plurals

1 Explain

Tell students that the plural endings *–s* and *–es* mean "more than one." Write the following spelling rules on the board, and read them aloud.

- Most words are made plural by adding *–s* to the end of the word, as in *hats*.
- Words that end in *–sh, -ch, -s, -ss,* or *–x* are made plural by adding *–es* to the end of the word, as in *lunches*.
- Words that end with a consonant and a *y* are usually made plural by changing the *y* to an *i* and adding *–es* to the end of the word, as in *copies*.

2 Model

Write the following on the board. Read each word aloud, and underline the plural ending.

–s:	plays, birds, shoes
–es:	bushes, couches, bosses, foxes
y changed to *i* + *es:*	ladies, duties, rubies

3 Guided Practice

Write the words below on the board. Ask students to underline the plural ending in each word. Then have them define each plural word. As you go through the list, remind students that these plural words all have a base word as well as a plural ending. After students define each plural word, have them identify the base word.

floors	noses	desks	dishes	catches
irises	compasses	taxes	cherries	families
cities	teachers	benches	axes	rashes

For practice with decoding and encoding, use **Practice Book** page 79 or online activities.

Read Multisyllabic Words

Transition to Longer Words Have students use what they know about plurals to decode and determine the meanings of words. Write the words below on the board. Ask students to read the words and then underline their plural endings.

Discuss any spelling changes required when plural endings are added. Model how to use the meaning of the base word to determine the meaning of the plural word. Make sure students do not allow the number of syllables in a word to prevent them from recognizing plural endings.

dress, dresses	variety, varieties	mix, mixes
certificate, certificates	giraffe, giraffes	country, countries
hostess, hostesses	carnival, carnivals	picture, pictures
principal, principals	library, libraries	stretcher, stretchers

OPTION
10 mins

Fluency

Accuracy and Expression

Explain/Model Tell students they can use their knowledge of plural endings to help them read more accurately. Remind them that using expression, or prosody, helps bring the text to life and makes it easier to understand. Read aloud the first three paragraphs of "Creating a Nation," **Reading/Writing Companion** page 128. Model using expression to build interest. Read carefully, emphasizing the plurals to clarify meaning.

Practice/Apply Have groups choral read the same passage, mimicking your careful reading and use of expression. Remind students that you will be listening for these qualities in their reading during the week. Explain that you will help them improve their reading by pointing out where they can increase accuracy and use expression more effectively.

Daily Fluency Practice

Automaticity Students can practice reading with accuracy and appropriate rate to develop automaticity using the online **Differentiated Genre Passage,** "Secret Help from Spain."

DIGITAL TOOLS

For more practice, have students use the phonics and fluency activities.

Word Study

Plurals

MULTIMODAL LEARNING

Write the plural endings *-s, -es,* and *-ies* on one set of note cards. On another set of cards, write a variety of singular nouns that can be made plural using *-s, -es,* or *-ies,* such as *pencil, fox,* and *city.* Ask partners to take turns putting together one plural ending card and one noun card to make a new plural word. Have them read their new word and tell its meaning.

FORMATIVE ASSESSMENT

❯ STUDENT CHECK-IN

Plurals Have partners share three plural words.

Multisyllabic Words Have partners add plurals to three multisyllabic words.

Fluency Ask partners to read "Secret Help from Spain" fluently.

Have partners reflect using the Check-In routine.

✔ CHECK FOR SUCCESS

Can students decode and determine the meanings of multisyllabic plural words? Can students read fluently?

❯ Small Group Instruction

If No:

● **Approaching** Reteach pp. T65, T68

● **ELL** Develop p. T65

If Yes:

● **On** Apply p. T70

● **Beyond** Apply p. T76

LESSONS 9-10

LEARNING GOALS

We can compare the photograph with the selections in this text set to build knowledge about what good problem solvers do.

OBJECTIVES

Integrate information from several texts on the same topic in order to write or speak about the subject knowledgeably.

Draw evidence from literary or informational texts to support analysis, reflection, and research.

Close Reading Routine

Read DOK 1–2

- Identify important ideas and details.
- Take notes and summarize.
- Use **A C T** prompts as needed.

Reread DOK 2–3

- Analyze the text, craft, and structure.
- Use the *Reading/Writing Companion*.

Integrate DOK 3–4

- Integrate knowledge and ideas.
- Make text-to-text connections.
- Use the Integrate/Make Connections lesson.
- Use *Reading/Writing Companion*, page 146.
- Complete the Show Your Knowledge task.
- Inspire action.

FORMATIVE ASSESSMENT

❯ STUDENT CHECK-IN

Ask partners to share their response on Reading/Writing Companion page 146. Then have them use the Check-In routine to reflect and fill in the bars.

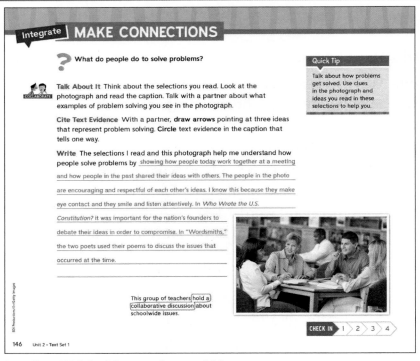

Reading/Writing Companion, p. 146

Integrate

🕙 Make Connections DOK 4

Talk About It

 Share and discuss students' responses to the "Meet Me in the Middle" Blast. Display the Build Knowledge anchor chart. Review the chart and have students read through their notes, annotations, and responses for each text. Then ask students to complete the Talk About It activity on **Reading/Writing Companion** page 146.

Cite Text Evidence

Guide students to see the connections between the photograph of the community board meeting on Reading/Writing Companion page 146 and the texts. Remind students to read the caption next to the photograph, and also the Quick Tip.

Write

Students should refer to their notes on the chart as they respond to the writing prompt at the bottom of the page. Then have groups share and discuss their responses.

📋 Build Knowledge: Make Connections

Talk About the Text Have partners discuss how people solve problems.

Write About the Text Have students add their ideas to their Build Knowledge pages of their reader's notebooks.

Anchor Chart Record any new ideas on the Build Knowledge anchor chart.

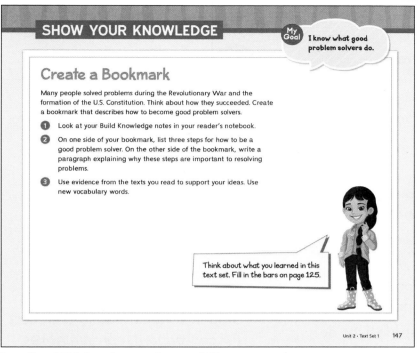

Reading/Writing Companion, p. 147

(10 mins) **Show Your Knowledge** DOK 4

Create a Bookmark

Explain to students that they will show how they built knowledge across the text set by creating a bookmark that describes how to become a good problem solver. Display the Build Knowledge anchor chart and ask: *What do good problem solvers do?*

Step 1 Guide partners to review the Build Knowledge anchor chart in their reader's notebook to discuss the prompt.

Step 2 Have students list three steps for how to be a good problem solver on one side of the bookmark. On the other side, they should write a paragraph explaining why these steps are important.

Step 3 Remind students to use evidence from the texts, video, and listening passage to support their ideas. Prompt students to use words from their Build Knowledge vocabulary list.

Inspire Action

Share Your Bookmark Have students present their bookmarks. Ask students in the audience to use sticky notes to post comments under the bookmarks on display. Presenters can read the comments and post sticky note responses.

What Are You Inspired to Do? Encourage partners to think of another way to respond to the texts. Ask: *What else do the texts inspire you to do?*

LEARNING GOALS

- We can build and expand on new vocabulary words.
- We use context clues to figure out unfamiliar words.
- We can write using new vocabulary words.

OBJECTIVES

Determine the meaning of general academic and domain-specific words and phrases in a text relevant to a grade 5 topic or subject area.

Use combined knowledge of all letter-sound correspondences, syllabication patterns, and morphology to read accurately unfamiliar multisyllabic words in context and out of context.

Use context as a clue to the meaning of a word or phrase.

Consult reference materials, both print and digital, to find the pronunciation and determine or clarify the precise meaning of key words and phrases.

DIGITAL TOOLS

Word Study   **Vocabulary Activities**

ELL ENGLISH LANGUAGE LEARNERS

Pair students of different language proficiency levels to practice vocabulary. Have partners discuss different shades of meaning in words with similar meanings, such as *proposal* and *suggestion*.

FORMATIVE ASSESSMENT

❯ STUDENT CHECK-IN

After each lesson, have partners share and reflect using the Check-In routine.

LESSON 1 Connect to Words

Practice the target vocabulary.

1. Why do people form **committees**?
2. What **conventions** have you read or heard about?
3. What is a topic you might **debate**?
4. What information might you include in a **proposal**?
5. What do **representatives** do?
6. How do you **resolve** problems with your friends?
7. Describe a funny **situation** that happened to you.
8. What advantages might people in a **union** have?

OPTION LESSON 6 Build Vocabulary

- Display *consequently, convince,* and *individuals.*
- Define each word and discuss the meanings with students.
- Write *consequence* under *consequently*. Have partners write other words with the same root and define them. Then have partners ask and answer questions using the words.
- Repeat with *convince* and *individuals.*

OPTION LESSON 2 Content Words

Help students create different forms of target words by changing inflectional endings.

- Write *committee* in the first column of a T-chart and *committees* in the second column. Read the words aloud.
- Have students share sentences using each form of *committee.*
- Students should add to the chart for *convention, representatives, situation, union,* and *proposal.* Then share sentences using the different forms of the words.
- Have students copy the chart in their reader's notebook.

See **Practice Book** page 71.

LESSON 7 Using a Dictionary

- Define *present* in this context: *The group will present its proposal.*
- Explain that a dictionary definition is a denotation, or literal meaning. A word's connotation implies the feeling it evokes. Have pairs discuss the connotation of *present.*
- Have pairs use a print or digital dictionary to verify other meanings and pronunciations of *present* as well as its syllabication.
- Have students use a print or digital resource to determine the word origin of *present.*

See **Practice Book** page 83.

LESSON 3 · Spiral Review · **Reinforce the Words**

Have students orally complete each sentence stem to review words.

1. You might find ____ at a <u>convention</u> about health.

2. Lisa was unfamiliar with the <u>situation</u>, so she ____.

3. Ed wants to visit every state in the <u>union</u> because ____.

4. <u>Committees</u> often are made up of people who ____.

5. Ann can <u>resolve</u> the fight with her sister by ____.

6. <u>Representatives</u> met to ____.

Display the previous vocabulary: *access, advance, cite, reasoning, drawbacks, data.* Have pairs ask and answer questions using the words.

See **Practice Book** page 72.

LESSON 8 · **Context Clues**

Use definitions and restatements to figure out unfamiliar words.

- Display On Level **Differentiated Genre Passage** "Secret Help from Spain." Read the second paragraph. Model figuring out the meaning of *revolt.*

- Have pairs use context clues to figure out meanings of other unfamiliar words in the passage.

- Partners can confirm meanings in a print or an online dictionary.

See **Practice Book** page 84.

OPTION LESSON 4 · **Connect to Writing**

- Have students write sentences in their reader's notebook using the target vocabulary.

- Tell them to write sentences that provide context to show what the words mean.

- **ELL** Provide the Lesson 3 sentence stems 1–6 for students needing extra support.

Write Using Vocabulary

Have students write something they learned from this text set's target words in their reader's notebook. For example, they might write about why *conventions* are held or about how *committees* help people accomplish tasks.

OPTION LESSON 9 · **Shades of Meaning**

Help students generate words related to *resolve.* Draw a T-chart with the labels "Synonyms" and "Antonyms."

- Have partners generate words to add to the T-chart. Encourage students to use a thesaurus.

- Add words not included, such as synonyms (e.g., *settle*) and antonyms (e.g., *waver, disagree*).

- Ask students to copy the words in their reader's notebook.

OPTION LESSON 5 · **Word Squares** · MULTIMODAL

Ask students to create Word Squares for each vocabulary word.

- In the first square, students write the word (e.g., *debate*).

- In the second square, students write their own definition of the word and any related words, such as synonyms (e.g., *argue, discuss, dispute*).

- In the third square, students draw an illustration that will help them remember the word (e.g., two people facing off, both talking).

- In the fourth square, students write nonexamples, including antonyms for the word (e.g., *lecture, conversation*).

Have partners discuss their squares.

OPTION LESSON 10 · **Morphology**

Use *convention* as a springboard to learn more words. Draw a three-column chart with *convention* on the left.

- In the right two columns, write *-ed* and *-ing.* Discuss how the suffixes change the meaning or part of speech of *convene.*

- Have students add suffixes to the base word of *situation: situate.*

- Ask partners to do a search for other words with these suffixes.

Write Using Vocabulary

Have students use vocabulary words in their extended writing.

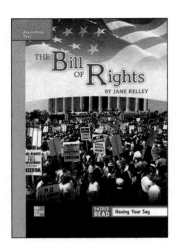

Lexile 820L

OBJECTIVES

Explain the relationships or interactions between two or more individuals, events, ideas, or concepts in a historical, scientific, or technical text based on specific information in the text.

Compare and contrast the overall structure (e.g., chronology, comparison, cause/effect, problem/solution) of events, ideas, concepts, or information in two or more texts.

Read grade-level text with purpose and understanding.

Determine or clarify the meaning of unknown and multiple-meaning words and phrases based on grade 5 reading and content, choosing flexibly from a range of strategies.

Use context (e.g., cause/effect relationships and comparisons in text) as a clue to the meaning of a word or phrase.

ELA ACADEMIC LANGUAGE

• *expository text, problem, solution, context clues*

• Cognates: *texto expositivo, problema, solución*

●Approaching Level

Leveled Reader: *The Bill of Rights*

Preview and Predict

Read the Essential Question: *What do good problem solvers do?*

Have students preview the title, introduction, and text features of *The Bill of Rights* to make predictions about the selection. Then discuss the predictions.

Review Genre: Expository Text

Remind students that expository text gives facts, examples, and explanations about a topic. It may also include text features such as charts, graphs, diagrams, or timelines to organize information. Have students identify the text features in *The Bill of Rights*.

Close Reading

Note Taking Ask students to use a copy of the online Problem and Solution **Graphic Organizer 4** as they read.

Pages 2–3 *Turn to a partner and explain what decision the colonists had to make after the American Revolution.* (They had to decide how to form a new government.) *At the convention in Philadelphia, how did the delegates share their ideas?* (through speeches)

Pages 4–6 *What context clues on page 4 help you identify the meaning of* Federalists*? Reread the second paragraph to find the answer.* (The word *federal* describes a central government where states still have control of some laws; people who wanted a strong central government were called Federalists.) **Have students add this word to their reader's notebook.** *How did James Madison solve the states' problem?* (He came up with a compromise. He promised that if Virginia ratified the Constitution and elected him to Congress, he would work to add a bill of rights.)

Pages 7–9 Point out the sidebar on page 8. *What information does the text give you?* (how amendments are made) *Why might the delegates who wrote the Constitution have created a way to amend, or change, it in the future?* (They realized ideas about rights would shift over time.)

Pages 10–12 *The author includes a timeline on page 10. When did Madison introduce the Bill of Rights?* (April 1789) *Reread the last paragraph on page 12. Paraphrase the problem the Third Amendment solved.* (The British could force people to give soldiers food or a place to sleep. The Third Amendment says that soldiers needed permission.)

Pages 13–15 *Reread page 13. What problem did the Fourth Amendment solve?* (British soldiers could no longer search or arrest people without a reason.) *What information do the headings provide?* (They tell what each section of text is about.)

Pages 16–17 *How can people today solve their problems the same way as when the Bill of Rights was developed?* (People can discuss their problems and find compromises.)

Respond to Reading Revisit the Essential Question and ask students to complete the Text Evidence questions on page 18.

 Write About Reading Check that students have correctly identified the problem and solution described on page 6.

Fluency: Accuracy and Rate

Model Model reading page 5 with accuracy and at an appropriate rate. Next, read the passage aloud and have students read along with you.

Apply Have students practice reading the passage with a partner.

Paired Read: "Having Your Say"

 Make Connections: Write About It

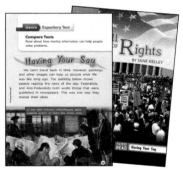

Before reading, ask students to note that the genre of this text is also expository text. Then discuss the Essential Question. After reading, ask students to write about connections between *The Bill of Rights* and "Having Your Say."

Leveled Reader

Build Knowledge

Talk About the Text Have partners discuss how people solve problems.

Write About the Text Have students add their ideas to the Build Knowledge pages of their reader's notebooks.

 FOCUS ON SOCIAL STUDIES

Students can extend their knowledge of compromising by completing the social studies activity on page 24.

LITERATURE CIRCLES

Ask students to conduct a literature circle using the Thinkmark questions to guide the discussion. You may wish to have a whole-class discussion, based on information in both selections in the Leveled Reader, about how people can solve problems through compromise.

 **LEVEL** UP

IF students read the Approaching Level fluently and answered the questions,

THEN pair them with students who have proficiently read the On Level and have students

- echo-read the On Level main selection.

- use self-stick notes to mark ways problems were solved.

 **Access Complex Text**

The On Level challenges students by including more **domain-specific words** and **complex sentence structures.**

Lexile 730L

OBJECTIVES

Explain the relationships or interactions between two or more individuals, events, ideas, or concepts in a historical, scientific, or technical text based on specific information in the text.

Compare and contrast the overall structure (e.g., chronology, comparison, cause/effect, problem/ solution) of events, ideas, concepts, or information in two or more texts.

Integrate information from several texts on the same topic in order to write or speak about the subject knowledgeably.

Determine or clarify the meaning of unknown and multiple-meaning words and phrases based on grade 5 reading and content, choosing flexibly from a range of strategies.

Use context (e.g., cause/effect relationships and comparisons in text) as a clue to the meaning of a word or phrase.

ELA ACADEMIC LANGUAGE

• *problem, solution, headings, connection, details*

• Cognates: *problema, solución, conexión, detalles*

●Approaching Level

Genre Passage: "Secret Help from Spain"

Build Background

Read aloud the Essential Question: *What do good problem solvers do?* Ask students to compare how two people they read about in this text set were able to solve a problem effectively. Use these sentence starters:

> *I read that good problem solvers . . .*
> *This helps me understand that solutions . . .*

Let students know that the online **Differentiated Genre Passage** "Secret Help from Spain" discusses the financial backing American colonists received from both Spain and France during the American Revolution. Explain that other countries often supply goods or money to help one country win a war. Discuss why this might be helpful to both countries.

Review Genre: Expository Text

Reiterate that expository text includes facts, details, and explanations about a topic. Expository texts may include text features, such as headings, that tell what a section of a text is mostly about. Text structures are used to organize information and present it in a logical order.

Close Reading

Note Taking As students read the passage the first time, ask them to annotate the text. Have them note key ideas and details, unfamiliar words, and questions they have. Then read again and use the following questions.

Problem and Solution Read paragraph 2 on page A1. *What did Spain agree to do to help the American colonists?* (give the colonists money) *What problem did this help the colonists solve?* (The colonists needed money to buy weapons and supplies in order to fight the war.)

Genre: Expository Text Read the rest of page A1. *Find a fact in paragraph 4.* (Possible answer: Grimaldi and Floridablanca were aristocrats.)

Problem and Solution Read paragraph 1 on page A2. *Why did Spain fear a new American nation?* (It might want land that Spain had already claimed.) *How might the war with England prevent this?* (Americans would be tired of war. They would not want to enter into another war with Spain.)

Text Features: Headings Read the heading on page A2. *What can you expect to read about below the heading?* (I can expect to read about the money and supplies the Spanish sent to the Americans.)

Context Clues Read paragraph 2. *What does the word* funds *mean?* (money) *How do you know?* (The author restates the meaning of *funds* as "*money.*")

 Summarize Have students use their notes to summarize how the Spanish helped the American patriots during the revolution.

Reread

Use the questions on page A3 to guide rereading.

Author's Craft Reread the section titled "National Self-Interests." *Why is this a good heading?* (National Self-Interests" is a good heading because the section explains that Spain helped the American rebels only because it helped Spain too.)

Author's Craft Reread paragraph 4 on page A1. *Why do you think the author used the word* oddly *in the first sentence?* (I think the author used the word to show that it might seem strange that Spanish aristocrats would give money to people they didn't support.)

Author's Craft Reread paragraph 2 on page A2. *How does the author help you understand how much Spain helped the American rebels?* (The author gives details about the supplies Spain gave. For example, Spain gave more than 200 cannons, 4,000 tents, and up to 30,000 uniforms. The text also says Spain gave funds.)

Integrate

 Make Connections Guide students to make connections between "Secret Help from Spain" and another selection they have read. Support pairs as they cite text evidence and respond to this question: *How do the authors help you understand how problems get solved?*

Compare Texts Display a Venn diagram labeled with the two texts students examined. Help pairs complete it with details that tell what each text shared about how to solve problems.

Build Knowledge

Talk About the Text Have partners discuss how people solve problems.

Write About the Text Have students add their ideas to the Build Knowledge pages of their reader's notebooks.

Differentiate and Collaborate

 Be inspired Have students think about "Secret Help From Spain" and other selections they have read. Ask: *What do the texts inspire you to do?* Use the following activities or have pairs of students think of a way to respond to the texts.

Make a Diorama Think of a time you were asked to help solve a problem. Create a diorama showing some of the steps you took to reach a solution.

Create a Public Service Advertisement Write a 30-second advertisement explaining why problem-solving is important. Draw a poster with a diagram outlining the steps problem solvers use. Label each step. Share your advertisement.

Readers to Writers

Supporting Details Remind students that authors use details, such as facts, definitions, examples, or quotations, to support a central idea. Ask students to reread the section titled "Money and Supplies" on page A2. Ask: *What supporting details does the author include? What additional details might the author add? How do the details help you better understand the central idea?*

LEVEL UP

IF students read the Approaching Level fluently and answered the questions,

THEN pair them with students who have proficiently read the On Level passage. Have them

- partner read the On Level passage.
- summarize a problem described in the text and identify the solution.

Approaching Level

Phonics/Decoding

REVIEW THE DIPHTHONG /oi/

OBJECTIVES

Know and apply grade-level phonics and word analysis skills in decoding words.

Decode words with the diphthong /oi/.

I Do Review with students that a diphthong is a blend of vowel sounds in the same syllable. Display the *boy* **Sound-Spelling Card** for /oi/. Point to the card and run your finger under the letters *oi* and *oy* that make the /oi/ sound. Read the word aloud, and write it on the board. Then write the word *coil* on the board. Run your finger under the /oi/ diphthong as you say the word. Point out that the same sound can be spelled in different ways.

We Do Write the words *toy* and *boil* on the board. Run your finger under the letters that make the /oi/ sound and say the word *toy*. Have students repeat the word after you. Then have students read the word *boil* as you run your finger under the letters that make the same vowel sound.

You Do Add the following examples to the board: *joy, spoil, oiled, employ*. Have students say each word with you as you point to it. Repeat several times.

PRACTICE WORDS WITH /ô/, /oi/, AND /ou/

OBJECTIVES

Know and apply grade-level phonics and word analysis skills in decoding words.

Use combined knowledge of all letter-sound correspondences, syllabication patterns, and morphology (e.g., roots and affixes) to read accurately unfamiliar multisyllabic words in context and out of context.

Decode words with variant vowel /ô/ and diphthongs /oi/, /ou/.

I Do Write the words *fought, coin,* and *couch* on the board. Read the words aloud, running your finger under the letters that designate the /ô/, /oi/, or /ou/ sound as you say them. Identify the letters for the /ô/, /oi/, or /ou/ sound in each word. Point out that these sounds can be spelled differently.

We Do Display word pairs *ought, talk; spoiled, joyful;* and *proud, growl*. Model how to say the first two words. Guide students as they say the rest and identify the /ô/, /oi/, or /ou/ sounds. Display the following words. Read aloud the first word. Identify the /ou/ sound.

| found | fall | boiling | prowler | frown |
| void | dawn | thoughtful | tall | join |

You Do Have students read aloud the rest of the words and list them in a three-column chart beneath the headings /ô/, /oi/, and /ou/. Afterward, point to the words in random order for students to read chorally.

REVIEW PLURAL WORDS

TIER 2

OBJECTIVES

Know and apply grade-level phonics and word analysis skills in decoding words.

Use combined knowledge of all letter-sound correspondences, syllabication patterns, and morphology (e.g., roots and affixes) to read accurately unfamiliar multisyllabic words in context and out of context.

Decode plural words.

I Do Display word pairs *desk, desks; box, boxes;* and *ruby, rubies.* Remind students that you can add *-s* to nouns to make them plural, as in *desk/desks.* Review adding *-es* to nouns that end in *-sh, -ch, -s, -ss,* or *-x* to make them plural, as in *box, boxes.* Then remind students that words ending with a *-y* are usually made plural by changing *y* to *i* and adding *-es,* as in *ruby, rubies.* Point to each pair as you read aloud, running your finger under the letter or letters that form the plural.

We Do Write the words *tank, tanks; lady, ladies;* and *beach, beaches* on the board. Say each singular word and its plural, and have students repeat after you. Help them identify the letter or letters that form the plurals.

You Do Add these words to the board: *couch, couches; flower, flowers; city, cities.* Have students read each singular word and its plural aloud as you point to it. Then have them identify the letter or letters that form the plural. Repeat.

PRACTICE PLURAL WORDS

OBJECTIVES

Know and apply grade-level phonics and word analysis skills in decoding words.

Use combined knowledge of all letter-sound correspondences, syllabication patterns, and morphology (e.g., roots and affixes) to read accurately unfamiliar multisyllabic words in context and out of context.

Decode plural words.

I Do Display the words *drills, wishes, coaches, babies,* and *foxes.* Remind students that plural endings can be spelled in different ways. Identify the plural ending in each word.

We Do Write the word pairs *skirt, skirts; branch, branches;* and *baby, babies.* Pronounce the first two words, then guide students to say the rest and identify plural endings. Repeat with the word pairs *pony, ponies; guess, guesses; bench, benches; wax, waxes; sash, sashes;* and *instruction, instructions.*

You Do Have students list words in a three-column chart labeled *-s, -es, -ies.* Point to the words in the list in random order for students to chorally read aloud. Ask them to supply more examples of regular plural pairs.

ELL For **ELL** students who need phonics and decoding practice, define words and help them use the words in sentences, scaffolding to ensure their understanding. See the **Language Transfers Handbook** for phonics elements that may not transfer from students' native languages.

●Approaching Level

Vocabulary

REVIEW HIGH-FREQUENCY WORDS

OBJECTIVES
Acquire and use accurately grade-appropriate general academic and domain-specific words and phrases, including those that signal contrast, addition, and other logical relationships (e.g., *however, although, nevertheless, similarly, moreover, in addition*).

I Do Use **High-Frequency Word Cards** 41–60. Display one word at a time, following the routine:
Display the word. Read the word. Then spell the word.

We Do Ask students to state the word and spell the word with you. Model using the word in a sentence and have students repeat the sentence after you.

You Do Display the word. Ask students to say the word then spell it. When completed, quickly flip through the word card set as students chorally read the words. Provide opportunities for students to use the words in speaking and writing. For example, provide sentence starters such as *After his bath, the dog was _____*. Ask students to write each word in their reader's notebook.

REVIEW ACADEMIC VOCABULARY

OBJECTIVES
Acquire and use accurately grade-appropriate general academic and domain-specific words and phrases, including those that signal contrast, addition, and other logical relationships (e.g., *however, although, nevertheless, similarly, moreover, in addition*).

I Do Display each **Visual Vocabulary Card** and state the word. Explain how the photograph illustrates the word. State the example sentence and repeat the word.

We Do Point to the word on the card and read the word with students. Ask them to repeat the word. Engage students in structured partner talk about the image as prompted on the back of the vocabulary card.

You Do Display each visual in random order, hiding the word. Have students match the definitions and context sentences of the words to the visuals displayed.

 You may wish to review high-frequency words with ELL students using the lesson above.

IDENTIFY RELATED WORDS

OBJECTIVE

Use the relationship between particular words (e.g., synonyms, antonyms, homographs) to better understand each of the words.

I Do Display the *committees* **Visual Vocabulary Card** and say aloud the word set: *committees, wings, groups.*

Point out that *groups* means almost the same thing as *committees.*

We Do Display the vocabulary card for *convention.* Say aloud the word set: *convention, invention, meeting.* With students, identify the word that has almost the same meaning as *convention* and discuss why.

You Do Have students work in pairs to choose the word that means almost the same as the first word in the group.

resolve, rest, settle   situation, circumstance, invitation

representatives, spokespeople, troops   union, partnership, separation

debate, argue, plan   proposal, positive, suggestion

Have students pick words from their reader's notebook and use an online thesaurus to find synonyms and a dictionary to check their pronunciation.

CONTEXT CLUES

OBJECTIVE

Use context to confirm or self-correct word recognition and understanding, rereading as necessary.

Determine or clarify the meaning of unknown and multiple meaning words and phrases based on grade 5 reading and content, choosing flexibly from a range of strategies.

Use context (e.g., cause/ effect relationships and comparisons in text) as a clue to the meaning of a word or phrase.

I Do Display the Approaching Level of "Secret Help from Spain" in the online **Differentiated Genre Passage.** Read aloud the fourth paragraph on page A1. Point to the word *Aristocrats.* Explain to students that authors may define or restate the meaning of an unfamiliar word by using commas or the clue word "or."

Think Aloud I am not sure what *aristocrats* are, but I see a comma and the words "or nobles" right after it. These context clues help me figure out that *aristocrats* are nobles.

We Do Ask students to find the word *funds* in paragraph 2 on page A2. Discuss with students how to use the comma and the clue words "or money" to figure out the meaning of *funds.*

You Do Have students find the meaning of *obtain* (page A2, paragraph 2) using clues from the passage. Then have students write the definition in their reader's notebook. They can use a dictionary to confirm the meaning of the word.

Approaching Level

Fluency/Comprehension

FLUENCY

OBJECTIVES

Read with sufficient accuracy and fluency to support comprehension.

Read grade-level prose and poetry orally with accuracy, appropriate rate, and expression on successive readings.

Use context to confirm or self-correct word recognition and understanding, rereading as necessary.

I Do Explain that good readers recognize words and read them accurately. They vary their reading rate, or speed, slowing down to understand more complex text. They use context to help with word recognition. Read the first two paragraphs of "Secret Help from Spain" in the Approaching Level online **Differentiated Genre Passage** page A1. Tell students to monitor your accuracy and listen for how you vary your reading rate.

We Do Read the rest of the page aloud and have students repeat each sentence after you, matching your reading rate. Explain that you monitored your rate, reading neither too fast or too slow, to ensure that you also read accurately. Demonstrate how to self-correct or confirm word recognition.

You Do Have partners take turns reading sentences from the passage. Remind them to focus on their accuracy and rate. Listen in and, as needed, provide corrective feedback by modeling proper fluency.

IDENTIFY IMPORTANT EVENTS

OBJECTIVES

Explain the relationships or interactions between two or more individuals, events, ideas, or concepts in a historical, scientific, or technical text based on specific information in the text.

Identify important events in an informational text.

I Do Read aloud the first paragraph of "Secret Help from Spain" in the online Approaching Level **Differentiated Genre Passage** page A1. Model identifying an important event described in this paragraph: a French secret service agent wrote to Spain's foreign minister and requested that Spain help the American colonists.

We Do Continue reading the first page of the passage. After reading the second and third paragraphs, ask: *What important events do these paragraphs describe?* Help students understand that the paragraphs describes how Spain agreed to give money to the American rebels, and how these secret payments continued throughout the Revolutionary War.

You Do Have students read the rest of the passage. After each paragraph, have them summarize the important events. Review their lists and help them explain why the events they chose are important. Then have them use these events to identify the overall problem discussed in the text.

REVIEW PROBLEM AND SOLUTION

OBJECTIVES

Explain the relationships or interactions between two or more individuals, events, ideas, or concepts in a historical, scientific, or technical text based on specific information in the text.

Describe the overall structure of events ideas, concepts, or information in a text or part of a text.

Link opinion and reasons using words, phrases, and clauses.

I Do Remind students that when authors use the problem-and-solution text structure, they state a problem and then describe the steps taken to solve that problem. Signal words and phrases such as *consequently, as a result,* and *therefore* can help readers identify the solution.

We Do Read the first paragraph of "Secret Help from Spain" in the online Approaching Level **Differentiated Genre Passage** page A1 with students. Help them identify the problem it reveals: France is providing money to the American colonists fighting against England, and Spain is considering if it should do the same. Then read the next two paragraphs with students, and help them describe how each paragraph provides more information about the problem.

You Do Have students keep track of other problems and solutions described in the text that are related to the overall problem. Then have them identify how the overall problem was finally solved.

SELF-SELECTED READING

OBJECTIVES

Explain the relationships or interactions between two or more individuals, events, ideas, or concepts in a historical, scientific, or technical text based on specific information in the text.

Reread difficult sections of text to increase understanding.

Independent Reading

In this text set, students focus on these key aspects of informational text: how text structures, such as problem and solution, and text features, such as headings and timelines, contribute to the meaning of a text. Guide students to transfer what they have learned in this text set as well as in previous lessons as they read.

Have students choose an informational text for sustained silent reading. Students can check the online **Leveled Reader Library** for selections. Remind students that

- informational texts often present a problem and then describe the steps taken to solve the problem.
- they should reread as necessary, and look at headings, timelines, and other text features, to help them better understand the information in the text.

Have students continue to read or reread the book independently, using the Reading **Center Activity Cards** as a resource. Students can conduct a book talk with their group using their responses from the Respond to Reading and Make Connections prompts.

Lexile 920L

OBJECTIVES

Explain the relationships or interactions between two or more individuals, events, ideas, or concepts in a historical, scientific, or technical text based on specific information in the text.

Compare and contrast the overall structure (e.g., chronology, comparison, cause/effect, problem/solution) of events, ideas, concepts, or information in two or more texts.

Read grade-level text with purpose and understanding.

Determine or clarify the meaning of unknown and multiple-meaning words and phrases based on grade 5 reading and content, choosing flexibly from a range of strategies.

Use context (e.g., cause/effect relationships and comparisons in text) as a clue to the meaning of a word or phrase.

ACADEMIC LANGUAGE

• *expository text, problem, solution, timeline, paraphrase*
• Cognates: *texto expositivo, problema, solución*

●On Level

Leveled Reader: *The Bill of Rights*

Preview and Predict

Have students read the Essential Question: *What do good problem solvers do?*

Next have them preview the title, opening pages, and text features for *The Bill of Rights* to make a prediction about the selection. Have students discuss their predictions.

Review Genre: Expository Text

Remind students that expository text gives facts, examples, and explanations about a topic. Explain that expository text may also include text features such as charts, graphs, diagrams, or timelines that organize information. Have students identify features of expository text in *The Bill of Rights*.

Close Reading

Note Taking Ask students to use a copy of online Problem and Solution **Graphic Organizer 4** as they read.

Pages 2–3 *What context clues help you understand the word* delegates *on page 3?* (The phrase *people they had chosen to represent them* is a context clue.) Have students add this word to their reader's notebook. *Reread page 3 to identify how many states had to vote yes in order for the United States to have a set of laws and a way to choose a government.* (Nine of the thirteen states had to vote yes.)

Pages 4–7 *Paraphrase the disagreement between the Federalists and the Anti-Federalists. How did each group feel about a strong central government? How did James Madison help solve the problem?* (The Federalists wanted a strong central government. The Anti-Federalists did not. James Madison helped the two groups reach a compromise by promising that if Virginia ratified the Constitution and elected him to Congress, he would work to develop a bill of rights to protect individuals' and states' rights.)

Pages 8–10 *Turn to a partner and discuss the timeline on page 10. What information does the timeline give you?* (It gives the dates on which different states ratified the Bill of Rights.)

Pages 11–17 *How does the author organize the text on these pages?* (The author uses logical order and lists each amendment as it appears in the Bill of Rights, followed by an explanation of the amendment and its purpose.) *Reread the conclusion of the text on page 17. Turn to your partner and discuss the process delegates used to solve their problems that still works today.* (They discussed their problems and reached compromises in order to solve them.)

Respond to Reading Revisit the Essential Question and ask students to complete the Text Evidence questions on page 18.

 Write About Reading Check that students have correctly identified a problem and solution from the text.

Fluency: Accuracy and Rate

Model Model reading page 6 with accuracy and at an appropriate rate. Next, read the passage aloud and have students read along with you.

Apply Have students practice reading the passage with a partner.

Paired Read: "Having Your Say"

 Make Connections: Write About It

Before reading, ask students to note that the genre of this text is also expository text. Then discuss the Essential Question. After reading, ask students to write about connections between the problems and solutions explored in *The Bill of Rights* and "Having Your Say."

Leveled Reader

Build Knowledge

Talk About the Text Have partners discuss how people solve problems.

Write About the Text Have students add their ideas to the Build Knowledge pages of their reader's notebooks.

 **FOCUS ON SOCIAL STUDIES**

Students can extend their knowledge of compromising by completing the social studies activity on page 24.

LITERATURE CIRCLES

Ask students to conduct a literature circle using the Thinkmark questions to guide the discussion. You may wish to have a whole-class discussion, based on information in both selections in the Leveled Reader, about how people can solve problems through compromise.

LEVEL UP

IF students read the On Level fluently and answered the questions,

THEN pair them with students who have proficiently read the Beyond Level and have students

- partner-read the Beyond Level main selection.
- summarize a problem described in the text and identify its solution.

 Access Complex Text

The Beyond Level challenges students by including more **domain-specific words** and **complex sentence structures**.

"Secret Help from Spain"
Lexile 800L

OBJECTIVES

Explain the relationships or interactions between two or more individuals, events, ideas, or concepts in a historical, scientific, or technical text based on specific information in the text.

Compare and contrast the overall structure (e.g., chronology, comparison, cause/effect, problem/solution) of events, ideas, concepts, or information in two or more texts.

Integrate information from several texts on the same topic in order to write or speak about the subject knowledgeably.

Determine or clarify the meaning of unknown and multiple-meaning words and phrases based on grade 5 reading and content, choosing flexibly from a range of strategies.

Use context (e.g., cause/effect relationships and comparisons in text) as a clue to the meaning of a word or phrase.

ELA ACADEMIC LANGUAGE

• *problem, solution, headings, connection, details*
• Cognates: *problema, solución, conexión, detalles*

● On Level

Genre Passage: "Secret Help from Spain"

Build Background

Read aloud the Essential Question: *What do good problem solvers do?* Ask students to compare how two people they read about in this text set were able to solve a problem effectively. Use these sentence starters:

> *I read that good problem solvers . . .*
> *This helps me understand that solutions . . .*

Let students know that the online **Differentiated Genre Passage** "Secret Help from Spain" discusses the financial backing American colonists received from both Spain and France during the American Revolution. Explain that other countries often supply goods or money to help one country win a war. Discuss why this might be helpful to both countries.

Review Genre: Expository Text

Reiterate that expository text includes facts, details, and explanations about a topic. Expository texts may include text features, such as headings, that tell what a section of a text is mostly about. Text structures are used to organize information and present it in a logical order.

Close Reading

Note Taking As students read the passage the first time, ask them to annotate the text. Have them note key ideas and details, unfamiliar words, and questions they have. Then read again and use the following questions.

 Read

Genre: Expository Text Read paragraphs 1 and 2 on page O1. *How do these paragraphs help you know this is expository text?* (The author gives facts and a quotation and uses an introduction and headings to organize information.)

Problem and Solution Read paragraphs 2–4 on page O1. *Why does Grimaldi agree to give the patriots money?* (Grimaldi says that it is desirable for the Americans to keep fighting against the British.) *How might this help solve a problem for Spain?* (Britain was a longtime enemy of Spain, and Spain thought a war with the Americans would weaken Britain's army.)

Text Features: Headings Read the heading on page O2. *How does it prepare you to read the section that follows?* (It lets me know that I can expect to read about the money and supplies that the Spanish sent to the American rebels.)

Context Clues Read paragraph 4 on page O2. *What does* currency *mean?* (money) *How do you know?* (The author uses a synonym directly after the word.)

Problem and Solution Read the last paragraph on page O2. *Why does the author say that Spain giving money was "a fair trade"?* (The American victory helped solve a problem for Spain by weakening its enemy, Britain.)

 Summarize Have students use their notes to summarize how the Spanish helped the American patriots during the revolution.

Reread

Use the questions on page O3 to guide rereading.

Author's Craft Reread "National Self-Interests." *Is this a good heading for this section? Explain.* (Yes, because Spain helped the American rebels only because this helped Spain.)

Author's Craft Reread paragraph 4 on page O1. *Why do you think the author used the word* oddly *in the first sentence?* (It seemed strange that Spanish aristocrats would give money to people they didn't support.)

Author's Craft Reread paragraph 2 on page O2. *How does the author help you understand how much Spain helped the American rebels?* (The author gives details about what the supplies were and how much money Spain gave. For example, Spain gave more than 200 cannons. The text also says that Spain gave funds. The funds and equipment were enough to keep the war going.)

Integrate

 Make Connections Have pairs explore connections between "Secret Help from Spain" and another selection they have read. Have them cite evidence and respond to this question: *How do the authors help you understand how problems get solved?*

Compare Texts Have pairs draw a Venn diagram labeled with the texts they reviewed and add details that tell what each text shared about how to solve problems.

Build Knowledge

Talk About the Text Have partners discuss how people solve problems.

Write About the Text Have students add their ideas to the Build Knowledge pages of their reader's notebooks.

Differentiate and Collaborate

 Be inspired Have students think about "Secret Help from Spain" and other selections they have read. Ask: *What do the texts inspire you to do?* Use the following activities or have pairs of students think of a way to respond to the texts.

Make a Diorama Think of a time you were asked to help solve a problem. Create a diorama showing some of the steps you took to reach a solution.

Create a Public Service Advertisement Write a 30-second advertisement explaining why problem-solving is important. Draw a poster with a diagram outlining the steps problem solvers use. Label each step. Share your advertisement.

Readers to Writers

Supporting Details Remind students that authors use details, such as facts, definitions, examples, or quotations, to support a central idea. Ask students to reread the section titled "Money and Supplies" on page O2. Ask: *What supporting details does the author include? What additional details might the author add? How do the details help you better understand the central idea?*

LEVEL UP

IF students read the On Level fluently and answered the questions,

THEN pair them with students who have proficiently read the Beyond Level. Have them

- partner read the Beyond Level passage.

- summarize a problem described in the text and identify its solution.

● On Level

Vocabulary/Comprehension

REVIEW ACADEMIC VOCABULARY

OBJECTIVES

Acquire and use accurately grade-appropriate general academic and domain-specific words and phrases, including those that signal contrast, addition, and other logical relationships (e.g., *however, although, nevertheless, similarly, moreover, in addition*).

I Do Use the **Visual Vocabulary Cards** to review the key selection words *committees, convention, representatives, resolve, situation,* and *union.* Point to each word, read it aloud, and have students chorally repeat it.

We Do Ask these questions and help students record and explain their answers:
- What are some *committees* you have at your school?
- What is something people might hold a *convention* to talk about?
- Why do people act as *representatives* for large groups?

You Do Have students work in pairs to discuss these questions:
- How do you *resolve* a disagreement with a friend?
- What is a *situation* you would like to be in?
- Why might people form a *union* for something they believe in?

Have students choose words from their reader's notebook and use an online thesaurus to find synonyms.

CONTEXT CLUES

OBJECTIVES

Use context to confirm or self-correct word recognition and understanding, rereading as necessary.

Determine or clarify the meaning of unknown and multiple meaning words and phrases based on grade 5 reading and content, choosing flexibly from a range of strategies.

Use context (e.g., cause/effect relationships and comparisons in text) as a clue to the meaning of a word or phrase.

I Do Read aloud the fourth paragraph on page O1 of On Level online **Differentiated Genre Passage** "Secret Help from Spain."

Think Aloud I want to know the meaning of *aristocrats* in the second paragraph. Right next to it, I see the words *or nobles* set off by commas. This restatement is followed by a definition: "people born into high social positions." The restatement and definition help me understand what *aristocrats* are.

We Do Have students read paragraph 2 on page O2 and determine the meaning of the word *funds.* Have students look for the definition or restatement of "money."

You Do Have students work in pairs to determine the meaning of the words *obtaining* (page O2, paragraph 2) and *currency* (page O2, paragraph 4).

REVIEW PROBLEM AND SOLUTION

OBJECTIVES

Explain the relationships or interactions between two or more individuals, events, ideas, or concepts in a historical, scientific, or technical text based on specific information in the text.

Describe the overall structure of events, ideas, concepts, or information in a text or part of a text.

I Do Remind students that when authors use the problem-and-solution text structure, they state a problem and then tell how it is solved. In a text that describes an overall problem and solution, individual sections may discuss other, related problems and their solutions.

We Do Have a volunteer read the first paragraph on page O1 of On Level online **Differentiated Genre Passage** "Secret Help from Spain." Help students identify the problem it reveals: France is providing money to the American colonists fighting against England and wants Spain to do the same. Then read the next two paragraphs. Discuss how they provide more information about the problem.

You Do As they read the rest of the passage, have partners identify additional, related problems discussed in the text and their solutions. Then have them retell how the overall problem was finally solved.

SELF-SELECTED READING

OBJECTIVES

Explain the relationships or interactions between two or more individuals, events, ideas, or concepts in a historical, scientific, or technical text based on specific information in the text.

Reread difficult sections to increase understanding.

Independent Reading

In this text set, students focus on how text structures, such as problem and solution, and text features, such as headings and timelines, contribute to the meaning of a text. Guide students to transfer what they have learned in this text set as well as in previous lessons as they read.

Have students choose an informational text for sustained silent reading. Students can check the online **Leveled Reader Library** for selections. Remind students that

- informational texts often present a problem and then describe the steps taken to solve the problem.
- they should reread as necessary, and look at headings, timelines, and other text features, to help them better understand the information in the text.

Have students read the book independently using the Reading **Center Activity Cards** as a resource. Students can conduct a book talk with their group using their responses from the Respond to Reading and Make Connections prompts.

 You may want to include **ELL** students in On Level vocabulary and comprehension lessons. Offer language support as needed.

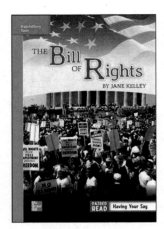

Lexile 1000L

OBJECTIVES

Explain the relationships or interactions between two or more individuals, events, ideas, or concepts in a historical, scientific, or technical text based on specific information in the text.

Compare and contrast the overall structure (e.g., chronology, comparison, cause/effect, problem/ solution) of events, ideas, concepts, or information in two or more texts.

Integrate information from several texts on the same topic in order to write or speak about the subject knowledgeably.

Read grade-level text with purpose and understanding.

Determine or clarify the meaning of unknown and multiple-meaning words and phrases based on grade 5 reading and content, choosing flexibly from a range of strategies.

Use context (e.g., cause/effect relationships and comparisons in text) as a clue to the meaning of a word or phrase.

ELA ACADEMIC LANGUAGE

• expository text, problem, solution, timeline, paraphrase

• Cognates: *texto expositivo, problema, solución*

●Beyond Level

Leveled Reader: *The Bill of Rights*

Preview and Predict

Read the Essential Question: *What do good problem solvers do?*

Have students preview the title, table of contents, and the opening pages of *The Bill of Rights*. Students should use information in the text and the text features to predict what they think the selection will be about.

Review Genre: Expository Text

Remind students that expository text gives facts, examples, and explanations about a topic. It may also include text features such as charts, graphs, diagrams, and timelines that organize information. Have students identify the text features in *The Bill of Rights*.

Close Reading

Note Taking Ask students to use a copy of the online Problem and Solution **Graphic Organizer 4** as they read.

Pages 2–7 *Turn to a partner and describe the problems faced by delegates to the Constitutional Convention in 1787.* (They had to create a new system of government and determine which rights belonged to individuals, to the states, and to the central government.) *Use the context clues in the first paragraph on page 6 to identify the meaning of* ratify. (*Ratify* means to approve. The words *or approve* appear right after the word *ratify*.) **Have students add this word to their reader's notebooks.**

Pages 8–10 *Reread the sidebar on page 8. How is the Constitution amended?* (Amendments must be approved by two-thirds of Congress and three-quarters of the states.) *According to the timeline, when did Congress send the Bill of Rights to the states?* (September 1789)

Pages 11–12 *What problem does the Bill of Rights attempt to solve?* (It protects individuals' rights and prevents future oppression.) *Paraphrase the problem the Third Amendment solved. Reread to find the answer.* (Before the Bill of Rights, the British army could force people to give soldiers food or a place to sleep. The Third Amendment prohibits the army from lodging soldiers without the homeowner's permission.)

Pages 13–15 *What problem did the Fourth Amendment solve?* (Before the Bill of Rights, British soldiers could search or arrest people without a reason. The Fourth Amendment indicated that people could not be searched or arrested without a good reason.) *Which amendment helps people who argue over property or money solve their disagreements?* (the Seventh Amendment)

Pages 16–17 *What does the text teach you about how people can solve problems today?* (People can discuss their problems and find solutions through compromising.)

Respond to Reading Revisit the Essential Question and ask students to complete the Text Evidence Questions on page 18 after they have finished reading.

 Write About Reading Check that students have correctly identified how the Federalists and Anti-Federalists reached a compromise.

Fluency: Accuracy and Rate

Model Model reading page 6 with accuracy and at an appropriate rate. Next, read the passage aloud and have students read along with you.

Apply Have students practice reading the passage with a partner.

Paired Read: "Having Your Say"

 Make Connections: Write About It

Before reading, ask students to note that the genre of this text is also expository text. Then discuss the Essential Question. After reading, ask students to make connections between *The Bill of Rights* and "Having Your Say."

Leveled Reader

Build Knowledge

Talk About the Text Have partners discuss how people solve problems.

Write About the Text Have students add their ideas to the Build Knowledge pages of their reader's notebooks.

 FOCUS ON SOCIAL STUDIES

Students can extend their knowledge of compromising by completing the social studies activity on page 24.

LITERATURE CIRCLES

Ask students to conduct a literature circle using the Thinkmark questions to guide the discussion. You may wish to have a whole-class discussion, based on information in both selections in the Leveled Reader, about how people solve problems through compromise.

⭐ **GIFTED AND TALENTED**

Synthesize Have students choose one amendment from the selection and explain how the amendment personally affects United States citizens today. Students should clearly identify the amendment, tell what it means, and offer a detailed explanation of the impact this amendment has on how people in this country express their views, interact with the government, or deal with conflicts.

"Secret Help from Spain"
Lexile 880L

OBJECTIVES

Explain the relationships or interactions between two or more individuals, events, ideas, or concepts in a historical, scientific, or technical text based on specific information in the text.

Compare and contrast the overall structure (e.g., chronology, comparison, cause/effect, problem/solution) of events, ideas, concepts, or information in two or more texts.

Integrate information from several texts on the same topic in order to write or speak about the subject knowledgeably.

Determine or clarify the meaning of unknown and multiple-meaning words and phrases based on grade 5 reading and content, choosing flexibly from a range of strategies.

Use context (e.g., cause/effect relationships and comparisons in text) as a clue to the meaning of a word or phrase.

ELA ACADEMIC LANGUAGE

- *problem, solution, headings, connection, details*
- Cognates: *problema, solución, conexión, detalles*

●Beyond Level

Genre Passage: "Secret Help from Spain"

Build Background

Read aloud the Essential Question: *What do good problem solvers do?* Ask students to compare how two people they read about in this text set were able to solve a problem effectively. Use these sentence starters:

> *I read that good problem solvers . . .*
> *This helps me understand that solutions . . .*

Let students know that the online **Differentiated Genre Passage** "Secret Help from Spain" discusses the financial backing American colonists received during the revolution. Explain that other countries often supply goods or money to help one country win a war. Discuss how this might help both countries.

Review Genre: Expository Text

Reiterate that expository text includes facts, details, and explanations about a topic. Expository texts may include text features, such as headings, that tell what a section of a text is mostly about. Text structures are used to organize information and present it in a logical order.

Close Reading

Note Taking As students read the passage the first time, ask them to annotate the text. Have them note key ideas and details, unfamiliar words, and questions they have. Then read again and use the following questions.

> Read

Genre: Expository Text *How do you know the selection is expository text?* (The author presents information organized with an introduction and headings and supports ideas with facts.)

Problem and Solution Read paragraphs 2–4 on page B1. *Why does Grimaldi agree to give the patriots money?* (Grimaldi says that it is desirable for the Americans to keep fighting against the British.) *How might this help solve a problem for Spain?* (Britain was a longtime enemy of Spain, so Spain thought a war with the Americans would weaken Britain's army.)

Context Clues Read the last paragraph on page B1. *What are* aristocrats? (people who are born into high social positions) *What is another word for* aristocrats? (nobles) *How do you know?* (The author provides a synonym after the word.)

Problem and Solution Read paragraph 1 on page B2. *What additional problem did the Spanish ministers think the war might solve? Explain.* (It would exhaust the British and the colonists and reduce the chance of attacks on Spanish holdings.)

Text Features: Headings Read the heading on page B2. *What does it indicate about the section below it?* (It indicates the section will be about the money and supplies that Spain sent to the Americans.)

Summarize Have students use their notes to summarize how the Spanish helped the American patriots during the revolution.

Reread

Use the questions on page B3 to guide rereading.

Author's Craft Reread "National Self-Interests." *Is this a good heading for this section? Explain.* (It is a good heading because the section explains that Spain helped the American rebels only because this helped Spain too. They didn't want America to win. They wanted the war to continue to weaken both sides.)

Author's Craft Reread paragraph 4 on page B1. *Why do you think the author used the word* oddly*?* (It seemed strange that Spanish aristocrats would give money to people they didn't support. Many might think that Spanish officials gave money because they believed in the Americans' cause.)

Author's Craft Reread paragraph 2 on page B2. *How does the author help you understand how much Spain helped the American rebels?* (The author gives details about what the supplies were and how much money Spain gave. These were enough to keep the war going.)

Integrate

Make Connections Have pairs connect "Secret Help from Spain" to another text they have read and respond to this question: *How do the authors help you understand how problems get solved?*

Compare Texts Have pairs draw a Venn diagram labeled with the texts they reviewed and add details that tell what each text shared about problem solving.

Build Knowledge

Talk About the Text Have partners discuss how people solve problems.

Write About the Text Have students add their ideas to the Build Knowledge pages of their reader's notebooks.

Differentiate and Collaborate

Be inspired Have students think about "Secret Help from Spain" and other selections they have read. Ask: *What do the texts inspire you to do?* Use the following activities or have pairs think of a way to respond to the texts.

Make a Diorama Think of a time you were asked to help solve a problem. Create a diorama showing some of the steps you took to reach a solution.

Create a Public Service Advertisement Write a 30-second advertisement explaining why problem-solving is important. Draw a poster with a diagram outlining the steps problem solvers use. Label each step. Share your advertisement.

Readers to Writers

Supporting Details Remind students that authors use details, such as facts, definitions, examples, or quotations, to support a central idea. Ask students to reread the section titled "Money and Supplies" on page B2. Ask: *What supporting details does the author include? What additional details might the author add? How do the details help you better understand the central idea?*

⭐ GIFTED AND TALENTED

Independent Study Have students synthesize information from their notes and the selections they read to create an illustrated problem-solving guide. Encourage them to choose a format that interests them (e.g., art, music, computer). Then have students think of a problem they need to solve and apply the steps. Ask them to self-evaluate and revise if necessary.

●Beyond Level

Vocabulary/Comprehension

REVIEW DOMAIN-SPECIFIC WORDS

OBJECTIVES
Acquire and use accurately grade-appropriate general academic and domain-specific words and phrases, including those that signal contrast, addition, and other logical relationships.

Model Use the **Visual Vocabulary Cards** to review the meanings of the words *debate* and *proposal*. Write social studies–related sentences on the board using the words.

Write the words *treaty* and *territory* on the board and discuss the meanings with students. Then help students write a context sentence for each word.

Apply Have students work in pairs to discuss the meanings of *compromise* and *amendments*. Then have partners write sentences using the words.

CONTEXT CLUES

OBJECTIVES
Use context to confirm or self-correct word recognition and understanding, rereading as necessary.

Determine or clarify the meaning of unknown and multiple meaning words and phrases based on grade 5 reading and content, choosing flexibly from a range of strategies.

Use context (e.g., cause/effect relationships and comparisons in text) as a clue to the meaning of a word or phrase.

Model Read aloud the fourth paragraph of "Secret Help from Spain" on Beyond Level online **Differentiated Genre Passage** page B1.

Think Aloud When I read this paragraph, I want to understand the meaning of *aristocrats*. I see a restatement that helps me. The words "or nobles" tell me that *aristocrats* means "nobles."

With students, discuss how the next part of the sentence builds on the meaning of *aristocrats*. Help them see that the text defines the term as "people born into high social positions."

Apply Have pairs read the rest of the passage. Ask them to use restatements to define *funds* (page B2, paragraph 2) and *currency* (page B2, paragraph 4). Then challenge pairs to find additional context clues that help them define *transaction* (page B1, paragraph 3), *rebellious* (page B1, paragraph 4), and *historians* (page B2, paragraph 3).

 Shades of Meaning Explain that many restatement clues are synonyms. Have students choose one of the words above and use a thesaurus to list numerous synonyms. Then have them choose the synonym that has the closest meaning and the synonym that has the furthest meaning from the original word and use them in sentences to show shades of meaning.

Have students repeat the activity by finding words in their reader's notebook and using an online thesaurus to look for synonyms.

REVIEW PROBLEM AND SOLUTION

OBJECTIVES

Explain the relationships or interactions between two or more individuals, events, ideas, or concepts in a historical, scientific, or technical text based on specific information in the text.

Compare and contrast the overall structure (e.g., chronology, comparison, cause/effect, problem/ solution) of events, ideas, concepts, or information in two or more texts.

Model Review that when authors use the problem-and-solution text structure, they state a problem and then tell how it is solved. Individual sections may discuss problems and solutions that are connected to an overall problem and solution described in the text.

Have students read the first paragraph of "Secret Help from Spain" on Beyond Level online **Differentiated Genre Passage** page B1. Ask open-ended questions to facilitate discussion, such as *How does this paragraph help us understand a problem? Why was this issue so important to both France and Spain?* Students should support their responses with details found in the text.

Apply Have students identify other related problems and solutions in the rest of the passage as they independently fill in a copy of online Problem and Solution **Graphic Organizer 4.** Then have partners use their work to summarize the selection, explaining the overall problem discussed in the text and how it was solved.

SELF-SELECTED READING

OBJECTIVES

Explain the relationships or interactions between two or more individuals, events, ideas, or concepts in a historical, scientific, or technical text based on specific information in the text.

Reread difficult sections of text to increase understanding.

Independent Reading

In this text set, students focus on how text structures, such as problem and solution, and text features, such as headings and timelines, contribute to the meaning of a text. Guide students to transfer what they have learned in this text set as well as in previous lessons as they read.

Have students choose an informational text for sustained silent reading. Students can check the online **Leveled Reader Library** for selections. Remind students that

- informational texts often present a problem and then describe the steps taken to solve the problem.
- they should reread as necessary, and look at headings, timelines, and other text features, to help them better understand the information in the text.

Have students read the book independently using the Reading **Center Activity Cards** as a resource. Students can conduct a book talk with their group using their responses from the Respond to Reading and Make Connections prompts.

 You may wish to assign the third Be Inspired! activity from the lesson plan as an Independent Study.

Student Outcomes

✓ Tested in *Wonders* Assessments

FOUNDATIONAL SKILLS

Phonics and Word Analysis

- Decode words with inflectional endings
- Decode words using knowledge of contractions

Fluency

- Read grade-level texts with accuracy, appropriate rate, expression, and automaticity

READING

Reading Literature

- ✓ Analyze how setting contributes to the plot in a literary text
- ✓ Explain the development of stated or implied theme(s) throughout a literary text
- ✓ Describe how an author develops a character's perspective in a literary text
- Read and comprehend texts in the grades 4–5 text complexity band

Reading Informational Text

- ✓ Explain how a sequential text structure contributes to the overall meaning of a text
- Summarize a text to enhance comprehension
- Write in response to text

Compare Texts

- Compare and contrast how authors present information on the same topic or theme

COMMUNICATION

Writing

Write to Sources

- ✓ Write expository texts about a topic using multiple sources and including an organizational structure and relevant elaboration
- With guidance and support from peers and adults, develop and strengthen writing as needed by planning, revising, and editing

Speaking and Listening

- Report on a topic or text or present an opinion, sequencing ideas; speak clearly at an understandable pace

Conventions

Grammar

- ✓ Identify plural nouns
- ✓ Use plural forms and appositives correctly
- ✓ Identify possessive nouns
- ✓ Add -s or -'s to form possessive nouns correctly

Spelling

- Spell words with inflectional endings
- Spell words using knowledge of contractions

Researching

- Conduct short research projects that build knowledge through investigation of different aspects of the topic

Creating and Collaborating

- Add audio recordings and visual displays to presentations when appropriate
- With some guidance and support from adults, use technology to produce and publish writing

VOCABULARY

Academic Vocabulary

- Acquire and use grade-appropriate academic vocabulary

Vocabulary Strategy

- ✓ Explain the use of personification

CONTENT AREA LEARNING

 Interdependence

- Collect and record information using detailed observations and accurate measuring. **Science**
- Describe the flow of energy within a food web, including the roles of the Sun, producers, consumers, and decomposers. **Science**

ELL Scaffolded supports for English Language Learners are embedded throughout the lessons, enabling students to communicate information, ideas, and concepts in English Language Arts and for social and instructional purposes within the school setting.

See the **ELL Small Group Guide** for additional support of the skills for the text set.

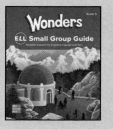

FORMATIVE ASSESSMENT

For assessment throughout the text set, use students' self-assessments and your observations.

Use the Data Dashboard to filter class, group, or individual student data to guide group placement decisions. It provides recommendations to enhance learning for gifted and talented students and offers extra support for students needing remediation.

DATA DASHBOARD

Develop Student Ownership

To build student ownership, students need to know what they are learning and why they are learning it, and to determine how well they understood it.

Students Discuss Their Goals

READING

TEXT SET GOALS

- I can read and understand a folktale.
- I can use text evidence to respond to a folktale.
- I know how following a plan can help people accomplish a task.

Have students think about what they know and fill in the bars on **Reading/Writing Companion** page 150.

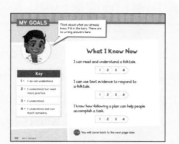

WRITING

EXTENDED WRITING GOALS

Extended Writing 2:

- I can write an expository essay.
- I can synthesize information from three sources.

Have students think about what they know and fill in the bars on Reading/Writing Companion page 198.

Students Monitor Their Learning

LEARNING GOALS

Specific learning goals identified in every lesson make clear what students will be learning and why. These smaller goals provide stepping stones to help students reach their Text Set and Extended Writing Goals.

CHECK-IN ROUTINE

The Check-In Routine at the close of each lesson guides students to self-reflect on how well they understood each learning goal.

Review the lesson learning goal.
Reflect on the activity.
Self-Assess by
- filling in the bars in the Reading/Writing Companion
- holding up 1, 2, 3, or 4 fingers
Share with your teacher.

Students Reflect on Their Progress

READING

TEXT SET GOALS

After completing the Show Your Knowledge task for the text set, students reflect on their understanding of the Text Set Goals by filling in the bars on Reading/Writing Companion page 151.

WRITING

EXTENDED WRITING GOALS

After completing both extended writing projects for the unit, students reflect on their understanding of the Extended Writing Goals by filling in the bars on Reading/Writing Companion page 199.

TEXT SET 2

Build Knowledge

Shared Read
Reading/Writing Companion p. 152

Anchor Text
Literature Anthology p. 118

Paired Selection
Literature Anthology p. 134

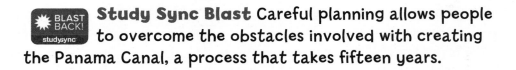

Essential Question
When has a plan helped you accomplish a task?

Video Having a plan and following it is important to consider when building a house.

Study Sync Blast Careful planning allows people to overcome the obstacles involved with creating the Panama Canal, a process that takes fifteen years.

Interactive Read Aloud The younger of two brothers comes up with a clever plan to defeat a dragon and save his town, and it works.

Shared Read Ping follows a plan to recover a lost brocade and is handsomely rewarded for following through with it.

Anchor Text Prince Alfonso trusts Blancaflor and successfully completes the three tasks by following her directions.

Paired Selection Recipes lay out a plan that help us make delicious food in the kitchen.

Make Connections The Wright brothers create detailed plans to make their flying machine.

Differentiated Sources

Leveled Readers

The Lion's Whiskers Alitash devises and follows a plan to get lion whiskers needed for a potion.

The Riddle of the Drum: A Tale from Mexico The prince sets out to find others who will help him solve the king's riddle.

Clever Manka Manka successfully devises a clever plan to win back her husband's love.

Differentiated Genre Passages

The snail creates a plan to outwit the fox but realizes it is important to be honest because honesty is usually rewarded.

Build Knowledge Routine

After reading each text, ask students to document what facts and details they learned to help answer the Essential Question of the text set.

 Talk About the source.

 Write About the source.

 Add to the Class Anchor Chart.

- Add to your Vocabulary List.

Show Your Knowledge

Create a Recipe for Success

Have students show how they built knowledge across the text set by creating a recipe for success. They should begin by thinking about the Essential Question: *When has a plan helped you accomplish a task?* Students will create a recipe for success with three steps necessary for accomplishing a task.

Social Emotional Learning

Planning and Social Problem-Solving

Anchor Text: It is vital to student success that they learn to follow a plan and problem solve. Discuss how Prince Alfonso trusts someone else to come up with a plan in *Blancaflor*.

Paired Selection: Baking is a great example of the need to follow a plan step-by-step. Ask: *Why must the recipe be followed precisely?*

Roundtable Discussion: In each folktale read in the text set, the story presents a sequence of problems a character must navigate in order to solve a problem or to reach a goal. Ask: *How are some of the problems found in the plot alike or different?*

TEXT SET 2

Explore the Texts

Essential Question: When has a plan helped you accomplish a task?

Access Complex Text (ACT) boxes throughout the text set provide scaffolded instruction for seven different elements that may make a text complex.

Teacher's Edition	Reading/Writing Companion	Literature Anthology	

"Lost Lake and the Golden Cup" Interactive Read Aloud p. T89 Folktale	**"The Magical Lost Brocade"** Shared Read pp. 152–155 Folktale	*Blancaflor* Anchor Text pp. 118–131 Folktale	**"From Tale to Table"** Paired Selection pp. 134–137 Expository Text

Qualitative

Meaning/Purpose Low Complexity **Structure** Moderate Complexity **Language** Moderate Complexity **Knowledge Demands** Low Complexity	**Meaning/Purpose** Moderate Complexity **Structure** Moderate Complexity **Language** Moderate Complexity **Knowledge Demands** Low Complexity	**Meaning/Purpose** Moderate Complexity **Structure** Moderate Complexity **Language** High Complexity **Knowledge Demands** Moderate Complexity	**Meaning/Purpose** Low Complexity **Structure** Moderate Complexity **Language** Low Complexity **Knowledge Demands** Moderate Complexity

Quantitative

Lexile 870L	**Lexile** 740L	**Lexile** 870L	**Lexile** 990L

Reader and Task Considerations

Reader Students will not need background knowledge or cultural details to understand the tale.	**Reader** Students will not need substantial background information. Explain that folktales often include magical elements, other settings and time periods, and patterns of three.	**Reader** Students will not need substantial background information. Explain that folktales often include magical elements, other settings and time periods, and patterns of three.	**Reader** Students will not need background knowledge to understand the text.

Task The questions for the read aloud are supported by teacher modeling. The tasks provide a variety of ways for students to begin to build knowledge and vocabulary about the text set topic. The questions and tasks provided for the other texts are at various levels of complexity, ensuring that all students can interact with the text in meaningful ways.

Additional Texts

Classroom Library
Mufaro's Beautiful Daughters
Genre: Folktale
Lexile: 790L

Where the Mountain Meets the Moon
Genre: Folktale
Lexile: 810L
See **Classroom Library Lessons**

Content Area Reading BLMs
Additional online texts related to grade-level Science, Social Studies, and Arts content

Leveled Readers

(A) *The Lion's Whiskers*

(O) *The Riddle of the Drum: A Tale from Mexico*

(B) *Clever Manka*

(ELL) *The Riddle of the Drum: A Tale from Mexico*

Qualitative

Meaning/Purpose Moderate Complexity	**Meaning/Purpose** Moderate Complexity	**Meaning/Purpose** Moderate Complexity	**Meaning/Purpose** Moderate Complexity
Structure Moderate Complexity	**Structure** Moderate Complexity	**Structure** Moderate Complexity	**Structure** Moderate Complexity
Language Moderate Complexity	**Language** Moderate Complexity	**Language** High Complexity	**Language** Low Complexity
Knowledge Demands Low Complexity	**Knowledge Demands** Moderate Complexity	**Knowledge Demands** Moderate Complexity	**Knowledge Demands** Low Complexity

Quantitative

Lexile 760L	**Lexile** 810L	**Lexile** 860L	**Lexile** 570L

Reader and Task Considerations

Reader Students might not be familiar with the country of Ethiopia. Show students where Ethiopia is on a map and images of its landscape.	**Reader** Students might not be familiar with the country of Mexico. Show students images of Mexico and where it is on a map.	**Reader** Students will not need background knowledge to understand the story.	**Reader** Students might not be familiar with the country of Mexico. Show students images of Mexico and where it is on a map.

Task The questions and tasks provided for the Leveled Readers are at various levels of complexity, ensuring that all students can interact with the text in meaningful ways.

Differentiated Genre Passages

(A) "The Fox and the Snail"

(O) "The Fox and the Snail"

(B) "The Fox and the Snail"

(ELL) "The Fox and the Snail"

Qualitative

Meaning/Purpose Moderate Complexity	**Meaning/Purpose** Moderate Complexity	**Meaning/Purpose** Moderate Complexity	**Meaning/Purpose** Moderate Complexity
Structure Moderate Complexity	**Structure** Low Complexity	**Structure** Low Complexity	**Structure** Low Complexity
Language Low Complexity	**Language** Moderate Complexity	**Language** High Complexity	**Language** Low Complexity
Knowledge Demands Low Complexity	**Knowledge Demands** Low Complexity	**Knowledge Demands** Moderate Complexity	**Knowledge Demands** Low Complexity

Quantitative

Lexile 700L	**Lexile** 770L	**Lexile** 840L	**Lexile** 710L

Reader and Task Considerations

Reader Students will not need background knowledge to understand the text.	**Reader** Students will not need background knowledge to understand the text.	**Reader** Students will not need background knowledge to understand the text.	**Reader** Students will not need background knowledge to understand the text.

Task The questions and tasks provided for the Differentiated Genre Passages are at various levels of complexity, ensuring that all students can interact with the text in meaningful ways.

Week 3 Planner

Customize your own lesson plans at
my.mheducation.com

LESSON 1   **LESSON 2**

60+ mins Reading Suggested Daily Time

READING LESSON GOALS

- I can read and understand a folktale.
- I can use text evidence to respond to a folktale.
- I know how following a plan can help people accomplish a task.

SMALL GROUP OPTIONS
The designated lessons can be taught in small groups. To determine how to differentiate instruction for small groups, use Formative Assessment and Data Dashboard.

30+ mins Writing Suggested Daily Time

WRITING LESSON GOALS

- I can write an expository essay.
- I can synthesize information from three sources.

Reading

LESSON 1

Introduce the Concept, T86–T87
Build Knowledge

Listening Comprehension, T88–T89
"Lost Lake and the Golden Cup"

Shared Read, T90–T93
Read "The Magical Lost Brocade"
Quick Write: Summarize

Vocabulary, T94–T95
Academic Vocabulary
Personification

Expand Vocabulary, T138

LESSON 2

Shared Read, T90–T93
Reread "The Magical Lost Brocade"

Minilessons, T96–T103
Make Predictions
Plot: Setting
Theme
⟫ Craft and Structure

⟫ **Respond to Reading, T104–T105**

⟫ **Phonics, T106–T107**
Inflectional Endings

Fluency, T106
Expression and Phrasing

⟫ **Research and Inquiry, T108–T109**

Expand Vocabulary, T138

Writing

Extended Writing 1: T238-T239 Analyze the Prompt	**Extended Writing 1: T240-T241** Analyze the Sources
⟫ **Writing Lesson Bank: Craft Minilessons, T266–T269**	
Teacher and Peer Conferences	
Grammar Lesson Bank, T274 More Plural Nouns Talk About It	**Grammar Lesson Bank, T274** More Plural Nouns Talk About It
Spelling Lesson Bank, T284 Inflectional Endings	⟫ **Spelling Lesson Bank, T284** Inflectional Endings

Teacher-Led Instruction

Differentiated Reading
Leveled Readers
- *The Lion's Whiskers,* T140–T141
- *The Riddle of the Drum: A Tale from Mexico,* T150–T151
- *Clever Manka,* T156–T157

Differentiated Skills Practice
● **Approaching Level**
Phonics/Decoding, T144
- Decode Words with Inflectional Endings ②
- Practice Words with Inflectional Endings

Vocabulary, T146
- Review High-Frequency Words ②
- Review Academic Vocabulary ②

Fluency, T148
- Expression and Phrasing ②

Comprehension, T148–T149
- Theme ②
- Self-Selected Reading

SMALL GROUP

Independent/Collaboratve Work   See pages T85G–T85H.

Reading
Comprehension
- Folktale
- Theme
- Make Predictions

Fluency

Independent Reading

Phonics/Word Study
Phonics/Decoding
- Inflectional Endings

Vocabulary
- Personification

Writing
Extended Writing 1: Expository Writing

Self-Selected Writing

Grammar
- More Plural Nouns

Spelling
- Inflectional Endings

Handwriting

ACADEMIC VOCABULARY
assuring, detected, emerging, gratitude, guidance, outcome, previous, pursuit

SPELLING
jogging, dripping, skimmed, accepted, amusing, easing, regretted, forbidding, referred, injured, deserved, applied, relied, renewing, complicated, qualified, threatening, gnarled, envied, fascinated

Review *difficulties, notches, rodeos*
Challenge *adoring, diaries*
See pages T284–T285 for Differentiated Spelling Lists.

 LESSON 3

 LESSON 4

 LESSON 5

Reading

Lesson 3	Lesson 4	Lesson 5
Anchor Text, T110–T125 Read *Blancaflor* Take Notes About Text **Expand Vocabulary, T139**	**Anchor Text, T110–T125** Read *Blancaflor* Take Notes About Text **Expand Vocabulary, T139**	**Anchor Text, T110–T125** Reread *Blancaflor* **Expand Vocabulary, T139**

Writing

Lesson 3	Lesson 4	Lesson 5
Extended Writing 1, T240–T241 Analyze the Sources	**Extended Writing 1, T240–T241** Analyze the Sources	**Extended Writing 1, T242–T243** Plan: Organize Ideas

Writing Lesson Bank: Craft Minilessons, T266–T269

Teacher and Peer Conferences

Lesson 3	Lesson 4	Lesson 5
Grammar Lesson Bank, T275 More Plural Nouns Talk About It	**Grammar Lesson Bank, T275** More Plural Nouns Talk About It	**Grammar Lesson Bank, T275** More Plural Nouns Talk About It
Spelling Lesson Bank, T285 Inflectional Endings	**Spelling Lesson Bank, T285** Inflectional Endings	**Spelling Lesson Bank, T285** Inflectional Endings

● **On Level**
Vocabulary, T154
- Review Academic Vocabulary
- Personification
Comprehension, T155
- Review Theme
- Self-Selected Reading
● **Beyond Level**

Vocabulary, T160
- Review Domain-Specific Words
- Personification
Comprehension, T161
- Review Theme
- Self-Selected Reading GIFTED and TALENTED

 ● **English Language Learners**
See ELL Small Group Guide, pp. 60–71

Content Area Connections

Content Area Reading
- Science, Social Studies, and the Arts
Research and Inquiry
- Accomplishing a Task
Inquiry Space
- Options for Project-Based Learning

 ● **English Language Learners**
See ELL Small Group Guide, pp. 60–71

Week 4 Planner

Customize your own lesson plans at
my.mheducation.com

LESSON 6 / LESSON 7

60+ mins — **Reading** Suggested Daily Time

READING LESSON GOALS

- I can read and understand a folktale.
- I can use text evidence to respond to a folktale.
- I know how following a plan can help people accomplish a task.

SMALL GROUP OPTIONS
The designated lessons can be taught in small groups. To determine how to differentiate instruction for small groups, use Formative Assessment and Data Dashboard.

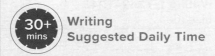

30+ mins — **Writing** Suggested Daily Time

WRITING LESSON GOALS

I can write an expository essay.

Reading

LESSON 6	LESSON 7
Anchor Text, T110–T125 ⟫ Reread *Blancaflor* ⟫ **Respond to Reading, T126–T127** **Expand Vocabulary, T138**	**Paired Selection, T128–T131** Read "From Tale to Table" **Expand Vocabulary, T138**

Writing

	Extended Writing 1, T244–T245 Draft: Elaboration
⟫ **Writing Lesson Bank: Craft Minilessons, T266–T269**	
Teacher and Peer Conferences	
Grammar Lesson Bank, T276 Possessive Nouns Talk About It	**Grammar Lesson Bank, T276** Possessive Nouns Talk About It
Spelling Lesson Bank, T286 Contractions	⟫ **Spelling Lesson Bank, T286** Contractions

Teacher-Led Instruction

Differentiated Reading
Differentiated Genre Passages
- "The Fox and the Snail," T142–T143
- "The Fox and the Snail," T152–T153
- "The Fox and the Snail," T158–T159

Differentiated Skills Practice
● **Approaching Level**
Phonics/Decoding, T145
- Decode Words with Contractions
  ⊞ 2
- Practice Words with Contractions

Vocabulary, T147
- Identify Related Words
- Personification

Fluency, T148
- Rate ⊞ 2

Comprehension, T149
- Review Theme
- Self-Selected Reading

SMALL GROUP

Independent/Collaborative Work See pages T85G–T85H.

Reading
Comprehension
- Folktale
- Theme
- Make Predictions

Fluency
Independent Reading

Phonics/Word Study
Phonics/Decoding
- Contractions

Vocabulary
- Personification

Writing
Extended Writing 1: Expository Writing
Self-Selected Writing
Grammar
- Possessive Nouns

Spelling
- Contractions

Handwriting

ACADEMIC VOCABULARY
assuring, detected, emerging, gratitude, guidance, outcome, previous, pursuit

SPELLING
you've, she'd, that's, what's, doesn't, there's, you're, wasn't, we'll, we've, we're, couldn't, I've, didn't, they're, shouldn't, wouldn't, he'd, don't, isn't

Review *dripping, applied, diaries*
Challenge *won't, aren't*
See pages T286–T287 for Differentiated Spelling Lists.

LESSON 8

LESSON 9

LESSON 10

Reading

Lesson 8	Lesson 9	Lesson 10
Paired Selection, T128–T131 Reread "From Tale to Table" **Author's Craft, T132–T133** Text Structure: Sequence **Phonics, T134–T135** Contractions **Expand Vocabulary, T139**	**Fluency, T135** Rate **Make Connections, T136** **Expand Vocabulary, T139**	**Show Your Knowledge, T137** **Progress Monitoring, T85I–T85J** **Expand Vocabulary, T139**

Writing

Lesson 8	Lesson 9	Lesson 10
	Extended Writing 1, T246–T247 Revise: Peer Conferences	

Writing Lesson Bank: Craft Minilessons, T266-T269

Teacher and Peer Conferences

Lesson 8	Lesson 9	Lesson 10
Grammar Lesson Bank, T277 Possessive Nouns Talk About It **Spelling Lesson Bank, T287** Contractions	**Grammar Lesson Bank, T277** Possessive Nouns Talk About It **Spelling Lesson Bank, T287** Contractions	**Grammar Lesson Bank, T277** Possessive Nouns Talk About It **Spelling Lesson Bank, T287** Contractions

● **On Level**
Vocabulary, T154
• Review Academic Vocabulary
• Personification
Comprehension, T155
• Review Theme
• Self-Selected Reading

● **Beyond Level**
Vocabulary, T160
• Review Domain-Specific Words
• Personification
Comprehension, T161
• Review Theme
• Self-Selected Reading GIFTED and TALENTED

 ● **English Language Learners**
See ELL Small Group Guide, pp. 60–71

Content Area Connections

Content Area Reading
• Science, Social Studies, and the Arts
Research and Inquiry
• Accomplishing a Task
Inquiry Space
• Options for Project-Based Learning

 ● **English Language Learners**
See ELL Small Group Guide, pp. 60–71

TEXT SET 2

Independent and Collaborative Work

As you meet with small groups, the rest of the class completes activities and projects that allow them to practice and apply the skills they have been working on.

Student Choice and Student Voice

- Print the My Independent Work blackline master and review it with students. Identify the "Must Do" activities.
- Have students choose additional activities that provide the practice they need.
- Remind students to reflect on their learning each day.

My Independent Work BLM

Reading

Independent Reading Texts

Students can choose a Center Activity Card to use while they read independently.

Classroom Library
Mufaro's Beautiful Daughters
Genre: Folktale
Lexile: 790L

Where the Mountain Meets the Moon
Genre: Fairy Tale
Lexile: 810L

Unit Bibliography
Have students self-select independent reading texts about people who have achieved a goal.

Leveled Texts Online
- Additional Leveled Readers in the **Leveled Reader Library Online** allow for flexibility.
- Six leveled sets of **Differentiated Genre Passages** in diverse genres are available.
- **Differentiated Texts** offer ELL students more passages at different proficiency levels.

Additional Literature
Literature Anthology
Where the Mountain Meets the Moon, p. 162
Genre: Fairy Tale

"The Princess and the Pea," p. 178
Genre: Fairy Tale

Center Activity Cards

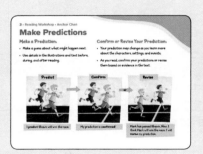
Make Predictions Card 3

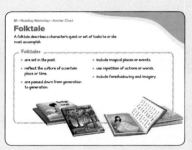
Folktale Card 31

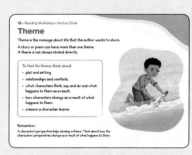
Theme Card 15

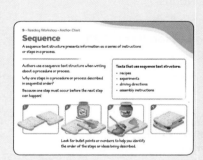
Sequence Card 9

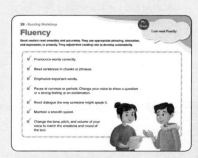
Fluency Card 38

Digital Activities

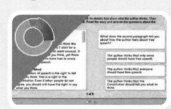
Comprehension

Phonics/Word Study

Center Activity Cards

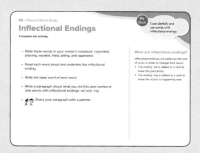

Inflectional Endings Card 98

Personification Card 75

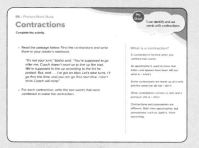

Contractions Card 99

Practice Book BLMs

Phonics: pages 91–91B, 94, 103–103B, 106

Vocabulary: pages 95–96, 107–108

Digital Activities

Phonics   **Vocabulary**

Writing

Center Activity Cards

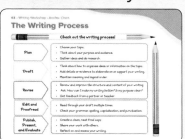

Writing Process Card 43

Elaboration Card 53

Self-Selected Writing

Share the following prompts.
- Imagine that you had magical powers. What would you use them to do?
- Write about a hero faced with an impossible task.
- Think about a famous building or structure. Describe how you think it was built.
- Describe your favorite dish?
- Research a famous battle. Describe the causes and effects of the battle.

Extended Writing

Have students continue developing their **expository essays.**

Practice Book BLMs

Grammar: pages 85–89, 97–101
Spelling: pages 90–94, 102–106
Handwriting: pages 361–396

Digital Activities

Grammar   **Spelling**

Content Area Connections

Content Area Reading Blackline Masters
- Additional texts related to Science, Social Studies, and the Arts

Research and Inquiry
- Accomplishing a Task

Inquiry Space
- Choose an activity

Progress Monitoring
Moving Toward Mastery

FORMATIVE ASSESSMENT

> **STUDENT CHECK-IN**

✓ **CHECK FOR SUCCESS**

For ongoing formative assessment, use students' self-assessments at the end of each lesson along with your own observations.

Assessing skills along the way . . .

SKILLS	HOW ASSESSED	
Comprehension **Vocabulary**	Digital Activities, Rubrics	
Text-Based Writing	Reading/Writing Companion: Respond to Reading	
Grammar, Mechanics, Phonics, Spelling	Practice Book, Digital Activities including word sorts	
Listening/Presenting/Research	Checklists	
Oral Reading Fluency (ORF) Fluency Goal: 111–131 words correct per minute (WCPM) Accuracy Rate Goal: 95% or higher	Fluency Assessment	

At the end of the text set . . .

SKILLS	HOW ASSESSED	
Plot: Setting **Theme** **Text Structure: Sequence**	Progress Monitoring	
Personification		

Making the Most of Assessment Results

Make data-based grouping decisions by using the following reports to verify assessment results. For additional student support options refer to the reteaching and enrichment opportunities.

ONLINE ASSESSMENT CENTER
- *Gradebook*

DATA DASHBOARD
- *Recommendations Report*
- *Activity Report*
- *Skills Report*
- *Progress Report*
- *Grade Card Report*

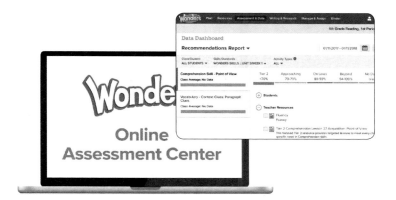

 Assign practice pages online for auto-grading.

Reteaching Opportunities with Intervention Online PDFs

IF STUDENTS SCORE . . .	THEN ASSIGN . . .
below 70% in **comprehension** . . .	lessons 28–30 on Setting in **Comprehension PDF**, lessons 34–36 on Theme in **Comprehension PDF**, and/or lessons 70–72 on Sequence in **Comprehension PDF**
below 70% in **vocabulary** . . .	lesson 119 on Personification in **Vocabulary PDF**
102–110 WCPM in **fluency** . . .	lessons from Section 1 or 7–10 of **Fluency PDF**
0–74 WCPM in **fluency** . . .	lessons from Sections 2–6 of **Fluency PDF**

Use the **Phonics/Word Study PDF** *and* **Foundational Skills Kit** *for additional reteaching opportunities.*
Use the **Foundational Skills Kit** *for students who need support with phonemic awareness and other early literacy skills.*

GIFTED and TALENTED

Enrichment Opportunities

Beyond Level small group lessons and resources include suggestions for additional activities in these areas to extend learning opportunities for gifted and talented students:

- *Leveled Readers*
- *Genre Passages*
- *Vocabulary*
- *Comprehension*
- *Leveled Reader Library Online*
- *Center Activity Cards*

OBJECTIVES

Engage effectively in a range of collaborative discussions (one-on-one, in groups, and teacher-led) with diverse partners on grade 5 topics and texts, building on others' ideas and expressing their own clearly.

Follow agreed-upon rules for discussions and carry out assigned roles.

Pose and respond to specific questions by making comments that contribute to the discussion and elaborate on the remarks of others.

ELA ACADEMIC LANGUAGE

• *plan, accomplish, task*

DIGITAL TOOLS

Show the image during class discussion.

Discuss Concept

Watch Video

Discuss Images

 VOCABULARY

task *(tarea)* a job

complete *(completar)* to finish

plan *(plan)* a set of actions to get something done

 10 mins

Build Knowledge

 MULTIMODAL

 Essential Question
When has a plan helped you accomplish a task?

Read the Essential Question on **Reading/Writing Companion** page 148. Tell students that they will read folktales that focus on accomplishing tasks and they will build knowledge on the topic. Students will learn and use words to read, write, and talk about the importance of following plans that provide the guidance needed to complete tasks and accomplish goals.

Watch the Video Play the video without sound first. Have partners narrate what they see. Then replay the video with sound as students listen.

Talk About the Video Have partners discuss how following a plan helps people complete tasks.

Write About the Video Have students add their ideas to their Build Knowledge pages of their reader's notebooks.

Anchor Chart Begin a Build Knowledge anchor chart. Write the Essential Question at the top of the chart. Have volunteers share what they learned about accomplishing tasks and record their ideas. Explain that students will add to the anchor chart after reading each text.

Build Knowledge

Discuss the photograph on the opener with students. Focus on how the sculptor is creating art. Ask: *What is the sculptor doing in this photo? What do his actions tell you?* Have students discuss in pairs or groups.

Build Vocabulary

Model using the graphic organizer to write down new words related to accomplishing tasks. Have partners continue the discussion and add the graphic organizer and new words to their reader's notebooks. Students will add words to the Build Knowledge pages in their notebooks as they read about following plans and accomplishing tasks throughout the text set.

 Collaborative Conversations

Take Turns Talking As students engage in discussions, have them take on roles to keep the discussion on track. Roles can include

- a questioner who asks questions to keep everyone involved.
- a recorder who takes notes and later reports to the class.
- a discussion monitor who keeps the group on topic and makes sure everyone gets a turn to talk.

Reading/Writing Companion, pp. 148–149

 BLAST BACK! studysync

Share the "Stand By Your Plan" Blast assignment with students. Point out that you will discuss their responses about following plans in the Make Connections lesson at the end of this text set.

 ## English Language Learners

Use the following scaffolds to build knowledge and vocabulary. Teach the ELL Vocabulary, as needed.

Beginning
Describe the photograph of the sculptor with students. Clarify the meaning of *sculptor*. Ask: *Is the sculptor working on a task?* (yes) *What is he creating?* (art) Help students generate a list of words and phrases to describe how the sculptor will complete the task. Then have partners discuss using: He follows a plan to complete a task.

Intermediate
Use the photograph to talk about what the sculptor is creating. Ask: *Is the sculptor working on a task?* (yes) *What is the sculptor creating?* The sculptor is creating art. Have partners generate a list of words and phrases to describe how the sculptor will complete the task. Then have them discuss using: He follows a plan to complete the task. The plan gives him guidance.

Advanced/Advanced High
Have partners discuss how a plan could help the sculptor complete his sculpture. Then have partners tell how a plan has helped them achieve a successful outcome and complete the graphic organizer.

 NEWCOMERS

To help students develop oral language and build vocabulary, use **Newcomer Cards 20–24** and the accompanying materials in the **Newcomer Teacher's Guide**. For thematic connection, use **Newcomer Card 8** with the accompanying materials.

MY GOALS ROUTINE

What I Know Now

Read Goals Have students read the goals on Reading/Writing Companion page 150.

Reflect Review the key. Ask students to reflect on each goal and fill in the bars to show what they know now. Explain they will fill in the bars on page 151 at the end of the text set to show their progress.

LESSON 1

  # Interactive Read Aloud

LEARNING GOALS

We can actively listen to learn about how following plans can help people accomplish tasks.

OBJECTIVES

Quote accurately from a text when explaining what the text says explicitly and when drawing inferences from the text.

Explain different characters' perspectives in a literary text.

Determine the meaning of words and phrases as they are used in a text, including figurative language such as metaphors and similes.

Summarize a written text read aloud or information presented in diverse media and formats, including visually, quantitatively, and orally.

Identify characteristics of folktales.

ELA ACADEMIC LANGUAGE
• *folktale, foreshadowing, predict*
• Cognate: *predecir*

DIGITAL TOOLS
Read or play the Interactive Read Aloud.

Interactive Read Aloud

FORMATIVE ASSESSMENT

❯ STUDENT CHECK-IN
Have partners talk about how the brothers were able to accomplish their task. Ask them to use the Check-In Routine.

Connect to Concept: A Plan of Action

Explain that accomplishing a task or overcoming an obstacle often requires a plan. Tell students that the story you will be reading aloud is about someone who sets out on a journey with a plan of action.

Preview Folktale

 Anchor Chart Explain that the passage you will read aloud is a type of folktale. Begin a Folktale anchor chart that includes the characteristics below. Review the characteristics, eliciting examples of texts students have read that include these characteristics:

• set in the past

• describes a hero or heroine's quest, or a set of tasks he or she must accomplish

• often includes foreshadowing and imagery

Ask them to think about other texts that they have read in class or independently that were folktales.

Read and Respond

Read the text aloud to students. Then reread it using the Teacher Think Alouds and Student Think Alongs on page T89 to build knowledge and model comprehension and the vocabulary strategy Personification.

Summarize Have students determine the plot and theme of "Lost Lake and the Golden Cup." Then have them summarize the text in their own words to enhance their comprehension.

Build Knowledge: Make Connections

 Talk About the Text Have partners discuss how following plans can help people accomplish tasks.

Write About the Text Have students add their ideas to their Build Knowledge pages of their reader's notebooks.

Anchor Chart Record any new ideas on the Build Knowledge anchor chart.

Add to the Vocabulary List Have students write down any words they learned about accomplishing tasks in their reader's notebooks.

Lost Lake and the Golden Cup

It hadn't rained in months, and the town needed water desperately. The only hope was that someone could get the golden cup from the edge of the Lost Lake, for it held an endless supply of water, or so the people believed. No one was sure because no one had ever actually held the cup, much less poured water from it. ∘∘①

Many adventurers had tried to find the golden cup. Each had returned telling of a huge dragon that guarded the cup and kept anyone from getting too close. Two brothers decided they would try to succeed where so many had failed. The older brother was sure that if they found the golden cup, he could snatch it and run like the wind back to town. The younger one, however, realized that they needed a plan to defeat the dragon. After a great deal of thought, he made what he called his "secret shield" and put it in a sack he would carry. He was sure it would protect them. ∘∘②

The next day, the two brothers set out. After many hours of climbing, they came to a ledge with a wide view. Just below them, they saw a hidden pool. Its emerald green water danced in the sun. Surely, it was Lost Lake! The brothers hiked down to the shore and began to search along it. Suddenly the older brother spotted a golden cup, shining in the sun. As they drew nearer, the lake became angry. Suddenly, it broke open, and a huge dragon loomed over them! As it opened its mighty jaws and bellowed a hideous roar, the younger brother opened his sack and removed his "secret shield." It was a pouch filled with honey and pine sap. He threw the pouch into the creature's mouth. As the dragon bit down on it, its jaws were stuck tightly together. All it could do was thrash about in the water trying to get them unstuck. The boys grabbed the cup and ran, fast as the wind, back to town. No matter how much water spilled out of the cup as they ran, it remained completely full. ∘∘③

When they arrived in the town, the townspeople cheered both brothers wildly. But the older brother gave the younger one the credit. "If he hadn't been so prepared," the older brother said, "we would have failed. His 'secret shield' saved us!"

---

①∘∘ **Teacher Think Aloud**

When reading fiction, I pay close attention to plot development, such as the conflict. The conflict refers to the problem that characters face. Paying attention to the conflict helps me increase my understanding of the story.

Student Think Along

Pay attention to the conflict as I reread the first paragraph. What problem does the town face? Listen for text evidence. Make a prediction about what kind of plan the town may create to solve their problem. Share your prediction with a partner.

---

②∘∘ **Teacher Think Aloud**

As I continue reading, I will look for more clues related to the plot. I see that two brothers have come up with a plan to get the golden cup from the dragon. I wonder if their plan will work.

Student Think Along

Think about the prediction you made after the first paragraph. Was it correct? Listen as I reread the paragraph. Turn to a partner and discuss whether or not you think the plan will help the two brothers accomplish the task.

---

③∘∘ **Teacher Think Aloud**

I know that personification means to give human characteristics to animals and objects. So when I read that the "emerald green water danced," I understand that this must be an example of personification because water can't actually dance.

Student Think Along

Pay attention as I reread this paragraph. What other example of personification do you hear? Raise your hand when you hear it. Turn to a partner and discuss why it is an example of personification.

LESSON 1

"The Magical Lost Brocade"

Lexile 740L

LEARNING GOALS

We can read and understand folktales.

OBJECTIVES

Determine a theme of a story, drama, or poem from details in the text, including how characters in a story or drama respond to challenges or how the speaker in a poem reflects upon a topic; summarize the text.

Compare and contrast two or more characters, settings, or events in a story or drama, drawing on specific details in the text (e.g., how characters interact).

By the end of the year, read and comprehend literature, including stories, dramas, and poetry, at the high end of the grade-level text complexity band independently and proficiently.

Use context to confirm or self-correct word recognition and understanding, rereading as necessary.

Demonstrate understanding of figurative language, word relationships, and nuances in word meanings.

Close Reading Routine

Read DOK 1–2

· Identify important ideas and details.
· Take notes and summarize.
· Use ⒶⒸⓉ prompts as needed.

Reread DOK 2–3

· Analyze the text, craft, and structure.
· Use the **Reread minilessons** and **prompts**.

Integrate DOK 3–4

· Integrate knowledge and ideas.
· Make text-to-text connections.
· Use the **Integrate** lesson.
· Complete the Show Your Knowledge task.
· Inspire action.

Reading/Writing Companion, pp. 152–153

Set a Purpose Before reading, have students connect to the Essential Question by considering what the title and illustrations indicate about a task the characters might have to accomplish. Have them set a purpose for reading. Students should use the left column on page 152 to note questions and to list words and details.

Focus on the **Read** prompts now. For additional support, use the extra prompts not included in the **Reading/Writing Companion.** Use the **Reread** prompts during the Craft and Structure lesson on pages T102–T103. Preteach the vocabulary to students who need more support.

⊙ DIFFERENTIATED READING

Approaching Level Review note-taking techniques and interesting words. As a group, complete all Read prompts.

On Level Ask students to read the selection and complete the Read prompts.

Beyond Level Share partners' responses to the Read prompts. Analyze how the setting and events influence the plot.

🎧 **English Language Learners** Preteach the vocabulary. Have Beginning and Early-Intermediate ELLs listen to the summary of the selection, available in multiple languages, and use the **Scaffolded Shared Read.** See also **ELL Small Group Guide.**

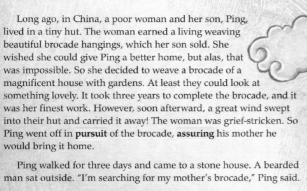

Long ago, in China, a poor woman and her son, Ping, lived in a tiny hut. The woman earned a living weaving beautiful brocade hangings, which her son sold. She wished she could give Ping a better home, but alas, that was impossible. So she decided to weave a brocade of a magnificent house with gardens. At least they could look at something lovely. It took three years to complete the brocade, and it was her finest work. However, soon afterward, a great wind swept into their hut and carried it away! The woman was grief-stricken. So Ping went off in **pursuit** of the brocade, **assuring** his mother he would bring it home.

Ping walked for three days and came to a stone house. A bearded man sat outside. "I'm searching for my mother's brocade," Ping said.

"A brocade flew by three days ago," said the man. "Now it's in a palace far away. I'll explain how you can get there and lend you my horse." Ping thanked the man and bowed deeply to express his **gratitude.**

"First, you must ride through Fire Valley," said the man. "You must cross over it regardless of the scorching heat, without uttering a word. If you utter even a single sound, you'll burn!" He continued, "After you've crossed Fire Valley, you'll arrive at Ice Ocean. You must ride through the icy waters without shivering. If you shiver even once, the **outcome** will be terrible! The sea will swallow you up!" The old man paused before concluding, "When you emerge from the sea, you'll be facing the Mountain of the Sun. The mountain is as steep as a straight line up to the sky! The palace sits on top of the mountain, and the brocade is in the palace."

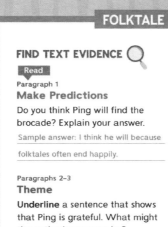

FOLKTALE

FIND TEXT EVIDENCE 🔍

Read

Paragraph 1
Make Predictions

Do you think Ping will find the brocade? Explain your answer.

Sample answer: I think he will because

folktales often end happily.

Paragraphs 2–3
Theme

Underline a sentence that shows that Ping is grateful. What might the author's message be?

Sometimes we have to accept the help

of others in order to succeed.

Paragraph 4
Plot: Setting

Circle the places that tell what kind of story this is.

Reread

Author's Craft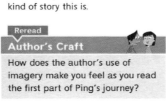

How does the author's use of imagery make you feel as you read the first part of Ping's journey?

Unit 2 • Text Set 2   153

Make Predictions DOK 2

Paragraph 1: *Do you think Ping will find the brocade? Explain your answer.*

Clarify students' understanding of a brocade before discussing why it is believable that a brocade hanging would blow away.

Think Aloud The title of the story tells me that the lost brocade is "magical." That makes me think that whatever magic it has will help Ping find it in the end. But since the story says that "a great wind" carried the brocade away, I'm guessing that it traveled pretty far. I think it will take a long time for Ping to find the brocade and that he will have some adventures along the way.

Theme DOK 2

Paragraphs 2–3: *Which sentence shows that Ping is grateful? What might the author's message be?*

Think Aloud Ping tells the man, "I'm searching for my mother's brocade." When the man offers to help him, Ping bows deeply to show that he is thankful for the man's help. I think the author's message might be that sometimes we have to accept the help of others in order to succeed. **Have students underline the sentence that shows Ping's gratitude towards the man.**

Plot: Setting DOK 2

Paragraph 4: Read the fourth paragraph and have students circle the locations that identify the story as a folktale. Ask: *What do all the places along Ping's journey have in common?* (They are very difficult to travel through.) *Why would a folktale feature a character traveling through such difficult places?* (Characters in folktales usually face challenges that are difficult to accomplish. It will be very hard for Ping to travel through Fire Valley and Ice Ocean and climb Mountain of the Sun in order to find the brocade.)

Check for Understanding DOK 2

Page 153: Monitor students' understanding of the story's characters and the problems they face. Ask: *Why is it so important that Ping's mother get her brocade back?* (She spent a long time weaving it. Also, she and her son are poor, and the brocade is the only valuable thing they own.) Have students summarize what Ping does to help her. (He goes looking for the brocade. He talks to a man who tells him it's in a palace and that he must travel a long way through difficult conditions to get it back.)

ELL Spotlight on Language

Page 153, Paragraph 4: Point out the verb phrases *must cross* and *must ride* in the first two sentences. Say: *The helping verb* must *tells readers that Ping has to do these things. He does not have a choice.* Guide students to use the helping verb *must* to form verb phrases and describe the remaining tasks Ping must accomplish. Then, have pairs use the word *must* to state tasks that students have to do.

Theme DOK 2

Paragraph 1: Read the first paragraph. Ask: *How does Ping describe the journey and what he will do?* (He says it will be extremely difficult. He says he will do his very best.) *What does this help you understand about the author's message?* (that people can do their best even when tasks seem impossible) Discuss how Ping's description connects to the author's message.

Context Clues DOK 2

Paragraph 2: Read the second sentence. Ask: *What words and phrases in the paragraph help you to understand the meaning of* frigid? (The body of water is called Ice Ocean and the word *icy* also appears in the paragraph, so I think *frigid* means "really cold.") *How does knowing the meaning help you understand why the horse would need "gentle guidance" from Ping?* (The horse would not want to get into water that is really cold. Ping would need to guide him.)

Personification DOK 2

Paragraph 2: Read the second paragraph and have students identify the use of personification. Ask: *Why do you think the author chose these words to describe the ocean?* (The words "touched" and "icy fingers" make the ocean seem like a villain.) *What effect does the personification have on your understanding of the ocean's dangers?* (Giving the ocean human qualities makes it seem menacing and alive, as though it intends to hurt Ping.)

 Access Complex Text

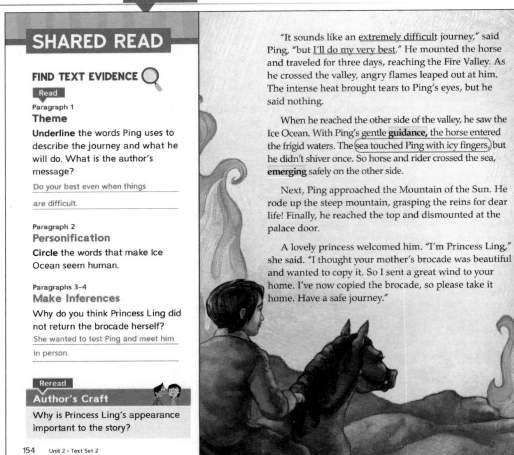

Reading/Writing Companion, pp. 154–155

Make Inferences DOK 2

Paragraphs 3–4: Read the third and fourth paragraphs. Ask: *What do you know about the hero of a folktale?* (He/She must complete a quest or challenge of some kind.) *How might the story have been different if the princess had gone to Ping's house to get the brocade?* (Ping never would have made the journey or faced the challenges he did.) Discuss with students what the princess learns about Ping by making him face so many challenges. (She learns that he is brave.)

Organization

Point out that this story has a sequence of events common to many folktales and fairy tales. Ask: *What problem is described at the beginning of the story?* (A wind carries away Ping's mother's brocade, and he must find it.) *What steps does the main character take in the middle to solve the problem?* (Ping goes on a journey and faces many challenges.) *How is the problem solved?* (Ping finds the brocade. It turns into a beautiful house with the princess inside. He marries the princess.)

Genre

In order to help students better understand and appreciate the folktale, guide them to identify additional genre features within it. Ask: *What is Ping's quest?*

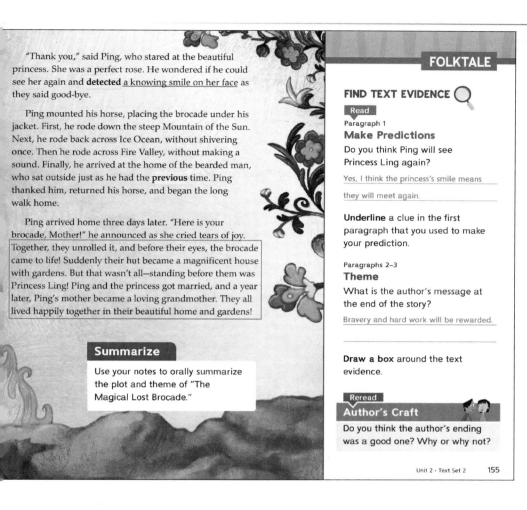

"Thank you," said Ping, who stared at the beautiful princess. She was a perfect rose. He wondered if he could see her again and **detected** <u>a knowing smile on her face</u> as they said good-bye.

Ping mounted his horse, placing the brocade under his jacket. First, he rode down the steep Mountain of the Sun. Next, he rode back across Ice Ocean, without shivering once. Then he rode across Fire Valley, without making a sound. Finally, he arrived at the home of the bearded man, who sat outside just as he had the **previous** time. Ping thanked him, returned his horse, and began the long walk home.

Ping arrived home three days later. "Here is your brocade, Mother!" he announced as she cried tears of joy. Together, they unrolled it, and before their eyes, the brocade came to life! Suddenly their hut became a magnificent house with gardens. But that wasn't all—standing before them was Princess Ling! Ping and the princess got married, and a year later, Ping's mother became a loving grandmother. They all lived happily together in their beautiful home and gardens!

Summarize

Use your notes to orally summarize the plot and theme of "The Magical Lost Brocade."

FOLKTALE

FIND TEXT EVIDENCE 🔍

Read

Paragraph 1
Make Predictions

Do you think Ping will see Princess Ling again?

Yes, I think the princess's smile means

they will meet again.

Underline a clue in the first paragraph that you used to make your prediction.

Paragraphs 2-3
Theme

What is the author's message at the end of the story?

Bravery and hard work will be rewarded.

Draw a box around the text evidence.

Reread

Author's Craft

Do you think the author's ending was a good one? Why or why not?

Unit 2 · Text Set 2   155

Make Predictions DOK 2

Paragraph 1: Read the first paragraph. Ask: *What does it mean that Princess Ling has "a knowing smile on her face"?* (It means that she's aware of something that Ping probably isn't aware of.) *What do you think this indicates about whether or not Ping will ever see her again?* (I think she knows she and Ping will meet again.) Remind students to check and confirm their predictions as they read.

(Ping's quest is to find and return his mother's lost brocade.) *What magical characters and situations does the folktale contain?* (The princess sends the wind to capture the brocade, transports herself in it, and brings it to life.) *What actions are repeated?* (The steps on Ping's quest are repeated three times.)

Theme DOK 2

Paragraphs 2-3: Reread paragraphs 2-3. Ask: *What is the outcome of Ping's journey?* (He completes every task, returns the brocade to his mother, and comes back to find a new home and Princess Ling.) *What message might this convey?* (Possible response: Bravery and hard work will be rewarded.)

Check for Understanding DOK 2

Paragraphs 2–3: Read the second and third paragraphs again. Ask: *What happens when Ping returns home with the brocade?* (The setting in the brocade becomes real. Princess Ling appears, and she and Ping get married and have a child.) *What does this indicate about the challenges Ping faced on his journey?* (The challenges were worth it; his bravery and hardwork were rewarded.) Discuss how these ideas contribute to the plot.

Summarize DOK 2

Analytical Writing **Quick Write** After their initial reads, have partners summarize the selection orally using their notes. Then have them write a summary in their reader's notebooks. Remind them to include only the most important events. Students may decide to digitally record presentations of summaries.

ELL Spotlight on Language

Page 155, Paragraph 2 Help students examine the use of sequence words in the second paragraph. *The author uses the word* first *to describe the first thing Ping does: First, he rode down the steep mountain.* Help students identify the next three sequence words in the paragraph. (next, then, finally) Have pairs use these words to describe the steps of an everyday task.

FORMATIVE ASSESSMENT

❯ **STUDENT CHECK-IN**

Have partners share their summaries from page 155. Ask them to reflect using the Check-In routine.

- We can use new vocabulary words to read and understand folktales.
- We can identify and explain the use of personification.

OBJECTIVES

Demonstrate understanding of figurative language, word relationships, and nuances in word meanings.

Interpret figurative language, including similes and metaphors, in context.

Acquire and use accurately grade-appropriate general academic and domain-specific words and phrases, including those that signal contrast, addition, and other logical relationships.

ELA ACADEMIC LANGUAGE

- *personification*
- Cognate: *personificación*

DIGITAL TOOLS

Visual Vocabulary Cards

▷ TEACH IN SMALL GROUP

Academic Vocabulary

⬤⬤ ⬤ **Approaching Level** and **ELL** Preteach the words before students begin the Shared Read.

⬤ **On Level** Have students look up each word in the online **Visual Glossary**.

⬤ **Beyond Level** Have partners write an original context sentence for each vocabulary word.

Reread

🕙 10 mins Academic Vocabulary

Use the routines on the **Visual Vocabulary Cards** to introduce each word.

When you are **assuring**, you are making someone feel certain or sure about something.

If you **detected** the smell of smoke, you discovered it or noticed it.

If something is **emerging**, it is coming into view and can be seen.

Gratitude is a feeling of thankfulness.
Cognate: *gratitud*

Guidance is leadership or direction.

An **outcome** is a result or consequence.

Previous means "before or earlier."
Cognate: *previo*

A **pursuit** is a chase.

Encourage students to use their newly acquired vocabulary in their discussions and written responses about the texts in this text set.

🕙 10 mins Personification

1 Explain

Remind students that folktales often include figurative language like personification, or the act of giving human qualities to animals or objects. Personification helps readers better picture animals, objects, or events in a story. If feelings or actions refer to animals or objects instead of people, then the author is using personification. Begin a Personification anchor chart. Have volunteers add points to the chart.

2 Model

Model finding an example of personification in the last paragraph on page 153 in the **Reading/Writing Companion**. Point out that *swallow* is an action that people usually perform. In this story, however, the author has the sea perform this action.

3 Guided Practice

Using the sentence provided from the text, help students work in pairs to identify how personification is used in the sentence on page 154. Encourage partners to explain how the use of personification shows human qualities and helps them picture and understand the event in the story.

Reading/Writing Companion, pp. 156–157

English Language Learners

Use the following scaffolds with **Guided Practice**. For small group support, see the **ELL Small Group Guide**.

Beginning

Read the first paragraph on page 154 with students. Point to the word *leaped* and clarify its meaning. *What leaped out at Ping?* (angry flames) *Are the angry flames a person?* (no) Help partners discuss why this is an example of personification. Then have them respond using: The words *angry* and *leaped* show personification. The flames act like a person.

Intermediate

Have partners read the first paragraph on page 154. Ask partners to describe the flames of Fire Valley. The flames of Fire Valley are angry just like people get angry. Say: *This is personification. The fire acts like a person. What is another word that shows the fire doing a human action?* (leap) Guide partners as they describe the fire using *angry* and *leap*. Allow them to mime and gesture to represent the flames.

Advanced/Advanced High

Have students reread to identify examples of personification on pages 153 and 154. Guide them with questions: *Can the sea really swallow someone? Can flames get angry and leap? What does the comparison tell you about the sea and the fire?* Have pairs describe these images using words from the text in their descriptions.

BUILD YOUR WORD LIST

Students might choose *deeply* from page 153. Have them use a print or online dictionary to find words that are related.

FORMATIVE ASSESSMENT

⊘ STUDENT CHECK-IN

Academic Vocabulary Ask partners to share two answers from Reading/Writing Companion pages 156–157.

Personification Ask partners to share their Your Turn responses on page 157.

Have students use the Check-In routine to reflect and fill in the bars.

✓ CHECK FOR SUCCESS

Rubric Use your online rubric to record student progress.

Can students identify and explain how personification helps them picture the event?

⟫ Small Group Instruction

If No:

● **Approaching** Reteach p. T147

If Yes:

● **On** Review p. T154

● **Beyond** Extend p. T160

LEARNING GOALS

We can make predictions to understand folktales.

OBJECTIVES

Quote accurately from a text when explaining what the text says explicitly and when drawing inferences from the text.

Explain different characters' perspectives in a literary text.

Read grade-level text with purpose and understanding.

Make, confirm, and revise predictions based on evidence in the text.

ELA ACADEMIC LANGUAGE

• *prediction, confirm, revise*

• Cognates: *predicción, confirmar, revisar*

Reread

Make Predictions

1 Explain

Explain that when they make predictions, students should use information in the text to determine what might happen in the plot.

- First, students should look for details in the text and illustrations about what the main character says, does, or thinks. They should also look for clues about how other characters respond to the main character.

- Then they should make a prediction about what events are likely to happen during the rising action, climax, and falling action of the plot, based on this text evidence.

- Students can also use what they know about the characteristics of a particular genre to make a prediction. For example, knowing that a folktale often features a character who embarks on a quest or adventure can help readers predict what the character might experience.

Point out that a prediction made early in the story may change as students learn more about the characters, settings, and events. Students should use new evidence in the text to confirm or revise their original predictions. Confirming and/or revising predictions will help students monitor and support their understanding of a text.

 Anchor Chart Begin a Make Predictions anchor chart. Have a volunteer add details about the strategy to the chart.

2 Model

Model how using evidence in the text can help you make a prediction about the story. Reread the first paragraph on **Reading/Writing Companion** page 154 of "The Magical Lost Brocade." Explain that you predict that Ping will succeed, because the text says that Ping promises that he will do his very best. Continue to read the next two paragraphs, pointing out details that indicate your prediction was correct.

3 Guided Practice

Guide pairs to share one prediction they made after Ping left the Mountain of the Sun and to explain the evidence that helped them make it. Have pairs tell whether they were able to confirm their predictions, and if not, what they did to revise them.

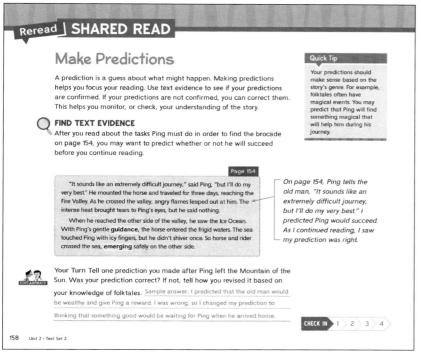

Reading/Writing Companion, p. 158

 # English Language Learners

Use the following scaffolds with **Guided Practice**. For small group support, see the **ELL Small Group Guide**.

Beginning

Read with students the first paragraph on **Reading/Writing Companion** page 155. *The princess smiles. She knows something. Do you think Ping will see the princess again?* Help pairs make predictions: I think that Ping will/will not see the princess again. Read the last paragraph. Help pairs discuss their predictions: *Was your prediction correct?* My prediction was/was not correct.

Intermediate

Have partners reread the first paragraph on **Reading/Writing Companion** page 155. What does Ping wonder? He wonders if he will see the princess again. *What word describes the princess's smile?* (knowing) *She smiles because she knows something. Do you think Ping will see the princess again?* I predict that Ping _____. Ask them to read the last paragraph to check their predictions: My prediction was _____.

Advanced/Advanced High

Have partners read paragraph 1 on page 155. Then ask guiding questions to help them as they predict Ping's future: *What does a knowing smile show? Do you think Ping will see the princess again?* Have pairs reread the last paragraph to check their predictions.

HABITS OF LEARNING

I use a variety of strategies when I read.

Making predictions is one of a variety of reading strategies that enables students to interact with the text. Explain that making predictions helps them to reach deeper into a text. Remind them to ask themselves: *What do I think will happen next? Why do I think this?*

FORMATIVE ASSESSMENT

❯ STUDENT CHECK-IN

Ask partners to share their Your Turn responses on Reading/Writing Companion page 158. Have them use the Check-In routine to reflect and fill in the bars.

✓ CHECK FOR SUCCESS

Do students make predictions about plot events? Do they revise predictions if they cannot be confirmed?

❯ Small Group Instruction

If No:

● **Approaching** Reteach p. T140

If Yes:

● **On** Review p. T150

● **Beyond** Extend p. T156

LESSON 2

10 mins

Plot: Setting

LEARNING GOALS

We can identify and analyze the setting to understand folktales.

OBJECTIVES

Quote accurately from a text when explaining what the text says explicitly and when drawing inferences from the text.

Explain different characters' perspectives in a literary text.

By the end of the year, read and comprehend literature, including stories, dramas, and poetry, independently and proficiently.

ELA ACADEMIC LANGUAGE

- *folktale, foreshadowing, setting, historical, cultural*
- Cognates: *histórico, cultural*

1 Explain

Tell students that a **folktale** is a story that is common to a specific culture. More and more people become familiar with the story as it is passed down, often by word of mouth.

Share with students the following key characteristics of a folktale:

- The hero or heroine in a folktale often goes on a quest or faces a challenge that he or she must accomplish. The quest or challenge usually involves a set of tasks that are difficult to complete.

- A folktale often includes magical or cultural settings, situations, or characters that advance the plot. The setting can reflect a historical time period or the land specific to a place where the people who first told the story lived.

- A folktale often includes foreshadowing, imagery, and the repetition of actions and words.

- A folktale usually contains a lesson or reflects a universal theme.

2 Model

Model identifying literary elements in "The Magical Lost Brocade."

Setting Point out the setting introduced in the first sentence on **Reading/Writing Companion** page 153: "Long ago, in China . . ." Explain that as students read the story, they can look for details that show how historical and cultural aspects of ancient China influence the story's plot.

Foreshadowing Remind students that foreshadowing gives readers clues about the outcome of events to come. Point out that the fourth paragraph on page 153, in which the old man describes challenges Ping will face on his quest, is an example of foreshadowing.

Anchor Chart Have a volunteer add details about setting and foreshadowing to the Folktale chart.

COLLABORATE

3 Guided Practice

Circulate as students work with partners to list two details that show "The Magical Lost Brocade" is a folktale and to identify examples that give clues about the historical and cultural setting. Partners should discuss how each example contributes to the plot of the folktale. Ask pairs to share their work with the class.

Independent Practice Have students read the online **Differentiated Genre Passage** "The Fox and the Snail."

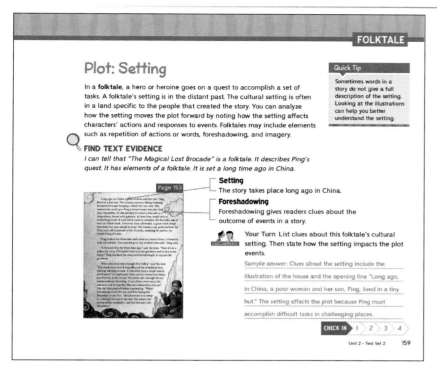

Reading/Writing Companion, p. 159

 English Language Learners

Use the following scaffolds with **Guided Practice**. For small group support, see the **ELL Small Group Guide**.

Beginning

Remind students of key characteristics of folktales: *In a folktale, the main character faces a challenge. What is the challenge, or problem, that Ping faces?* Ping has to find the <u>brocade</u>. *Check students' understanding of "setting." The setting of a folktale is in the distant, or long ago, past. What is the setting for this folktale?* The first line of this folktale tells that the setting is <u>long ago in China</u>.

Intermediate

Review folktale characteristics: *In a folktale, the main character faces a challenge. What challenge does Ping face?* Ping has to <u>find the brocade</u>. Check understanding of setting. Then ask: *How do you know the setting of this folktale?* The first line of this folktale tells where and when the <u>story takes place</u>. The setting is <u>long ago in China</u>.

Advanced/Advanced High

Have volunteers take turns naming the main characteristics of folktales. Then have partners choose two historical and cultural characteristics of the folktale's setting. Help partners practice presenting their findings to each other before presenting to the group.

LESSON 2

10 mins

Theme

LEARNING GOALS

We can read and understand folktales by identifying the theme.

OBJECTIVES

Determine a theme of a story, drama, or poem from details in the text, including how characters in a story or drama respond to challenges or how the speaker in a poem reflects upon a topic; summarize the text.

Describe how a narrator's or speaker's point of view influences how events are described. Explain different characters' perspectives in a literary text.

Describe how an author develops a character's perspective in a literary text.

ELA ACADEMIC LANGUAGE

• *theme, summarize, infer perspective*

• Cognates: *tema, inferir, perspectiva*

DIGITAL TOOLS

To differentiate instruction for key skills, use the results of the activity.

1 Explain

Explain to students that the theme of a story is a big idea or message about life that the author wants to share with readers.

• Tell students that the theme of a story is usually not stated directly. Readers must use details in the text to infer the implied theme. It is often possible to identify more than one theme in a story.

• Explain that students can analyze text details that describe the relationships between and conflicts among the characters, along with their words and actions, to help them identify the theme of the story.

• Point out that the way an author develops a character's perspective, or attitude, may also lead to the development of a theme. Analyzing multiple perspectives in a text allows readers to see things from different points of view because they are based on each character's personal experiences and background.

 Anchor Chart Begin a Theme anchor chart and have a volunteer add details to the chart.

2 Model

Identify Ping's words and actions that result from the promise he makes to his mother in the first paragraph on **Reading/Writing Companion** page 153 and list them in the graphic organizer. Then model using this information to begin forming ideas about how the author develops the theme of the story. Say: *One way the author develops the theme is through what Ping says and does. He tells her he will find her brocade and sets off on a journey to find it. Another way the theme is developed is through Ping's perspective, or attitude. His relationship with his mother is important to him, and he cares about her. He doesn't want her to be sad. I can infer that the theme is about how family members care about and help one another.*

3 Guided Practice

Circulate as partners work to complete a graphic organizer for "The Magical Lost Brocade." Have students record what Ping thinks, says, and does as well as his perspective. Remind them to consider each character's perspective, or point of view, as they determine additional themes.

Analytical Writing **Write About Reading: Summary** Ask pairs to work together to summarize one of the story's themes. Select pairs of students to share their summaries with the class.

Reread | SHARED READ

FOLKTALE

Theme

The theme of a story is an overall idea or message about life that the author wants to share. Themes may be stated directly or implied. To find an implied theme, think about the plot, setting, and what the characters think, say, or do. A character's perspective can help to develop a theme.

FIND TEXT EVIDENCE

At the end of the first paragraph on page 153, Ping assures his mother he will find her brocade. I know Ping cares about his mother and wants to make her feel better. I can use Ping's perspective to find the theme.

What Does the Character Think, Say, or Do?	What Is the Character's Perspective?
Ping assures his mother he will find her lost brocade and goes off to search for it.	Ping cares about his mother and doesn't want her to be sad about her lost brocade.

Theme
Family members care about and help each other.

Quick Tip
Many times, a reader can infer multiple themes in a story. For example, one theme you may infer after reading the first paragraph on page 153 is, "Family members help each other." Make sure you use text evidence to infer a possible theme.

COLLABORATE

Your Turn Reread "The Magical Lost Brocade." Complete the graphic organizer on page 161 to determine another theme of the story. Record what Ping thinks, says, and does and then his perspective. State the theme you inferred.

CHECK IN 1 2 3 4

160 Unit 2 • Text Set 2

Sample answers shown.

What Does the Character Think, Say, or Do?	What Is the Character's Perspective?
Ping tells the bearded man, "I'll do my best," and travels to Fire Valley. He doesn't say anything when he crosses the intense heat.	Ping doesn't want to risk not finding his mother's brocade. He is careful about following the instructions, even though they are difficult.
Ping gently guides the horse as he crosses Ice Ocean. Ping does not shiver when he crosses the icy cold ocean.	Ping not only cares about his mother, but also his horse. He is patient and determined. He continues to follow the instructions.

Theme
If you are determined and follow instructions, you will succeed at your tasks.

Unit 2 • Text Set 2 161

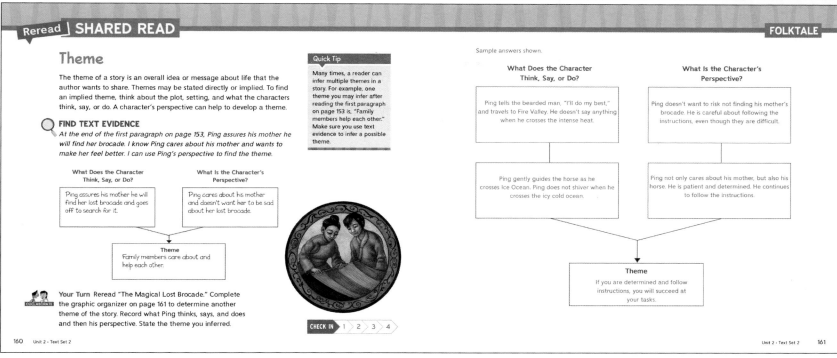

Reading/Writing Companion, pp. 160–161

English Language Learners

Use the following scaffolds with **Guided Practice**. For small group support, see the **ELL Small Group Guide**.

Beginning

Help students describe what Ping thinks, says, and does as well as his perspective. Say: *Ping wants to get the brocade. Why?* (to help his mother) *He has a difficult journey.* (cognate: *difícil*) Read with students the last paragraph on page 153 of "The Magical Lost Brocade." *Does Ping follow the instructions?* (yes) Then discuss the theme with students and help them fill in their graphic organizer.

Intermediate

Guide partners to describe what Ping thinks, says, and does as well as his perspective: *What does Ping want?* Ping wants to get the brocade back. *What challenge does Ping face?* He has to complete a difficult journey. Have them reread the last paragraph on page 153 and the first paragraph on page 154 of "The Magical Lost Brocade." Help students describe the theme: *Does Ping follow the man's instructions?* (yes) When you follow instructions, you can get what you want.

Advanced/Advanced High

Have pairs to describe what Ping thinks, says, and does as well as his perspective by asking: *What does Ping want? Why? What challenge does he face? How does he respond to the challenge?* Then have them discuss the theme and complete the graphic organizer.

FORMATIVE ASSESSMENT

STUDENT CHECK-IN

Ask partners to share their graphic organizers on Reading/Writing Companion page 161. Have them use the Check-In routine to reflect and fill in the bars.

CHECK FOR SUCCESS

Rubric Use your online rubric to record student progress.

Can students list details about a character's thoughts, words, actions and perspective? Can they use the details to infer a second theme in the story?

Small Group Instruction

If No:

- **Approaching** Reteach p. T149

If Yes:

- **On** Review p. T155
- **Beyond** Extend p. T161

LESSON
2

LEARNING GOALS

We can reread to analyze craft and structure in folktales.

OBJECTIVES

Quote accurately from a text when explaining what the text says explicitly and when drawing inferences from the text.

Explain different characters' perspectives in a literary text.

Determine a theme of a story, drama, or poem from details in the text, including how characters in a story or drama respond to challenges or how the speaker in a poem reflects upon a topic; summarize the text.

Demonstrate understanding of figurative language, word relationships, and nuances in word meanings.

ELA ACADEMIC LANGUAGE

• *craft, analyze, technique, mood, imagery*
• Cognates: *analizar, técnica, personificación, imaginería*

⟫ TEACH IN SMALL GROUP

● **Approaching Level** Use the scaffolded questions to guide students as they reread "The Magical Lost Brocade." Have them note relevant text evidence in the margins.

● **On Level** Work with partners to complete the Reread prompts and share their responses.

● **Beyond Level** Allow partners to answer the Reread prompts on their own.

● **ELL** Have Beginning and Early-Intermediate ELLs use the **Scaffolded Shared Read.**

 Reread

⏱ 10 mins
Craft and Structure

Tell students that they will now reread parts of "The Magical Lost Brocade" and analyze the techniques the author used in writing the selection. The use of imagery and descriptive language allows authors to help readers visualize the magical settings, events, conflicts, and characters common to folktales. It also helps authors convey a specific mood.

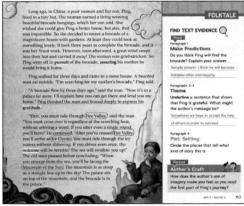

Reading/Writing Companion, p. 153

AUTHOR'S CRAFT DOK 2

Reread the last paragraph on page 153 with students. Ask: *What are the names of the places Ping must journey across to find the brocade?* ("Fire Valley," "Ice Ocean," "Mountain of the Sun") *What do these names suggest?* (They suggest Ping's journey will be dangerous.)

ELL As needed, use gestures or pantomime to define *scorching* and *shiver.* Then support partners as they talk about important ideas conveyed by the imagery and dialogue in the paragraph. Fire Valley is very <u>hot</u>. Walking through it would <u>hurt</u>. It would be hard to be <u>quiet</u>. Ice Ocean is very <u>cold</u>. It would be hard to cross it and not <u>shiver</u>. The bearded man tells Ping that he cannot <u>make noise</u> in Fire Valley or <u>shiver</u> in Ice Ocean. If he does, he will <u>die</u>.

How does the author's use of imagery make you feel as you learn about the first part of Ping's journey? (Possible response: Imagery such as "scorching heat" and "icy waters" helps me realize how dangerous the places are. The author then uses the bearded man's dialogue to warn Ping that he will die if he makes a noise in the burning Fire Valley or shivers in the frigid Ice Ocean—both of which would be nearly impossible to avoid doing. This makes me fear for Ping's safety.)

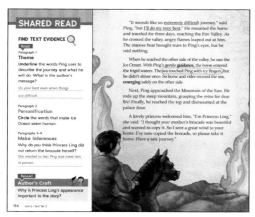

Reading/Writing Companion, p. 154

AUTHOR'S CRAFT DOK 3

Reread the last paragraph on page 154 and the first paragraph on page 155. Ask: *How does the author describe Princess Ling?* (She is described as "lovely.") *How do you know she wants Ping to be successful?* (She says, "Have a safe journey.")

ELL Read the last paragraph on page 154. *What words show that Princess Ling is friendly?* (lovely, welcomed, Have a safe journey) Read the first paragraph on page 155. *Talk to your partner about how the princess makes Ping feel.* Work with partners to identify evidence of Ping's feelings.

Why is Princess Ling's appearance important to the story? (Princess Ling's appearance shows a turning point in the story. Ling has finally recovered the brocade. She represents hope that Ping will return safely.)

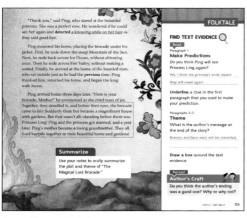

Reading/Writing Companion, p. 155

AUTHOR'S CRAFT DOK 2

Reread the last paragraph on page 155. Ask: *How is Ping rewarded for what he has done for his mother?* (The princess magically appears, and the brocade becomes a house and gardens.) *How is this ending like that of other folktales and fairy tales you have read?* (The ending is similar because it is happy. The main characters get what they wanted.)

ELL Read the final paragraph on page 155. *Does the story have a happy ending?* (yes) *What is the happy ending?* (The hut becomes a house and garden; Ping and Ling get married and have children; they all live happily together.)

Do you think the author's ending was a good one? Why or why not? (Possible answer: The ending was good because it was happy. Ping was rewarded for helping his mother. Also, an unhappy ending would have felt strange, because folktales usually end with a positive outcome.)

MAKE INFERENCES

Explain that when you make inferences, you use information in the text and what you already know to draw a conclusion about characters or events. By making inferences, you can gain insight into characters' feelings and attitudes.

Think Aloud By paying close attention to the manner in which Princess Ling speaks to Ping and what she says to him on page 154, I can make an inference about her attitude toward Ping. She treats him well, and she seems to like and respect him.

BUILD KNOWLEDGE: MAKE CONNECTIONS

Talk About the Text Have partners discuss how following a plan helped Ping accomplish an important task.

Write About the Text Have students add their ideas to their Build Knowledge pages of their reader's notebooks.

Anchor Chart Record any new ideas on the Build Knowledge anchor chart.

Add to the Vocabulary List Have students write down any words they learned about accomplishing a task in their reader's notebooks.

FORMATIVE ASSESSMENT

❯ STUDENT CHECK-IN

Have partners share their responses to one of the Reread prompts on Reading/Writing Companion pages 153-155. Ask them to reflect using the Check-In routine.

Reread

Write About the Shared Read

LEARNING GOALS

We can use text evidence to respond to a folktale.

OBJECTIVES

Describe how a narrator's or speaker's point of view influences how events are described.

Explain different characters' perspectives in a literary text.

Describe how an author develops a character's perspective in a literary text.

Demonstrate understanding of figurative language, word relationships, and nuances in word meanings.

Draw evidence from literary or informational texts to support analysis, reflection, and research.

ELA ACADEMIC LANGUAGE

• prompt, evidence, imagery, visualize, reaction

• Cognates: evidencia, imaginería, reacción

TEACH IN SMALL GROUP

● **Approaching Level** Have partners work together to determine their main points, order their ideas logically, and gather text evidence.

● **On Level** Have pairs work together to write their responses and exchange feedback.

● **Beyond Level** After writing their responses, have partners provide each other with feedback and revision suggestions.

● **ELL** Group students of mixed proficiency levels to discuss and respond to the prompt.

Analyze the Prompt DOK 3

Read the prompt aloud. *Why do we care about Ping and what happens to him on his dangerous journey?* Ask: *What is the prompt asking?* (to explain why readers care about Ping as he completes his journey) Say: *Let's reread to see how the author describes what happens to Ping and how he responds. As we review the story, we can note text evidence. Doing this will help you make inferences to aid you in your response.*

Analyze Text Evidence

Remind students that an author often uses descriptive language and imagery to help readers visualize a story's setting, events, and characters. Students should look for words and phrases in the text that help them picture Ping and the challenges he encounters on his journey. In the **Reading/Writing Companion,** have students reread the first paragraph on page 154. Ask: *How does the intense heat of Fire Valley affect Ping?* (It makes his eyes tear up.) *What is Ping's reaction?* (He says nothing.) *How does this characterize him?* (Possible answers: brave, courageous, determined) Have students continue looking for examples of imagery and descriptions in the text that help them characterize Ping. As they look for text evidence, remind them to consider Ping's perspective, or point of view, and to infer how his situation might make the average person feel.

Respond

Direct student pairs to the sentence starters on **Reading/Writing Companion** page 162. Ask: *How does examining the use of imagery in the story help you care about Ping?* As needed, model a response.

Think Aloud By analyzing the imagery the author uses to describe Ping's actions, I can see just how frightening and challenging his journey was. He faced scorching hot fires, icy waters, and steep mountains, but he did it all bravely and without showing fear in order to help his mom. He knew the brocade was important to his mother, and he was willing to take risks to get it back. Using the author's descriptions to visualize Ping's actions made me admire his bravery and strength and to root for him to succeed.

Analytical Writing Students should use the phrases in the sentence starters to form their responses. They should use text evidence to support their answers. Students may continue their responses on a separate piece of paper.

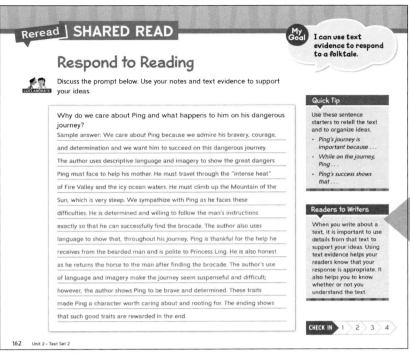

Reading/Writing Companion, p. 162

 # English Language Learners

Use the following scaffolds with **Respond**.

Beginning

Read the prompt with students and discuss what they will write about. Review the meaning of *dangerous* and *brave* with students. Ask: *Does Ping show fear during his dangerous journey?* (no) *Does the author use descriptive language and imagery to show Ping is brave?* (yes) Help partners discuss why Ping's journey is important and respond using: Ping's journey is important. It shows that Ping is brave.

Intermediate

Read the prompt with students and discuss what they will write about. Ask: *What does Ping do when he sees the angry flames and feels the icy fingers of the sea?* (keeps going) *Does the author use descriptive language and imagery to describe Ping's actions?* (yes) *What does it show about Ping?* It shows Ping is brave/determined. Have partners discuss why Ping's journey is important and respond using: Ping's journey is important because _____.

Advanced/Advanced High

Review the prompt and sentence starters on page 162 with students. Guide students to describe how the author uses imagery to show that Ping is brave. Then have partners discuss why Ping's journey is important and have them respond using the sentence starters.

ELL NEWCOMERS

Have students listen to the summaries of the **Shared Read** in their native language and then in English to help them access the text and develop listening comprehension. Help students ask and answer questions with a partner. Use these sentence frames: What is Ping's problem? Ping's problem is ___. Then continue the lessons in the **Newcomer Teacher's Guide**.

FORMATIVE ASSESSMENT

❯ STUDENT CHECK-IN

Ask partners to share their response on Reading/Writing Companion page 162. Have them use the Check-In routine to reflect and fill in the bars..

LESSON 2

LEARNING GOALS

- **We can identify and use words with inflectional endings.**
- **We can identify and read multisyllabic words.**
- **We can read fluently with expression and phrasing.**

OBJECTIVES

Use combined knowledge of all letter-sound correspondences, syllabication patterns, and morphology (e.g., roots and affixes) to read accurately unfamiliar multisyllabic words in context and out of context.

Read with sufficient accuracy and fluency to support comprehension.

Read grade-level text with purpose and understanding.

Expand vocabulary by adding inflectional endings.

- Rate: 111–131 WCPM

ELA ACADEMIC LANGUAGE

- *expression, phrasing*
- Cognates: *expresión, fraseo*

 **TEACH IN SMALL GROUP**

Word Study

⬤ **Approaching Level** and **ELL** Use Tier 2 activity on page T144 before the lesson.

⬤ **On Level** As needed, use the Guided Practice section.

⬤ **Beyond Level** As needed, use Multisyllabic Words only.

⬤ **ELL** See page 5 of the **Language Transfers Handbook** for guidance in identifying sounds and symbols that may not transfer for speakers of certain languages, and support in accommodating those students.

 OPTION 10 mins

Inflectional Endings

1 Explain

Tell students that the inflectional endings *–ed* or *–ing* can be added to verbs. The endings change the tense of the verb. The *–ed* ending means the action happened in the past. The *–ing* ending means the action is happening right now. Then explain the following:

- For many base words, adding *–ed* or *–ing* does not change the spelling of the base word (e.g., *cough: coughed, coughing*).

- For a base word that ends with a consonant and *e*, drop the final *e* before adding *–ed* or *–ing* (e.g., *bake: baked, baking*).

- For most words that end with a vowel and a consonant, double the final consonant before adding *–ed* or *–ing* (e.g., *sip: sipped, sipping*).

- For words that end in *y*, change the *y* to *i* before adding *–ed* (e.g., *hurry: hurried*).

2 Model

Write the following on the board. Read each word series aloud, and underline the inflectional endings. Give the meaning of each word with an inflectional ending (for example, *washed in the past, is washing now*).

- wash: washed, washing
- hike: hiked, hiking
- zip: zipped, zipping
- carry: carried, carrying

3 Guided Practice

Write the words below on the board. Ask students to underline the inflectional endings and identify any spelling change. Then have students chorally read the words.

top	topping	miss	missed
hit	hitting	rope	roped
worked	working	stray	straying
paved	paving	zoned	zoning
napped	napping	petted	petting
hurried	carried	readied	worried

For practice with decoding and encoding, use **Practice Book** page 91 or online activities.

Read Multisyllabic Words

Transition to Longer Words Have students use what they know about inflectional endings to decode multisyllabic words. Ask students to read the words, then underline the inflectional endings. Discuss any spelling changes required when inflectional endings are added. Make sure students do not allow the number of syllables in a word to prevent them from applying what they learned about inflectional endings.

overcorrect	overcorrected	overcorrecting
disapprove	disapproved	disapproving
regret	regretted	regretting
decrease	decreased	decreasing
compliment	complimented	complimenting
beautify	beautified	beautifying
petrify	petrified	petrifying

Fluency

Expression and Phrasing

Explain/Model Remind students that phrasing is the way readers group words together. Explain that fluent readers group words into meaningful chunks, or phrases. Review that readers stop briefly when they reach a period or other mark of end punctuation. They pause briefly when they see a comma or a dash. Correct phrasing helps readers add expression, or prosody, to their reading. Read aloud the first two paragraphs of "The Magical Lost Brocade," **Reading/Writing Companion** pages 152–155. Model using expression and phrasing as you read.

Practice/Apply Have groups choral read the same passage, modeling your phrasing and use of expression. Remind students that you will be listening for these qualities in their reading during the week. Explain that you will help them improve their reading by giving them multiple opportunities to read the same text in order to improve their phrasing.

Daily Fluency Practice

Automaticity Students can practice reading with accuracy and appropriate rate to develop automaticity using the online **Differentiated Genre Passage** "The Fox and the Snail."

DIGITAL TOOLS

For more practice, use the word study and fluency activities.

Word Study — **Inflectional Endings**

 MULTIMODAL LEARNING

Use self-stick notes to mark the beginning and end of a short section of a reading passage. Choose sentences that have words with inflectional endings *-ed* and *-ing*, if possible. Have partners read the section aloud to each other. As they read, have students underline words with the inflectional endings. After reading, have partners take turns saying the underlined words aloud.

FORMATIVE ASSESSMENT

⊙ **STUDENT CHECK-IN**

Inflectional Endings Have partners share three words with inflectional endings.

Multisyllabic Words Have partners read the following words: *overcorrecting, regretted,* and *decreased.*

Fluency Ask partners to read "The Magical Lost Brocade" fluently.

Then have partners use the Check-In routine to reflect.

✔ **CHECK FOR SUCCESS**

Can students decode multisyllabic words with inflectional endings? Can students read with expression and phrasing?

▷ **Small Group Instruction**

If No:

● **Approaching** Reteach pp. T144, T148

● **ELL** Develop pp. T144

If Yes:

● **On** Apply p. T150

● **Beyond** Apply p. T156

LESSON
2

- **We can use the research process to create an illustrated food web.**
- **We can develop a logical research plan.**

OBJECTIVES

Follow agreed-upon rules for discussions and carry out assigned roles.

Include multimedia components (e.g., graphics, sound) and visual displays in presentations when appropriate to enhance the development of main ideas or themes.

Conduct short research projects that use several sources to build knowledge through investigation of different aspects of a topic.

Develop a logical research plan.

 Collect and record information using detailed observations and accurate measuring.

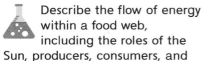 Describe the flow of energy within a food web, including the roles of the Sun, producers, consumers, and decomposers.

ELA ACADEMIC LANGUAGE

- *resources, credible, cite, illustrated, labels*
- Cognates: *recursos, citar, ilustrada*

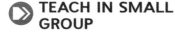 **TEACH IN SMALL GROUP**

You may wish to teach the Research and Inquiry lesson during Small Group time. Have groups of mixed abilities complete the page and work on the food web.

 Accomplishing a Task
10 mins

Explain to students that for the next two weeks they will work collaboratively in groups to research food webs. They will create an illustrated food web of their own. Discuss the meanings of *producers, consumers,* and *decomposers* with students. Share a few examples of illustrated food webs. Point out that illustrated food webs typically include the following features:

- *illustrations* that may depict plants, animals, water, the sun, and the earth
- *labels* to identify the illustrations
- *arrows* to show the relationship between producers, consumers, and decomposers

Develop a Logical Plan Before students begin, point out that a good research plan should list a purpose, materials, and logical steps to follow. Support them as they look at the sample plan and go through each step in the Research Process as outlined on **Reading/Writing Companion** page 163.

STEP 1 **Set a Goal** Explain to students that every environment will have multiple food webs in it, so there are many ways to create an illustrated food web. Tell groups to consider an environment they'd like to research as they find producers, consumers, and decomposers to include in their webs. Offer feedback as students generate questions and decide what to include on their webs. Have them use a **Layered Book Foldable®**, available online, to help organize their information. Remind them to create and define roles for each member of the group.

STEP 2 **Identify Sources** Brainstorm with groups the kinds of digital and print resources they can use for their research. Remind them to use credible sources. Discuss plagiarism with students and explain the importance of not copying someone else's work and presenting it as their own.

STEP 3 **Find and Record Information** Review with students how to take notes and cite the sources they use to gather information for their illustrated food webs. Remind them that each plant and animal in their web should have a relationship with at least one other plant or animal.

STEP 4 **Organize and Synthesize Information** Show students how to organize the information that they want to include in their webs. Have them sketch out their webs into a flowchart.

STEP 5 **Create and Present** Review with students the details and illustrations they should include on their food webs. Discuss options for presenting their webs. Model how to present the food webs using one of the samples you presented at the beginning of the activity.

Reading/Writing Companion, p. 163

 ## English Language Learners

Use the following scaffold with **Step 3**.

Beginning

Review the features of a food web with students and check their understanding of *producers, consumers,* and *decomposers.* Guide partners to research information about the relationship between producers, consumers, and decomposers for their food web. Ask: *Does each plant or animal have a relationship with one other plant or animal?* (yes/no) Model how to take notes and cite sources. Review the students' notes and provide feedback.

Intermediate

Review the features of a food web with students. Ask: *What should each plant or animal have a relationship with in your food web?* They should have a relationship with at least one other plant or animal. Help partners take notes about the relationship between producers, consumers, and decomposers for their food web. Then guide them on how to cite sources. Review the students' notes and provide feedback.

Advanced/Advanced High

Discuss the features of a food web with students. Allow partners to research and take notes about the relationship between producers, consumers, and decomposers for their food web. Remind them to cite their sources.

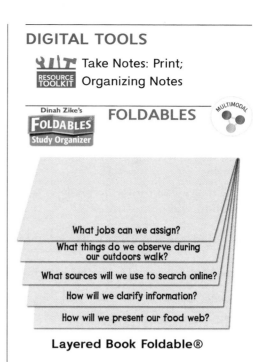

DIGITAL TOOLS

Take Notes: Print;
Organizing Notes

Dinah Zike's **FOLDABLES** Study Organizer

FOLDABLES MULTIMODAL

What jobs can we assign?

What things do we observe during our outdoors walk?

What sources will we use to search online?

How will we clarify information?

How will we present our food web?

Layered Book Foldable®

◉ STUDENT CHECK-IN

Food Web Ask students to share their illustrated food webs.

Logical Plan Have students share how they followed a logical research plan to create their food webs.

Have them use the Check-In routine to reflect and fill in the bars on Reading/Writing/Companion page 163.

Blancaflor

Lexile 870L

Read We can apply strategies and skills to read folktales.

Reread We can reread to analyze text, craft, and structure and compare texts.

Have students apply what they learned as they read.

ACT *What makes this text complex?*

▶ **Genre**

▶ **Sentence Structure**

▶ **Connection of Ideas**

▶ **Specific Vocabulary**

Close Reading Routine

▼

Read DOK 1–2

• Identify important ideas and details.
• Take notes and summarize.
• Use **ACT** prompts as needed.

▼

Reread DOK 2–3

• Analyze the text, craft, and structure.
• Use *Reading/Writing Companion*, pp. 164–166.

▼

Integrate DOK 3–4

• Integrate knowledge and ideas.
• Make text-to-text connections.
• Use the Integrate lesson.
• Complete the Show Knowledge task.
• Inspire action.

Genre • Folktale

Blancaflor

by Alma Flor Ada
Illustrated by Beatriz Vidal

? Essential Question

When has a plan helped you accomplish a task?

Read about how Blancaflor's plan helps a prince.

Go Digital!

118

Literature Anthology, pp. 118–119

⟩ DIFFERENTIATED READING

You may wish to read the full selection aloud once with minimal stopping before you begin using the Read prompts.

Approaching Level Have students listen to the selection summary. Use the Reread prompts during Small Group time.

On Level and **Beyond Level** Pair students or have them independently complete the Reread prompts on **Reading/ Writing Companion** pages 164–166.

🎧 **English Language Learners** Have ELLs listen to the summary of the selection, available in multiple languages. See also **ELL Small Group Guide**.

A young prince had gone riding very early in the morning, before the sunrise. Now, tired and sad, he sat under the branches of a large oak tree. He was thinking about his father, the king, who lay in the castle, sick with an illness no one knew how to cure.

Physicians had been called in from all the neighboring kingdoms, wizards had been consulted, and the queen had prepared with her own hands all the herbal medicines suggested. But nothing seemed to help the king, who grew weaker and weaker with each passing day.

The young prince had been sitting under the tree for a while, lost in thought, when he was surprised by a deep voice that seemed to come from the branches of the oak tree: "What would you be willing to give for your father's health?" The prince looked around, but could see no one.

"I would give anything and everything for my father's health," he responded, trying to disguise the fear in his voice.

"Then, in three years' time, you shall bring yourself to me, to the Three Silver Towers, in the Land of No Return. Do I have your promise?" the deep voice bellowed as every leaf of the oak tree quivered.

"Yes," agreed the young man. "I, Prince Alfonso, do solemnly promise that I will do as you ask, if my father is indeed cured."

119

Read

Set a Purpose Tell students to preview the text and set a purpose for reading. Remind them that setting a purpose can help them monitor their comprehension.

Note Taking: Use the Graphic Organizer

Analytical Writing Distribute copies of online Theme Graphic Organizer 5. Have students record details.

Reread

Author's Craft: Personification DOK 2

Reading/Writing Companion, p. 164

Reread the fifth paragraph on page 119. How does the author use personification to set the mood of the story? (The author says that "every leaf of the oak tree quivered." *Quiver* means "to shake with fear." The mood is fearful and suspenseful. The prince has made a dangerous promise with a mysterious being.)

Evaluate Information   DOK 2

Explain The author gives the leaves human qualities by making them quiver.

Discuss *Was it appropriate for the author to use human qualities to describe the leaves?* (Yes; it shows that even the leaves are fearful of the voice.)

Apply As they read, have students look for other examples of personification.

A C T Access Complex Text

Genre

Tell students that often in a folktale, the hero has a task to accomplish or a problem to solve. Help them identify the problem that sets the tale in motion.

- *What problem does the prince have?* (The prince's father is sick with an illness that no one can cure.)

- *What solution appears to the Prince?* (A voice offers to help in exchange for a promise to appear again in three years' time.)

- *Why might this solution lead to another problem?* (The prince does not know what exactly he is promising this voice, or what it will mean.)

Read

1 Theme DOK 1

On page 119 the prince makes a promise. What happens to the king on page 120 as a result of the prince's promise? (The king regains his health.) Add these events to your graphic organizer.

What Does the Character Think, Say and Do?	What is the Character's Perspective?
Prince Alfonso promises the voice that he will return in three years if his father is cured.	The prince is happy that his father recovered, but he is sad knowing he must keep his promise.

Build Vocabulary on page 120

Have students add the Build Vocabulary word to their reader's notebook.

cascading: falling quickly

placid: peaceful

prolonged: lasting a long time

seamstresses: people who sew for a living

coiffeurs: people who cut and style hair for a living

"Three years from today...," said the voice so loudly that all of the leaves fell, cascading down upon the startled prince. Shaking them off his shoulders, he jumped on his horse and back to the palace and to his father's room.

"Son!" His mother greeted him with a smile, the first he had seen on her loving face in many days. "Look at your father! He seems so much better." And, indeed, the sleeping king seemed to have regained all his color, and his sleep was sound and placid.

The king was completely healthy again in no time. But now the queen worried about her son. He seemed delighted, as was everyone, to see the kind king recover. And yet, once in a while, the queen detected a profound sadness in her son's eyes.

The king was determined that Prince Alfonso should marry. His prolonged illness had left him with a renewed urgency for life. "I want to see you start a family. I want to get to know my grandchildren."

Even though the prince insisted that he was not ready for marriage, the king ordered portraits of every marriageable princess brought in from all the neighboring kingdoms. When they all failed to interest the prince, the king organized banquets, dances, and outings to have the prince meet every noble girl he could possibly invite. But while the king managed to create a great deal of work for the seamstresses and coiffeurs of the kingdom, and while many young people had a wonderful time at the events, he could not get the prince to change his mind.

As time passed, the prince's behavior became stranger and stranger. He spent most of his time outside of the castle, riding his horse. During the evening he wrote poems and composed sweet, sad music on his lute. Finally, one morning, exactly one month before three years had gone by from the day on which he had heard the mysterious voice, he set out on his journey.

120

Literature Anthology, pp. 120–121

 Access Complex Text

Sentence Structure

Point out the ellipsis in the first sentence on page 120. Read the sentence aloud, trailing off at the end. Explain that the ellipsis is used to show that the speaker's voice has faded out, leaving something unsaid.

- *What does the speaker leave unsaid?* (The speaker doesn't say that the prince must travel to the Land of No Return.)

- *What feeling do the ellipsis and the unsaid words convey to the reader?* (They give a threatening or haunting feeling.)

He left behind a stack of poems that talked about his love for his mother, his **gratitude** toward his father, and his joy in everyone and everything. He also left a letter for his parents, asking forgiveness for causing them sorrow, but **assuring** them that he was leaving only because he needed to honor a promise.

The king could not understand the disappearance of his son. He was ready to send his knights and guards to comb the world until they found him. But the queen requested that he honor his son's wishes, just as his son was honoring his promise. Inside her mother's heart she sensed a connection between her husband's healing and her son's departure.

121

Read

2 Make, Correct, and Confirm Predictions DOK 1

Teacher Think Aloud I know that when I read the story, I can stay more connected to the text by making, correcting, and confirming predictions about what will happen to Prince Alfonso on his journey. On page 119, Alfonso says he "would give anything and everything" for his father's health. On page 121, he asks forgiveness for causing his parents sorrow. Based on this evidence, I predict that Alfonso faces great danger. As I continue reading, I will look for story details to either confirm my prediction or correct it.

Build Vocabulary on page 121

comb: search an area very carefully

departure: act of leaving, or setting out

Reread

Author's Craft: Word Choice DOK 2

Reread the third paragraph on page 120. Why did the author choose the words *delighted* and *profound* instead of other synonyms, such as *happy* and *great*? (*Delighted* and *profound* have a much stronger connotation and make it more clear how the prince feels.)

Connection of Ideas

In the fifth paragraph on page 120, the author uses a pronoun to refer to a noun mentioned earlier. Read aloud the first two sentences in the fifth paragraph.

- *The word* they *is a pronoun. What does* they *refer back to?* (the portraits of marriageable princesses)
- *Why did the author use a plural pronoun?* (because the noun it refers back to is a plural noun)

 Spotlight on Idioms

Page 121, Paragraph 1 Explain that *to honor a promise* means *to keep a promise. How is the prince* honoring a promise? (by traveling to the Land of No Return) Ask partners to tell each other about a time when they honored a promise: I honored a promise by _____.

Read

3 Confirm or Correct Predictions
DOK 2

Teacher Think Aloud I will look for evidence that either confirms my **prediction** that the Prince will face great danger, or leads me to correct it.

Prompt students to confirm or correct their predictions. Have them paraphrase the text they use to confirm or correct.

Student Think Aloud I read on page 123 that the Prince must win his life back, which confirms my prediction that he is in danger.

4 Theme DOK 1

Does the prince honor his promise to return to the Land of No Return? (yes) What happens to the prince when he reaches the Land of No Return? (The voice tells him that he must complete three tasks to win back his life.) Add these events to your organizer.

What Does the Character Think, Say, and Do?	What is the Character's Perspective?
Prince Alfonso keeps his promises and returns to the Land of No Return.	The prince believes that honoring one's word is important.

Young Prince Alfonso rode for many days, eating sparingly of the food he had taken with him. Several times he asked shepherds he met along the way for directions to the Land of No Return. They always pointed in the same direction, toward the setting sun. And when they wondered, "Why should anyone want to go there?" the prince would respond, "To honor my word."

On the seventh day of his journey the prince saw a white dove who seemed to signal him to follow her. And so he did. But after many hours of following the dove, he found himself facing a deep ravine. He stopped, puzzled, knowing well that he could not cross the gorge on horseback or on foot. Then a majestic eagle appeared in front of him and looked piercingly into his eyes.

"Might you carry me to the other side?" he asked the eagle.

"Only if you give me your chain," the eagle responded.

Young Alfonso took off the heavy gold chain that bore the eagle emblem of his kingdom and hung it around the eagle's neck.

122

Literature Anthology, pp. 122–123

A C T   Access Complex Text

Specific Vocabulary

Point out the word *ravine* in the second paragraph on page 122.

- *Identify context clues to figure out what* ravine *means.* ("he could not cross the gorge on horseback or on foot")

- *What is a* ravine? (A *ravine* is a deep, steep-sided valley, like a gorge or canyon.)

Genre

Point out that animals often play important roles in folktales, sometimes providing guidance to the hero.

- *What roles do the dove and the eagle play in the story?* (Both help the Prince on his journey. The dove signals to him, and the eagle carries him across a ravine.)

"It is only fitting," the prince said. "I have carried your image with me always. Now it should be yours." Then the eagle grasped him firmly by his leather belt and flew across the ravine.

The eagle released the young prince on the other side, where the land was deserted and barren. Basalt and obsidian rocks burned hot under the fierce sun. Far in the distance, high above the steep walls, three towers of silver glittered.

Alfonso had just taken a few steps toward the towers when he was stopped by a thundering voice: "Who dares step on my land?"

"I am here to honor my promise," the young prince answered.

"That is as it should be," the voice replied. "And to reward you, I will give you an opportunity to win your life back. If you fulfill the three tasks that I ask of you, you will stay here and marry one of my three daughters. But if you do not complete the tasks, you will be food for my hounds."

Alfonso took a deep breath. Squaring his shoulders and steadying his voice he asked, "What would you like me to do?"

"Take this sack of wheat. Walk up to the valley, plant it, harvest it, and mill it. With the flour, bake some bread and bring it to me tomorrow by eleven o'clock in the morning." To Alfonso's great surprise a small sack of wheat appeared before his eyes.

The young man lifted the sack and began to walk up the path among the rocks. What else could he do? His head hung low and his shoulders drooped because he knew there was no way he could fulfill his task. But he had not walked far when a young girl appeared in front of him.

123

Page 123, Paragraph 2 Point out the words that describe the landscape: *deserted, barren, basalt and obsidian rocks.* Explain that *deserted* and *barren* are adjectives, or words that describe. *What do these words describe?* (land) *They mean the land is empty. The land has basalt and obsidian rocks, which are rocks from volcanoes.* Use images or realia to clarify as needed. *Does this land seem attractive?* (no) *How do you think the prince feels when he gets here?* (possible answers: scared, curious)

✔ **STOP AND CHECK**   DOK 2

Make Predictions How will Alfonso accomplish the task? (Alfonso thinks there is "no way he could fulfill his task." However, the signal word "But" in the last sentence leads me to predict that he will, with the help of the young girl.)

Build Vocabulary on pages 122 and 123
emblem: a symbol that represents something
deserted: empty
barren: lifeless

Reread

Author's Craft: Imagery DOK 2
Reading/Writing Companion, p. 165
Reread page 123. How does the author use descriptive language to help you visualize what the prince is experiencing? (The author uses imagery to describe the barren land, the burnt rocks, and the fierce sun.) **How does this help you visualize the setting?** (The author describes a terrible place, so I visualize the deserted land, the dark rocks, and the steep walls and high towers. This visualization tells me that it seems unlikely that the prince will be able to survive the journey.)

✂ **Evaluate Information**   DOK 2

Explain Many folktales do not take place in modern times.

Discuss *When does this folktale take place?* (long ago) *What details tell you that this story does not take place today?* (There is no modern medicine for the king; there are no cars.)

Apply As students read, have them look for details that tell about the historical setting of the folktale. Have them analyze how the setting contributes to the plot.

LESSONS 3-6

5 Theme DOK 1

Whom does the prince meet? (The prince meets Blancaflor.) What must the prince do if he wants her to help him save his life? (The prince must trust Blancaflor.)

6 Make Inferences DOK 2

Why do you think Blancaflor leaves after she helps Alfonso? Support your inference with evidence from the text. (I think Blancaflor's father will be angry with Blancaflor and Alfonso if he discovers that Blancaflor is helping Alfonso. I can infer this from the text because Blancaflor says it is better if her father doesn't find her there when he comes for the bread.)

Build Vocabulary on page 124

ripe: fully grown

harvest: to pick crops

"What's wrong?" she asked him. "Why are you so sad?"

"I have been asked to do an impossible task. And my life depends on it."

5 "My father must be up to one of his tricks," she responded. "But do not worry. I will help you. Take this stick and poke the earth with it. Keep walking on a straight line and poke as you walk. I will drop the seeds and all will be well."

That afternoon, after all the wheat had been planted, they watched the sunset together. The young girl said, "My name is Blancaflor. And if you trust me, we will save your life. Now I have to go; otherwise they will miss me at dinner."

After she left, Alfonso went to sleep, resting his back against a large boulder. In the morning the valley was covered with ripe wheat, its golden spikes shining under the early sun.

Alfonso was still rubbing his eyes when Blancaflor appeared.

"It's time to harvest the grain, mill it, and bake bread with the flour," she said. And as she spoke the wheat flew out of its stalks and formed a golden mountain. A mill and an outdoor oven appeared next to the mountain of wheat.

124

Literature Anthology, pp. 124–125

A C T Access Complex Text

Genre

Explain that words and actions often repeat in folktales. Like people, characters learn through repetition. Identify examples.

- *What steps are repeated in Alfonso's first two tasks?* (He must plant something, harvest it, and make something from it. Each task must be completed by eleven o'clock the next morning.)

- *By repeatedly doing tasks that seem to be impossible, what is Alfonso learning from Blancaflor?* (Alfonso is learning to trust Blancaflor, who has the power to help him complete the tasks.)

"Keep fetching wood for the oven," Blancaflor told Alfonso. And while he did, the mill ground the wheat, and loaf upon loaf of bread dough appeared ready to be baked. When the smell of the recently baked bread filled the valley, Blancaflor disappeared. "It's better that my father doesn't find me here when he comes for his bread," she told Alfonso before leaving.

 6

Soon a thundering voice was heard: "Either you are a wizard or you have met Blancaflor."

Alfonso kept silent.

"Well, you still have two more tasks!" shouted the voice. "Better get started. Plant these grapevines and have the wine ready for me by eleven o'clock tomorrow morning." And while the loaves of bread moved through the air as if carried by giant hands, Alfonso found one hundred grapevine saplings at his feet.

It was not long before Blancaflor appeared again. And just as the pair had grown the wheat the **previous** day, now they planted the saplings. That evening, as they watched the sunset, Alfonso told Blancaflor about his mother and father and the promise he had made. And once again she asked him to trust her.

The next morning the valley was covered by fully grown grapevines loaded with ripe bunches of grapes. And it took only a few words from Blancaflor for the grapes to be harvested and crushed and for the wine to be stored in huge oak casks.

Just before eleven, after Blancaflor had already departed, the thundering voice was heard again: "Either you are a mighty wizard or you have been talking to Blancaflor."

Alfonso remained silent. But he shivered when he heard the voice laugh.

7 "Well, let's see how you do with your last task. You need to bring back the ring my great-great-grandmother lost in the ocean. And if you do not have it here by eleven o'clock tomorrow, you will be food for my hounds."

125

 Spotlight on Language

Page 124, Paragraph 7 Explain that *harvest the grain* means to pick the wheat after it has fully grown and it is ready to be eaten. Next, Alfonso has to mill the wheat, which means to grind it up into flour. Demonstrate milling by miming a grinding action. *Talk to your partner about how long you think it would take to plant, grow, harvest, and mill wheat. How is Alfonso able to do it in one day?* (He has help from Blancaflor.)

Read

7 Ask and Answer Questions
DOK 1

COLLABORATE After reading page 125, generate a question of your own about the story and share it with a partner. To find the answer, try reading on. The author may give more details or information. For example, you might ask, "Will the grapevine saplings grow overnight like the wheat did?" Paraphrase the part of the text that contains the answer. (Yes, when Alfonso wakes up the next morning he finds that the grapevines are completely grown and filled with ripe grapes.)

Build Vocabulary page 125
fetching: gathering
recently: a short while ago
saplings: small, young trees
casks: large wooden barrels

Reread

Author's Purpose DOK 2

Reread the last paragraph on page 125. How is the last task different from the first two? (The first two required Alfonso to grow something, harvest it, and make something. The last requires him to find something tiny in a very big place.) **Why does the author make the last task different?** (Making the last task the most challenging builds suspense.)

Read

8 Plot: Setting DOK 2

Describe the setting. (Prince Alfonso and Blancaflor are standing on high cliffs next to the ocean.) **How does this setting affect the mood?** (It creates a suspenseful mood filled with danger.) **How does the illustration relate to the setting?** (The illustration connects to the setting because it shows Blancaflor falling toward the ocean after slipping from Alfonso's hand.)

9 Theme DOK 1

What happens as a result of Alfonso deciding to trust Blancaflor? (He completes the three tasks and gets to choose Blancaflor as a wife.) **Add these events to your graphic organizer.**

What Does the Character Think, Say and Do?	What is the Character's Perspective?
Alfonso says, "This task will be impossible." Blancaflor tells him to trust her and let her go. He breaks her finger not letting go of her right away.	Alfonso is worried about completing the task and afraid of losing Blancaflor. He is relieved later when he chooses her for a bride.

When Blancaflor returned, there were tears in Alfonso's eyes. "I'm not afraid to die. But I hate to break my mother's heart. This task will be impossible," he told her.

"No, it won't be. But you will need to trust me even more," she replied.

Blancaflor led Alfonso to a set of high cliffs next to the ocean. There the prince spotted the eagle who had carried him across the gorge.

"The eagle will take us to the middle of the ocean, and then you must let go of me and let me fall in," Blancaflor instructed.

"But I will not be able to do that," he argued.

"Yes, you will. You must," insisted Blancaflor.

When they were high above the ocean, Blancaflor asked the prince to let her go. But at the last minute he held on desperately to her hand. As her fingers slipped from his, he heard a crack. Her little finger hung broken.

8

126

Literature Anthology, pp. 126–127

A C T   Access Complex Text

Connection of Ideas

Tell students that characters in folktales often undergo magical transformations, or changes of form. Point to the middle of page 127.

- *Why does Alfonso choose the dove with the broken wing?* (Alfonso connects the dove's broken wing to Blancaflor's broken finger.)

- *How did Alfonso connect the doves with the daughters?* (Alfonso has received many clues from Blancaflor. On page 124, she tells him that her father is up to his tricks, so Alfonso can infer that the voice belongs to Blancaflor's father. When Alfonso must choose a daughter, he can infer that the doves are the daughters.)

Alfonso felt his heart stop as he saw Blancaflor disappear under the water. His eyes filled with tears as the eagle flapped her wings. Before he knew it, he was standing in the meadow, next to the boulder against which he had slept the last two nights. There, on top of the boulder, was an extraordinary ring in the shape of a dragon with two emeralds for eyes.

He had not admired the ring for very long before he heard the thundering voice. "So you found the ring. Either you are the king of all wizards or you have been helped by Blancaflor."

Alfonso remained silent.

The voice continued, "Follow the path to the castle. Tonight you will meet my three daughters and choose one for your wife!"

When Alfonso reached the Three Silver Towers, the gates were open. He entered, and in the main banquet hall there were three white doves.

"Choose one, right now!" the voice echoed against the thick walls.

Alfonso studied the three doves. They looked identical. But he noticed that one had what looked like a broken wing. He remembered Blancaflor's little finger, hanging twisted from her hand.

"I choose this one," he said, and walked toward the dove with the broken wing. Suddenly Blancaflor stood in front of him surrounded by her sisters, who looked just like her. No one would have been able to tell them apart. But when Alfonso observed Blancaflor's hand, he could see that one of her little fingers had been bandaged.

"Take your wife," ordered the voice. "And let's all go to sleep now. We will celebrate the wedding tomorrow."

9

127

 Read

 STOP AND CHECK   DOK 1

Confirm or Correct Predictions How did Alfonso complete the tasks? (Possible answer: Alfonso was able to complete the tasks by accepting Blancaflor's help and trusting her. This confirms the prediction I made on page 123.)

Reread

Author's Craft: Figurative Language DOK 2

Reread the first sentence on page 127. Consider the phrase, "Alfonso felt his heart stop." Why is this an example of figurative language? (Alfonso's heart does not really stop.) Why is the phrase an effective way to show Alfonso's feelings? (It shows how frightened and upset he is about seeing Blancaflor disappear into the water.)

 Spotlight on Language

Page 127, Paragraph 1 Point out that the word *as* is used in the first two sentences. *The word* as *tells that two things are happening at the same time.* Explain that in the first sentence, there are two actions: The prince feels his heart stop and Blancaflor disappears under the water. *What are the two actions in the second sentence?* (his eyes fill with tears, and the eagle flaps her wings) Have partners work together to use *as* to tell a time when they did two actions at the same time.

 Newcomers

Use the **Newcomer Online Visuals** and their accompanying prompts to help students expand vocabulary and language about My Body (10a-e) and Clothing (11a-e). Use the Conversation Starters, Speech Balloons, and the Games in the **Newcomer Teacher's Guide** to continue building vocabulary and developing oral and written language.

LESSONS 3-6

Read

⑩ Make Predictions DOK 2

Do you think Alfonso made the right choice when he chose the younger and stronger horse? Use evidence from the text to predict what will happen.

Student Think Aloud I predict that Alfonso did not make the right choice because Blancaflor told him to take the older horse. I make this prediction because Blancaflor knows the horses, and so far Blancaflor has been very trustworthy.

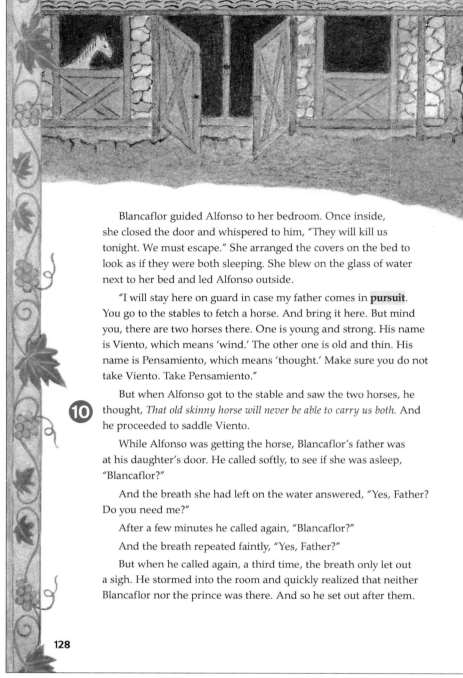

Blancaflor guided Alfonso to her bedroom. Once inside, she closed the door and whispered to him, "They will kill us tonight. We must escape." She arranged the covers on the bed to look as if they were both sleeping. She blew on the glass of water next to her bed and led Alfonso outside.

"I will stay here on guard in case my father comes in **pursuit**. You go to the stables to fetch a horse. And bring it here. But mind you, there are two horses there. One is young and strong. His name is Viento, which means 'wind.' The other one is old and thin. His name is Pensamiento, which means 'thought.' Make sure you do not take Viento. Take Pensamiento."

⑩ But when Alfonso got to the stable and saw the two horses, he thought, *That old skinny horse will never be able to carry us both.* And he proceeded to saddle Viento.

While Alfonso was getting the horse, Blancaflor's father was at his daughter's door. He called softly, to see if she was asleep, "Blancaflor?"

And the breath she had left on the water answered, "Yes, Father? Do you need me?"

After a few minutes he called again, "Blancaflor?"

And the breath repeated faintly, "Yes, Father?"

But when he called again, a third time, the breath only let out a sigh. He stormed into the room and quickly realized that neither Blancaflor nor the prince was there. And so he set out after them.

128

Literature Anthology, pp. 128–129

A C T Access Complex Text

Connection of Ideas

Remind students that an action in a folktale may seem mysterious at the time it occurs. Review with students that on page 128, Blancaflor blew on a glass of water. Point out that the significance of this action is revealed in the last paragraph on the page.

• *Why did Blancaflor breathe on the glass of water?* (She breathed on it so that it would answer her father when he called for her.)

• *How did this help Blancaflor and Alfonso escape?* (It gave them a head start before Blancaflor's father realized they were missing.)

Blancaflor was dismayed when Alfonso came to fetch her riding Viento, but seeing that her father was **emerging** from the castle, she jumped on the horse behind the prince and urged him to go on.

They had galloped across the valley for only a few minutes when they heard Pensamiento, carrying her father, catching up with them.

"If only we had taken Pensamiento instead of Viento," said Blancaflor, "my father would never have been able to keep up with us." Then she took the comb that held her hair and threw it on the road behind them.

129

Read

11 **Genre: Folktale** DOK 2

Review with students that repetition and pattern are often elements of folktales. What number has been repeated throughout this story? (three) How has the number three been repeated so far? (There are three tasks, three daughters, three doves, and the king calls for Blancaflor three times.) To escape from her father, Blancaflor throws a comb in the road. How many more things do you think she will throw behind her? Why? (She will throw two more things, for a total of three things, to match the pattern.)

Build Vocabulary on pages 128 and 129
fetch: get and bring back
dismayed: upset

ELL **English Language Learners**

Synonyms and Circumlocution Remind students they can use circumlocution, or paraphrasing, to clarify unfamiliar words to express ideas using words they know. Point to *mind you* on page 128. *Blancaflor says* mind you *to remind Alfonso there are two horses. The phrase tells him to keep something in mind.* Use gestures to clarify the idiom. Then have students brainstorm expressions they could use to convey a similar meaning. (possible answers: remember that, pay attention to, watch out)

Read

12 Personification DOK 2

In what ways does the author use personification to describe the wind? (The author describes the wind as "ripping the leaves off trees" and as "dying." These are human qualities.)

13 Theme DOK 2

Encourage students to use what they have learned about Alfonso's actions and his perspective to find the theme, or author's message, in this folktale. What is the theme? (If you honor your word and trust others, you can overcome challenges and find happiness.)
Add the theme to your organizer.

The comb turned into a chain of steep mountains that blocked the way and allowed them to gain a little distance. But very soon they heard the sound of Pensamiento's hooves approaching again.

Blancaflor took the gold pin that held her shawl and threw it on the road behind them.

The gold pin turned into a desert of very hot sand, and that allowed them to gain a little distance. But soon they heard Pensamiento's hooves again.

"If only we had taken Pensamiento instead of Viento," said Blancaflor. And she took her blue silk shawl and threw it on the road behind them.

The blue silk shawl turned into a large sea with high waves covered with foam.

Then Alfonso urged Viento, "Take on all my good thoughts— the thoughts of my mother's love, the thoughts of my father's kindness, my thoughts of love for Blancaflor. You can take these thoughts, Viento. Let them lighten your step."

130

Literature Anthology, pp. 130–131

ACT Access Complex Text

Specific Vocabulary

Point out the phrase *"lighten your step"* in the last sentence on page 130.

- *What does Alfonso want Viento to do?* (He wants Viento to move faster.) *What does "lighten your step" mean?* (It means to move more quickly.)

Point out the word *embrace* in the first paragraph on page 131.

- *Identify context clues to figure out what* embrace *means.* ("kind father," "loving mother," "held them") *What is another word for* embrace*?* (hug)

Point out the word *subsided* in the third paragraph.

- *Identify context clues to figure out what* subsided *means.* ("dying wind")

- *Did the wind get stronger or weaker?* (weaker)

Spurred by Alfonso's thoughts, Viento became as fast as Pensamiento. Before they knew it, the prince and Blancaflor were at the doors of Alfonso's own castle, being greeted by his kind father and his loving mother, who held them both in one embrace.

They were still holding one another when a terrible gust of wind began ripping the leaves off the trees, and they could see a black tornado approaching. Alfonso gathered all his courage and shouted into the wind, "My word has been honored! How about yours?"

The wind blew even more wildly for a moment, but then it subsided, and they heard in the dying wind a deep voice that sounded as though it came from far away, "You have proven to be wise, my daughter. Now...be happy!"

12

And this is the story of Blancaflor. It began with threads of silver and ended with threads of gold, all woven for you in the story I told. **13**

131

 Spotlight on Language

Page 131, Paragraph 4 *Is everyone happy at the end of the story?* (Yes.) *Which words tells you so?* (silver; gold) *What does it mean that the story began with threads of silver?* (It means that the story started out pretty happily.) *What does it mean that the story ended with threads of gold?* (It means that the story ended even happier than it began.)

✓ **STOP AND CHECK** DOK 1

Reread How do Blancaflor and Alfonso escape? (They escape from Blancaflor's father with the help of the magical obstacles that Blancaflor creates and Alfonso's good thoughts that spur on the horse.)

Return to Purpose Review students' purpose for reading. Then ask partners to share how setting a purpose helped them understand the text.

Reread

Author's Craft: Figurative Language DOK 2

Reading/Writing Companion, p. 166

Reread the last three paragraphs on page 130. How does the author use words and phrases to change the mood of the story? (The story reaches a climax when Alfonso shifts his attention to positive thoughts. He says to Viento, "Let them lighten your step." These words can have two meanings. One meaning is "run faster." As a second, figurative meaning, they show that Alfonso's spirit is no longer heavy; it has lightened and as a result, the story's mood has shifted.)

💡 **Make Inferences** DOK 2

Explain We can make inferences about characters by analyzing what they say and do in a story.

Discuss *What can you infer about Alfonso at the end of the story?* (Possible response: He is happy, relieved, and brave.)

Apply Have students identify clues in the text that support their inferences about Alfonso. Then have them make an inference about Blancaflor's father.

LESSONS 3-6

Read

Meet the Author DOK 2

Alma Flor Ada and Beatriz Vidal

Have students read the biographies of the author and illustrator. Ask:

- How might living in other countries have influenced Alma Flor Ada's writing?

- How do you think Beatriz Vidal's inspiration to become an artist might have led her to teach others to illustrate children's books?

- If you were an illustrator, what kind of book would you illustrate? Explain your response.

Reread

Author's Purpose DOK 2

To Entertain: Remind students that authors who write to entertain often have a message or lesson that they want to share with their readers. Students may say that the author is reminding readers that thoughtfulness and planning are often more important than speed when it comes to accomplishing a task.

Reread

Author's Craft: Dialogue DOK 2

How does the author's use of dialogue characterize Alfonso? (The dialogue lets us hear Alfonso's thoughts in his own words. For example, on page 119 Alfonso says, "I would give anything and everything for my father's health." This shows how deeply Alfonso loves his father and how selfless he is.)

Illustrator's Craft DOK 2

 Have partners discuss how Beatriz Vidal's illustrations add to the story's mood. Use the following sentence frame:

This illustration creates a _____ mood because . . .

About the Author and Illustrator

 Alma Flor Ada knew that she would be a writer by the time she was in fourth grade. "Most of my stories I told aloud before I ever wrote them down," she says. "And it was other people listening and other people being interested that gave me a motivation to write them."

Alma Flor Ada grew up in Cuba, but she has also lived in Spain and Peru. Today she makes her home in San Francisco, California. For Alma, knowing two languages—English and Spanish—has made her world richer. She believes that all children should be given the chance to learn two or more languages.

 **Beatriz Vidal** grew up in Argentina, but later traveled to New York. There, she met an artist who inspired her to begin a career as an artist, so she began to study painting and design. Soon, her work was shown in magazines and later books and exhibitions. Beatriz has won awards for her colorful work and has taught others to enrich children's books through illustration.

Author's Purpose

In the story, the author gives the horses names that are Spanish words: Viento and Pensamiento. Blancaflor tells Prince Alfonso to take Pensamiento, meaning "thought." What message is the author trying to send?

132

Literature Anthology, p. 132

ELL Spotlight on Language

Page 132, Paragraph 1 Point out the word *motivation* (cognate: *motivación*). Explain that motivation is what helps people work towards getting something done. Ask: *What motivated the author to write her stories?* (Other people listened and enjoyed her stories. That motivated her.) Have students discuss activities they enjoy doing and what motivates them to do the activities or to keep working at them.

Read

Summarize

Tell students they will use the events and details from their Theme Chart to summarize. As I read *Blancaflor*, I recorded important story events and details. To summarize, I will include the plot and theme.

Reread

Analyze the Text

After students read and summarize the selection, have them reread

Blancaflor to develop a deeper understanding of the text by answering the questions on **Reading/Writing Companion** pages 164–166. For students who need support in citing text evidence, use the Reread prompts on pages T111–T124.

Integrate

Build Knowledge: Make Connections

Talk About the Text Have partners discuss the Essential Question: *When has a plan helped you accomplish a task?*

Write About the Text Have students add their ideas to their Build Knowledge pages of their reader's notebooks.

Anchor Chart Record any new ideas on the Build Knowledge anchor chart.

Add to the Vocabulary List Have students write down any words they learned about accomplishing tasks in their reader's notebooks.

Compare Texts DOK 4

Have students compare how the authors present information on following plans to accomplish a task in "The Magical Lost Brocade" and *Blancaflor*. Ask: *How are Ping and the young prince from* Blancaflor *similar? How are they different? How is each of them able to accomplish tasks?*

FORMATIVE ASSESSMENT

⊙ STUDENT CHECK-IN

Read Have partners share their Theme charts and summaries. Have them reflect using the Check-In routine.

Reread Have partners share responses and text evidence on Reading/ Writing Companion pages 164-166. Then have them reflect using the Check-In routine to fill in the bars.

LEARNING GOALS

We can use text evidence to respond to a folktale.

OBJECTIVES

Quote accurately from a text when explaining what the text says explicitly and when drawing inferences from the text.

Describe how a narrator's or speaker's point of view influences how events are described.

Explain different characters' perspectives in a literary text.

Describe how an author develops a character's perspective in a literary text.

Apply grade 5 Reading standards to literature.

Write routinely over extended time frames and shorter time frames for a range of discipline-specific tasks, purposes, and audiences.

Demonstrate understanding of figurative language, word relationships, and nuances in word meanings.

Analyze a writing prompt.

ELA ACADEMIC LANGUAGE

- *mood, figurative language, personification, positive*
- Cognates: *personificación, positivo*

▶ TEACH IN SMALL GROUP

⬤⬤ **Approaching Level** and **On Level** Have partners work together to plan and complete the response to the prompt.

⬤ **Beyond Level** Ask students to respond to the prompt independently.

⬤ **ELL** Group students of mixed proficiency levels to discuss and respond to the prompt.

Reread

Write About the Anchor Text

10 mins

Analyze the Prompt DOK 3

Read the prompt aloud: *Why is it important for people to keep their word?* Ask: *What is the prompt asking?* (to describe why it is important for people to keep their word) Say: *Let's reread to see how the author sets the mood of the story. Doing this will help us make inferences about the characters that we can use to answer the prompt.*

Analyze Text Evidence

Remind students that the mood refers to the emotions a reader feels while reading a story. Mood can often point to a story's theme, or important message. Have students turn to **Literature Anthology** page 119. Reread the first two paragraphs aloud. Ask: *How is the prince feeling, and why does he feel this way?* (The prince is described as "tired and sad" because his father is sick with an illness that no one knows how to cure. The author's repetition of the words "weaker and weaker" emphasizes how sick his father is.) *How does this make you feel as a reader?* (Possible responses: sad, helpless, worried) Then turn to page 124 and have students reread it. Ask: *How does the story's mood begin to change?* (The mood changes after Blancaflor appears and helps the prince. Her dialogue is reassuring as she confidently tells the prince, "And if you trust me, we will save your life." The reader feels relieved and hopeful that Alfonso will succeed in his task.) *What does the story's change show about Alfonso keeping his word?* (Although keeping your word may be difficult, it is worth it to do so.) Encourage students to look for more examples of how the author's use of language conveys mood. Then have them craft a short response.

Respond

Review pages 164–166 of the **Reading/Writing Companion**. Have partners refer to and discuss their completed charts and writing responses from those pages. Then direct students' attention to the sentence starters on page 167. Have them use the sentence starters to guide their responses.

Analytical Writing Students should focus on the mood at the beginning of the story and how it changes as the plot develops. In their responses, students should include specific examples of descriptive and figurative language, including personification, that the author uses to convey the mood. Finally, students should note how the story's resolution and the author's use of language lighten the mood and end the story on a positive note. Remind students to vary sentence structure by combining short sentences and adding phrases and clauses to others. Students may use additional paper to complete the assignment if needed.

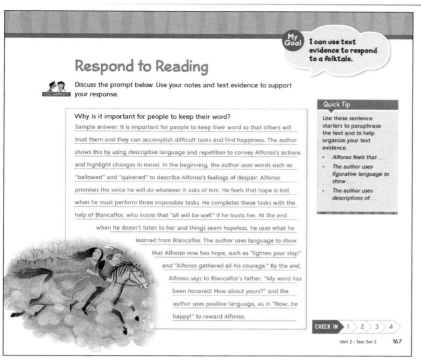

Reading/Writing Companion, p. 167

 English Language Learners

Use the following scaffolds with **Respond**.

Beginning

Read the prompt with students and discuss what they will write about. Clarify what it means when a person "keeps their word." Review the students' completed charts on **Reading/Writing Companion** pages 164-166. Ask: *Can you trust a person who keeps their word?* (yes) Help partners discuss why it is important for a people to keep their word and respond using: It is important for people to keep their <u>word</u> so that others will <u>trust</u> them.

Intermediate

Read the prompt with students. Have partners review their completed charts on **Reading/Writing Companion** pages 164-166. Guide partners to write their responses by asking: *What happens when people keep their word?* Other people will <u>trust them</u>. *Does Alfono's actions show this?* (yes) *What does the author use to describe Alfono's actions?* The author uses <u>descriptive details and repetition</u>.

Advanced/Advanced High

Review the prompt and the sentence starters on page 167 with students. Have partners use their completed charts on pages 164-166 and discuss why it is important for people to keep their word. Then have them respond using the sentence starters.

ELL NEWCOMERS

Have students listen to the summaries of the **Anchor Text** in their native language and then in English to help them access the text and develop listening comprehension. Help students ask and answer questions with a partner. Use these sentence frames: *Why is the prince scared? The prince is scared because _____.* Then have them complete the online **Newcomer Activities** individually or in pairs.

❯ STUDENT CHECK-IN

Ask partners to share their response on Reading/Writing Companion page 167. Have them reflect using the Check-In routine to fill in the bars.

LESSONS 7-8

"From Tale to Table"

Lexile 990L

LEARNING GOALS

Read We can apply skills and strategies to read expository text.

Reread We can reread to analyze text, craft, and structure, and to compare texts.

Have students apply what they learned as they read.

 Collect and record information using detailed observations and accurate measuring.

What makes this text complex?

▶ Prior Knowledge

▶ Connection of Ideas

Analytical Writing Compare Texts DOK 4

As students read and reread "From Tale to Table," encourage them to take notes and think about the Essential Question: *When has a plan helped you accomplish a task?* Students should discuss how this text is similar to and different from *Blancaflor.*

Read

1 Text Structure: Cause and Effect DOK 2

What effect does combining, stirring, kneading, and shaping have on the ingredients? (Combining, stirring, kneading, and shaping changes the separate ingredients into a mixture that has a different look and feel than each of the individual ingredients.)

Build Vocabulary on page 134

transformation: a complete change

Genre • Expository Text

Compare Texts
Read about how a recipe can help you accomplish a task.

From Tale to Table

Whether it's a princess turning into a dove or a frog turning into a prince, many folktales and fairy tales include a magical transformation of one thing into another. Though it seems like an impossible task that only a magician could do, transformations can in fact happen in real life—even in your own kitchen!

134

Literature Anthology, pp. 134–135

 Access Complex Text

Prior Knowledge

Read through the recipe with students. Point out the two parts that all recipes include: ingredients and steps. Discuss terms such as "floured surface" and "greased bowl" in step 4.

- *What do you think the author means by a "floured surface?"* (a surface on which a little flour has been sprinkled)

- *A surface is floured and a bowl is greased for the same reason. What do you think the reason is?* (to keep the dough from sticking)

A Wise Plan

Through the process of cooking and baking, individual ingredients can be transformed into something delicious. Did you know that the bread in the sandwich you had for lunch was probably made with only six basic ingredients: flour, water, oil, yeast, salt, and sugar? It may seem impossible, but by combining and heating these ingredients you can create something different: bread. It's not magic, but it does require a plan.

When you bake bread, or anything else, that plan is a *recipe*. A recipe includes a list of ingredients with amounts of each and steps to follow. The following recipe provides the `guidance` you need for making a loaf of bread. By combining, stirring, kneading, and shaping, you can change the separate ingredients into a mixture that has a different look and feel than each of the individual ingredients. After baking, this mixture will also have a different form, color, texture, and—of course—taste!

1

Recipe for Basic Bread

Ingredients:

1 cup warm water

1/4 cup sugar

2 teaspoons active dry yeast

1 teaspoon salt

3 cups all-purpose flour

2 tablespoons vegetable oil

1. In a bowl, combine the warm water and two teaspoons of sugar. Make sure the water is not hot. Sprinkle the yeast on top of the solution. Set the bowl aside. Then wait five minutes.
2. Stir the solution in the bowl. Then add the salt, oil, and the rest of the sugar.
3. Put flour in another bowl. Slowly pour in the solution and stir until the mixture comes together. Shape the dough with your hands to make it round.
4. Knead the dough on a floured surface for eight minutes. Then place it in a covered, greased bowl. Put it somewhere warm for an hour to rise. The dough should double in size.
5. Take out the dough and punch it down. Shape the dough into a loaf.
6. Place the loaf in a greased bread pan. Then cover the loaf. Wait for about an hour.
7. Remove the cover and bake the dough in the oven at 375 degrees Fahrenheit for 25-30 minutes. Check that the crust is golden brown.
8. Remove the pan from the oven. Let the pan cool.

135

Spotlight on Language

Page 134, Title The word *Tale* in the title refers to stories like fairy tales and folktales, such as *Blancaflor*. The word *Table* refers to food. "*From Tale to Table*" *makes a connection between tales and the making of food because there can be great changes in both.* Have partners discuss the changes in *Blancaflor* and the changes in food when it is made.

Reread

Author's Craft: Text Features
DOK 2

Reading/Writing Companion, p. 170

Reread pages 134–135. Think about what is involved in a recipe. What makes the creation of a new recipe so remarkable? (Recipes don't exist until people create them. In order to create them, people must experiment with many different ingredients and cooking techniques to find the perfect combination necessary to make something.) **Look at the title. Why is "From Tale to Table" a good title for this selection?** (It's a good title because the transformation of several ingredients into a new food, such as bread, is remarkable, just like transformations in folktales.)

Connect to Content

Changes in Matter

Matter, or the substance that things are made of, has the ability to change both physically and chemically. In many cases, temperature affects these changes. Page 136 tells that at the right temperature, yeast gives off gases. By releasing gases, yeast changes chemically. Have students discuss what might happen to the bread if the wrong temperature is used to bake it.

READING • PAIRED SELECTION

Read

❷ Central Idea and Relevant Details DOK 2

What is the central, or main, idea of the section "Too Hot, Too Cold, and Just Right"? (It's important to follow the steps of a recipe carefully to get the same result.) What relevant, or key, details support the central idea? (If you use hot water in the recipe, you can kill the yeast. If you use cold water, the yeast may create very little or no gas. Without the gas that the yeast produces, the dough will not rise.)

❸ Text Structure: Cause and Effect DOK 2

What will happen to your bread if you don't time each step correctly? (Your bread will not turn out correctly.)

Reread

Author's Craft: Text Features DOK 2

Reread the caption on page 136. How do the photographs support this text? (They show the steps in the bread-making process.) How can photographs help you better understand a recipe? (They provide a visual reference, making it easier to check that you are following the recipe correctly.)

A C T Access Complex Text

Connection of Ideas

On page 136, point out the details in the first paragraph that describe yeast and what it does. Help students make connections to understand that yeast is a living organism and the baking of bread relies on a series of connected processes.

Too Hot, Too Cold, and Just Right

❷ A recipe has usually been tried and tested previously, so it is important to follow the steps carefully to get the same result. Slight changes in temperature can affect the **outcome**. For example, in step 1, the water should be warm, not hot. Why? Though it's hard to tell by looking at it, yeast is a living organism. At the right temperature, it gives off gases that create bubbles in the dough. This is what makes the dough rise. If you use hot water in the recipe, you can kill the yeast. If you use cold water, the yeast may create very little or no gas. Without the gas that the yeast produces, the dough will not rise.

❸

First combine ingredients (top left). Next, shape the dough (top right). After kneading, let the dough rise (left). Ingredients must be at the right temperature and combined in the right order to make a dough that will rise.

136

Dave King/Dorling Kindersley/Getty Images

Literature Anthology, pp. 136–137

- *What are some examples of other living organisms?* (humans, plants, animals, bacteria)
- *All living organisms consume energy to survive. Yeast consumes sugar, and as a result, creates gas.*
- Reread page 136. *What factor affects the production of the gas?* (temperature)

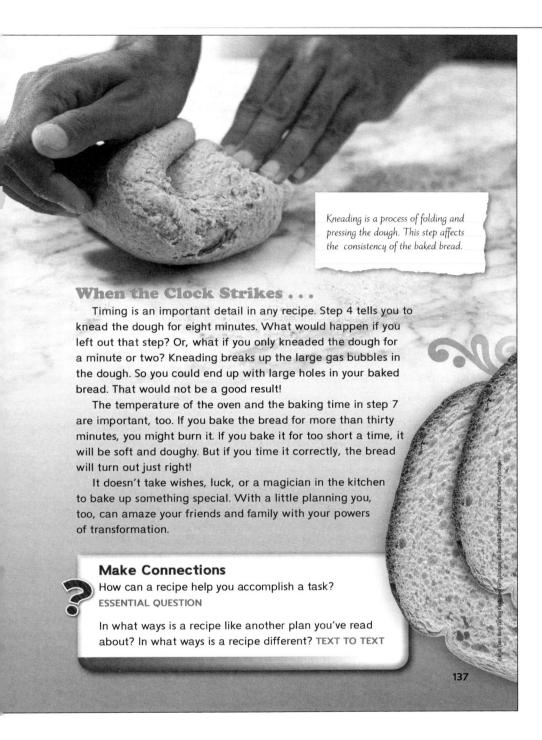

Kneading is a process of folding and pressing the dough. This step affects the consistency of the baked bread.

When the Clock Strikes . . .

Timing is an important detail in any recipe. Step 4 tells you to knead the dough for eight minutes. What would happen if you left out that step? Or, what if you only kneaded the dough for a minute or two? Kneading breaks up the large gas bubbles in the dough. So you could end up with large holes in your baked bread. That would not be a good result!

The temperature of the oven and the baking time in step 7 are important, too. If you bake the bread for more than thirty minutes, you might burn it. If you bake it for too short a time, it will be soft and doughy. But if you time it correctly, the bread will turn out just right!

It doesn't take wishes, luck, or a magician in the kitchen to bake up something special. With a little planning you, too, can amaze your friends and family with your powers of transformation.

Make Connections
How can a recipe help you accomplish a task?
ESSENTIAL QUESTION

In what ways is a recipe like another plan you've read about? In what ways is a recipe different? **TEXT TO TEXT**

137

ELL Spotlight on Idioms

Page 136, Paragraph 1 Read the paragraph with students. Reread the first sentence and explain that *tried and tested* means that something has been repeated many times to make sure that the results are always the same. *Why would you want a recipe to be tried and tested?* (so that the food will always taste good) *What are other things that you would want to be tried and tested?* (Possible answer: the brakes on a car or bicycle)

Read
Summarize

Guide students to summarize the selection. Remind them to include the central idea and relevant details.

Reread
Analyze the Text

After students read and summarize, have them reread and answer questions on pages 168-170 of the **Reading/Writing Companion**.

Integrate

📋 Build Knowledge: Make Connections

Talk About the Text Have partners discuss how recipes provide a plan for making food.

Write About the Text Have students add their ideas to their Build Knowledge pages of their reader's notebooks.

Anchor Chart Record any new ideas on the Build Knowledge anchor chart.

Add to the Vocabulary List Have students write down any words they learned about following plans in their reader's notebooks.

Compare Texts DOK 4

Text to Text <u>Answer</u>: Blancaflor's plan and recipes are sets of steps for completing tasks, similar to a recipe. <u>Evidence</u>: Alfonso gets to marry Blancaflor because they followed a plan. A recipe transforms ingredients into bread.

FORMATIVE ASSESSMENT

❯ STUDENT CHECK-IN

Read Ask partners to share their summaries. Then have them reflect using the Check-In routine.

Reread Ask partners to share their responses on Reading/Writing Companion pages 168-170. Then have them use the Check-In routine to reflect and fill in the bars.

We can identify a sequence text structure to help us read and understand expository text.

OBJECTIVES

Determine two or more central, or main, ideas of a text and explain how they are supported by relevant, or key, details; summarize the text.

Compare and contrast the overall structure (e.g., chronology, comparison, cause/effect, problem/solution) of events, ideas, concepts, or information in two or more texts.

Explain how an author uses reasons and evidence to support particular points in a text, identifying which reasons and evidence support which point(s).

Identify the author's purpose.

Pose and respond to specific questions by making comments that contribute to the discussion and elaborate on the remarks of others.

ELA ACADEMIC LANGUAGE

• *sequence, organization, procedure, process, relationship*

• Cognates: *organización, procedimiento, proceso, relación*

Reread

Text Structure: Sequence

10 mins

1 Explain

Have students turn to **Reading/Writing Companion** page 171. Reiterate that authors use text structure to organize ideas and information so that readers can identify and understand relationships between and among the ideas. Share with students the following key points of a sequence text structure that is organized according to order of importance or logical order:

• In a sequential order, ideas are organized logically so that one naturally follows from the next. Steps in a process or procedure are often described in a sequential order because one step must occur before the next step can happen. Texts that often use this kind of structure include recipes, experiments, driving directions, and assembly instructions.

• Texts organized sequentially often include bullet points or numbers to help readers follow the order of the steps or ideas being described.

• A sequence text structure can also reflect the importance of the ideas being discussed. An author might state an important idea, and then follow with an example that supports the idea.

2 Model

Model identifying and analyzing the sequence text structure in the second paragraph on page 168. Have students read the sentence. Point out that the author draws readers in by asking about something very familiar: bread used in a sandwich. The author then introduces a supporting idea: Bread is made with very few ingredients. As a group, discuss the connection between the two ideas, as well as how they logically lead to the ideas that follow.

COLLABORATE

3 Guided Practice

Now have partners work together to analyze sequential order in the text on **Reading/Writing Companion** page 169. Ask: *How does the author organize the text in a sequential order?* (The author states the importance of following the steps in a recipe carefully; then focuses on discussing one step.) *Why does this organizational pattern make sense?* (To explain the steps involved in making bread, it makes sense to start with step 1 and follow them in a logical order.)

Have partners discuss any additional aspects of the paragraph that reflect a sequential order as well as how the order helps readers understand the ideas. Have them share their findings with the class. Allow students time to enter their responses on page 171.

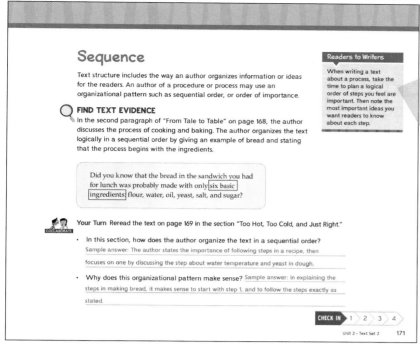

Reading/Writing Companion, p. 171

Readers to Writers

Reiterate that writing a procedural text involves thinking about a logical order of steps and the details necessary to understand each step. Have students reread step 4 on **Literature Anthology** page 135. Ask: *What does this step tell you to do?* (Knead the dough and put it in a bowl.) *How does the author share an idea that might be important?* (The author tells readers how to know when the dough has risen enough.)

 English Language Learners

Use the following scaffolds with **Guided Practice**.

Beginning

Read the first two sentences on **Reading/Writing Companion** page 169 with students. Point out to them that the author organizes the text in sequential order. Ask: *What does the author say about the steps in a recipe?* It is important to follow the steps carefully. *Does the author focus on discussing one step as an example?* (yes) Discuss with students why this organizational pattern makes sense and help them answer the questions on page 171.

Intermediate

Have partners read the paragraph on **Reading/Writing Companion** page 169. Guide them to discuss how the author organizes the text in sequential order by asking: *Does the author state that it is important to follow the steps in a recipe carefully?* (yes) *Then what does the author focus on?* The author focuses on discussing one step. Then have partners discuss why this organizational pattern makes sense and answer the questions on page 171.

Advanced/Advanced High

Have partners read the paragraph on page 169. Guide them to discuss how the author organizes the text in sequential order. Then have them discuss why this organizational pattern makes sense and answer the questions on page 171 using the terms *states, steps,* and *recipe.*

FORMATIVE ASSESSMENT

◯ STUDENT CHECK-IN

Ask partners to share their Your Turn responses on Reading/Writing Companion page 171. Then have them use the Check-In routine to reflect and fill in the bars.

AUTHOR'S CRAFT **T133**

Contractions

OPTION 10 mins

1 Explain

Tell students that two words are sometimes shortened to make one word. The shortened words are called **contractions.** An apostrophe takes the place of the missing letter or letters.

Some contractions are made up of a verb and the word *not:*

- *are not* becomes *aren't*
- *do not* becomes *don't*

Other contractions connect a pronoun and a verb:

- *she is* becomes *she's*
- *I am* becomes *I'm*

Emphasize the difference between possessives and contractions. Point out that both have apostrophes, but possessives, such as *Sam's,* show ownership.

2 Model

Write the following words and contractions on the board. Underline the letter or letters that are replaced by an apostrophe to create the contraction. Then model blending the contractions.

did not	didn't	have not	haven't
I am	I'm	we are	we're
he is	he's	you will	you'll

3 Guided Practice

Write the following contractions on the board. Help students underline the part of the word where a letter or letters have been left out. Then help them identify the two words each contraction stands for and the letter or letters that were left out and replaced with an apostrophe.

what's	you're	I'm	that's
he'd	we'll	it's	I'd
I'll	hadn't	he's	can't
they're	there's	isn't	I've

For practice with decoding and encoding, use **Practice Book** pages 103.

Read Multisyllabic Words

Transition to Longer Words Write the words below on the board. Have students read the word pairs in the first column. Following each word pair, model how to read the contraction in the second column formed from the two words. Have students tell which letters were replaced by the apostrophe in each contraction. Then have students chorally read the contractions.

would not	wouldn't	could not	couldn't
have not	haven't	does not	doesn't
what will	what'll	had not	hadn't
there will	there'll	would have	would've
should not	shouldn't	did not	didn't

Write the words *will not* and *won't* on the board. Explain that the contraction *won't* is irregular. It does not follow the same rule for replacing letters with an apostrophe as the others do.

Fluency

OPTION 10 mins

Rate

Explain/Model Remind students that it is important to read at an appropriate rate, or speed. Explain that the content of their reading will dictate their pace. For example, students would read a chapter from a science textbook more slowly than they would read an article in an entertainment magazine. Model reading at an appropriate rate as you read aloud the first three paragraphs of "The Magical Lost Brocade" on **Reading/Writing Companion** page 153.

Practice/Apply Have partners alternate reading sentences in the same passage, following the reading rate you established. Remind students that you will be listening for appropriate reading rates as you monitor their reading during the week.

Daily Fluency Practice

Automaticity Students can practice reading with accuracy and appropriate rate to develop automaticity using the online **Differentiated Genre Passage** "The Fox and the Snail."

DIGITAL TOOLS

For more practice, have students use the phonics and fluency activities.

Word Study

Contractions

MULTIMODAL LEARNING

In small groups, assign students the parts of the fox, the snail, and the narrator in the **Differentiated Genre Passage** "The Fox and the Snail." Ask them to use **Audio Recorder** to record themselves reading. Then have students listen to their recording as they track the print with a finger. Tell them to ask questions, such as *Did I pronounce the words correctly? Did I read at an appropriate speed?*

FORMATIVE ASSESSMENT

STUDENT CHECK-IN

Contractions Have partners identify and read contractions.

Multisyllabic Words Have partners read the following words: *wouldn't, what'll,* and *would've.*

Fluency Ask partners to read "The Fox and the Snail" fluently.

Have partners reflect using the Check-In routine.

CHECK FOR SUCCESS

Can students identify contractions when given word pairs? Can they identify word pairs in contractions? Can students read fluently?

Small Group Instruction

If No:

● **Approaching** Reteach pp. T145, T148

● **ELL** Develop p. T145

If Yes:

● **On** Apply p. T150

● **Beyond** Apply p. T156

LEARNING GOALS

We can compare the Wright Brothers' sketches with the selections in this text set to build knowledge about following plans to accomplish a task.

OBJECTIVES

Integrate information from several texts on the same topic in order to write or speak about the subject knowledgeably.

Draw evidence from literary or informational texts to support analysis, reflection, and research.

Close Reading Routine

Read DOK 1–2
- Identify important ideas and details.
- Take notes and summarize.
- Use prompts as needed.

Reread DOK 2–3
- Analyze the text, craft, and structure.
- Use the *Reading/Writing Companion.*

Integrate DOK 3–4
- Integrate knowledge and ideas.
- Make text-to-text connections.
- Use the Integrate/Make Connections lesson.
- Use *Reading/Writing Companion,* p. 172.
- Complete the Show Your Knowledge task.
- Inspire action.

FORMATIVE ASSESSMENT

❯ STUDENT CHECK-IN

Ask partners to share their response on Reading/Writing Companion page 172. Have them use the Check-In routine to reflect and fill in the bars.

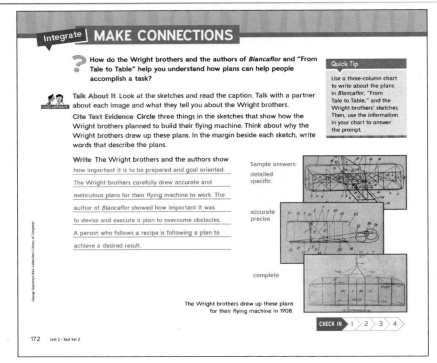

Reading/Writing Companion, p. 172

Integrate

10 mins

Make Connections DOK 4

Talk About It

COLLABORATE

Share and discuss students' responses to the "Stand by Your Plan" Blast. Display the Build Knowledge anchor chart. Review the chart and have students read through their notes, annotations, and responses for each text. Have them complete the Talk About It activity on **Reading/Writing Companion** page 172.

Cite Text Evidence

Guide students to see the connections between the Wright Brothers' sketches on page 172 and the selections. Remind students to read the caption and the Quick Tip on page 172.

Write

Students should refer to their notes on the chart as they respond to the writing prompt at the bottom of the page. Then have groups share and discuss their responses.

Build Knowledge: Make Connections

Talk About the Text Have partners discuss how following a plan can help people accomplish tasks.

Write About the Text Have students add their ideas to their Build Knowledge pages of their reader's notebooks.

Anchor Chart Record any new ideas on the Build Knowledge Anchor Chart.

Reading/Writing Companion, p. 173

Integrate

 ⏱ 10 mins

Show Your Knowledge DOK 4

Create a Recipe for Success

Discuss the meaning of the idiom, *recipe for success*. Explain to students that they will show how they built knowledge across the text set by creating a recipe for success based on what they read. Display the Build Knowledge anchor chart and ask: *How can following a plan help you accomplish a task?*

Steps 1 Guide partners to review the Build Knowledge anchor chart in their reader's notebook to discuss the prompt.

Step 2 Have students write a list of traits that help people become successful. Have them include examples from the texts, video, and listening passage. Prompt students to use words from their Build Knowledge vocabulary list in their reader's notebook.

Steps 3 Instruct students to use their list of character traits and words to create their recipes. Encourage them to be creative by designing their recipes in a manner similar to a cooking recipe.

Inspire Action

Share Your Recipe for Success Have partners present their recipes and display their work in the classroom. Ask students to place comments under each display using sticky notes. Students can choose to respond if they wish.

What Are You Inspired to Do? Have students talk about the texts they read this week. Ask: *What do these texts inspire you to do?*

LESSONS 1-10

LESSON 1 Connect to Words

Practice the target vocabulary.

1. Is **assuring** someone *encouraging or discouraging*?
2. If you **detected** a problem at school, what would you do?
3. What things start **emerging** in the spring?
4. For what do you feel **gratitude**?
5. Describe a time when you gave someone **guidance**.
6. Tell about a time that your actions had a positive **outcome.**
7. What did you do during the **previous** weekend?
8. If you are in **pursuit**, what would that look like? Show me.

OPTION LESSON 6 Build Vocabulary

- Display *intense, approached,* and *emerged.*
- Define each word and discuss the meanings with students.
- Write *intensity* under *intense.* Have partners write other words with the same root and define them. Then have partners ask and answer questions using the words.
- Repeat with *approached* and *emerged.*

OPTION LESSON 2 Related Words

Have students create different forms of target words by adding, changing, or removing inflectional endings.

- Draw a four-column chart on the board. Write *assuring* in the last column. Then write *assure, assures,* and *assured* in the first three columns. Read aloud the words with students.
- Have students share sentences using each form of *assure.*
- Students should add to the chart for *detected* and *emerging,* and then share sentences using the different forms of the words.
- Have students copy the chart in their reader's notebooks.

See **Practice Book** page 95.

LESSON 7 Roots (*geo, photo*)

Remind students that knowing the meaning of a root can help them figure out the meaning of a word.

- Tell students that *geo* is a Greek root meaning "Earth." For example, *geography* is the study of Earth's features.
- Point out that *photo* is a Greek root meaning "light." For example, *photocopy* is a copy that is made using light.
- Have students name other words that use the roots *geo* and *photo* and record them in their reader's notebook.

See **Practice Book** page 107.

Spiral Review

LESSON 3 Reinforce the Words

Have students orally complete each sentence stem to review words.

1. The <u>previous</u> day was rainy, so I feel <u>gratitude</u> that today the sky is ____.

2. The fox started his <u>pursuit</u>, <u>emerging</u> from ____ to chase the rabbit.

3. Isaac <u>detected</u> a sound in the basement, so he ____.

4. Pam spent a few moments <u>assuring</u> Jon when he ____.

Display the previous text set's vocabulary: *committees, convention, debate, proposal, representatives, resolve, situation,* and *union.* Have partners ask and answer questions using each word.

See **Practice Book** page 96.

 OPTION

LESSON 4 Connect to Writing

• Have students write sentences in their reader's notebooks using the target vocabulary.

• Tell them to write sentences that provide context to show what the words mean.

• **ELL** Provide the Lesson 3 sentence stems 1–4 for students needing extra support.

Write Using Vocabulary

Have students write something they learned from this text set's words in their reader's notebook. For example, they might write about reasons people seek *guidance* or how they express their *gratitude.*

 OPTION

LESSON 5 Word Squares

 MULTIMODAL

Ask students to create Word Squares for each vocabulary word.

• In the first square, students write the word (e.g., *detected*).

• In the second square, students write their own definition of the word and any related words, such as synonyms (e.g., *noticed, sensed, became aware of*).

• In the third square, students draw a simple illustration that will help them remember the word (e.g., a magnifying glass).

• In the fourth square, students write nonexamples, including antonyms (e.g., *missed, overlooked, failed to see*).

Have partners discuss their squares.

LESSON 8 Personification

Explain that personification means giving human qualities to an animal or object.

• Display On Level **Differentiated Genre Passage** "The Fox and the Snail." Read paragraph 7 on page O1. Focus on the phrase *claimed the fox.* Model identifying this phrase as personification.

• Have partners continue reading the folktale to find other examples of personification. Partners can keep a list in their reader's notebook.

See **Practice Book** page 108.

 OPTION

LESSON 9 Shades of Meaning

Help students generate words related to *gratitude.* Draw a T-chart. Head one column "Antonyms" and the other "Synonyms."

• Have partners use a thesaurus to find and add related words to the T-chart.

• Add words not included, such as synonyms (e.g., *appreciation, thankfulness*) and antonyms (e.g., *ingratitude, thanklessness*).

• Ask students to copy the words in their reader's notebooks.

 OPTION

LESSON 10 Morphology

Use *outcome* as a springboard for students to learn more words. Label a T-chart with *out* and *come.*

• Explain that *outcome* is a compound noun.

• Ask partners to find other compound words with the same word parts (e.g., *without, blackout, takeout, income, become, comeback, overcome*).

• Add the words to the T-chart. Review their meanings.

Write Using Vocabulary

Have students use vocabulary words in their extended writing.

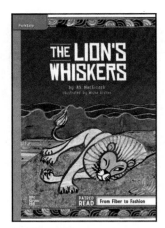

Lexile 760

OBJECTIVES

Determine a theme of a story, drama, or poem from details in the text, including how characters in a story or drama respond to challenges or how the speaker in a poem reflects upon a topic; summarize the text.

Read grade-level text with purpose and understanding.

Read grade-level prose and poetry orally with accuracy, appropriate rate, expression, and automaticity on successive readings.

Cite evidence to explain and justify reasoning.

ELA ACADEMIC LANGUAGE

• folktale, theme, make predictions, heroine, personification, paraphrase

• Cognates: *tema, predicciones*

●Approaching Level

Leveled Reader: *The Lion's Whiskers*

Preview and Predict

Read the Essential Question: *When has a plan helped you accomplish a task?*

Ask students to read the title and look at the illustrations for *The Lion's Whiskers* to make a prediction about what will happen.

Review Genre: Folktale

Tell students that this selection is a folktale. In a folktale, the hero or heroine often has a problem that he or she must solve. The setting of a folktale often takes place long ago in a land that is specific to the people who created the story. Foreshadowing, imagery, and repetition of words or actions are common elements in a folktale. As they read, have students identify genre characteristics of a folktale.

Close Reading

Note Taking Ask students to use a copy of online Theme **Graphic Organizer 5** as they read.

Pages 2–3 *What goal does the heroine of the story, Alitash, want to accomplish?* (Alitash wants Dawit, her stepson, to grow to love her.) *What obstacles does she face?* (Dawit misses his own mother and does not want Alitash to take her place.)

Pages 4–5 *Turn to a partner and discuss why Alitash visits the wise woman.* (She hopes the wise woman will give her a potion that will make Dawit love her.) *What does the wise woman want Alitash to do?* (She wants Alitash to get three whiskers from a live lion.)

Pages 6–7 *Which phrase on page 6 is an example of personification?* (*her thoughts just chased each other around in circles*) *To whom or what does it give a human quality?* (Her thoughts are personified.) Then read the last paragraph on page 7. *What clue in the text tells you Alitash is afraid?* (her legs are unwilling) *Although Alitash is afraid, why does she choose to approach the lion?* (Her determination to make Dawit love her is stronger than her fear of the lion.)

Pages 8–11 *Turn to a partner and paraphrase Alitash's plan.* (Alitash gains the lion's trust by feeding him meat every day. She gets closer and closer to him until she is finally able to cut three whiskers.) *Share a prediction with your partner.* (Alitash will bring the whiskers to the wise woman and get the potion.)

Pages 12–15 *What does Alitash learn from the wise woman?* (to put the same determination and patience into gaining Dawit's happiness and love as she did in gaining the lion's trust) *Review your previous predictions. Were they correct? Explain.* (Yes, but I did not realize that Alitash would have to win Dawit's love without the potion.) *Generate a question of your own about what you have just read and share it with a partner. Try to find the answer by rereading the text.*

Respond to Reading Revisit the Essential Question and ask students to complete the Text Evidence questions on page 16 after they have finished reading.

Write About Reading Check that students have incorporated the story's theme into their writing about the wise woman's message.

Analytical Writing

Fluency: Expression and Phrasing

Model Reread page 6. Model rereading the page with expression and appropriate phrasing to convey the character's thoughts. Next read the passage aloud and have students read along with you.

Apply Have students practice reading the passage with a partner.

Paired Read: "From Fiber to Fashion"

Make Connections: Write About It

Analytical Writing

Before reading, ask students to note that the genre of this selection is expository text. Then discuss the Essential Question. After reading, ask students to write about connections between the folktale *The Lion's Whiskers* and the expository text "From Fiber to Fashion." Have students use text evidence to compare how a plan accomplishes a task in a folktale and in expository text.

Leveled Reader

Build Knowledge

Talk About the Text Have partners discuss how following a plan can help people accomplish a task.

Write About the Text Have students add their ideas to the Build Knowledge pages of their reader's notebooks.

FOCUS ON GENRE

Have students complete the activity on page 20 to create a new challenge for Alitash.

LITERATURE CIRCLES

Ask students to conduct a literature circle using the Thinkmark questions to guide the discussion. You may wish to have a whole-class discussion, using both selections in the Leveled Reader, about how a plan can help a person accomplish a task.

LEVEL UP

IF students read the Approaching Level fluently and answered the questions,

THEN pair them with students who have proficiently read the On Level and have students

- echo-read the On Level main selection.

- list the problems and solutions they find in the folktale.

A C T Access Complex Text

The On Level challenges students by including more **figurative language** and **complex sentence structures**.

"The Fox and the Snail"
Lexile 700L

OBJECTIVES

Quote accurately from a text when explaining what the text says explicitly and when drawing inferences from the text.

Explain different characters' perspectives in a literary text.

Determine a theme of a story, drama, or poem from details in the text, including how characters in a story or drama respond to challenges or how the speaker in a poem reflects upon a topic; summarize the text.

Compare and contrast two or more characters, settings, or events in a story or drama, drawing on specific details in the text (e.g., how characters interact).

Demonstrate understanding of figurative language, word relationships, and nuances in word meaning.

ELA ACADEMIC LANGUAGE

• *theme, personification, setting, folktale*

• Cognates: *tema, personificación*

●Approaching Level

Genre Passage: "The Fox and the Snail"

Build Background

Read aloud the Essential Question: *When has a plan helped you accomplish a task?* Ask students to compare how two characters in this text set made a plan to achieve a goal. Use the following sentence starters to help focus discussion:

> *The character's plan succeeded because . . .*

> *This helps me understand that a successful plan . . .*

Read aloud the text under the title of the online **Differentiated Genre Passage** "The Fox and the Snail." Explain that *adapted* means that the story was first told by people in France, and that parts of it may have changed as different people told it over the years. Discuss why this might happen.

Review Genre: Folktale

Remind students that a folktale is a story common to a specific culture and is passed down through the years. Its setting can reflect the time period or culture of the place where it was first told. The main character must solve a challenge. Folktales often include personification, imagery, and foreshadowing.

Close Reading

Note Taking As students read the passage the first time, ask them to annotate the text. Have them note key ideas and details, unfamiliar words, and questions they have. Then read again and use the following questions. Encourage students to cite text evidence from the selection.

> **Read**

Plot: Setting Read the first paragraph on page A1. *When and where is the story set?* ("long, long ago" and "in the far-off land of Touleroo")

Genre: Folktale Read paragraphs 2–8. *What is the fox doing?* (telling the snail that he'll be the first to win a reward from the king) *What is the snail doing?* (asking the fox about his proof) *How do their actions tell you that this story is a folktale?* (The animals can talk and plan even though they are animals. The snail is the hero. He must outsmart the dishonest fox.)

Personification Read paragraphs 8–11. *Find two details that tell about the animals' human qualities.* (The fox grins slyly. The snail figures out the truth.)

Personification Read paragraphs 1–2 on page A2. *How does the snail trick the fox?* (He hides in the fox's tail.) *What does this trick help you understand about the snail?* (that he is more clever than the fox)

Theme Read the last four paragraphs. *What does the snail do?* (He tells the king the truth about the fox.) *How does the king respond?* (He rewards the snail.) *Based on these actions, what message do you think the author wants to share?* (Possible answer: It is important to be honest; honesty is usually rewarded.)

 Summarize Have students use their notes to summarize how the snail outwits the fox.

Reread

Use the questions on page A3 to guide students' rereading of the passage.

Author's Craft Reread the first paragraph on page A1. *How does the author create suspense?* (The author writes that the fox is hurrying along a seaside road. This makes me wonder why the fox is hurrying and where he is going.)

Author's Craft Reread paragraphs 1–2 on page A2. *How does the author foreshadow, or give a hint about, what will happen?* (The author writes that the snail smiles at what the fox says and makes a wager that he will get to the king first. Then the snail hides in the fox's tail. This helps me predict that the snail will go as fast as the fox.)

Author's Craft Reread the third paragraph on page A2. *Why do you think the author used the word "slipped" to describe the snail's action?* (The author uses the word "slipped" to show that the snail is being careful so the fox won't see him.)

Integrate

Make Connections Guide students to recognize connections between "The Fox and the Snail" and other folktales they've read. Have pairs gather evidence to answer this question: *What makes each character's plan successful?*

Compare Texts Display a three-column chart labeled *Character, Plan,* and *Reason for Success.* Help students compare reasons the characters' plans succeeded.

Build Knowledge

Talk About the Text Have partners discuss how following a plan can help people accomplish a task.

Write About the Text Have students add their ideas to the Build Knowledge pages of their reader's notebooks.

Differentiate and Collaborate

Be inspired Have students think about "The Fox and the Snail" and other selections they have read. Ask: *What do the texts inspire you to do?* Use the following activities or have pairs of students think of a way to respond to the texts.

Write a Folktale Think of a story you like to tell, and turn it into a folktale. Include a character who makes a plan to accomplish a challenging task. Illustrate your story and read it aloud to family or friends.

Design a Quest Work with a group to design a scavenger "quest" through your school. Come up with and hide clues that lead from one place to the next. Then challenge classmates to complete the quest. Award a prize to whomever finishes first.

Readers to Writers

Dialogue Remind students that dialogue is the words in quotation marks that characters speak. Authors use dialogue to help readers understand the characters and their relationships. Have students reread the dialogue in paragraphs 2–6 on page A1. Ask: *What do you learn about each character through dialogue? What do you learn about how the characters feel about each other?*

LEVEL UP

IF students read the Approaching Level fluently and answered the questions,

THEN pair them with students who have proficiently read the On Level. Have them

- partner read the On Level passage.
- summarize what the snail did to accomplish his goal.

Approaching Level

Word Study/Decoding

REVIEW INFLECTIONAL ENDINGS

OBJECTIVES

Know and apply grade-level phonics and word analysis skills in decoding words.

Use combined knowledge of all letter-sound correspondences, syllabication patterns, and morphology (e.g., roots and affixes) to read accurately unfamiliar multisyllabic words in context and out of context.

Decode words with inflectional endings.

I Do Write the words *end, ended,* and *ending* on the board. Review that adding *-ed* or *-ing* to many verbs changes their tense. The *-ed* ending typically indicates that an action happened in the past. The *-ing* ending indicates an ongoing action. Then write *add, added; shine, shining;* and *dry, dried* on the board. Review the rules for adding inflectional endings, including when to double the final consonant (*added*), when to drop the silent *e* (*shining*), and when to change *y* to *i* before adding the ending (*dried*).

We Do Write the words *chart, charted; flip, flipping;* and *brace, braced* on the board. Model how to say each verb with its inflectional ending. Have students repeat the word after you. Then help students identify which tense each inflectional ending forms.

You Do Add the following examples to the board: *yell, yelling; hope, hoped; clap, clapping.* Have students say each word, telling what tense the inflectional ending forms.

PRACTICE INFLECTIONAL ENDINGS

OBJECTIVES

Know and apply grade-level phonics and word analysis skills in decoding words.

Use combined knowledge of all letter-sound correspondences, syllabication patterns, and morphology (e.g., roots and affixes) to read accurately unfamiliar multisyllabic words in context and out of context.

Decode words with inflectional endings.

I Do Write the words *batted, seeing, chopping, raking,* and *relied* on the board. Read the words aloud, and identify the inflectional ending in each word as you run your fingers under the letters in the inflectional ending. Remind students that inflectional endings can be spelled in different ways.

We Do Write the word pairs *drained, draining; rinsed, rinsing; flapped, flapping;* and *fried, frying* on the board. Model how to decode the first two words; then guide students as they decode the remaining words.

Write the following word pairs on the board: *rippled, rippling; blushed, blushing; denied, denying; lapped, lapping; hurried, hurrying; skipped, skipping; outwitted, outwitting; multiplied, multiplying.* Read aloud the first word pair and identify the inflectional endings.

You Do Have students read aloud the remaining words. Ask them to identify the inflectional ending in each word and tell what tense it forms. Point to the words in random order for students to chorally read.

REVIEW CONTRACTIONS

OBJECTIVES

Know and apply grade-level phonics and word analysis skills in decoding words.

Use combined knowledge of all letter-sound correspondences, syllabication patterns, and morphology (e.g., roots and affixes) to read accurately unfamiliar multisyllabic words in context and out of context.

Decode contractions.

I Do Review with students that two words are sometimes shortened to make one word, which is called a contraction. In a contraction, an apostrophe takes the place of the missing letters. Point out that some contractions are made up of a verb and the word *not,* such as *don't (do* and *not)* and *won't (will* and *not).* Other contractions combine a pronoun and a verb, such as *he's (he* and *is)* and *she'll (she* and *will).*

We Do Write the contractions *wasn't* and *it's* on the board. Read the word *wasn't* and have students repeat it after you. Help them identify the two words it combines and tell what letter was removed. Repeat with the word *it's.* Stress the difference between the contraction *it's,* meaning "it is," and the possessive *its,* meaning "belonging to it."

You Do Add the following examples of contractions: *isn't, I'm, they're, haven't.* Have students say each contraction and tell which two words were combined.

PRACTICE CONTRACTIONS

OBJECTIVES

Know and apply grade-level phonics and word analysis skills in decoding words.

Use combined knowledge of all letter-sound correspondences, syllabication patterns, and morphology (e.g., roots and affixes) to read accurately unfamiliar multisyllabic words in context and out of context.

Decode contractions.

I Do Write the words *they have* and the contraction *they've* on the board. Read the words aloud, running your finger under the letters replaced by the apostrophe in the contraction. Remind students that apostrophes are also used to show possession. Provide examples and remind students to avoid confusing contractions and possessives.

We Do Write the words below on the board. Model matching *he would* in the first column with *he'd* in the second column.

he would	she'll
she will	would've
would have	won't
will not	he'd

You Do Have students match the remaining words with a contraction. They should identify the letters that were replaced by the apostrophe in each contraction. Point to the contractions in random order for students to chorally read.

ELL For **ELL** students who need phonics and decoding practice, define words and help them use the words in sentences, scaffolding to ensure their understanding. See the **Language Transfers Handbook** for phonics elements that may not transfer from students' native languages.

●Approaching Level

Vocabulary

REVIEW HIGH-FREQUENCY WORDS

TIER 2

OBJECTIVES

Acquire and use accurately grade appropriate general academic and domain specific words and phrases, including those that signal contrast, addition, and other logical relationships.

Review high-frequency words.

I Do Use **High-Frequency Word Cards** 61–80. Display one word at a time, following the routine:

Display the word. Read the word. Then spell the word.

We Do Ask students to state the word and spell the word with you. Model using the word in a sentence and have students repeat after you.

You Do Display the word. Ask students to say the word, and then spell it. When completed, quickly flip through the word card set as students chorally read the words. Provide opportunities for students to use the words in speaking and writing. For example, provide sentence starters, such as *You can get a funny _____.* Ask students to write each word in their reader's notebook.

REVIEW ACADEMIC VOCABULARY

 **TIER 2**

OBJECTIVES

Acquire and use accurately grade appropriate general academic and domain specific words and phrases, including those that signal contrast, addition, and other logical relationships.

I Do Display each **Visual Vocabulary Card** and state the word. Explain how the photograph illustrates the word. State the example sentence and repeat the word.

We Do Point to the word on the card and read the word with students. Ask them to repeat the word. Engage students in structured partner talk about the image as prompted on the back of the vocabulary card.

You Do Display each visual in random order, hiding the word. Have students match the definitions and context sentences of the words to the visuals displayed.

 ELL You may wish to review high-frequency words with ELL students using the lesson above.

IDENTIFY RELATED WORDS

OBJECTIVES

Demonstrate understanding off figurative language, word relationships, and nuances in word meanings.

Use the relationship between particular words (e.g., synonyms, antonyms, homographs) to better understand each of the words.

I Do Display the *gratitude* **Visual Vocabulary Card** and say aloud the word set *gratitude, appreciation, neglect.* Point out that the word *appreciation* means almost the same as *gratitude.*

We Do Display the vocabulary card for the word *previous.* Say aloud the word set *previous, earlier, following.* With students, identify the word that means almost the same as *previous* and discuss why it does.

You Do Using the word sets below, display the remaining cards one at a time, saying aloud the word set. Ask students which word means almost the same as the first word in each group.

pursuit, need, chase	*assuring, convincing, denying*
emerging, disappearing, rising	*detected, discovered, overlooking*
guidance, betrayal, advice	*outcome, cause, result*

Have students pick words from their reader's notebook and use a digital thesaurus to find a synonym for each word.

PERSONIFICATION

OBJECTIVES

Demonstrate understanding off figurative language, word relationships, and nuances in word meanings. Interpret figurative language, including similes and metaphors, in context.

Identify words that demonstrate personification.

I Do Read aloud the last paragraph of "The Fox and the Snail" in the Approaching Level online **Differentiated Genre Passage** page A1. Explain to students that writers sometimes use words in unusual ways to help readers better picture an animal, thing, or event in the story. Personification is when a writer gives human qualities to an animal or object.

Think Aloud I know that *grinned slyly* is an action that people usually perform. In this story, though, the fox is performing this action.

Explain that this action helps you picture the fox as he is boasting to the snail. This action helps you understand his dishonest character.

We Do Point to the word *astonished* in paragraph 2 on page A2. Discuss how the word personifies the fox and how it helps you picture what is happening.

You Do Have students identify and explain examples of personification in the words *slipped* (page A2, paragraph 3) and *called* (page A2, paragraph 3).

●Approaching Level

Comprehension

FLUENCY

OBJECTIVES

Read with sufficient accuracy and fluency to support comprehension.

Read grade-level prose and poetry orally with accuracy, appropriate rate, and expression on successive readings.

I Do Explain that reading with expression by changing your voice helps you convey a text's meaning to listeners. Reading with proper phrasing by pausing at punctuation marks helps distinguish ideas for your listeners. Read the first paragraph of "The Fox and the Snail" in the online Approaching Level **Differentiated Genre Passage** page A1. Tell students to listen for your expression and phrasing.

We Do Read the rest of the page aloud and have students repeat each sentence after you, using the same expression and phrasing. Explain that your voice changed for certain words and that you paused briefly for commas and longer for periods.

You Do Have partners take turns reading sentences from the passage. Remind them to focus on their expression and phrasing. Listen in and, as needed, provide corrective feedback by modeling proper fluency.

IDENTIFY DETAILS ABOUT CHARACTERS

OBJECTIVES

Determine a theme of a story, drama, or poem from details in the text, including how characters in a story or drama respond to challenges or how the speaker in a poem reflects upon a topic; summarize the text.

Identify details about the characters that point to the story's theme.

I Do Read paragraph 7 of "The Fox and the Snail" in the online Approaching Level **Differentiated Genre Passage** page A1. Point out what the fox says: "for I am the smartest of beasts." Help students understand that this detail tells readers that the fox is a boastful character.

We Do Read paragraph 8. Ask: *What does the snail say?* Remind students that identifying a character's words, thoughts, and actions is the first step to understanding that character. Then ask: *What is the character's perspective, or attitude, as a result of the snail's actions?* Explain that understanding this connection can help students figure out the theme.

You Do Have students read the rest of the passage and identify the snail's words, thoughts, actions, and perspective. Review students' lists with them and help them explain what these details reveal about the snail.

REVIEW THEME

OBJECTIVES

Determine a theme of a story, drama, or poem from details in the text, including how characters in a story or drama respond to challenges or how the speaker in a poem reflects upon a topic; summarize the text.

I Do Remind students that the theme is the big idea or message about life that the author wants to share with readers. The theme is not usually stated directly. Readers can identify the theme by thinking about what the characters think, say, do and their perspective, and asking themselves what the author's message might be.

We Do With students, read page A1 of "The Fox and the Snail" in the online Approaching Level **Differentiated Genre Passage**. Identify the animals' words and actions and list them on a copy of online Theme **Graphic Organizer 5**. Model using this information to begin to form ideas about the story's theme.

You Do Have students complete the organizer. Tell students to record details from the text about what the snail thinks, says, and does and its perspective. Remind students to wait until they have completed the organizers to state the theme of the passage.

SELF-SELECTED READING

OBJECTIVES

Determine a theme of a story, drama, or poem from details in the text, including how characters in a story or drama respond to challenges or how the speaker in a poem reflects upon a topic; summarize the text.

Make, confirm, and revise predictions based on details in the text.

Independent Reading

Have students choose a folktale for independent reading. Students can read a **Classroom Library** book or check the online **Leveled Reader Library** or **Unit Bibliography** for selections. Guide students to transfer what they have learned in this text set as they read. Remind them that

- the theme is the big idea, or message, about life that the author wants to share; characters' words and actions can help determine the theme;

- making, confirming, and revising predictions as they read is a good way to stay focused and keep track of what is happening in a story.

Have students record the character's words, actions, perspective, and the story's theme on online **Graphic Organizer 5** as they read independently. After they finish, they can conduct a book talk, each telling about the texts they read.

- Students can choose activities from the Reading **Center Activity Cards** to help them apply skills to the text as they read. After they finish, they can choose a Book Talk activity to talk about the texts they read.

- Offer assistance and guidance with self-selected assignments.

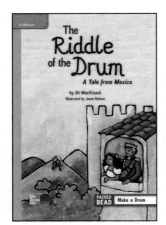

Lexile 810L

OBJECTIVES

Determine a theme of a story, drama, or poem from details in the text, including how characters in a story or drama respond to challenges or how the speaker in a poem reflects upon a topic; summarize the text..

Read grade-level text with purpose and understanding.

Read grade-level prose and poetry orally with accuracy, appropriate rate, and expression on successive readings.

Cite evidence to explain and justify reasoning.

ELA ACADEMIC LANGUAGE

• folktale, theme, make predictions, paraphrase, personification
• Cognates: *tema, predicciones*

●On Level

Leveled Reader: *The Riddle of the Drum*

Preview and Predict

Read the Essential Question: *When has a plan helped you accomplish a task?*

Ask students to read the title and preview the illustrations in *The Riddle of the Drum* in order to make predictions about what the folktale will be about.

Review Genre: Folktale

Tell students that in a folktale, the hero or heroine often has a problem or challenge that he or she must solve. The setting of a folktale often takes place long ago in a land that is specific to the people who created the story. Foreshadowing, imagery, and repetition of words or actions are common elements of a folktale. Have students identify genre characteristics as they read the folktale.

Close Reading

Note Taking Ask students to use a copy of online Theme **Graphic Organizer 5** as they read.

Pages 2–5 *Which words are repeated on pages 2 and 5?* (*clever, resourceful, capable, confident*) *Why do you think the author repeats these words?* (They are qualities that connect to the theme of the story.)

Pages 6–8 *Paraphrase what the prince does on pages 6–8.* (The prince sets out to find others who will help him solve the king's riddle. He finds people who have special skills that are useful.) *What do the prince's actions suggest about his perspective?* (He is determined to solve the riddle and follows a good plan to help him succeed.)

Pages 9–10 *Turn to a partner and share a prediction about whether the prince will solve the riddle. Explain your prediction.* (I predict that the prince's helpers, with their special skills, will help him solve the riddle of the drum.)

Pages 11–14 *Which phrase on page 14 is an example of personification?* (*the legs of the tables groaned*) *Why?* (The phrase makes it seem like the legs of the tables are alive and groaning in discomfort, like a person.)

Page 15 *What is the story's theme or message? Use details from the text to help you answer.* (Having a plan and being persistent are good ways of finding solutions to problems or challenges. The prince developed a plan and followed it in order to solve the riddle and accomplish the tasks set by the king.)

Generate a question of your own about what you have just read and share it with a partner. Try to find the answer by rereading the text.

Respond to Reading Revisit the Essential Question and ask students to complete the Text Evidence questions on page 16.

 Analytical Writing **Write About Reading** Check that students have explained how the prince's plan helped him obtain water. Students should mention at least two of the prince's obstacles and his successes and should connect these to the story's theme.

Fluency: Expression and Phrasing

Model Reread page 6. Model rereading the page with expression and appropriate phrasing to help readers keep track of important events. Next read the passage aloud and have students read along with you.

Apply Have students practice reading the passage with a partner.

Paired Read: "Make a Drum"

Analytical Writing **Make Connections: Write About It**

Before reading, ask students to note that the genre of this selection is expository text. Then discuss the Essential Question. After reading, ask students to write about connections between the folktale *The Riddle of the Drum* and the expository text "Make a Drum." Have students use text evidence to compare how a plan accomplishes a task in a folktale and in an expository text.

Leveled Reader

Build Knowledge

Talk About the Text Have partners discuss how following a plan can help people accomplish a task.

Write About the Text Have students add their ideas to the Build Knowledge pages of their reader's notebooks.

FOCUS ON GENRE

Have students complete the activity on page 20 to create a new challenge for the prince.

LITERATURE CIRCLES

Ask students to conduct a literature circle using the Thinkmark questions to guide the discussion. You may wish to have a whole-class discussion, using both selections in the Leveled Reader, about how having a plan can help accomplish a task.

LEVEL UP

IF students read the On Level fluently and answered the questions,

THEN pair them with students who have proficiently read the Beyond Level and have students

- partner-read the Beyond Level main selection.
- make, confirm, and revise predictions.
- identify examples of personification.

ACT Access Complex Text

The Beyond Level challenges students by including more **figurative language** and **complex sentence structures**.

"The Fox and the Snail"
Lexile 770L

OBJECTIVES

Quote accurately from a text when explaining what the text says explicitly and when drawing inferences from the text.

Explain different characters' perspectives in a literary text.

Determine a theme of a story, drama, or poem from details in the text, including how characters in a story or drama respond to challenges or how the speaker in a poem reflects upon a topic; summarize the text.

Compare and contrast two or more characters, settings, or events in a story or drama, drawing on specific details in the text (e.g., how characters interact).

Compare and contrast stories in the same genre (e.g., mysteries and adventure stories) on their approaches to similar themes and topics.

Demonstrate understanding of figurative language, word relationships, and nuances in word meaning.

ELA ACADEMIC LANGUAGE

- *theme, personification, setting, folktale*
- Cognates: *tema, personificación*

●On Level

Genre Passage: "The Fox and the Snail"

Build Background

Read aloud the Essential Question: *When has a plan helped you accomplish a task?* Ask students to compare how characters from two folktales they have read in this text set were able to develop a plan to achieve a goal. Use the following sentence starters to help focus discussion:

> *The character's plan succeeded because . . .*
>
> *This helps me understand that a successful plan . . .*

Read aloud the text under the title of the online **Differentiated Genre Passage** "The Fox and the Snail." Explain that *adapted* means that the story students will read was first told by people in France, and that parts of it may have changed as people told it over the years. Discuss why it might change over time as different people tell it.

Review Genre: Folktale

Remind students that a folktale is a story common to a specific culture and is passed down through the years. A folktale's setting can reflect the time period or culture of the place where it was first told. The main character must solve a challenge. Folktales often include personification, imagery, and foreshadowing.

Close Reading

Note Taking As students read the passage the first time, ask them to annotate the text. Have them note key ideas and details, unfamiliar words, and questions they have. Then read again and use the following questions. Encourage students to cite text evidence from the selection.

Read

Plot: Setting Read the first paragraph on page O1. *When and where does the folktale take place?* (long ago in the far-off land of Touleroo)

Genre: Folktale Read paragraphs 2–8. *What details indicate the story is a folktale?* (The snail is the hero. He must outsmart the dishonest fox. They can talk even though they are animals.)

Personification Read paragraphs 9–11. *What human qualities of the fox and snail do these paragraphs reveal?* (The fox is sly. He thinks he can win the reward by cheating. The snail is smart. He gets the fox to admit he didn't think of the proof.)

Personification Read paragraph 2 on page O2. *How does the snail trick the fox?* (He crawls into the fox's tail while the fox is counting.) *Why is this action an example of personification?* (The snail cleverly tricks the fox, as one person might trick another.)

Theme Read the last four paragraphs. *What themes are revealed?* (Possible answers: Honesty is important; honesty brings its own reward.) *What evidence supports these themes?* (The snail didn't prove Earth was round, but he is rewarded for honesty.)

Summarize Have students use their notes to summarize how the snail outsmarts the fox and what happens once they reach the king.

Reread

Use the questions on page O3 to guide students' rereading of the passage.

Author's Craft Reread the first paragraph on page O1. *How does the author create suspense?* (The author creates suspense by saying the fox is hurrying along a seaside road. The word "hurrying" makes me wonder why he is going fast. I also wonder where he needs to go so quickly.)

Author's Craft Reread paragraphs 1-2 on page O2. *How does the author use foreshadowing?* (The author writes that the snail smiles at what the fox says and makes a wager he will get to the king first. Then the snail hides in the fox's tail. I predict that he will go as fast as the fox and will get to the king first.)

Author's Craft Reread the third paragraph on page O2. *Why do you think the author uses the word "slipped" to describe the snail's action?* (The author uses the word "slipped" to show that the snail is being careful so that the fox won't see him.)

Integrate

Make Connections Have partners explore connections between "The Fox and the Snail" and other folktales they've read. They should gather text evidence to answer this question: *What makes each character's plan successful?*

Compare Texts Have pairs create a three-column chart labeled *Character, Plan,* and *Reason for Success,* and compare reasons why the characters' plans succeeded.

Build Knowledge

Talk About the Text Have partners discuss how following a plan can help people accomplish a task.

Write About the Text Have students add their ideas to the Build Knowledge pages of their reader's notebooks.

Differentiate and Collaborate

Be inspired Have students think about "The Fox and the Snail" and other selections they have read. Ask: *What do the texts inspire you to do?* Use the following activities or have pairs of students think of a way to respond to the texts.

Write a Folktale Think of a story you like to tell, and turn it into a folktale. Include a character who makes a plan to accomplish a task. Illustrate your story and read it aloud to family or friends.

Design a Quest Work with a group to design a scavenger "quest" through your school. Come up with and hide clues that lead from one place to the next. Then challenge classmates to complete the quest. Award a prize to whomever finishes first.

Readers to Writers

Dialogue Remind students that dialogue is the words in quotation marks that characters speak. Authors use dialogue to help readers understand the characters and their relationships. Have students reread the dialogue in paragraphs 2–6 on page O1. Ask: *What do you learn about each character through dialogue? What do you learn about how the characters feel about each other?*

LEVEL UP

IF students read the **On Level** fluently and answered the questions,

THEN pair them with students who have proficiently read the **Beyond Level**. Have them

- partner read the **Beyond Level** passage.
- summarize what the snail did to accomplish his goal.

●On Level

Vocabulary/Comprehension

REVIEW ACADEMIC VOCABULARY

OBJECTIVES

Acquire and use accurately grade-appropriate general academic and domain-specific words and phrases, including those that signal contrast, addition, and other logical relationships (e.g., *however, although, nevertheless, similarly, moreover, in addition*).

I Do Use the **Visual Vocabulary Cards** to review key selection words *assuring, detected, emerging, gratitude, previous,* and *pursuit.* Point to each word, read it aloud, and have students chorally repeat it.

We Do Ask these questions and help students respond and explain their answers.
- What are some *assuring* words you can say to a worried friend?
- What might happen if a virus is *detected* on a computer?
- Is something that is *emerging* beginning or ending?

You Do Have students work in pairs to respond to these questions and explain their answers.
- What is a way that someone can show *gratitude?*
- What is the fourth word on the *previous* page in this book?
- When have you participated in a *pursuit?*

PERSONIFICATION

OBJECTIVES

Demonstrate understanding of figurative language, word relationships, and nuances in word meanings.

Interpret figurative language, including similes and metaphors, in context.

I Do Display the last paragraph of "The Fox and the Snail" in the online On Level **Differentiated Genre Passage** page O1. Point out the words *smiled slyly.*

Think Aloud I know that *smiled slyly* is an action that people usually perform. In this story, though, the fox is performing this action.

Explain how this action helps you picture the fox as he is boasting to the snail. This action helps you understand his dishonest character.

We Do Point to the word *astonished* in paragraph 2 on page O2. Discuss how the word personifies the fox and how it helps you picture what is happening in this part of the story.

You Do Have students explain the personification in the words *slipped* (page O2, paragraph 3) and *squeezed* (page O2, paragraph 3). Have students repeat the activity by finding examples of personification in their reader's notebook.

REVIEW THEME

OBJECTIVES

Determine a theme of a story, drama, or poem from details in the text, including how characters in a story or drama respond to challenges or how the speaker in a poem reflects upon a topic; summarize the text.

I Do Remind students that the theme is the big idea, or message about life, that the author wants to share with readers. The theme is not usually stated directly. Readers can identify the theme by thinking about what the characters think, say, and do and their perspective, or attitude.

We Do Have volunteers read the first page of "The Fox and the Snail" in the online On Level **Differentiated Genre Passage**. Have students orally list characters and their words and actions. Then model how to fill in a copy of online Theme **Graphic Organizer 5** and determine the results of the characters' words, actions, and perspective, and what these suggest about the theme.

You Do Have partners identify the snail's actions and words in the rest of the passage. Have them determine the snail's perspective. Then ask them to use this information to determine the theme of the story.

SELF-SELECTED READING

OBJECTIVES

Determine a theme of a story, drama, or poem from details in the text, including how characters in a story or drama respond to challenges or how the speaker in a poem reflects upon a topic; summarize the text.

By the end of the year, read and comprehend literature, including stories, dramas, and poetry, at the high end of the grades 4-5 text complexity band independently and proficiently.

Make, confirm, and revise predictions based on details in the text.

Independent Reading

Have students choose a folktale for independent reading. Students can read a **Classroom Library** book or check the online **Leveled Reader Library** or **Unit Bibliography** for selections. Guide students to transfer what they have learned in this text set as they read. Remind them that

- what a character thinks, says, and does often reveals his or her perspective.
- stories often contain stated or implied themes, or messages.
- a story's setting contributes to the plot.

Before they read, have students preview the text, looking at illustrations and making predictions. Remind them to reread difficult sections as they read.

Students can choose activities from the Reading **Center Activity Cards** to help them apply skills to the text as they read. After they finish, they can choose a Book Talk activity to talk about the texts they read.

 You may want to include **ELL** students in On Level vocabulary and comprehension lessons. Offer language support as needed.

Clever Manka
Lexile 860L

OBJECTIVES

Determine a theme of a story, drama, or poem from details in the text, including how characters in a story or drama respond to challenges or how the speaker in a poem reflects upon a topic; summarize the text.

Read grade-level text with purpose and understanding.

Read grade-level prose and poetry orally with accuracy, appropriate rate, expression, and automaticity on successive readings.

Cite evidence to explain and justify reasoning.

ELA ACADEMIC LANGUAGE

• *folktale, theme, make predictions, foreshadowing, personification, paraphrase*
• Cognates: *tema, predicciones*

●Beyond Level

Leveled Reader: *Clever Manka*

Preview and Predict

Have students read the Essential Question: *When has a plan helped you accomplish a task?*

Then have them preview the title, illustrations, and opening pages of *Clever Manka* and make a prediction about what might happen in the folktale. Tell students to confirm or revise their predictions as they read on.

Review Genre: Folktale

Tell students that this selection is a folktale. In a folktale, the hero or heroine often has a problem or challenge that he or she must solve. The setting of a folktale often takes place long ago in a land that is specific to the people who created the story. A folktale also often includes foreshadowing, imagery, and repetition. Have students identify genre characteristics as they read.

Close Reading

Note Taking Ask students to use a copy of online Theme **Graphic Organizer 5** as they read.

Pages 2–5 *Which adjectives describe Manka on page 3?* (clever, honest, and determined) *Turn to a partner and discuss how her actions show these characteristics.* (She wants her father to see the mayor to make sure that he is not cheated by the farmer. She also plans to solve the mayor's riddle.)

Pages 6–10 *Read the last sentence on page 10. What literary element is this an example of?* (foreshadowing) *What does this sentence suggest about the next part of the story?* (They will not always be happy.)

Pages 11–13 *Read the following sentence on page 13:* "He felt sorrow put cold hands upon his heart." *Why is this an example of personification?* (Sorrow, which is a feeling, is given human characteristics.) *Share a prediction about what Manka might do after her husband tells her to return to her father's house.* (She will devise another clever plan to win his love again.)

Pages 14–15 *Was your prediction correct? Explain.* (Yes. Manka devises a clever plan to win back her husband's love.) *Paraphrase the ending of the story and explain what the story's theme, or message, might be.* (Manka's husband tells her to take what she holds most dear to her father's house. She gives her husband a sleeping potion and takes him to her father's house as he sleeps. When he wakes up, he realizes how lucky he is to have such a clever wife. A message might be that you can solve many problems if you have a good plan.) *Generate a question of your own about what you have just read and share it with a partner. Try to find the answer by rereading the text.*

Respond to Reading Revisit the Essential Question and ask students to complete the Text Evidence questions on page 16 after they have finished reading.

 Write About Reading Check that students have explained how Manka's plan helped her win her husband back. They should incorporate the story's theme into their writing.

Fluency: Expression and Phrasing

Model Model reading page 6 with expression and appropriate phrasing. Next read the passage aloud and have students read along with you.

Apply Have students practice reading the passage with a partner.

Paired Read: "From Bee to You"

 Make Connections: Write About It

Before reading, ask students to note that the genre of this selection is expository text. Then discuss the Essential Question. After reading, ask students to make connections between *Clever Manka* and "From Bee to You." Have students use text evidence to compare how a plan can accomplish a task in a folktale and in an expository text.

Leveled Reader

Build Knowledge

Talk About the Text Have partners discuss how following a plan can help people accomplish a task.

Write About the Text Have students add their ideas to the Build Knowledge pages of their reader's notebooks.

FOCUS ON GENRE

Have students complete the activity on page 20 to create a new challenge for Manka.

LITERATURE CIRCLES

Ask students to conduct a literature circle using the Thinkmark questions to guide the discussion. You may wish to have a whole-class discussion, using both selections in the Leveled Reader, about how having a plan can help individuals accomplish tasks.

⭐ **GIFTED AND TALENTED**

Synthesize Think about all the characters you have read about this week and the different plans they devise in order to accomplish a task. *What traits do these characters have in common? Which characters are most similar to Manka and her clever plans?* Draw a Venn diagram that compares and contrasts Manka with another character from this week's reading selections.

"The Fox and the Snail"
Lexile 840L

OBJECTIVES

Quote accurately from a text when explaining what the text says explicitly and when drawing inferences from the text.

Explain different characters' perspectives in a literary text.

Determine a theme of a story, drama, or poem from details in the text, including how characters in a story or drama respond to challenges or how the speaker in a poem reflects upon a topic; summarize the text.

Compare and contrast two or more characters, settings, or events in a story or drama, drawing on specific details in the text (e.g., how characters interact).

Compare and contrast stories in the same genre (e.g., mysteries and adventure stories) on their approaches to similar themes and topics.

Demonstrate understanding of figurative language, word relationships, and nuances in word meanings.

ELA ACADEMIC LANGUAGE

• *theme, personification, setting, folktale*
• Cognates: *tema, personificación*

●Beyond Level

Genre Passage: "The Fox and the Snail"

Build Background

Ask students to read the Essential Question: *When has a plan helped you accomplish a task?* Ask students to compare how characters from two folktales they have read in this text set were able to develop a plan to achieve a goal. Use the following sentence starters to help focus discussion:

> *The character's plan succeeded because . . .*
>
> *This helps me understand that a successful plan . . .*

Read aloud the text under the title of the online **Differentiated Genre Passage** "The Fox and the Snail." Explain that *adapted* means that the story students will read was first told by people in France, and that parts of the story may have changed as more people told it over the years. Discuss why it might change over time as different people tell it.

Review Genre: Folktale

Remind students that a folktale is a story common to a specific culture and is passed down through the years. A folktale's setting can reflect the time period or culture of the place where it was first told. The main character must solve a challenge. Folktales often include personification, imagery, and foreshadowing.

Close Reading

Note Taking As students read the passage the first time, ask them to annotate the text. Have them note key ideas and details, unfamiliar words, and questions they have. Then read again and use the following questions. Encourage students to cite text evidence from the selection.

Read

Plot: Setting Read the first paragraph on page B1. *When and where is the folktale set?* (long, long ago in the far-off land of Touleroo)

Genre: Folktale Read paragraphs 2–8. *What details indicate the story is a folktale?* (The snail is the hero. He must outsmart the dishonest fox. They can talk even though they are animals.)

Personification Read paragraphs 9–13. *What human qualities of the fox do these paragraphs reveal?* (The fox is sly and dishonest. He thinks he can give the king someone else's idea and win the reward for himself.)

Personification Read paragraphs 1–3 on page B2. *How does personification help you understand the snail?* (It helps me understand that the snail is very clever. He tricks the fox into taking him to the king.)

Theme Read the last four paragraphs. *What themes do these paragraphs reveal?* (Possible answers: Honesty is important; honesty brings its own reward.) *What evidence supports these themes?* (The snail told the truth, and he is rewarded for his honesty.)

 Summarize Have students use their notes to summarize how the snail outwits the fox and what happens once they reach the king.

Reread

Use the questions on page B3 to guide students' rereading of the passage.

Author's Craft Reread the first paragraph on page B1. *How does the author create suspense?* (by saying the fox is hurrying along a seaside road; The word "hurrying" makes me wonder why he is going fast. I also wonder where he needs to go so quickly.)

Author's Craft Reread the last paragraph on page B1 and the first paragraph on page B2. *How does the author use foreshadowing?* (The author writes that the snail smiles at what the fox says and makes a wager that he will get to the king first. Then the snail hides in the fox's tail. I predict that the snail will go as fast as the fox and will see the king first.)

Author's Craft Reread the third paragraph on page B2. *Why do you think the author used the word "slipped" instead of "went" to describe the snail's action?* (The author uses the word "slipped" to show that the snail is being careful so that the fox won't see him. The word "went" does not convey how carefully the snail moves from the fox's tail.)

Integrate

 Make Connections Have partners explore connections between "The Fox and the Snail" and other folktales they've read. They should gather text evidence to answer this question: *What makes each character's plan successful?*

Compare Texts Have pairs create a three-column chart labeled *Character, Plan,* and *Reason for Success,* and compare reasons why the characters' plans succeeded.

Build Knowledge

Talk About the Text Have partners discuss how following a plan can help people accomplish a task.

Write About the Text Have students add their ideas to the Build Knowledge pages of their reader's notebooks.

Differentiate and Collaborate

 **Be inspired** Have students think about "The Fox and the Snail" and other selections they have read. Ask: *What do the texts inspire you to do?* Use the following activities or have pairs of students think of a way to respond to the texts.

Write a Folktale Think of a story you like to tell, and turn it into a folktale. Include a character who makes a plan to accomplish a challenging task. Illustrate your story and read it aloud to family or friends.

Design a Quest Work with a group to design a scavenger "quest" through your school. Come up with and hide clues that lead from one place to the next. Then challenge classmates to complete the quest. Award a prize to whomever finishes first.

Readers to Writers

Dialogue Remind students that dialogue is the words in quotation marks that characters speak. Authors use dialogue to help readers get to know the characters and better understand their relationships. Have students reread the dialogue in paragraphs 2–7 on page B1. Ask: *What do you learn about each character through dialogue? What do you learn about the characters' perspectives?*

⭐ **GIFTED AND TALENTED**

Independent Study Have students synthesize their notes and the selections they read to create a planning checklist. Students' checklists should include step-by-step tips and instructions that can be used by someone who is crafting a plan to accomplish a goal or task. Encourage students to add photographs or illustrations. Have pairs exchange checklists and provide feedback.

●Beyond Level

Vocabulary/Comprehension

REVIEW DOMAIN-SPECIFIC WORDS

OBJECTIVES

Acquire and use accurately grade-appropriate general academic and domain-specific words and phrases, including those that signal contrast, addition, and other logical relationships (e.g., *however, although, nevertheless, similarly, moreover, in addition*).

Model Use the **Visual Vocabulary Cards** to review the meanings of the words *outcome* and *guidance*. Write science-related sentences on the board using the words.

Write the words *humble* and *judgment* on the board and discuss the meanings. Then help students write sentences using these words.

Apply Have partners review the meanings of the words *emerging* and *detected*. Then have them write sentences using the words.

PERSONIFICATION

OBJECTIVES

Demonstrate understanding of figurative language, word relationships, and nuances in word meanings.

Interpret figurative language, including similes and metaphors, in context.

Model Read aloud the second to last paragraph of "The Fox and the Snail" in the online Beyond Level **Differentiated Genre Passage** page B1. Point out the words *smiled slyly*.

Think Aloud I know that *smiled slyly* is an action that people usually perform. In this story, though, the fox is performing the action, so it is an example of personification. The words help me better picture the fox as he is boasting to the snail. This action helps me understand his dishonest character.

With students, read paragraph 1 on page B2. Help them explain how *astonished* is an example of personification.

Apply Have pairs of students read the rest of the passage. Ask them to explain how personification works in the words *slipped* (page B2, paragraph 4) and *squeezed* (page B2, paragraph 4).

★GIFTED and TALENTED **Synthesize** Have students perform research to learn about a famous plan in history that helped accomplish a task. Challenge students to write a two-to-three paragraph explanation of what they learned using words from their reader's notebook and present their findings to the class.

REVIEW THEME

OBJECTIVES

Determine a theme of a story, drama, or poem from details in the text, including how characters in a story or drama respond to challenges or how the speaker in a poem reflects upon a topic; summarize the text.

Model Remind students that the theme is the big idea or message about life that the author wants to share with readers. The theme is not usually stated directly. Readers can identify the theme by thinking about what the characters think, say, and do, and their perspective, and asking themselves what the author's message is.

Have students read the first page of "The Fox and the Snail" in the online Beyond Level **Differentiated Genre Passage** page B2. Ask open-ended questions to facilitate discussion, such as: *What do the characters think, say, and do on this page? What is the character's perspective? What possible theme can you infer?* Students should support their responses with details from the text.

Apply Have students read the rest of the passage as they independently fill in a copy of online Theme **Graphic Organizer 5**. Then have partners use their work to determine the theme of the passage.

SELF-SELECTED READING

OBJECTIVES

Determine a theme of a story, drama, or poem from details in the text, including how characters in a story or drama respond to challenges or how the speaker in a poem reflects upon a topic; summarize the text.

By the end of the year, read and comprehend literature, including stories, dramas, and poetry, at the high end of the grades 4-5 text complexity band independently and proficiently.

Make, confirm, and revise predictions based on details in the text.

Independent Reading

Have students choose a folktale for independent reading. Students can read a **Classroom Library** book or check the online **Leveled Reader Library** or **Unit Bibliography** for selections. Guide students to transfer what they have learned in this text set as they read by analyzing how the setting contributes to the plot, explaining the development of the theme, and describing how an author develops a character's perspective.

Students can choose activities from the Reading **Center Activity Cards** to help them apply skills to the text as they read. After they finish, they can choose a Book Talk activity to talk about the texts they read.

 Independent Study Challenge students to discuss how their books relate to the weekly theme of a plan of action. Have students compare the different ways characters formulate a plan and put it into action. *How do these plans help the characters with their tasks? Which plan do you feel was the most effective and why?*

Student Outcomes

✓ Tested in *Wonders* Assessments

FOUNDATIONAL SKILLS

Phonics and Word Analysis
- Decode words with closed syllables

Fluency
- Read grade-level texts with accuracy, appropriate rate, expression, and automaticity

READING

Reading Literature
✓ Identify the structure of narrative and free verse poetry
✓ Explain the development of stated or implied theme(s) throughout a literary text
✓ Explain how poetic elements such as form and line breaks work together in a poem
- Read and comprehend texts in the grades 4–5 text complexity band
- Summarize a text to enhance comprehension
- Write in response to text

Compare Texts
- Compare and contrast how authors present information on the same topic or theme

COMMUNICATION

Writing

Write to Sources
✓ Write expository texts about a topic using multiple sources and including an organizational structure, relevant elaboration, and varied transitions
- With guidance and support from peers and adults, develop and strengthen writing as needed by planning, revising, and editing.

Speaking and Listening
- Report on a topic or text or present an opinion, sequencing ideas; speak clearly at an understandable pace

Conventions

Grammar
✓ Identify prepositional phrases
✓ Punctuate titles and letters correctly

Spelling
- Spell words with closed syllables

Researching
- Conduct research projects that build knowledge through investigation of different aspects of the topic

Creating and Collaborating
- Add audio recordings and visual displays to presentations when appropriate
- With some guidance and support from adults, use technology to produce and publish writing

VOCABULARY

Academic Vocabulary
- Acquire and use grade-appropriate academic vocabulary

Vocabulary Strategy
✓ Use context clues to determine the meaning of multiple-meaning and unknown words and phrases, including homographs

CONTENT AREA LEARNING

Civic and Political Participation
- Use primary and secondary sources to identify the contributions of prominent individuals or groups who contributed to a state's history. **Social Studies**

ELL Scaffolded supports for English Language Learners are embedded throughout the lessons, enabling students to communicate information, ideas, and concepts in English Language Arts and for social and instructional purposes within the school setting.

See the **ELL Small Group Guide** for additional support of the skills for the text set.

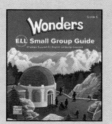

FORMATIVE ASSESSMENT

For assessment throughout the text set, use students' self-assessments and your observations.

Use the Data Dashboard to filter class, group, or individual student data to guide group placement decisions. It provides recommendations to enhance learning for gifted and talented students and offers extra support for students needing remediation.

DATA DASHBOARD

Develop Student Ownership

To build student ownership, students need to know what they are learning and why they are learning it, and to determine how well they understood it.

Students Discuss Their Goals

TEXT SET GOALS

- I can read and understand poetry.
- I can use text evidence to respond to poetry.
- I know what motivates people to accomplish a goal.

Have students think about what they know and fill in the bars on **Reading/Writing Companion** page 176.

EXTENDED WRITING GOALS

Extended Writing 2:
- I can write an expository essay.
- I can synthesize information from three sources.

Have students think about what they know and fill in the bars on Reading/Writing Companion page 198.

Students Monitor Their Learning

LEARNING GOALS

Specific learning goals identified in every lesson make clear what students will be learning and why. These smaller goals provide stepping stones to help students reach their Text Set and Extended Writing Goals.

CHECK-IN ROUTINE

The Check-In Routine at the close of each lesson guides students to self-reflect on how well they understood each learning goal.

Review the lesson learning goal.
Reflect on the activity.
Self-Assess by
- filling in the bars in the Reading/Writing Companion
- holding up 1, 2, 3, or 4 fingers

Share with your teacher.

Students Reflect on Their Progress

TEXT SET GOALS

After completing the Show Your Knowledge task for the text set, students reflect on their understanding of the Text Set Goals by filling in the bars on Reading/Writing Companion page 177.

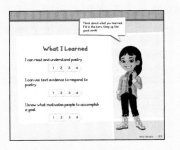

EXTENDED WRITING GOALS

After completing both extended writing projects for the unit, students reflect on their understanding of the Extended Writing Goals by filling in the bars on Reading/Writing Companion page 199.

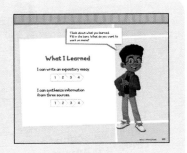

Build Knowledge

Shared Read
Reading/Writing Companion p. 178

Anchor Text
Literature Anthology p. 138

Paired Selection
Literature Anthology p. 142

Essential Question
What motivates you to accomplish a goal?

 Video Different things, such as winning a race or performing on stage, motivate people to accomplish their goals.

Study Sync Blast Boyan Slat is attempting a cleanup of the Great Pacific Garbage Patch that will remove plastic from the ocean without harming marine life.

Interactive Read Aloud A boy is motivated to make friends, so he asks his brother for advice about how to make friends.

Shared Read In "A Simple Plan," Jack makes little changes to the world by helping others with their chores and inspires his brother to be better. In "Rescue," the narrator witnesses an oil spill and neighbors rushing to help.

Anchor Text In "Stage Fright," the speaker overcomes his fear of performing in front of a large crowd. In "Catching Quiet," the speaker accomplishes a goal of appreciating the small periods of quiet that occasionally appear in city life.

Paired Selection A basketball player accomplishes his goal of helping his team as the crowds cheer him on.

 Make Connections Soccer demonstrates how a crowd can motivate players.

Differentiated Sources

Leveled Readers

Clearing the Jungle The need to be organized in order to accomplish and address responsibilities motivates Joe to become organized.

I Want to Ride! Ariela learns that accomplishing a dream takes planning and responsibility.

Changing Goals Although Maggie can't participate in the basketball games, she helps in another way.

Differentiated Genre Passages

In "Blue Ribbon Dreams," a girl practices riding her horse for a State Fair competition. In "Sammy's Day Out," a wolf cub sneaks snacks from the refrigerator.

Build Knowledge Routine

After reading each text, ask students to document what facts and details they learned to help answer the Essential Question of the text set.

 Talk About the source.

 Write About the source.

 Add to the Class Anchor Chart.

- Add to your Vocabulary List.

Show Your Knowledge

Write a Poem

Have students show how they built knowledge across the text set by writing a poem. They should begin by thinking about the Essential Question: *What motivates you to accomplish a goal?* Students will write a free verse poem about what motivates people to accomplish a goal.

Social Emotional Learning

Creativity

Anchor Text: Help students understand how to express creative thinking. Discuss the range of emotions of the young boy in the first poem and how it connects to retelling his entire experience.

Paired Selection: Being able to make connections is an important aspect of creativity. Ask students to tell of a time when they have been in a similar position as the boy shooting a foul shot and what happened.

Roundtable Discussion: One of the lines in "Stage Fright" by Lee Bennett Hopkins is "...my mind simply snapped..." Ask: *How does it relate to the line "You have to be quick." in "Catching Quiet" by Marci Ridlon? In what ways were Lee and Marci creative as they crafted their poems?*

Explore the Texts

TEXT SET 3

Essential Question: What motivates you to accomplish a goal?

Access Complex Text (ACT) boxes throughout the text set provide scaffolded instruction for seven different elements that may make a text complex.

ACT

Teacher's Edition	Reading/Writing Companion	Literature Anthology	

"How to Make a Friend" Interactive Read Aloud p. T169 Poetry	**"A Simple Plan," "Rescue"** Shared Read pp. 178–181 Poetry	**"Stage Fright," "Catching Quiet"** Anchor Text pp. 138–141 Poetry	**"Foul Shot"** Paired Selection pp. 142–143 Poetry

Qualitative

Meaning/Purpose Moderate Complexity	**Meaning/Purpose** Moderate Complexity	**Meaning/Purpose** High Complexity	**Meaning/Purpose** High Complexity
Structure Moderate Complexity	**Structure** Moderate Complexity	**Structure** High Complexity	**Structure** High Complexity
Language Low Complexity	**Language** High Complexity	**Language** High Complexity	**Language** High Complexity
Knowledge Demands Moderate Complexity	**Knowledge Demands** Low Complexity	**Knowledge Demands** Moderate Complexity	**Knowledge Demands** Moderate Complexity

Quantitative

Lexile NP	**Lexile** NP	**Lexile** NP	**Lexile** NP

Reader and Task Considerations

Reader Students should not need much background knowledge to understand the poem.	**Reader** Students should not need much background knowledge. Support includes explaining causes and effects of oil spills on wildlife and the environment.	**Reader** Students should not need much background knowledge to understand the poems. Some explanation about stage fright may be beneficial.	**Reader** Students should not need much background knowledge to understand the poem. Some explanation about basketball may be beneficial.

Task The questions for the read aloud are supported by teacher modeling. The tasks provide a variety of ways for students to begin to build knowledge and vocabulary about the text set topic. The questions and tasks provided for the other texts are at various levels of complexity, ensuring that all students can interact with the text in meaningful ways.

Additional Texts

Content Area Reading BLMs

Additional online texts related to grade-level Science, Social Studies, and Arts content

Leveled Readers

(A) *Clearing the Jungle*

(O) *I Want to Ride!*

(B) *Changing Goals*

(ELL) *I Want to Ride!*

Qualitative

(A) Clearing the Jungle

Meaning/Purpose Moderate Complexity
Structure Low Complexity
Language Low Complexity
Knowledge Demands Moderate Complexity

(O) I Want to Ride!

Meaning/Purpose Moderate Complexity
Structure Low Complexity
Language Moderate Complexity
Knowledge Demands Moderate Complexity

(B) Changing Goals

Meaning/Purpose High Complexity
Structure Low Complexity
Language High Complexity
Knowledge Demands High Complexity

(ELL) I Want to Ride!

Meaning/Purpose Moderate Complexity
Structure Low Complexity
Language Low Complexity
Knowledge Demands Moderate Complexity

Quantitative

Lexile 650L

Lexile 730L

Lexile 860L

Lexile 600L

Reader and Task Considerations

Reader Students will not need background knowledge to understand the story.

Reader Students will not need background knowledge to understand the story.

Reader Students will not need background knowledge to understand the story.

Reader Students will not need background knowledge to understand the story.

Task The questions and tasks provided for the Leveled Readers are at various levels of complexity, ensuring that all students can interact with the text in meaningful ways.

Differentiated Genre Passages

(A) "Blue Ribbon Dreams," "Sammy's Day Out"

(O) "Blue Ribbon Dreams," "Sammy's Day Out"

(B) "Blue Ribbon Dreams," "Sammy's Day Out"

(ELL) "Blue Ribbon Dreams," "Sammy's Day Out"

Qualitative

Meaning/Purpose Moderate Complexity
Structure Moderate Complexity
Language Low Complexity
Knowledge Demands Moderate Complexity

Meaning/Purpose Moderate Complexity
Structure Moderate Complexity
Language Low Complexity
Knowledge Demands Moderate Complexity

Meaning/Purpose Moderate Complexity
Structure Moderate Complexity
Language Low Complexity
Knowledge Demands Moderate Complexity

Meaning/Purpose Moderate Complexity
Structure Moderate Complexity
Language Low Complexity
Knowledge Demands Moderate Complexity

Quantitative

Lexile NP

Lexile NP

Lexile NP

Lexile NP

Reader and Task Considerations

Reader Students may need some background knowledge about county fairs.

Reader Students may need some background knowledge about county fairs.

Reader Students may need some background knowledge about county fairs.

Reader Students may need some background knowledge about county fairs.

Task The questions and tasks provided for the Differentiated Genre Passages are at various levels of complexity, ensuring that all students can interact with the text in meaningful ways.

TEXT SET 3

Week 5 Planner

Customize your own lesson plans at
my.mheducation.com

 LESSON 1   **LESSON 2**

 60+ mins Reading
Suggested Daily Time

Reading

LESSON 1	LESSON 2
Introduce the Concept, T166–T167 Build Knowledge	**Shared Read, T170–T173** Reread "A Simple Plan," "Rescue"
Listening Comprehension, T168–T169 "How to Make a Friend"	**Minilessons, T176–T183** Poetic Elements: Repetition and Rhyme Poetry: Narrative and Free Verse Theme 〉 Craft and Structure
Shared Read, T170–T173 Read "A Simple Plan," "Rescue" Quick Write: Make Connections	〉 **Respond to Reading, T184–T185**
Vocabulary, T174–T175 Academic Vocabulary Homographs	〉 **Phonics, T186–T187** Closed Syllables
Expand Vocabulary, T202	**Fluency, T186** Expression and Phrasing
	〉 **Research and Inquiry, T188–T189**
	Expand Vocabulary, T202

READING LESSON GOALS

- **I can read and understand poetry.**
- **I can use text evidence to respond to poetry.**
- **I know what motivates people to accomplish a goal.**

〉 **SMALL GROUP OPTIONS**
The designated lessons can be taught in small groups. To determine how to differentiate instruction for small groups, use Formative Assessment and Data Dashboard.

Writing

Extended Writing 2: Expository Essay	**Extended Writing 2, T248–T249** Analyze the Rubric

 30+ mins Writing
Suggested Daily Time

WRITING LESSON GOALS

I can write an expository essay.

〉 **Writing Lesson Bank: Craft Minilessons, T266–T269**	
Teacher and Peer Conferences	
〉 **Grammar Lesson Bank, T278** Prepositional Phrases Talk About It	〉 **Grammar Lesson Bank, T278** Prepositional Phrases Talk About It
〉 **Spelling Lesson Bank, T288** Closed Syllables	〉 **Spelling Lesson Bank, T288** Closed Syllables

---

Teacher-Led Instruction

Differentiated Reading
Leveled Readers
- ● *Clearing the Jungle*, T204–T205
- ● *I Want to Ride!*, T214–T215
- ● *Changing Goals*, T220–T221

Differentiated Genre Passages
- ● "Blue Ribbon Dreams,"... T206–T207
- ● "Blue Ribbon Dreams,"... T216–T217
- ● "Blue Ribbon Dreams,"... T222–T223

Differentiated Skills Practice
- ● **Approaching Level**
Phonics/Decoding, T208–T209
  - Decode and Build Words with Closed Syllables
  - Practice Words with Closed Syllables
Vocabulary, T210–T211
  - Review High-Frequency Words

Review Academic Vocabulary
- Answer Yes/No Questions
- Homographs
Fluency, T212
- Expression and Phrasing
Comprehension, T212–T213
- Identify and Review Theme
- Self-Selected Reading

 SMALL GROUP

Independent/Collaborative Work   See pages T165E–T165F.

Reading
Comprehension
- Narrative Poetry
- Theme
- Poetic Elements: Repetition and Rhyme
Fluency
Independent Reading

Phonics/Word Study
Phonics/Decoding
- Closed Syllables
Vocabulary
- Homographs

Writing
Extended Writing 2: Expository Essay
Self-Selected Writing
Grammar
- Prepositional Phrases
Spelling
- Closed Syllables
Handwriting

ACADEMIC VOCABULARY
ambitious, memorized, satisfaction, shuddered, free verse, narrative, repetition, rhyme

SPELLING
dentist, jogger, fifteen, flatter, submit, mustang, absent, hollow, empire, blizzard, culture, goggles, summon, excite, kennel, valley, fragment, gallop, vulture, pigment

Review *won't, shouldn't, we're*
Challenge *clammy, hammock*
See pages T288–T289 for Differentiated Spelling Lists.

LESSON 3

LESSON 4

LESSON 5

Reading

Anchor Text, T190–T193 Read and Reread "Stage Fright," "Catching Quiet" Take Notes About Text ▶ **Respond to Reading, T194–T195** **Expand Vocabulary, T203**	**Paired Selection, T196–T197** Read and Reread "Foul Shot" **Author's Craft, T198–T199** Poetic Elements: Form and Line Breaks **Expand Vocabulary, T203**	**Make Connections, T200** **Show Your Knowledge, T201** **Progress Monitoring, T165G–T165H** **Expand Vocabulary, T203**

Writing

Extended Writing 2, T250–T251 Academic Vocabulary	**Extended Writing 2, T252–T253** Analyze the Student Model	**Extended Writing 2, T254–T255** Analyze the Student Model

▶ **Writing Lesson Bank: Craft Minilessons, T266–T269**

Teacher and Peer Conferences

▶ **Grammar Lesson Bank, T279** Prepositional Phrases Talk About It	▶ **Grammar Lesson Bank, T279** Prepositional Phrases Talk About It	▶ **Grammar Lesson Bank, T279** Prepositional Phrases Talk About It
▶ **Spelling Lesson Bank, T289** Closed Syllables	▶ **Spelling Lesson Bank, T289** Closed Syllables	**Spelling Lesson Bank, T289** Closed Syllables

● **On Level**
Vocabulary, T218
• Review Vocabulary Words
• Homographs
Comprehension, T219
• Review Theme
• Self-Selected Reading

● **Beyond Level**
Vocabulary, T224
• Review Domain-Specific Words
• Homographs 🌟**GIFTED and TALENTED**
Comprehension, T225
• Review Theme
• Self-Selected Reading 🌟**GIFTED and TALENTED**

● **English Language Learners**
See ELL Small Group Guide, pp. 72–83

Content Area Connections
Content Area Reading
• Science, Social Studies, and the Arts
Research and Inquiry
• Achieving Goals
Inquiry Space
• Options for Project-Based Learning

● **English Language Learners**
See ELL Small Group Guide, pp. 72–83

TEXT SET 3

Independent and Collaborative Work

As you meet with small groups, the rest of the class completes activities and projects that allow them to practice and apply the skills they have been working on.

Student Choice and Student Voice

- Print the My Independent Work blackline master and review it with students. Identify the "Must Do" activities.
- Have students choose additional activities that provide the practice they need.
- Remind students to reflect on their learning each day.

My Independent Work BLM

Reading

Independent Reading Texts

Students can choose a Center Activity Card to use while they read independently.

Classroom Library
Mufaro's Beautiful Daughters
Genre: Folktale
Lexile: 790L

Where the Mountain Meets the Moon
Genre: Fairy Tale
Lexile: 810L

Unit Bibliography
Have students self-select independent reading texts about people setting goals for themselves.

Leveled Texts Online
- Additional Leveled Readers in the **Leveled Reader Library Online** allow for flexibility.
- Six leveled sets of **Differentiated Genre Passages** in diverse genres are available.
- **Differentiated Texts** offer ELL students more passages at different proficiency levels.

Additional Literature
Differentiated Genre Passages
Genres: Personal Narrative, Social Studies Article, Fable, Myth, Legend, Tall Tale

Center Activity Cards

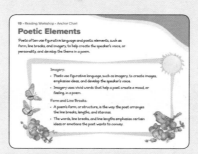

Poetic Elements Card 19

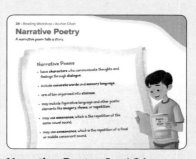

Narrative Poetry Card 34

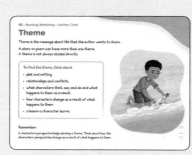

Theme Card 15

Free Verse Poetry Card 35

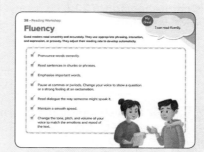

Fluency Card 38

Digital Activities

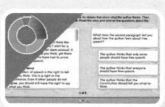

Comprehension

Phonics/Word Study

Center Activity Cards

Open and Closed Syllables Card 101

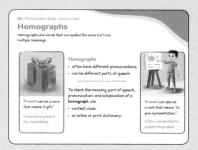

Homographs Card 69

Practice Book BLMs

Phonics: pages 115–115B, 118

Vocabulary: pages 119–120

Digital Activities

Phonics

Vocabulary

Writing

Center Activity Cards

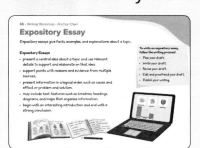

Expository Essay Card 45

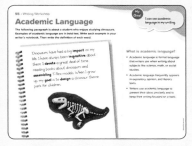

Academic Language Card 55

Self-Selected Writing

Share the following prompts.
- Describe a time where you overcame a fear. How did you do it?
- What are some things that motivate you to achieve a goal?
- Write about a person who overcame a challenge.
- Write about a goal that you have. Why do you want to accomplish this goal?
- Think about a time when you worked hard to complete a difficult task. How did completing this task make you feel?

Extended Writing

Have students continue developing their **expository essays**.

Practice Book BLMs

Grammar: pages 109–113
Spelling: pages 114–118
Handwriting: pages 361–396

Digital Activities

Grammar

Spelling

Content Area Connections

Content Area Reading Blackline Masters
- Additional texts related to Science, Social Studies, and the Arts

Research and Inquiry
- Achieving Goals

Inquiry Space
- Choose an activity

Progress Monitoring
Moving Toward Mastery

FORMATIVE ASSESSMENT

→ STUDENT CHECK-IN

✓ CHECK FOR SUCCESS

For ongoing formative assessment, use students' self-assessments at the end of each lesson along with your own observations.

Assessing skills along the way . . .

SKILLS	HOW ASSESSED	
Comprehension **Vocabulary**	Digital Activities, Rubrics	
Text-Based Writing	Reading/Writing Companion: Respond to Reading	
Grammar, Mechanics, Phonics, Spelling	Practice Book, Digital Activities including word sorts	
Listening/Presenting/Research	Checklists	
Oral Reading Fluency (ORF) Fluency Goal: 111–131 words correct per minute (WCPM) Accuracy Rate Goal: 95% or higher	Fluency Assessment	

At the end of the text set . . .

SKILLS	HOW ASSESSED	
Poetic Elements: Repetition and Rhyme **Theme** **Poetic Elements: Form and Line Breaks**	Progress Monitoring	
Homographs		

Making the Most of Assessment Results

Make data-based grouping decisions by using the following reports to verify assessment results. For additional student support options refer to the reteaching and enrichment opportunities.

ONLINE ASSESSMENT CENTER

- *Gradebook*

DATA DASHBOARD

- *Recommendations Report*
- *Activity Report*
- *Skills Report*
- *Progress Report*
- *Grade Card Report*

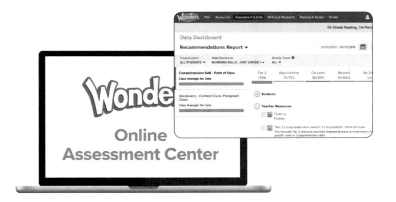

 Assign practice pages online for auto-grading.

Reteaching Opportunities with Intervention Online PDFs

IF STUDENTS SCORE . . .	THEN ASSIGN . . .
below 70% in **comprehension** . . .	lessons 117 and 118 on Rhyme and Repetition in **Comprehension PDF,** lessons 34–36 on Theme in **Comprehension PDF,** and/or lesson 122 on Stanzas and Line Breaks in **Comprehension PDF**
below 70% in **vocabulary** . . .	lesson 122 on Homographs and Homophones in **Vocabulary PDF**
102–110 WCPM in **fluency** . . .	lessons from Section 1 or 7–10 of **Fluency PDF**
0–74 WCPM in **fluency** . . .	lessons from Sections 2–6 of **Fluency PDF**

Use the **Phonics/Word Study PDF** *and* **Foundational Skills Kit** *for additional reteaching opportunities.*
Use the **Foundational Skills Kit** *for students who need support with phonemic awareness and other early literacy skills.*

GIFTED and TALENTED

Enrichment Opportunities

Beyond Level small group lessons and resources include suggestions for additional activities in these areas to extend learning opportunities for gifted and talented students:

- *Leveled Readers*
- *Genre Passages*
- *Vocabulary*

- *Comprehension*
- *Leveled Reader Library Online*
- *Center Activity Cards*

LESSON 1

OBJECTIVES

Engage effectively in a range of collaborative discussions (one-on-one, in groups, and teacher-led) with diverse partners on grade 5 topics and texts, building on others' ideas and expressing their own clearly.

Follow agreed-upon rules for discussions and carry out assigned roles.

Pose and respond to specific questions by making comments that contribute to the discussion and elaborate on the remarks of others.

ELA ACADEMIC LANGUAGE

• *goal, motivated*

• Cognate: *motivado*

DIGITAL TOOLS

Show the images during class discussion.

Discuss Concept

Watch Video

 ELL VOCABULARY

focused (*concentrado*) keeping your attention on something

ambitious (*ambicioso*) having or showing a strong wish to succeed

rehearse (*ensayar*) to practice over and over

accomplished (*realizó*) reached a goal

---

 10 mins # Build Knowledge MULTIMODAL

 ## Essential Question

What motivates you to accomplish a goal?

Read the Essential Question on page 174 of the **Reading/Writing Companion**. Tell students they will read poems and build knowledge about people who set goals for themselves and how they achieve those goals. They will use words to read, write, and talk about what motivates people to accomplish a goal.

Watch the Video Play the video without sound first. Have partners narrate what they see. Then replay the video with sound as students listen.

Talk About the Video Have partners discuss what motivates people to accomplish a goal.

Write About the Video Have students add their ideas to their Build Knowledge pages of their reader's notebooks.

Anchor Chart Begin a Build Knowledge anchor chart. Write the Essential Question at the top of the chart. Have volunteers share what they learned about what motivates people to accomplish a goal. Explain that students will add to the anchor chart after they read each text.

Build Knowledge

Discuss the photograph with students. Focus on the satisfaction that comes from working hard to achieve a goal. Ask: *What is an ambitious goal that you have had? What motivated you to accomplish it?* Have students discuss in pairs or groups.

Build Vocabulary

Model using the graphic organizer to write down new words related to achieving a goal. Have partners continue the discussion and add the graphic organizer and new words to their reader's notebooks. Students will add words to the Build Knowledge pages in their notebooks as they read about accomplishing goals throughout the text set.

 ## Collaborative Conversations

Listen Carefully As students engage in partner, small-group, and whole-class discussions, encourage them to follow discussion rules by actively listening to speakers. Remind students to

• ask relevant questions and make pertinent comments.

• always look at the person who is speaking.

• respect others by not interrupting them.

Reading/Writing Companion, pp. 174–175

Share the "Reaching a Goal" Blast assignment with students. Point out that you will discuss their responses in the Make Connections lesson at the end of this text set.

 English Language Learners

Use the following scaffolds to build knowledge and vocabulary. Teach the ELL Vocabulary, as needed.

Beginning

Have students look at the photo of the dancers. Say: *These dancers are working hard. They want to be great dancers. Is this easy or hard?* (hard) *Are they ambitious?* (yes) Help pairs state a goal they have had and talk about how it is ambitious: My goal is to _____. It is ambitious because I have to _____.

Intermediate

Use the photograph to guide students to describe the dancers: *What is their ambitious goal?* They want to be _____. *Will they feel good when they perform really well?* Yes, they will feel <u>satisfaction</u>. Help pairs state a goal they have and explain why it is ambitious: My goal is to _____. I will practice _____.

Advanced/Advanced High

Have pairs discuss these questions as you guide them to complete the graphic organizer: *Have you accomplished an ambitious goal? What was your goal? What did you have to do? How did you feel?*

ELL NEWCOMERS

To reinforce students' development of oral language and vocabulary, review **Newcomer Cards 15–24** and the accompanying materials in the **Newcomer Teacher's Guide**.

MY GOALS ROUTINE

What I Know Now

Read Goals Have students read the goals on Reading/Writing Companion page 176.

Reflect Review the key. Ask students to reflect on each goal and fill in the bars to show what they know now. Explain they will fill in the bars on page 177 at the end of the text set to show their progress.

LESSON 1

LEARNING GOALS

We can actively listen to learn about what motivates people to accomplish goals.

OBJECTIVES

Explain how a series of chapters, scenes, or stanzas fits together to provide the overall structure of a particular story, drama, or poem.

Summarize a written text read aloud or information presented in diverse media and formats, including visually, quantitatively, and orally.

Use the relationship between particular words (e.g., synonyms, antonyms, homographs) to better understand each of the words.

Listen for a purpose.

Identify characteristics of narrative poems.

ELA ACADEMIC LANGUAGE

• *narrative poem, theme, stanza, reread*

• Cognates: *poema, tema*

DIGITAL TOOLS

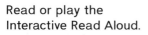

Read or play the Interactive Read Aloud.

Interactive Read Aloud

FORMATIVE ASSESSMENT

❯ STUDENT CHECK-IN

Have partners discuss how one brother accomplishes a goal in the poem. Ask them to reflect using the Check-In routine.

Interactive Read Aloud

10 mins

Connect to Concept: Making It Happen

Tell students that making something happen and working toward a goal takes determination and, sometimes, a willingness to follow advice. Explain that you will be reading aloud a narrative poem in which a boy heeds his older brother's advice about making a new friend.

Preview Poetry

Anchor Chart Explain that the text you will read aloud is poetry, specifically a narrative poem. Start a Poetry anchor chart, and ask students to add characteristics of the genre. Students should add characteristics to the chart as they read more kinds of poetry. Review the characteristics of narrative poetry, including:

• tells a story

• has characters and dialogue

• may rhyme

Ask students to think about other texts they have read aloud or they have read independently that were poetry.

Respond to Reading

Read the text aloud to students. Then reread it using the Teacher Think Alouds and Student Think Alongs on page T169 to build knowledge and model comprehension and the vocabulary strategy, Homographs.

Summarize Have students identify the characters and explain the message of "How to Make a Friend." Then have them summarize the poem in their own words to enhance their comprehension.

Build Knowledge: Make Connections

Talk About the Text Have partners discuss what sort of things might motivate someone to accomplish a goal.

Write About the Text Have students add their ideas to their Build Knowledge pages of their reader's notebooks.

Anchor Chart Record any new ideas on the Build Knowledge anchor chart.

Add to the Vocabulary List Have students write down any words they learned about motivation in their reader's notebooks.

How to Make a Friend

Two brothers were walking home from school.
The younger one asked, "Is there a rule
for making friends? We've been here a week
and I still can't get up the nerve to speak
when anyone looks at me at all.
Mostly I blend into the walls.
With other kids, though, I don't blend.
So, tell me, how do you make a friend?"

The older brother scratched his head.
"Make a friend? That sounds," he said,
"like something a mad scientist might
do in a lab on a stormy night!
Okay, I know, it's a common expression,
But it kind of leaves the wrong impression.
You don't 'make' friends out of thin air.
You find friends who are already there!" **1**

They waited for a traffic light
to change. A line of cars turned right.
A van drove past them down the street
And someone waved from the far back seat.

"In other words," explained the older
brother, "You don't need to be *bolder*—
or smarter or funnier or cooler
or measure yourself with some kind of ruler—"

They crossed the street. "You're qualified!
It's up to you to decide
which person is your friend-to-be.
So look around. He or she
is out there somewhere. Don't be rude:
Start a conversation, dude!
Pretty soon, your search will end.
And that is how you make a friend." **2**

They took a shortcut through the park
and suddenly they heard a bark—
a dog raced by, chasing a squirrel
and chasing the dog was a red-haired girl
from the younger boy's class, and in the breeze
of her running past, he seized
a moment of confidence and laughter.
"I'll help you!" he hollered, running after. **3**

---

1 **Teacher Think Aloud**
Rereading helps me monitor my comprehension. As I reread the first stanza, I see that the younger brother is struggling to make a friend. I wonder if his older brother's talk will motivate him.

Student Think Along
What does the older brother say to help motivate his younger brother? Listen as I reread the second stanza. Make an inference about how you think the younger brother might respond.

2 **Teacher Think Aloud**
I know that the word *right* is a homograph that has multiple meanings and parts of speech. When I reread the fourth stanza, I find context clues, such as "car turned," that help me see that *right* is a noun referring to direction.

Student Think Along
Listen as I reread stanza 4. Raise your hand when you hear a homograph. With a partner, find its other meanings and parts of speech in a dictionary.

3 **Teacher Think Aloud**
The events of the last stanza happen very quickly. Let's reread it to make sure we understand how the younger brother "seized the moment" to accomplish his goal of making a friend.

Student Think Along
What happens at the end of the poem? Does the younger brother take his older brother's advice? Turn and talk to a partner about what motivates the younger brother.

"A Simple Plan" and "Rescue"

Lexile NP

LEARNING GOALS

We can read and understand poetry.

OBJECTIVES

Determine a theme of a story, drama, or poem from details in the text, including how characters in a story or drama respond to challenges or how the speaker in a poem reflects upon a topic; summarize the text.

Use context to confirm or self-correct word recognition and understanding, rereading as necessary.

Determine or clarify the meaning of unknown and multiple-meaning words and phrases, choosing flexibly from a range of strategies.

Use context (e.g., cause/ effect relationships and comparisons in text) as a clue to the meaning of a word or phrase.

Demonstrate understanding of figurative language, word relationships, and nuances in word meanings.

Close Reading Routine

Read   DOK 1–2

• Identify important ideas and details.
• Take notes and summarize.
• Use Ⓐ Ⓒ Ⓣ prompts as needed.

Reread   DOK 2–3

• Analyze the text, craft, and structure.
• Use the **Reread minilessons** and **prompts**.

Integrate   DOK 3–4

• Integrate knowledge and ideas.
• Make text-to-text connections.
• Use the Integrate lesson.
• Complete the Show Your Knowledge task.
• Inspire action.

Read

SHARED READ

My Goal — I can read and understand poetry.

TAKE NOTES
Make note of interesting words and important details.

A Simple Plan

Each morning when Jack rises,
He schemes a simple plot:
"I think I'll change the world," says he,
"A little, not a lot."
For neighbors he might mow a lawn
Before they know he's done it,
Or lead a soccer match at school,
And not care which team won it.
Some kids would laugh,
but Jack would smile
And look for more to do.
He'd walk your dog or tell a joke,
Or play a song for you.
Jack's brother John just didn't see
What Jack was all about.
John shuddered at Jack's crazy ways,
But Jack had not one doubt.

Essential Question

What motivates you to accomplish a goal?

Read how two poets describe unusual goals and why they matter.

178   Unit 2 · Text Set 3

Reading/Writing Companion, pp. 178–179

Set a Purpose Before students begin, have them think about the Essential Question and what motivates someone to reach a goal. Then set a purpose for reading. After previewing the poems and images, have students make predictions about each poem in the left column on page 178. As they read, they can take notes.

Focus on the **Read** prompts now. For additional support, use the extra prompts not included in the **Reading/Writing Companion**. Use the **Reread** prompts during the Craft and Structure lesson on pages T182–T183. Consider preteaching vocabulary to some students.

⊗ DIFFERENTIATED READING

Approaching Level Model using the images to make a prediction about each poem. Complete Read prompts together.

On Level Have pairs preview the poems and make predictions, and then complete the Read prompts before you meet.

Beyond Level Have pairs share responses to the Read prompts. Talk about the impact the images had on their understanding.

🎧 **English Language Learners** Preteach the vocabulary. Have Beginning and Early-Intermediate ELLs listen to the selection summary, available in multiple languages, and use the **Scaffolded Shared Read**. See also **ELL Small Group Guide**.

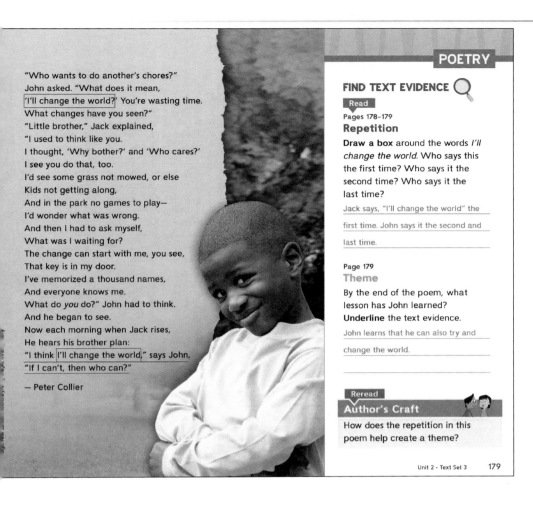

"Who wants to do another's chores?"
John asked. "What does it mean,
'I'll change the world?' You're wasting time.
What changes have you seen?"
"Little brother," Jack explained,
"I used to think like you.
I thought, 'Why bother?' and 'Who cares?'
I see you do that, too.
I'd see some grass not mowed, or else
Kids not getting along,
And in the park no games to play—
I'd wonder what was wrong.
And then I had to ask myself,
What was I waiting for?
The change can start with me, you see,
That key is in my door.
I've memorized a thousand names,
And everyone knows me.
What do *you* do?" John had to think.
And he began to see.
Now each morning when Jack rises,
He hears his brother plan:
"I think I'll change the world," says John,
"If I can't, then who can?"

— Peter Collier

POETRY

FIND TEXT EVIDENCE 🔍

Read
Pages 178–179
Repetition

Draw a box around the words *I'll change the world*. Who says this the first time? Who says it the second time? Who says it the last time?

Jack says, "I'll change the world" the first time. John says it the second and last time.

Page 179
Theme

By the end of the poem, what lesson has John learned? **Underline** the text evidence.

John learns that he can also try and change the world.

Reread
Author's Craft

How does the repetition in this poem help create a theme?

Unit 2 · Text Set 3   179

Poetic Elements: Repetition DOK 2

Pages 178–179: *Who says* I'll change the world *the first time? Who says it the second time? Who says it the last time?*

Think Aloud: I'm going to reread the poem slowly to locate each instance of the phrase. I see that it first appears in line 3. I'll read those first three lines again. *Jack rises. He schemes a simple plot. "I think I'll change the world," says he.* The pronoun *he* in the dialogue refers to Jack, so Jack is the one who says it the first time. I'll keep reading and looking for hints in the dialogue that tell me who else says this phrase the other two times. **Discuss with students what the characters mean by "change the world."**

Theme DOK 2

Page 179: *By the end of the poem, what lesson has John learned? How is this theme developed?*

Think Aloud: I'm going to look back over the poem to see how John's attitude changes. At the top of page 169, I see that John says to Jack, "You're wasting time." But when Jack points out the things he does to help others and then asks John, "What do *you* do?," John realizes he doesn't do enough. So by the end, he decides to help "change the world," or do more to help others, just like Jack. **Have students name some of the feelings Jack might have triggered in John through his actions.**

Check for Understanding DOK 2

Page 179: Monitor students' understanding of Jack's "simple plan" and how his relationship with his brother evolves. Ask: *What is Jack's "simple plan" in the poem?* (He wants to make little changes to the world by doing things like walking people's dogs or mowing their lawns for them.) Have students explain how Jack's relationship with his brother John changes in the poem. (At first John doesn't understand why Jack does the things he does. But then he gets inspired by Jack's actions and decides that he should be more like him.)

ELL Spotlight on Language

Page 179: Clarify the use of pronouns in the lines 5–16 on page 179: *Jack uses the pronouns* I *and* me *as he talks.* Jack uses the pronouns *I* and *me* to talk about himself. *Do* I *and* me *stand for Jack or John?* (Jack) *Which word or phrase shows who Jack is talking to?* (Little brother) *Jack uses the pronoun* you *as he talks. Does* you *stand for Jack or John?* (John) Jack is talking to John. Jack uses the pronoun *you* to talk about what John does. Clarify the meaning of the use of the italicized *you* in line 19 of the poem: *When a word is in italics, it can tell the reader to emphasize it, or show that it is important.* Read the line aloud with appropriate phrasing and volume to demonstrate. Then have students repeat.

Homographs DOK 2

Page 180: Read lines 2–4. Ask: *What are two different meanings for* tipped*?* (*Tipped* can mean "fell over" or "gave extra money to someone.") *What clues help you determine which meaning is correct in line 3?* (The speaker says that "syrup" is tipped "onto a tablecloth," so I know that "fell over" is the correct meaning.) **Discuss the feeling the speaker conveys by the descriptive language in these lines.** (It is easy to visualize the mess that would result from sticky syrup tipped onto a tablecloth. The descriptive language conveys a feeling of concern and seriousness.)

Context Clues DOK 2

Page 180: Read lines 6–9 aloud. Ask: *What words and phrases help you define the word* sodden *in line 7?* (The birds are "bogged down" and "coated" in oil. I know that oil is a thick liquid, so I think that *sodden* means "really wet" or "heavy with liquid.") *Why do you think the poet chose this word to describe the sea birds?* (Possible response: The initial sounds in *sodden* and *sea birds* create alliteration and make the image of the wet, oil-covered birds stand out.)

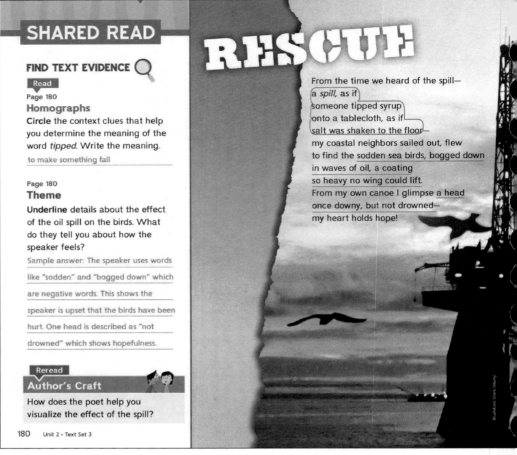

Reading/Writing Companion, pp. 180–181

Theme DOK 2

Page 180: Read lines 7–12. Ask: *What words and phrases does the author use to describe the birds in lines 7–9?* (The author describes the birds as "sodden" and "bogged down in waves of oil.") *How do lines 10–11 help you understand how the spill has affected the birds?* (The words "once downy, but not drowned" indicate that the birds are covered with thick oil and that it is weighing them down in the water.) **Discuss with students why, despite this, the speaker still says that "my heart holds hope!"** (The speaker is focused on the fact that the bird is alive. Despite the spill, he or she is hopeful that the bird can be saved.)

ⒶⒸⓉ Access Complex Text

Connection of Ideas

The reasons behind a speaker's actions in each poem may not be clear to students. Guide them in connecting details to determine each speaker's motivation. Reread "A Simple Plan" on pages 178–179. Ask: *What makes Jack decide to change the world?* (He wonders why no one is doing anything to help. Then he realizes that he can make a difference.) **Next, reread the end of**

"Rescue" on page 180. Ask: *Why did the speaker and his or her neighbors take out their boats?* (to save birds from an oil spill)

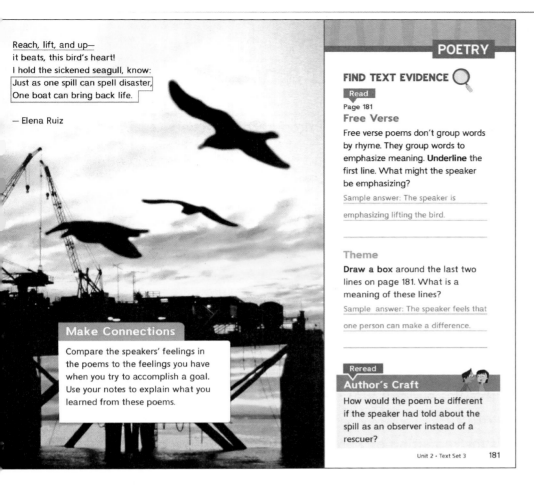

Reach, lift, and up—
it beats, this bird's heart!
I hold the sickened seagull, know:
Just as one spill can spell disaster,
One boat can bring back life.

— Elena Ruiz

Make Connections

Compare the speakers' feelings in the poems to the feelings you have when you try to accomplish a goal. Use your notes to explain what you learned from these poems.

POETRY

FIND TEXT EVIDENCE 🔍

Read
Page 181
Free Verse

Free verse poems don't group words by rhyme. They group words to emphasize meaning. **Underline** the first line. What might the speaker be emphasizing?

Sample answer: The speaker is

emphasizing lifting the bird.

Theme

Draw a box around the last two lines on page 181. What is a meaning of these lines?

Sample answer: The speaker feels that

one person can make a difference.

Reread
Author's Craft

How would the poem be different if the speaker had told about the spill as an observer instead of a rescuer?

Unit 2 · Text Set 3   181

Poetry: Free Verse DOK 2

Page 181: Read the first line. Ask: *If the speaker is in the canoe and the bird is in the water, what might this line be referring to?* (Possible answer: I think it's referring to the speaker reaching over the side of the boat to lift the bird up and out of the water.) Have students explain how the title of the poem supports this action. (Possible answer: The speaker is rescuing the bird from the water.)

Genre

Help students identify the elements of free verse poetry by using clues in the poem. Have students look at the visual arrangement of "Rescue." Ask: *Is the poem separated into stanzas?* (no) *What do you notice about the line lengths?* (The lengths have no pattern.) *Does the poet use rhyme?* (no) Explain that free verse poems are open-ended in their form and do not have the same rules that other poems do.

Theme DOK 2

Page 181: Read the last two lines of the poem. Ask: *How does the speaker think his or her actions can help?* (Possible answer: even though the speaker is just one person, his or her actions can help save the birds from dying.) Discuss with students how this seems to make the speaker feel. (Possible answer: It makes the speaker feel useful because he or she is helping to save a life.)

Check for Understanding DOK 2

Pages 180–181: Look at the photograph on these pages. Ask: *What is happening in the photograph?* (Birds are flying around what looks like a machine used to drill oil.) *What message might the poet be trying to convey through the details in the photograph?* (Possible answer: It is important for people in industries such as oil drilling to protect nearby wildlife so that they can safely coexist.)

Make Connections DOK 2

Analytical Writing **Quick Write** After their initial reads of the poems, ask partners to connect the feelings of each speaker to those they have when they try to accomplish a goal. Have students write their responses in their reader's notebook.

ELL Spotlight on Language

Page 180: *In which line does the word* spill *look different?* (line 2) *The poet uses italic text* (cognate: *itálica*) *to show that this oil spill is different than a syrup spill. Which kind of spill is a big problem?* An <u>oil spill</u> is a big problem. A syrup spill is a <u>small problem</u>. Model emphasizing *spill* as you read lines 1–2 aloud.

FORMATIVE ASSESSMENT

▶ STUDENT CHECK-IN

Have partners share their responses from Reading/ Writing Companion page 181. Ask them to reflect using the Check-In routine.

LEARNING GOALS

- We can use new vocabulary words to read and understand poetry.
- We can use context clues to figure out the meaning of homographs.

OBJECTIVES

Use context to confirm or self-correct word recognition and understanding, rereading as necessary.

Demonstrate understanding of figurative language, word relationships, and nuances in word meanings.

Use the relationship between particular words (e.g., synonyms, antonyms, homographs) to better understand each of the words.

ELA ACADEMIC LANGUAGE

- *homograph, context*
- Cognates: *homógrafo, contexto*

DIGITAL TOOLS

Visual Vocabulary Cards

TEACH IN SMALL GROUP

Academic Vocabulary

● ● **Approaching Level** and **ELL** Preteach the words before students begin the Shared Read.

● **On Level** Have students look up each word in the online **Visual Glossary**.

● **Beyond Level** Have pairs write an example for each poetry term.

---

 10 mins

Academic Vocabulary

 MULTIMODAL

Use the **Visual Vocabulary Cards** to introduce each vocabulary word.

If you are **ambitious**, you have a strong desire to succeed at something.
Cognate: *ambicioso*

If you **memorized** something, you learned it by heart.
Cognate: *memorizar*

Satisfaction is feeling pleased when you accomplish something.
Cognate: *satisfacción*

If you **shuddered**, you shook or trembled from fear or cold.

Poetry Terms

Free verse poems do not have rhyme.

A **narrative** poem is a poem that tells a story.
Cognate: *narrativo*

Repetition is the repeating of words, phrases, or lines in a poem.
Cognate: *repetición*

A poem with **rhyme** has lines that end with the same sound.
Cognate: *rima*

Encourage students to use their newly acquired vocabulary in their discussions and written responses about the texts in this text set.

10 mins

Homographs

1 Explain

Homographs are words that are spelled the same but have different meanings. They may or may not have the same pronunciation. Students can use context clues or a dictionary to find which meaning of a homograph is correct. Add to the Homographs anchor chart.

2 Model

Model using context clues to determine the appropriate meaning of the word *park* in the eleventh line on **Reading/Writing Companion** page 179 of "A Simple Plan."

 COLLABORATE

3 Guided Practice

Have partners reread "Rescue" on pages 180–181 and use context clues to figure out the meanings of *down* and *spell*. Have them verify meaning and pronunciation using a print or online dictionary.

POETRY

Vocabulary

Use the example sentences to talk with a partner about each word. Then answer the questions.
Sample answers shown.

ambitious
Paulo is an **ambitious** bike rider and always looks for challenges.

What makes someone ambitious?

Wanting to be very good at something can make a person ambitious.

memorized
Pat **memorized** the poem and recited it perfectly for the class.

What is the name of a poem or song that you memorized?

I memorized "America the Beautiful" a few years ago.

satisfaction
Participating in sports, such as basketball, gave Jason great **satisfaction**.

What activity gives you great satisfaction?

I get great satisfaction from baking bread for my family.

shuddered
Jill **shuddered** as she bit into the tart, juicy lemon.

What is a synonym for *shuddered*?

A synonym for *shuddered* is *shivered*.

Poetry Terms

narrative
I like to read **narrative** poems because they tell a story.

What story would you like to tell in a narrative poem?

I would like to tell about my first day in a new school in a narrative poem.

repetition
The **repetition** of words, phrases, or lines is used for emphasis.

What is the repetition of a word or phrase that you would use to emphasize happiness?

I laughed and laughed, and then laughed some more.

free verse
A **free verse** poem does not have a set rhyming pattern.

What topic would you choose for a free verse poem?

I would like to write a free verse poem about swimming.

rhyme
A poem with **rhyme** contains words that end with the same sound.

Can you think of three words that rhyme with *funny*?

Three words that rhyme with *funny* are *money*, *honey*, and *sunny*.

Build Your Word List Reread "Rescue" on pages 180–181. Underline three adjectives. In your reader's notebook, write the three words. Use an online or print thesaurus to find two synonyms for each word. Write the synonyms next to each adjective.

Homographs

Homographs are words that are spelled the same but have different meanings and may or may not have the same pronunciation. You can use context clues to help figure out which meaning is correct.

FIND TEXT EVIDENCE
In "A Simple Plan," I see the word *park*. I know that *park* can be a verb meaning "to place or leave something" and it can also be a noun meaning "land set apart for recreation." The phrase "games to play" is a clue that *park* has the second meaning.

> I'd see some grass not mowed, or else
> Kids not getting along,
> And in the park no games to play—
> I'd wonder what was wrong.

Your Turn Reread the homographs *down* and *spell* in the poem "Rescue." Identify clues that help you figure out the meaning. Use a print or digital dictionary to check your work.

Bogged and *in waves of oil* are clues that the meaning of *down* is "sink in." *Spill* and *disaster* are clues that *spell* means "lead to" or "means."

CHECK IN 1 2 3 4

182 Unit 2 • Text Set 3

Unit 2 • Text Set 3 183

Reading/Writing Companion, pp. 182–183

English Language Learners

Use the following scaffolds with **Guided Practice**. For small group support, see the **ELL Small Group Guide**.

Beginning

Check understanding of *homograph*. Write the word *spell* on the board. Read aloud line 4 on page 181 with students. *What can an oil spill do?* An oil spill can spell disaster. Say: *To* spell *can also mean "to cause something."* Help partners restate the sentence: An oil spill can cause a disaster. *Use a dictionary to look up the word* spell *to verify meaning and pronunciation.* Repeat for *down* on page 180.

Intermediate

Have partners read the first four lines on page 181. *What is the effect of an oil spill?* A spill of oil into the water can spell disaster. *What does that mean?* An oil spill can cause disaster. Have partners use a dictionary to check for meaning and pronunciation, then use *spell* to write other sentences describing cause and effect: A/an _____ can spell _____. Repeat for *down* on page 180.

Advanced/Advanced High

Have partners reread the poem on page 181 and find the word *spell*. Guide them to look for words in the poem that help them figure out the meaning of *spell*. *Use a dictionary with your partner to verify meaning and pronunciation.* Repeat for *down* on page 180.

BUILD YOUR WORD LIST

Students might choose *match* from page 178. Have them use a dictionary to determine its multiple meanings and parts of speech.

FORMATIVE ASSESSMENT

❯ STUDENT CHECK-IN

Academic Vocabulary Ask partners to share two answers from Reading/Writing Companion pages 182–183.

Homographs Ask partners to share their Your Turn responses on page 183

Have students use the Check-In routine to reflect and fill in the bars.

✔ CHECK FOR SUCCESS

Rubric Use your online rubric to record student progress.

Can students find context clues within "Rescue" to determine the correct meanings of *down* and *spell*?

❯ **Small Group Instruction**

If No:
● **Approaching** Reteach p. T211

If Yes:
● **On** Review p. T218
● **Beyond** Extend p. T224

LESSON 2

LEARNING GOALS

We can identify repetition and rhyme in poetry.

OBJECTIVES

Expain how a series of chapters, scenes, or stanzas fits together to provide the overall structure of particlar story, drama, or poem.

Read grade-level text with purpose and understanding.

Explain major differences between poems, drama, and prose, and refer to the structural elements of poems (e.g., verse, rhythm, meter) and drama (e.g., casts of characters, settings, descriptions, dialogue, stage directions) when writing or speaking about a text.

ELA ACADEMIC LANGUAGE

- *poem, emphasize, distinction*
- Cognates: *poema, enfatizar, distinción*

Reread

⏱ **10 mins**

Poetic Elements: Repetition and Rhyme

1 Explain

Explain to students that poets often use poetic elements such as **repetition** and **rhyme** to achieve certain effects.

- A poet may repeat words, phrases, or sounds. The repetition of the final sound in two or more words is called rhyme.

- Repeating a word, phrase, or sentence style can help the poet emphasize certain details, ideas, or feelings in a poem that connect to its meaning and theme.

Point out that recognizing and understanding how a poet uses repetition and rhyme can help students better understand a poem and can make reading it more interesting and enjoyable.

 Anchor Chart Have a volunteer add details about repetition and rhyme to the Poetry anchor chart.

2 Model

Reread the poem "Rescue" and draw students' attention to the first four lines on **Reading/Writing Companion** page 180. Model identifying the repetition of the words *spill* and *as if*. Explain that the repetition emphasizes an important event—the spill—and an important distinction the poet is trying to make—that the spill described in the poem is much worse than a syrup or salt spill, even though the same word is used in all three contexts and seems to suggest that they are comparable.

COLLABORATE

3 Guided Practice

Support pairs as they look for and identify two examples of repetition in "A Simple Plan." Then guide students to explain the ideas these examples emphasize. (Possible response: "Each morning when Jack rises" emphasizes that Jack continues to work toward his goals; "kids" emphasizes a group of people John wants to help)

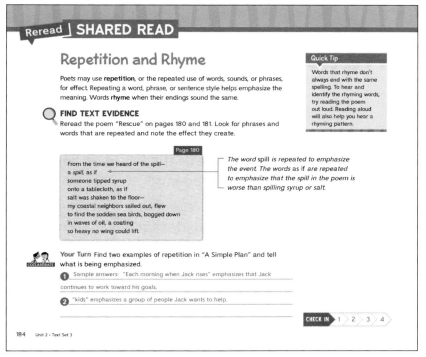

Reading/Writing Companion, p. 184

English Language Learners

Use the following scaffolds with **Guided Practice**. For small group support, see the **ELL Small Group Guide**.

Beginning

Read the first three lines of pages 178 and 179 of "A Simple Plan" with students. Then read the last two lines of page 179. *Each time the phrase* I'll change the world *appears, who is speaking?* (Jack, John, John) Help students understand that John repeats what Jack says: *How many times does the poet use this phrase?* (three) *Who wants to change the world first?* (Jack) *Who wants to change the world at the end?* (John)

Intermediate

Have pairs find the phrase *I'll change the world* in "A Simple Plan" and identify who says it each time. (Jack, John, John) Then have pairs discuss the repetition: *How many times does the poet use the sentence?* (three) *Who wants to change the world at the beginning?* (Jack) *What happens at the end?* John wants to change the world.

Advanced/Advanced High

Have pairs find the phrase the poet repeats three times in "A Simple Plan." Provide the following questions to guide them to discuss the repetition: *Who says it each time? What happens at the end? What does repetition emphasize about Jack and John?*

FORMATIVE ASSESSMENT

> **STUDENT CHECK-IN**

Ask partners to share their Your Turn responses on Reading/Writing Companion page 184. Have them use the Check-In routine to reflect and fill in the bars.

> **CHECK FOR SUCCESS**

Can students identify two examples of repetition in "A Simple Plan"? Can they explain what the repetition emphasizes?

> **Small Group Instruction**

If No:
- **Approaching** Reteach p. T204

If Yes:
- **On** Review p. T214
- **Beyond** Extend p. T220

SHARED READ **T177**

LESSON 2

Reread

Poetry: Narrative and Free Verse

10 mins

LEARNING GOALS

We can identify the characteristics of a narrative and a free verse poem to understand poetry.

OBJECTIVES

Expain how a series of chapters, scenes, or stanzas fits together to provide the overall structure of particlar story, drama, or poem.

By the end of the year, read and comprehend literature, including stories, dramas, and poetry, at the high end of the text complexity band independently and proficiently.

Explain major differences between poems, drama, and prose, and refer to the structural elements of poems (e.g., verse, rhythm, meter) and drama (e.g., casts of characters, settings, descriptions, dialogue, stage directions) when writing or speaking about a text.

ELA ACADEMIC LANGUAGE

• *narrative, free verse, dialogue, rhyme, rhythm, speaker*

• Cognates: *poema narrativo, diálogo, rima, ritmo*

1 Explain

Remind students that poets carefully choose and arrange words to express feelings and ideas. Share with students the following key characteristics of **narrative** and **free verse** poems.

- A narrative poem tells a story. It contains characters who may communicate their thoughts, feelings, and ideas to each other and to the reader through dialogue. A narrative poem may or may not rhyme.

- A free verse poem shares feelings and ideas with no regular patterns of rhyme or rhythm. It has no set line length; the lines can be a mix of short and long lines. The visual arrangement of lines in a free verse poem may give added meaning to the poem.

Point out that while a poet is the writer of a poem, the feelings and ideas the poet expresses are those of the poem's speaker, or narrator. They do not necessarily reflect the poet's own feelings.

2 Model

Model how the first few lines on **Reading/Writing Companion** page 179 can be used to identify "A Simple Plan" as a narrative poem that tells a story. Point out the characters, Jack and John, and the quotation marks that indicate their dialogue, or the exact words they speak to each other. Point out that this narrative poem rhymes. Then explain that "Rescue" is a free verse poem because there is no set line length or rhyming pattern.

 Anchor Chart Have a volunteer add elements of narrative and free verse poems to the Poetry anchor chart.

3 Guided Practice

Help students work in pairs to reread the poems "A Simple Plan" and "Rescue." Ask them to explain how each author's choice to rhyme or not to rhyme affects his or her poem as well as students' reactions to it. Have students share and compare their ideas with the class.

Independent Practice Have students read the online **Differentiated Genre Passage**, "Blue Ribbon Dreams."

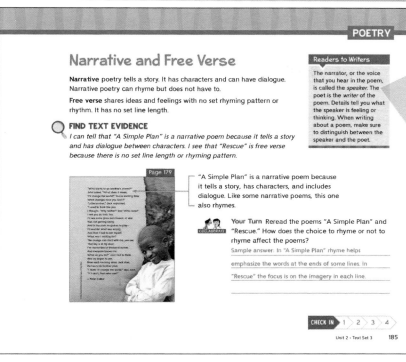

Reading/Writing Companion, p. 185

Readers to Writers

Reiterate the differences between the poet, or writer of a poem, and the speaker, or "voice" that narrates the poem. *Think about writing a story about another person's experiences. You might not share your own thoughts or feelings in that story. In a poem, the speaker's words and thoughts are his or her own—they are not always those of the poet.* Remind students to distinguish between the speaker and the poet as they complete their work.

 # English Language Learners

Use the following scaffolds with **Guided Practice**. For small group support, see the **ELL Small Group Guide**.

Beginning

Review the meaning of *rhyme* with students. Reread "A Simple Plan" and "Rescue" with them. Help partners point out and say the rhyming words in the first four lines of "A Simple Plan." (plot, lot) Ask: *Does this poem have rhyme?* (yes) *Are the rhyming words at the end of the lines?* (yes) *Does the poem* "Rescue" *have rhyme?* (no)

Intermediate

Review rhyme in narrative and free verse poems with students. Have partners reread the poem "A Simple Plan" and "Rescue." Guide partners to look for rhyming words in the poems. Ask: *Which poem has rhyme?* ("A Simple Plan") *What are the rhyming words?* (plot, lot) Then have partners discuss how this affects the poem and respond using: In "A Simple Plan" the rhyme helps _____.

Advanced/Advanced High

Have pairs reread the poems "A Simple Plan" and "Rescue." Provide guiding questions to have them compare the poems and discuss how the author's choice to rhyme or not rhyme affects the poems: *Does the poem rhyme? What are the rhyming words? What does the rhyme emphasize?*

FORMATIVE ASSESSMENT

❯ STUDENT CHECK-IN

Ask partners to share their Your Turn responses on Reading/Writing Companion page 185. Have them use the Check-In routine to reflect and fill in the bars.

✔ CHECK FOR SUCCESS

Can students explain how the poet's choice of whether or not to include rhyme affects the narrative poem "A Simple Plan" and the free verse poem "Rescue"?

❯ **Small Group Instruction**

If No:

● **Approaching** Reteach p. T206

If Yes:

● **On** Review p. T216

● **Beyond** Extend p. T222

LEARNING GOALS

We can read and understand poetry by analyzing the theme.

OBJECTIVES

Determine a theme of a story, drama, or poem from details in the text, including how characters in a story or drama respond to challenges or how the speaker in a poem reflects upon a topic; summarize the text.

Read with sufficient accuracy and fluency to support comprehension.

ELA ACADEMIC LANGUAGE

• theme, details, summarize, interpretation

• Cognates: tema, detalles, interpretación

DIGITAL TOOLS

To differentiate instruction for key skills, use the results of the activity.

Reread

Theme

10 mins

1 Explain

Explain to students that a poem's **theme** is the message that the poet wishes to communicate to readers. Most poems have one big idea, but may include many smaller themes.

• Considering the speaker and the poet's word choice and use of important, or key, details can help readers identify a poem's theme.

• Reading a poem aloud can help reveal its rhythm and the feelings it evokes, which are important to understanding theme.

• Point out to students that by rereading a poem several times, they may notice important details they did not notice after the first reading.

Anchor Chart Have a volunteer add details to the Theme anchor chart.

2 Model

Explain that both poems are about accomplishing goals, but each has a specific theme. Model using important details from the narrative poem "A Simple Plan" on **Reading/Writing Companion** pages 178–179 to determine its theme. Point out that the dialogue contains many of the poem's important details.

Explain to students that one reason that reading poetry can be so interesting is that a poem's theme can be interpreted in different ways. As long as an interpretation can be supported by important details in the text, it is valid. Model how to use the graphic organizer to interpret the theme in "A Simple Plan."

3 Guided Practice

Guide pairs as they reread the free verse poem "Rescue." Ask them to consider the poem's speaker and record important details from the text in the graphic organizer. Encourage students to look for details that describe events and how the speaker feels about them. Partners should then work together to infer a theme.

Analytical Writing **Write About Reading: Summary** Have pairs summarize how the speaker and his or her neighbors responded to a challenge and what the speaker learns as a result. Ask volunteers to include an explanation of how the poet developed the theme.

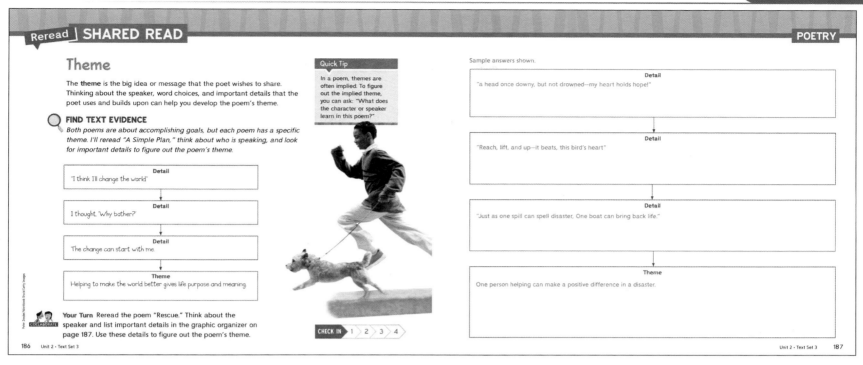

Reading/Writing Companion, pp. 186-187

 # English Language Learners

Use the following scaffolds with **Guided Practice.** For small group support, see the **ELL Small Group Guide**.

Beginning

Direct students' attention to the last three lines on page 180. Clarify the meaning of *glimpse: To glimpse something means to see it very quickly.* Act out the action. Then read the lines slowly and with expression. Ask: *What does the speaker glimpse?* The speaker glimpses a <u>head</u>. *Which word tells you how the speaker feels?* (hope) Ask a volunteer to write *hope* in the graphic organizer.

Intermediate

Have partners take turns rereading "Rescue" on pages 180–181. Then ask them to work together to identify important events and tell how the speaker feels about them: *What happened to the water in the ocean?* (oil spill) *What happened to the birds in the water?* They can't move or <u>fly</u>. *Why does the speaker feel hope?* She sees the <u>head</u> of a bird that was not <u>drowned</u>. Model filling in the graphic organizer.

Advanced/Advanced High

Have partners take turns rereading "Rescue" on pages 180–181. Provide guiding questions as they use details from the text to discuss the speaker's feelings: *What happened to the birds? How do the speaker and her neighbors feel? How do you know?* Have partners work to record details in the graphic organizer.

FORMATIVE ASSESSMENT

❯ STUDENT CHECK-IN

Ask partners to share their graphic organizers on Reading/Writing Companion page 187. Have them use the Check-In routine to reflect and fill in the bars.

✔ CHECK FOR SUCCESS

Rubric Use your online rubric to record student progress.

Do students identify important details that describe how the speaker of "Rescue" feels about events? Can they use these details to infer a theme of the poem?

❯ **Small Group Instruction**

If No:
● **Approaching** Reteach p. T213

If Yes:
● **On** Review p. T219
● **Beyond** Extend p. T225

LESSON 2

 10 mins

Craft and Structure

LEARNING GOALS

We can reread to analyze craft and structure in poetry.

OBJECTIVES

Determine the meaning of words and phrases as they are used in a text.

Draw evidence from literary or informational texts to support analysis, reflection, and research.

Apply grade 5 Reading standards to literature.

ELA ACADEMIC LANGUAGE

• *technique, repetition, theme, visualize*

• Cognates: *técnica, repetición, tema, visualizar*

▶ TEACH IN SMALL GROUP

● **Approaching Level** Use the scaffolded questions provided to guide students as they reread and interpret specific portions of the poems using text evidence.

● **On Level** Have partners collect evidence and respond to the Reread prompts together.

● **Beyond Level** Have partners independently answer the Reread prompts and share their responses with the group.

● **ELL** Have Beginning and Early-Intermediate ELLs use the **Scaffolded Shared Read**.

Tell students that they will now reread parts of "A Simple Plan" and "Rescue" and analyze the techniques the poets used in writing the poems. Remind students that poets often incorporate repetition, rhyme, and other poetic elements into their poems to emphasize important ideas and help readers visualize the actions and events the speaker is describing.

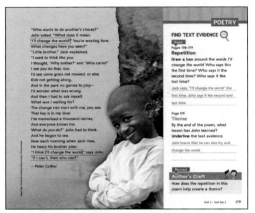

Reading/Writing Companion p. 179

AUTHOR'S CRAFT

Review repetition and reread page 179 with students. Have students locate the three instances in which "I'll change the world" is repeated. Ask: *Why do you think this phrase is repeated over and over?* (The repetition reminds readers of the intent that Jack initially states at the beginning of the poem: that he will change the world "a little, not a lot.") *What meaning do these words add to the poem?* (Possible answer: They emphasize how even a small action can "change the world" by having a positive effect on people.)

ELL Discuss what Jack means by the phrase "I'll change the world": *Jack knows he cannot really change the whole world in a big way. But he can help people he knows. Who does Jack help?* Jack helps his <u>neighbors</u> mow their lawn. Jack helps his friends at school <u>play soccer</u>. He helps people in <u>small/little</u> ways. Have pairs brainstorm examples of small actions they could do in their community to change people's lives for the better.

How does the repetition in this poem help create a theme? **DOK 3**

(Repeating the phrase "I'll change the world" reminds readers of the idea that even small actions can make a difference. This helps the poem convey the theme that each individual person is capable of making the world a better place.)

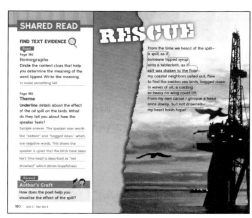

Reading/Writing Companion p. 180

AUTHOR'S CRAFT DOK 2

Reread page 180 with students. Ask: *How do the descriptions of the birds in lines 7–9 help you understand the danger they were in?* (Possible answer: "Sodden sea birds" "bogged down in waves of oil," and "coating so heavy no wing could lift" help me picture a thick coating of oil that made moving, and probably even breathing, difficult for the birds.)

ELL Clarify the descriptive language in lines 7–9: *Which words or phrases describe the sea birds?* (*Sodden sea birds, bogged down in waves of oil, coating so heavy no wing could lift*) Clarify the meanings of *sodden* and *bogged down. How do the descriptions explain that the birds are in danger?* (They show that the birds can't move.)

How does the poet help you visualize the effect of the spill? (The poet includes descriptive details like "sodden sea birds," "bogged down in waves of oil," and "coating so heavy no wing could lift" to help me visualize the effect of the spill and how dangerous it was for the birds.)

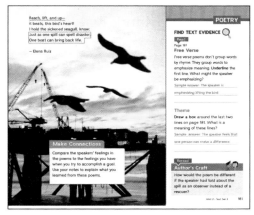

Reading/Writing Companion p. 181

AUTHOR'S CRAFT DOK 3

Reread page 181 with students. Ask: *What lines in this part of the poem help you understand the speaker's feelings?* (The second line—"it beats, this bird's heart!"— tells me that the speaker is excited to find the bird still alive. The last line, "One boat can bring back life," tells me how happy and relieved the speaker is to have helped.)

ELL Have students point to the punctuation mark at the end of line 2. Ask: *What is this mark called?* (an exclamation point) *What does it tell you about the speaker's feelings?* The speaker is <u>excited</u>.

How would the poem be different if the speaker had told about the spill as an observer instead of a rescuer? (It would not convey what it felt like to rescue a bird. As an observer, the speaker wouldn't have had the experience of knowing that his or her actions were responsible for the bird's survival.)

Integrate

📋 BUILD KNOWLEDGE: 🔗 MAKE CONNECTIONS

Talk About the Text Have partners discuss what motivated the speaker of "Rescue" to save the seagull.

Write About the Text Have students add their ideas to their Build Knowledge pages of their reader's notebooks.

Anchor Chart Record any new ideas on the Build Knowledge anchor chart.

Add to the Vocabulary List Have students write down any words they learned about accomplishing a goal in their reader's notebooks.

FORMATIVE ASSESSMENT

❯ STUDENT CHECK-IN

Have partners share their responses to one of the Reread prompts on Reading/Writing Companion pages 179–181. Ask them to reflect using the Check-In routine.

Reread

Write About the Shared Read

LEARNING GOALS

We can use text evidence to respond to poetry.

OBJECTIVES

Compare and contrast stories in the same genre on their approaches to similar themes and topics.

Produce clear and coherent writing in which the development and organization are appropriate to task, purpose, and audience.

Draw evidence from literary or informational texts to support analysis, reflection, and research.

Analyze a writing prompt.

Write routinely over extended time frames and shorter time frames for a range of discipline-specific tasks, purposes, and audiences.

ELA ACADEMIC LANGUAGE

• *details, imagery, visualize, speaker, poet*
• Cognates: *detalles, visualizar, poeta*

⟫ TEACH IN SMALL GROUP

● **Approaching Level** As a group, review the poems to gather text evidence that will support students' responses.

● **On Level** Have pairs gather text evidence and then work independently to respond.

● **Beyond Level** Have students exchange their responses with a partner for feedback.

● **ELL** Group students of mixed proficiency levels to discuss and respond to the prompt.

Analyze the Prompt DOK 3

Read the prompt aloud: *How do the poems "A Simple Plan" and "Rescue" motivate readers to action? Do you think they are inspiring? Why or why not?* Ask: *What is the prompt asking?* (to describe how the poems motivate readers and explain why they are or aren't inspiring) Say: *Let's reread to see how the poets use descriptive details and imagery to convey the idea of accomplishing a goal. We'll review the poems and note text evidence to support your response.*

Analyze Text Evidence

Remind students of the difference between a poet and a speaker: The poet is the writer of a poem, while the speaker is the poem's narrator, or "voice." Explain that poets often use descriptive details and imagery to help readers visualize the thoughts, feelings, and actions described by the speaker or the characters in a poem. Students should look for words and phrases that help them picture the characters and the events that are taking place. In the **Reading/Writing Companion**, have students skim page 179 of "A Simple Plan" for examples of those who might benefit from Jack's help. Ask: *What details does the poet include to help you visualize how Jack responds?* (Jack describes "grass not mowed" and "kids not getting along." These are simple problems he can help fix.) **What does the phrase "That key is in my door" say about Jack's attitude?** (It tells me that Jack feels that he has the power to "change the world" by doing things for others.) Have students look for descriptive details and imagery that the poet of "Rescue" uses to help readers picture the accomplishment of goals.

Respond

Direct pairs to the sentence starters on Reading/Writing Companion page 188. Ask: How are the poems motivational? Model a response.

Think Aloud In "Rescue," the poet describes the birds the speaker sees as "sodden" and "bogged down" by the effects of the oil spill. Those details help me picture the unsafe and dangerous environment the oil spill has caused. But the speaker is determined to save the birds. When the speaker lifts a bird out of the water, saying, "it beats, this bird's heart!," I can visualize his or her relief that the bird is still alive.

Analytical Writing Students should use the phrases in the sentence starters to form their responses. They may continue their responses on a separate piece of paper.

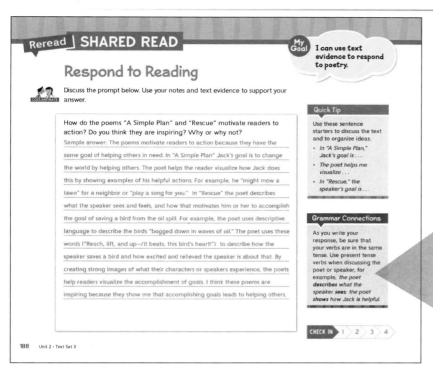

Reading/Writing Companion, p. 188

 # English Language Learners

Use the following scaffolds with **Respond**.

Beginning

Read the prompt with students and explain what they will write about. Clarify the meaning of *motivate* and *goal* with students. Ask: *What is Jack's goal in "A Simple Plan"?* Jack's goal is to look for more to do. *What is the speaker's goal in "Rescue"? The speaker's goal is to save the* birds. Help partners discuss how the poems motivate readers. Then have them respond using: The poems have the same goal of helping others in need.

Intermediate

Read the prompt with students. Ask: *What is Jack's goal in "A Simple Plan"?* In "A Simple Plan" Jack's goal is to change the world by helping others. *What is the speaker's goal in "Rescue"?* In "Rescue" the speaker's goal is to save birds from the oil. *Do you think the poems are inspiring?* (yes/no) Have partners discuss their responses and write using: The poems motivate readers to action because _____. I think the poems are inspiring/not inspiring because _____.

Advanced/Advanced High

Review the prompt and sentence starters on page 188 with students. Have pairs discuss Jack's goal in "A Simple Plan" and the speaker's goal in "Rescue." Then have them respond using the sentence starters.

 NEWCOMERS

Have students listen to the summaries of the **Shared Read** in their native language and then in English to help them access the text and develop listening comprehension. Help students ask and answer questions with a partner. Use these sentence frames: *What does the poem's speaker do? The speaker ____.* Then continue the lessons in the **Newcomer Teacher's Guide**.

FORMATIVE ASSESSMENT

❯ **STUDENT CHECK-IN**

Ask partners to share their response on 188. Have them use the Check-In routine to reflect and fill in the bars.

LESSON **2**

LEARNING GOALS

- We can decode words with closed syllables.
- We can identify and read multisyllabic words.
- We can read fluently with expression and phrasing.

OBJECTIVES

Know and apply grade-level phonics and word analysis skills in decoding words.

Use combined knowledge of all letter-sound correspondences, syllabication patterns, and morphology (e.g. roots and affixes) to read accurately unfamiliar multisyllabic words in context and out of context.

Read with sufficient accuracy and fluency to support comprehension.

Read grade-level text with purpose and understanding.

- Rate: 111–131 WCPM

ELA ACADEMIC LANGUAGE

- expression, phrasing
- Cognates: *espresión, fraseo*

 **TEACH IN SMALL GROUP**

Phonics

🔘 ⚫ **Approaching Level** and **ELL** Use the Tier 2 activity on page T208 before teaching the lesson.

🔘 **On Level** As needed, use the Guided Practice section.

🔘 **Beyond Level** As needed, use the Multisyllabic Words section only.

⚫ **ELL** See page 5 in the **Language Transfers Handbook** for guidance in identifying sounds and symbols that may not transfer for speakers of certain languages, and support in accommodating those students.

 OPTION 10 mins

Closed Syllables

1 Explain

Review with students that every syllable in a word has one vowel sound. Write the word *pencil* on the board. Draw a slash between the *n* and the *c* and pronounce each syllable: *pen/cil*. Point out that when a syllable ends in one or more consonants and has a short vowel sound spelled with a single vowel, it is called a closed syllable. *Pen* is a closed syllable. Remind students that some words have one closed syllable and one VC*e* syllable, such as *update* or *empire*. The syllables divide between the two consonants in both *update* and *empire*.

2 Model

Write the following words on the board: *tender, rustic, mistake,* and *custom*. Read each word aloud. Model identifying the closed syllable or syllables in each word. Draw a line under the closed syllables *ten, rus, mis,* and *cus*. Point out that these syllables are closed syllables. Emphasize that the vowel in each closed syllable has a short vowel sound.

3 Guided Practice

Write the following closed syllables on the board and read each one aloud. Then have students chorally read the sample words as you point to them.

bas as in *basket*	*win* as in *winter*
dis as in *distant*	*mit* as in *mitten*
plan as in *planet*	*sus* as in *suspect*
west as in *western*	*trans* as in *transfer*
con as in *conclude*	*en* as in *engage*

Underline the syllables *bas* and *ket* in *basket*. Identify each syllable as closed. Then have students underline the closed syllable or syllables in the remaining words.

For practice with decoding and encoding, use **Practice Book** page 115 or online activities.

Read Multisyllabic Words

Transition to Longer Words Help students transition to reading multisyllabic words with closed syllables. Write the following closed syllables and sample words on the board. Read aloud the first closed syllable and identify the vowel sound as short. Then model reading the related sample word in the second column. Have students chorally read each remaining closed syllable and its related word in the second column. Finally, draw students' attention to the longer words in the third column. Model reading the longer words. Then have students read the longer words chorally as you point to them.

den	dentist	dentistry
splen	splendid	splendidly
con	contact	contacted
help	helpful	helpfulness
mag	magnet	magnetism
ran	random	randomly
prob	problem	problematic

Fluency

Expression and Phrasing

Explain/Model Tell students that reading with expression, or prosody, helps create interest and clarify ideas in poems. Paying attention to phrasing, which is indicated by punctuation, also helps make the meaning of the poem clear. Emphasize the use of proper expression and phrasing as you model reading "A Simple Plan" **on Reading/Writing Companion** pages 178–179.

Practice/Apply Have partners take turns reading the poem, modeling the expression and phrasing you used. Remind students that you will also be listening for their use of expression and phrasing as you monitor their reading during the week.

Daily Fluency Practice

Automaticity Students can practice reading with accuracy and appropriate rate to develop automaticity using the online **Differentiated Genre Passage**, "Blue Ribbon Dreams."

DIGITAL TOOLS

For more practice, have students use the phonics and fluency activities.

Closed Syllables

MULTIMODAL LEARNING

Write two-syllable words with one closed syllable, such as *open, bonus,* and *student,* on strips of paper or index cards. Have students read the words aloud and then fold the paper or index cards to divide the syllables. Ask students to display their strips or index cards so that only closed syllables are visible.

FORMATIVE ASSESSMENT

⊙ STUDENT CHECK-IN

Closed Syllables Have partners share three words with closed syllables.

Read Multisyllabic Words Have partners read the following words and identify the first syllable: *splendidly, helpfulness,* and *magnetism.*

Fluency Ask partners to read "Blue Ribbon Dreams" fluently.

Have partners reflect using the Check-In routine.

✓ CHECK FOR SUCCESS

Rubric Can students identify closed syllables? Do students read with expression and phrasing?

⊘ Small Group Instruction

If No:

● **Approaching** Reteach pp. T208, T212

● **ELL** Develop p. T208

If Yes:

● **On** Apply p. T214

● **Beyond** Apply p. T220

LEARNING GOALS

- **We can use the research process to create a comic strip.**
- **We can use primary and secondary sources to conduct research.**

OBJECTIVES

Analyze multiple accounts of the same event or topic, noting important similarities and differences in the point of view they represent.

Conduct short research projects that use several sources to build knowledge through investigation of different aspects of a topic.

Recall relevant information from experiences or gather relevant information from print and digital sources; summarize or paraphrase information in notes and finished work, and provide a list of sources.

Report on a topic or text or present an opinion, sequencing ideas logically and using appropriate facts and relevant, descriptive details to support main ideas or themes; speak clearly at an understandable pace.

Adapt speech to a variety of contexts and tasks, using formal English when appropriate to task and situation.

🌐 Use primary and secondary sources to identify the contributions of prominent individuals or groups who contributed to a state's history.

ELA ACADEMIC LANGUAGE

- *primary, secondary, firsthand, secondhand*
- Cognates: *primaria, secundaria*

▶ TEACH IN SMALL GROUP

You may wish to teach the Research and Inquiry lesson during Small Group time. Have groups of mixed abilities complete the page and work on the comic strip.

⏱ 10 mins Achieving Goals

Explain to students that for the next two weeks they will work collaboratively with a partner to create a comic strip.

Primary and Secondary Sources Students will conduct research to identify a prominent person or group from their state's history. Students will then create a comic strip that shows how that person or group was able to achieve an important goal. Discuss examples of primary and secondary sources with students:

- Primary sources are firsthand accounts of an event. Examples of primary sources might include photographs, letters, diaries, journals, or speeches. It can also include official state or historical documents.
- Secondary sources are secondhand accounts of an event. Encyclopedias and textbooks are examples of secondary sources.

As students research prominent people or groups in their state's history, have them consider their motivations for achieving the goals. Support them as they go through each step in the Research Process as outlined in the **Reading/Writing Companion** page 189 to create their comic strips.

STEP 1 Set a Goal Guide students as they brainstorm a list of famous people or groups from their state's history. Explain that generating questions may help them determine who to pick from the brainstormed list and what to include in their comic strips. Have students use a **Layered Book Foldable®**, available online, to help organize their information.

STEP 2 Identify Sources Brainstorm with groups the kinds of digital and print resources they can use for their research. Remind them to use credible primary and secondary sources. Model how to locate historical documents or photographs online.

STEP 3 Find and Record Information Review with students how to take notes and cite the sources they use to gather information for their comic strips. Have students take notes specific to the goal that was achieved by the person or group they chose to research. Review photographs or other visuals to use as reference materials when sketching out the comic strips.

STEP 4 Organize and Synthesize Information Show students how to organize the places and information that they want to add to their comic strips. Discuss which primary and secondary sources were most informative and interesting to include, and analyze the information gathered to help students sketch a story map.

STEP 5 Create and Present Review with students what they should include in their comic strips. Encourage them to add details to their sketches to emphasize or clarify important ideas or motivations they researched. Refer students to the online Presentation Checklists and Rubrics.

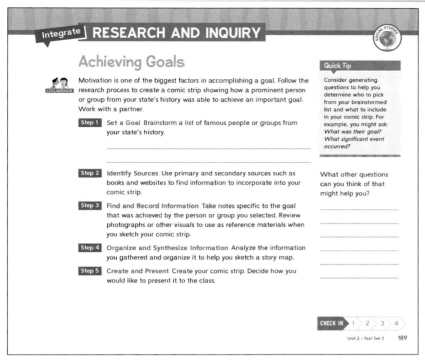

Reading/Writing Companion, p. 189

DIGITAL TOOLS

DIGITAL TOOLS

RESOURCE TOOLKIT — Evaluate Sources for Reliability; Organizing Notes

Dinah Zike's **FOLDABLES** Study Organizer — **FOLDABLES** — MULTIMODAL

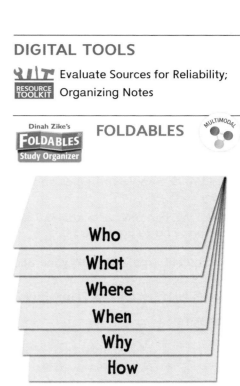

Layered Book Foldable®

English Language Learners

Use the following scaffold with **Step 3**.

Beginning

Review examples of primary and secondary sources with students. Guide partners to research information about a famous person in history and the goal he or she achieved. Ask: *Is the information from a primary or secondary source?* (primary/secondary source) Model how to take notes in the **Layered Book Foldable®** and cite sources. Review the students' notes and provide feedback.

Intermediate

Review examples of primary and secondary sources with students. Help partners research about a famous person or group in history from primary and secondary sources. Ask: *Is the information about the goal that was achieved by the person/group?* (yes/no) Then have partners take notes in the **Layered Book Foldable®** and cite sources. Review the students' notes and provide feedback.

Advanced/Advanced High

Discuss examples of primary and secondary sources with students. Have partners research and take notes specific to the goal that was achieved by the person or group. Then have partners take notes in the **Layered Book Foldable®** and cite sources.

FORMATIVE ASSESSMENT

❯ STUDENT CHECK-IN

Comic Strip Ask students to share their comic strips.

Primary and Secondary Sources Have students share an example of a primary and a secondary source that they used.

Have students use the Check-In routine to reflect and fill in the bars on Reading/Writing Companion page 189.

LESSON 3

"Stage Fright" and "Catching Quiet"

Lexile NP

LEARNING GOALS

Read We can apply strategies and skills to read poetry.

Reread We can reread to analyze text, craft, and structure, and to compare texts.

Have students apply what they learned as they read.

ACT *What makes this text complex?*
▶ **Genre**

Close Reading Routine

Read DOK 1–2

• Identify important ideas and details.
• Take notes and summarize.
• Use **ACT** prompts as needed.

Reread DOK 2–3

• Analyze the text, craft, and structure.
• Use *Reading/Writing Companion*, pp. 190–191.

Integrate DOK 3–4

• Integrate knowledge and ideas.
• Make text-to-text connections.
• Use the Integrate lesson.
• Complete the Show Your Knowledge task.
• Inspire action.

Genre • Poetry

Stage Fright

I wanted the role.
The Prince.

The Prince.

I got it.
Knew it.
I was totally convinced.

I memorized each line.
Learned them by heart.
I studied and studied
my perfect Prince-part.

But—
when I took center stage
    I stammered
    stuttered
    hemmed
    hawed
    suddenly shuddered.

Essential Question
What motivates you to accomplish a goal?
Read about how ambitious people can accomplish their goals.

Go Digital!

138

Literature Anthology, pp. 138–139

DIFFERENTIATED READING

You may wish to read the full selection aloud once with minimal stopping before you begin using the Read prompts.

Approaching Level Have students listen to the selection summary. Use the Reread prompts during Small Group time.

On Level and **Beyond Level** Have students independently complete the Reread prompts on **Reading/Writing Companion** pages 190–191.

🎧 **English Language Learners** Have ELLs listen to the summary of the poem, available in multiple languages. See also the **ELL Small Group Guide**.

My heart skipped a beat.
Face turned bright red.
Until finally
Prince-words popped back in my head.

Though I'll always know
my mind simply snapped
I still got a thrill
when I took my last bow
as my classmates
    stood up
    shouted
    and
    clapped.

    ①

— *Lee Bennett Hopkins*

139

 **Spotlight on Language**

Page 138, Lines 13–17 Read the lines aloud. *Which words are the speaker's actions?* (*stammered, stuttered, hemmed, hawed, suddenly shuddered*) Act out the words to clarify their meanings. *How do you think the speaker feels? Why do you think he feels this way?* (He is frightened to be in front of an audience.) Have partners define each of the speaker's actions and describe a time when they stammered, stuttered, hemmed and hawed, or shuddered.

Read

Set a Purpose Tell students that they will read poems about accomplishing goals. Remind them that setting a purpose can help them monitor their comprehension.

Note Taking: Use the Graphic Organizer

Analytical Writing Distribute copies of online Theme Graphic Organizer 6. Remind students to take notes as they read.

① Theme DOK 2

What is the theme of "Stage Fright"? (It's worthwhile to perform, even when your performance is not perfect.) **Add important details along with the theme to your organizer.**

Reread

Author's Craft: Poetic Elements
DOK 2

Reading/Writing Companion, p. 190
How does the poet use visual arrangement to help you understand how the speaker feels before and after he performs? (Two stanzas have indented lines. The first stanza shows how nervous the speaker feels when he first performs. The second one shows how the crowd enjoyed the show despite the speaker's imperfect performance, and this makes the speaker happy.)

Evaluate Information   DOK 2

Explain Poets use line length to create meaning in their poems.

Discuss *Notice that the lines at the end of each page are indented and short. What is happening in these lines?* (They show the speaker's nervousness and the crowd's reaction.)

Apply Have students tell how the lines call attention to the poem's theme.

Read

2 Homographs DOK 2

The word *long* can refer to a period of time, or it can also mean "to want or desire something." Which meaning of *long* is used in line 4 of "Catching Quiet"? How do you know? (It refers to a period of time. The line before it says, *"you have to be quick,"* meaning the quiet won't be around for a long time.)

Reread

Author's Craft: Poetic Elements
DOK 3

Reading/Writing Companion, p. 191

Reread the poem. Why does the poet use repetition? Cite specific evidence in your answer. (Repetition helps the poet emphasize the theme that peace and quiet in the city is rare and should be cherished. The poet repeats the words *before* and *after* to emphasize that a person can find quiet in the city between two sounds if they wait patiently for it.) Why do you think the poet reverses the usual order of *before* and *after*? (The poet wants to show the noisiness of the city by making the point that quietness occurs *after* one sound and *before* another.)

 Spotlight on Idioms

Page 140, Title and Line 16 Explain that the title is an example of an idiom: *Idioms mean something different from the exact meaning of the individual words. What does* catch *mean?* (grab, capture) *Can you catch quiet like you can catch a ball?* (No.) Help partners define the expression. (find a quiet moment) Have pairs define "stick it in your heart." (keep something in your memory) Then have them brainstorm times when cities are quiet. (possible answers: late at night; during storms)

Catching Quiet

It's hard to catch quiet
In the city.
You have to be quick.

2 It isn't around long.
You might find it
after the roar of a truck,
before a jet flies by.
You might find it
after the horns stop honking,
before the sirens start.
You might find it
after the ice cream man's bell,
before your friends call you
to play.
But when you find it,
stick it in your heart fast.
Keep it there.
It's a bit of the sky.

— *Marci Ridlon*

140

Literature Anthology, pp. 140–141

 Access Complex Text

Genre

Poetry often includes concrete imagery. Guide students to understand that the poem "Catching Quiet" treats the abstract noun *quiet* as a concrete noun to help readers experience it.

- *When does quiet appear? Describe it.* (Quiet appears after noisy events, such as roaring trucks, flying jets, and honking horns.) *How is quiet "a bit of the sky"?* (It's open and still.)

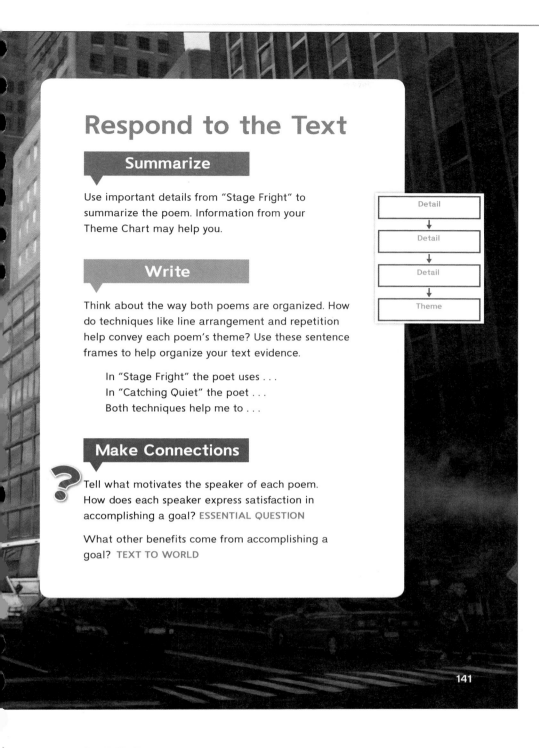

Respond to the Text

Summarize

Use important details from "Stage Fright" to summarize the poem. Information from your Theme Chart may help you.

Detail
↓
Detail
↓
Detail
↓
Theme

Write

Think about the way both poems are organized. How do techniques like line arrangement and repetition help convey each poem's theme? Use these sentence frames to help organize your text evidence.

In "Stage Fright" the poet uses . . .
In "Catching Quiet" the poet . . .
Both techniques help me to . . .

Make Connections

Tell what motivates the speaker of each poem. How does each speaker express satisfaction in accomplishing a goal? ESSENTIAL QUESTION

What other benefits come from accomplishing a goal? TEXT TO WORLD

141

Read

Return to Purpose Review students' purposes for reading. Then ask partners to share how setting a purpose helped them understand the text.

Summarize

Tell students that they will use details from their Theme Chart to summarize "Stage Fright." As I read each poem, I wrote down important details. I can use these details to summarize the theme of the poem.

Reread

Analyze the Text

After students summarize, have them reread to develop a deeper understanding of the poems and answer questions on **Reading/Writing Companion** pages 190–191. For students who need support in citing text evidence, use the Reread prompts on pages T191–T192.

Integrate

Compare Texts DOK 4

Have students compare how the poets present information on accomplishing goals in the poems you have read in this text set.

Ask: *What is similar about the way the speakers of "Rescue" and "Stage Fright" accomplish their goals? What is different?*

Integrate

Build Knowledge: Make Connections

Talk About the Text Have partners discuss the Essential Question: *What motivates you to accomplish a goal?*

Write About the Text Have students add their ideas to their Build Knowledge page of their reader's notebook.

Anchor Chart Record any new ideas on the Build Knowledge anchor chart.

Add to the Vocabulary List Have students write down any words they learned about motivation in their reader's notebooks.

FORMATIVE ASSESSMENT

❯ STUDENT CHECK-IN

Read Have partners share their charts and summaries. Then have them reflect using the Check-In routine.

Reread Have partners share their responses and text evidence on Reading/Writing Companion pages 190-191. Then have them use the Check-In routine to reflect and fill in the bars.

LESSON 3

LEARNING GOALS

We can use text evidence to respond to poetry.

OBJECTIVES

Determine a theme of a story, drama, or poem from details in the text, including how characters in a story or drama respond to challenges or how the speaker in a poem reflects upon a topic; summarize the text.

Compare and contrast stories in the same genre (e.g., mysteries and adventure stories) on their approaches to similar themes and topics.

Produce clear and coherent writing in which the development and organization are appropriate to task, purpose, and audience.

Draw evidence from literary or informational texts to support analysis, reflection, and research.

ELA ACADEMIC LANGUAGE

• *poetry, arrangement, repetition, theme*
• Cognates: *poesía, repetición, tema*

⟫ TEACH IN SMALL GROUP

●● **Approaching Level** and **On Level** Have partners work together to plan and complete the response to the prompt.

● **Beyond Level** Ask students to respond to the prompt independently.

● **ELL** Group students of mixed proficiency levels to discuss and respond to the prompt.

Reread

Write About the Anchor Text

10 mins

Analyze the Prompt DOK 3

Read the prompt aloud: *What is the poet's message in each poem? How does that message motivate you to accomplish a goal?* Ask: *What is the prompt asking?* (to describe each poet's message and how it motivates people to accomplish a goal) Say: *Let's reread and pay attention to how each poet uses repetition, line length, and arrangement to convey a theme.*

Analyze Text Evidence

Remind students that a poem's theme is the big message or idea that the poet wishes to share with readers. Poets often use specific techniques and devices to emphasize certain ideas and convey the poem's theme. Have students turn to **Literature Anthology** page 138–139 and reread "Stage Fright." Ask: *How is the poem organized? How does this relate to the poet's message?* (The line lengths are different in the stanzas to show the change in the speaker's feelings. The lines get shorter when the speaker is nervous and again at the end of the poem when the audience is cheering. The differences in line length emphasize the theme that you can enjoy and be proud of your accomplishments, even when you make mistakes.) Then turn to page 140 and read aloud "Catching Quiet." Ask: *Where does this scene take place?* (in a large city) *What repetition do you hear?* (The phrase "You might find it" is repeated three times.) *What idea does the repetition emphasize?* (It emphasizes that there are certain places where you might find quiet in the city.) Have students look for more repetition and organizational patterns in the poems that relate to the themes of the poems. Encourage them to consider how each poem's message motivates them to accomplish a goal.

Respond

Review pages 190-191 of the **Reading/Writing Companion**. Have partners or small groups refer to and discuss their completed charts and responses from those pages. Then direct students' attention to the sentence starters on page 192. Have them use sentence starters to guide their responses.

Analytical Writing Students should focus on how the poet's use of poetic elements through line arrangement help convey the theme of "Stage Fright." They should contrast that with the use of poetic elements in "Catching Quiet" and explain how the repetition of the speaker's words helps the poet convey a theme. Remind students to vary sentence structure by combining short sentences and adding phrases and clauses to others. Students may use additional paper to complete the assignment if needed.

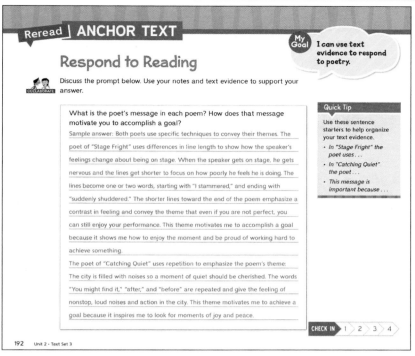

Reading/Writing Companion, p. 192

 # English Language Learners

Use the following scaffolds with **Respond.**

Beginning

Read the prompt with students and discuss what they will write about. Review the students' completed charts on **Reading/Writing Companion** pages 190-191. Identify with students the theme, or message in each poem. Help partners discuss how the message motivates them to accomplish a goal and respond using: The message in "Stage Fright" motivates me to be proud of working hard. The message in "Catching Quiet" motivates me to look for peace.

Intermediate

Read the prompt with students. Review the students' completed charts on **Reading/Writing Companion** pages 190-191. Help partners describe the theme, or message in each poem. Then have them discuss how the message motivates them to accomplish a goal and respond using: The message in "Stage Fright" motivates me to ____. The message in "Catching Quiet" motivates me to ____.

Advanced/Advanced High

Review the prompt and sentence starters on page 192 with students. Have partners discuss their completed charts on pages 190-191 and describe the theme in each poem. Then have them discuss how the message motivates them to accomplish a goal and respond using the sentence starters.

ELL NEWCOMERS

Have students listen to the summaries of the **Anchor Text** in their native language and then in English to help them access the text and develop listening comprehension. Help students ask and answer questions with a partner. Use these sentence frames: What is the poem about? The poem is about ____. Then have them complete the online **Newcomer Activities** individually or in pairs.

FORMATIVE ASSESSMENT

❯ STUDENT CHECK-IN

Ask partners to share their response on Reading/Writing Companion page 192. Have them use the Check-In routine to reflect and fill in the bars.

"Foul Shot"

Lexile NP

LEARNING GOALS

Read We can apply strategies and skills to read poetry.

Reread We can reread to analyze text, craft, and structure, and to compare texts.

Have students apply what they learned as they read.

Analytical Writing **Compare Texts** DOK 4

As students read and reread "Foul Shot," encourage them to take notes and think about the Essential Question: *What motivates you to accomplish a goal?* Students should discuss how this poem, "Stage Fright," and "Catching Quiet" are similar and different.

Read

1 Genre: Narrative and Free Verse Poetry DOK 2

What kind of poem is "Foul Shot"? (It is both narrative and free verse.) **How do you know?** (It tells a story, but it does not have any set rhyme, rhythm, or line length.)

Reread

Author's Craft: Personification DOK 2

Reading/Writing Companion, p. 193

How does the poet use personification to help you understand how the boy feels? (The poet uses personification to slow down the moment and create suspense. The poet's words help the reader visualize the boy, tense and focused, as he throws the basketball toward the hoop and scores.)

Genre • Poetry

Compare Texts
Read how an ambitious player accomplishes a goal.

FOUL SHOT

With two 60's stuck on the scoreboard
And two seconds hanging on the clock,
The solemn boy in the center of eyes,
Squeezed by silence,
Seeks out the line with his feet,
Soothes his hands along his uniform,
Gently drums the ball against the floor
Then measures the waiting net,
Raises the ball on his right hand,
Balances it with his left,
Calms it with fingertips,
Breathes,
Crouches,
Waits,
And then through a stretching of stillness,
Nudges it upward.

142

Literature Anthology, pp. 142–143

 Spotlight on Language

Page 143 Read aloud the first 8 lines. Point out that the whole page is one sentence. *What is the subject of the sentence?* (the ball) *What words describe the movement of the ball?* (*wavers, hesitates, exasperates*) Define the words, emphasizing that each action involves feeling and choice. *Does a ball have feelings or make choices?* (No) *Who or what normally does these actions?* (people) Remind students that giving human actions and emotions to an object is called personification. *Why does the poet say that the ball does these things?* It helps readers understand that the <u>boy</u> and the <u>audience</u> feel <u>nervous</u>.

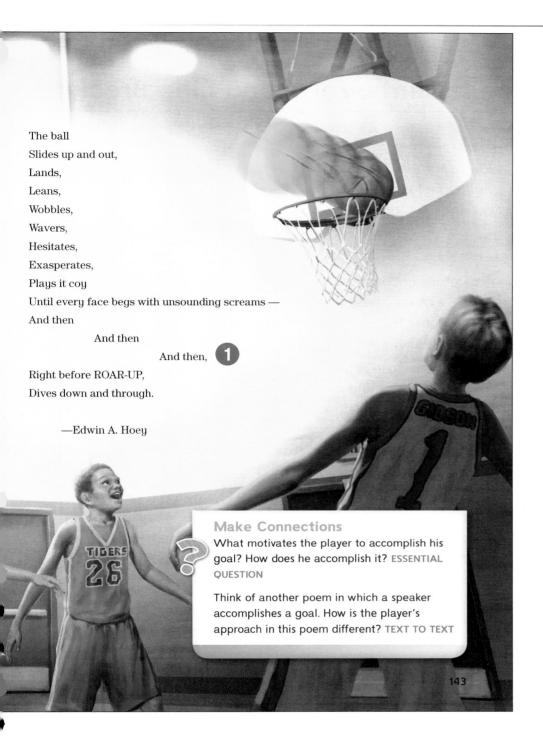

The ball
Slides up and out,
Lands,
Leans,
Wobbles,
Wavers,
Hesitates,
Exasperates,
Plays it coy
Until every face begs with unsounding screams —
And then
　　　　And then
　　　　　　And then, ❶
Right before ROAR-UP,
Dives down and through.

　　　—Edwin A. Hoey

Make Connections
What motivates the player to accomplish his goal? How does he accomplish it? ESSENTIAL QUESTION

Think of another poem in which a speaker accomplishes a goal. How is the player's approach in this poem different? TEXT TO TEXT

143

Integrate

Build Knowledge: Make Connections

Talk About the Text Have partners discuss what motivates the player to meet his goal.

Write About the Text Have students add their ideas to their Build Knowledge pages of their reader's notebooks.

Anchor Chart Record any new ideas on the Build Knowledge anchor chart.

Add to the Vocabulary List Have students write down any words they learned about accomplishing a goal in their reader's notebook.

Read

Summarize

Guide students to summarize the poem.

Reread

Author's Craft: Word Choice DOK 2

Reading/Writing Companion, p. 194

How does the poet's word choice create suspense in the poem? (The words *wavers, hesitates, exasperates, lands, leans, wobbles,* and the repetition of *and then* create suspense. Everyone is anxious to see if the ball will go into the basket.)

Analyze the Text

Have students reread the text to develop a deeper understanding of the text by annotating and answering questions on pages 193-194 of the **Reading/Writing Companion**.

Integrate

Compare Texts DOK 4

Text to Text Answer: The boy in "Stage Fright" is confident at first, but stammers on stage. The player in "Foul Shot" is calm the entire time and makes his shot. Evidence: Page 138 of "Stage Fright" describes how the boy freezes up when he is on stage. Page 142 of "Foul Shot" describes the calm movements of the player.

FORMATIVE ASSESSMENT

❯ **STUDENT CHECK-IN**

Read Ask partners to share their summaries. Then have them reflect using the Check-In routine.

Reread Ask students to share their responses on Reading/Writing Companion pages 193–194. Then have them use the Check-In routine to reflect and fill in the bars.

Reread

10 mins

Poetic Elements: Form and Line Breaks

LEARNING GOALS

We can identify form and line breaks to help us read and understand poetry.

OBJECTIVES

Determine the meaning of words and phrases as they are used in a text.

Explain how a series of chapters, scenes, or stanzas fits together to provide the overall structure of a particular story, drama, or poem.

Adapt speech to a variety of contexts and tasks, using formal English when appropriate to task and situation.

Demonstrate understanding of figurative language, word relationships, and nuances in word meanings.

ELA ACADEMIC LANGUAGE

• voice, tone, rhythm, repetition

• Cognates: voz, tono, ritmo, repetición

1 Explain

Have students turn to **Reading/Writing Companion** page 195. Share with students the following key poetic elements:

• In poetry, the voice telling the poem belongs to the speaker. Voice can give the speaker a specific personality and show how the speaker feels.

• A poet carefully chooses words to help him or her develop the specific voice of the speaker and thus the speaker's personality and feelings. The poet may use figurative language or imagery to express the speaker's attitude toward his or her readers.

• The poet may also use repetition to emphasize a feeling. Visual arrangement, such as line length, line position, punctuation, and capitalization, can also help to convey the speaker's voice.

2 Model

Model analyzing the effect of using word repetition and line breaks in "Foul Shot" on **Literature Anthology** page 143. Read the poem aloud, drawing out the repeated "And then" for effect. Ask: *Why did I read the lines that way?* (Each time the phrase is said, it appears on a new line, so readers are forced to read more slowly.) Discuss the effect of the arrangement of the lines as well as the repetition. Ask: *How does the repetition contribute to the voice in the poem?* (Repeating "And then" shows the speaker is excited and anticipating what will happen.) As a group, discuss how the voice might have changed had the poet left out this repetition.

COLLABORATE

3 Guided Practice

Now have students analyze the effect of visual arrangement at the end of the poem. Have partners read aloud the last two lines. Ask: *What do you notice about the words* ROAR-UP? (They are set in capital letters.) *What do these words represent?* (the cheers of the crowd) *Why do you think the poet chose to write these words this way?* (They are meant to resemble the loud cheering a crowd would make.)

Have partners discuss the speaker's voice at the end of the poem and how the lines contribute to the speaker's voice. Remind students to pay attention to the visual arrangement as well as word choice, and then share their work with the class.

Allow students time to enter their responses on **Reading/Writing Companion** page 195.

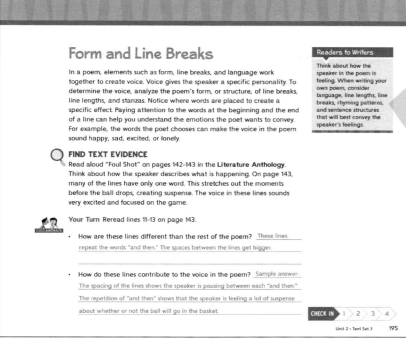

Reading/Writing Companion, p. 195

 # English Language Learners

Use the following scaffolds with **Guided Practice**.

Beginning

Reread the last two lines of "Foul Shot" with students. Write *roar-up* and *ROAR-UP* on the board and explain to students that "roar-up" refers to people cheering. Use gestures as you read each to convey the different meanings. Guide students in explaining how each version of the phrase is read: When the phrase is in lower case letters, I read it in a <u>normal</u> voice. When it is in capital letters, I read it in a <u>loud</u> voice, or yell it.

Intermediate

Have partners reread the last two lines of "Foul Shot." Have them point to the words *ROAR-UP*. Help pairs take turns reading each with the corresponding volume. Ask: *Are the words set in lowercase or capital letters?* (capital) *Do the capital letters show the cheers of the crowd?* (yes) *Talk to your partner about how this adds to what you know about the speaker's voice.*

Advanced/Advanced High

Have students read the last two lines of the poem. Provide questions to have partners discuss: *What does "roar-up" refer to? Why does the poet write it in capital letters? Talk to your partner about how this adds to the speaker's voice. Share your conclusion with the class.*

FORMATIVE ASSESSMENT

STUDENT CHECK-IN

Ask partners to share their Your Turn responses on Reading/Writing Companion page 195. Then have them use the Check-In routine to reflect and fill in the bars.

AUTHOR'S CRAFT **T199**

LESSON
5

We can compare the photograph with the selections in this text set to build knowledge about how people accomplish goals.

OBJECTIVES

Compare and contrast stories in the same genre (e.g., mysteries and adventure stories) on their approaches to similar themes and topics.

Draw evidence from literary or informational texts to support analysis, reflection, and research.

Close Reading Routine

Read DOK 1–2

- Identify important ideas and details.
- Take notes and summarize.
- Use ACT prompts as needed.

Reread DOK 2–3

- Analyze the text, craft, and structure.
- Use the *Reading/Writing Companion*.

Integrate DOK 3–4

- Integrate knowledge and ideas.
- Make text-to-text connections.
- Use the Integrate/Make Connections lesson.
- Use *Reading/Writing Companion*, p. 196.
- Complete the Show Your Knowledge task.
- Inspire action.

❯ STUDENT CHECK-IN

Ask partners to share their response on Reading/Writing Companion page 196. Then have them use the Check-In routine to reflect and fill in the bars.

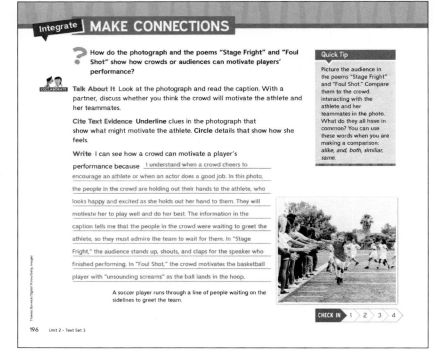

Reading/Writing Companion, p. 196

Integrate

(10 mins)
Make Connections DOK 4

Talk About It

COLLABORATE

Share and discuss students' responses to the "Reaching a Goal" blast. Display the Build Knowledge anchor chart. Review the chart and have students read through their notes, annotations, and responses for each text. Then ask students to complete the Talk About It activity on **Reading/Writing Companion** page 196.

Cite Text Evidence

Guide students to see the connections between the photograph on Reading/Writing Companion page 196 and the poems. Remind students to reread the caption and the Quick Tip.

Write

Students should refer to their notes on the chart as they respond to the writing prompt on the page. When students have finished writing, have groups share and discuss their responses.

Build Knowledge: Make Connections

Talk About the Text Have partners discuss what motivates people to accomplish a goal.

Write About the Text Have students add their ideas to their Build Knowledge pages of their reader's notebooks.

Anchor Chart Record any new ideas on the Build Knowledge anchor chart.

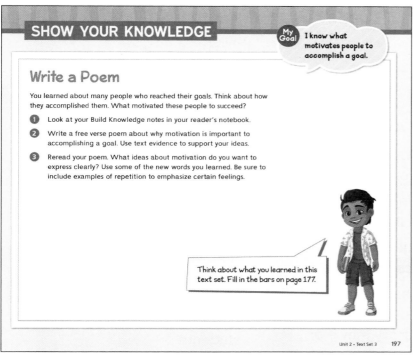

Reading/Writing Companion, p. 197

Integrate

Show Your Knowledge DOK 4

Write a Poem

Explain that students will show how they built knowledge across the text set by writing a poem about what motivates people to reach their goals. Display the Build Knowledge anchor chart and ask: *What motivates you to accomplish a goal?*

Steps 1 Guide partners to review the Build Knowledge anchor chart in their reader's notebook to discuss the prompt.

Step 2 Have students brainstorm three things that can motivate people to accomplish a goal. Then have them write a free verse poem about why motivation is important to accomplishing a goal. Have students use text evidence to support their ideas.

Step 3 Have students reread their poems. Have them consider what ideas about motivation they want to express. Prompt students to use words from their Build Knowledge vocabulary list in their poems.

Inspire Action

Share Your Poem Have partners present and display their poems. Ask students in the audience to write down things they found interesting or questions they have for the presenters on sticky notes. Presenters can read the comments and post sticky note responses.

What Are You Inspired to Do? Encourage partners to think of another way to respond to the texts. Ask: *What else do the texts inspire you to do?*

LEARNING GOALS

We can write a poem to show the knowledge we built about what motivates people to accomplish goals.

OBJECTIVES

Report on a topic or text or present an opinion, sequencing ideas logically and using appropriate facts and relevant, descriptive details to support main ideas or themes; speak clearly at an understandable pace.

Adapt speech to a variety of contexts and tasks, using formal English when appropriate to task and situation.

Demonstrate command of the conventions of standard English grammar and usage when writing or speaking.

ELA ACADEMIC LANGUAGE

• *motivate, goal, resolve, succeed*

• Cognates: *motivar, resolver*

DIGITAL TOOLS

Show Your Knowledge Rubric

ELL ENGLISH LANGUAGE LEARNERS

Provide the sentence frames for support. *Three things that can motivate people to accomplish a goal are ___. Motivation is important because ___.*

MY GOALS ROUTINE

What I Learned

Review Goals Have students turn back to page 177 of the Reading/Writing Companion and review the goals for the text set.

Reflect Have students think about the progress they've made toward the goals. Review the key. Have students reflect and fill in the bars.

LEARNING GOALS

- **We can build and expand on new vocabulary words.**
- **We can use context clues to determine the meaning of homographs.**
- **We can write using new vocabulary words.**

OBJECTIVES

Determine or clarify the meaning of unknown and multiple-meaning words and phrases, choosing flexibly from a range of strategies.

Expand vocabulary by adding inflectional endings and suffixes.

DIGITAL TOOLS

Word Study

Vocabulary Activities

 **ENGLISH LANGUAGE LEARNERS**

According to their language proficiency, students should contribute to discussions by using short phrases, asking questions, and adding relevant details.

FORMATIVE ASSESSMENT

❯ STUDENT CHECK-IN

After each lesson, have partners share and reflect using the Check-In routine.

 LESSON 1 Connect to Words

Practice the target vocabulary.

1. Which is **ambitious**—doing ten chores in a day, or doing one?
2. What is something you have **memorized**? Recite it.
3. What action might give a baseball player **satisfaction**?
4. Who is likely to have **shuddered**—the person who watched a scary movie or the one who heard a funny joke?

Build Vocabulary

Discuss important academic words.

- Display *repetition* and *rhyme*.
- Define the words and discuss their meanings.
- Display *repeat* and *repetition*. Have partners look up and define related words. Write the related words on the board.
- Ask partners to generate examples of *repetition* and *rhyme*.

 OPTION LESSON 2 Related Words

Help students generate different forms of this week's words by adding, changing, or removing inflectional endings.

- Draw a four-column chart on the board. Write *memorized* in the third column. Then write *memorize, memorizes,* and *memorizing* in the other columns. Read aloud the words with students.
- Have students share sentences using each form of *memorize*.
- Students can fill in the chart for *shuddered,* and then share sentences using different forms of the word.
- Have students copy the chart in their reader's notebook.

See **Practice Book** page 119.

Similes And Metaphors

- Remind students that similes and metaphors compare two unlike things. Similes use *like* or *as;* metaphors do not.
- Provide and discuss the simile *The mother's touch was as soft as a cloud.*
- Have partners write similes or metaphors using the vocabulary words. For example, ____ *was as ambitious as* ____, or *He shuddered like a* ____. Ask pairs to present examples to the class.

Spiral Review

LESSON 3 — Reinforce the Words

Have students orally complete each sentence stem.

1. The <u>ambitious</u> singer felt <u>satisfaction</u> when ____.
2. In preparation for the test, Rosa <u>memorized</u> ____.
3. I <u>shuddered</u> when ____.
4. Kayla left the house, <u>assuring</u> her parents that ____.
5. The police <u>detected</u> fingerprints at the ____.
6. The baby bird is <u>emerging</u> from ____.
7. I felt <u>gratitude</u> for ____.
8. Teo likes the <u>previous</u> album better than ____.
9. The hungry cat was in <u>pursuit</u> of the ____.

See **Practice Book** page 120.

Homographs

Remind students to use context clues or a print or online dictionary to distinguish homographs.

- Display On Level **Differentiated Genre Passage** "Blue Ribbon Dreams." Read the first ten lines on page O1. Model how to figure out the meaning of "stall."
- Have students find other homographs in the passage.
- Ask students to record these homographs in their reader's notebook and explain how they used context clues to figure out the meaning of each one.

OPTION — LESSON 4 — Connect to Writing

- Have students write sentences in their reader's notebook using the target vocabulary.
- Tell them to write sentences that provide context to show what the words mean.
- **ELL** Provide the Lesson 3 sentence stems 1–9 for students needing extra support.

Write Using Vocabulary

Have students write something they learned from this text set's target vocabulary in their reader's notebook. For example, they might write about how an *ambitious* person set goals and then felt *satisfaction* after achieving them.

Shades of Meaning

Help students generate synonyms and antonyms of the word *ambitious*. Draw an antonym/synonym scale.

- Remind students that similar words can have slightly different meanings. This is called "nuance."
- Have partners generate and sequence words in order of intensity.
- Ask each pair to post its scale and present it to the class. Stop to discuss differences among the scales.
- Ask students to copy the scales into their reader's notebook.

OPTION — LESSON 5 — Word Squares

 MULTIMODAL

Ask students to create Word Squares for each vocabulary word.

- In the first square, students write the word (e.g., *shuddered*).
- In the second square, students write a definition and any related words, such as synonyms (e.g., *quivered, trembled*).
- In the third square, students draw a simple sketch that will help them remember the word (e.g., squiggly lines to show a person shuddering).
- In the fourth square, students write nonexamples, including antonyms for the word (e.g., *relaxed, loosened up*).
- Have partners share and discuss their squares.

Morphology

Use a T-chart to teach the Latin root *mem*, meaning "mind."

- In the right column, write *memorized*. In the left column, write a definition that includes the word *mind*.
- Have students define *memorial* and *remember*.
- Tell students to record the charts in their reader's notebook.

Write Using Vocabulary

Have students use vocabulary words in their extended writing.

Lexile 650L

OBJECTIVES

Determine a theme of a story, drama, or poem from details in the text, including how characters in a story or drama respond to challenges or how the speaker in a poem reflects upon a topic; summarize the text.

Read grade-level prose and poetry orally with accuracy, appropriate rate, and expression on successive readings.

Read grade-level text with purpose and understanding.

ELA ACADEMIC LANGUAGE

• theme, realistic fiction, poetry, homograph

• Cognates: *tema, poesía, homógrafo*

●Approaching Level

Leveled Reader: *Clearing the Jungle*

Preview and Predict

Read the Essential Question: *What motivates you to accomplish a goal?*

Have students preview the title, table of contents, and first page of *Clearing the Jungle*. Students should use details in the text and images to predict what the story might be about.

Review Genre: Realistic Fiction

Tell students that this selection is realistic fiction. The characters and settings are like real people and places, and the events could actually happen. As students preview the book, have them identify features of realistic fiction in *Clearing the Jungle*.

Close Reading

Note Taking Ask students to use a copy of the online Theme **Graphic Organizer 6** as they read.

Page 2 Point to the word *live* in the sentence "It's a wonder that jungle animals don't live in there with you." *Is this word an adjective, meaning "alive," or a verb, meaning "reside"?* (a verb, meaning "reside") Ask students to identify the part of speech and meaning of the word *live* in "but I'm sure there aren't any live animals." (adjective, meaning "alive") Have students add this word to their reader's notebook. *How does the comparison between Ethan's room and a jungle help you understand the setting of the story?* (The comparison shows readers that Ethan's bedroom is wild, tangled, and unorganized.)

Pages 3–4 *Reread to find details that reinforce the idea that Ethan's room is messy.* (Books and papers covered the desk; runaway socks peeked out from underneath his bed; a stack of board games crashed down from the top shelf.)

Pages 5–8 *Ethan's library book is overdue. His science project is unfinished, and he doesn't have his field trip permission slip. Also, his planner is missing. With a partner, discuss one possible lesson Ethan might learn by the end of the story based on these details. This lesson may be one theme of the story.* (Ethan will learn to be more responsible.)

Pages 9–11 *How does Ethan's older brother, Joe, help him?* (Joe helps Ethan get started by identifying a goal and steps to take.)

Pages 12–13 *What actions does Ethan take to "tame the jungle" and be more responsible? Reread to help you answer the question.* (He cleans and organizes his room, pins a calendar to his bulletin board, and enters important dates into his planner. At school, he turns in his permission slip and offers ideas for the project.)

Pages 14–15 *What is the theme of this story? With a partner, identify details from the story to support your idea.* (Staying organized can help people be more responsible. Organizing his room helps Ethan find his lost library book and permission slip and complete his projects.)

Respond to Reading Revisit the Essential Question and ask students to complete the Respond to Reading section on page 16.

 Write About Reading Check that students have described how Ethan's friends and teacher respond differently to him in Chapter 4. Be sure they have explained how this change supports the story's theme.

Fluency: Expression and Phrasing

Model Model reading page 11 with proper expression and phrasing. Next reread the page aloud and have students read along with you.

Apply Have students practice reading the passage with a partner.

Paired Read: "Just for Once"

Analytical Writing **Make Connections: Write About It**

Before reading, ask students to note that the genre of this text is poetry. Then discuss the Essential Question. After reading, ask students to write about connections between the themes of *Clearing the Jungle* and "Just for Once."

Leveled Reader

Build Knowledge

Talk About the Text Have partners discuss what motivates people to accomplish a goal.

Write About the Text Have students add their ideas to the Build Knowledge pages of their reader's notebooks.

FOCUS ON LITERARY ELEMENTS

Students can extend their knowledge of rhyme and repetition by completing the genre activity on page 20.

LITERATURE CIRCLES

Ask students to conduct a literature circle using the Thinkmark questions to guide the discussion. You may wish to have a whole-class discussion, using both selections in the Leveled Reader, about what motivates people to accomplish a goal.

LEVEL UP

IF students read the Approaching Level fluently and answered the questions,

THEN pair them with students who have proficiently read the On Level and have students

- echo-read the On Level main selection.

- use self-stick notes to identify details that may be important to the story's theme.

 **Access Complex Text**

The On Level challenges students by including more **domain-specific words** and **complex sentence structures**.

"Blue Ribbon Dreams"
"Sammy's Day Out"

OBJECTIVES

Quote accurately from a text when explaining what the text says explicitly and when drawing inferences from the text.

Explain different characters' perspectives in a literary text.

Determine a theme of a story, drama, or poem from details in the text, including how characters in a story or drama respond to challenges or how the speaker in a poem reflects upon a topic; summarize the text.

Explain how a series of chapters, scenes, or stanzas fits together to provide the overall structure of a particular story, drama, or poem.

Demonstrate understanding of figurative language, word relationships, and nuances in word meanings.

Use the relationship between particular words (e.g., synonyms, antonyms, homographs) to better understand each of the words.

ELA ACADEMIC LANGUAGE

- poetry, speaker, repetition, rhyme, theme, homograph, nonliteral
- Cognates: *poesía, repetición, rima, tema, homógrafo*

Approaching Level

Genre Passage: "Blue Ribbon Dreams" and "Sammy's Day Out"

Build Background

Read aloud the Essential Question: *What motivates you to accomplish a goal?* Have pairs compare how the speakers of the poems they read in this text set were motivated to reach a goal. Use sentence starters.

> *The speaker acted because . . .*
>
> *This helps me understand that goals . . .*

Review Genre: Poetry

Review that poems express the thoughts and feelings of a speaker who is not necessarily the poet. Narrative poems tell a story and may include characters and dialogue. In free verse poems, a speaker shares thoughts and feelings directly with readers. Devices such as description, repetition, rhyme, and line organization allow a poem to convey a theme, or important idea.

Close Reading

Note Taking As students first read the poems, have them annotate key ideas and details, unfamiliar words, and questions they have. Then read again and use the following questions. Remind students to cite evidence from the text.

> **Read**

Poetic Elements: Rhyme Read the first four lines of "Blue Ribbon Dreams" on page A1. *What do you notice about each pair of lines?* (The final words in each pair rhyme.) *How does this affect the poem?* (The rhyme adds rhythm and makes the lines sound fun to read.)

Homographs Read line 13. *The homograph* fair *can be an adjective meaning "honest" or a noun meaning "carnival." How is it used in line 13? Use context clues to explain.* (The speaker is talking about being judged badly because of her size, so it is being used as an adjective meaning "honest.") Have students add this word to their reader's notebook.

Theme Read lines 13–16. *What feelings does the speaker share?* (She wants to prove to people that she can succeed despite her small size.) *Read the last four lines. What might they suggest about a theme of the poem?* (The theme might be that anyone can accomplish a goal if they work hard enough.)

Summarize Have students use their notes to summarize how the speaker works to accomplish a goal.

Genre: Narrative Poetry Read the first stanza of "Sammy's Day Out" on page A3. *What type of poem is this? How do you know?* (It's a narrative poem. The poem tells a story about a wolf cub named Sammy.)

Theme Read aloud the last two stanzas. *What does Sammy learn?* (He should have listened to his parents.) *What does this suggest about doing whatever you want?* (Possible answer: Sometimes listening to others is a good thing.)

Summarize Have students use their notes to summarize what Sammy does and what happens as a result.

Reread

Use the questions on pages A2 and A3 to guide rereading of the poems.

Author's Craft Reread lines 1 and 2 of "Blue Ribbon Dreams" on page A1. *What words or phrases tell you how the girl feels?* (The girl says she is "trudging" and her feet are "like lead." This lets me know she is tired as she walks to the barn.)

Author's Craft Reread line 19 of "Blue Ribbon Dreams." *Why do you think the poet repeats the word "again"?* (The poet wants to show that training Little Red means doing the same thing over and over again and is hard work.)

Author's Craft Reread the second stanza of "Sammy's Day Out," *Why do you think the poet uses the word "crept"?* (The poet uses the word "crept" to show that Sammy doesn't want anyone to hear him.)

Integrate

Make Connections Guide students to recognize connections between "Blue Ribbon Dreams," "Sammy's Day Out," and other poems they have read. Have pairs work together to gather text evidence and answer this question: *What do the themes of the poems help you understand about why people work toward a goal?*

Compare Texts Display a three-column chart labeled *Poem, Theme,* and *What I Learned.* Help students compare how the poems' themes share a lesson about achieving a goal.

Build Knowledge

Talk About the Text Have partners discuss what motivates people to accomplish a goal.

Write About the Text Have students add their ideas to the Build Knowledge pages of their reader's notebooks.

Differentiate and Collaborate

Be Inspired Have students think about poems they have read, such as "Blue Ribbon Dreams" and "Sammy's Day Out." Ask: *What do the poems inspire you to do?* Use these activities or have pairs think of a way to respond to the poems.

Make a 7-Day Plan Think of a goal you would like to accomplish in a week. Using a calendar, write one thing you will do each day to reach your goal. Post the calendar and check off each task as you accomplish it.

Conduct an Interview Interview someone you know who has successfully achieved a goal. Ask questions about what motivated the person and how they were able to accomplish what they wanted.

Readers to Writers

Nonliteral Language Remind students that the meaning of nonliteral language is different from its dictionary definition. Nonliteral language can create a certain effect or help readers visualize what is being described. Have students reread line 22 on page A1. *What does the speaker mean when she says she breaks out into song? What effect does this nonliteral language have?*

LEVEL UP

IF students read the Approaching Level fluently and answered the questions,

THEN pair them with students who have proficiently read the On Level. Have them

- partner read the On Level passage.
- summarize what motivates the speakers of each poem.

● Approaching Level

Phonics/Decoding

REVIEW WORDS WITH CLOSED SYLLABLES

OBJECTIVES

Know and apply grade-level phonics and word analysis skills in decoding words.

Use combined knowledge of all letter-sound correspondences, syllabication patterns, and morphology (e.g., roots and affixes) to read accurately unfamiliar multisyllabic words in context and out of context.

Decode words with closed syllables.

I Do Review with students that every syllable has one vowel sound. Write the word *witness* on the board. Draw a line between the *t* and the *n*, and pronounce each syllable separately. Remind students that when a syllable ends with a consonant and has a short vowel sound spelled with a single vowel, it is called a closed syllable. *Wit* and *ness* are closed syllables.

We Do Write the words *suspect, contact,* and *basket* on the board. Read the words aloud and divide them into syllables. Then model identifying the closed syllables in each word. Draw a circle around the closed syllables *sus, pect, con, tact, bas,* and *ket*. Explain that all are closed syllables because they end in consonants and contain a short vowel sound spelled with one vowel.

You Do Add the words *dentist* and *flatbed* to the list and read them aloud. Have students identify the closed syllables in these words. Then have them chorally read the words aloud.

BUILD WORDS WITH CLOSED SYLLABLES

OBJECTIVES

Use combined knowledge of all letter-sound correspondences, syllabication patterns, and morphology (e.g., roots and affixes) to read accurately unfamiliar multisyllabic words in context and out of context.

Build words with closed syllables.

I Do Tell students that they will be building longer words from closed syllables. Display the **Word-Building Cards** *mag, net, con,* and *sent*. Read aloud the syllable on each card.

We Do Work with students to combine the Word-Building Cards to create two-syllable words with closed syllables. Have them chorally read the words *magnet* and *consent*. Draw a line under each syllable and point out that they are all closed syllables because they end with a consonant and have a short vowel sound spelled with a single vowel.

You Do Display the Word-Building Cards *sub, com, self, ment, let,* and *less*. Have partners combine them to build new words and identify the closed syllables in each. Then have pairs of students read the words chorally as you point to them.

PRACTICE WORDS WITH CLOSED SYLLABLES

OBJECTIVES

Know and apply grade-level phonics and word analysis skills in decoding words.

Use combined knowledge of all letter-sound correspondences, syllabication patterns, and morphology (e.g., roots and affixes) to read accurately unfamiliar multisyllabic words in context and out of context.

Decode words with closed syllables.

I Do Write these words on the board: *planet, suspect, distant,* and *transmit.* Read the words aloud, and identify the closed syllables in each word.

We Do Write the words *rabbit, mitten,* and *consist* on the board. Model how to decode the first word. Identify both closed syllables in the word. Then have students decode the remaining words. As necessary, help them identify the closed syllables.

To provide additional practice, write the words below on the board. Read aloud the first word, underlining the letters in the closed syllable with your finger.

conduct	mascot	submit
admit	problem	discuss
contest	fossil	fragment
fitness	bandit	splendid

You Do Have students read aloud the remaining words. Ask them to identify the closed syllables in each word. Afterward, point to the words in the list in random order for students to read chorally.

ELL For **ELL** students who need phonics and decoding practice, define words and help them use the words in sentences, scaffolding to ensure their understanding. See the **Language Transfers Handbook** for phonics elements that may not transfer from students' native languages.

Approaching Level

Vocabulary

REVIEW HIGH-FREQUENCY WORDS

TIER 2

OBJECTIVES

Acquire and use accurately grade-appropriate general academic and domain-specific words and phrases, including those that signal contrast, addition, and other logical relationships (e.g., *however, although, nevertheless, similarly, moreover, in addition*).

Review high-frequency words.

I Do Choose review words from **High-Frequency Word Cards** 41–80. Display one word at a time, following the routine:

Display the word. Read the word. Then spell the word.

We Do Ask students to state the word and spell the word with you. Model using the word in a sentence and have students repeat after you.

You Do Display the word. Ask students to say the word and then spell it. When completed, quickly flip through the word card set as students chorally read the words. Provide opportunities for students to use the words in speaking and writing. For example, provide sentence starters such as *I like to draw pictures of ____*. Ask students to write each word in their reader's notebook.

REVIEW ACADEMIC VOCABULARY

MULTIMODAL **TIER 2**

OBJECTIVES

Acquire and use accurately grade-appropriate general academic and domain-specific words and phrases, including those that signal contrast, addition, and other logical relationships (e.g., *however, although, nevertheless, similarly, moreover, in addition*).

I Do Display each **Visual Vocabulary Card** and state the word. Explain how the photograph illustrates the word. State the example sentence and repeat the word.

We Do Point to the word on the card and read the word with students. Ask them to repeat the word. Engage students in structured partner talk about the image as prompted on the back of the vocabulary card.

You Do Display each visual in random order, hiding the word. Have students match the definitions and context sentences of the words to the visuals displayed.

 ELL You may wish to review high-frequency words with ELL students using the lesson above.

UNDERSTAND ACADEMIC VOCABULARY

OBJECTIVES

Acquire and use accurately grade-appropriate general academic and domain-specific words and phrases, including those that signal contrast, addition, and other logical relationships (e.g., *however, although, nevertheless, similarly, moreover, in addition*).

I Do Display the *ambitious* **Visual Vocabulary Card** and ask: *When have you been* ambitious*?* Give a sample answer: *I was* ambitious *when I practiced every day to make the basketball team.*

We Do Ask students to describe something they have memorized. Help them respond and explain their answers.

You Do Have pairs respond to these questions and explain their answers.

- What is something that might give you great *satisfaction*?
- If you had a dog that *shuddered*, what could you do to comfort it?

Have students pick words from their reader's notebook and write the definition of the word and a sentence using the word.

HOMOGRAPHS

OBJECTIVES

Use context to confirm or self-correct word recognition and understanding, rereading as necessary.

Demonstrate understanding of figurative language, word relationships, and nuances in word meanings.

Use the relationship between particular words (e.g., synonyms, antonyms, homographs) to better understand each of the words.

I Do Remind students that homographs are words that are spelled the same but have different meanings. They can use context clues to figure out which meaning of a homograph is correct. Display "Blue Ribbon Dreams" in the online Approaching Level **Differentiated Genre Passage** page A1. Choral-read the first two lines. Point to the word *lead*.

Think Aloud I am not sure which meaning of *lead* is correct: "a heavy, blue-gray metal" or "show the way." The word *Trudging* at the beginning of the line means "Walking slowly." I think if the narrator's feet were like lead, they felt heavy. So I can tell that "a heavy, blue-gray metal" is the correct meaning of *lead* in this example.

We Do Ask students to point to the word *fair* in the fourth line. Give two meanings for *fair*: "a festive gathering for the purpose of exhibition" and "by the rules." Point out the context clues *barn* (line 2) and *County* (line 4). Ask students which meaning is correct in the sentence.

You Do Have students use context clues to determine the correct meanings to use for the words *entrance* (line 5), *entrances* (line 9), *fair* (lines 13, 24, and 25), and *lead* (line 20). They should explain which context clues they used to help them determine the correct meaning.

Approaching Level

Fluency/Comprehension

FLUENCY

OBJECTIVES

Read with sufficient accuracy and fluency to support comprehension.

Read grade-level prose and poetry orally with accuracy, appropriate rate, and expression on successive readings.

I Do Explain that readers should read with expression by changing the sound of their voices to show the meaning of what they read. Phrasing means grouping words into meaningful chunks. Punctuation marks are clues that help readers read with good expression and correct phrasing. Read the first six lines of "Blue Ribbon Dreams" in the online Approaching Level **Differentiated Genre Passage** page A1. Tell students to listen for the way you group the words and use expression to show meaning or to place emphasis.

We Do Read the rest of the poem aloud and have students repeat each line after you while imitating your expression and phrasing. Point out that you grouped words that go together and used your voice to add expression.

You Do Have partners take turns reading lines from the passage. Remind them to focus on reading in phrases and with good expression. Listen in and provide corrective feedback as needed by modeling proper fluency.

IDENTIFY IMPORTANT DETAILS

OBJECTIVES

Determine a theme of a story, drama, or poem from details in the text, including how characters in a story or drama respond to challenges or how the speaker in a poem reflects upon a topic; summarize the text.

I Do Remind students that poets often include many important, or key, details to help readers understand the theme or meaning of a poem. By rereading the poem several times, readers may notice details they did not notice the first time.

We Do Read the first ten lines of "Blue Ribbon Dreams" in the online Approaching Level **Differentiated Genre Passage** page A1. Point out important details about the speaker and setting. You might mention that details reveal that the speaker loves his or her horse, Little Red, and is training hard to win first place at the fair. The setting at the beginning of the poem is Little Red's barn.

You Do Have student pairs read the rest of the poem. After each five lines, have them write down the important details they find. Review their lists with them and help them explain why the details they chose are important.

REVIEW THEME

OBJECTIVES

Determine a theme of a story, drama, or poem from details in the text, including how characters in a story or drama respond to challenges or how the speaker in a poem reflects upon a topic; summarize the text.

I Do Remind students that the theme in a poem is the important idea or message the poet wants to share with readers. Identifying the poet's word choice and use of details can help readers identify a poem's theme.

We Do Echo-read lines 1–16 of "Blue Ribbon Dreams" in the online Approaching Level **Differentiated Genre Passage** page A1. Discuss with students any interesting or powerful words they notice when the poem is read aloud—for example, *entrances* creates a strong sense of the speaker's feelings about his or her horse. Then have students refer to the list of details they compiled earlier. Model how to use the poet's choice of words and key details to offer ideas about the theme of the poem so far.

You Do Have partners take turns reading the rest of the poem aloud. Ask them to review and add to the list of key details they have been creating. Then have students consider all of these details in order to determine the theme of the poem as a whole.

SELF-SELECTED READING

OBJECTIVES

Determine a theme of a story, drama, or poem from details in the text, including how characters in a story or drama respond to challenges or how the speaker in a poem reflects upon a topic; summarize the text.

By the end of the year, read and comprehend literature, including stories, dramas, and poetry, at the high end of the grades 4–5 text complexity band independently and proficiently.

Reread to increase understanding.

Independent Reading

In this text set, students focus on these key aspects of literary text: how an author develops a theme and how figurative language and poetic elements work together in narrative and free verse poetry. Guide students to transfer what they have learned in this text set as they read.

Have students choose a narrative or free verse poem for sustained silent reading. Students can check the online **Leveled Reading Library** for selections. Remind them that:

- the theme of a poem is the big idea or message that the poet wants to share with readers.
- they should reread to identify relevant, or key, details in the poem and use these details to determine the theme.

Have students read the book independently, using the Reading **Center Activity Cards** as a resource. Students can conduct a book talk with their group using their responses from the Respond to Reading and Make Connections prompts.

Lexile 730L

OBJECTIVES

Determine a theme of a story, drama, or poem from details in the text, including how characters in a story or drama respond to challenges or how the speaker in a poem reflects upon a topic; summarize the text.

Read grade-level text with purpose and understanding.

Read grade-level prose and poetry orally with accuracy, appropriate rate, and expression on successive readings.

Draw evidence from literary or informational texts to support analysis, reflection, and research.

Apply grade 5 Reading standards to literature.

ELA ACADEMIC LANGUAGE

• *theme, realistic fiction, poetry, paraphrase*

• Cognates: *tema, ficción realista, poesía*

●On Level

Leveled Reader: *I Want to Ride!*

Preview and Predict

Read the Essential Question: *What motivates you to accomplish a goal?*

Have students preview the title, table of contents, and first page of *I Want to Ride!* Students should use details in the text and illustrations to predict what the story might be about.

Review Genre: Realistic Fiction

Tell students that this selection is realistic fiction. The characters and settings are like real people and places, and the events could actually happen in real life. As they preview the book, have students identify features of realistic fiction in *I Want to Ride!*

Close Reading

Note Taking Ask students to use a copy of online Theme **Graphic Organizer 6** as they read.

Page 2 *Notice that the narrator uses first-person pronouns such as* I *and* me. *Ariela is telling her own story. What important information does Ariela tell readers about herself?* (She loves horses and dreams of having a mare named Dawn Princess. She reads a lot about horses and really wants to learn to ride one.)

Pages 3–4 *In the sentence "I was on the ground," is the word* ground *a noun, meaning "surface," or a verb, meaning "crushed into particles"?* (noun, meaning "surface") *How has Drew's accident affected Ariela?* (Her mom is concerned about safety and doesn't want her to ride her bike.)

Pages 5–7 *Reread the dialogue between Ariela and Mrs. Murphy. What is one possible theme of this story that appears directly in the dialogue?* ("With effort and persistence, dreams can become reality!")

Pages 8–11 *Reread to find clues about why Ms. Miller does not offer to help Ariela during their first visit.* (Ms. Miller thinks that Ariela might not understand the responsibility of horse riding.) *Why does Ms. Miller change her mind about helping Ariela?* (Mrs. Murphy tells Ms. Miller that Ariela is hardworking and reliable.)

How does Ariela's mom respond when Ariela asks if she can go with Mrs. Miller to the riding club? (She doesn't think riding horses is safe.) *What changes her mind?* (Drew convinces her that it is a great opportunity for Ariela. He points out that Ariela will have excellent instructors and will use safety gear.)

Pages 12–13 *What jobs does Ms. Miller show Ariela how to do?* (how to brush the horse's coat, check his hooves for stones, put on his saddle) *Is Ariela disappointed or excited after visiting the club? Explain.* (She is excited. She is eager to work so she can spend time with the horses.)

Pages 14–15 *What does Ariela learn about making a dream come true? Discuss your ideas with a partner and paraphrase text details to support your thoughts.* (Ariela learns that accomplishing a dream takes planning and responsibility. In order to get riding lessons, she has to do Internet research, talk to Ms. Miller and her mom, and be willing to work hard.)

Respond to Reading Revisit the Essential Question and ask students to complete the Respond to Reading section on page 16.

 Write About Reading Check that students identify the relationship between Ms. Miller's change in attitude and the story's theme.

Fluency: Expression and Phrasing

Model Model reading page 6 with proper expression and phrasing. Next, reread the page aloud and have students read along with you.

Apply Have students practice reading the passage with a partner.

Paired Read: "Home Run"

 **Make Connections: Write About It**

Before reading, ask students to note that the genre of this text is poetry. Then discuss the Essential Question. After reading, ask students to write about connections between the themes of *I Want to Ride!* and "Home Run." **Leveled Reader**

Build Knowledge

Talk About the Text Have partners discuss what motivates people to accomplish a goal.

Write About the Text Have students add their ideas to the Build Knowledge pages of their reader's notebooks.

FOCUS ON LITERARY ELEMENTS

Students can extend their knowledge of rhyme and repetition by completing the genre activity on page 20.

LITERATURE CIRCLES

Ask students to conduct a literature circle using the Thinkmark questions to guide the discussion. You may wish to have a whole-class discussion, using both selections in the Leveled Reader, about what motivates people to accomplish a goal.

LEVEL UP

IF students read the On Level fluently and answered the questions,

THEN pair them with students who have proficiently read the Beyond Level and have students

- partner-read the Beyond Level main selection.

- identify details about the characters and events that point to the story's theme.

A C T Access Complex Text

The Beyond Level challenges students by including more **domain-specific words** and **complex sentence structures**.

"Blue Ribbon Dreams"
"Sammy's Day Out"

OBJECTIVES

Quote accurately from a text when explaining what the text says explicitly and when drawing inferences from the text.

Explain different characters' perspectives in a literary text.

Determine a theme of a story, drama, or poem from details in the text, including how characters in a story or drama respond to challenges or how the speaker in a poem reflects upon a topic; summarize the text.

Explain how a series of chapters, scenes, or stanzas fits together to provide the overall structure of a particular story, drama, or poem.

Demonstrate understanding of figurative language, word relationships, and nuances in word meanings.

Use the relationship between particular words (e.g., synonyms, antonyms, homographs) to better understand each of the words.

Produce clear and coherent writing in which the development and organization are appropriate to task, purpose, and audience.

ELA ACADEMIC LANGUAGE

• *poetry, speaker, repetition, rhyme, theme, homograph, verse, nonliteral*

• Cognates: *poesía, repetición, rima, tema, homógrafo, verso*

●On Level

Genre Passage: "Blue Ribbon Dreams" and "Sammy's Day Out"

Build Background

Read aloud the Essential Question: *What motivates you to accomplish a goal?* Have pairs compare how the speakers of the poems they read in this text set were motivated to reach a goal. Use these sentence starters.

> *The speaker acted because . . .*
>
> *This helps me understand that goals . . .*

Review Genre: Poetry

Review that poems express the thoughts and feelings of a speaker who is not necessarily the poet. Narrative poems tell a story and may include characters and dialogue. In free verse poems, the speaker shares thoughts and feelings directly with readers. A poet can use devices such as description, repetition, rhyme, and line organization to allow the speaker to convey a theme, or important idea.

Close Reading

Note Taking As students first read the poems, have them annotate important ideas and details, unfamiliar words, and questions they have. Then read again and use the following questions. Remind students to cite evidence from the text.

 Read

Theme Read lines 3, 4, 23, and 24 of "Blue Ribbon Dreams" on page O1. *How are these lines different from the others?* (They are printed in italic type; lines 3 and 4 are indented.) *What idea does this difference emphasize?* (It emphasizes the speaker's goal: to compete at the County Fair with her horse.)

Homographs Read lines 2 and 20. *The word* lead *can mean "a kind of metal" or "guide." Use context clues to explain how it is used in each line.* (In line 2, *lead* means "a kind of metal," because the speaker is saying that her feet feel heavy. In line 20, it means "guide," because she is guiding the horse around the pen.) Have students add this word to their reader's notebook.

Theme Read the last five lines. *What feelings does the speaker share?* (She thinks she and her horse are winners—even without a blue ribbon.) *Read the remaining poem. What is the theme?* (The speaker works to succeed despite her size. The theme is that anyone can accomplish a goal if they work hard enough.)

 Summarize Have students use their notes to summarize how the speaker works to accomplish a goal.

Read

Genre: Narrative and Free Verse Poetry Read aloud the first stanza of "Sammy's Day Out" on page O3. *Is this a narrative poem or free verse?* (narrative) *Explain.* (It tells a story about a wolf cub named Sammy. It has characters and dialogue.)

Theme Read the rest of the poem. *What might be a theme of this poem?* (Making your own choices is harder than it seems.) *What details support this?* (Sammy is excited to have free time, but it ends up hurting him when he chooses to eat lots of junky food.)

 Summarize Have students use their notes to summarize what the speaker learns.

Reread

Use the questions on pages O2 and O3 to guide rereading.

Author's Craft Reread the first two lines of "Blue Ribbon Dreams" on page O1. *How do you know how the girl feels as she is walking to the barn?* (The girl says she is "trudging" and her feet are "like lead." This lets me know she is tired as she walks to the barn.)

Author's Craft Reread line 19. *What does the repetition of "again" help express?* (Repeating the word "again" expresses that training Little Red means doing the same thing many times is hard work.)

Author's Craft Reread the second stanza of "Sammy's Day Out" on page O3. *Why might the poet have chosen the word "crept" instead of "walked"?* ("Crept" is a specific way of moving. It shows that Sammy is moving carefully so that no one can hear him. The word "walked" is less specific.)

Integrate

Make Connections Guide students to connect "Blue Ribbon Dreams," "Sammy's Day Out," and other poems they have read. Have pairs gather text evidence and answer this question: *What do the themes of the poems help you understand about why people work toward a goal?*

Compare Texts Label a three-column chart *Poem, Theme,* and *What I Learned.* Have pairs compare how the poems share lessons about achieving goals.

Build Knowledge

Talk About the Text Have partners discuss what motivates people to accomplish a goal.

Write About the Text Have students add their ideas to the Build Knowledge pages of their reader's notebooks.

Differentiate and Collaborate

Be Inspired Have students think about poems they have read, such as "Blue Ribbon Dreams" and "Sammy's Day Out." Ask: *What do the poems inspire you to do?* Use these activities or have pairs think of a way to respond to the poems.

Make a 7-Day Plan Think of a goal you would like to accomplish in a week. Using a calendar, write one thing you will do each day to reach your goal. Post the calendar and check off each task as you accomplish it.

Conduct an Interview Interview someone you know who has successfully achieved a goal. Ask questions about what motivated the person and how they were able to accomplish what they wanted.

Readers to Writers

Nonliteral Language Remind students that the meaning of nonliteral language is different from its dictionary definition. Nonliteral language can create a certain effect or help readers visualize what is being described. Have students reread line 22 on page O1. *What does the speaker mean when she says she breaks out into song? What effect does this nonliteral language have?*

LEVEL UP

IF students read the On Level fluently and answered the questions,

THEN pair them with students who have proficiently read the Beyond Level. Have them

- partner read the Beyond Level passage.
- summarize what motivates the speakers of each poem.

On Level

Vocabulary/Comprehension

REVIEW ACADEMIC VOCABULARY

OBJECTIVES

Acquire and use accurately grade-appropriate general academic and domain-specific words and phrases, including those that signal contrast, addition, and other logical relationships (e.g., *however, although, nevertheless, similarly, moreover, in addition*).

I Do Use the **Visual Vocabulary Cards** to review the key selection words *ambitious, memorized, satisfaction,* and *shuddered.* Point to each word, read it aloud, and have students chorally repeat it.

We Do Ask these questions and help students respond.
- What goal have you set that shows you are *ambitious*?
- If you *memorized* something, what strategies did you use?

You Do Have students work in pairs to respond to these questions.
- What is something you achieved that gave you great *satisfaction*?
- If someone *shuddered* from the cold, how might you help them?

Have students choose words from their reader's notebook and write a definition for each word and use the word in a sentence.

HOMOGRAPHS

OBJECTIVES

Use context to confirm or self-correct word recognition and understanding, rereading as necessary.

Demonstrate understanding of figurative language, word relationships, and nuances in word meanings.

Use the relationship between particular words (e.g., synonyms, antonyms, homographs) to better understand each of the words.

I Do Remind students to use context clues to figure out which meaning of a homograph is correct. Display "Blue Ribbon Dreams" in the On Level online **Differentiated Genre Passage** page O1. Read aloud the second line.

Think I am not sure which meaning of *lead* to use: "a heavy metal" or "showed the way." The word *Trudging* at the beginning of the line means "walking slowly." I think the speaker's feet felt heavy enough to slow her down. So the correct meaning here is "a heavy metal."

We Do Point out *fair* in the fourth line. Use the context clues "training every day" (line 3) and *"County"* (line 4) to help identify the correct meaning. Guide students to state the meaning of *fair*.

You Do Have students work in pairs to identify the context clues to determine the correct meaning of *entrance* (line 5), *entrances* (line 9), *fair* (lines 13, 24, 25), and *might* (lines 14, 18). Have them define the words and explain the context clues they used.

REVIEW THEME

OBJECTIVES

Determine a theme of a story, drama, or poem from details in the text, including how characters in a story or drama respond to challenges or how the speaker in a poem reflects upon a topic; summarize the text.

I Do Remind students that the theme in a poem is the message that the poet wants to share. Rereading and identifying details in the poem and considering the poet's word choice can help readers identify the theme.

We Do Have volunteers read lines 1–16 of "Blue Ribbon Dreams" in the On Level online **Differentiated Genre Passage** page O1. Help students identify details about the speaker. Encourage students to reread in order to identify any additional powerful words the poet uses. Model using these details and words to suggest the theme of the poem so far.

You Do Have partners take turns reading the rest of the poem aloud. Ask them to review and add to the lists of key details and word choices. Then have them determine the theme of the poem as a whole.

SELF-SELECTED READING

OBJECTIVES

Determine a theme of a story, drama, or poem from details in the text, including how characters in a story or drama respond to challenges or how the speaker in a poem reflects upon a topic; summarize the text.

By the end of the year, read and comprehend literature, including stories, dramas, and poetry, at the high end of the grades 4–5 text complexity band independently and proficiently.

Reread to increase understanding.

Independent Reading

In this text set, students focus on how an author develops a theme and how figurative language and poetic elements work together in narrative and free verse poetry. Guide students to transfer what they have learned in this text set as they read.

Have students choose a narrative or free verse poem for sustained silent reading. Students can check the online **Leveled Reading Library** for selections. Remind students that:

- the theme of a poem is the big idea or message that the poet wants to share with readers.
- they should reread to identify relevant, or key, details in the poem and use these details to determine the theme.

Have students read the book independently using the Reading **Center Activity Cards** as a resource. Students can conduct a book talk with their group using their responses from the Respond to Reading and Make Connections prompts.

 You may want to include **ELL** students in On Level vocabulary and comprehension lessons. Offer language support as needed.

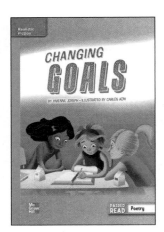

Lexile 860L

OBJECTIVES

Determine a theme of a story, drama, or poem from details in the text, including how characters in a story or drama respond to challenges or how the speaker in a poem reflects upon a topic; summarize the text.

Read grade-level text with purpose and understanding.

Read grade-level prose and poetry orally with accuracy, appropriate rate, and expression on successive readings.

Draw evidence from literary or informational texts to support analysis, reflection, and research.

Apply grade 5 Reading standards to literature.

ELA ACADEMIC LANGUAGE

• theme, realistic fiction, poetry
• Cognates: *tema, poesía*

●Beyond Level

Leveled Reader: *Changing Goals*

Preview and Predict

Read the Essential Question: *What motivates you to accomplish a goal?*

Have students preview the title, table of contents, and first page of *Changing Goals.* Students should use details in the text and illustrations to predict what the story might be about.

Review Genre: Realistic Fiction

Tell students that this selection is realistic fiction. The characters and settings are like real people and places, and the events could actually happen in real life. As they preview the book, have students identify features of realistic fiction in *Changing Goals.*

Close Reading

Note Taking Ask students to use a copy of the online Theme **Graphic Organizer 6** as they read.

Page 2 *Reread to find clues about why Maggie feels frustrated at the beginning of the story.* (She is unable to dribble around Lori, and she is unable to stop Lori from dribbling around her.) *Does Maggie give up?* (no) *What happens as a result?* (She successfully blocks Lori.)

Page 3 *Why does the author of the story compare the way Maggie memorizes defensive moves to the way a dancer memorizes steps? Discuss with a partner.* (Both activities require grace and practiced movements.)

Pages 4–5 *During the game, Maggie falls and hurts her right arm. Read this sentence: "It's going to need a cast." As it is used here, does the word* cast *mean "a mold to set a broken bone" or "actors who perform in a play"?* ("a mold to set a broken bone") Have students add this word to their reader's notebook.

Pages 6–7 *What ideas for helping the team does Maggie brainstorm?* (help out at practice, organize a pizza party, make posters and signs) *What does she finally decide to do?* (raise money for new uniforms) *Although Maggie cannot play basketball, she still participates. With a partner, discuss how this choice may cause Maggie to learn a lesson and may represent a possible theme in the story.* (Maggie may learn not to give up when faced with challenging circumstances.)

Pages 8–9 *How does Maggie plan to raise money for the uniforms?* (by baking and selling cookies) *Does she plan to work alone or ask for help? Why is this a good idea?* (ask for help; More people can get more done.) *How will the girls purchase ingredients?* (They will each chip in money.)

Pages 10–15 *How does Maggie feel the night before the sale?* (She worries that something will go wrong.) *Reread the text to identify the obstacle the group overcomes.* (The van breaks down, but two of the moms load the cookies into their cars instead.) *Describe the outcome of the sale.* (The team sells all the cookies by noon and raises more money than the boys' team.) *What does Maggie learn about goal-setting?* (Sometimes one has to change one's goals to fit new circumstances.)

Respond to Reading Revisit the Essential Question and ask students to complete the Respond to Reading section on page 16.

 Write About Reading Check that students understand how Maggie's experiences in Chapter 1, before her accident, help communicate the theme of the story.

Fluency: Expression and Phrasing

Model Model reading page 2 with proper expression and phrasing. Next, reread the page aloud and have students read along with you.

Apply Have students practice reading the passage with partners.

Paired Read: "Today's Lesson"

 Make Connections: Write About It

Before reading, ask students to note that the genre of this text is poetry. Then discuss the Essential Question. After reading, ask students to write about connections between the themes of *Changing Goals* and "Today's Lesson."

Leveled Reader

Build Knowledge

Talk About the Text Have partners discuss what motivates people to accomplish a goal.

Write About the Text Have students add their ideas to the Build Knowledge pages of their reader's notebooks.

FOCUS ON LITERARY ELEMENTS

Students can extend their knowledge of rhyme and repetition by completing the literary elements activity on page 20.

LITERATURE CIRCLES

Ask students to conduct a literature circle using the Thinkmark questions to guide the discussion. You may wish to have a whole-class discussion, using both selections in the Leveled Reader, about what motivates people to accomplish a goal.

⭐ GIFTED AND TALENTED

Synthesize Have students consider the Leveled Reader selections and their own wants and needs and then make a list of goals. These goals might be academic, athletic, or philanthropic. Ask volunteers to share their ideas. Then have each student choose one goal from his or her list and write it in the center of a web diagram. In the radiating circles, the student should write what motivates him or her to accomplish it and what steps he or she might take to achieve it.

"Blue Ribbon Dreams"
"Sammy's Day Out"

OBJECTIVES

Quote accurately from a text when explaining what the text says explicitly and when drawing inferences from the text.

Explain different characters' perspectives in a literary text.

Determine a theme of a story, drama, or poem from details in the text, including how characters in a story or drama respond to challenges or how the speaker in a poem reflects upon a topic; summarize the text.

Explain how a series of chapters, scenes, or stanzas fits together to provide the overall structure of a particular story, drama, or poem.

Demonstrate understanding of figurative language, word relationships, and nuances in word meanings.

Use the relationship between particular words (e.g., synonyms, antonyms, homographs) to better understand each of the words.

ELA ACADEMIC LANGUAGE

• poetry, speaker, repetition, rhyme, theme, homograph, nonliteral
• Cognates: poesía, repetición, rima, tema, homógrafo

● Beyond Level

Genre Passage: "Blue Ribbon Dreams" and "Sammy's Day Out"

Build Background

Read aloud the Essential Question: *What motivates you to accomplish a goal?* Have pairs compare how the speakers of the poems they read in this text set were motivated to reach a goal. Use sentence starters.

> *The speaker acted because . . .*
>
> *This helps me understand that goals . . .*

Review Genre: Poetry

Review that poems express the thoughts and feelings of a speaker who is not necessarily the poet. Narrative poems tell a story and may include characters and dialogue. In free verse poems, the speaker shares thoughts and feelings directly with readers. A poet can use devices such as description, repetition, rhyme, and line organization to allow the speaker to convey a theme, or important idea.

Close Reading

Note Taking As students first read the poems, have them annotate important ideas and details, unfamiliar words, and questions they have. Then read again and use the following questions. Remind students to cite evidence from the text.

> **Read**

Theme Read lines 3, 4, 23, and 24 of "Blue Ribbon Dreams" on page B1. *How does the poet emphasize an idea in these lines?* (The use of italic type emphasizes the speaker's goal: to compete with her horse at the County Fair.)

Homographs Read lines 5 and 9. *Use context clues to explain how* entrance *should be pronounced in each line.* (In line 5, *entrance* should be pronounced EN-trance because it means "doorway." In line 9, it should be pronounced en-TRAN-ces because it means "captivates.") Check your answer with a print or digital resource. Have students add these words to their reader's notebook.

Theme Read the poem. *How do the speaker's feelings change from the beginning to the end?* (At first the speaker is tired and doesn't want to go to the barn. But once she works with her horse, she feels motivated to show everyone what they can do—even if they don't win.) *What theme does this suggest?* (Having a goal can motivate you even when things seem too tough.)

 Summarize Have students use notes to summarize how the speaker works to accomplish a goal.

Read

Genre: Narrative and Free Verse Poetry Read aloud the first stanza of "Sammy's Day Out" on page B3. *What kind of poem is this? Explain.* (It is a narrative poem. It tells a story about a wolf cub named Sammy using characters and dialogue.)

Theme Read the rest of the poem. *Explain two themes the poem suggests.* (1. It's good to be honest even if you know you will get in trouble. 2. Making your own choices is harder than it seems.)

 Summarize Have students use their notes to summarize what the speaker learns.

Reread

Use the questions on pages B2 and B3 to guide rereading.

Author's Craft Reread the first two lines of "Blue Ribbon Dreams" on page B1. *How does the poet help you understand the speaker's mood?* (The speaker says she is "trudging" and her feet are "like lead." This helps me understand that she is very tired and not enthusiastic as she walks to the barn.)

Author's Craft *Find an example of repetition in the poem. What idea does it help emphasize?* (An example of repetition is "again, again, and yet again." The repetition emphasizes the idea that the training is a lot of work because the speaker has to lead Little Red around the pen many times.)

Author's Craft *In "Sammy's Day Out," how do we know Sammy knows he is doing something he shouldn't be doing?* (*Lest he be caught* shows Sammy is doing something he shouldn't be doing.)

Integrate

Make Connections Guide students to connect these poems and others they have read. Have pairs use evidence to respond: *What do the themes of the poems help you understand about why people work toward a goal?*

Compare Texts Label a three-column chart *Poem, Theme,* and *What I Learned.* Have pairs compare how the poems share lessons about achieving goals.

Build Knowledge

Talk About the Text Have partners discuss what motivates people to accomplish a goal.

Write About the Text Have students add their ideas to the Build Knowledge pages of their reader's notebooks.

Differentiate and Collaborate

Be Inspired Have students think about "Blue Ribbon Dreams," "Sammy's Day Out," and other poems they have read. Ask: *What do the poems inspire you to do?* Use the following activities or have pairs of students think of a way to respond to the poems.

Make a Seven-Day Plan Think about a goal you would like to accomplish in a week's time. Using a calendar, write one thing you will do each day to reach your goal. Post the calendar and check off each task as you accomplish it.

Conduct an Interview Interview someone you know who has successfully achieved a goal. Ask questions about what motivated the person and how he or she accomplished said goal. Videotape the interview and play it for your class.

Readers to Writers

Nonliteral Language Remind students that words and phrases in nonliteral language have a meaning that is different from their dictionary definitions. Nonliteral language can create a certain effect or help readers visualize what the poet is describing. Have students reread line 22 on page B1. Ask: *What does the speaker mean when she says she breaks out into song? What effect does this use of nonliteral language have on readers?*

⭐ GIFTED AND TALENTED

Independent Study Have students synthesize their notes and the selections they read to create a guide to getting motivated. Students' guides can include anecdotes that describe times they've had to motivate themselves to reach a goal, as well as tips for helping others get "unstuck" in their own motivation. Have partners read each other's guides and discuss how they will incorporate their partner's tips into their own lives.

●Beyond Level

Vocabulary/Comprehension

REVIEW DOMAIN-SPECIFIC WORDS

OBJECTIVES

Acquire and use accurately grade-appropriate general academic and domain-specific words and phrases, including those that signal contrast, addition, and other logical relationships.

Model Use the **Visual Vocabulary Cards** to review the meanings of the words *ambitious* and *satisfaction*. Write genre-related sentences on the board using the words.

Write the words *intend* and *demonstrate* on the board and read them aloud. Discuss the meanings with students. Then help students write sentences using these words.

Apply Have students work in pairs to review the meanings of the words *motivated, confirmed,* and *pursuit.* Then have partners write sentences using these words.

HOMOGRAPHS

OBJECTIVES

Demonstrate understanding of figurative language, word relationships, and nuances in word meanings.

Use the relationship between particular words (e.g., synonyms, antonyms, homographs) to better understand each of the words.

Use context to confirm or self-correct word recognition and understanding, rereading as necessary.

Model Read aloud the second line of "Blue Ribbon Dreams" in the Beyond Level online **Differentiated Genre Passage** page B1.

Think Aloud I am not sure which meaning of *lead* to use: "a heavy, blue-gray metal" or "showed the way." The word *Trudging* at the beginning of the line means "walking slowly." I think if the narrator's feet were like lead, they felt heavy. So the correct meaning here is "a heavy, blue-gray metal."

With students, read aloud the fourth line and point out the word *fair*. Ask students to give two meanings for the word and find context clues to determine the correct meaning.

Apply Have pairs of students read the rest of the passage. Ask them to use context clues to determine the meanings of *entrance* (line 5), *entrances* (line 9), *fair* (lines 13, 24, and 25), *might* (lines 14 and 18), and *lead* (line 20). Have them explain which context clues they used.

 Analyze Challenge students to identify a pair of homographs they have not yet explored, define each homograph, and then write two sentences in which each homograph is used correctly. Have pairs read their sentences and identify the correct meanings from context. Have students repeat the activity by finding homographs in their reader's notebook.

REVIEW THEME

OBJECTIVES

Determine a theme of a story, drama, or poem from details in the text, including how characters in a story or drama respond to challenges or how the speaker in a poem reflects upon a topic; summarize the text.

Model Review that the theme in a poem is the important idea or message that the poet wishes to convey to readers. Identifying the author's choice of words and use of key details may help readers identify a poem's theme.

Have student volunteers read aloud lines 1–16 of "Blue Ribbon Dreams" in the Beyond Level online **Differentiated Genre Passage** page B1. Work with them to listen for powerful words and identify key details. Remind them to reread as necessary. Then guide students to use the words and key details to offer some ideas about the poem's theme thus far.

Apply Have partners read aloud the rest of the poem to identify key details. Remind them to listen for word choices and to reread as necessary. They can independently fill out a copy of online Details and Theme **Graphic Organizer 6** and identify the theme. Then have students share their completed organizers with the class.

SELF-SELECTED READING

OBJECTIVES

Determine a theme of a story, drama, or poem from details in the text, including how characters in a story or drama respond to challenges or how the speaker in a poem reflects upon a topic; summarize the text.

By the end of the year, read and comprehend literature, including stories, dramas, and poetry, at the high end of the grades 4–5 text complexity band independently and proficiently.

Reread to increase understanding.

Independent Reading

In this text set, students focus on how an author develops a theme and how figurative language and poetic elements work together in narrative and free verse poetry. Guide students to transfer what they have learned in this text set as they read.

Have students choose a narrative or free verse poem for sustained silent reading. Students can check the online **Leveled Reading Library** for selections.

- As they read, have them fill a copy of online Details and Theme **Graphic Organizer 6.**
- Remind students that the theme of a poem is the big idea or message that the poet wants to share with readers.
- Tell students to reread to identify relevant, or key, details in the poem and use these details to determine the theme.

Have students read the book independently using the Reading **Center Activity Cards** as a resource. Students can conduct a book talk with their group using their responses from the Respond to Reading and Make Connections prompts.

 You may wish to assign the third Be Inspired! activity from the lesson plan as an Independent Study.

Notes

WRITING Communicate Effectively Through Writing

Extended Writing 1

Expository Essay

Writing to Sources

Writing Prompt: Write an expository essay to explain to your class about how inventors improved society.

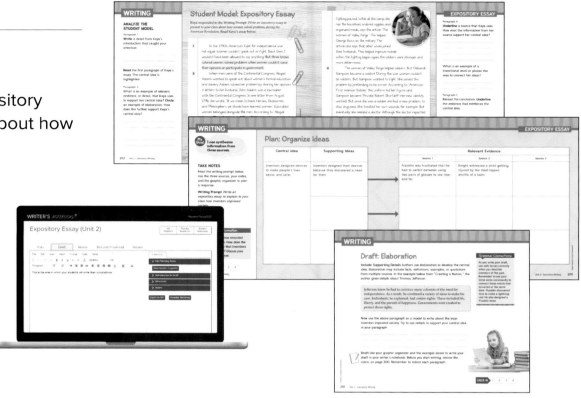

Extended Writing 2

Expository Essay

Writing to Sources

Writing Prompt: Write an expository essay to print in your school newspaper about the ways humans protect the environment.

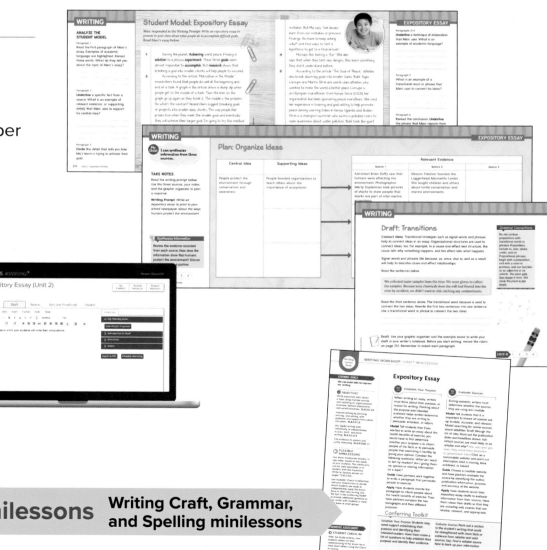

Flexible Minilessons — Writing Craft, Grammar, and Spelling minilessons

PROJECT 1

Extended Writing: Write to Sources
Expository Essay

Extended Writing Goals

- I can write an expository essay.
- I can synthesize information from three sources.

Start off each Extended Writing Project with a Writing Process minilesson, or choose a Craft minilesson from the Writing Craft Lesson Bank. As you confer with students, the rest of your students write independently or collaboratively or confer with peers.

Writing Process Minilessons

During Writing Process minilessons, students first analyze a rubric and student model and then answer a writing prompt, going through each step of the writing process to develop an expository essay.

- Analyze the Rubric
- Central Idea
- Analyze the Student Model
- Analyze the Prompt
- Analyze the Sources
- Plan: Organize Ideas
- Draft: Elaboration
- Revise: Peer Conferences

Independent and Collaborative Writing

- Provide time during writing for students to work on their writing both collaboratively with partners and independently.
- Use this time for teacher and peer conferencing.

Flexible Minilessons

Choose from the following minilessons to focus on areas where your students need support.

Writing Craft Lesson Bank

Establish Your Purpose T266
Evaluate Sources T266
Avoid Plagiarism T267
Add Examples or Definitions T267
Use a Powerful Quotation T267
Organize Information T268
Use Prepositions and Prepositional Phrases T268
Combine Sentences T269
Establish Voice and Tone T269
Use Digital Tools T269

Grammar Lesson Bank

Kinds of Nouns T270
Capitalizing Proper Nouns T271
Singular and Plural Nouns T272
Forming Plural Nouns T273
More Plural Nouns T274
Plural Nouns and Appositives T275
Possessive Nouns T276
Adding -s or -'s T277

Spelling Lesson Bank

Variant Vowel /ô/; Diphthongs /oi/, /ou/ T280–T281
Plurals T282–T283
Differentiated Spelling Lists T280, T282
Inflectional Endings T284–T285
Contractions T286–T287
Differentiated Spelling Lists T284, T286

Suggested Pacing

Students can develop their writing over four weeks, taking time to deconstruct a student model and then work with sources to write their own expository essay. Adjust the pacing to address your students' needs.

Weeks 1–2 ANALYZE A STUDENT MODEL

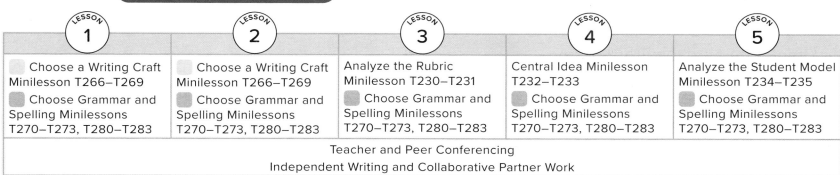

LESSON 1
Choose a Writing Craft Minilesson T266–T269
Choose Grammar and Spelling Minilessons T270–T273, T280–T283

LESSON 2
Choose a Writing Craft Minilesson T266–T269
Choose Grammar and Spelling Minilessons T270–T273, T280–T283

LESSON 3
Analyze the Rubric Minilesson T230–T231
Choose Grammar and Spelling Minilessons T270–T273, T280–T283

LESSON 4
Central Idea Minilesson T232–T233
Choose Grammar and Spelling Minilessons T270–T273, T280–T283

LESSON 5
Analyze the Student Model Minilesson T234–T235
Choose Grammar and Spelling Minilessons T270–T273, T280–T283

Teacher and Peer Conferencing
Independent Writing and Collaborative Partner Work

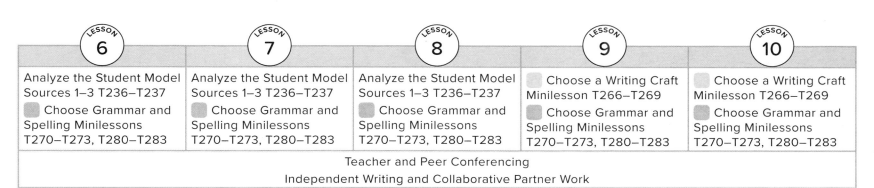

LESSON 6
Analyze the Student Model Sources 1–3 T236–T237
Choose Grammar and Spelling Minilessons T270–T273, T280–T283

LESSON 7
Analyze the Student Model Sources 1–3 T236–T237
Choose Grammar and Spelling Minilessons T270–T273, T280–T283

LESSON 8
Analyze the Student Model Sources 1–3 T236–T237
Choose Grammar and Spelling Minilessons T270–T273, T280–T283

LESSON 9
Choose a Writing Craft Minilesson T266–T269
Choose Grammar and Spelling Minilessons T270–T273, T280–T283

LESSON 10
Choose a Writing Craft Minilesson T266–T269
Choose Grammar and Spelling Minilessons T270–T273, T280–T283

Teacher and Peer Conferencing
Independent Writing and Collaborative Partner Work

Weeks 3–4 DEVELOP EXPOSITORY ESSAYS

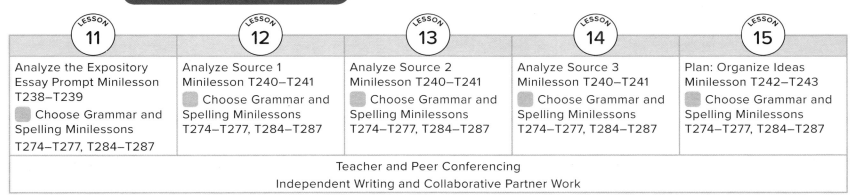

LESSON 11
Analyze the Expository Essay Prompt Minilesson T238–T239
Choose Grammar and Spelling Minilessons T274–T277, T284–T287

LESSON 12
Analyze Source 1 Minilesson T240–T241
Choose Grammar and Spelling Minilessons T274–T277, T284–T287

LESSON 13
Analyze Source 2 Minilesson T240–T241
Choose Grammar and Spelling Minilessons T274–T277, T284–T287

LESSON 14
Analyze Source 3 Minilesson T240–T241
Choose Grammar and Spelling Minilessons T274–T277, T284–T287

LESSON 15
Plan: Organize Ideas Minilesson T242–T243
Choose Grammar and Spelling Minilessons T274–T277, T284–T287

Teacher and Peer Conferencing
Independent Writing and Collaborative Partner Work

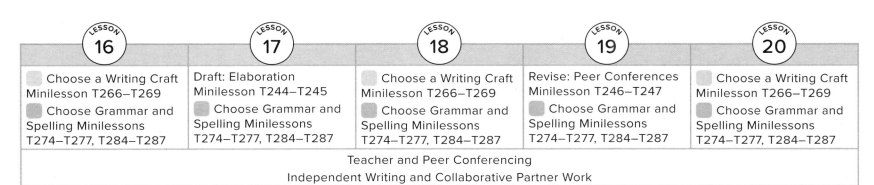

LESSON 16
Choose a Writing Craft Minilesson T266–T269
Choose Grammar and Spelling Minilessons T274–T277, T284–T287

LESSON 17
Draft: Elaboration Minilesson T244–T245
Choose Grammar and Spelling Minilessons T274–T277, T284–T287

LESSON 18
Choose a Writing Craft Minilesson T266–T269
Choose Grammar and Spelling Minilessons T274–T277, T284–T287

LESSON 19
Revise: Peer Conferences Minilesson T246–T247
Choose Grammar and Spelling Minilessons T274–T277, T284–T287

LESSON 20
Choose a Writing Craft Minilesson T266–T269
Choose Grammar and Spelling Minilessons T274–T277, T284–T287

Teacher and Peer Conferencing
Independent Writing and Collaborative Partner Work

Extended Writing: Write to Sources
Expository Essay

Extended Writing Goals

- I can write an expository essay.
- I can synthesize information from three sources.

Start off each Extended Writing Project with a Writing Process minilesson, or choose a Craft minilesson from the Writing Craft Lesson Bank. As you confer with students, the rest of your students write independently or collaboratively or confer with peers.

Writing Process Minilessons

During Writing Process minilessons, students first analyze a rubric and student model and then answer a writing prompt, going through each step of the writing process to develop an expository essay.

- Analyze the Rubric
- Academic Language
- Analyze the Student Model
- Analyze the Prompt
- Analyze the Sources
- Plan: Organize Ideas
- Draft: Transitions
- Revise: Peer Conferences

Independent and Collaborative Writing

- Provide time during writing for students to work on their writing both collaboratively with partners and independently.
- Use this time for teacher and peer conferencing.

Flexible Minilessons

Choose from the following minilessons to focus on areas where your students need support.

Writing Craft Lesson Bank	Grammar Lesson Bank	Spelling Lesson Bank
Establish Your Purpose T266	Prepositional Phrases T278	Closed Syllables T288–T289
Evaluate Sources T266	Punctuating Titles and Letters T279	Differentiated Spelling List T288
Avoid Plagiarism T267		
Add Examples or Definitions T267		
Use a Powerful Quotation T267		
Organize Information T268		
Use Prepositions and Prepositional Phrases T268		
Combine Sentences T269		
Establish Voice and Tone T269		
Use Digital Tools T269		

Suggested Pacing

Students can develop their writing over two weeks, taking time to deconstruct a student model and then work with sources to write their own expository essay. Adjust the pacing to address your students' needs.

Week 5 — ANALYZE A STUDENT MODEL

LESSON 1	LESSON 2	LESSON 3	LESSON 4	LESSON 5
☐ Choose a Writing Craft Minilesson T266–T269 ☐ Choose Grammar and Spelling Minilessons T278–T279, T288–T289	Analyze the Rubric Minilesson T248–T249 ☐ Choose Grammar and Spelling Minilessons T278–T279, T288–T289	Academic Language Minilesson T250–T251 ☐ Choose Grammar and Spelling Minilessons T278–T279, T288–T289	Analyze the Student Model Minilesson T252–T253 ☐ Choose Grammar and Spelling Minilessons T278–T279, T288–T289	Analyze the Student Model Minilesson T254–T255 ☐ Choose Grammar and Spelling Minilessons T278–T279, T288–T289
Teacher and Peer Conferencing Independent Writing and Collaborative Partner Work			

Week 6 — DEVELOP EXPOSITORY ESSAYS

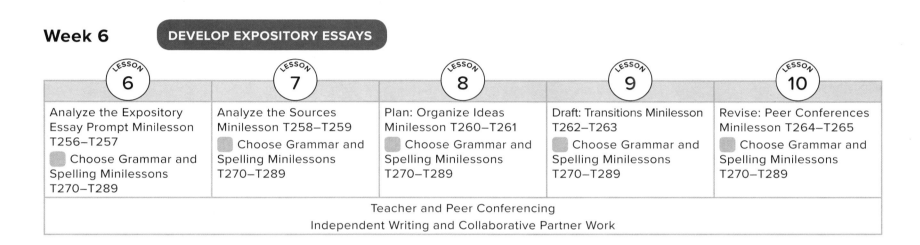

LESSON 6	LESSON 7	LESSON 8	LESSON 9	LESSON 10
Analyze the Expository Essay Prompt Minilesson T256–T257 ☐ Choose Grammar and Spelling Minilessons T270–T289	Analyze the Sources Minilesson T258–T259 ☐ Choose Grammar and Spelling Minilessons T270–T289	Plan: Organize Ideas Minilesson T260–T261 ☐ Choose Grammar and Spelling Minilessons T270–T289	Draft: Transitions Minilesson T262–T263 ☐ Choose Grammar and Spelling Minilessons T270–T289	Revise: Peer Conferences Minilesson T264–T265 ☐ Choose Grammar and Spelling Minilessons T270–T289
Teacher and Peer Conferencing Independent Writing and Collaborative Partner Work			

LEARNING GOALS

We can use a rubric to understand what makes a strong expository essay.

OBJECTIVES

Explain how an author uses reasons and evidence to support particular points in a text, identifying which reasons and evidence support which point(s).

Write informative/explanatory texts to examine a topic and convey ideas and information clearly.

Use knowledge of language and its conventions when writing, speaking, reading, or listening.

Analyze a rubric used to evaluate argumentative essays.

ELA ACADEMIC LANGUAGE

• *expository, central idea, evidence, rubric*

• Cognates: *idea central, evidencia*

---

10 mins Analyze the Rubric

Expository Writing Rubric

Students will use the Expository Writing rubric to first evaluate a student model and then write their own expository essays. Remind students that a rubric helps writers know what to include. Students can also use the rubric to identify parts of their essays that are successful and those that need work. Remind students that this section of the rubric shows the highest scores and criteria. Point out each category and the score of 4 on the rubric on **Reading/Writing Companion** page 200.

Have partners discuss how a writer's awareness of purpose, focus, and organization would help a reader understand an expository essay. (The purpose would help the reader understand why the essay is being written. The focus would help the reader understand the main points. The organization puts ideas in a logical order for the reader.)

Purpose, Focus, and Organization

Tell students that an effective essay must have a clear purpose, focus, and organization. Students will analyze the second bullet in the rubric. Understanding this bullet will help students include a central, or main, idea in their own essays.

Analytical Writing Read aloud the highlighted bullet. Ask: *What is a central idea?* (A central idea is the most important idea; it tells what the essay is about.) Have students write their response on page 200. Then ask: *Why should writers include a central idea?* (so readers can understand the topic of an essay; so that the writer can stay focused on the topic of the essay) Remind students that a central idea provides a focus for the essay and helps writers choose details that support that focus. The central idea also keeps the essay organized. Students will examine a central idea in a student model and then develop their own.

Evidence and Elaboration

Remind students that a strong essay includes evidence. This part of the rubric identifies how evidence should be incorporated and what kinds of evidence can be used. Review all of the bullets with students.

Analytical Writing Reread the first bullet. Ask: *How are facts and details connected to the central idea?* (Facts and details support the central idea.) Have students write their response on page 200. Then have students review the rubric and underline the word in the second bullet that tells where the evidence comes from. (*multiple sources*)

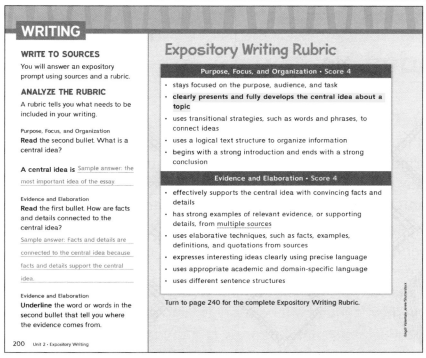

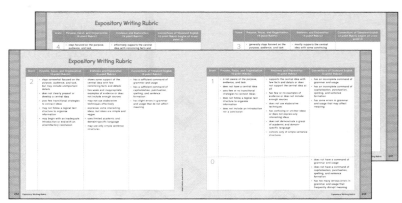

For the full Expository Writing Rubric, see **Reading/Writing Companion,** pages 240–243.

Reading/Writing Companion, p. 200

ELL English Language Learners

Use the following scaffolds with **Purpose, Focus, and Organization.**

Beginning

Review with students that a rubric gives information about what writers need to have in their writing. Point to "Purpose, Focus, and Organization," and explain that writers need to have a reason for writing (purpose), a central idea (focus), and an order that makes sense (organization). Read the highlighted bullet in the rubric with students. Say: *A strong central idea tells about the most important idea.* Help partners describe using the following: A central idea is the most important idea. It tells what the essay is about. It answers the writing prompt.

Intermediate

Review the two parts of the rubric in the chart with students. Then read the highlighted bullet in the rubric with them. Discuss how a strong central idea answers the prompt and tells the most important idea. Explain that writers choose information to support the central idea. Have partners describe using the following: A central idea is the most important idea. It answers the prompt and tells readers what the essay is about.

Advanced/Advanced High

Review the rubric with students. Remind them that an effective essay has a strong central idea. Discuss with them what a strong central idea tells about. Then have partners read the highlighted bullet in the rubric and discuss why writers should include a central idea.

ELL NEWCOMERS

To help students develop their writing, display the **Newcomer Cards** and **Newcomer Online Visuals,** and ask questions to help them discuss the images. Provide sentence starters. For example: What do you see? I see a/an ___. What are they doing? They are ___. Have students point to the image as they ask and answer. Then have them write the sentences in their notebooks. Throughout the extended writing project, help students develop their writing by adding to and revising their sentences.

FORMATIVE ASSESSMENT

⊘ STUDENT CHECK-IN

Have partners share their responses. Then ask them to reflect using the Check-In routine.

LEARNING GOALS

We can identify a central idea and supporting details.

OBJECTIVES

Determine two or more central, or main, ideas of a text and explain how they are supported by relevant, or key, details; summarize the text.

Introduce a topic clearly, provide a general observation and focus, and group related information logically; include formatting (e.g., headings), illustrations, and multimedia when useful to aiding comprehension.

Recall relevant information from experiences or gather relevant information from print and digital sources; summarize or paraphrase information in notes and finished work, and provide a list of sources.

Quote accurately from a text when explaining what the text says explicitly and when drawing inferences from the text. Identify the author's purpose.

Identify the author's purpose.

ELA ACADEMIC LANGUAGE

• *expository, connect, focus, maintained*

• Cognates: *expositivo, conectar*

DIGITAL TOOLS

 Student Model Sources

 Purpose of Expository Writing

 Central Idea
10 mins

Presenting the Central Idea

Tell students that the central, or main, idea of an expository essay is the essay's most important idea. A strongly maintained central idea is supported throughout the essay by relevant, or key, details that connect back to it. Read aloud the paragraph on **Reading/Writing Companion** page 201.

Think Aloud I see that the central idea is, "Their plan had an immediate effect on the rubber industry." The writer includes information about how the United States needed foreign rubber and how Thomas Edison, Henry Ford, and Harvey Firestone worried that rubber would run out someday. The writer also tells how they founded a laboratory for Edison to test rubber plant samples in Florida. I understand that the laboratory is part of "their plan" to save the industry. This helps me understand the focus of the essay.

 Have students think about the focus of the essay and respond to the question on page 201.

Relevant Details

Discuss how writers use relevant, or related, details to maintain their central idea. These details keep the essay focused and help readers to better understand the central idea.

Reread **Literature Anthology** page 97. Have students identify the central idea of the paragraph. (With a sense of urgency, state leaders gathered for a convention in Philadelphia to discuss what could be done to keep the nation together.) Explain that unimportant or unrelated information in essays can confuse readers or stop them from reading on. Unimportant details also prevent writers from fulfilling the purpose and task of expository writing. Ask: *How do the details in the paragraph keep the essay focused on the central idea?* (They tell the time period and what was happening in America leading up to the convention. The details inform readers of what they need to know to understand the central idea.)

Have students reread the paragraph on **Reading/Writing Companion** page 201 and cross out the unimportant detail that does not help focus the writer's central idea. (The laboratory often had many visitors.)

Apply

For more practice with identifying the central idea, have partners read the three student model sources in the **Online Writer's Notebook** and identify the central idea in one or more sources.

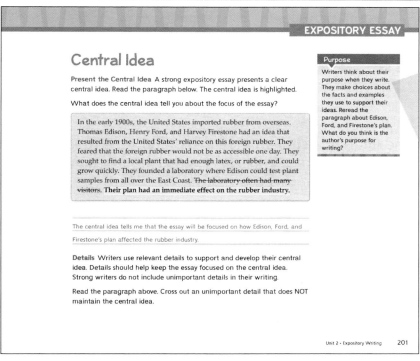

Reading/Writing Companion, p. 201

 English Language Learners

Use the following scaffolds with **Presenting the Central Idea**. For additional support, see **ELL Small Group Guide**.

Beginning

Read the central idea on page 201. Explain that an *industry* is a group of businesses that make a type of product, such as rubber. Then read the paragraph together and help students retell: The United States bought rubber from other countries in the 1900s. Thomas Edison started a laboratory to make rubber from plants. Discuss how these sentences support the central idea. Help partners answer the question on page 201 using the following: The central idea is the main idea. The paragraph is about how the rubber industry changed.

Intermediate

Review central idea with students and read the paragraph on page 201. Discuss the meaning of *industry*, using examples. Have students retell the other sentences and explain how they support the central idea. Have partners respond to the question on page 201 using the following: The central idea tells me that the focus of the essay is why and how the rubber industry changed in the 1900s.

Advanced/Advanced High

Have students describe what a central idea is. Read the paragraph on page 201 with students and have them identify the central idea. Have students retell the other sentences and explain how they support the central idea. Have partners respond to the question on page 201 using the term *central idea*.

FORMATIVE ASSESSMENT

❯ STUDENT CHECK-IN

Have partners share their responses. Then have them reflect using the Check-In routine.

EXTENDED WRITING 1

We can use a rubric to evaluate a student model.

OBJECTIVES

Determine two or more central, or main, ideas of a text and explain how they are supported by relevant, or key, details; summarize the text.

Quote accurately from a text when explaining what the text says explicitly and when drawing inferences from the text.

Identify the author's purpose.

Draw evidence from literary or informational texts to support analysis, reflection, and research.

Apply grade 5 Reading standards to informational texts.

Analyze a model and apply a rubric to understand the elements of an effective expository essay.

Analyze a writing prompt.

ELA ACADEMIC LANGUAGE

• *prompt, solve, relevant, elaboration*

• Cognates: *resolver, relevante, elaboración*

DIGITAL TOOLS

 Student Model Sources

Analyze the Student Model

10 mins

Expository Essay

Students will read and analyze a student model and apply the rubric to explain why Keya scored a 4 for "Purpose, Focus, and Organization" on her essay. Complete the routine below for Keya's prompt.

ANALYZE THE PROMPT ROUTINE

Read aloud the prompt.

Identify the purpose. *Is the purpose to inform or persuade?*

Identify the audience. *Who is the audience?*

Identify the type of writing the prompt is asking for. *What is the prompt asking the writer to do?*

At the completion of the routine, students should understand that Keya's purpose is to inform, her audience is the students in her class, and the prompt asks Keya to tell how women solved problems during the American Revolution.

Discuss the Student Model

As you read Keya's model with students, ask them to look for ways that Keya uses relevant details to keep her essay focused. Have them look for examples, definitions, and quotations that support the central idea. Have students note interesting words and questions they have as they read.

Paragraph 1 Ask students to write one detail from Keya's introduction that caught their attention and made them want to read more about the topic. Ask: *What were the lives of colonial women like before the American Revolution?* (They did not have a voice in government and could not fight.) Remind students that the central idea in an expository essay is contained in one or two sentences. These sentences answer the prompt and reveal the main focus of the essay.

Paragraph 2 Ask: *What relevant evidence does Keya use in this paragraph?* (a quotation from a letter written by Abigail Adams to John Adams, sent in August of 1776) *What is an example of elaboration?*

Think Aloud I see that Keya cites a letter Abigail Adams sent to John Adams that states: "If we mean to have Heroes, Statesmen, and Philosophers, we should have learned women." This evidence provides an example to support the central idea that colonial women solved problems. This reinforces the idea that Abigail Adams couldn't speak up in the government, but she could speak up with her husband. Keya then paraphrases this quote in her own words as a way to elaborate.

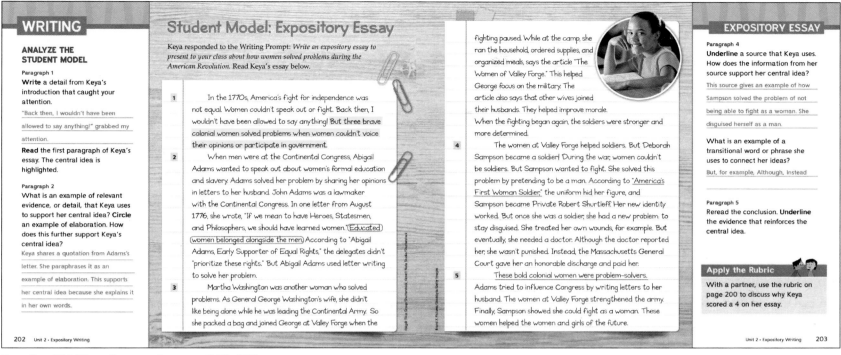

Reading/Writing Companion, pp. 202–203

 Have partners circle more examples of relevant evidence that Keya uses. Ask them to write their responses on page 202.

Paragraph 3 Remind students that effective essays use relevant elaboration to help support the central idea. Elaboration can include definitions, paraphrased information, and examples. Have students reread the paragraph and then underline an example of elaboration that Keya uses. (The article also says that other wives joined their husbands.)

Paragraph 4 Have students circle the phrase that tells what Deborah Sampson did to solve a problem. (by pretending to be a man) Ask: *What source does Keya use in this paragraph?* ("America's First Woman Soldier")

 Have partners discuss how the information from the source supports Keya's central idea. Have them write their responses on page 203.

Ask: *What is an example of a transitional word or phrase Keya uses to connect her ideas?* (During, But, for example, Although, instead) Have students write their answers on page 203.

Paragraph 5 Read the conclusion to the essay. Remind students that a conclusion should reinforce the central idea and continue to maintain the focus of the essay. Have students underline the sentence that reinforces the central idea.

Apply the Rubric

Have pairs of students discuss what was effective in Keya's essay and what needs to be improved. Have them use the rubric on page 200 and these sentence starters:

Keya supports her central idea by using . . .

Her essay includes . . .

TEACH IN SMALL GROUP

● **English Language Learners** For support with reading the student model and analyzing three sources, see **ELL Small Group Guide**.

CLASSROOM CULTURE

We respect and value each other's experiences. To create a classroom culture where students value each other's efforts and topics of interest, remind them to listen as others share their work. Encourage them to make positive comments. Ask: *How can you show you're listening as you work with a partner?*

FORMATIVE ASSESSMENT

STUDENT CHECK-IN

Have partners share their responses to Apply the Rubric on Reading/Writing Companion page 203. Then ask them to reflect using the Check-In routine.

EXTENDED WRITING 1

Student Model Sources

LEARNING GOALS

We can analyze student model essay sources.

OBJECTIVES

Quote accurately from a text when explaining what the text says explicitly and when drawing inferences from the text.

Identify the author's purpose.

Determine two or more central, or main, ideas of a text and explain how they are supported by relevant, or key, details; summarize the text.

By the end of the year, read and comprehend informational texts, including history/social studies, science, and technical texts, at the high end of the grades 4–5 text complexity band independently and proficiently.

Analyze a model and apply a rubric to understand the elements of an effective expository essay.

ELA ACADEMIC LANGUAGE

• *maintain, purpose, focus, annotate*

• Cognates: *mantener, propósito*

DIGITAL TOOLS

Student Model Sources

Analyze the Student Model

10 mins

Analyze the Student Model Sources

Explain that Keya read three sources to write her expository essay. Use copies of the online Student Model Sources to show how Keya developed a central, or main, idea supported by evidence. Also, examine how Keya used information from the sources to produce a focused essay. Remind students that Keya answered the prompt: *Write an expository essay to present to your class about how women solved problems during the American Revolution.*

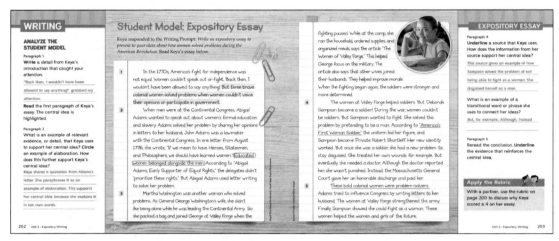

Reading/Writing Companion, pp. 202–203

SOURCE 1 — "Abigail Adams, Early Supporter of Equal Rights"

After reading Source 1, read aloud Keya's second paragraph. Have students compare the information they read in this paragraph to the information found in Source 1. Ask: *How does Keya include information from Source 1 in this paragraph?*

Think Aloud I see that Keya uses a quote from this source about giving women opportunities for education. She also tells that Abigail Adams shared her ideas about women's education and slavery with her husband, John, and that he respected those ideas.

Explain that using quotations and examples from sources can help the writer to support the central idea. These relevant, or key, details can also help the writer maintain the purpose of the essay: to inform. When students read sources to write their own expository essays, they can keep in mind which examples and quotations will best inform their audience. Point out how Keya references her sources in the essay to avoid plagiarism.

Have partners find other examples from Source 1 in paragraph 2.

SOURCE 2 "America's First Woman Soldier"

After reading Source 2, read aloud Keya's fourth paragraph. Ask: *What information does Keya include that supports her central idea?* (She includes relevant information about how Deborah Sampson disguised herself as a young man to fight in the war.)

Have partners read Source 2 to find details that Keya does not use. **COLLABORATE** Have students write down two of these details. (Sample responses: Sampson's age, whom she married after the war) Discuss why some facts might be left out of the expository essay. (These facts did not directly support the central idea.) Explain that including all facts could make an essay too long and not as focused.

SOURCE 3 "The Women of Valley Forge"

After reading Source 3, read aloud Keya's third paragraph. Ask: *What information does Keya include that supports her central idea?* (She uses information about the way Martha Washington got to Valley Forge. She lists how Martha Washington took action to help her husband and his soldiers.)

Have partners annotate the Student Model on **Reading/Writing** **COLLABORATE** **Companion** page 203 by circling more relevant facts and details from Source 3 in Keya's essay. Ask: *Where does Keya use these facts and details in her essay?* (paragraphs 3 and 5) *How does Keya use these facts and details?* (She uses them as evidence to support her central idea that colonial women found new ways to solve problems during the American Revolution.)

Synthesize Information

Reread Keya's central idea, highlighted on page 202. Explain that Keya develops her central idea after reading and thinking about all three sources. Remind students that Keya also analyzes the prompt and reads the sources to find relevant information about the actions colonial women took to solve problems during the American Revolution. Have partners find similarities among the three sources. Then have partners look back at their notes and use their writer's notebook to answer the question, *How does Keya develop her central idea by synthesizing information from all three sources?* (All sources describe how different women solved different problems within the time period of the American Revolution. Keya notes the actions of these women and uses them to conclude that colonial women found new and unusual ways to solve problems.)

Point out how Keya references where the information comes from in her essay to avoid plagiarism. Discuss grade-appropriate expectations for citing sources with students prior to writing their own expository essays.

▷ TEACH IN SMALL GROUP

● **Approaching Level** Read each online source aloud. Help students identify a central idea and relevant facts in each source.

● **On Level** Read the online sources with students. Have partners work to identify the central idea and relevant facts in each source. Discuss how Keya used the sources to write her essay.

● **Beyond Level** Have students read the online sources. Ask them to pick out relevant details they would use to most effectively support Keya's central idea.

● **English Language Learners** Help students understand what Keya's task was. Then read through one online source and work with them to identify the central idea and relevant details. For additional support, see the **ELL Small Group Guide**.

FORMATIVE ASSESSMENT

▶ STUDENT CHECK-IN

Have partners share their responses. Then ask them to reflect using the Check-In routine.

LEARNING GOALS

We can set a purpose for reading sources to answer a prompt.

OBJECTIVES

Write informative/explanatory texts to examine a topic and convey ideas and information clearly.

Link ideas within and across categories of information using words, phrases, and clauses (e.g., *in contrast, especially*).

Follow agreed-upon rules for discussions and carry out assigned roles

Adapt speech to a variety of contexts and tasks, using formal English when appropriate to task and situation.

Produce clear and coherent writing in which the development and organization are appropriate to task, purpose, and audience.

Analyze a writing prompt.

Analyze voice and tone.

ELA ACADEMIC LANGUAGE

• *prompt, audience, purpose*
• Cognates: *audiencia, propósito*

DIGITAL TOOLS

 Skim and Scan

 ## Analyze the Prompt
(10 mins)

Writing Prompt

Follow the Analyze the Prompt Routine on page T234. Read the writing prompt on **Reading/Writing Companion** page 204 aloud: *Write an expository essay to explain to your class about how inventors improved society.* Guide students to identify the purpose and audience. Then ask: *What is the prompt asking you to do?* (to write an expository essay about how inventors improved society)

 Anchor Chart Review the features of an expository essay and add any new ones to the expository essay anchor chart.

• It includes a central, or main, idea supported by facts and specific details.

• It provides relevant, or key, evidence from multiple sources.

• It has a varied sentence structure with transitional words and phrases to link ideas.

Purpose, Audience, and Task

Explain that thinking about their purpose and audience will help students plan and organize their writing. Ask students to identify the appropriate purpose of expository essays: to inform. Point out that in this writing prompt, the audience is identified. Ask: *Who are you writing this expository essay for?* (my classmates) Have them consider who will read what they write, such as their teacher and classmates.

Remind students that the task is the type of writing they are being asked to do and the topic is what they are being asked to write about. Reread the prompt. Ask: *What words in the prompt tell you about the task?* Have students underline three key words in the prompt on **Reading/Writing Companion** page 204. Then have them think about whether they will use formal or informal language in their essay. Remind students that their language choices depend on their audience and their task. Ask students to write their responses to the questions.

Set a Purpose for Reading Sources

Tell students that before they write their essays, they will read, annotate, and answer questions about three sources. Encourage them to look at the source on page 205. Have them read the title and make a note of the graphic feature. (a sketch of glasses) Explain that noticing graphic features can help them get a better idea about what they are going to read.

 Have students turn to a partner and say the writing prompt in their own words. Then ask them to look at the sketch and to skim "Benjamin Franklin's Bifocals" on page 205. Tell students to think of a question and write it on page 204.

WRITING

Analyze the Prompt

Writing Prompt

Write an expository essay to explain to your class about how inventors improved society.

My Goal: I can write an expository essay.

Purpose, Audience, and Task Reread the writing prompt. What is your purpose for writing? My purpose is to _____

Who will your audience be? My audience will be _____

What type of writing is the prompt asking for? _____

Set a Purpose for Reading Sources Asking questions about the ways inventors improved society will help you figure out your purpose for reading. It also helps you understand what you already know about the topic. Before you read the following passage set about inventions, write a question here.

_____
_____
_____
_____

204 Unit 2 • Expository Writing

Reading/Writing Companion, p. 204

English Language Learners

Use the following scaffolds with the **Writing Prompt**. For additional support, see the **ELL Small Group Guide**.

Beginning

Read the prompt with students and discuss the meaning. Explain that when you *improve* something, you make it better and that *society* is the world we live in. Explain that *inventors* are people who make *inventions* or new things and these inventions make changes in society. Discuss examples of important inventions with students, and talk about the ways they helped society. Help partners describe the prompt using: I will write about how <u>inventors</u> helped <u>society</u>.

Intermediate

Read the prompt with students, and discuss what they will write about. To reinforce the meaning of the prompt, have students describe what it means to improve society. Discuss with students how certain people invented things that made society better. Point to the first part of the prompt, and elicit that they will write an expository essay to inform their classmates. Have partners describe the prompt using the following: I will write about how inventors <u>made society a better place</u>.

Advanced/Advanced High

Read the prompt with students. Have them give examples of how inventors have improved society. Point to the first part of the prompt, and discuss the purpose, audience, and task of the prompt. Then have partners describe what they will write about using the terms *inventors, improve,* and *society.*

CLASSROOM CULTURE

We respect and value each other's experiences.

To create a classroom culture where students value each other's efforts and topics of interest, remind them to listen thoughtfully as others share their ideas. After setting a purpose for reading, ask students: *What questions will help your partner think more about the sources?*

FORMATIVE ASSESSMENT

❯ STUDENT CHECK-IN

Have partners share the purpose they set for reading the sources. Then ask them to reflect using the Check-In routine.

EXTENDED WRITING 1

LEARNING GOALS

We can take notes to find relevant evidence to answer a prompt.

OBJECTIVES

Draw on information from multiple print or digital sources, demonstrating the ability to locate an answer to a question quickly or to solve a problem efficiently.

Explain how an author uses reasons and evidence to support particular points in a text, identifying which reasons and evidence support which point(s).

Explain an author's perspective, or point of view, toward a topic in an informational text.

Integrate information from several texts on the same topic in order to write or speak about the subject knowledgeably.

Draw evidence from literary or informational texts to support analysis, reflection, and research.

Write routinely over extended time frames and shorter time frames for a range of discipline-specific tasks, purposes, and audiences.

ELA ACADEMIC LANGUAGE

• central idea, details, source
• Cognates: *idea central, detalles*

TEACH IN SMALL GROUP

● **Approaching Level** Help students understand each source's central idea. Complete the questions with the group.

● **On Level** Have partners identify the sources' central ideas and complete the questions.

● **Beyond Level** Ask students to paraphrase the sources' central ideas. Discuss how relevant details keep the essay focused.

● **ELL** For support having students read the sources, see **ELL Small Group Guide.**

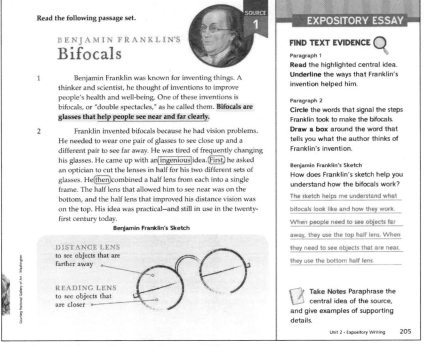

Reading/Writing Companion, p. 205

⏱ Analyze the Sources
10 mins

Find Text Evidence

As students read the source passages, ask them to note important ideas and details, interesting or unfamiliar words, and any questions they may have in their writer's notebooks. Use the questions below. Remind students to cite text evidence.

 SOURCE 1 **"Benjamin Franklin's Bifocals"**

Paragraph 1 *How did Franklin's invention help people?* (It helped people see clearly near and far.)

Paragraph 2 *How did Franklin create bifocals?* (He put the tops and bottoms of two different pairs of glasses into a single frame.) *What words signal the steps Franklin took to accomplish this?* (First; then) Have students talk about what the author thinks of Franklin's invention.

Benjamin Franklin's Sketch *How does the sketch help the audience understand how the bifocals worked?* (It shows how the top and bottom lenses were put together and tells what each part did.)

 Analytical Writing **Take Notes** Have students paraphrase the central idea of the source. Ask them to use their notes and these sentence starters to give examples of supporting details.

> *I read that Benjamin Franklin . . .*

> *The author supports this central idea with details like . . .*

Reading/Writing Companion Pages 206–207

WRITING

FIND TEXT EVIDENCE 🔍

Paragraph 3
Underline the central idea. The details that help focus the essay are highlighted.

Paragraph 4
Circle an example of a transitional word or phrase that links two ideas.

Paragraph 5
How did Knight's bag-making machine improve society?

Knight's bag-making machine made people's lives easier. Her machine cut, folded, and glued paper bags quickly and efficiently.

Paragraph 6
Draw a box around the detail that tells you how successful Knight was.

📝 **Take Notes** Paraphrase the central idea of the source, and give examples of supporting details.

206   Unit 2 • Expository Writing

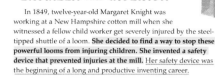

SOURCE 2
Margaret Knight, ENGINEER AND INVENTOR

3   In 1849, twelve-year-old Margaret Knight was working at a New Hampshire cotton mill when she witnessed a fellow child worker get severely injured by the steel-tipped shuttle of a loom. **She decided to find a way to stop these powerful looms from injuring children. She invented a safety device that prevented injuries at the mill.** Her safety device was the beginning of a long and productive inventing career.

4   Knight had always been fascinated with machines. To create the safety device for the loom, she methodically tested and experimented with different machines. She finally made a device that worked successfully. As a result, it was installed in all of the looms in the mill.

5   Knight didn't stop inventing after she developed the safety device for the loom. In 1867, while working at a paper bag factory, she had another brilliant idea. At the time, paper bags didn't have flat bottoms. They were also made by hand. She designed and built a model of an automatic bag-making machine. Her machine could cut, fold, and glue bags with flat bottoms. In no time, her machine made the bag-making process run much more efficiently.

6   Throughout her lifetime, Knight developed ninety other inventions. Her engineering skills were advanced for her time, and her inventions improved the lives of many people.

HENRY FORD and the MODEL T

SOURCE 3

7   "I will build a car for the great multitude. It will be large enough for the family, but small enough for the individual to run and take care of. It will be constructed of the best materials, by the best men to be hired, after the simplest designs that modern engineering can devise. But it will be so low in price that no man making a good salary will be unable to own one."

8   Automobile manufacturer Henry Ford famously spoke these words when he introduced his Model T car in 1908. Ford's success in creating a reliable, affordable car transformed the way Americans traveled. Previously, only the wealthy could afford cars. With its improved traction, the Model T was a reliable option, as it could handle rough dirt roads.

9   In 1913, Ford also pioneered new manufacturing processes. The Model T was mass-produced on a moving assembly line. Ford and his team followed basic principles of mass production. One job flowed into the next, so work moved continuously.

10   Ford's processes reduced factory costs. In less than a year, assembly time for each car frame, or structure, dropped from twelve hours to ninety-three minutes. The price of a new Model T dropped, too, from $950 in 1908 to $290 in 1927.

11   For the first time, more Americans, including the working-class, could travel as never before. They had more freedom to travel outside their homes.

EXPOSITORY ESSAY

FIND TEXT EVIDENCE 🔍

Paragraphs 7–8
Underline the central idea. Draw a box around the details that support the idea that the Model T transformed travel.

Paragraph 9
What is another way that the Model T changed American society?

The Model T was the first car to be mass-produced on an assembly line. This changed American industrial production.

Paragraph 10
Circle the fact and detail that provide strong evidence for the central idea.

Paragraph 11
Draw a box around the group that was most affected by the Model T.

📝 **Take Notes** Paraphrase the central idea of the source and give examples of supporting details.

Unit 2 • Expository Writing   207

Reading/Writing Companion, pp. 206–207

SOURCE 2
"Margaret Knight, Engineer and Inventor"

Paragraph 3 *Which sentence is the central idea?* (Her safety device was the beginning of a long and productive inventing career.) *Why did Knight invent a safety device?* (to stop the looms from injuring children)

Paragraph 4 *Which word or phrase links two ideas?* (As a result)

Paragraph 5 *What invention did Knight come up with at the paper bag factory?* (an automatic bag-making machine) Have students discuss how the bag-making machine improved society and write their responses on page 206.

Paragraph 6 *What detail reinforces the central idea?* (She developed ninety inventions.)

Analytical Writing **Take Notes** Have students paraphrase the central idea of the source. Ask them to use their notes to give examples of relevant evidence.

SOURCE 3
"Henry Ford and the Model T"

Paragraphs 7–8 *What source does the author use to introduce the essay and provide details that focus on a topic?* (a quotation from Henry Ford) *What relevant details support the idea that the Model T transformed travel?* (Most people couldn't afford cars. With its improved traction, the Model T could handle rough dirt roads.)

Paragraph 9 *What new manufacturing process did the Model T pioneer?* (mass production on an assembly line)

Paragraph 10 *How did Ford's manufacturing processes affect the Model T's price?* (The price of a Model T dropped from $950 in 1908 to $290 in 1927.)

Paragraph 11 *What group was most affected by the Model T?* (working-class)

Analytical Writing **Take Notes** Have students paraphrase the central idea of the source. Ask them to use their notes to identify supporting details.

MULTIMODAL LEARNING

As students read and reread the source, ask them to note important words and phrases on index cards. Then have them write the central idea of each paragraph in their own words on another card. With a partner, have students arrange the cards to show the relevant details that support the central ideas in each paragraph.

FORMATIVE ASSESSMENT

❯ STUDENT CHECK-IN

Have partners share their responses. Then ask them to reflect using the Check-In routine.

EXTENDED WRITING 1

We can synthesize information from three sources to plan and organize an expository essay.

OBJECTIVES

Introduce a topic clearly, provide a general observation and focus, and group related information logically; include formatting (e.g., headings), illustrations, and multimedia when useful to aiding comprehension.

Develop the topic with facts, definitions, concrete details, quotations, or other information and examples related to the topic.

Produce clear and coherent writing in which the development and organization are appropriate to task, purpose, and audience.

Draw evidence from literary or informational texts to support analysis, reflection, and research.

Apply Grade 5 Reading standards to informational texts.

Organize notes from sources to plan an expository essay.

ELA ACADEMIC LANGUAGE

• *relevant, evidence, synthesize*
• Cognates: *relevante, evidencia*

DIGITAL TOOLS

 Model Graphic Organizer

 Organizing Notes

Plan: Organize Ideas

10 mins

Take Notes

Remind students that they will write an expository essay about how inventors improved society. They will synthesize information from each source to form their response to the prompt.

Say: *When you write your expository essay, you are not simply summarizing the information you read in the sources. You should choose relevant evidence from each source to craft your answer to the prompt. Think about how these details come together to help you understand how inventors have improved society.*

Graphic Organizer

Tell students that before writing their expository essay, they will organize the notes they took from each source in the graphic organizer on **Reading/Writing Companion** pages 208–209. Some of the graphic organizer has been filled in. Help students understand how to complete the graphic organizer.

Central idea Remind students that the central, or main, idea tells the focus of the essay. It answers the prompt directly.

Supporting Ideas These ideas, or details, strongly support the central idea in different ways. Students analyze important information from sources to determine supporting details.

Relevant Evidence Students record evidence taken from sources that expand on or explain the supporting details. Remind students that strong, expository essays do not include information unrelated to the central idea. Tell students that they may not find evidence from all three sources for each supporting detail.

 Have students complete the graphic organizer.

Analytical Writing

 Synthesize Information

Explain that when writers synthesize information, they connect details from sources to create a new understanding. One way to help synthesize information is to use relevant facts and details from two or more sources to answer a question. Have partners review their completed graphic organizers and answer the question, *How did inventions improve society?* Partners can provide feedback on whether or not the facts and details are relevant to the central idea.

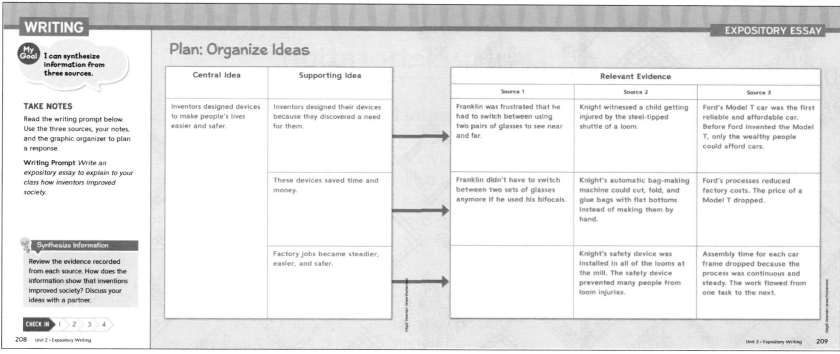

WRITING

EXPOSITORY ESSAY

My Goal: I can synthesize information from three sources.

Plan: Organize Ideas

TAKE NOTES

Read the writing prompt below. Use the three sources, your notes, and the graphic organizer to plan a response.

Writing Prompt Write an expository essay to explain to your class how inventors improved society.

Synthesize Information

Review the evidence recorded from each source. How does the information show that inventions improved society? Discuss your ideas with a partner.

CHECK IN 1 2 3 4

208   Unit 2 • Expository Writing

Central Idea	Supporting Idea	Relevant Evidence		
		Source 1	Source 2	Source 3
Inventors designed devices to make people's lives easier and safer.	Inventors designed their devices because they discovered a need for them.	Franklin was frustrated that he had to switch between using two pairs of glasses to see near and far.	Knight witnessed a child getting injured by the steel-tipped shuttle of a loom.	Ford's Model T car was the first reliable and affordable car. Before Ford invented the Model T, only the wealthy people could afford cars.
	These devices saved time and money.	Franklin didn't have to switch between two sets of glasses anymore if he used his bifocals.	Knight's automatic bag-making machine could cut, fold, and glue bags with flat bottoms instead of making them by hand.	Ford's processes reduced factory costs. The price of a Model T dropped.
	Factory jobs became steadier, easier, and safer.		Knight's safety device was installed in all of the looms at the mill. The safety device prevented many people from loom injuries.	Assembly time for each car frame dropped because the process was continuous and steady. The work flowed from one task to the next.

Unit 2 • Expository Writing   209

Reading/Writing Companion, pp. 208–209

ELL English Language Learners

Use the following scaffolds with the **Graphic Organizer**. For additional support, see the **ELL Small Group Guide**.

Beginning

Help students complete the graphic organizer. Point out how evidence from Sources 1 and 2 in the first row adds to the supporting idea that inventors made things to fill a need. Then have students add Source 3 information about Henry Ford and his Model T car. Help partners describe using the following: Ford saw that poor people could not buy cars. He made cars that were low in price. Have partners look at their notes and continue filling in the chart.

Intermediate

Explain and discuss parts of the graphic organizer with students. Read the evidence from Sources 1 and 2 in the first row, and discuss how it adds to the supporting idea that inventors made things to fill a need. Then have students fill in information from Source 3 that supports the same idea in the first row. Help partners describe the following: Ford wanted to make cars that working people could buy. Have students look at their notes to continue filling in the chart.

Advanced/Advanced High

Have students complete the first row of the graphic organizer. Have them review their notes and describe the information they can use. Then have partners brainstorm another supporting idea and find evidence to fill in the second row.

FORMATIVE ASSESSMENT

❯ STUDENT CHECK-IN

Have partners share their graphic organizer on Reading/Writing Companion pages 208–209. Ask them to use the Check-In routine to reflect and fill in the bars.

LEARNING GOALS

We can use our graphic organizer to write a draft.

OBJECTIVES

Come to discussions prepared, having read or studied required material; explicitly draw on that preparation and other information known about the topic to explore ideas under discussion.

Develop the topic with facts, definitions, concrete details, quotations, or other information and examples related to the topic.

Produce clear and coherent writing in which the development and organization are appropriate to task, purpose, and audience

Use elaboration to draft an effective expository text.

ELA ACADEMIC LANGUAGE

• *facts, details, relevant, elaborate*
• Cognates: *detalles, relevante*

DIGITAL TOOLS

 Student Model Draft

DIFFERENTIATED WRITING

● **Approaching Level** Review for supporting details.

● **On Level** Partners can review for supporting details.

● **Beyond Level** Partners can make suggestions for supporting details.

● **ELL** For support on writing a draft, see **ELL Small Group Guide**.

---

10 mins Draft: Elaboration

Include Supporting Details

Tell students that writers use elaboration to develop the central idea in an expository essay. Writers may elaborate, or expand on, the central idea by including facts, definitions, examples, descriptions, anecdotes, or quotations that directly support the central idea. These details should be relevant to help the reader connect them to the central idea and to keep the essay focused on the topic.

Read the sentence from Keya's essay on **Reading/Writing Companion** page 202: *Adams solved her problem by sharing her opinions in letters to her husband.* Point out that this detail supports Keya's central idea that three colonial women, including Abigail Adams, solved problems when women had few rights. Say: *When you choose relevant evidence, you need to look for information that can specifically support the central idea. In this example, Keya elaborates by providing a detail that shows how one colonial woman was able to find a way to express her ideas about politics when she didn't have a voice in government.*

Read aloud the paragraph on page 210. Ask: *What is the central idea of this paragraph?* (Jefferson knew he had to convince many colonists of the need for independence.) Have students look at how the writer elaborates on and supports this central idea using relevant evidence in the paragraph. Then have students use the paragraph as a model to craft a central idea supported by relevant evidence for their own expository essays.

 Have partners read their paragraphs aloud and explain how the details support the central idea.

Draft

 Have students write an expository essay about how inventors improved society. Before students begin drafting, have them review the rubric on page 200, the evidence they recorded in the graphic organizer, and the notes they took in their writer's notebook.

Remind students that one feature of a strong essay is an introduction in which the central idea is clearly stated. Encourage them to use relevant evidence to support and elaborate on the central idea of the essay.

Make sure students write their drafts legibly in print or cursive in their writer's notebook or type accurately on-screen. If students choose to write their essays in cursive, guide them to produce legible works within the same timeframe as they would for writing in print. Circulate to assist and check their progress. Remind them to indent each paragraph.

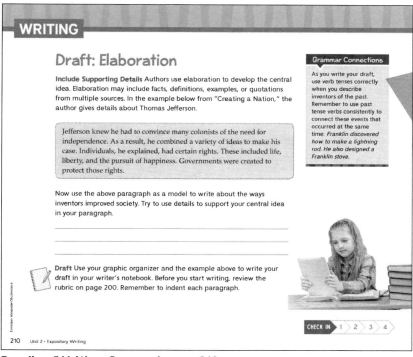

Reading/Writing Companion, p. 210

ELL English Language Learners

Use the following scaffolds with **Include Supporting Details**.

Beginning
Remind students that supporting details are facts, definitions, examples, or quotations that support the central idea. Read the paragraph on page 210 with students, and discuss the central idea: Jefferson knew he had to convince many colonists of the need for independence. Explain that colonists were people who settled into a new country. Then help partners identify facts that tell more about how he convinced colonists: Jefferson explained that people had certain rights.

Intermediate
Review with students that writers support their central ideas with facts, definitions, examples, or quotations. Read the paragraph on page 210, and have students determine the central idea of the paragraph: Jefferson knew he had to convince many colonists of the need for independence. Then help partners describe how Jefferson convinced people of this need with facts: Jefferson explained that individuals had certain rights. He combined a variety of ideas to make his case.

Advanced/Advanced High
Have students discuss what they can include to support a central idea. Have them identify the central idea and the facts that support it in the paragraph about Jefferson on page 210. Then have partners discuss and write another supporting detail for the paragraph.

TEACHER CONFERENCES
As students draft, hold teacher conferences with individual students.

Step 1: Talk About Strengths
Point out strengths in the essay: *The central idea is clear and tells the focus of the essay.*

Step 2: Focus on Skills
Give feedback on how the student uses supporting details: *The example in this sentence provides a detail that seems unnecessary. Replace this example with one that supports the central idea.*

Step 3: Make Concrete Suggestions
Provide specific direction to help students draft, such as making sure the central idea is clear and appears at the beginning of the essay. Have students meet with you to review progress.

FORMATIVE ASSESSMENT

STUDENT CHECK-IN
Have partners share their draft. Then have them use the Check-In routine to reflect and fill in the bars on Reading/Writing Companion page 210.

EXTENDED
WRITING
1

LEARNING GOALS

We can revise our writing to make it stronger.

OBJECTIVES

Engage effectively in a range of collaborative discussions (one-on-one, in groups, and teacher-led) with diverse partners on grade 5 topics and texts, building on others' ideas and expressing their own clearly.

Follow agreed-upon rules for discussions and carry out assigned roles.

Use knowledge of language and its conventions when writing, speaking, reading, or listening.

Link ideas within and across categories of information using words, phrases, and clauses (e.g., *in contrast, especially*).

With guidance and support from peers and adults, develop and strengthen writing as needed by planning, revising, and editing.

ELA ACADEMIC LANGUAGE

• *feedback, conference*

• Cognate: *conferencia*

DIFFERENTIATED WRITING

Check student progress at this stage during Small Group time.

● **Approaching Level** Review students' drafts for supporting details in Small Group time.

● **On Level** Partners can focus on details that support the central idea as they read their drafts.

● **Beyond Level** As students review each other's drafts, they can identify sentences where supporting details can be made clearer for their audience.

● **ELL** For support with revising the drafts, see **ELL Small Group Guide**.

Revise: Peer Conferences

Review a Draft

Explain to partners that they will review and give feedback on each other's drafts. Remind them that a well-written expository essay begins with a focused introduction that states the central idea. Before students review each other's drafts, remind them to think about some features of an organized and focused essay:

• sources, facts, details, and examples that support the central idea

• transitional words to link ideas together or to clarify ideas

• proper verb tense when describing events

• varied sentence structure by starting with a question or adding punctuation for emphasis

Review with students the routine for peer review of writing:

• **Step 1:** Listen carefully as the writer reads his or her work aloud.

• **Step 2:** Avoid calling attention away from or interrupting the writer.

• **Step 3:** Ask questions afterward to help you make sense of anything that is unclear.

• **Step 4:** Take note of the things you liked about the writing.

Model using sentence starters on **Reading/Writing Companion** page 211. Say: *I like the evidence you used to support the central idea because . . .* and finish the sentence. Discuss the steps of the peer-conferencing routine. Ask: *Why is it important to listen actively?* (to show respect and to comment on the writing) *Why should we ask questions afterward?* (to make sure we understand; to clarify how ideas are connected)

 Circulate and observe as partners review and give feedback on **COLLABORATE** each other's drafts. Ensure that partners are following the routine and the agreed-upon rules of listening actively and taking notes. Remind them to consider the varying sentence beginnings, consistent verb tense, and specific facts and details that are relevant to the topic. Have students reflect on partner feedback and record on page 211 the suggestion that they found most helpful.

Revision

Review the Revising Checklist on page 211 and the features of the rubric on pages 240–243. Explain that a rubric has scores that add up to a maximum of 10. Point out the score in the left column and the three categories in the right column. Then have students use the rubric to score their essays on page 211.

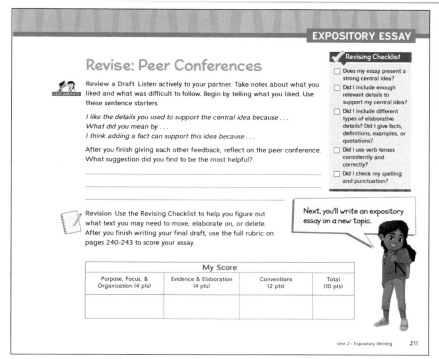

Reading/Writing Companion, p. 211

ELL English Language Learners

Use the following scaffolds with **Review a Draft**.

Beginning

Pair students with more proficient readers. Have students ask for clarification and provide feedback using: *What does the word _____ mean? What did you mean by _____?* and *I like _____.* Students may need to see the draft as well as hear it. Have partners complete the Partner Feedback on page 211. Help students check their drafts for the last two items on the Revising Checklist. Help them revise their drafts using consistent verb tenses.

Intermediate

Pair students with more proficient speakers. Have students ask for clarification and provide feedback, using: *I like the part about _____. Can you explain _____?* Have partners complete the Partner Feedback on page 211. Have students use the last three items on the Revising Checklist to identify the revisions they want to make. Have them use consistent verb tenses. Check their revisions and provide feedback as needed.

Advanced/Advanced High

Have partners provide feedback using the sentence starters on page 211 and read each other's responses to check that their partner understood them correctly. Have students use the Revising Checklist to identify the features that appear in their writing.

 TEACHER CONFERENCES

As students revise, hold teacher conferences with individual students.

Step 1: Talk About Strengths
Point out strengths in the essay: *You used strong transitions in your opening paragraph that help me understand the relationship between inventors and society.*

Step 2: Focus on Skills
Give feedback on how the student uses transitions: *Be sure to use transitions when you are relating one idea to another.*

Step 3: Make Concrete Suggestions
Provide specific direction to help students revise, such as making the link between two or more ideas more clear. Have students revise and then meet with you to review progress.

 DIGITAL TOOLS
Revised Student Model

Revise Checklist (Expository), Revise Conferencing Checklist (Expository), Peer Conferencing (Collaborative Conversations Video)

FORMATIVE ASSESSMENT

▶ **STUDENT CHECK-IN**

Have partners share their drafts and give feedback. Ask them to reflect using the Check-In routine and rubric on Reading/Writing page 211.

LEARNING GOALS

We can use a rubric to understand what makes a strong expository essay.

OBJECTIVES

Link ideas within and across categories of information using words, phrases, and clauses (e.g., *in contrast, especially*).

Provide logically ordered reasons that are supported by facts and details.

With guidance and support from peers and adults, develop and strengthen writing as needed by planning, revising, and editing.

Demonstrate command of the conventions of standard English grammar and usage when writing or speaking.

Analyze a rubric used to evaluate expository essays.

ELA ACADEMIC LANGUAGE

• *transitional, strategies, logical, progression*

• Cognates: *estrategias, logico, progresión*

10 mins Analyze the Rubric

Expository Writing Rubric

Students will use the Expository Writing Rubric to first evaluate a student model and then to write their own expository essays. Remind students that they can use the rubric to understand what to include in their essays and to identify parts of an essay that are successful and those that need work. Point out each category and the score of 4 on the rubric.

COLLABORATE Have partners read the full rubric. Then have them summarize the bullet points in Purpose, Focus, and Organization and Evidence and Elaboration. (Purpose, Focus, and Organization tells that an essay should include a central idea, transitions, and a logical organization with an introduction and conclusion. Evidence and Elaboration tells that an essay should include evidence, elaboration, academic language, and sentence variety.)

Purpose, Focus, and Organization

Remind students that an effective essay must have a clear purpose, focus, and organization. Review all the bullets with students. Then read aloud the third bullet. Remind students that transitions are words and phrases that link ideas. Explain that a logical expression of ideas helps the reader follow the writer's ideas and understand the essay. Transitional strategies help signal their progression of ideas. Ask: *Why is it important for a writer to use transitional strategies in an essay?* (Transitional strategies help the reader follow along with the writer's thinking.) *What is the connection between transitional strategies and a logical text structure?* (The transitional words help readers follow the writer's logical progression of ideas.)

Analytical Writing Have students write their response on **Reading/Writing Companion** page 212. Ask: *What are transitional strategies?* (the use of transitional words or phrases to connect information and ideas)

Evidence and Elaboration

This part of the rubric identifies how evidence should be incorporated and what kinds of evidence can be used. Students will analyze the fifth bullet. Understanding this bullet will help them include academic and domain-specific language in their own essays. Read aloud the highlighted bullet. Ask: *What is academic language?* (words that are uncommon in informal conversation but that express ideas clearly) *What is domain-specific language?* (words that are directly related to a particular subject area)

Analytical Writing Have partners underline the words in the fifth bullet that tell what kind of vocabulary belongs in an expository essay. Have students write their responses on page 212.

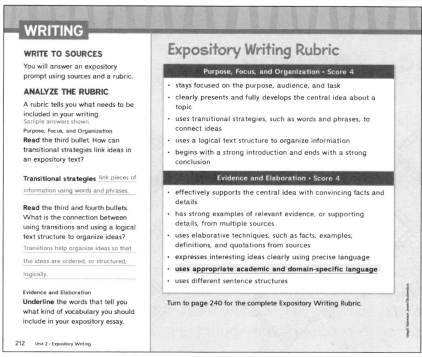

Reading/Writing Companion, p. 212

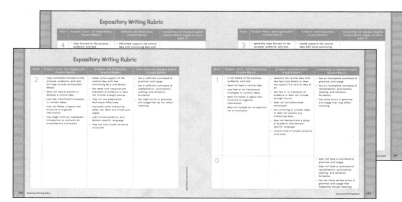

For the full Expository Writing Rubric, see **Reading/Writing Companion,** pages 240–243.

English Language Learners

Use the following scaffolds with **Evidence and Elaboration.**

Beginning

Review with students that a rubric tells what to have in their writing. Read the highlighted bullet and say: *Academic language clearly shows your ideas. These are words you may not use speaking naturally.* Compare sentences using academic and nonacademic words: I *watch* a movie. I *observe* an experiment. Then explain domain-specific language: *Domain-specific words are about a subject like math or social studies.* Have partners describe: Use academic language to write clear information. Use domain-specific language to write about a subject.

Intermediate

Review the rubric with students and focus on the meaning of academic and domain-specific language. Discuss how essays for school often have these words: Academic language adds clarity and domain-specific language is important for writing about subjects. Read the highlighted bullet and help students retell: Strong writers use academic and domain-specific language that fits the essay's content and audience. Have partners share academic and domain-specific words.

Advanced/Advanced High

Review the rubric and have students read the highlighted bullet with you. Have students define academic and domain-specific language and describe how it focuses writing. Then have partners describe why this kind of language needs to be appropriate for the audience and purpose.

NEWCOMERS

To help students develop their writing, display the **Newcomer Cards** and **Newcomer Online Visuals,** and ask questions to help them discuss the images. Provide sentence starters. For example: What do you see? I see a/an ___. What are they doing? They are ___. Have students point to the image as they ask and answer. Then have them write the sentences in their notebooks. Throughout the extended writing project, help students develop their writing by adding to and revising their sentences.

FORMATIVE ASSESSMENT

STUDENT CHECK-IN

Have partners share their responses. Then ask them to reflect using the Check-In routine.

LEARNING GOALS

We can identify academic language.

OBJECTIVES

With guidance and support from peers and adults, develop and strengthen writing as needed by planning, revising, editing, rewriting, or trying a new approach.

Acquire and use accurately grade-appropriate general academic and domain-specific words and phrases, including those that signal contrast, addition, and other logical relationships (e.g., *however, although, nevertheless, similarly, moreover, in addition*).

Use academic language in an expository essay.

Draw evidence from literary or informational texts to support analysis, reflection, and research.

ELA ACADEMIC LANGUAGE

• *precise, formal, signal, indicate*

• Cognates: *preciso, formal, indicar*

DIGITAL TOOLS

 Student Model Sources

 Purpose of Expository Writing

---

 10 mins

Academic Language

Choose Appropriate Words

Tell students that academic language is formal language that they can use when writing about subjects like science, math, or social studies. Academic language frequently appears in expository, argumentative, and literary texts. To present their ideas precisely and to keep their writing focused on a topic, writers use academic language.

Reread the first paragraph under the heading "Lucy Terry Prince" on **Literature Anthology** page 114. Point out examples of academic language, such as *activist*, *conflict*, and *colonial*. Explain that these words help readers understand more about Lucy Terry Prince, the focus of the paragraph. Say: *The language tells readers precise details about Lucy Terry Prince and her poem "Bars Fight."*

Read aloud the paragraph on **Reading/Writing Companion** page 213.

Think Aloud I see that the writer uses the word *supported* in the first sentence of the paragraph. I know the word *support* means "to give assistance to" or "to help function or act." The writer chose this word to precisely describe Alexander Hamilton's attitude toward ratifying the Constitution. If the writer had used the phrase *agreed with*, for example, the text would have been less precise. The choice of words helps me understand the central idea of the paragraph.

Reread the paragraph on **Reading/Writing Companion** page 213. Have students identify the central idea. (*The Federalist Papers* had a direct impact on the delegates.) Ask: *What language in the central idea helps you understand the focus of the paragraph?* (impact) Ask: *What caused* The Federalist Papers *to have a direct impact on the delegates?* (Hamilton and others encouraged delegates to ratify the Constitution when they wrote *The Federalist Papers.*)

COLLABORATE Have partners reread the paragraph on **Reading/Writing Companion** page 213 and discuss how the highlighted examples of academic language make the paragraph more precise.

Apply

For more practice with academic language, have partners read the three student model sources in the **Online Writer's Notebook** and identify examples of academic language in one or more source.

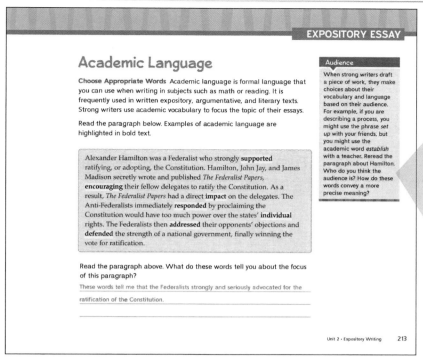

Reading/Writing Companion, p. 213

 English Language Learners

Use the following scaffolds with **Choose Appropriate Words**. For additional support, see **ELL Small Group Guide**.

Beginning

Discuss with students how writers use academic language to present ideas in a precise, or detailed way. Read the paragraph on page 213, and point out the academic words *supported* and *encouraging*. Review the meanings, and discuss how the academic words help the writer express ideas precisely. Help students retell using the following: Alexander Hamilton supported the Constitution. *The Federalist Papers* encouraged delegates to ratify, or approve, the Constitution.

Intermediate

Discuss with students how writers use academic language. Read the paragraph on page 213 with them, pointing out how *support* and *encourage* add precise meaning. Have partners retell the first two sentences and discuss how the academic words clarify ideas. Have partners respond to the question on page 213 using: The academic words convey how Alexander Hamilton supported the Constitution and *The Federalist Papers* encouraged delegates to ratify the Constitution.

Advanced/Advanced High

Have students discuss how writers use academic language. Read the paragraph on page 213 with them. Have students retell the first two sentences and discuss why the writer includes academic language. Have partners answer the question on page 213 and discuss examples of other academic language.

> STUDENT CHECK-IN

Have partners share their responses. Then have them reflect using the Check-In routine.

EXTENDED
WRITING
2

LEARNING GOALS

We can use a rubric to evaluate
a student model.

OBJECTIVES

Link ideas within and across
categories of information using
words, phrases, and clauses (e.g.,
in contrast, especially).

Use precise language and
domain-specific vocabulary to
inform about or explain the topic.

With guidance and support from
peers and adults, develop and
strengthen writing as needed by
planning, revising, and editing.

Analyze a writing prompt.

Analyze a model of an expository
essay.

ELA ACADEMIC LANGUAGE

• *introduction, example,
  elaboration, paragraph*

• Cognates: *introducción, ejemplo,
  elaboración, párrafo*

DIGITAL TOOLS

Student Model Sources

Analyze the Student Model

10
mins

Expository Essay

Students will read and analyze a student model and apply the rubric to
examine why Marc scored a 4 for Purpose, Focus, and Organization on his
essay. Complete the routine below for Marc's prompt.

ANALYZE THE PROMPT ROUTINE

Read aloud the prompt.

Identify the purpose. *Is the purpose to inform or persuade?*

Identify the audience. *Who is the audience?*

Identify the type of writing the prompt is asking for. *What is the prompt
asking the writer to do?*

At the completion of the routine, students should understand that Marc's
purpose is to inform, his audience is his class, and the prompt is asking Marc
to explain what people do to accomplish difficult goals.

Discuss the Student Model

As you read Marc's essay with students, ask them to look for the academic
language Marc uses to precisely express his ideas and the ways Marc uses
transitional strategies to indicate a logical order in his essay. Have students
note interesting words and questions they have as they read.

Paragraph 1 Remind students an expository essay will include academic
language. Ask students to write one academic word from Marc's
introduction that caught their attention and helped them understand Marc's
topic. (Sample response: He uses the word *achieving*, which means
"reaching a result due to effort, skill, or courage.") Ask: *What is the central
idea of Marc's essay?* (Research shows that breaking a goal into smaller
chunks will help people to succeed.)

Paragraph 2 Marc supports his central idea by citing an article titled
"Motivation in the Middle." Ask: *How does this source support Marc's central
idea?*

Think Aloud In this paragraph, Marc states that people don't perform as
well during the middle of a big project as they do at the beginning or the
end. His research says breaking a goal into smaller chunks will help people
to succeed. This provides relevant evidence that supports his central idea.

Have students circle more examples of relevant evidence that Marc
uses on **Reading/Writing Companion** page 214.

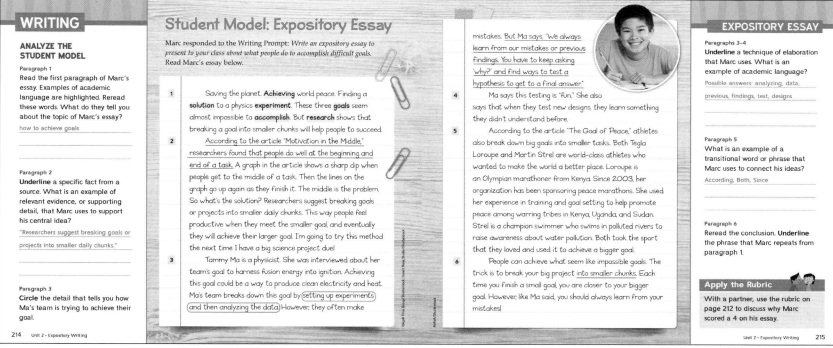

Reading/Writing Companion, pp. 214-215

Paragraphs 3-4 Point out that these paragraphs provide another example to explain how people can break a goal into smaller chunks to be successful. Ask: *What academic or domain-specific language does Marc use in paragraph 3?* (harness, fusion energy, ignition, experiments, hypothesis, data) Point out the academic language *achieving* and *experiments*. Ask: *How do these words help you understand what Ma is doing to ensure success?* (The word *achieving* tells me Ma's intention. The word *experiments* tells me precisely what she is doing to reach her goal.)

Have partners circle more examples of academic language.

Paragraph 5 Ask: *What group of people does Marc include in Paragraph 5 to support his central idea?* (athletes) Ask students to identify examples of transitional words or phrases that Marc uses to connect ideas about the two athletes. (According, Both, Since)

Paragraph 6 Have students underline the phrase that Marc repeats from Paragraph 1. ("break your big project into smaller chunks")

Apply the Rubric

Have pairs of students discuss what was effective in Marc's essay and what needs to be improved. Have them use the rubric on page 212 and these sentence starters.

Marc supports his central idea by using . . .

His essay could be improved by . . .

TEACH IN SMALL GROUP

● **ELL** For support reading the student model and analyzing the three sources, see the **ELL Small Group Guide**.

CLASSROOM CULTURE

We learn through modeling and practice.

A classroom that provides access to different resources, or models of expository essays, improves the students' understanding of the task and helps them in their writing. Ask: *How do examples of academic language improve your writing?*

FORMATIVE ASSESSMENT

❯ STUDENT CHECK-IN

Have partners share their responses to Apply the Rubric on Reading/Writing Companion page 215. Then ask them to reflect using the Check-In routine.

EXTENDED WRITING 2

Student Model Sources

LEARNING GOALS

We can analyze student model essay sources.

OBJECTIVES

Explain how an author uses reasons and evidence to support particular points in a text, identifying which reasons and evidence support which point(s).

Read grade-level text with purpose and understanding.

With guidance and support from peers and adults, develop and strengthen writing as needed by planning, revising, and editing.

Analyze sources to understand the elements of an effective argumentative essay.

Cite evidence to explain and justify reasoning.

ELA ACADEMIC LANGUAGE

• *elaboration, support*
• Cognate: *elaboración*

DIGITAL TOOLS

 Student Model Sources

Analyze the Student Model

(10 mins)

Analyze the Student Model Sources

Explain that Marc used three sources to write his expository essay. Use copies of the online Student Model Sources to show how Marc developed a central idea, used elaboration, and chose academic language. Remind students that Marc answered the prompt: *Write an expository essay to present to your class about what people do to accomplish difficult goals.*

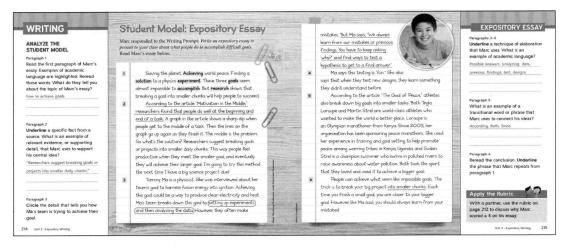

Reading/Writing Companion, pp. 214-215

SOURCE 1 **"Interview with an Experimental Physicist"**
After reading Source 1, read aloud Marc's third and fourth paragraphs. Have students compare the information they read in Marc's paragraphs to the information found in Source 1. Ask: *How does Marc include information from Source 1 in his third and fourth paragraphs?*

Think aloud I see that Marc includes information from Source 1 about how Ma and her team accomplish their goals. He paraphrases information from the source to explain Ma's goal and how the team accomplishes the goal by setting up experiments and analyzing data. He also says Ma's team sometimes makes mistakes. To show how they overcome such obstacles, he quotes Ma as saying, "We always learn from our mistakes or previous findings." The paraphrased and quoted information elaborates on the example that Ma's team breaks their goal into experiments.

COLLABORATE Have partners annotate the Student Model on **Reading/Writing Companion** pages 214-215 by citing examples of the scientists' actions that tell how they accomplished their goals.

SOURCE 2 **"The Goal of Peace"**

After reading Source 2, read aloud Marc's fifth paragraph. Have students compare the information they read in Marc's paragraph to the information found in Source 2. Ask: *How do the actions of Tegla Loroupe and Martin Strel support Marc's central idea?* (Marc uses their training and goal-setting experience as examples of how people have accomplished difficult goals.) Have students consider how the names and actions of important people in a source can be used as examples to support a central idea.

COLLABORATE Have partners identify how Marc used details from Source 2 to introduce his topic in his first paragraph. Have them compare the academic language in Marc's first paragraph with the language in Source 2.

SOURCE 3 **"Motivation in the Middle"**

After reading Source 3, read aloud Marc's first paragraph. Have students compare the information they read in Marc's paragraph to the information found in Source 3. Ask: *How does Marc include information from Source 3 in his first paragraph?* (He uses the research findings from the source to provide evidence for the benefits of breaking a large goal into smaller tasks.)

COLLABORATE Have students annotate the Student Model on **Reading/Writing Companion** pages 214-215 by circling facts and details from Source 3 in Marc's essay.

Synthesize Information

Reread Marc's central idea in paragraph 1: *But research shows that breaking a goal into smaller chunks will help people to succeed.* Explain that Marc developed his central idea after reading and thinking about all three sources. Marc read the sources to find things people do to reach big goals. Marc read about breaking a goal into smaller chunks in one source but synthesized information from all the sources to support his central idea.

COLLABORATE Have partners find similarities among the three sources. Have partners look back at their notes and then use their writer's notebook to answer the following question: *How did Mark develop his central idea by synthesizing information from all three sources?* (All sources tell about achieving goals. Two sources provide examples of specific people who accomplish difficult goals. One source tells about research on accomplishing goals. Mark combined ideas from all three sources to come up with the focus of his essay. He uses details and examples from all the sources to support the conclusion that breaking a goal into smaller chunks will help people to succeed.)

TEACH IN SMALL GROUP

● **Approaching Level** Read each online source aloud. Help students identify the academic language in each.

● **On Level** Reread the online sources aloud. Ask students to work with a partner to identify the academic language in each. Talk about how Marc used the sources to write his essay.

● **Beyond Level** Ask students to note how Marc clearly and effectively expresses his ideas. Have them use the online sources to identify academic language Marc used in his essay.

● **ELL** Help students understand what Marc's task was. Then read one online source aloud and work with students to identify important academic language. For additional support, see the **ELL Small Group Guide**.

FORMATIVE ASSESSMENT

STUDENT CHECK-IN

Have partners share their responses. Then ask them to reflect using the Check-In routine.

EXTENDED
WRITING
2

We can set a purpose for reading sources to answer a prompt.

OBJECTIVES

Provide logically ordered reasons that are supported by facts and details.

Introduce a topic clearly, provide a general observation and focus, and group related information logically; include formatting (e.g., headings), illustrations, and multimedia when useful to aiding comprehension.

Use precise language and domain-specific vocabulary to inform about or explain the topic.

With guidance and support from peers and adults, develop and strengthen writing as needed by planning, revising, editing, rewriting, or trying a new approach.

Analyze a writing prompt.

ELA ACADEMIC LANGUAGE

• *expository essay, source, passage*

• Cognates: *ensayo expositivo, pasaje*

Analyze the Prompt

Writing Prompt

Follow the Analyze the Prompt Routine on page T252. Read the writing prompt on **Reading/Writing Companion** page 216 aloud: *Write an expository essay to print in your school newspaper about the ways humans protect the environment.* Guide students to identify the purpose and audience. Then ask: *What is the prompt asking you to do?* (to write an expository essay about the way humans protect the environment)

Anchor Chart Review the features of an expository essay and add any new details to the Expository Essay anchor chart.

• It has a central idea supported by relevant evidence from sources.

• It includes academic language to keep the essay focused and formal.

• It uses transitional words and phrases to connect ideas.

Purpose, Audience, and Task

Remind students that thinking about their purpose and audience will help them plan and organize their writing. Reread the writing prompt and ask: *What is your purpose for writing?* (to inform readers) *Who will your audience be?* (people who read my school newspaper—students at my school, teachers, and parents) *What type of writing is the prompt asking for?* (writing that provides information about ways humans protect the environment) Given the purpose and audience, have them think about whether they will use formal or informal language in their essay.

Remind students that the prompt helps determine their task, or what they will write. Reread the prompt. Ask: *What words in the prompt tell you what you will write about?* Have students underline four key words in the prompt on page 216. Ask students to then write their responses to the questions on page 216.

Set a Purpose for Reading Sources

Tell students that before they write their essays, they will read, annotate, and answer questions about three sources. Have them look at the source on page 217, read the title, and skim the text. Remind students that when they skim, they will not read every word. They will read quickly for the central, or main, ideas and relevant details. Skimming the first source passage will help them write a question and set a purpose for reading the three sources.

Have students turn to a partner and say the writing prompt in their own words. Then tell students to think of a question that will help them set a purpose for reading, and have them write the question on page 216.

WRITING

Analyze the Prompt

My Goal: I can write an expository essay.

Writing Prompt

Write an expository essay to print in your school newspaper about the ways humans protect the environment.

Purpose, Audience, and Task Reread the writing prompt. What is your purpose for writing? My purpose is to _____

Who will your audience be? My audience will be _____

What type of writing is the prompt asking for? _____

Set a Purpose for Reading Sources Asking questions about the different ways humans protect the environment will help you figure out your purpose for reading. It also helps you understand what you already know about the topic. Before you read the passage set about the ways humans care for nature and wildlife, write a question here.

_____
_____
_____

216 Unit 2 • Expository Writing

Reading/Writing Companion, p. 216

ELL English Language Learners

Use the following scaffolds with **Writing Prompt**. For additional support, see the **ELL Small Group Guide**.

Beginning

Read the prompt with students and discuss what they will write about. Explain that the *environment* refers to the world around us, including the animals, plants, oceans, and air. Discuss examples of how people can protect the environment, such as cleaning up a beach or reducing air pollution. Then have students tell you the audience, or for whom the essay is written, and have them discuss why it matters. Help partners describe the prompt using the following: I will write about the ways people protect the environment.

Intermediate

Read the prompt with students and discuss what they will write about. To reinforce the meaning of the prompt, have students give examples of how people can protect the environment. Point to the first part of the prompt, and elicit from students that they will write an expository essay that will be printed in their school newspaper. Have partners describe the prompt using the following: I will write about the ways that people protect the environment. My audience is other students at school.

Advanced/Advanced High

Review the prompt with students, and discuss what they will write about. Have students give examples of how people protect the environment. Point to the prompt and have partners restate it, including the purpose and audience.

FORMATIVE ASSESSMENT

❯ STUDENT CHECK-IN

Have partners share the purpose they set for reading the sources. Then ask them to reflect using the Check-In routine.

EXTENDED WRITING 2

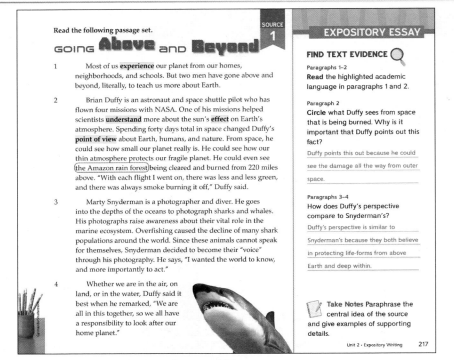

Reading/Writing Companion, p. 217

LEARNING GOALS

We can take notes to find relevant evidence to answer a prompt.

OBJECTIVES

Explain how an author uses reasons and evidence to support particular points in a text, identifying which reasons and evidence support which point(s).

Engage effectively in a range of collaborative discussions (one-on-one, in groups, and teacher-led) with diverse partners, building on others' ideas and expressing their own clearly.

Analyze multiple accounts of the same event or topic, noting important similarities and differences in the point of view they represent.

Read grade-level text with purpose and understanding.

Obtain and combine information about ways individual communities use science ideas to protect the Earth's resources and environment.

ELA ACADEMIC LANGUAGE

- *quotation, point of view, compare, paraphrase*
- Cognates: *comparar, parafrasear*

TEACH IN SMALL GROUP

● **Approaching Level** Help students find words that support the focus of the sources. Complete the questions with the group.

● **On Level** Have partners note words that support the sources and complete the questions.

● **Beyond Level** Ask students to identify information they will be able to use in their essays. Discuss why this information is relevant.

● **ELL** For support reading the sources, see the **ELL Small Group Guide**.

10 mins Analyze the Sources

Find Text Evidence

As students read the source passages, ask them to note key ideas and details, interesting or unfamiliar words, and any questions they may have in their writer's notebooks. Use the questions below. Remind students to cite text evidence.

SOURCE 1 **"Going Above and Beyond"**

Paragraphs 1–2 Have students read the highlighted academic language. Ask: *What did Bryan Duffy see from space?* (He saw the Amazon rain forest being cleared and burned.) *Why is this fact important?* (It shows that Duffy could see the damage all the way from space.)

Paragraphs 3–4 *What caused the decline of many shark populations around the world?* (overfishing) *What did Snyderman decide to do about the decline?* (take and share photographs of sharks to tell people about the problem) Have students tell how Duffy's and Snyderman's perspectives are similar and write their responses on page 217.

Analytical Writing **Take Notes** Have students reread paragraphs 2 and 3. Ask them to use information from these paragraphs to paraphrase the central idea and relevant details of the source.

SOURCE 2 **"The Turtle Lady of Juno Beach"**

Paragraph 5 *Why is honey put in turtles' wounds?* (It bonds well with water and helps the turtles heal.) *What does the Loggerhead Marinelife Center do when its turtles are healthy again?* (It releases them back to the sea.)

Reading/Writing Companion, pp. 218–219

WRITING

FIND TEXT EVIDENCE 🔍

Paragraph 5
Draw a box around the detail that tells what unusual ointment the Loggerhead Marinelife Center gives to wounded turtles.

Paragraph 6
Reread this paragraph. Examples of academic language are highlighted. What do these words tell you about the focus of this passage?
These words tell me that the topic is about research and education.

Paragraph 7
Circle the signal words or phrase that links the ideas in paragraphs 6 and 7.

Paragraph 8
Underline the details that tell how the center protects the environment.

✏️ **Take Notes** Paraphrase the central idea of the source, and give examples of supporting details.

218 Unit 2 • Expository Writing

SOURCE 2

THE TURTLE LADY OF Juno Beach

5 When people think of honey, they usually think of a sweet snack, but for a facility in Florida that treats wounded sea turtles, honey is used as a medicine! The Loggerhead Marinelife Center rescues and rehabilitates sea turtles. When the turtles are healthy, they are released back to the sea. Sometimes they leave with honey in their wounds, which bonds well with water and helps them heal.

6 The center was **founded** by "the Turtle Lady" Eleanor Fletcher. Fletcher and her husband worked in real estate in Juno Beach. Sea turtles nested on the shore below their office. Fletcher saw hatchlings move toward land instead of toward the sea. She **researched** and learned that the turtles were walking toward land because of the bright lights that people had built along the beaches. The lights confused the hatchlings, so Fletcher put a stop to them. Then she started **educating** children and adults about turtle conservation and protection.

7 At first she did a lot of the work herself. She opened her home to visitors, giving tours and showing marine specimens. She taught herself how to categorize and count turtle nests. She even confronted poachers and chased them away.

8 Eventually, she founded the Loggerhead Marinelife Center. The center welcomes school field trips, outreach programs, and summer camps. Over 300,000 guests come each year to view the exhibits and visit the turtle hospital. The facility has an outdoor classroom, research labs, a resource center, a park, and a store. The exhibits and programs highlight South Florida's wildlife and marine environments.

SOURCE 3

COMMUNITY BIRD SCIENTIST

9 In 1896, Harriet Hemenway and Minna Hall founded the Massachusetts Audubon Society to help protect waterbirds from future harm. Their efforts helped shape the national Audubon Society, which continues to protect birds and their habitats.

10 One of the society's programs is the Great Backyard Bird Count (GBBC). The GBBC is a global event over a weekend in February. It is run by the society and the Cornell Lab of Ornithology. First participants register on the GBBC website. These "community scientists" are then asked to go bird-watching in their backyards for fifteen minutes or more during that weekend. Bird-watchers use field guides and bird-watching apps to identify each bird species they've seen. People all over the world complete checklists. They record their local bird sightings on the GBBC eBird database. Ornithologists still use this data to help with bird conservation.

Top 5 State Bird Count Listings

State	Number of Species	Number of Checklists
California	373	8,530
Texas	361	6,785
New York	171	6,520
Pennsylvania	145	5,953
Florida	290	5,612

Data totals as of March 14, 2018.

Unit 2 • Expository Writing 219

EXPOSITORY ESSAY

FIND TEXT EVIDENCE 🔍

Paragraph 9
Underline the detail that tells why Hemenway and Hall founded the Audubon Society.

Paragraph 10
Circle the signal words that list the steps in the order in which participants complete checklists.

Top 5 State Bird Count Listings
What do you notice about the number of species and the number of checklists when you compare the findings across these five states?
The number of checklists increases from bottom to top. The number of species is greater in California, Texas, and Florida than in New York and Pennsylvania.

✏️ **Take Notes** Paraphrase the central idea of the source, and give examples of supporting details.

Paragraph 6 Point out the highlighted academic language. Ask: *Why were turtle hatchlings moving toward land instead of toward water?* (They were confused by the bright lights people had built along the beaches.) *What did Eleanor Fletcher do to help the young turtles?* (She put a stop to the bright lights.) *How does the academic language support the focus of the source?* (It tells readers that the focus is about the turtle lady's research and education.)

Paragraphs 7–8 *What signal word or phrase links ideas in paragraph 7?* ("At first") *What did Fletcher and the center do to protect young turtles?* (She confronted poachers and chased them away. The center educates visitors and has a hospital for turtles.)

 Analytical Writing **Take Notes** Have students paraphrase why Fletcher wanted to protect animals like young turtles.

SOURCE 3 ## "Community Bird Scientist"

Paragraphs 9–10 *Why did Harriet Hemenway and Minna Hall found the Massachusetts Audubon Society?* (to protect birds from being harmed) *What is the Great Backyard Bird Count?* (a program that asks people to go bird-watching and turn in their notes) Have students underline examples of academic language and circle signal words that tell the order in which participants complete checklists.

Top 5 State Bird Count Listings Have students compare the number of checklists and number of species across the five states. *Which state has the most checklists?* (California)

 Analytical Writing **Take Notes** Have students paraphrase how the Great Backyard Bird Count can help protect birds.

MULTIMODAL LEARNING

As students read and reread the sources, ask them to draw simple pictures related to the sources. After all three sources have been read, have students share their completed pictures with a partner and explain how each one relates to a source.

FORMATIVE ASSESSMENT

➤ **STUDENT CHECK-IN**

Have partners share their responses. Then ask them to reflect using the Check-In routine.

LEARNING GOALS

We can synthesize information from three sources to plan and organize an expository essay.

OBJECTIVES

Write informative/explanatory texts to examine a topic and convey ideas and information clearly.

Introduce a topic or text clearly, state an opinion, and create an organizational structure in which ideas are logically grouped to support the writer's purpose.

Recall relevant information from experiences or gather relevant information from print and digital sources; summarize or paraphrase information in notes and finished work, and provide a list of sources.

Organize notes from sources to plan an expository essay.

ELA ACADEMIC LANGUAGE

• *response, organize, review, record*
• Cognates: *respuesta, organizar, revista*

DIGITAL TOOLS

 Model Graphic Organizer

 Paraphrase the Idea

Plan: Organize Ideas

10 mins

Take Notes

Remind students that they will write an expository essay about the ways humans protect the environment. They will synthesize information from the three sources to develop their response to the prompt.

Say: *When you write your expository essay, stay focused on your topic and include relevant details and examples from the sources to support your ideas. Think about how the details and examples in the sources will help your readers understand how people protect the environment.*

Graphic Organizer

Tell students that before writing their expository essay, they will organize the notes they took from each source in the graphic organizer on **Reading/Writing Companion** pages 220–221. Some of the graphic organizer has already been filled in. Help students understand how to complete the graphic organizer.

Central Idea Remind students that the central idea is the main idea of their essay. One central idea is that people protect the environment through conservation and awareness. Point out that students can develop a different central idea or come up with other ideas to support the provided central idea.

Supporting Ideas Students should include supporting ideas, or details, for the central idea in their essay. Remind students that they will find supporting details based on information from the sources. Each paragraph in their essay will have a supporting detail.

Relevant Evidence Remind students that they should support each detail with evidence from the sources. They don't have to use evidence from all three sources for every detail, but they should use evidence from at least one source for each detail. Remind students that each time they use evidence from a source, they should name the source.

 Have students complete the graphic organizer.

 Synthesize Information

Remind students that one way writers can synthesize information is by using information from different sources to create a logical progression of ideas. For example, a writer could say how people protect the environment in both big and small ways. Have partners share their graphic organizers and discuss how evidence from the sources shows how people protect the environment in different ways.

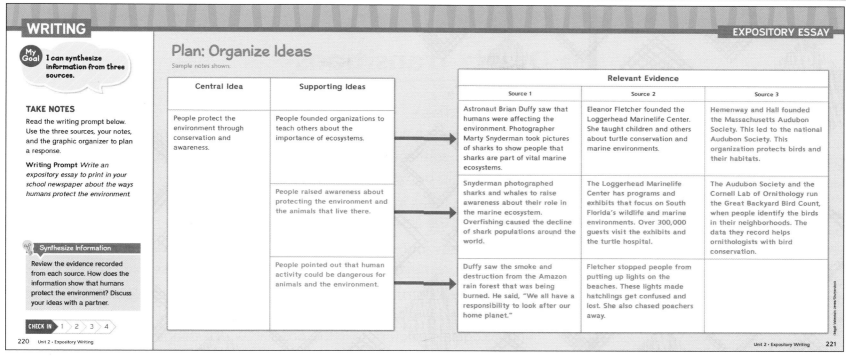

Reading/Writing Companion, pp. 220–221

ELL English Language Learners

Use the following scaffolds with **Graphic Organizer**. For additional support, see the **ELL Small Group Guide**.

Beginning

Explain to students how the graphic organizer is set up. Each row in the Relevant Evidence section supplies evidence from the sources for a supporting idea. The supporting ideas all focus on the central idea. Help students fill in the information. For example, help them look at notes to find evidence from Source 3 to complete the first row. They can write: Harriet Hemenway and Minna Hall founded the Massachusetts Audubon Society to help protect and save birds.

Intermediate

Discuss with students how the graphic organizer is arranged with sections for the central idea, supporting ideas, and relevant evidence they need to include for their draft. Have students fill in the top row for Source 3. Then have students use their notes and find information to fill in a second supporting idea. Have partners use the following: People can help animals by protecting their habitats. Then have them find supporting evidence from the sources and fill it in the second row.

Advanced/Advanced High

Provide help as students fill in the graphic organizer. Have them use information from their notes to complete the first row and fill in a second supporting idea with relevant evidence in the second row.

FORMATIVE ASSESSMENT

⊙ **STUDENT CHECK-IN**

Have partners share their graphic organizer on Reading/Writing Companion pages 220-221. Ask them to use the Check-In routine to reflect and fill in the bars.

EXTENDED
WRITING
2

LEARNING GOALS

We can use our graphic organizers to write a draft.

OBJECTIVES

Link ideas within and across categories of information using words, phrases, and clauses.

Use precise language and domain-specific vocabulary to inform about or explain the topic.

With guidance and support from peers and adults, develop and strengthen writing as needed by planning, revising, and editing.

With some guidance and support from adults, use technology, including the Internet, to produce and publish writing as well as to interact and collaborate with others; demonstrate sufficient command of keyboarding skills to type a minimum of two pages in a single sitting.

Demonstrate fluent and legible cursive writing skills.

ELA ACADEMIC LANGUAGE

- *linking words, structure, connect*
- Cognates: *estructura, conectar*

▶ DIFFERENTIATED WRITING

● **Approaching Level** Review students' drafts for transitions and linking words.

● **On Level** Partners can review drafts for transitions and linking words.

● **Beyond Level** Partners can make suggestions about adding or improving transitions and linking words.

● **English Language Learners** For support on writing a draft, see **ELL Small Group Guide**.

DIGITAL TOOLS

Student Model Draft

Outline to Draft

⏱ 10 mins

Draft: Transitions

Connect Ideas

Tell students that linking words and phrases are transitional strategies that writers use to connect their ideas. Linking words and transitions also signal the relationship between ideas. Share with students the information below.

- Connecting ideas in a logical way makes it easier for readers to understand the information in an essay.

- Linking words and phrases, such as *especially, however, in contrast, when, finally, before starting,* and *for this reason,* can be used to connect ideas.

- Organizational structures can also be used to connect ideas. A cause-and-effect structure tells why something happens and the effect it has. A chronological structure tells the order in which things happen.

Read the sentences on **Reading/Writing Companion** page 222, focusing on the last sentence: *Because toxic chemicals from the mill had flowed into the river by accident, we didn't want to risk catching any contaminants.* Ask: *What linking word or phrase do you see in this sentence?* (Because) Ask: *What ideas does it connect?* (It connects what happened to the toxic chemicals and the reason why the people wore gloves.) *What type of text structure does the linking word* because *signal?* (a cause-and-effect text structure) Explain that the sentence tells the effect of toxic chemicals entering the river.

Have partners work together to combine the first two sentences **COLLABORATE** into one sentence that uses linking words to connect the two ideas. (Sample response: When we collected water samples from the river, we wore gloves). Have them write their responses on page 222.

Draft

Have students write an expository essay about how humans protect the environment. Before students begin drafting, have them review the rubric on page 212, the information they recorded in their graphic organizer, and the notes they took in their writer's notebook.

Remind students to choose and include academic language that conveys ideas clearly and precisely. Also, remind students that their essay should include transitions that connect ideas and indicate a logical order.

Make sure students write their drafts legibly in print or cursive, or type accurately on-screen in their online writer's notebook. Circulate to assist and check their progress. Remind them to indent each paragraph.

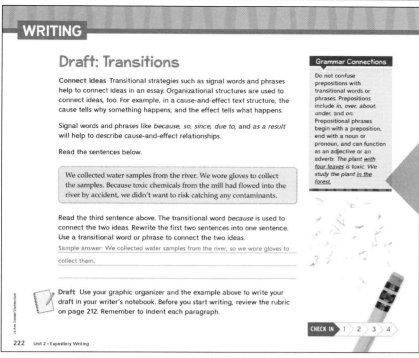

Reading/Writing Companion, p. 222

ELL English Language Learners

Use the following scaffolds with **Connect Ideas**.

Beginning

Review with students that it is good for writers to use linking words and phrases to connect their ideas. Explain that it makes it easier to understand the writing. Review common linking words and phrases such as *however, also, for example, next, if, or, at first,* and *when.* Then read the first two sentences in the text box on page 222 with students. Help partners use the word *when* to combine these sentences: <u>When</u> we collected water samples from the river, we wore gloves.

Intermediate

Review with students that using linking words and phrases to connect their ideas is a good idea. It makes their writing easier to understand. Review common linking words such as *yet, also, for example, next, when, or,* and *second.* Read the first two sentences in the text box on page 222 with students. Then have students combine the sentences using the word *when.* (When we collected water samples from the river, we wore gloves.)

Advanced/Advanced High

Have students reread the first two sentences in the text box on page 222. Then have partners work together to use *when* to combine the sentences in two different ways. (When we collected water samples from the river, we wore gloves. We wore gloves when we collected water samples from the river.)

TEACHER CONFERENCES

As students draft, hold teacher conferences with individual students.

Step 1: Talk About Strengths
Point out strengths in the essay: *The academic language you used helps the readers of the school newspaper understand the focus of your essay.*

Step 2: Focus on Skills
Give feedback on how the student includes relevant evidence: *In this paragraph, you could provide stronger evidence for your supporting detail. Include an example of how humans protect the environment.*

Step 3: Make Concrete Suggestions
Provide specific direction to help students: *Your word choice could be more precise. Instead of saying "this is a good thing," you could say "this is an exciting solution."* Have students draft and then meet with you to review progress.

FORMATIVE ASSESSMENT

❯ STUDENT CHECK-IN

Have partners share their draft. Then have them use the Check-In routine to reflect and fill in the bars on Reading/Writing page 222.

LEARNING GOALS

We can revise our writing to make it stronger.

OBJECTIVES

Provide a concluding statement or section related to the information or explanation presented.

Engage effectively in a range of collaborative discussions (one-on-one, in groups, and teacher-led) with diverse partners on grade-level topics and texts, building on others' ideas and expressing their own clearly.

Follow agreed-upon rules for discussions and carry out assigned roles.

Review the key ideas expressed and draw conclusions in light of information and knowledge gained from the discussions.

Adapt speech to a variety of contexts and tasks, using formal English when appropriate to task and situation.

ELA ACADEMIC LANGUAGE

• *review, draft, evidence, revise*
• Cognates: *revista, evidencia, revisar*

▶ DIFFERENTIATED WRITING

Check student progress at this stage during Small Group time.

● **Approaching Level** Review students' drafts for academic language and a focused controlling idea.

● **On Level** Partners can focus on academic language and a focused central idea.

● **Beyond Level** Students should suggest alternative words to improve language and focus.

● **ELL** For support to help students revise their drafts, see the **ELL Small Group Guide**.

⏱ 10 mins Revise: Peer Conferences

Review a Draft

Remind students that well-written expository essays follow the criteria of the rubric. Remind them to think about the following from Purpose, Focus, and Organization and Evidence and Elaboration:

• A clearly stated and strongly maintained central idea
• A variety of transitional strategies to clarify the relationships between and among ideas
• A logical progression of ideas from beginning to end, and a satisfying conclusion
• Relevant evidence with references to sources
• Precise, academic, and domain-specific language appropriate for the audience and purpose

Review with students the routine for peer review of writing.

• Step 1: Listen carefully as the writer reads his or her work aloud.
• Step 2: Avoid calling attention away from the writer.
• Step 3: Ask a question that will help you understand anything that is unclear.
• Step 4: Take note of things you liked about the writing.

Model using the sentence starters on **Reading/Writing Companion** page 223. Say: *I like the evidence you used to support the central idea because . . .* and finish the sentence. Discuss the steps of the peer conferencing routine. Ask: *Why is it important to listen carefully as your partner reads his or her work?* (to show respect for the writer and their work, and so you will be able to offer helpful feedback)

COLLABORATE Circulate and observe as partners review and give feedback on each other's drafts. Remind students to think about being focused on the central idea, good transitions between and among ideas, and using precise word choice. Have them reflect on partner feedback and write on page 223 about the most helpful suggestion.

Revision

Review the Revising Checklist on page 223 and the features of the rubric on pages 240–243. Explain that this is a rubric with scores that add up to a maximum of 10. Point out the score in the left column and the three categories in the right column. After students complete their final drafts, have them score themselves using the My Score boxes on page 223.

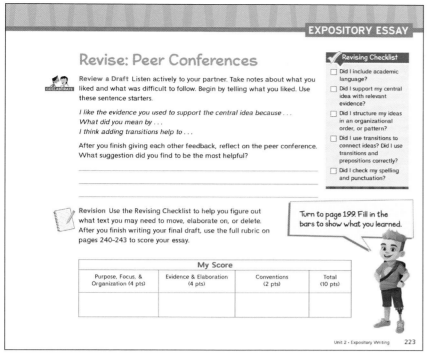

Reading/Writing Companion, p. 223

ELL English Language Learners

Use the following scaffolds with **Review a Draft**.

Beginning

Pair students with more proficient readers. Have partners ask for clarification using the following: *What is the central idea? Can you reread ___? What did you mean by ___?* Provide feedback using the following: *I liked the way you ___.* Students may need to see the draft as well as hear it. Have students complete the Partner Feedback on page 223. Then help them check their draft for the first two items on the Revising Checklist. If necessary, help them revise to strengthen or clarify their central idea or include additional relevant evidence.

Intermediate

Pair students with more proficient speakers. Have partners ask for clarification using the following: *Can you explain ___? What do you mean when you say ___?* Provide feedback using: *I thought you did a great job with ___.* Have students complete the Partner Feedback on page 223. Have students use the last three items on the Revising Checklist to identify revisions they want to make. Have them check to see that their evidence is relevant to the topic and supports their central idea. Check their revisions and provide feedback as needed.

Advanced/Advanced High

Have partners provide feedback using the sentence starters on page 223 and read each other's responses to check that their partner understood them correctly. Have students review the Revising Checklist with their partner to be sure they have addressed these elements in their essay.

TEACHER CONFERENCES

As students revise, hold teacher conferences with individual students.

Step 1: Talk About Strengths

Point out strengths in the essay: *The evidence you paraphrased from your sources is relevant and fully supports your central idea.*

Step 2: Focus on Skills

Give feedback on how the student uses linking words: *Add a stronger linking word or phrase between these two paragraphs to show the connection between the ideas.*

Step 3: Make Concrete Suggestions

Provide specific direction to help students revise: *Use academic language to make your writing more formal. Instead of saying "He talked to someone about the problem," you could say "He consulted with an environmental expert to resolve the issue."* Have students revise and then meet with you to review progress.

DIGITAL TOOLS

 Revised Student Model

Revise Checklist (Expository); Peer Conferencing Checklist (Expository); Peer Conferencing (Collaborative Conversations Video)

MY GOALS ROUTINE

What I Learned

Read Have students turn back to page 199 of the Reading/Writing Companion.

Reflect Have students think about the progress they've made toward the goals. Review the key, if needed. Then have students fill in the bars.

LEARNING GOALS

We can build skills to improve our writing.

OBJECTIVES

Develop the topic with facts, definitions, concrete details, quotations, or other information and examples related to the topic.

With some guidance and support from adults, use technology, including the Internet, to produce and publish writing as well as to interact and collaborate with others; demonstrate sufficient command of keyboarding skills to type a minimum of two pages in a single sitting.

Conduct short research projects that use several sources to build knowledge through investigation of different aspects of a topic.

Report on a topic, sequencing ideas logically and using appropriate facts and relevant, descriptive details to support main ideas or themes; speak clearly at an understandable pace.

▶ FLEXIBLE MINILESSONS

Use these minilessons flexibly, in any order, based on the needs of your students. The minilessons can be used separately or in tandem with the Expository Write to Sources lessons on pages T230–T265.

Use students' Check-In reflections and your observations to decide which students are ready to independently apply the lesson focus to their own writing. Use the tips in the Conferring Toolkit to provide additional guidance as you confer with students or meet with them in small groups.

FORMATIVE ASSESSMENT

▶ STUDENT CHECK-IN

After the Guide activity, have students reflect on their understanding of the lesson focus. Have them reflect using the Check-In routine.

Expository Essay

 Establish Your Purpose

When writing an essay, writers must think about their purpose, or reason for writing. Thinking about the purpose and intended audience helps writers determine whether they are writing to persuade, entertain, or inform.

Model Tell students that if you wanted to write an essay about the health benefits of exercise, you would have to first determine whether your purpose is to inform people of the facts or to persuade people that exercising is healthy by giving your opinion. Consider the following questions: *What do I want to tell my readers? Am I giving them my opinion or sharing information on a topic?*

Guide Have partners work together to write a paragraph that persuades people to exercise.

Apply Have students rewrite the paragraph to inform people about the health benefits of exercise. Then have partners compare the two paragraphs and their different purposes.

10 mins Evaluate Sources

During research, writers must determine whether the sources they are using are credible.

Model Tell students that it is important to ensure all sources are up-to-date, accurate, and relevant. Model searching for online sources about satellites. Scroll through the list of sites. Point out the publication dates and headlines shown. Ask: *Which sources are most likely to be reliable and why?* (the .edu and .gov ones; they come from education or government sites) Click on a noncredible website and point out information that is missing, false, outdated, or biased.

Guide Choose a credible website and have partners evaluate the source by identifying the author, publication information, purpose, and accuracy of the website.

Apply Have students revisit their expository essay drafts to evaluate information from their sources. Have them revise their drafts so that they are including only sources that are reliable, relevant, and appropriate.

Conferring Toolkit

Establish Your Purpose Students may need support establishing their purpose and identifying their intended readers. Have them make a list of questions to help establish their purpose and identify their audience.

Evaluate Sources Point out a section in the student's writing that could be strengthened with more facts or evidence from reliable and valid sources. Say: *Find a reliable source here to back up your information.*

Avoid Plagiarism

When taking notes, students should write relevant information and important details in their own words or as direct quotations. They must also cite source information.

Model Read aloud information about a topic of your choice from a textbook or credible website. Write the topic as a heading. Next write the title of the source and its author. Then model writing the information in your own words using short phrases instead of full sentences. Ask students to discuss how you avoided plagiarism. (wrote in your own words; didn't copy from source; noted source information)

Guide Have partners take notes from a short passage from a textbook or credible website. Remind them to write the information in their own words to avoid plagiarism.

Apply Have students reread their notes for their expository essays to see where they need to rewrite the information in their own words or cite direct quotations to avoid plagiarism. Ask students to share examples of the changes they made.

 Add Examples or Definitions

Elaboration means to explain or provide additional information about a topic. Elaborative techniques include using examples or definitions to help support and expand your ideas.

Model Write the following statement on the board: *When skateboarding, I wear safety gear*. Point out how this statement could be improved by elaborating. Then write, *When skateboarding, I wear safety gear, such as wrist guards, knee pads, and a helmet*. Have students discuss the difference between the two statements and how using examples elaborated and strengthened the sentence.

Guide Have partners rewrite the following sentence using an example or definition to elaborate. *Some animals make great pets*. (Cats, dogs, and hamsters make great pets because they are easy to care for.)

Apply Have students look for places in their draft where they can elaborate using examples or definitions. Ask students to share examples of the changes they made.

 Use a Powerful Quotation

Authors choose powerful quotations to support or provide additional information about a topic. These quotations should be profound and important, not information that is common knowledge.

Model Text Read aloud the first paragraph of the online Student Model Source 1, "Abigail Adams, Early Supporter of Equal Rights." Model identifying the last sentence as a powerful quotation and show students how to introduce and format it in a sentence. Ask students whether the first sentence in the next paragraph would be a powerful quotation and why or why not. (No, because it's common knowledge.)

Guide Have partners identify another quotation from the Student Model Source and write an expository paragraph that includes it.

Apply Have students remove weak quotations and add powerful ones to their expository essay drafts. Be sure they cite their sources.

Avoid Plagiarism

Point out sentences or paragraphs that may be worded too closely to the original source. Ask: *In which source did you find this information? How can we say this in your own words?*

 Add Examples or Definitions

Discuss the difference between adding definitions and examples to elaborate. Suggest places where students can add examples or definitions. In paragraph__, I added an example/definition because __.

Use a Powerful Quotation

Guide students in identifying strong quotations in their sources. Ask: *Would someone's birthdate or words they said be an example of a strong quotation? Why?*

LEARNING GOALS

We can build skills to improve our writing.

OBJECTIVES

Introduce a topic clearly, provide a general observation and focus, and group related information logically; include formatting (e.g., headings), illustrations, and multimedia when useful to aiding comprehension.

With some guidance and support from adults, use technology, including the Internet, to produce and publish writing as well as to interact and collaborate with others; demonstrate sufficient command of keyboarding skills to type a minimum of two pages in a single sitting.

Explain the function of conjunctions, prepositions, and interjections in general and their function in particular sentences.

▶ FLEXIBLE MINILESSONS

Use these minilessons flexibly, in any order, based on the needs of your students. The minilessons can be used separately or in tandem with the Expository Write to Sources lessons on pages T230–T265.

Use students' Check-In reflections and your observations to decide which students are ready to independently apply the lesson focus to their own writing. Use the tips in the Conferring Toolkit to provide additional guidance as you confer with students or meet with them in small groups.

FORMATIVE ASSESSMENT

● STUDENT CHECK-IN

After each lesson, have students reflect on their ability to apply the lesson focus in their writing. Have them use the Check-In routine.

Expository Essay

Organize Information (10 mins)

When organizing information by problem and solution, the writer presents a problem and then provides the solution. When organizing information by cause and effect, the writer tells why and how something happens.

Model Text Read aloud the first two paragraphs of online Student Model Source 2, "America's First Woman Soldier." Point out how the writer introduces the problem that Deborah Sampson faces and how this helps to inform the structure of the rest of the essay.

Guide Have partners read the rest of "America's First Woman Soldier" and discuss how the problem-and-solution text structure supports the author's purpose.

Apply Have students reread their expository essays and identify where they can revise a paragraph using a problem-and-solution or cause-and-effect text structure.

Use Prepositions and Prepositional Phrases (5 mins)

Tell students that prepositions include words such as *in, over, on,* and *about.* Prepositional phrases are groups of words that begin with a preposition and end with a noun or pronoun.

Model Text Read aloud the first paragraph of online Student Model Source 1, "Interview with an Experimental Physicist." Point out the prepositional phrases and discuss how they are used to show direction, time, place, location, and relationships between objects.

Guide Have partners create a T-chart: Prepositions and Nouns. Ask students to list six prepositions and nouns in the correct columns. Then have them write sentences that contain prepositional phrases using the prepositions and nouns from the columns.

Apply Have students revise their expository essays to ensure they are using prepositions and prepositional phrases correctly.

Conferring Toolkit

Organize Information

Students may need support in identifying a paragraph to revise. Have them think about their research. Ask: *Did any of the people you researched face a challenge or solve a problem? How can you organize this information?*

Use Prepositions

Point out a section in the student's writing that could be improved by using prepositional phrases to show direction, time, place, location, or relationships between things. Ask: *When and where did this event occur?*

Combine Sentences (5 mins)

Writers often combine short, simple sentences to form longer, compound and complex sentences. When combining sentences, they use a comma and a conjunction, such as *and, but, yet,* or *so.*

Model Write these sentences: *Crocodiles are reptiles. They live on land and in water. They have webbed feet. Their feet help them navigate through the water. They have scales. Their scales help protect them.* Model how the sentences can be combined into compound and complex sentences. (Crocodiles are reptiles that live on land and in water. Their webbed feet help them navigate through the water, and their scales protect them against predators.)

Guide Have partners work together to find other ways to combine the sentences in the model you provided.

Apply Have students revise their expository essays to combine sentences. Ask them to share examples of the changes they made.

 Establish Voice and Tone (10 mins)

Voice and tone are created through the writer's use of language. Explain that writers use an appropriate tone based on their audience and purpose. The tone of an essay might be sad, cheerful, excited, or serious.

Model Text Read aloud the first and second paragraphs of online Student Model Source 2, "The Goal of Peace." Discuss how the author's use of language, or word choice, helps create a specific tone and voice. (The text is about an athlete who overcame obstacles to achieve her goals and help others. The author uses terms, such as *strive, impossible, astounded,* and *benefit,* to create a serious and respectful tone.)

Guide Have partners read the rest of "The Goal of Peace" and discuss how word choice helps the author set the tone of the text.

Apply Have partners exchange essays and discuss the word choice. Then have students revise their essays to have a formal tone.

 Use Digital Tools (10 mins)

Spell checkers and online dictionaries can be useful tools when revising and editing essays on a computer.

Model Type the following sentence on a computer for students to see: *Located in Coconut Groove, Florida, The Campong is a botanicle garden with exotik plants from around the word.* Model how to proofread the sentence using a spell check feature or online dictionary. Show students how to use a reliable website to check the spellings of unfamiliar places.

Guide Have partners correct this sentence: *Each year, milions off people visit the Kenedy Space Center, located on Merrit Island.* (Each year, millions of people visit the Kennedy Space Center, located on Merritt Island.)

Apply Have students use a spell checker and online dictionary to proofread and revise their drafts. Encourage them to check their original sources for the correct spellings of people and places.

ELL Combine Sentences

Review how students can use the conjunctions to combine sentences. Suggest places where students can combine sentences. Provide the following sentence frames to discuss: In paragraph __, I used the conjunctions __ to combine sentences.

Establish Voice and Tone

Students may have trouble understanding how their word choice creates a specific tone. Guide them in identifying words that give their expository essays an informal tone. Ask: *What's a more formal way of saying that someone is "awesome"?*

Use Digital Tools

Remind students that while there are many digital resources, they will still need to read through their work carefully for errors. Point out how online spelling checkers and dictionaries cannot tell them if they used homophones correctly, for example.

LEARNING GOALS

We can identify and use different kinds of nouns.

OBJECTIVES

Demonstrate command of the conventions of standard English grammar and usage when writing or speaking.

Explain the function of nouns, pronouns, verbs, adjectives and adverbs in general and their functions in particular sentences.

Use abstract nouns.

Capitalize proper nouns correctly.

Proofread sentences.

DAILY LANGUAGE ACTIVITY

Use the online review for grammar, practice, and usage.

 TEACH IN SMALL GROUP

You may wish to use the Talk About It activities during Small Group time.

⬤⬤⬤ **Approaching Level, On Level,** and **Beyond Level** Pair students of different proficiency levels.

⬤ **ELL** According to their language proficiency, students should contribute to discussions by using short phrases, asking questions, and adding relevant details.

FORMATIVE ASSESSMENT

❯ **STUDENT CHECK-IN**

After completing each Practice Book page, have partners share. Ask them to reflect using the Check-In routine.

Kinds of Nouns

 Teach

Introduce Common, Proper, Collective Nouns

- A **common noun** names any person, place, thing, or event.

- A **proper noun** names a specific person, place, or thing and begins with a capital letter: *Thursday, August, Memorial Day.*

- A **collective noun** names a group of individuals: *family, public, class.* When a collective noun refers to an entire group, use the singular form of a verb after it. *Our club meets on Thursdays.* When a collective noun refers to individual members of a group, use the plural form of a verb. *The jury discuss the evidence.*

See **Practice Book** page 61 or online activity.

 Teach

Review Common, Proper, Collective Nouns

Ask students to explain the difference between common, proper, and collective nouns.

Introduce Concrete and Abstract Nouns

- A **concrete noun** names a person, place, or thing. It is something you can sense: *sunset, music, aroma, peach, fabric.*

- An **abstract noun** is an idea or concept. You cannot see, hear, smell, taste, or feel it: *love, courage, idea, trust, happiness.*

See **Practice Book** page 62.

 **Talk About It**

The Name Game

Have small groups sit in a circle. Give each group a general topic (e.g., *nature, hobbies, music*). Have each student in the group name a common noun, a proper noun, and a collective noun related to the topic. Go around several times.

Noun Pairs 1

Have partners come up with pairs of common and proper nouns, such as *girl/Marie, school/Park Elementary, city/Boston.* Have partners trade words and form sentences with each pair. For example: *Boston is a large city.*

3 Mechanics and Usage

Capitalizing Proper Nouns

- A proper noun always begins with a capital letter.

- When proper nouns contain more than one word, capitalize each important word: *The Wizard of Oz, Big Bend National Park.*

- Capitalize the names of days, months, historical events, places, organizations, nationalities: *Friday, Memorial Day, Battle of Gettysburg, World Health Organization.*

- Capitalize abbreviations of days and months, too: *Fri., Jan.*

- Capitalize the letters in initials and acronyms: *A.M., John F. Kennedy, NASA, NBA.*

See **Practice Book** page 63 or online activity.

 OPTION **4** Proofread and Write

Proofread

Have students identify and correct errors in the story:

Uncle mike and aunt mary are taking my friend, t.j., and me to a movie at the grand theater. The movie is about the lewis and clark expedishon. There team of pioneers inspire me. (1: Mike; 2: Aunt Mary; 3: T.J.; 4: Grand Theater; 5: Lewis and Clark Expedition; 6: Their; 7: inspires)

Write

Have students find a piece of their own writing in their writer's notebook and correct capitalization errors. For additional practice, have students write a paragraph about an organization. Then have them check their work to make sure that any organizations, abbreviations, initials, and acronyms they included use proper punctuation and capitalization.

See **Practice Book** page 64.

 OPTION **5** Assess and Reteach

Assess

Use the Daily Language Activity and **Practice Book** page 65 for assessment.

Rubric Use your online rubric to record student progress.

Reteach

Use the online **Grammar Handbook** page 455 and **Practice Book** pages 61–64 for additional reteaching. Remind students to use nouns correctly as they speak and write.

Check students' writing for use of the skill and listen for it in their speaking. Assign grammar revision assignments in their writer's notebooks as needed.

Noun Pairs 2

Have groups list pairs of related concrete and abstract nouns, such as *school/education, heart/love, painting/beauty.* Have groups trade words and form sentences with each pair. Supply a list of abstract words to help students if needed.

Twenty Questions

Have partners play Twenty Questions. Partner A thinks of a noun. Partner B asks up to 20 questions to guess what the noun is. Encourage students to ask whether the noun is common, proper, collective, abstract, or concrete.

Word Association

Give small groups an abstract noun as a topic word (e.g., *wisdom, joy, hope*). Have each group list other nouns they think of when they hear the topic word. Have them identify each noun as common, proper, collective, concrete, or abstract.

Singular and Plural Nouns

LEARNING GOALS

We can identify and use singular and plural nouns.

OBJECTIVES

Demonstrate command of the conventions of standard English grammar and usage when writing or speaking.

Form and use regular and irregular plural nouns.

Distinguish between singular and plural nouns.

Proofread sentences.

DAILY LANGUAGE ACTIVITY

Use the online review for grammar, practice, and usage.

▶ TEACH IN SMALL GROUP

You may wish to use the Talk About It activities during Small Group time.

●●● **Approaching Level, On Level,** and **Beyond Level** Pair students of different proficiency levels.

● **ELL** According to their language proficiency, students should contribute to discussions by using short phrases, asking questions, and adding relevant details.

FORMATIVE ASSESSMENT

▶ STUDENT CHECK-IN

After completing each Practice Book page, have partners share. Ask them to reflect using the Check-In routine.

 6 Teach

Introduce Singular and Plural Nouns

Present the following:

- A **singular noun** names one person, place, idea, or thing.
- A **plural noun** names more than one person, place, idea, or thing.
- Most plural nouns are formed by adding -s or -es.
- A singular or plural noun can function in a sentence as a subject, a direct object of an action verb, or an object of a preposition. *The <u>band</u> performed <u>concerts</u> in twelve <u>cities</u>.*

See **Practice Book** page 73 or online activity.

 7 Teach

Review Singular and Plural Nouns

Nouns and plural nouns can be subjects, direct objects, or objects of prepositions.

Irregular Plural Nouns

- Add -es to form the plural of singular nouns that end in s, sh, ch, or x: *grass, grasses; dish, dishes; branch, branches; box, boxes.*
- For nouns ending in a consonant and the letter y, change the y to i and add -es: *sky, skies.*
- For nouns ending in a vowel and y, add -s: *key, keys; birthday, birthdays.*

See **Practice Book** page 74.

 OPTION **Talk About It** MULTIMODAL

Use Plural Nouns

Ask partners to use plural nouns to talk about characters from fairy tales, stories, or favorite films (e.g., three wishes, seven dwarves, magic seeds, talking animals). As they talk, students should listen to be sure they use plural nouns.

Pick the Plural

On index cards, write one singular noun and two plural forms of the same noun, one correct and one incorrect. Have partners identify the correct plural. Have each student write a sentence using the correct plural noun.

LESSON 8 Mechanics and Usage

Forming Plural Nouns

- Add -*s* to form the plural of most nouns. Add -*es* to form the plural of singular nouns that end in *s, sh, ch,* or *x*.
- To form the plural of nouns ending in a consonant and the letter *y*, change the *y* to *i* and add -*es*.
- To form the plural of nouns ending in a vowel and *y*, add -*s*.

See **Practice Book** page 75 or online activity.

 OPTION LESSON 9 Proofread and Write

Proofread

Have students correct errors in the story:

Four baseballes landed in the bushs. My brother's pitchs were high and wide. He needs lessones, I thought, as I crawled through the branchs to retrieve his tossies. Maybe he needs some new hobbys. (1: baseballs; 2: bushes; 3: pitches; 4: lessons; 5: branches; 6: tosses; 7: hobbies)

Write

Have students find a piece of their own writing in their writer's notebook and correct plural noun errors.

See **Practice Book** page 76.

 OPTION LESSON 10 Assess and Reteach

Assess

Use the Daily Language Activity and **Practice Book** page 77 for assessment.

Rubric Use your online rubric to record student progress.

Reteach

Use the online **Grammar Handbook** page 456 and **Practice Book** pages 73–76 for reteaching. Remind students that it is important to use singular and plural nouns correctly as they speak and write.

Check students' writing for use of the skill and listen for it in their speaking. Assign grammar revision assignments in their writer's notebooks as needed.

Replace the Nouns

Ask each student to write two sentences using plural nouns. Have partners read their sentences aloud. The listening partner repeats the sentence, replacing any plural noun with other plural nouns that make sense in the context.

Spelling Challenge

Display a list of singular nouns that form the plural in different ways (e.g., *country, box, wish, key, house*). Have partners take turns choosing a word, spelling its plural, and forming a sentence with it. Partners check each other's spellings.

Crazy Plural World

Ask students in small groups to imagine that there are two or more of everything in the world (e.g., two Eiffel Towers, three Japans, two of each student). Have students take turns describing this world using plural nouns.

GRAMMAR LESSON BANK

LEARNING GOALS

We can identify and use different kinds of plural nouns.

OBJECTIVES

Demonstrate command of the conventions of standard English grammar and usage when writing or speaking.

Explain the function of nouns, pronouns, verbs, adjectives and adverbs in general and their functions in particular sentences.

Distinguish between plural nouns and collective nouns.

Identify and use appositives.

Proofread sentences.

DAILY LANGUAGE ACTIVITY

Use the online review for grammar, practice, and usage.

▷ TEACH IN SMALL GROUP

You may wish to use the Talk About It activities during Small Group time.

⬤⬤⬤ **Approaching Level, On Level,** and **Beyond Level** Pair students of different proficiency levels.

⬤ **ELL** According to their language proficiency, students should contribute to discussions by using short phrases, asking questions, and adding relevant details.

FORMATIVE ASSESSMENT

▷ STUDENT CHECK-IN

After completing each Practice Book page, have partners share. Ask them to reflect using the Check-In routine.

More Plural Nouns

 LESSON 1 Teach

Introduce More Plural Nouns and Collective Nouns

- To form the plural of some nouns ending in *f* or *fe*, change the *f* to *v* and add *-es*: *loaf, loaves.*
- To form the plural of nouns ending in a vowel followed by *o*, add *-s*: *rodeo, rodeos; zoo, zoos.*
- To form the plural of nouns ending in a consonant followed by *o*, add *-s* or *-es*: *echoes.*
- Some nouns, like *crew, council,* and *class,* name a group. These nouns are called **collective nouns.** A collective noun can be considered singular or plural. *The crew is on the boat.* The singular verb form *is* lets you know to think of *crew* as a group not as individuals. *The crew are receiving their orders.* The plural verb form *are* lets you know to think of each member of the crew.

See **Practice Book** page 85 or online activity.

 LESSON 2 Teach

Review More Plural Nouns

Have students explain how to form plural nouns that do not end in *-s* or *-es*. Remind students that a collective noun can be singular or plural. When a collective noun is singular, use a the singular verb form. When a collective noun is plural, use the plural verb form. *The class needs a teacher.* (e.g., class: singular) *The class have volunteered at a shelter.* (e.g., class: plural)

Introduce Irregular Plural Nouns

- Some nouns have a special plural form that does not end in *-s*: *ox/oxen; tooth/teeth; foot/feet; woman/women; child/children.*
- Some nouns stay the same whether singular or plural: *trout, moose, deer, fish, sheep, swine.*
- Remember to check a dictionary for the spelling of irregular plurals.

See **Practice Book** page 86.

 ^{OPTION} **Talk About It** ^{MULTIMODAL}

Use Plural Nouns

Ask partners to use complete sentences to talk about animals in nature. Partners should help each other form complete sentences, using a variety of plural nouns. Display words such as *mice* and *wolves* to prompt students.

Use Collective Nouns

Display several collective nouns, such as *choir, herd, cast* (of actors), and *audience.* In small groups, have students come up with singular and plural uses for each word. *The cast of the play practices daily. The cast are trying on their costumes.*

Mechanics and Usage

Plural Nouns and Appositives

- Some nouns have a special plural form that does not end in *-s or -es: child/children; foot/ feet; goose/geese.*

- Some nouns stay the same whether singular or plural: *herd, salmon.*

- Appositives tell more about the nouns they follow.

- Commas set off many appositives. *Mr. Jackson, our principal, has been at our school for twenty years.* In this sentence, *our principal* is an appositive. The phrase *our principal* tells more about Mr. Jackson.

See **Practice Book** page 87 or online activity.

 Proofread and Write

Proofread

Have students correct these sentences:

1. The rest of my girl scout troops was sound asleep. (troop)

2. I could hear many childs snoring quietly. (children)

3. I heard branch snapping and was sure it was wolf. (1: branches; 2: wolves)

4. Koalaes a kind of marsupial sleep during the day. (1: Koalas,: 2: marsupial,)

Write

Have students find a piece of their own writing in their writer's notebook and correct errors in plural nouns usage. Remind students that collective nouns usually have a singular verb because they refer to a group as a whole.

See **Practice Book** page 88.

 Assess and Reteach

Assess

Use the Daily Language Activity and **Practice Book** page 89 for assessment.

Rubric Use your online rubric to record student progress.

Reteach

Use online **Grammar Handbook** page 456 and **Practice Book** pages 85–88 for additional reteaching. Remind students that it is important to use plural nouns correctly as they speak and write.

Check students' writing for use of the skill and listen for it in their speaking. Assign grammar revision assignments in their writer's notebook as needed.

Replace the Nouns

Have students write two sentences using singular nouns. Partners read their sentences aloud to each other. Have the listening partner repeat the sentence, replacing the singular noun with its plural form and changing the verb as needed.

Spelling Challenge

Display singular nouns that form the plural in different ways (e.g., *knife, radio, potato, child, goose, deer*). Have partners check each other's work as they take turns choosing a word, spelling its plural, and writing a sentence with it.

Plurals in the Garden

Have groups make a list of plants used for food (e.g., *corn, tomato, potato, squash, cherry, peach*) and then use a dictionary to find out how to form the plural. Have students write each plural form and use the plurals in sentences.

GRAMMAR LESSON BANK

Possessive Nouns

Teach — LESSON 6

Introduce Possessive Nouns

- A **possessive noun** is a noun that shows who or what owns or has something. *Mary's book is on the shelf.* In this sentence, *Mary's* is a possessive noun.

- A **singular possessive noun** is a singular noun that shows ownership: *John's telescope.*

- Form a singular possessive noun by adding an apostrophe (') and an -s to a singular noun: *the horse's mane, Aaron's music.*

- A person's name or a collective noun that ends in -s also has an apostrophe (') and an -s in the possessive: *Bess's skateboard, the class's schedule.*

- Remember, an apostrophe (') and -s added to a noun shows possession.

See **Practice Book** page 97 or online activity.

Teach — LESSON 7

Review Singular Possessive Nouns

Elicit from students how to form a possessive noun.

Introduce Plural Possessive Nouns

- A **plural possessive noun** is a plural noun that shows ownership.

- To form the possessive of a plural noun that ends in -s, add an apostrophe: *the citizens' concerns.* (*Citizens* is plural, so only an apostrophe (') is added following the -s. Do not add an apostrophe (') -s following a plural noun ending in -s.)

- To form the possessive of a plural noun that does not end in -s, add an apostrophe and an -s: *the mice's nest, geese's wings.*

See **Practice Book** page 98.

OPTION • Talk About It • MULTIMODAL

Whose Is It?	Use Possessive Nouns
Have partners describe unnamed objects in the room. Partner A gives clues, and Partner B guesses who owns the object. For example: A: *It's red, and it has a sports logo on it.* B: *Is it Matt's sweatshirt?* Then have partners switch roles.	Have partners use possessive nouns to talk about accomplishing a plan. As they talk, partners write down the possessive noun phrases they hear (e.g., *Jamie's suggestion, Dad's idea*). Have partners check the form of each possessive noun.

Mechanics and Usage

Adding –s or –'s

- When a singular noun ends in *-s,* show the possessive form by adding an apostrophe and an *-s: bus's driver.*

- The plural form of a noun that ends in *-s* will only need an apostrophe: *buses' drivers.*

- To form the possessive of a plural noun that does not end in *-s,* add an apostrophe with an *-s: children's activities.*

- Do not confuse plurals with possessives: *Scientists* is plural; *scientist's* is singular possessive, and *scientists'* is plural possessive as shown in these sentences:

  The scientists wrote a report.

  The scientist's experiment is part of the report.

  The scientists' results were ground-breaking.

See **Practice Book** page 99 or online activity.

 Proofread and Write

Proofread

Have students identify and correct errors in the story:

Jans favorite after-school program is Circus Arts. The classes teacher, Chris, is a juggler and mime. Chris' skills include stilt walking, which Jan loves. The stilts's height made her nervous at first, but the other childrens laughter reassured her. Now she loves that she walks as high as birds' fly! (1: Jan's; 2: class's; 3: Chris's; 4: stilts'; 5: children's; 6: birds)

Write

Have students find a piece of their own writing in their writer's notebook and correct possessives.

See **Practice Book** page 100.

 Assess and Reteach

Assess

Use the Daily Language Activity .and **Practice Book** page 101 for assessment.

Rubric Use your online rubric to record student progress.

Reteach

Use the online **Grammar Handbook** page 457 and **Practice Book** pages 97–100 for additional reteaching. Remind students that it is important to use possessive nouns correctly as they speak and write.

Check students' writing for use of the skill and listen for it in their speaking. Assign grammar revision assignments in their writer's notebook as needed.

Use Plural Possessives

Have each student write two sentences with plural possessives. Have partners read their sentences to each other. The listener writes down the plural possessive phrases and checks them with the speaker (e.g., *girls' coats, children's toys*).

Describe Objects

Display a list of several common objects (e.g., *clothing, books, pencils*). Have partners take turns choosing an object and making a possessive sentence. For example: *hat + friend = My friend's favorite hat is a yellow baseball cap.*

Spelling Bee

Have small groups each make a list of 10 possessive words. Group A reads a word for Group B to spell. If Group B is correct, they get a point. Take turns until all words are spelled.

GRAMMAR
LESSON
BANK

Prepositional Phrases

We can identify and use prepositional phrases.

OBJECTIVES

Demonstrate command of the conventions of standard English grammar and usage when writing or speaking.

Explain the function of conjunctions, prepositions, and interjections in general and their function in particular sentences.

Use underlining, quotation marks, or italics to indicate titles of works.

Proofread sentences.

DAILY LANGUAGE ACTIVITY

Use the online review for grammar, practice, and usage.

 TEACH IN SMALL GROUP

You may wish to use the Talk About It activities during Small Group time.

●●● **Approaching Level, On Level,** and **Beyond Level** Pair students of different proficiency levels.

● **ELL** According to their language proficiency, students should contribute to discussions by using short phrases, asking questions, and adding relevant details.

FORMATIVE ASSESSMENT

❯ **STUDENT CHECK-IN**

After completing each Practice Book page, have partners share. Ask them to reflect using the Check-In routine.

 Teach

Introduce Prepositional Phrases

- A **prepositional phrase** is a group of words that tells more about an important part of a sentence.

- A prepositional phrase begins with a **preposition** such as *about, during, in, near, under,* or *with.* It ends with a noun.

- A prepositional phrase can function as an adjective or an adverb. *The girl <u>with blue shoes</u> reads many books.* (This prepositional phrase functions as an adjective that tells more about the girl.) *The girl reads <u>at the library</u>.* (The prepositional phrase functions as an adverb that answers the question *where*?)

See **Practice Book** page 109 or online activity.

 Teach

Review Prepositional Phrases

Review how prepositional phrases function as modifiers in sentences. Have students write sentences using prepositional phrases as adjectives and adverbs. Then have students underline each prepositional phrase.

Introduce Nouns in Prepositional Phrases

- The object of a prepositional phrase is the noun or pronoun that follows the preposition: *in the <u>room</u>, for <u>her</u>.*

- The most important word in a prepositional phrase is often the noun or pronoun at the end: *across the <u>hall</u>, over the <u>door</u>, by <u>him</u>.*

See **Practice Book** page 110.

 **Talk About It**

Tour the Classroom

Have students role-play a scenario where a new family is considering their school. Ask different students to take the family on a tour and to narrate it, using prepositional phrases. For example: *The drawings <u>on the wall</u> are made <u>by the students</u>.*

Tell a Story

List prepositions and nouns separately. Have students choose a word from each list. Ask a student to begin a made-up story, using a prepositional phrase with the chosen words. The next student continues the story doing the same.

LESSON 3 Mechanics and Usage

Punctuating Titles and Letters

Present the following:

- Use quotation marks around the title of a song, part of a book, or a short story. *The chapter is "Dog Days of Summer."*

- Use italics or underlining with the title of a long work, such as a book: *I read <u>Old Yeller</u>.*

- Italics or underlining can also be used for emphasis in writing: *I had a <u>great</u> time at the park! I'll never eat that again!*

- Use commas after the greeting and closing in a friendly letter and in the date and address. In a business letter, use a colon after the greeting. Examples:

    Dear Aunt Sue,
    Yours truly,

    Dear Mr. Smith:

    Yours sincerely,

See **Practice Book** page 111 or online activity.

 OPTION **LESSON 4** Proofread and Write

Proofread

Have students correct errors in these sentences:

1. Dara loves the song Windy. (1. song,; 2. "Windy.")

2. Have you read the book Shiloh? (*Shiloh*/<u>Shiloh</u>)

3. I'm so happy right now! (*happy*/<u>happy</u>)

4. The dog of the shaggy fur chased the cat. (with)

5. The school is in the lake. (near/by/beside)

6. I was born on August, 14 2004. (August 14, 2004)

7. Dear Dr. Simpson, (Simpson:)

Write

Have students correct prepositional phrases, punctuation of titles, and emphasis in a piece of their own writing in their writer's notebooks. Students should try using both italics and underlining.

See **Practice Book** page 112.

OPTION **LESSON 5** Assess and Reteach

Assess

Use the Daily Language Activity and **Practice Book** page 113 for assessment.

Rubric Use your online rubric to record student progress.

Reteach

Use the online **Grammar Handbook** pages 457, 472, 480 and **Practice Book** pages 109–112 for additional practice with prepositional phrases and punctuation within titles and letters. Remind students that it is important to use grammar correctly as they speak and write.

Check students' writing for use of these skills and listen for them in speaking. Assign grammar revision assignments in their writer's notebook as needed.

Sort Sentences

Create a T-chart: *Adjective* and *Adverb*. Ask each student to write a sentence that contains a prepositional phrase. Ask students to take turns posting the prepositional phrases from the sentences in the correct columns and explaining their placements.

Search a Story

Have students search stories for sentences that contain prepositional phrases. Ask students to take turns posting their sentences in the correct column of the T-chart from Lesson 3 and explaining their placements.

Add It

Have partners each write a sentence without a prepositional phrase. Ask them to exchange sentences. Partners will take turns reading each other's sentences and will add a prepositional phrase to their partner's sentence.

LEARNING GOALS

We can read, sort and use spelling words with variant vowels and diphthongs.

OBJECTIVES

Use combined knowledge of all letter-sound correspondences, syllabication patterns, and morphology (e.g., roots and affixes) to read accurately unfamiliar multisyllabic words in context and out of context.

▷ DIFFERENTIATED SPELLING

Go online for Dictation Sentences for differentiated spelling lists.

●● On Level and ELL

joint	counter	sprouts
foul	brought	cautious
coil	bawl	turmoil
hoist	fountain	scrawny
stout	sprawls	foundation
dawdle	douse	turquoise
mouthful	clause	

Review work, thirst, squirm
Challenge buoyant, renown

● Approaching Level

joint	counter	sprouts
foul	brought	cause
coil	hawks	turmoil
join	fountain	scrawny
round	straws	bounce
dawn	south	point
mouthful	sauce	

● Beyond Level

loiter	council	scour
outnumber	wrought	cautious
poise	bawl	turmoil
hoist	fountain	scrawny
stout	sprawls	foundation
dawdle	douse	renowned
mouthful	clause	

FORMATIVE ASSESSMENT

❯ STUDENT CHECK-IN

After completing each Practice Book page, have partners share. Ask them to reflect using the Check-In routine.

Variant Vowel /ô/; Diphthongs /oi/, /ou/

 LESSON 1 Assess Prior Knowledge

Read the spelling words aloud, drawing out the vowel sounds.

Point out the variant vowel /ô/ sound in *dawdle*. Draw a line under *aw* as you say the word. Explain that not all words with the variant vowel /ô/ sound are spelled in the same way. Point out the /oi/ and /ou/ diphthongs in this week's lesson as well. Explain that diphthongs are gliding vowel sounds; they combine two vowel sounds into one syllable.

Sort a few of the spelling words under the key words *bawl, coil,* and *sprouts*. Point out the variant vowel and diphthong sounds in each word.

Use the Dictation Sentences from Lesson 5 to give the pretest. Say the underlined word, read the sentence, and repeat the word. Have students write the words and check their papers.

See **Practice Book** page 66 for a pretest.

 OPTION LESSON 2 Spiral Review

Review the *r*-controlled vowel sounds in *work, thirst,* and *squirm*. Read each sentence below, repeat the review word, and have students write the word.

1. I <u>work</u> hard at school.
2. I had a <u>thirst</u> for water.
3. The movie made me <u>squirm</u>.

Have students trade papers.

Challenge Words

Review this week's variant vowel /ô/ sound and the /oi/ and /ou/ diphthongs. Read each sentence, repeat the challenge word, and have students write them.

1. We felt <u>buoyant</u> at festival time.
2. He was a man of great <u>renown</u>.

Have students check their spellings and write the words in their writer's notebooks.

 Word Sorts MULTIMODAL

OPEN SORT

Have students cut apart the **Spelling Word Cards** available online and initial the back of each card. Have them read the words aloud with partners. Then have partners do an open sort. Have them record their sorts in their writer's notebooks.

PATTERN SORT

Complete the pattern sort from Lesson 1 by using the boldfaced key words on the Spelling Word Cards. Point out the variant vowel and diphthong sounds. Partners should compare and check their sorts. See **Practice Book** pages 67, 67A, and 67B for differentiated practice.

Word Meanings

Have students copy the three analogies below into their word study notebooks. Say the sentences aloud. Then ask students to fill in the blanks with a spelling word.

1. *Hot* is to *cold* as ____ is to *hurry*. (dawdle)

2. *Flowers* is to *bunch* as *food* is to ____. (mouthful)

3. *Book* is to *paper* as ____ is to *water*. (fountain)

Challenge students to create analogies for their other spelling, review, or challenge words. Encourage them to use synonyms and antonyms. Have students post their analogies on the board.

See **Practice Book** page 68 or online activity.

 Proofread and Write

Write these sentences on the board. Have students circle and correct each misspelled word. Have students use a print or digital dictionary to check and correct their spellings.

1. I mixed cement to repair the joynt in the foundatien. (joint, foundation)

2. We were cawtious as we began to hoyst the heavy desk. (cautious, hoist)

3. Joel was glad he had brawt gear for the fowl weather. (brought, foul)

Error Correction Point out that the *oi* spelling never appears at the end of a word or syllable, but the *oy* spelling can, as in *boy*.

Apply to Writing Have students correct a piece of their own writing.

See **Practice Book** page 69.

 Assess

Use the Dictation Sentences for the posttest. Have students list the misspelled words in their writer's notebooks. Look for students' use of these words in their writing.

See **Practice Book** page 66 for a posttest. Use page 70 for review.

Dictation Sentences

1. The pain is in my elbow joint.
2. A foul smell filled the room.
3. Coil the rope so nobody will trip.
4. Just hoist the basket over.
5. She was a stout woman.
6. Let's not dawdle along the way.
7. He chewed a mouthful of food.
8. They ordered ice cream at the counter.
9. The mailman brought letters.
10. The baby started to bawl.
11. We got a drink at the fountain.
12. The cat sprawls in the doorway.
13. Douse your hands in water.
14. Check the clause in the contract.
15. Grass sprouts from the lawn.
16. It could be dangerous, so be cautious.
17. There was turmoil in the streets.
18. The scrawny dog was always hungry.
19. The house has a firm foundation.
20. Emma lost her turquoise ring.

Have students self-correct their tests.

SPEED SORT

Have partners do a speed sort to see who is fastest. Then have them do a word hunt in this week's readings to find words with the same vowel sounds as the spelling words. Have them record the words in their writer's notebooks.

BLIND SORT

Have partners do a blind sort: one reads a Spelling Word Card; the other tells under which key word it belongs. Have students explain how they sorted the words. Then have partners use their word cards to play Go Fish, using this week's spelling patterns as the "fish."

LEARNING GOALS

We can read, sort and use spelling words with plural endings.

OBJECTIVES

Spell grade appropriate words correctly, consulting references as needed.

▶ DIFFERENTIATED SPELLING

Go online for Dictation Sentences for differentiated spelling lists.

●● On Level and ELL

rattlers	reptiles	identities
fangs	surroundings	losses
countries	beliefs	possibilities
liberties	difficulties	notches
potatoes	batches	zeroes
rodeos	abilities	eddies
taxes	lashes	

Review brought, counter, coil
Challenge mangoes, sinews

● Approaching Level

rattlers	reptiles	families
fangs	snakes	losses
babies	beliefs	berries
liberties	enemies	bunches
couches	batches	zeroes
rodeos	cities	trophies
taxes	lashes	

● Beyond Level

rattlers	reptiles	identities
molecules	surroundings	losses
countries	beliefs	possibilities
calamities	difficulties	notches
potatoes	crutches	zeroes
canopies	mangoes	eddies
geniuses	mosquitoes	

FORMATIVE ASSESSMENT

❯ STUDENT CHECK-IN

After completing each Practice Book page, have partners share. Ask them to reflect using the Check-In routine.

Plurals

LESSON 6 Assess Prior Knowledge

Read the spelling words aloud, segmenting each word syllable by syllable.

Draw a line under the plural spelling -ies in liber_ties_. Point out that the y in liberty changes to an i before the plural ending -es is added. Point out additional plural spellings: adding -s and adding -es.

Demonstrate sorting the spelling words by pattern under the key words beliefs, taxes, and countries. Sort a few words. Point out the different plural spellings.

Use the Dictation Sentences from Lesson 10 to give the pretest. Say the underlined word, read the sentence, and repeat the word. Have students write the words. Then have students check their papers.

See **Practice Book** page 78 for a pretest.

OPTION LESSON 7 Spiral Review

Review the /ô/, /oi/, and /ou/ sounds in brought, coil, and counter. Read each sentence below, repeat the review word, and have students write the word.

1. I brought cups to the picnic.
2. The counter is filled with dishes.
3. The coil curves around and around.

Have students trade papers and check their spellings.

Challenge Words

Review this week's plural spellings. Read each sentence below, repeat the challenge word, and have students write the word.

1. I like mangoes that are ripe.
2. Relax your muscles and sinews.

Have students check and correct their spellings and write the words in their writer's notebooks.

 Word Sorts MULTIMODAL

OPEN SORT

Have students cut apart the **Spelling Word Cards** in the Online Resource Book and initial the back of each card. Have them read the words aloud with partners. Then have partners do an open sort. Have them record their sorts in their writer's notebooks.

PATTERN SORT

Complete the pattern sort from Lesson 6 by using the boldfaced key words on the Spelling Word Cards. Partners should compare and check their sorts and record them in their writer's notebooks. See **Practice Book** pages 79, 79A, and 79B for differentiated practice.

Word Meanings

OPTION LESSON 8

Have students research and write the word origin for each word below. Have students use a print or digital dictionary for their research.

1. potatoes (1560s from the Spanish word *patata*; from the Taino word *batata* which means "sweet potato")

2. reptiles (late 14th century from the Old French word *reptile*; from the late Latin word *rēptilis* which means "creeping, crawling")

3. fangs (from 1550s Old English word *fōn*, which means "to seize")

Challenge students to find origins for other spelling words. Then have students record the word histories in their writer's notebooks.

See **Practice Book** page 80 or online activity.

Proofread and Write

OPTION LESSON 9

Write these sentences on the board. Have students circle and correct each misspelled word. Have students use a print or digital dictionary to check and correct their spellings.

1. Not all countrys have the same libertees that we do. (countries, liberties)

2. A bag of patatoes offers many menu possabilites. (potatoes, possibilities)

3. Harsh suroundings bring many difficultys. (surroundings, difficulties)

Error Correction Some students will need additional practice adding plurals to words ending in *y*. Review the rule of changing *y* to *i* when a consonant appears before the *y*.

Apply to Writing Have students correct a piece of their own writing.

See **Practice Book** page 81.

Assess

LESSON 10

Use the Dictation Sentences for the posttest. Have students list the misspelled words in their writer's notebooks. Look for students' use of these words in their writing.

See **Practice Book** page 78 for a posttest. Use page 82 for review.

Dictation Sentences

1. **Rattlers** shake their tails.
2. Their **fangs** are powerful tools.
3. I want to visit different **countries**.
4. We give up certain **liberties** at school.
5. Mashed **potatoes** are my favorite.
6. We saw cowboys at the **rodeos**.
7. My parents pay **taxes** every year.
8. Snakes are also **reptiles**.
9. Be aware of your **surroundings**.
10. Sandy has strong **beliefs**.
11. We faced a lot of **difficulties**.
12. I baked three **batches** of cookies.
13. Dancing is one of her best **abilities**.
14. **Lashes** protect our eyes.
15. A spy can have many **identities**.
16. Our win makes up for all our **losses**.
17. Let's explore all the **possibilities**.
18. The **notches** in the tree were made by a woodpecker.
19. How many **zeroes** are in a million?
20. Fish hide in the river's **eddies**.

Have students self-correct their tests.

SPEED SORT

Have partners do a speed sort to see who is fastest. Then have them do a word hunt in this week's readings to find words with plural spellings for each spelling pattern. Have them record the words in their writer's notebooks.

BLIND SORT

Have partners do a blind sort: one reads a Spelling Word Card; the other tells under which key word it belongs. Have partners compare their sorts. Then have partners use one set of word cards to play Word Match. Two words with the same spelling pattern make a match.

SPELLING LESSON BANK

LEARNING GOALS

We can read, sort, and use words with inflectional endings.

OBJECTIVES

Spell grade-appropriate words correctly, consulting references as needed.

▶ DIFFERENTIATED SPELLING

Go online for Dictation Sentences for differentiated spelling lists.

●● ● On Level and ELL

jogging	forbidding	complicated
dripping	referred	qualified
skimmed	injured	threatening
accepted	deserved	gnarled
amusing	applied	envied
easing	relied	fascinated
regretted	renewing	

Review difficulties, notches, rodeos
Challenge adoring, diaries

● Approaching Level

jogging	swimming	dared
dripping	referred	studied
skimmed	injured	awaiting
raking	deserved	checked
amusing	applied	pitied
saving	relied	traced
flipped	renewing	

● Beyond Level

accepted	forbidding	complicated
shredding	referred	qualified
skimmed	portrayed	threatening
recognizing	dedicated	gnarled
amusing	applied	envied
easing	unified	fascinated
regretted	soothing	

FORMATIVE ASSESSMENT

◯ STUDENT CHECK-IN

After completing each Practice Book page, have partners share. Ask them to reflect using the Check-In routine.

Inflectional Endings

LESSON 1 Assess Prior Knowledge

Read the spelling words aloud, segmenting each word syllable by syllable.

Explain that spelling rules dictate that word spellings can change when -ed and -ing are added. Model adding -ing to amuse. Point out that the e is dropped.

Demonstrate sorting the spelling words by pattern under the key words amusing, dripping, applied, and threatening. Sort a few words. Point out the different orthographic rules as you sort the words.

Use the Dictation Sentences from Lesson 5 to give the pretest. Say the underlined word, read the sentence, and repeat the word. Have students write the words. Then have students check their papers.

See **Practice Book** page 90 for a pretest.

OPTION LESSON 2 Spiral Review

Review spelling plurals with *difficulties, notches,* and *rodeos.* Read each sentence below, repeat the review word, and have students write the word.

1. The trip was without <u>difficulties</u>.
2. <u>Notches</u> were carved on the floor.
3. I see cowboys at <u>rodeos</u>.

Have students trade papers and check their spellings.

Challenge Words

Review this week's inflectional endings and spellings. Read each sentence below, repeat the challenge word, and have students write the word.

1. She waved to her <u>adoring</u> fans.
2. People's <u>diaries</u> are personal.

Have students check and correct their spellings and write the words in their writer's notebooks.

Word Sorts

MULTIMODAL

OPEN SORT

Have students cut apart the **Spelling Word Cards** in the Online Resource Book and initial the back of each card. Have them read the words aloud with partners. Then have partners do an open sort. Have them record their sorts in their writer's notebooks.

PATTERN SORT

Complete the pattern sort from Lesson 1 by using the boldfaced key words on the Spelling Word Cards. Point out the inflectional endings. Partners should compare and check their sorts. Have them record their sorts in their writer's notebooks. See **Practice Book** pages 91, 91A, and 91B for differentiated practice.

Word Meanings

Have students copy the words below in their writer's notebooks. Say the words aloud. Then ask students to identify the spelling word that is a synonym for each word.

1. running (jogging)
2. difficult (complicated)
3. hurt (injured)

Challenge students to identify synonyms for their other spelling, review, or challenge words. Have students write the spelling words and the synonyms in their writer's notebooks.

See **Practice Book** page 92 or online activity.

Proofread and Write

Write these sentences on the board. Have students circle and correct each misspelled word. Have students use a print or digital dictionary to check and correct their spellings.

1. I enjured my foot joging on the rocky path. (injured, jogging)
2. May desserved to be accepted into the art program. (deserved, accepted)
3. The amussing play fascanated us. (amusing, fascinated)
4. Rinewing his license was a complicatted process. (renewing, complicated)

Error Correction Review the rules that determine when different spelling changes occur when inflectional endings are added. Remind students that sometimes no change is made to a word when an ending is added. Have students edit errors in inflectional endings and spelling patterns in their writer's notebook.

See **Practice Book** page 93.

Assess

Use the Dictation Sentences for the posttest. Have students list the misspelled words in their writer's notebooks. Look for students' use of these words in their writings.

See **Practice Book** page 90 for a posttest. Use page 94 for review.

Dictation Sentences

1. I like <u>jogging</u> in the park.
2. Please fix the <u>dripping</u> faucet.
3. Julie <u>skimmed</u> the chapter.
4. I <u>accepted</u> the trophy for my team.
5. The comedy show was <u>amusing</u>.
6. We began <u>easing</u> into our seats.
7. He <u>regretted</u> saying mean things.
8. His mom was <u>forbidding</u> him to play with us.
9. He <u>referred</u> to the dictionary.
10. The <u>injured</u> player needs surgery.
11. The team <u>deserved</u> to win.
12. We <u>applied</u> for a scholarship.
13. She <u>relied</u> on their help.
14. I'm <u>renewing</u> the book for a week.
15. This machine is <u>complicated</u>.
16. Maya is <u>qualified</u> for the job.
17. That squirrel gave me a <u>threatening</u> look.
18. We sat under a <u>gnarled</u> tree.
19. The class <u>envied</u> her talent.
20. The stars <u>fascinated</u> him.

Have students self-correct their tests.

SPEED SORT

Have partners do a speed sort to see who is fastest. Then have one partner randomly draw a Spelling Word Card and orally create a sentence. The other partner draws a card and creates a sentence that is related to the first one. Partners continue until all words are used.

BLIND SORT

Have partners do a blind sort: one reads a Spelling Word Card; the other tells under which key word it belongs. Have students write a reflection of how they sorted the words.

SPELLING LESSON BANK

LEARNING GOALS

We can read, sort, and use contractions.

OBJECTIVES

Spell grade-appropriate words correctly, consulting references as needed.

DIFFERENTIATED SPELLING

Go online for Dictation Sentences for differentiated spelling lists.

●● On Level and ELL

you've	wasn't	they're
she'd	we'll	shouldn't
that's	we've	wouldn't
what's	we're	he'd
doesn't	couldn't	don't
there's	I've	isn't
you're	didn't	

Review dripping, applied, diaries
Challenge won't, aren't

● Approaching Level

you've	wasn't	they're
she'd	we'll	shouldn't
that's	we've	wouldn't
what's	we're	he'd
doesn't	couldn't	don't
there's	I've	isn't
you're	didn't	

● Beyond Level

you've	wasn't	they're
she'd	we'll	shouldn't
that's	we've	wouldn't
what's	we're	he'd
doesn't	couldn't	don't
there's	I've	isn't
you're	didn't	

FORMATIVE ASSESSMENT

STUDENT CHECK-IN

After completing each Practice Book page, have partners share. Ask them to reflect using the Check-In routine.

Contractions

LESSON 6 Assess Prior Knowledge

Read the spelling words aloud.

Model spelling the word *you've*. Explain that *you've* is the contraction for the words *you have*. Say *you have* aloud and have students listen for the sounds of the letters replaced by the apostrophe.

Demonstrate sorting the spelling words that are formed from the words *have, had, is, are, will,* and *not*. Sort a few words. Point out any words that have homophones, such as *they're/their* and *you're/your*.

Use the Dictation Sentences from Lesson 10 to give the pretest. Say the underlined word, read the sentence, and repeat the word. Have students write the words. Then have students check their papers.

See **Practice Book** page 102 for a pretest.

OPTION LESSON 7 Spiral Review

Review the inflectional endings in *dripping, applied,* and *diaries*. Read each sentence below, repeat the review word, and have students write the word.

1. Water was <u>dripping</u> off the roof.
2. He <u>applied</u> for a new job.
3. Our <u>diaries</u> are full of funny stories.

Have students trade papers and check their spellings.

Challenge Words

Review this week's contraction spellings. Read each sentence below, repeat the challenge word, and have students write the word.

1. We <u>won't</u> be drawing today.
2. We <u>aren't</u> getting a new pet.

Have students check and correct their spellings and write the words in their writer's notebooks.

Word Sorts · MULTIMODAL

OPEN SORT

Have students cut apart the **Spelling Word Cards** in the Online Resource Book and initial the back of each card. Have them read the words aloud with partners. Then have partners do an open sort. Have them record their sorts in their writer's notebooks.

PATTERN SORT

Complete the pattern sort from Lesson 6. Point out the contraction spellings. Partners should compare, check, and record their sorts in their writer's notebooks. Or have partners use **Practice Book** page 103. See Practice Book pages 103A and 103B for differentiated practice.

OPTION LESSON 8 Word Meanings

Have students copy the words below in their writer's notebooks. Read the words aloud. Then ask students to identify a spelling word that is opposite in meaning for each word.

1. was _____ (wasn't)
2. does _____ (doesn't)
3. do _____ (don't)

Challenge students to identify related words for their other spelling, review, or challenge words. Have students discuss the related words they identified with a partner.

See **Practice Book** page 104 or online activity.

OPTION LESSON 9 Proofread and Write

Write these sentences on the board. Have students circle and correct each misspelled word. Have students use a print or digital dictionary to check and correct their spellings.

1. Wel'l make sure there is't a leak in the hose. (We'll, isn't)
2. There're going to make sure wev'e received the tickets. (they're, we've)
3. She could'nt believe he woodn't share. (couldn't, wouldn't)
4. We do'nt know wha'ts wrong with the television. (don't, what's)

Error Correction Remind students that an apostrophe should never be placed in a contraction where no letters are being removed.

Apply to Writing Have students correct a piece of their own writing.

See **Practice Book** page 105.

LESSON 10 Assess

Use the Dictation Sentences for the posttest. Have students list the misspelled words in their writer's notebooks. Look for students' use of these words in their writings.

See **Practice Book** page 102 for the posttest. Use page 106 for review.

Dictation Sentences

1. I know <u>you've</u> eaten already.
2. I think <u>she'd</u> like to go with us.
3. <u>That's</u> a beautiful sweater!
4. <u>What's</u> your middle name?
5. He <u>doesn't</u> like to swim.
6. <u>There's</u> a large boat in the lake.
7. <u>You're</u> going to like that present.
8. I <u>wasn't</u> sure if I should leave.
9. I think <u>we'll</u> have a sandwich for lunch.
10. <u>We've</u> never been late for recess.
11. <u>We're</u> going on a fun field trip.
12. I <u>couldn't</u> open that jar.
13. <u>I've</u> been wanting to go to a movie.
14. We <u>didn't</u> like that last movie.
15. <u>They're</u> playing soccer tomorrow.
16. We <u>shouldn't</u> be late for school.
17. I <u>wouldn't</u> like pickles in my soup.
18. I know <u>he'd</u> rather not play today.
19. We <u>don't</u> need to throw that away.
20. Mrs. Sanchez <u>isn't</u> sick today.

Have students self-correct their tests.

SPEED SORT

Have partners do a speed sort to see who is fastest. Then have them have a conversation about things that have happened recently in school, noting the contractions each other uses in their writer's notebooks.

BLIND SORT

Have partners do a blind sort: one reads a Spelling Word Card, the other tells under which spelling pattern it belongs. Then have partners write a reflection of how they sorted the words.

SPELLING LESSON BANK

We can read, sort, and use spelling words with closed syllables.

OBJECTIVES

Spell grade-appropriate words correctly, consulting references as needed.

 DIFFERENTIATED SPELLING

Go online for Dictation Sentences for differentiated spelling lists.

● ● On Level and ELL

dentist	hollow	kennel
jogger	empire	valley
fifteen	blizzard	fragment
flatter	culture	gallop
submit	goggles	vulture
mustang	summon	pigment
absent	excite	

Review won't, shouldn't, we're
Challenge clammy, hammock

● Approaching Level

garden	arrow	injure
jogger	empire	valley
fifteen	blizzard	fragment
bottom	corner	gallop
basket	goggles	vulture
mustang	dinner	clatter
absent	checkers	

● Beyond Level

swerving	hollow	kennel
jogger	clammy	canyon
cinder	suspend	fragment
flattery	culture	gallop
muttered	stallion	vulture
stubble	summon	pigment
whimper	whinnied	

▶ STUDENT CHECK-IN

After completing each Practice Book page, have partners share. Ask them to reflect using the Check-In routine.

Closed Syllables

 LESSON 1 Assess Prior Knowledge

Read the spelling words aloud, sounding out each syllable.

Point out the spelling pattern in *submit*. Draw a line to separate the syllables (*sub/mit*) and say each one. Point out that both syllables are closed syllables. Remind students that when a syllable ends in one or more consonants and has a short vowel, it is a closed syllable.

Demonstrate sorting the spelling words by pattern under the key words *valley* and *absent*. Point out the double consonant in *valley*.

Use the Dictation Sentences from Lesson 5 to give the pretest. Say the underlined word, read the sentence, and repeat the word. Have students write the words. Then have students check their papers.

See **Practice Book** page 114 for a pretest.

 Word Sorts MULTIMODAL

OPEN SORT

Have students cut apart the **Spelling Word Cards** in the Online Resource Book and initial the back of each card. Have them read the words aloud with partners. Then have partners do an open sort. Have them record their sorts in their writer's notebooks.

 OPTION LESSON 2 Spiral Review

Review the contractions *won't, shouldn't,* and *we're.* Read each sentence below, repeat the review word, and have students write the word.

1. We <u>won't</u> wear masks.
2. We <u>shouldn't</u> hide our faces.
3. <u>We're</u> wearing hats instead.

Have students trade papers and check their spellings.

Challenge Words

Review this week's closed syllable pattern. Read each sentence below, repeat the challenge word, and have students write the word.

1. In the cave, my skin felt <u>clammy</u>.
2. I lay in the <u>hammock</u> under the tree.

Have students check and correct their spellings and write the words in their writer's notebook.

PATTERN SORT

Complete the pattern sort from Lesson 1 by using the boldfaced key words on the Spelling Word Cards. Point out the closed syllable patterns. Partners should compare and check their sorts. See **Practice Book** pages 115, 115A, and 115B for differentiated practice.

Word Meanings

Have students copy the three analogies below into their writer's notebooks. Say the sentences aloud. Then ask students to fill in the blanks with a spelling word.

1. *Mustang* is to *corral* as *dog* is to ____. (kennel)

2. *Summon* is to *call* as ____ is to *runner*. (jogger)

3. *Absent* is to *present* as *insult* is to ____. (flatter)

Challenge students to create analogies for their other spelling words. Encourage them to use word relationships. Have students post their analogies on the board.

See **Practice Book** page 116 or online activity.

 Proofread and Write

Write these sentences on the board. Have students circle and correct each misspelled word. Remind them to use a print or digital dictionary to check and correct their spellings.

1. I found the fragmint of a paintbrush in the pigmint. (fragment, pigment)

2. Tad wore gogles as he hiked through the snowy valey. (goggles, valley)

3. The animal trainer will summun the vulcher. (summon, vulture)

4. If you are absint one day, come fiffteen minutes early the next. (absent, fifteen)

Error Correction Point out that suffix spellings such as *-ment* remain consistent with all words.

Apply to Writing Have students correct a piece of their own writing.

See **Practice Book** page 117.

 Assess

Use the Dictation Sentences for the posttest. Have students list the misspelled words in their writer's notebooks. Look for students' use of these words in their writings.

See **Practice Book** page 114 for a pretest. Use page 118 for review.

Dictation Sentences

1. The <u>dentist</u> examined Lisa's teeth.
2. A <u>jogger</u> ran through the park.
3. Joe turns <u>fifteen</u> on Tuesday.
4. <u>Flatter</u> her with compliments.
5. Please <u>submit</u> the library card application on Monday.
6. Bob could tell the horse was a <u>mustang</u>.
7. Kate was <u>absent</u> from school.
8. The owl made a home in the <u>hollow</u> tree.
9. The <u>empire</u> fell after the attack.
10. The lights failed during the <u>blizzard</u>.
11. Each <u>culture</u> has its own traditions.
12. He wore <u>goggles</u> to swim.
13. He yelled to <u>summon</u> the horse.
14. The game will <u>excite</u> me.
15. The dog stayed at the <u>kennel</u>.
16. A river curled through the <u>valley</u>.
17. I swept up the <u>fragment</u> of broken glass.
18. The horse took off at a <u>gallop</u>.
19. The <u>vulture</u> circled its prey.
20. The painter mixed <u>pigment</u> into the paint.

Have students self-correct their tests.

SPEED SORT

Have partners do a speed sort to see who is fastest. Then have them do a word hunt in this week's readings to find words with closed syllables. Have them record the words in their writer's notebooks.

BLIND SORT

Have partners do a blind sort: one reads a Spelling Word Card; the other tells under which key word it belongs. Then have partners use one set of word cards to play Concentration. Have them match words with the same pattern.

From Good to Great

OBJECTIVES

Engage effectively in a range of collaborative discussions (one-on-one, in groups, and teacher-led) with diverse partners on grade 5 topics and texts, building on others' ideas and expressing their own clearly.

Pose and respond to specific questions by making comments that contribute to the discussion and elaborate on the remarks of others.

Review the key ideas expressed and draw conclusions in light of information and knowledge gained from the discussions.

Report on a topic or text or present an opinion, sequencing ideas logically and using appropriate facts and relevant, descriptive details to support main ideas or themes; speak clearly at an understandable pace.

Adapt speech to a variety of contexts and tasks, using formal English when appropriate to task and situation.

DIGITAL TOOLS

To help students improve their writing, use the **RESOURCE TOOLKIT** Online Grammar Handbook, Digital writing activities, and Center Activity Cards.

PORTFOLIO CHOICE

Ask students to select one finished piece of writing from their writing portfolio. Have them consider a piece that they would like to improve.

Teacher Conference Choose students to conference with, or have them talk with a partner, about their writing to figure out one thing that can be improved. As you conference with each student:

✓ Identify at least one or two things you like about the writing. *The descriptive details you included in the first paragraph help me visualize _____.*

✓ Focus on how the student uses the writing trait. *The supporting details you used help me understand _____.*

✓ Make concrete suggestions for revisions.

✓ Have students work on their writing and then meet with you to review their progress.

Use the following strategies and tips to provide specific direction to help focus writers.

✓ Purpose, Focus, and Organization

- Read the essay and target one sentence for revision. *Rewrite this sentence to eliminate unimportant details.*

- Underline a section that needs to be revised. Provide specific suggestions. *The ideas in this section are related to one another. What transitions or linking words can you use to connect your ideas?*

- Have students reread their writing and think of a more interesting way to introduce their topic. *Is the controlling idea stated as clearly as it could be? Can you think of a good way to grab the reader's attention?*

- Ask students to choose one thing that can be improved. *What can you add or change to give your readers some examples of what you're talking about?*

Have students choose two sentences with similar ideas and read them aloud. *Is there a transition or linking word you can use to connect these sentences?*

✓ Evidence and Elaboration

- Point out places where students could add more relevant evidence. *Reread the sources and find evidence to support the statement that _____.*

- Circle a word that could be more precise. Provide specific suggestions. *You use the word _____ here. Can you think of a word that would make this idea more precise? Look up ____ in the dictionary and see if you can think of a more precise word.*

- If the student includes an irrelevant detail, point it out and underline it. *Does this detail really relate to the controlling idea?*

- If the student repeats the same word, say: *You use the word ___ here and here. Can you think of a different word you can use the second time?*

- Read the writing and target one sentence for revision. *This sentence provides an example of what you're talking about, but it doesn't _____.*

 Help students show a contrast between ideas using a word. *These two ideas are contrasted by _____, because _____. What word or phrase can you use to compare different ideas?*

✓ Conventions

- Underline a sentence fragment. Read it aloud with the student. *This is missing a _____. How can you rewrite this fragment so that it's a complete sentence?*

- Circle a verb that's in the wrong tense. *You've been writing in the _____ tense, but this verb is in the ___ tense. How can you write this verb so that the tenses are consistent?*

- Read the writing and target missing or incorrect punctuation. *What is this punctuation used for? What punctuation should be here instead?*

 Have students listen as you read their writing. Help them identify sentences that are not clear or complete. *Which part is not clear? What words can you add or change in this sentence?*

✓ Apply the Rubric

COLLABORATE Have students apply the rubric as they revise their writing. Ask them to read their writing to a partner. Use these sentence starters to focus their discussion:

You supported the controlling idea by . . .

The ideas are in a logical order because . . .

CLASSROOM CULTURE

We respect and value each other's experiences.

To create a classroom culture where students value each other's efforts and topics of interest, remind them to listen carefully as others share their work. Encourage them to make positive comments. Ask: *What questions will help your partner improve their writing?*

Notes

Extend

Reading Digitally

Reader's Theater

Level Up with Leveled Readers

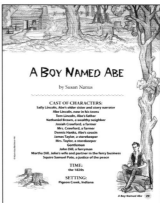

Connect

Connect to Science

Connect to Social Studies

Content Area Reading Options

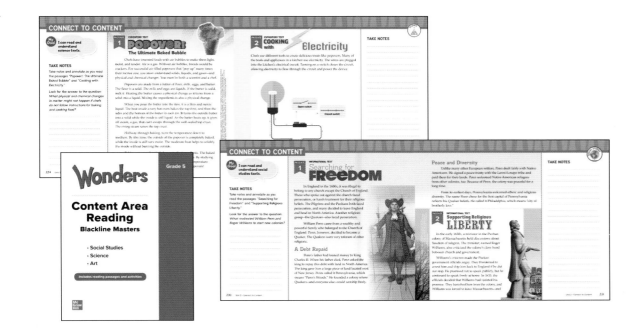

Assess

Reflect on Learning

Unit Assessment

Fluency Assessment

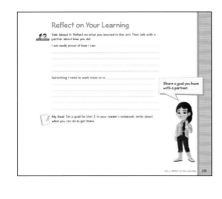

Presentation Options Reader's Theater, Inquiry Space, Writing

FOUNDATIONAL SKILLS

Fluency
- Read grade-level texts with accuracy, appropriate rate, expression, and automaticity

READING

Reading Informational Text
- ✓ Explain how text features contribute to the understanding of a text
- ✓ Explain how text structures contribute to the overall meaning of texts
- ✓ Explain how relevant, or key, details support the central, or main, idea(s), implied or explicit
- Read and comprehend texts in the grades 4–5 text complexity band
- Summarize a text to enhance comprehension
- Write in response to texts

Compare Texts
- Compare and contrast how authors present information on the same topic or theme

COMMUNICATION

Writing

Write to Sources
- ✓ Write an expository text about a topic using multiple sources and including an organizational structure and varied transitions
- With guidance and support from peers and adults, develop and strengthen writing as needed by planning, revising, and editing

Speaking and Listening
- Report on a topic or text or present an opinion, sequencing ideas; speak clearly at an understandable pace

Researching
- Conduct short research projects that build knowledge through investigation of different aspects of the topic

Creating and Collaborating
- Add audio recordings and visual displays to presentations when apppropriate
- With some guidance and support from adults, use technology to produce and publish writing

VOCABULARY

Academic Vocabulary
- Acquire and use grade-appropriate academic vocabulary

Vocabulary Strategy
- ✓ Use context clues and/or background knowledge to determine the meaning of multiple-meaning and unknown words and phrases, appropriate to grade level

CONTENT AREA LEARNING

Scientific Inquiry and Processes
- Make observations and measurements to identify materials based on their properties. **Science**
- Collect and record information using detailed observations and accurate measreuemnts. **Science**

Civic and Political Participation
- Identify the contributions of significant individuals in American history. **Social Studies**

ELL Scaffolded supports for English Language Learners are embedded throughout the lessons, enabling students to communicate information, ideas, and concepts in English Language Arts and for social and instructional purposes within the school setting.

Extend, Connect, and Assess

Extend

TIME KiDS
Reading Digitally

"The Long Road"
Genre: Online Article

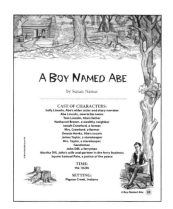

Reader's Theater

A Boy Named Abe
Genre: Play

Connect

Science

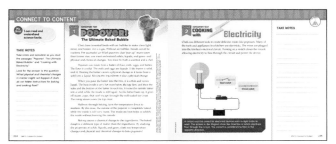

Reading/Writing Companion pp. 224–229

- "Popover! The Ultimate Baked Bubble"
- "Cooking with Electricity"
- Compare the Passages, Make Observations, Explain Your Observations

Social Studies

Reading/Writing Companion pp. 230–234

- "Searching for Freedom"
- "Supporting Religious Liberty"
- Compare the Passages, Make a Timeline

Assess

Unit Assessments

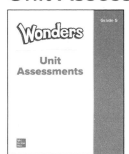

Unit 2 Test

Unit 2 Test Online

Fluency

EVALUATE STUDENT PROGRESS

Use the *Wonders* online assessment reports to evaluate student progress and help you make decisions about small-group instruction and assignments.

Self-Assess Have students complete Reflect on Your Learning and note any areas where they need improvement.

LESSON 1

LESSON 2

Reading

60+ mins
Reading
Suggested Daily Time

READING LESSON GOALS

- I can read and understand science text.
- I can read and understand social studies text.

SMALL GROUP OPTIONS
The designated lessons can be taught in small groups. To determine how to differentiate instruction for small groups, use Formative Assessment and Data Dashboard.

30+ mins
Writing
Suggested Daily Time

WRITING LESSON GOALS

- I can write an expository essay.
- I can synthesize information from three sources.

LESSON 1 — Reading

Reading Digitally, T294–T295
Read "The Long Road" TIME·KiDS

Reader's Theater, T296–T297
A Boy Named Abe
Read the Play and Model Fluency

Connect to Content: Science, T298–T299
Read "Popover!: The Ultimate Baked Bubble," "Cooking with Electricity"

LESSON 2 — Reading

Reading Digitally, T294–T295
Reread "The Long Road" TIME·KiDS

Reader's Theater, T296–T297
A Boy Named Abe
Assign Roles and Practice the Play

Connect to Content: Science, T300–T301
Compare the Passages, Make Observations, Explain Your Observations

Writing

Extended Writing 2: Expository Essay, T256–T257
Analyze the Prompt

Extended Writing 2: Expository Essay, T258–T259
Analyze the Sources

Writing Lesson Bank: Craft Minilessons, T268–T269

Teacher and Peer Conferences

Teacher-Led Instruction

Level Up with Leveled Readers
● ● **Approaching Level to On Level, T314**
The Bill of Rights

Level Up with Leveled Readers
● ● **On Level to Beyond Level, T315**
The Bill of Rights

Level Up with Leveled Readers
● ● **ELL Level to On Level, T316**
The Bill of Rights

SMALL GROUP

Independent/Collaborative Work

Reading

Comprehension
- Make Inferences
Fluency
- Reader's Theater
Independent Reading

Reader's Theater Card 39

Make Inferences Card 40

Writing

Extended Writing 2:
Expository Essay

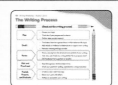
Writing Process Card 43

Transitions Card 56

Get Ready for Assessment

Before administering the unit assessment, identify any gaps in students' understanding using the Data Dashboard. Use resources from the unit or your own resources to differentiate Small Group Teacher-Led Instruction and to provide Independent/Collaborative Work options.

 LESSON 3

 LESSON 4

 LESSON 5

Reading

Reader's Theater, T296–T297 *A Boy Named Abe* Practice the Play and Extend	**Reader's Theater, T296–T297** *A Boy Named Abe* Perform and Reread the Play	**Unit Wrap Up, T306–T307** Make Connections Reflect on Your Learning
Connect to Content: Social Studies, T302–T303 Read "Searching for Freedom," "Supporting Religious Liberty"	**Connect to Content: Social Studies, T304–T305** Compare the Passages, Make a Timeline	**Presentation Options, T308–T313** Speaking and Listening Publish and Present Inquiry Space Present Writing
		Summative Assessment and Next Steps, T318–T320

Writing

Extended Writing 2: Expository Essay, T260–T261 Plan	**Extended Writing 2: Expository Essay, T262–T263** Draft	**Extended Writing 2: Expository Essay, T264–T265** Revise: Peer Conferences

Writing Lesson Bank: Craft Minilessons, T268–T269

Teacher and Peer Conferences

Level Up with Leveled Readers
● **Beyond Level to Self-Selected Trade Book, T317**
The Bill of Rights

Level Up Writing
●●●● **From Good to Great, T290–T291**
- Purpose, Focus, and Organization
- Evidence and Elaboration
- Conventions
- Apply the Rubric

 ● **English Language Learners**
See ELL Small Group Guide, pp. 90–91

Content Area Connections

Content Area Reading
- Science, Social Studies, and the Arts

Inquiry Space
- Options for Project-Based Learning

LESSONS 1-2

We can use interactive features to read an online text.

OBJECTIVES

Draw on information from multiple print or digital sources, demonstrating the ability to locate an answer to a question quickly or to solve a problem efficiently.

Integrate information from several texts on the same topic in order to write or speak about the subject knowledgeably.

Provide a concluding statement or section related to the information or explanation presented.

Review the key ideas expressed and draw conclusions in light of information and knowledge gained from the discussions.

Summarize a written text read aloud or information presented in diverse media and formats, including visually, quantitatively, and orally.

ELA ACADEMIC LANGUAGE
- access, *hyperlinks*
- Cognate: *accesar*

⏩ DIFFERENTIATED READING

⬤⬤ **Approaching Level** and **ELL** Read the text with students. Have partners work together to complete the graphic organizers and summarize the text orally.

⬤⬤ **On Level** and **Beyond Level** Have students read the text and access the interactive features independently. Complete the Reread activities during Small Group time.

TIME KiDS

The Long Road

Before Reading

Introduce the Genre Discuss the features of an online article. Scroll through "The Long Road" at <u>my.mheducation.com</u>. Clarify how to navigate through the article. Point out the interactive features, such as **hyperlinks** and **pop-up windows**.

Close Reading Online

Read

Take Notes Scroll back to the top. As you read the article aloud, ask questions to focus students on the problem of conserving the Serengeti and how people worked to solve it. Have students take notes using **Graphic Organizer 4**. After each section, have partners paraphrase the central ideas, giving text evidence. Make sure students understand words with Greek and Latin suffixes, such as *ecology* and *migration*.

Access Interactive Features Help students access the interactive features. Discuss what information these elements add to the text.

Summarize Review students' graphic organizers. Model using the information to summarize "The Long Road." Ask students to write a summary of the article, stating the problem and the actions people took to solve it. Partners should discuss their summaries.

Reread

Craft and Structure Have students reread parts of the article paying attention to text structure and author's craft. Discuss these questions.

- What text structure does the author use to organize the information?
- For what purpose did the author add the hyperlink?

Author's Perspective Tell students they will now reread to help them answer this question: *According to the author, why is the Serengeti important?* Have students skim the text and find reasons the Serengeti is important to humans and animals. Have partners share findings and discuss whether they agree with the author's perspective, or point of view.

Integrate

Make Connections

Text Connections Have students compare what they learned about putting plans into action with what they have learned about other plans in texts they have read in this unit.

Research Online

Navigate Links to Information Remind students that online texts may include **hyperlinks**, colored or underlined text on a Web page that connects to another Web page with related information. Have students generate questions they'd like answered about the Serengeti. Do an online search about the Serengeti. Model using a hyperlink to jump to another Web page. Discuss the information on the new Web page. Examine the information and list relevant facts, opinions, and details. Help students clarify their questions as needed.

Choosing Reliable Sites Tell students that finding credible primary and secondary sources is important. Explain that the last three letters in a URL can help them determine if a site is reliable. For example, government sites end in .gov and are usually credible. Tell students that .org are run by organizations. Some .org sites offer unbiased and helpful information, but many are biased. Guide students to find a .org Web site related to the topic of the Serengeti, and point out indicators of bias. Encourage students to scan Web sites for potential bias. Have them compare and contrast the sources they find.

Inspire Action

Protecting Wildlife Have students write about the question: *Why is it sometimes difficult for people to protect wildlife?* Have students make an outline of possible reasons and do research online to find facts supporting those reasons. Point out that often people must give up something to protect wildlife:

- The government of Tanzania gave up building a highway through the Serengeti.
- Some Maasai wanted the road for commerce and for access to medical care.

As students write, remind them to cite sources used and to end with a strong conclusion.

Independent Study

Choose a Topic Students should brainstorm questions related to the article. For example: *How have people implemented plans to conserve natural areas?* Have them choose a question to research. Help them clarify what they want to learn.

Conduct Research Remind students to use only reliable, unbiased sources. Encourage them to track the sources so they can cite them in a bibliography.

Present Have groups conduct a roundtable discussion on how people put plans into action.

ELL ENGLISH LANGUAGE LEARNERS

Author's Perspective Read the question with students and elicit the information they need to answer the question. *Did the author use the word* important *or similar words to talk about the Serengeti?* Discuss words or phrases, such as *significant* or *essential,* and review the meanings. *Where did you read about them?* As needed, have students look for the words in the second, fourth, and sixth paragraphs and reread the sentences around the words. *Does the information tell you why the Serengeti is important?* As needed, have students restate the reasons using: The author thinks the Serengeti is important because _____. For Beginning students use: I read about _____. The Serengeti is important for _____. *Do you agree with the author's perspective?* Have students express their opinions using: I agree/disagree with the author because _____.

🖉 READERS TO WRITERS

Encourage students to think about how they might use interactive features and hyperlinks in their own writing.

FORMATIVE ASSESSMENT

❯ STUDENT CHECK-IN

Have partners share something they learned using an online interactive feature. Then have them reflect using the Check-In routine.

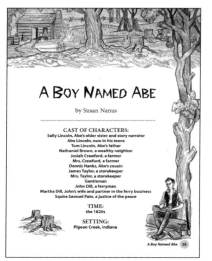

LEARNING GOALS

We can read fluently to perform a play.

OBJECTIVES

By the end of the year, read and comprehend literature, including stories, dramas, and poetry, at the high end of the grades 4–5 text complexity band independently and proficiently.

Read grade-level prose and poetry orally with accuracy, appropriate rate, expression, and automaticity on successive readings.

Use context to confirm or self-correct word recognition and understanding, rereading as necessary.

Review the key ideas expressed and draw conclusions in light of information and knowledge gained from the discussions.

Read, practice, and perform a play.

TEACH IN SMALL GROUP

You may wish to teach the Reader's Theater lesson during Small Group time and then have groups present their work to the class.

A Boy Named Abe

Introduce the Genre

Explain that *A Boy Named Abe* is a play set in Indiana in the 1820s that focuses on Abraham Lincoln's early years. It dramatizes stories from Lincoln's life and highlights his most famous qualities. Distribute the Elements of Drama handout and scripts from **Reader's Theater** pages 2–3 and 5–13.

- Review the features of a play.

- Review the cast of characters, time, and setting. Mention that plays about a real person may dramatize both true and made-up stories.

- Point out the stage directions that provide a summary of Lincoln's life.

Read the Play and Model Fluency

Model reading the play as students follow along in their scripts. As you read each part, state the name of the character and read the part, reading accurately and using appropriate phrasing and expression, or prosody.

Focus on Vocabulary Stop and discuss any vocabulary words that students may not know. You may wish to teach:

- deed
- quill
- merchandise
- gavel
- reverently

Monitor Comprehension As you read, check that students are understanding the characters, setting, and plot.

- Highlight Lincoln's birth in a log cabin and his love of reading.

- After reading the part of Sally, the narrator, ask students to identify what information she gives about the play.

- After reading each character part, ask partners to note the character's traits. Model how to find text evidence that tells them about the characters.

Assign Roles

You may wish to split the class into two groups. If necessary, you can assign the same role to more than one student.

Practice the Play

Allow students time to practice their parts in the play. Pair fluent readers with less fluent readers. Pairs can echo read or chorally read their parts. Work with less fluent readers to mark pauses in their scripts using one slash for a short pause and two slashes for longer pauses.

Throughout the week have students work on the Reader's Theater activities on **Reader's Theater Center Activity Card 39**.

Once students have practiced reading their parts, allow students time to practice performing the script. Remind them that nonverbal communication is an important part of portraying a character and provide examples.

Extend: Dress the Part

Costumes and props can add to a performance and make it more interesting for the audience. Have students work in small groups to come up with one prop or costume for each character.

Ask students to think about props and costumes relevant to each character. The prop or costume should help reveal what the character is like. Have students discuss how a character's prop or costume might help an actor convey that character's personality and other characteristics to the audience through nonverbal messages.

Perform the Reader's Theater

- At the end of the week, have students perform the play in small groups or for the whole class.
- Discuss how performing a play aloud is different from reading it silently. Have students interpret both the verbal and nonverbal messages they saw during the play.
- Lead a class discussion on what it is like to be a particular character. What is that character thinking? Encourage students to make personal and emotional connections to the story and its characters.

Reread the Play

Remind students that a play's setting affects the characters and their actions. Characters may act differently depending on their location or time period. Reread *A Boy Named Abe* and pay attention to the setting and when it changes. Then discuss the following questions with students:

1. When and where does the play take place?
2. The scenes take place in different settings within Pigeon Creek, Indiana, in the 1820s. What are these settings?
3. How is the setting of each scene indicated?
4. What quality or ability of Abraham Lincoln's does each scene highlight?

ELL ENGLISH LANGUAGE LEARNERS

Practice the Play Review the features of a play with Beginning students: characters, setting, dialogue, stage directions. Have all students read aloud the lines for their roles. Listen to each student practice their lines and ask: Which words or phrases do you find difficult to pronounce? Model the words and phrases slowly for students as they practice them. Then review the stage directions and ask them to think about whether they are saying the lines correctly.

FORMATIVE ASSESSMENT

STUDENT CHECK-IN

Have partners reflect on how fluently they read their lines.

LESSONS 1-2

"Popover!: The Ultimate Baked Bubble"

"Cooking with Electricity"

LEARNING GOALS

We can read and understand science texts.

OBJECTIVES

Determine two or more central, or main, ideas of a text and explain how they are supported by relevant, or key, details; summarize the text.

Compare and contrast the overall structure (e.g., chronology, comparison, cause/effect, problem/solution) of events, ideas, concepts, or information in two or more texts.

Analyze multiple accounts of the same event or topic, noting important similarities and differences in the point of view they represent.

Explain an author's perspective, or point of view, toward a topic in an informational text.

Use context (e.g., cause/effect relationships and comparisons in text) as a clue to the meaning of a word or phrase.

 Collect and record information using detailed observations and accurate measuring.

FORMATIVE ASSESSMENT

❯ STUDENT CHECK-IN

Have partners summarize the texts. Then have them reflect using the Check-In routine.

CONNECT TO CONTENT

My Goal I can read and understand science texts.

TAKE NOTES

Take notes and annotate as you read the passages "Popover!: The Ultimate Baked Bubble" and "Cooking with Electricity."

Look for the answer to the question: *What physical and chemical changes in matter might not happen if chefs do not follow instructions for baking and cooking food?*

_____

_____

_____

_____

_____

_____

_____

_____

_____

PASSAGE 1 EXPOSITORY TEXT

POPOVER!
The Ultimate Baked Bubble

Chefs have invented foods with air bubbles to make them light, moist, and tender. Air is a gas. Without air bubbles, breads would be crackers. For successful air-filled popovers that "pop up" many times their former size, you must understand solids, liquids, and gases—and physical and chemical changes. You must be both a scientist and a chef.

Popovers are made from a batter of flour, milk, eggs, and butter. The flour is a solid. The milk and eggs are liquids. If the butter is solid, melt it. Heating the butter causes a physical change as it turns from a solid into a liquid. Mixing the ingredients is also a physical change.

When you pour the batter into the tins, it is a thin and runny liquid. The heat inside a very hot oven bakes the top first, and then the sides and the bottom of the batter in each tin. It turns the outside batter into a solid while the inside is still liquid. As the batter heats up, it gives off steam, a gas, that can't escape through the well-sealed top crust. The rising steam raises the top crust.

Halfway through baking, turn the temperature down to medium. By this time, the outside of the popover is completely baked, while the inside is still very moist. The moderate heat helps to solidify the inside without burning the outside.

Baking causes a chemical change to the ingredients. The baked dough is a different type of matter than the ingredients. By studying the properties of solids, liquids, and gases, chefs use temperature changes and physical and chemical changes to bake popovers!

224 Unit 2 · Connect to Content

Reading/Writing Companion, p. 224

Take Notes Tell students they will be reading two passages that tell about cooking and baking. Explain that they will read independently using the Close Reading Routine. Remind them to annotate the text as they read and use the side columns to make notes.

For students who need more support, use the Read prompts to help them understand the text, and the Reread prompts to analyze the text, craft, and structure of each passage.

 Read

Cause and Effect DOK 1

What is an effect of baking popovers at a very high temperature to start? (The top, sides, and bottom bake while the inside is still liquid.)

Reread

Author's Purpose DOK 2

What is the author's purpose for writing "Popover!: The Ultimate Baked Bubble"? (The author's purpose is to explain why and how popovers pop up.)

A C T Access Complex Text

Specific Vocabulary

"Cooking with Electricity" includes science vocabulary that students may not know. Review strategies for finding the meaning of unfamiliar words, such as using context clues, word parts, or a dictionary. Point out the words *circuit, electrons, current,*

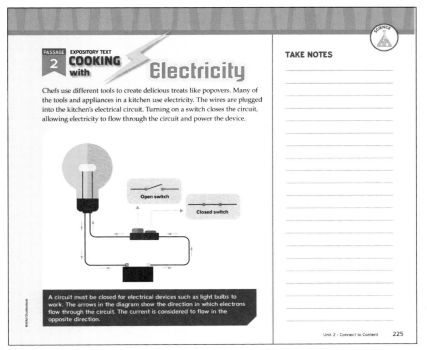

Reading/Writing Companion, p. 225

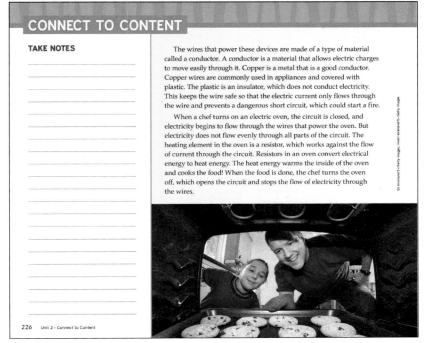

Reading/Writing Companion, p. 226

Read

Reread DOK 1

What happens when a switch is turned on in an electrical circuit? Reread the first paragraph to determine the answer. (The circuit closes, and electricity flows through to power a device.)

Read

Cause and Effect DOK 1

What causes an electric oven to warm up so it can cook food? (The resistor changes electrical energy to heat energy.)

Reread

Print and Graphic Features DOK 2

How does the diagram on page 225 help you understand the text? (The diagram shows how electrons flow through a circuit and how a switch opens and closes the circuit.)

conductor, and *resistors.* Have students use strategies to define each word.

• *What is a conductor?* (A conductor is material that allows electric charges to move through it easily.)

• *What happens when a circuit is closed?* (Electricity can flow through and power a device.)

ELL ENGLISH LANGUAGE LEARNERS

"Popover!: The Ultimate Baked Bubble"
Preteach vocabulary: *solid, liquid, gas, popover, steam, crust, chemical and physical changes* (Cognates: *sólido, líquido, gas, químico, físico*) Read the passage with students. After each paragraph, ask questions to help them identify and discuss key concepts. *What happens when the batter heats up?* (It gives off steam that cannot escape.) *What does the steam do to the top crust of the popover?* (It makes the top crust rise.)

"Cooking with Electricity"
Preteach vocabulary: *appliances, device, copper, energy, electricity, circuit, switch* (Cognate: *energía*) Read the passage with students and restate any challenging sentences. After each paragraph, ask questions to help them identify and discuss key concepts. *What are the wires of an electrical device plugged into in the kitchen?* (They are plugged into the kitchen's electrical circuit.) *What does the diagram on page 224 show?* (It shows how electrons flow through a circuit. A switch opens and closes the circuit. When a circuit is closed, electricity can flow through.)

CONNECT TO CONTENT • SCIENCE

- **We can compare two texts about cooking and baking.**
- **We can apply what we've learned to make and explain scientific observations.**

OBJECTIVES

Draw on information from multiple print or digital sources, demonstrating the ability to locate an answer to a question quickly or to solve a problem efficiently.

Summarize a written text read aloud or information presented in diverse media and formats, including visually, quantitatively, and orally.

 Make observations and measurements to identify materials based on their properties.

ELA ACADEMIC LANGUAGE

- *observations, causes, effects*
- Cognates: *observación, causa, efecto*

FORMATIVE ASSESSMENT

❯ STUDENT CHECK-IN

Compare Have partners share their Venn diagrams and responses on Reading/Writing Companion page 227.

Make Observations Have partners share their cause-and-effect charts.

Ask students to use the Check-In routine to reflect and fill in the bars.

COMPARE THE PASSAGES

Review your notes from "Popover!: The Ultimate Baked Bubble" and "Cooking with Electricity." Use your notes and the Venn diagram below to record how the information in both texts is alike and different.

Alike

Popover!: The Ultimate Baked Bubble
- If chefs don't turn down the temperature from high to medium halfway through baking, the popovers won't be baked correctly.
- The inside of the popovers will not be moist, and the outside of the popovers can become burned.
- If the butter isn't melted, the batter might not be thin and runny enough to bake properly.

Chefs must understand how heat changes ingredients when we make food.

Cooking with Electricity
- Chefs must understand when and how to use an electric oven.
- If a chef does not turn off an electric oven, the flow of electricity continues and may overcook the food in the oven.

Synthesize Information
Think about both texts. What information in both texts helps you understand how chefs use scientific principles in the kitchen? Write your response in your reader's notebook.

CHECK IN   1   2   3   4

Unit 2 • Connect to Content   227

Reading/Writing Companion, p. 227

Integrate

Compare the Passages

Explain Remind students that both of the passages they read are expository text and both give information about cooking and baking. Tell students they will complete a Venn diagram to show how the two passages are alike and different.

 Talk About It Have students work in small groups or with a partner to talk about the two texts and their similarities and differences. Have them review the characteristics of the genre. Partners or group members should share ideas with one another about the different ways each text presents information about cooking and baking.

Apply Have students use the notes they made on **Reading/Writing Companion** pages 224–226 and their Talk About It discussion to complete the Venn diagram and answer the Synthesize Information question on page 227.

✂ **Synthesize Information**   DOK 2

Explain Remind students that when they tell how the passages are alike they are synthesizing information. Students can use the middle of the Venn diagram to understand that information from both passages tells how heat helps cooks in the kitchen.

Model Point out that information in the last paragraph of "Popover!: The Ultimate Baked Bubble" and the last paragraph of "Cooking with Electricity" both explain how chefs use science principles in the kitchen.

Apply Have students cite evidence from both passages that helps them understand how chefs use science principles to prepare food. They can record their evidence in the center of the Venn diagram.

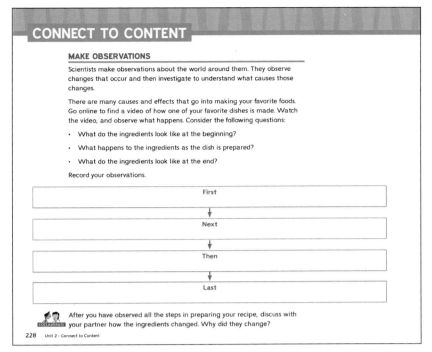

Reading/Writing Companion, p. 228

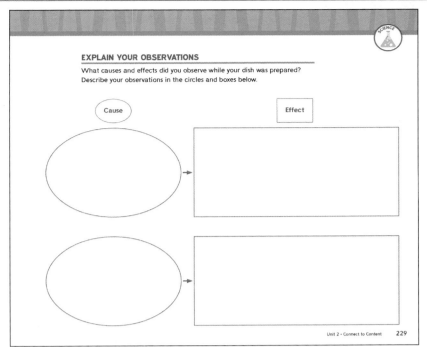

Reading/Writing Companion, p. 229

Make Observations

Explain Explain to students that they will observe the changes that happen when their favorite food is being made. For example, ask students to picture an egg frying in a pan. As it cooks, the liquid egg becomes solid. The clear white changes from transparent to a solid white color.

Talk About It Have partners review and discuss their understanding, making their observations on **Reading/Writing Companion** page 228. Have them discuss what they will be looking for in the video.

Apply Have partners independently watch the video of their dish being prepared and answer the questions about how the ingredients look at the beginning and the end and what happened to the ingredients. Have them complete their observations of each step. Then have partners discuss how and why the ingredients changed.

Explain Your Observations

Explain Remind students that they will explain what caused the changes they observed as the dish was prepared.

Guided Practice Have students work in pairs to discuss how they might explain their observations using causes and effects.

Analytical Writing **Apply** Have students fill in their cause-and-effect chart independently. Remind them to use their observations and the ideas they shared with their partner as they complete the chart.

ELL ENGLISH LANGUAGE LEARNERS

Synthesize Information Provide sentence frames for students to share text evidence they used to synthesize information. In "Popover!: The Ultimate Baked Bubble," we read that <u>liquid</u> ingredients become <u>solid</u> when they bake. There are both <u>physical</u> and <u>chemical</u> changes in popovers when we bake them with heat energy. In "Cooking with Electricity," we read that some chefs bake with an <u>electric</u> oven. When the chef turns it on, the circuit <u>closes</u>. Electricity flows through the <u>wires</u>. Then resistors turn this energy into <u>heat</u> energy.

Explain Observations, Apply Have students share their cause-and-effect charts. Review how specific words can express the cause-and-effect relationship in their observations such as *because*, *since*, *due to*, and *so*. Then have them restate cause and effect and express their observations in a cause-and-effect relationship: A <u>cause</u> leads to an effect. The result of a cause is the <u>effect</u>. Because <u>the cake was in the oven too long, the</u> effect was that <u>it burned</u>.

LESSONS 3-4

"Searching for Freedom"
"Supporting Religious Liberty"

LEARNING GOALS

We can read and understand social studies texts.

OBJECTIVES

Determine two or more central, or main, ideas of a text and explain how they are supported by relevant, or key, details; summarize the text.

Compare and contrast the overall structure (e.g., chronology, comparison, cause/effect, problem/solution) of events, ideas, concepts, or information in two or more texts.

Explain how an author uses reasons and evidence to support particular points in a text, identifying which reasons and evidence support which point(s).

Identify the author's purpose.

By the end of the year, read and comprehend informational texts, including history/social studies, science, and technical texts, at the high end of the grades 4–5 text complexity band independently and proficiently.

 Identify the contributions of significant individuals in American history.

FORMATIVE ASSESSMENT

⊘ STUDENT CHECK-IN

Have partners summarize the texts. Then have them reflect using the Check-In routine.

> ### CONNECT TO CONTENT
>
> **My Goal** I can read and understand social studies texts.
>
> #### TAKE NOTES
> Take notes and annotate as you read the passages "Searching for Freedom" and "Supporting Religious Liberty."
>
> Look for the answer to the question: *What motivated William Penn and Roger Williams to start new colonies?*
>
> _____
> _____
> _____
> _____
> _____
> _____
> _____
> _____
> _____
> _____
>
> #### INFORMATIONAL TEXT
> PASSAGE 1
> ## Searching for FREEDOM
>
> In England in the 1600s, it was illegal to belong to any church except the Church of England. Those who spoke out against the church faced persecution, or harsh treatment for their religious beliefs. The Pilgrims and the Puritans both faced persecution, and many decided to leave England and head to North America. Another religious group—the Quakers—also faced persecution.
>
> William Penn came from a wealthy and powerful family who belonged to the Church of England. Penn, however, decided to become a Quaker. The Quakers were very tolerant of other religions.
>
> ##### A Debt Repaid
> Penn's father had loaned money to King Charles II. When his father died, Penn asked the king to repay this debt with land in North America. The king gave him a large piece of land located west of New Jersey. Penn called it Pennsylvania, which means "Penn's Woods." He founded a colony where Quakers—and everyone else—could worship freely.
>
> 230   Unit 2 • Connect to Content

Reading/Writing Companion, p. 230

Take Notes Tell students they will be reading two passages that tell about establishing new colonies. Explain that they will read independently using the Close Reading Routine. Remind them to annotate the text as they read and use the side columns to make notes.

For students who need more support, use the Read prompts to help them understand the text, and the Reread prompts to analyze the text, craft, and structure of each passage.

Read

Problem and Solution DOK 1

What problem caused the Pilgrims and the Puritans to leave England? (They were persecuted for their religious beliefs and wanted religious freedom.)

Reread

Print and Graphic Features DOK 2

What text feature does the author include in "Searching for Freedom"? (The author includes headings that tell what each section is about.)

 Access Complex Text

Connection of Ideas

Help students understand the connection between William Penn's religious beliefs and his actions in "Searching for Freedom" using these questions:

• *Why did William Penn start a new colony in America?* (He

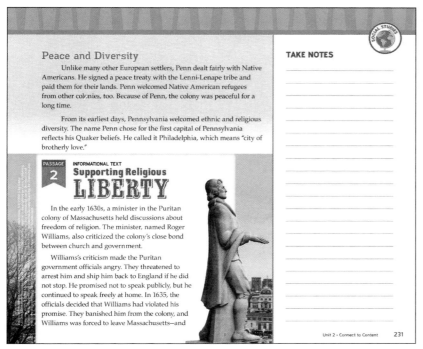

Peace and Diversity

Unlike many other European settlers, Penn dealt fairly with Native Americans. He signed a peace treaty with the Lenni-Lenape tribe and paid them for their lands. Penn welcomed Native American refugees from other colonies, too. Because of Penn, the colony was peaceful for a long time.

From its earliest days, Pennsylvania welcomed ethnic and religious diversity. The name Penn chose for the first capital of Pennsylvania reflects his Quaker beliefs. He called it Philadelphia, which means "city of brotherly love."

PASSAGE 2 · INFORMATIONAL TEXT
Supporting Religious LIBERTY

In the early 1630s, a minister in the Puritan colony of Massachusetts held discussions about freedom of religion. The minister, named Roger Williams, also criticized the colony's close bond between church and government.

Williams's criticism made the Puritan government officials angry. They threatened to arrest him and ship him back to England if he did not stop. He promised not to speak publicly, but he continued to speak freely at home. In 1635, the officials decided that Williams had violated his promise. They banished him from the colony, and Williams was forced to leave Massachusetts—and

TAKE NOTES

Unit 2 - Connect to Content 231

Reading/Writing Companion, p. 231

CONNECT TO CONTENT

TAKE NOTES

his family.

Williams then traveled south of Boston and bought land from the Narragansett Native Americans. In 1636, he established a colony in what is now Rhode Island.

In 1644, Williams's colony took the revolutionary step of granting liberty to all of its inhabitants, including Jews, Native Americans, and other non-Christians. The colonial charter promised that no person would be "punished, disquieted, or called in question for any differences in opinion on matters of religion."

Rhode Island was also the first American colony to guarantee separation of church and state. Williams's colony remained a sanctuary for people of all faiths throughout the colonial era.

Roger Williams was forced to leave his family when he was banished from the colony of Massachusetts in 1635.

232 Unit 2 - Connect to Content

Reading/Writing Companion, p. 232

Read

Cause and Effect DOK 1

What happened as a result of the way William Penn treated Native Americans and people of all religions and ethnic groups? (The colony of Pennsylvania was peaceful for a long time.)

Read

Ask and Answer Questions DOK 2

What question might you ask to better understand what made Rhode Island different from other American colonies? (Sample response: *What kinds of people were interested in Roger Williams's colony?*)

Reread

Author's Purpose DOK 2

What is the author's purpose in "Supporting Religious Liberty"? (The author's purpose is to tell how the colony of Rhode Island was founded as a place where all religions were allowed.)

needed a place where he and other Quakers could worship freely.)

• *How did Quaker beliefs about other religions affect Pennsylvania?* (Since the Quakers were tolerant of other religions, the colony was diverse.)

• *How did Quaker beliefs affect Penn's treatment of Native Americans?* (Penn treated Native Americans fairly as the Quakers welcomed diversity.)

ELL ENGLISH LANGUAGE LEARNERS

"Searching for Freedom"
Preteach vocabulary: *persecution, debt, worship, ethnic, religious, colony* (Cognates: *persecucion, étnico*) Read the passage with students and restate challenging sentences, as needed. After each paragraph, ask questions to help them identify and discuss key concepts. *What is this first section about?* (King Charles II paid back a loan from William Penn's father with land in America. William went to live there.) *What is the next section about?* (peace and diversity in the colony of Pennsylvania)

"Supporting Religious Liberty"
Preteach vocabulary: *liberty, banished, guarantee, inhabitants, disquieted, sanctuary* (Cognates: *garantía, habitante, santuario*) Read the passage with students. After each paragraph, ask questions to help them identify and discuss key concepts. *What did Roger Williams do when he was forced to leave Massachusetts?* (He started the new colony of Rhode Island.) *Who came to live in Rhode Island?* (Jews and non-Christians who were persecuted for their religion.) *Why did they come to Rhode Island?* (for religious freedom)

LEARNING GOALS

- We can compare two social studies texts about how and why people established American colonies.

- We can apply what we've learned to make a timeline.

OBJECTIVES

Determine two or more central, or main, ideas of a text and explain how they are supported by relevant, or key, details; summarize the text.

Draw on information from multiple print or digital sources, demonstrating the ability to locate an answer to a question quickly or to solve a problem efficiently.

Integrate information from several texts on the same topic in order to write or speak about the subject knowledgeably.

Write routinely over extended time frames (time for research, reflection, and revision) and shorter time frames (a single sitting or a day or two) for a range of discipline-specific tasks, purposes, and audiences.

Identify the contributions of significant individuals in American history.

ELA ACADEMIC LANGUAGE

- *timeline, vertical, horizontal, digital, hyperlinks, captions*
- Cognates: *vertical, horizontal, digital*

FORMATIVE ASSESSMENT

❯ STUDENT CHECK-IN

Compare Have partners share their Venn diagrams and responses on Reading/Writing Companion page 233.

Make a Timeline Have partners share their timelines.

Ask students to use the Check-In routine to reflect and fill in the bars.

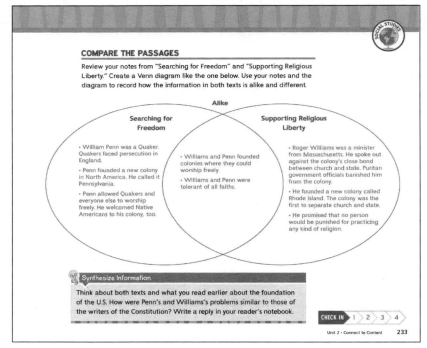

Reading/Writing Companion, p. 233

Compare the Passages

Explain Remind students that both the passages they read are expository texts and both give information about how and why people established new American colonies. Tell students they will complete a Venn diagram to show how the two passages are alike and different.

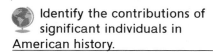

Talk About It Have students work in small groups or with a partner to talk about the two texts and their similarities and differences. Have them review the characteristics of the genre. Partners or group members should share ideas with one another about the different ways each text presents information about how and why people established new American colonies.

Apply Have students use the notes they made on **Reading/Writing Companion** pages 230–232 and their Talk About It discussion to complete the Venn diagram and answer the Synthesize Information question on page 233.

Synthesize Information   DOK 2

Explain Readers can think about information from two passages and connect the ideas to provide the answer to a question.

Model *I can use information from both passages to answer the question, How were the problems of Penn and Williams similar to those of the writers of the U.S. Constitution?* Point out the mention of the Puritans in the first paragraph of "Searching for Freedom" on page 230. Then have students reread what the Puritan colony of Massachusetts was like in the first paragraph of "Supporting Religious Liberty" on page 231.

Apply Have students cite more evidence from both passages that helps them understand how Penn and Williams faced problems similar to the people who wrote the U.S. Constitution.

CONNECT TO CONTENT

MAKE A TIMELINE

Williams's and Penn's colonies weren't the only ones that offered religious choice. In 1632, the Catholic-practicing George Calvert, the 1st Lord Baltimore, was granted a charter by England's King Charles I for a North American settlement. In this settlement, people could worship freely.

In 1634, his son, Cecil Calvert, the 2nd Lord Baltimore, established the colony of Maryland. This colony was a haven for Catholics who fled England's religious persecution. The Calverts offered religious freedom to all Christian settlers, Protestant or Catholic. These rights were confirmed in 1649 by the Act of Toleration, considered a milestone of religious liberty. Unfortunately, the act proved to be short-lived. When Anglicans outnumbered Catholics in Maryland, the colony's new Anglican leaders repealed the act in 1654.

A timeline shows the order in which key events happened during a certain time period. Timelines can be vertical or horizontal.

- Research the key events that occurred between 1634 and 1681. Include events that relate to Williams, Penn, and the 2nd Lord Baltimore.

- Create a digital timeline that includes photographs and hyperlinks. Or make an illustrated poster with captions about each event.

Something I learned while working on this timeline is

_____

_____

_____

_____

2nd Lord Baltimore establishes the colony of Maryland.

◆1634

1654

◆1681

234   Unit 2 • Connect to Content

Reading/Writing Companion, p. 234

Make a Timeline

Explain and Model Remind students that a timeline organizes events chronologically, or in the order in which they happened. Review the dates mentioned in the text on page 234 and what happened on each one. Add the event that took place in 1649 (the Act of Toleration gave religious freedom to all Christians) to the timeline on the right side of the page.

Talk About It Have partners or small groups of students share their research plans for learning more about the early years of the Maryland colony. Then have them discuss how they plan to present their findings.

Apply After their discussions, have students complete the timeline on **Reading/Writing Companion** page 234.

Additional Content Area Reading

For more content-area reading, use these resources.

Content Area Reading Blackline Masters

Additional texts and activities related to grade-level Science, Social Studies, and Arts topics.

Online Component

If You Lived at the Time of the American Revolution

An expository text about America's fight for independence.

Classroom Library

The Boy Who Drew Birds

A biography of naturalist and ornithologist John James Audubon, the great painter of birds.

Literature Anthology, pp. 144–155

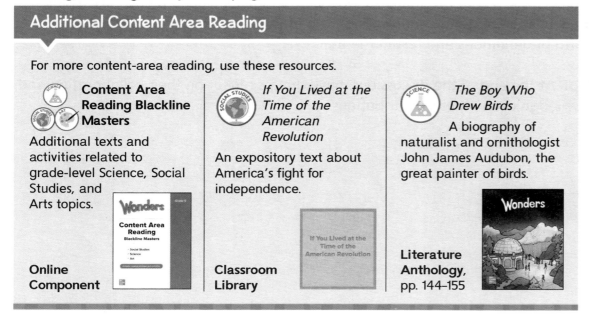

Make a Timeline, Apply Help students write sentences for adding events to their timelines. Review the event from 1634 as described on page 234, explaining the meaning of words such as *haven* and *persecution*. Show the event in the timeline on the page. Then ask: *What happened in 1654?* (New Anglican leaders of Maryland repealed the Act of Toleration.) Remind students to write short sentences to complete the timeline. *How can we write what happened in 1654 in a shorter way for the timeline?* (The Act of Toleration was repealed.)

LEARNING GOALS

We synthesize information from multiple texts.

OBJECTIVES

By the end of the year, read and comprehend literature, including stories, dramas, and poetry, at the high end of the grades 4–5 text complexity band independently and proficiently.

By the end of the year, read and comprehend informational texts, including history/social studies, science, and technical texts, at the high end of the text complexity band independently and proficiently.

Engage effectively in a range of collaborative discussions (one-on-one, in groups, and teacher-led) with diverse partners on grade 5 topics and texts, building on others' ideas and expressing their own clearly.

Come to discussions prepared, having read or studied required material; explicitly draw on that preparation and other information known about the topic to explore ideas under discussion.

Follow agreed-upon rules for discussions and carry out assigned roles.

Review the key ideas expressed and draw conclusions in light of information and knowledge gained from the discussions.

FORMATIVE ASSESSMENT

⊙ STUDENT CHECK-IN

Have students reflect on how well they synthesized the unit's information. Then have them reflect using the Check-In routine.

MULTIMODAL

Make Connections

Connect to a Big Idea

Text to Text Write this Big Idea question on the board: *What does it take to put a plan into action?* Divide the class into small groups. Each group will compare the information they learned during the course of the unit in order to answer the Big Idea question. Model how to compare this information by using examples from the **Leveled Readers** and this unit's selections.

Collaborative Conversations Have students review their notes and organizers before they begin their discussions. Have each group pick one student to take notes. Explain that each group will use an Accordion Foldable® to record their ideas. You may wish to model how to use an Accordion Foldable® to record comparisons of texts.

Dinah Zike's
FOLDABLES
Study Organizer

Present Ideas and Synthesize Information When students finish their discussions, ask for a volunteer from each group to read their notes aloud. After each group has presented their ideas, ask: *What are the five most important things we have learned about putting a plan into action?* Lead a class discussion and list students' ideas on the board. Have students share any personal or emotional connections they felt to the texts they read and listened to over the course of the unit.

Building Knowledge Encourage students to continue building knowledge about the Big Idea. Display the online Unit Bibliography and have students search online for articles and other resources related to the Big Idea. After each group has presented their ideas, ask: *What are the consequences of inaction?* Lead a class discussion asking students to use the information from their charts to answer the question in the form of definitions and restatements.

Reflect At the end of the discussions, have groups reflect on their collaboration and acknowledge each other's contributions.

Reflect on Your Learning

Talk About It Reflect on what you learned in this unit. Then talk with a partner about how you did.

I am really proud of how I can _____

_____

_____

Something I need to work more on is _____

_____

> Share a goal you have with a partner.

My Goal Set a goal for Unit 3. In your reader's notebook, write about what you can do to get there.

Unit 2 · Reflect on Your Learning   235

Reading/Writing Companion, p. 235

Reflect on Your Learning

Talk About It

Remind students that one meaning of reflect is to think carefully about **COLLABORATE** something you have done. Give students time to reflect on what they have learned in Unit 1. Ask: *How did the skills and strategies you learned help you with reading and writing in this unit? How can the things you learned help you do other things?* Have partners answer these questions together, using their reader's and writer's notebooks to support their discussion.

Then guide partners to discuss what they did in Unit 1 that made them feel proud and what they need to continue working on. Have students complete the sentence starters on page 235 of the **Reading/Writing Companion**. Encourage them to review their work and feedback they received throughout the unit. They can also review their completed My Goals bars on pages 125, 151, 177, and 199 of the Reading/Writing Companion.

Review students' reflections and guide them in forming a plan to continue developing skills they need to work on.

Set a Unit 3 Goal

 Have students set their own learning goal for the next unit. Have partners or small groups flip through Unit 3 of the Reading/Writing Companion to get an idea of what to expect. Pairs can discuss their goals and plans for achieving them. Point out that sharing goals with others can help us achieve them. Then have students record their goal and plan in their reader's notebook.

LEARNING GOALS

We can reflect on our learning and set our own learning goals.

OBJECTIVES

Engage effectively in a range of collaborative discussions (one-on-one, in groups, and teacher-led) with diverse partners on grade 5 topics and texts, building on others' ideas and expressing their own clearly.

Reflect on learning.

HABITS OF LEARNING

I am a part of a community of learners.

Ask students to reflect on the unit's Habit of Learning and connect the habit to their life outside of school. Ask:

- Why is it important to be able to share information with others?
- How are out-of-school activity groups, such as sports teams or scouting groups, also "communities of learners"?
- Why is it important to listen actively and build on others' thoughts as a member of one of those groups?

FORMATIVE ASSESSMENT

❯ **STUDENT CHECK-IN**

Have students share one thing they are proud of learning. Then have them reflect using the Check-In routine.

LEARNING GOALS

- We can use effective speaking strategies.
- We can use effective listening strategies.

OBJECTIVES

Pose and respond to specific questions by making comments that contribute to the discussion and elaborate on the remarks of others.

Report on a topic or text or present an opinion, sequencing ideas logically and using appropriate facts and relevant, descriptive details to support main ideas or themes; speak clearly at an understandable pace.

Summarize the points a speaker or media source makes and explain how each claim is supported by reasons and evidence, and identify and analyze any logical fallacies.

Adapt speech to a variety of contexts and tasks, using formal English when appropriate to task and situation.

DIGITAL TOOLS

Students may use these tools:

How to Give a Presentation (Collaborative Conversations Video)

Presentation Checklist

FORMATIVE ASSESSMENT

STUDENT CHECK-IN

Speaking Have students use the Presentation Rubric to reflect on their presentations.

Listening Have partners share key ideas they heard during the presentations.

Then have students reflect using the Check-In routine.

TEACHER CHOICE

As you wrap up the unit, invite students to present their work to small groups, the class, or a larger audience. Choose from among these options:

✓ **Reader's Theater:** Have students perform the play on page T296.

✓ **Research and Inquiry Projects:** Small groups can share their completed projects. See page T26, T108, and T188.

✓ **Inquiry Space:** Students can give multimodal presentations of the work that they developed using Inquiry Space. See page T310.

✓ **Publishing Celebrations:** Have students share one of the pieces of writing they worked on throughout the unit. See page T312.

Use the Speaking and Listening minilesson below to help students prepare.

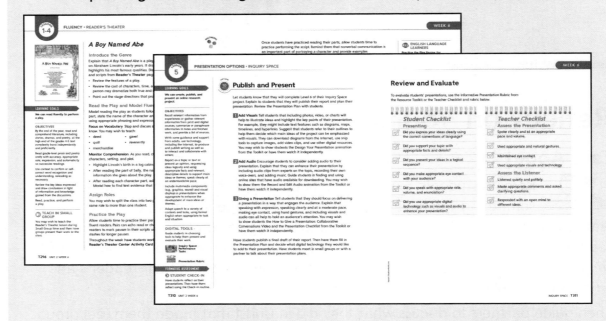

OPTION 10 mins

Speaking

Explain to students that when orally giving a formal presentation to a large audience, such as a whole class, they should remember these strategies:

- Rehearse the presentation in front of a friend and ask for feedback.
- Speak slowly and clearly, using correct pronunciation and an appropriate speaking rate, volume, and tone.
- Emphasize points nonverbally, using appropriate hand gestures or facial expressions, so that the audience can follow important ideas.
- Stand up straight and make eye contact with the audience.

Remind students to time themselves during practice sessions to allow enough time for questions from the audience following the presentation.

Listening

Use the strategies to encourage participation and develop oral proficiency:

- Give students ample time to present and respond.
- Give positive confirmation. Repeat correct responses in a clear, loud voice and at a slower pace to motivate students.
- Repeat responses to model the proper form for incorrect grammar or pronunciation.

Remind students that an effective listener

- listens for facts and key ideas about the topic;
- stays focused on the speaker's presentation and ignores distractions;
- listens without interruption but is prepared to ask questions and provide constructive feedback after the presentation is finished;
- listens carefully to evaluate the speaker's point of view;
- articulates thoughts clearly and builds upon the ideas of others.

After the presentation, invite students to write down any questions they have during the presentation. Guide a discussion, asking some students to paraphrase or summarize the key ideas. You may wish to have students complete the Listening Checklist from the Resource Toolkit.

Discuss how listeners would strive to maintain respect and careful attention in whatever setting the presentation took place.

Presentation Rubric

4 Excellent	3 Good	2 Fair	1 Unsatisfactory
• presents the information clearly • includes many facts and details • presents ideas in a logical sequence • includes sophisticated observations	• presents the information adequately • provides adequate facts and details • sequences ideas adequately • includes relevant observations	• attempts to present information • offers few or vague facts and details • struggles with sequencing ideas • includes few or irrelevant personal observations	• shows little grasp of the informative task • presents irrelevant information • lacks a logical sequence of ideas • reflects extreme difficulty with research or presentation

LESSON 5

Publish and Present

LEARNING GOALS

We can create, publish, and present an online research project.

OBJECTIVES

Recall relevant information from experiences or gather relevant information from print and digital sources; summarize or paraphrase information in notes and finished work, and provide a list of sources.

With some guidance and support from adults, use technology, including the Internet, to produce and publish writing as well as to interact and collaborate with others;

Report on a topic or text or present an opinion, sequencing ideas logically and using appropriate facts and relevant, descriptive details to support main ideas or themes; speak clearly at an understandable pace.

Include multimedia components (e.g., graphics, sound) and visual displays in presentations when appropriate to enhance the development of main ideas or themes.

Adapt speech to a variety of contexts and tasks, using formal English when appropriate to task and situation.

DIGITAL TOOLS

Guide students in choosing tools to help them present and evaluate their work.

Inquiry Space Performance Tasks

Presentation Rubric

FORMATIVE ASSESSMENT

❯ STUDENT CHECK-IN

Have students reflect on their presentations. Then have them reflect using the Check-In routine.

Let students know that they will complete Level 6 of their Inquiry Space project. Explain to students that they will publish their report and plan their presentation. Review the Presentation Plan with students.

1 Add Visuals Tell students that including photos, video, or charts will help to illustrate ideas and highlight the key points of their presentation. For example, they might include text features such as diagrams, maps, timelines, and hyperlinks. Suggest that students refer to their outlines to help them decide which main ideas of the project can be emphasized with visuals. They can download diagrams from the Internet, use snip tools to capture images, add video clips, and use other digital resources. You may wish to show students the Design Your Presentation animation from the Toolkit or have them watch it independently.

2 Add Audio Encourage students to consider adding audio to their presentation. Explain that they can enhance their presentation by including audio clips from experts on the topic, recording their own voice-overs, and adding music. Guide students in finding and using online sites that have audio available for downloading. You may wish to show them the Record and Edit Audio animation from the Toolkit or have them watch it independently.

3 Giving a Presentation Tell students that they should focus on delivering a presentation in a way that engages the audience. Explain that speaking with expression, speaking clearly and at a moderate pace, making eye contact, using hand gestures, and including visuals and audio can all help to hold an audience's attention. You may wish to show students the How to Give a Presentation: Collaborative Conversations Video and the Presentation Checklist from the Toolkit or have them watch it independently.

Have students publish a final draft of their report. Then have them fill in the Presentation Plan and decide what digital technology they would like to add to their presentation. Have students meet in small groups or with a partner to talk about their presentation plans.

Review and Evaluate

To evaluate students' presentations, use the Informative Presentation Rubric from the Resource Toolkit or the Teacher Checklist and rubric below.

Student Checklist

Presenting

☑ Did you express your ideas clearly using the correct conventions of language?

☑ Did you support your topic with appropriate facts and details?

☑ Did you present your ideas in a logical sequence?

☑ Did you make appropriate eye contact with your audience?

☑ Did you speak with appropriate rate, volume, and enunciation?

☑ Did you use appropriate digital technology such as visuals and audio to enhance your presentation?

Teacher Checklist

Assess the Presentation

☑ Spoke clearly and at an appropriate pace and volume.

☑ Used appropriate and natural gestures.

☑ Maintained eye contact.

☑ Used appropriate visuals and technology.

Assess the Listener

☑ Listened quietly and politely.

☑ Made appropriate comments and asked clarifying questions.

☑ Responded with an open mind to different ideas.

LESSON 5

Present Writing

LEARNING GOALS

- We can use effective strategies to present our writing.
- We can use effective strategies to listen to presentations.

OBJECTIVES

Analyze how visual and multimedia elements contribute to the meaning, tone, or beauty of a text.

With some guidance and support from adults, use technology, including the Internet, to produce and publish writing as well as to interact and collaborate with others.

Summarize the points a speaker makes and explain how each claim is supported by reasons and evidence.

Report on a topic or text or present an opinion, sequencing ideas logically and using appropriate facts and relevant, descriptive details to support main ideas or themes; speak clearly at an understandable pace.

Include multimedia components and visual displays in presentations when appropriate to enhance the development of main ideas or themes.

Adapt speech to a variety of contexts and tasks, using formal English when appropriate to task and situation.

 TEACH IN SMALL GROUP

You may wish to arrange groups of various abilities to complete their presentations, evaluate each other's work, and discuss portfolio choices.

FORMATIVE ASSESSMENT

 STUDENT CHECK-IN

Presenting Have partners use the Presentation Rubric to reflect on their presentations.

Listening Have partners share key ideas they heard during presentations.

Have students reflect using the Check-In routine.

Select the Writing

Now is an opportunity for students to share one of the pieces of writing that they have worked on through the unit. Have them review their writing and select one piece to present. You may wish to invite parents or students from other classes to the Publishing Celebrations.

Preparing for Presentations

Tell students that they will need to prepare in order to best present their writing. Allow students time to rehearse their presentations. Encourage them to reread their writing a few times. This will help them become more familiar with their pieces so that they will not have to read word by word as they present.

Students should consider any visuals or digital elements that they may want to use to present their writing. Discuss a few possible options with students.

- Can they show any objects that relate to their topics?
- Are there photographs, charts, tables, maps, or graphs that would give the audience additional information about the topic?
- Have they created any materials that might provide additional information about the topic?

Students can practice presenting to a partner in the classroom. They can also practice with family members at home, or in front of a mirror. Share the following checklist with students to help them focus on important parts of their presentation as they rehearse. Discuss each point on the checklist.

✓ Speaking Checklist

Review the Speaking Checklist with students as they practice.

- ☐ Have all of your notes and visuals ready.
- ☐ Take a few deep breaths.
- ☐ Stand up straight.
- ☐ Look at the audience.
- ☐ Speak loudly enough so everyone can hear.
- ☐ Speak with enthusiasm to generate interest.
- ☐ Use appropriate gestures.
- ☐ Hold your visual aids so everyone can see them.
- ☐ Point to relevant features of the visual aids as you speak.

Listening to Presentations

Remind students that they will be part of the audience for other students' presentations. A listener serves an important role. Review with students the following Listening Checklist.

✓ Listening Checklist

DURING THE PRESENTATION

☐ Listen to the speaker carefully.

☐ Pay attention to how the speaker organizes information logically.

☐ Notice how the speaker supports the topic with relevant, descriptive details.

☐ Write one question or comment you have about the information presented.

AFTER THE PRESENTATION

☐ Summarize the speaker's main points.

☐ Tell why you liked the presentation.

☐ Ask a question or share a comment you have based on the information presented.

☐ Draw conclusions based on class discussion about the information.

Portfolio Choice

Ask students to select one finished piece of writing, as well as two revisions, to include in their writing portfolio. As students consider their choices, have them use the questions below.

FINISHED WRITING	WRITING ENTRY REVISIONS
Does your writing	**Do your revisions show**
• clearly state your topic and provide details related to the topic? • use the correct voice (formal or informal) based on the audience? • follow standard English conventions with little to no spelling or grammatical errors? • use precise language, concrete words, and figurative language as warranted? • demonstrate neatness when published? • demonstrate legible cursive writing skills, if handwritten?	• a stronger opening and closing? • a clear organizational structure or sequence? • added facts, examples, and details? • ideas that transition naturally? • only information that supports the topic? • improved cursive writing, if handwritten, so that it can be read easily by others?

Explain that students will also have the opportunity to improve their finished writing. Use the suggestions on the Level Up Writing lesson on pages T290–T291 to meet students' individual needs.

Leveled Reader

OBJECTIVES

Explain the relationships or interactions between two or more individuals, events, ideas, or concepts in a historical, scientific, or technical text based on specific information in the text.

Determine the meaning of general academic and domain-specific words and phrases in a text relevant to a grade 5 topic or subject area.

By the end of the year, read and comprehend informational texts, including history/social studies, science, and technical texts, at the high end of the grades 4–5 text complexity band independently and proficiently.

Review the key ideas expressed and draw conclusions in light of information and knowledge gained from the discussions.

Approaching Level
to On Level

The Bill of Rights

Preview Discuss what students remember about the Bill of Rights. Tell them they will be reading a more challenging version of *The Bill of Rights*.

Vocabulary Use the Visual Vocabulary Cards and routine to review.

▶ **Specific Vocabulary** Review with students the following social studies words that are new to this title. Model how to use context clues or the glossary to determine the meanings of *personal liberties, independent,* and *persecution.*

▶ **Connection of Ideas** Students may need help connecting how the information in the text features, such as sidebars and timelines, connects to the information on the page. See pages 8, 10, and 11. With students, summarize the information in the text. Then compare with the information in the text feature.

▶ **Sentence Structure** Students may need help understanding the difference between rhetorical questions and questions the author poses to the reader. See pages 2 and 17. Chorally read the last paragraph on page 2 with students and ask them to state what the paragraph is about. Have students find the sentence before the questions. Then ask: *Are these the colonists' questions or the narrator's questions to the reader?* (the colonists' questions) *Why does the author include them?* (to show readers what kind of decisions the colonists will need to make) Repeat a similar procedure for the other questions.

Ask students to complete the Respond to Reading on page 18. Have students complete the Paired Read and hold Literature Circles.

On Level
to Beyond Level

The Bill of Rights

Leveled Reader

Preview Discuss what students remember about the Bill of Rights. Tell them they will be reading a more challenging version of *The Bill of Rights*.

Vocabulary Use the Visual Vocabulary Cards and routine to review.

▶ **Specific Vocabulary** Review the following social studies words that are new to this title: *pre-revolution, negotiation,* and *compensated.* Model using vocabulary strategies, such as word parts, context clues, or using a glossary.

▶ **Connection of Ideas** Students may need help connecting and synthesizing ideas from page to page and section to section. After reading page 4, model for students how to use text structure to connect the information they just read to the information from page 3. As students continue reading, have partners talk about how the information they read in one section relates or connects to information from a previous section.

▶ **Sentence Structure** Explain that sometimes the narrator of an expository text will interrupt the flow of information to pose a question to readers. Readers should try to answer this question for themselves before continuing to read. Point out the question in the first paragraph on page 17, and read it aloud with students: *Can you name any of these other amendments?* Before students read on, encourage them to answer the question, thinking about what they have learned about amendments.

Ask students to complete the Respond to Reading on page 18. Have students complete the Paired Read and hold Literature Circles.

OBJECTIVES

Determine the meaning of general academic and domain-specific words and phrases in a text relevant to a grade 5 topic or subject area.

Determine the meaning of general academic and domain-specific words and phrases in a text relevant to a grade 5 topic or subject area.

Compare and contrast the overall structure of events, ideas, concepts, or information in two or more texts.

By the end of the year, read and comprehend literature, including stories, drama, and poetry, at the high end of the grades 4–5 text complexity band independently and proficiently.

By the end of the year, read and comprehend informational texts, including history/social studies, science, and technical texts, at the high end of the grades 4–5 text complexity band independently and proficiently.

Leveled Reader

OBJECTIVES

Explain the relationships or interactions between two or more individuals, events, ideas, or concepts in a historical, scientific, or technical text based on specific information in the text.

Determine the meaning of general academic and domain-specific words and phrases in a text relevant to a grade 5 topic or subject area.

By the end of the year, read and comprehend informational texts, including history/social studies, science, and technical texts, at the high end of the grades 4–5 text complexity band independently and proficiently.

English Language Learners to On Level

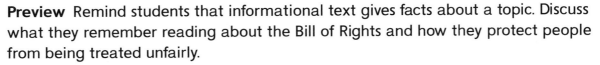

The Bill of Rights

Preview Remind students that informational text gives facts about a topic. Discuss what they remember reading about the Bill of Rights and how they protect people from being treated unfairly.

Vocabulary Use the Visual Vocabulary Cards and routine to review the vocabulary. Point out cognates: *comités, debatía, representantes, resolver, situación, unión.*

▶ **Specific Vocabulary** Show students how to identify context clues that will help them figure out difficult words, such as *merchants* in the second paragraph on page 4. Point out the context clue "business interests" in the following sentence and use it to help students state a definition. Repeat for other words.

▶ **Connection of Ideas** Help students understand how information in the sidebars connects to the content on the page. With students, summarize the information in the text. Then compare the information in the sidebar. For example, in the main text on page 9, the author explains what the Bill of Rights is. Then, in the sidebar, the author clarifies the information by explaining that the Bill of Rights is not a separate document.

▶ **Sentence Structure** Point out complex text structures as you read, such as the original amendment text on page 11. Explain to students that the amendment reflects a style of writing that is more formal than what we use today. The language is legal language of the time. Paraphrase the amendment for students.

Ask students to complete the Respond to Reading on page 18. Have students complete the Paired Read and hold Literature Circles.

Beyond Level
to Self-Selected Trade Book

Independent Reading

Leveled Reader | Advanced Level Trade Book

Together with students, identify the particular focus of their reading based on the text they choose. Students who have chosen the same title will work in groups to closely read the selection.

Taking Notes Assign a graphic organizer for students to use to take notes as they read. Reinforce a specific comprehension focus from the unit by choosing one of the graphic organizers that best fits the book.

EXAMPLES	
Fiction	**Informational Text**
Theme	Text Structure: Problem and Solution
Graphic Organizer 5	Graphic Organizer 4

Ask and Answer Questions Remind students to ask questions as they read. Suggest that they use self-stick notes to record and mark their questions. As students meet, have them discuss the section that they have read. They can discuss the questions they noted and work together to find text evidence to support their answers. You may want to have students write the responses to their questions.

EXAMPLES	
Fiction	**Informational Text**
What is the theme of this story?	Identify key details from the text. See how they are connected. Use them to find the main idea.

Literature Circles Suggest that students hold Literature Circles and share interesting facts or favorite parts from the books they read.

OBJECTIVES

By the end of the year, read and comprehend literature, including stories, dramas, and poetry, at the high end of the grades 4–5 text complexity band independently and proficiently.

By the end of the year, read and comprehend informational texts, including history/social studies, science, and technical texts, at the high end of the grades 4–5 text complexity band independently and proficiently.

Summative Assessment

Online Assessment Center

Wonders Unit Assessments

Unit 2 Tested Skills

COMPREHENSION	VOCABULARY	GRAMMAR	WRITING
• Plot: Setting • Theme • Poetic Elements: Form and Line Breaks • Poetic Elements: Repetition and Rhyme • Text Structure: Problem and Solution • Text Structure: Sequence • Text Features: Headings and Timelines • Comparative Reading	• Personification • Context Clues • Homographs	• Kinds of Nouns • Plural Forms and Appositives • Possessive Nouns • Prepositional Phrases	• Expository Writing Prompt

Additional Assessment Options

Fluency

Conduct assessments individually using the differentiated passages in **Fluency Assessment**. Students' expected fluency goal for this unit is 111–131 words correct per minute (WCPM) with an accuracy rate of 95% or higher.

ELL Assessment

Assess English Language Learner proficiency and track student progress using the **English Language Development Assessment**. This resource provides unit assessments and rubrics to evaluate students' progress in the areas of listening and reading comprehension, vocabulary, grammar, speaking, and writing. These assessments can also be used to determine the language proficiency levels for subsequent sets of instructions.

Making the Most of Assessment Results

Make data-based grouping decisions by using the following reports to verify assessment results. For additional student support options refer to the reteaching and enrichment opportunities.

ONLINE ASSESSMENT CENTER

- *Gradebook*

DATA DASHBOARD

- *Recommendations Report*
- *Activity Report*
- *Skills Report*
- *Progress Report*
- *Grade Card Report*

 Assign practice pages online for auto-grading.

Reteaching Opportunities with Intervention Online PDFs

IF STUDENTS SCORE . . .	THEN ASSIGN . . .
below 70% in **comprehension** . . .	tested skills using the **Comprehension PDF**
below 70% in **vocabulary** . . .	tested skills using the **Vocabulary PDF**
below 8 on **writing prompt** . . .	tested skills using the **Writing and Grammar PDF**
0–110 WCPM in **fluency** . . .	tested skills using the **Fluency PDF**

Use the **Phonics/Word Study PDF** *and* **Foundational Skills Kit** *for additional reteaching opportunities.*

Enrichment Opportunities

Beyond Level small group lessons and resources include suggestions for additional activities in the following areas to extend learning opportunities for gifted and talented students:

- *Leveled Readers*
- *Genre Passages*
- *Vocabulary*
- *Comprehension*
- *Leveled Reader Library Online*
- *Center Activity Cards*

Next Steps

NEXT STEPS FOR YOUR STUDENTS' PROGRESS . . .

Interpret the data you have collected from multiple sources throughout this unit, including formal and informal assessments.

Data Dashboard

Who — Regrouping Decisions

- Check student progress against your interpretation of the data, and regroup as needed.
- Determine how English Language Learners are progressing.
- Consider whether students are ready to Level Up or Accelerate.

What — Target Instruction

- Analyze data from multiple measures to decide whether to review and reinforce particular skills or concepts or whether you need to reteach them.
- Target instruction to meet students' strengths/needs.
- Use Data Dashboard recommendations to help determine which lessons to provide to different groups of students.

Coach and Classroom Videos

Methodology

How — Modify Instruction

- Vary materials and/or instructional strategies.
- Address students' social and emotional development.
- Provide students with opportunities for self-reflection and self-assessment.

AUTHOR INSIGHT

"The many essential decisions that educators make to help every student succeed should be informed by multiple sources of information, including daily observations of each student's performance, along with progress checks provided by progress monitoring and unit assessments."
—Dr. Jan Hasbrouck

NEXT STEPS FOR YOU . . .

As you prepare your students to move on to the next unit, don't forget to take advantage of the many opportunities available in your online course for self-evaluation and professional development.

PROFESSIONAL DEVELOPMENT

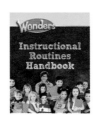

Instructional Routines

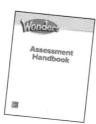

Manage Assessments

Program Author Whitepapers

Research Base

Roger Pelissier

Contents

Additional Digital Resources

my.mheducation.com

- Unit Bibliography

- Word Lists

- More Resources

Scope and Sequence

Text Set Focus	Read Aloud	Shared Read	Literature Anthology	Leveled Readers	Vocabulary
Text Set 1: **Weeks 1 and 2** **Essential Question:** How can experiencing nature change the way you think about it? **Genre:** Narrative Nonfiction *Differentiated Genre Passages available*	**Interactive Read Aloud:** "Capturing the Natural World" **Genre:** Narrative Nonfiction	"A Life in the Woods" **Genre:** Narrative Nonfiction **Lexile:** 770L *ELL Scaffolded Shared Read available*	**Anchor Text** *Camping with the President* **Genre:** Narrative Nonfiction **Lexile:** 760L **Paired Selection** "A Walk with Teddy" **Genre:** Autobiography **Lexile:** 910L	**Main Selections** **Genre:** Narrative Nonfiction ● *Save This Space!* **Lexile:** 750L ● *Save This Space!* **Lexile:** 960L ● *Save This Space!* **Lexile:** 730L ● *Save This Space!* **Lexile:** 980L **Paired Selections** **Genre:** Expository Text ● "The Journey of Lewis and Clark" ● "The Journey of Lewis and Clark" ● "The Journey of Lewis and Clark" ● "The Journey of Lewis and Clark"	**Academic Vocabulary:** debris, emphasis, encounter, generations, indicated, naturalist, sheer, spectacular Homographs Prefixes
Text Set 2: **Weeks 3 and 4** **Essential Question:** How do we get the things we need? **Genre:** Realistic Fiction *Differentiated Genre Passages available*	**Interactive Read Aloud:** "Finding a Way" **Genre:** Realistic Fiction	"A Fresh Idea" **Genre:** Realistic Fiction **Lexile:** 760L *ELL Scaffolded Shared Read available*	**Anchor Text** *One Hen* **Genre:** Realistic Fiction **Lexile:** 810L **Paired Selection** "Reading Between the Dots" **Genre:** Personal Narrative **Lexile:** 910L	**Main Selections** **Genre:** Realistic Fiction ● *Parker's Plan* **Lexile:** 680L ● *Can-do Canines* **Lexile:** 790L ● *Can-do Canines* **Lexile:** 570L ● *Cleaning Up the Competition* **Lexile:** 970L **Paired Selections** **Genre:** Expository Text ● "Taking Care of Your Money" ● "You Can Bank on It" ● "You Can Bank on It" ● "Growing Money"	**Academic Vocabulary:** afford, loan, profit, prosper, risk, savings, scarce, wages Context Clues: Sentence Clues Suffixes
Text Set 3: **Week 5** **Essential Question:** What are the positive and negative effects of new technology? **Genre:** Argumentative Text *Differentiated Genre Passages available*	**Interactive Read Aloud:** "Electronic Books: A New Way to Read" **Genre:** Argumentative Text	"Are Electronic Devices Good for Us?" **Genre:** Argumentative Text **Lexile:** 900L *ELL Scaffolded Shared Read available*	**Anchor Text** *The Future of Transportation* **Genre:** Argumentative Text **Lexile:** 870L **Paired Selection** "Getting from Here to There" **Genre:** Technical Text **Lexile:** 890L	**Main Selections** **Genre:** Expository Text ● *What About Robots?* **Lexile:** 740L ● *What About Robots?* **Lexile:** 840L ● *What About Robots?* **Lexile:** 760L ● *What About Robots?* **Lexile:** 990L **Paired Selections** **Genre:** Persuasive Text ● "No Substitute" ● "No Substitute" ● "No Substitute" ● "No Substitute"	**Academic Vocabulary:** access, advance, analysis, cite, counterpoint, data, drawbacks, reasoning Greek and Latin Prefixes

Week 6	Reading Digitally	Fluency	Connect to Content: Science	Connect to Content: Social Studies	Writing	Presentation Options
Extend, Connect, and Assess	**Genre:** Online Article "Take It from Nature"	**Reader's Theater:** *It Couldn't Be Done*	**Passages** **Genre:** Narrative Nonfiction "A Protector of Nature" **Genre:** Narrative Nonfiction "Children Save the Rain Forest" **Genre:** Realistic Fiction "Solutions, Not Complaints" **Activities** Compare the Passages Complete a Map Write an Essay	**Passages** "The NYC Subway: An Interview with a Transit Supervisor" "Solutions, Not Complaints" **Activities** Compare the Passages Write a Letter	**Writing Process** Write to Sources: Argumentative Writing Analyze the Prompt Analyze the Sources: "Honoring Black Women Inventors of the Past," "Morse Code Is Safe and Reliable," "All Aboard on America's Rail System" Plan: Organize Ideas Draft: Elaboration Revise: Peer Conferences	**Reader's Theater** **Inquiry Space** **Writing**

Comprehension	Phonics and Spelling	Fluency	Writing and Grammar	Research and Inquiry
Ask and Answer Questions Primary and Secondary Sources Text Structure: Cause and Effect Author's Perspective	**Week 1** Short Vowels **Week 2** Long Vowels *Differentiated Spelling Lists available*	**Week 1** Accuracy and Expression **Week 2** Intonation and Rate	**Respond to Reading** **Writing Process** Write to Sources: Argumentative Writing Analyze the Rubric Rubric Minilesson: Make a Claim Analyze the Student Model **Grammar and Mechanics** **Week 1:** Sentences; Punctuating Sentences **Week 2:** Subjects and Predicates; Commas	**Project:** Experiencing Nature **Product:** Promotional Map **Blast:** "Protecting Our Parks"
Reread Plot: Conflict and Resolution Plot: Events Text Structure: Chronology	**Week 3** Words with /ū/, /ů/, and /ü/ **Week 4** *r*-controlled Vowels /är/, /âr/, /ôr/ *Differentiated Spelling Lists available*	**Week 3** Expression and Phrasing **Week 4** Rate	**Respond to Reading** **Writing Process** Write to Sources: Argumentative Writing Analyze the Prompt Analyze the Sources: "Landmark Deal Approved!," "Fund Florida Forever!," "Revitalize Florida's Downtowns" Plan: Organize Ideas Draft: Relevant Evidence Revise: Peer Conferences **Grammar and Mechanics** **Week 3:** Compound Sentences; Punctuation in Compound Sentences **Week 4:** Complex Sentences; Commas	**Project:** Meeting Needs **Product:** Compare/Contrast Chart **Blast:** "Clothing, Food, and Shelter"
Reread Headings and Graphs Author's Claim Author's Purpose	**Week 5** *r*-controlled Vowel /ûr/ *Differentiated Spelling Lists available*	**Week 5** Accuracy and Phrasing	**Respond to Reading** **Writing Process** Write to Sources: Argumentative Writing Analyze the Rubric Rubric Minilesson: Strong Introduction Analyze the Student Model **Grammar and Mechanics** **Week 5:** Run-on Sentences; Correcting Run-on Sentences	**Project:** Technology **Product:** Debate **Blast:** "Riding Technology's Rollercoaster"

Scope and Sequence

Text Set Focus	Read Aloud	Shared Read	Literature Anthology	Leveled Readers	Vocabulary
Text Set 1: Weeks 1 and 2 **Essential Question:** What do good problem solvers do? **Genre:** Expository Text *Differentiated Genre Passages available*	**Interactive Read Aloud:** "The Haudenosaunee Confederacy" **Genre:** Expository Text	"Creating a Nation" **Genre:** Expository Text **Lexile:** 690L *ELL Scaffolded Shared Read available*	**Anchor Text** *Who Wrote the U.S. Constitution?* **Genre:** Expository Text **Lexile:** 760L **Paired Selection** "Wordsmiths" **Genre:** Expository Text **Lexile:** 970L	**Main Selections** **Genre:** Expository Text ● *The Bill of Rights* **Lexile:** 820L ● *The Bill of Rights* **Lexile:** 920L ● *The Bill of Rights* **Lexile:** 840L ● *The Bill of Rights* **Lexile:** 1000L **Paired Selections** **Genre:** Expository Text ● "Having Your Say" ● "Having Your Say" ● "Having Your Say" ● "Having Your Say"	**Academic Vocabulary:** committees, convention, debate, proposal, representatives, resolve, situation, union Context Clues Dictionary and Glossary
Text Set 2: Weeks 3 and 4 **Essential Question:** When has a plan helped you accomplish a task? **Genre:** Folktale *Differentiated Genre Passages available*	**Interactive Read Aloud:** "Lost Lake and the Golden Cup" **Genre:** Folktale	"The Magical Lost Brocade" **Genre:** Folktale **Lexile:** 740L *ELL Scaffolded Shared Read available*	**Anchor Text** *Blancaflor* **Genre:** Folktale **Lexile:** 870L **Paired Selection** "From Tale to Table" **Genre:** Expository Text **Lexile:** 990L	**Main Selections** **Genre:** Folktale ● *The Lion's Whiskers* **Lexile:** 760L ● *The Riddle of the Drum: A Tale from Mexico* **Lexile:** 810L ● *The Riddle of the Drum: A Tale from Mexico* **Lexile:** 570L ● *Clever Manka* **Lexile:** 860L **Paired Selections** **Genre:** Expository Text ● "From Fiber to Fashion" ● "Make a Drum" ● "Make a Drum" ● "From Bee to You"	**Academic Vocabulary:** assuring, detected, emerging, gratitude, guidance, outcome, previous, pursuit Personification Roots
Text Set 3: Week 5 **Essential Question:** What motivates you to accomplish a goal? **Genre:** Poetry *Differentiated Genre Passages available*	**Interactive Read Aloud:** "How to Make a Friend" **Genre:** Narrative Poetry	"A Simple Plan," "Rescue" **Genre:** Narrative and Free Verse Poetry **Lexile:** NP *ELL Scaffolded Shared Read available*	**Anchor Text** "Stage Fright," "Catching Quiet" **Genre:** Narrative and Free Verse Poetry **Lexile:** NP **Paired Selection** "Foul Shot" **Genre:** Free Verse Poetry **Lexile:** NP	**Main Selections** **Genre:** Realistic Fiction ● *Clearing the Jungle* **Lexile:** 650L ● *I Want to Ride!* **Lexile:** 730L ● *I Want to Ride!* **Lexile:** 600L ● *Changing Goals* **Lexile:** 860L **Paired Selections** **Genre:** Poetry ● "Just for Once" ● "Home Run" ● "Smash!" ● "Today's Lesson"	**Academic Vocabulary:** ambitious, memorized, satisfaction, shuddered **Poetry Terms:** narrative, repetition, free verse, rhyme Homographs

Week 6	Reading Digitally	Fluency	Connect to Content: Science	Connect to Content: Social Studies	Writing	Presentation Options
Extend, Connect, and Assess	**Genre:** Online Article "The Long Road"	**Reader's Theater:** *A Boy Named Abe*	**Passages** "Popover! The Ultimate Baked Bubble" "Cooking with Electricity" **Activities** Compare the Passages Make Observations Explain Your Observations	**Passages** "Searching for Freedom" "Supporting Religious Liberty" **Activities** Compare the Passages Make a Timeline	**Writing Process** Write to Sources: Expository Writing Analyze the Prompt Analyze the Sources: "Going Above and Beyond," "The Turtle Lady of Juno Beach," "Community Bird Scientist" Plan: Organize Ideas Draft: Transitions Revise: Peer Conferences	**Reader's Theater** **Inquiry Space** **Writing**

Comprehension	Phonics and Spelling	Fluency	Writing and Grammar	Research and Inquiry
Reread Headings and Timelines Text Structure: Problem and Solution Print and Graphic Features	**Week 1** Variant Vowel /ô/; Diphthongs /oi/, /ou/ **Week 2** Plurals *Differentiated Spelling Lists available*	**Week 1** Accuracy and Rate **Week 2** Accuracy and Expression	**Respond to Reading** **Writing Process** Write to Sources: Expository Writing Analyze the Rubric Rubric Minilesson: Central Idea Analyze the Student Model **Grammar and Mechanics** **Week 1:** Kinds of Nouns; Capitalizing Proper Nouns **Week 2:** Singular and Plural Nouns; Forming Plural Nouns	**Project:** Founders Solve Problems **Product:** Multimedia Slideshow **Blast:** "Meet Me in the Middle"
Make Predictions Plot: Setting Theme Text Structure: Sequence	**Week 3** Inflectional Endings **Week 4** Contractions *Differentiated Spelling Lists available*	**Week 3** Expression and Phrasing **Week 4** Rate	**Respond to Reading** **Writing Process** Write to Sources: Expository Writing Analyze the Prompt Analyze the Sources: "Benjamin Franklin's Bifocals," "Margaret Knight, Engineer and Inventor," "Henry Ford and the Model T" Plan: Organize Ideas Draft: Elaboration Revise: Peer Conferences **Grammar and Mechanics** **Week 3:** More Plural Nouns; Plural Forms and Appositives **Week 4:** Possessive Nouns; Adding -s or -'s	**Project:** Accomplishing a Task **Product:** Illustrated Food Web **Blast:** "Stand by Your Plan"
Repetition and Rhyme Narrative and Free Verse Theme Form and Line Breaks	**Week 5** Closed Syllables *Differentiated Spelling Lists available*	**Week 5** Expression and Phrasing	**Respond to Reading** **Writing Process** Write to Sources: Expository Writing Analyze the Rubric Rubric Minilesson: Academic Language Analyze the Student Model **Grammar and Mechanics** **Week 5:** Prepositional Phrases; Punctuating Titles and Letters	**Project:** Achieving Goals **Product:** Comic Strip **Blast:** "Reaching a Goal"

Scope and Sequence

Text Set Focus	Read Aloud	Shared Read	Literature Anthology	Leveled Reader	Vocabulary
Text Set 1: **Weeks 1 and 2** **Essential Question:** What can learning about different cultures teach us? **Genre:** Realistic Fiction *Differentiated Genre Passages available*	**Interactive Read Aloud:** "Foods for Thought" **Genre:** Realistic Fiction	"A Reluctant Traveler" **Genre:** Realistic Fiction **Lexile:** 770L *ELL Scaffolded Shared Read available*	**Anchor Text** *They Don't Mean It!* **Genre:** Realistic Fiction **Lexile:** 870L **Paired Selection** "Where Did That Come From?" **Genre:** Expository Text **Lexile:** 940L	**Main Selections** **Genre:** Realistic Fiction ● *All the Way from Europe* **Lexile:** 690L ● *Dancing the Flamenco* **Lexile:** 790L ● *Dancing the Flamenco* **Lexile:** 510L ○ *A Vacation in Minnesota* **Lexile:** 950L **Paired Selections** **Genre:** Expository Text ● "A Sporting Gift" ● "Flamenco" ● "Flamenco" ○ "The Scandinavian State?"	**Academic Vocabulary:** appreciation, blurted, complimenting, congratulate, contradicted, critical, cultural, misunderstanding Context Clues: Cause and Effect Adages
Text Set 2: **Weeks 3 and 4** **Essential Question:** What benefits come from people working as a group? **Genre:** Expository Text *Differentiated Genre Passages available*	**Interactive Read Aloud:** "Teamwork in Space" **Genre:** Expository Text	"Gulf Spill Superheroes" **Genre:** Expository Text **Lexile:** 860L *ELL Scaffolded Shared Read available*	**Anchor Text** *Winter's Tail* **Genre:** Expository Text **Lexile:** 940L **Paired Selection** "Helping Hands" **Genre:** Expository Text **Lexile:** 1040L	**Main Selections** **Genre:** Expository Text ● *The Power of a Team* **Lexile:** 740L ● *The Power of a Team* **Lexile:** 900L ● *The Power of a Team* **Lexile:** 800L ○ *The Power of a Team* **Lexile:** 1010L **Paired Selections** **Genre:** Expository Text ● "Hands on the Wheel" ● "Hands on the Wheel" ● "Hands on the Wheel" ○ "Hands on the Wheel"	**Academic Vocabulary:** artificial, collaborate, dedicated, flexible, function, mimic, obstacle, techniques Latin Roots Similes and Metaphors
Text Set 3: **Week 5** **Essential Question:** How do we explain what happened in the past? **Genre:** Argumentative Text *Differentiated Genre Passages available*	**Interactive Read Aloud:** "Stonehenge: Puzzle from the Past" **Genre:** Argumentative Text	"What Was the Purpose of the Inca's Knotted Strings?" **Genre:** Argumentative Text **Lexile:** 920L *ELL Scaffolded Shared Read available*	**Anchor Text** *Machu Picchu: Ancient City* **Genre:** Argumentative Text **Lexile:** 990L **Paired Selection** "Dig This Technology!" **Genre:** Expository Text **Lexile:** 970L	**Main Selections** **Genre:** Expository Text ● *The Ancestral Puebloans* **Lexile:** 820L ● *The Ancestral Puebloans* **Lexile:** 920L ● *The Ancestral Puebloans* **Lexile:** 840L ○ *The Ancestral Puebloans* **Lexile:** 990L **Paired Selections** **Genre:** Persuasive Text ● "The Ancestral Puebloans Were Astronomers" ● "The Ancestral Puebloans Were Astronomers" ● "The Ancestral Puebloans Were Astronomers" ○ "The Ancestral Puebloans Were Astronomers"	**Academic Vocabulary:** archaeologist, era, fragments, historian, intact, preserved, reconstruct, remnants Sentence Clues

Week 6	Reading Digitally	Fluency	Connect to Content: Social Studies	Connect to Content: Science	Writing	Presentation Options
Extend, Connect, and Assess	**Genre:** Online Article "Animal Survivors"	**Reader's Theater:** *A Thousand Miles to Freedom*	**Passages** **Genre:** Expository Text "Teamwork and Destiny" "U.S. Space School" **Activities** Compare the Passages Share and Reflect Make a Teamwork Poster	**Passages** **Genre:** "To Be an Archaeologist" "Digging into the Past" **Activities** Compare the Passages Make Observations of Footprints	**Writing Process** Write to Sources: Argumentative Analyze the Prompt Analyze the Sources: "Remember St. Helena's Role," "Collaboration at Angel Mounds," "No Digging Allowed" Plan: Organize Ideas Draft: Sentence Structure Revise: Peer Conferences	**Reader's Theater** **Inquiry Space** **Writing**

Comprehension	Phonics and Spelling	Fluency	Writing and Grammar	Research and Inquiry
Summarize Plot: Characterization Theme Author's Purpose	**Week 1** Open Syllables **Week 2** Open Syllables (V/V) *Differentiated Spelling Lists available*	**Week 1** Intonation **Week 2** Expression and Phrasing	**Respond to Reading** **Writing Process** Write to Sources: Argumentative Writing Analyze the Rubric Rubric Minilesson: Precise Language Analyze the Student Model **Grammar and Mechanics** **Week 1:** Action Verbs; Subject-Verb Agreement **Week 2:** Verb Tenses; Avoid Shifting Tenses	**Project:** Learning About Different Cultures **Product:** Pamphlet **Blast:** "A Special Day"
Ask and Answer Questions Text Structure: Problem and Solution Central Idea and Relevant Details Literal and Figurative Language	**Week 3** Vowel Team Syllables **Week 4** Consonant + *le* Syllables *Differentiated Spelling Lists available*	**Week 3** Accuracy and Rate **Week 4** Rate	**Respond to Reading** **Writing Process** Write to Sources: Argumentative Writing Analyze the Prompt Analyze the Sources: "Parents Say No to Study Abroad," "The Benefits of Study Abroad Programs," "U.S. Students Study Abroad" Plan: Organize Ideas Draft: Logical Order Revise: Peer Conferences **Grammar and Mechanics** **Week 3:** Main and Helping Verbs; Special Helping Verbs; Contractions; Troublesome Words **Week 4:** Linking Verbs; Punctuating Titles and Product Names	**Project:** Working Together **Product:** Television Segment **Blast:** "Two Heads Are Better Than One"
Summarize Text Structure: Compare and Contrast Author's Claim Figurative Language	**Week 5** *r*-controlled Vowel Syllables *Differentiated Spelling Lists available*	**Week 5** Accuracy and Rate	**Respond to Reading** **Writing Process** Write to Sources: Argumentative Writing Analyze the Rubric Rubric Minilesson: Strong Conclusion Analyze the Student Model **Grammar and Mechanics** **Week 5:** Irregular Verbs; Correct Verb Usage	**Project:** Investigating the Past **Product:** Multimedia Presentation **Blast:** "Remnants of the Past"

Scope and Sequence

Text Set Focus	Read Aloud	Shared Read	Literature Anthology	Leveled Reader	Vocabulary
Text Set 1: **Weeks 1 and 2** **Essential Question:** What can people do to bring about a positive change? **Genre:** Biography *Differentiated Genre Passages available*	**Interactive Read Aloud:** "Fighting for Change" **Genre:** Biography	"Frederick Douglass: Freedom's Voice" **Genre:** Biography **Lexile:** 830L *ELL Scaffolded Shared Read available*	**Anchor Text** *Rosa* **Genre:** Biography **Lexile:** 860L **Paired Selection** "Our Voices, Our Votes" **Genre:** Expository Text **Lexile:** 920L	**Main Selections** **Genre:** Biography ● *Jane Addams: A Woman of Action* **Lexile:** 700L ● *Jane Addams: A Woman of Action* **Lexile:** 910L ● *Jane Addams: A Woman of Action* **Lexile:** 710L ● *Jane Addams: A Woman of Action* **Lexile:** 1000L SS.5.C.2.5 **Paired Selections** **Genre:** Expository Text ● "Gus García Takes on Texas" ● "Gus García Takes on Texas" ● "Gus García Takes on Texas" ● "Gus García Takes on Texas"	**Academic Vocabulary:** anticipation, defy, entitled, neutral, outspoken, reserved, sought, unequal Prefixes and Suffixes Hyperbole
Text Set 2: **Weeks 3 and 4** **Essential Question:** What can you discover when you give things a second look? **Genre:** Drama *Differentiated Genre Passages available*	**Interactive Read Aloud:** "The Mystery Riddle" **Genre:** Drama (Mystery Play)	"Where's Brownie?" **Genre:** Drama (Mystery Play) **Lexile:** NP *ELL Scaffolded Shared Read available*	**Anchor Text** *A Window Into History: The Mystery of the Cellar Window* **Genre:** Drama (Mystery Play) **Lexile:** NP **Paired Selection** "A Boy, a Horse, and a Fiddle" **Genre:** Legend **Lexile:** 950L	**Main Selections** **Genre:** Drama ● *The Mysterious Teacher* **Lexile:** NP ● *The Unusually Clever Dog* **Lexile:** NP ● *The Unusually Clever Dog* **Lexile:** NP ● *The Surprise Party* **Lexile:** NP **Paired Selections** **Genre:** Realistic Fiction ● "The Case of the Missing Nectarine" ● "The Gift Basket" ● "The Gift Basket" ● "The Clothes Thief"	**Academic Vocabulary:** astounded, concealed, inquisitive, interpret, perplexed, precise, reconsider, suspicious Adages and Proverbs Synonyms and Antonyms
Text Set 3: **Week 5** **Essential Question:** How do you express something that is important to you? **Genre:** Poetry *Differentiated Genre Passages available*	**Interactive Read Aloud:** "I'm a Swimmer" **Genre:** Free Verse Poetry	"How Do I Hold the Summer?," "Catching a Fly," "When I Dance" **Genre:** Lyric and Free Verse Poetry **Lexile:** NP *ELL Scaffolded Shared Read available*	**Anchor Text** "Words Free as Confetti," "Dreams" **Genre:** Free Verse and Lyric Poetry **Lexile:** NP **Paired Selection** "A Story of How a Wall Stands" **Genre:** Free Verse Poetry **Lexile:** NP	**Main Selections** **Genre:** Realistic Fiction ● *Tell Me the Old, Old Stories* **Lexile:** 650L ● *From Me to You* **Lexile:** 810L ● *From Me to You* **Lexile:** 580L ● *Every Picture Tells a Story* **Lexile:** 990L **Paired Selections** **Genre:** Poetry ● "Family Ties" ● "Dear Gina" ● "Sssh!" ● "The Eyes of a Bird"	**Academic Vocabulary:** barren, expression, meaningful, plumes **Poetry Terms:** lyric, alliteration, meter, stanza Similes and Metaphors

Week 6	Reading Digitally	Fluency	Connect to Content: Social Studies	Connect to Content: Science	Writing	Presentation Options
Extend, Connect, and Assess	**Genre:** Online Article "Droughtbusters"	**Reader's Theater:** *The Golden Door*	**Passages** "Cesar Chavez: Hero at Work" "Army of Helpers" **Activities** Compare the Passages Analyze a Quote Create a Brochure	**Passages** "Colorful Chameleons" "Changing Their Look" **Activities** Compare the Passages Research Mimicry	**Writing Process** Write to Sources: Expository Writing Analyze the Prompt Analyze the Sources: "A Life in Color," "The Federal Art Project," "William Bartram: One with Nature" Plan: Organize Ideas Draft: Strong Conclusion Revise: Peer Conferences	**Reader's Theater** **Inquiry Space** **Writing**

Comprehension	Phonics and Spelling	Fluency	Writing and Grammar	Research and Inquiry
Summarize Photographs and Captions Author's Perspective Text Structure: Chronology	**Week 1** Words with Final /əl/ and /ən/ **Week 2** Prefixes *Differentiated Spelling Lists available*	**Week 1** Expression **Week 2** Accuracy and Rate	**Respond to Reading** **Writing Process** Write to Sources: Expository Writing Analyze the Rubric Rubric Minilesson: Relevant Evidence and Sources Analyze the Student Model **Grammar and Mechanics** **Week 1:** Pronouns and Antecedents; Pronoun-Antecedent Agreement **Week 2:** Kinds of Pronouns; Quotation Marks in Dialogue	**Project:** Positive Change **Product:** Plaque **Blast:** Liberty and Justice for All
Visualize Play Character Perspective Similes and Metaphors	**Week 3** Homographs **Week 4** Words with /chər/ and /zhər/ *Differentiated Spelling Lists available*	**Week 3** Phrasing **Week 4** Accuracy and Expression	**Respond to Reading** **Writing Process** Write to Sources: Expository Writing Analyze the Prompt Analyze the Sources: "Building a Better World," "The Power of Words," "A War at Home and Abroad" Plan: Organize Ideas Draft: Strong Introduction Revise: Peer Conferences **Grammar and Mechanics** **Week 3:** Pronoun-Verb Agreement; Abbreviations **Week 4:** Possessive Pronouns; Apostrophes, Possessives, and Reflexive Pronouns	**Project:** A Second Look **Product:** Formal Letter **Blast:** A Second Glance
Stanza and Meter Lyric and Free Verse Theme Imagery	**Week 5** Suffixes -ance and -ence *Differentiated Spelling Lists available*	**Week 5** Expression and Rate	**Respond to Reading** **Writing Process** Write to Sources: Expository Writing Analyze the Rubric Rubric Minilesson: Logical Text Structure Analyze the Student Model **Grammar and Mechanics** **Week 5:** Pronouns and Homophones; Punctuating Poetry	**Project:** What Is Important to You? **Product:** Timeline **Blast:** Expressions of Freedom

Scope and Sequence

Text Set Focus	Read Aloud	Shared Read	Literature Anthology	Leveled Reader	Vocabulary
Text Set 1: **Weeks 1 and 2** **Essential Question:** How can scientific knowledge change over time? **Genre:** Expository Text *Differentiated Genre Passages available*	**Interactive Read Aloud:** "The Sun: Our Star" **Genre:** Expository Text	"Changing Views of Earth" **Genre:** Expository Text **Lexile:** 910L *ELL Scaffolded Shared Read available*	**Anchor Text** *When Is a Planet Not a Planet?* **Genre:** Expository Text **Lexile:** 980L **Paired Selection** "The Crow and the Pitcher" **Genre:** Fable **Lexile:** 640L	**Main Selections** **Genre:** Expository Text ● *Mars* **Lexile:** 700L ● *Mars* **Lexile:** 900L ● *Mars* **Lexile:** 700L ● *Mars* **Lexile:** 970L **Paired Selections** **Genre:** Science Fiction ● "Zach the Martian" ● "Zach the Martian" ● "Zach the Martian" ● "Zach the Martian"	**Academic Vocabulary:** approximately, astronomical, calculation, criteria, diameter, evaluate, orbit, spheres Greek Roots Thesaurus
Text Set 2: **Weeks 3 and 4** **Essential Question:** How do shared experiences help people adapt to change? **Genre:** Historical Fiction *Differentiated Genre Passages available*	**Interactive Read Aloud:** "Starting Over" **Genre:** Historical Fiction	"The Day the Rollets Got Their Moxie Back" **Genre:** Historical Fiction **Lexile:** 900L *ELL Scaffolded Shared Read available*	**Anchor Text** *Bud, Not Buddy* **Genre:** Historical Fiction **Lexile:** 950L **Paired Selection** "Musical Impressions of the Great Depression" **Genre:** Expository Text **Lexile:** 990L	**Main Selections** **Genre:** Historical Fiction ● *The Picture Palace* **Lexile:** 710L ● *Hard Times* **Lexile:** 830L ● *Hard Times* **Lexile:** 520L ● *Woodpecker Warriors* **Lexile:** 900L **Paired Selections** **Genre:** Expository Text ● "The Golden Age of Hollywood" ● "Chicago: Jazz Central" ● "Chicago: Jazz Central" ● "A Chance to Work"	**Academic Vocabulary:** assume, guarantee, nominate, obviously, rely, supportive, sympathy, weakling Idioms Puns
Text Set 3: **Week 5** **Essential Question:** How do natural events and human activities affect the environment? **Genre:** Argumentative Text *Differentiated Genre Passages available*	**Interactive Read Aloud:** "Dams: Harnessing the Power of Water" **Genre:** Argumentative Text	"Should Plants and Animals from Other Places Live Here?" **Genre:** Argumentative Text **Lexile:** 930L *ELL Scaffolded Shared Read available*	**Anchor Text** *The Case of the Missing Bees* **Genre:** Argumentative Text **Lexile:** 950L **Paired Selection** "Busy, Beneficial Bees" **Genre:** Expository Text **Lexile:** 980L	**Main Selections** **Genre:** Expository Text ● *The Great Plains* **Lexile:** 760L ● *The Great Plains* **Lexile:** 910L ● *The Great Plains* **Lexile:** 830L ● *The Great Plains* **Lexile:** 1020L **Paired Selections** **Genre:** Persuasive Text ● "Save the Great Plains Wolves" ● "Save the Great Plains Wolves" ● "Save the Great Plains Wolves" ● "Save the Great Plains Wolves"	**Academic Vocabulary:** agricultural, declined, disorder, identify, probable, thrive, unexpected, widespread Root Words

Week 6	Reading Digitally	Fluency	Connect to Content: Science	Connect to Content: Social Studies	Writing	Presentation Options
Extend, Connect, and Assess	**Genre:** Online Article "Is Anybody Out There?"	**Reader's Theater:** *Jane Addams and Hull House*	**Passages** "Sir Isaac Newton" "Gravity" **Activities** Compare the Passages Investigate Newton's Laws Record Your Data	**Passages** "Wind in the Great Plains" "Dusting Off with Humor" **Activities** Compare the Passages Write a 1-2-3 Report on Environment	**Writing Process** Personal Narrative Revise: Strong Conclusion Peer Conferencing Edit and Proofread Publish, Present, and Evaluate	**Reader's Theater** **Inquiry Space** **Writing**

Comprehension	Phonics and Spelling	Fluency	Writing and Grammar	Research and Inquiry
Ask and Answer Questions Diagrams Central Idea and Relevant Details Imagery	**Week 1** Suffixes **Week 2** Homophones *Differentiated Spelling Lists available*	**Week 1** Expression **Week 2** Accuracy and Phrasing	**Respond to Reading** **Writing Process** Research Report Expert Model Plan: Relevant Evidence Draft: Elaboration **Grammar and Mechanics** **Week 1:** Clauses; Appositives **Week 2:** Complex Sentences; Commas with Clauses	**Project:** Scientific Knowledge Grows **Product:** Podcast **Blast:** "A Better World with Satellites"
Make, Confirm, and Revise Predictions Plot: Characterization Plot: Conflict Text Structure: Compare and Contrast	**Week 3** Prefixes **Week 4** Suffixes *-less* and *-ness* *Differentiated Spelling Lists available*	**Week 3** Rate **Week 4** Accuracy	**Respond to Reading** **Writing Process** Research Report Revise: Sentence Structure Peer Conferencing Edit and Proofread Publish, Present, and Evaluate **Grammar and Mechanics** **Week 3:** Adjectives; Capitalization and Punctuation **Week 4:** Adjectives That Compare; Using *More* and *Most*	**Project:** Supporting One Another **Product:** Collage **Blast:** "Shared Experiences"
Ask and Answer Questions Charts and Headings Author's Perspective Puns	**Week 5** Suffix *-ion* *Differentiated Spelling Lists available*	**Week 5** Accuracy and Rate	**Respond to Reading** **Writing Process** Personal Narrative Expert Model Plan: Sequence Draft: Description **Grammar and Mechanics** **Week 5:** Comparing with *Good* and *Bad*; Irregular Comparative Forms	**Project:** Environmental Changes **Product:** Mock Blog Report **Blast:** "Leaving a Trace"

Scope and Sequence

Text Set Focus	Read Aloud	Shared Read	Literature Anthology	Leveled Reader	Vocabulary
Text Set 1: **Weeks 1 and 2** **Essential Question:** How do different groups contribute to a cause? **Genre:** Historical Fiction *Differentiated Genre Passages available*	**Interactive Read Aloud:** "Hope for the Troops" **Genre:** Historical Fiction	"Shipped Out" **Genre:** Historical Fiction **Lexile:** 810L *ELL Scaffolded Shared Read available*	**Anchor Text** *The Unbreakable Code* **Genre:** Historical Fiction **Lexile:** 640L **Paired Selection** "Allies in Action" **Genre:** Expository Text **Lexile:** 870L	**Main Selections** **Genre:** Historical Fiction ● *Mrs. Gleeson's Records* **Lexile:** 730L ● *Norberto's Hat* **Lexile:** 770L ● *Norberto's Hat* **Lexile:** 640L ● *The Victory Garden* **Lexile:** 900L **Paired Selections** **Genre:** Expository Text ● "Scrap Drives and Ration Books" ● "The Bracero Program" ● "The Bracero Program" ● "Gardening for Uncle Sam"	**Academic Vocabulary:** bulletin, contributions, diversity, enlisted, intercept, operations, recruits, survival Homophones Literal and Figurative Language
Text Set 2: **Weeks 3 and 4** **Essential Question:** How are living things adapted to their environment? **Genre:** Expository Text *Differentiated Genre Passages available*	**Interactive Read Aloud:** "Bacteria: They're Everywhere" **Genre:** Expository Text	"Mysterious Oceans" **Genre:** Expository Text **Lexile:** 980L *ELL Scaffolded Shared Read available*	**Anchor Text** *Survival at 40 Below* **Genre:** Expository Text **Lexile:** 990L **Paired Selection** "Why the Evergreen Trees Never Lose Their Leaves" **Genre:** Pourquoi Story **Lexile:** 850L	**Main Selections** **Genre:** Expository Text ● *Cave Creatures* **Lexile:** 760L ● *Cave Creatures* **Lexile:** 900L ● *Cave Creatures* **Lexile:** 750L ● *Cave Creatures* **Lexile:** 1010L **Paired Selections** **Genre:** Pourquoi Story ● "Why Bat Flies at Night" ● "Why Bat Flies at Night" ● "Why Bat Flies at Night" ● "Why Bat Flies at Night"	**Academic Vocabulary:** adaptation, agile, cache, dormant, forage, frigid, hibernate, insulates Context Clues: Paragraph Clues Sound Devices
Text Set 3: **Week 5** **Essential Question:** What can our connections to the world teach us? **Genre:** Poetry *Differentiated Genre Passages available*	**Interactive Read Aloud:** "The Beat" **Genre:** Lyric Poetry	"To Travel!," "Wild Blossoms" **Genre:** Lyric and Narrative Poetry **Lexile:** NP *ELL Scaffolded Shared Read available*	**Anchor Text** "You Are My Music (Tú eres mi música)," "You and I" **Genre:** Lyric and Narrative Poetry **Lexile:** NP **Paired Selection** "A Time to Talk" **Genre:** Lyric Poetry **Lexile:** NP	**Main Selections** **Genre:** Realistic Fiction ● *Your World, My World* **Lexile:** 730L ● *Flying Home* **Lexile:** 790L ● *Flying Home* **Lexile:** 610L ● *Helping Out* **Lexile:** 940L **Paired Selections** **Genre:** Poetry ● "Do I Know You?" ● "Tell Me, Show Me" ● "Fun and Play" ● "A Journalistic Journey"	**Academic Vocabulary:** blares, connection, errand, exchange **Poetry Terms:** personification, assonance, consonance, imagery Personification

Week 6		Reading Digitally	Fluency	Connect to Content: Social Studies	Connect to Content: Science	Writing	Presentation Options
Extend, Connect, and Assess	**Genre:** Online Article "The Tortoise and the Solar Plant"		**Reader's Theater:** *'Round the World with Nellie Bly*	**Passages** "Sarah Winnemucca: Word Warrior" "Sequoyah's Gift" **Activities** Compare the Passages Research Historical Information Write About a Memory	**Passages** "Wonders of the Water Cycle" "An Ocean of Adaptations" **Activities** Compare the Passages Observe Water Molecules in Action	**Writing Process** Narrative Poem Revise: Concrete Words and Sensory Language Peer Conferences Edit and Proofread Publish, Present, and Evaluate	**Reader's Theater** **Inquiry Space** **Writing**

Comprehension	Phonics and Spelling	Fluency	Writing and Grammar	Research and Inquiry
Summarize Plot: Flashback Theme Print and Graphic Features	**Week 1** Words with Greek Roots **Week 2** Words with Latin Roots *Differentiated Spelling Lists available*	**Week 1** Expression and Phrasing **Week 2** Intonation	**Respond to Reading** **Writing Process** Historical Fiction Expert Model Plan: Characters Draft: Develop Plot **Grammar and Mechanics** **Week 1:** Adverbs; Capitalization and Abbreviations in Letters and Formal E-mails **Week 2:** Adverbs That Compare; Using *good, well; more, most; -er, -est*	**Project:** World War II **Product:** Cause/Effect Chart **Blast:** "Outstanding Contributions"
Ask and Answer Questions Maps Text Structure: Cause and Effect Character Perspective	**Week 3** Words from Mythology **Week 4** Number Prefixes *uni-, bi-, tri-, cent-* *Differentiated Spelling Lists available*	**Week 3** Accuracy and Rate **Week 4** Expression and Phrasing	**Respond to Reading** **Writing Process** Historical Fiction Revise: Dialogue and Pacing Peer Conferences Edit and Proofread Publish, Present, and Evaluate **Grammar and Mechanics** **Week 3:** Negatives; Correct Double Negatives **Week 4:** Sentence Combining; Commas and Colons	**Project:** Animal Adaptations **Product:** Slideshow **Blast:** "Blending In"
Assonance and Consonance Lyric and Narrative Point of View and Perspective Imagery	**Week 5** Suffixes *-ible, -able* *Differentiated Spelling Lists available*	**Week 5** Expression and Phrasing	**Respond to Reading** **Writing Process** Narrative Poem Expert Model Plan: Characters, Setting, and Plot Draft: Figurative Language **Grammar and Mechanics** **Week 5:** Prepositional Phrases; Pronouns in Prepositional Phrases	**Project:** Connections **Product:** Email **Blast:** "Be Nice"

Social Emotional Development

Emotional Self Regulation
Maintains feelings, emotions, and words with decreasing support from adults

$\ggg$

As the child collaborates with a partner, the child uses appropriate words calmly when disagreeing.

$\ggg$

Behavioral Self Regulation
Manages actions, behaviors, and words with decreasing support from adults

$\ggg$ $\ggg$

Rules and Routines
Follows classroom rules and routines with increasing independence

Transitioning from one activity to the next, the child follows established routines, such as putting away materials, without disrupting the class.

$\ggg$

Working Memory
Maintains and manipulates distinct pieces of information over short periods of time

$\ggg$ $\ggg$ $\ggg$

Focus Attention
Maintains focus and sustains attention with minimal adult support

$\ggg$

During Center Time, the child stays focused on the activity assigned and is able to stop working on the activity when it is time to move on to a different task.

Relationships and Prosocial Behaviors
Engages in and maintains positive relationships and interactions with familiar adults and children

$\ggg$

Social Problem Solving
Uses basic problem solving skills to resolve conflicts with other children

$\ggg$ $\ggg$

Self Awareness
Recognizes self as a unique individual as well as belonging to a family, community, or other groups; expresses confidence in own skills

$\ggg$

Creativity
Expresses creativity in thinking and communication

$\ggg$

Initiative
Demonstrates initiative and independence

$\ggg$

When working independently, the child understands when to ask for help and gets the help needed.

$\ggg$

Task Persistence
Sets reasonable goals and persists to complete the task

$\ggg$

Logic and Reasoning
Thinks critically to effectively solve a problem or make a decision

$\ggg$

Planning and Problem Solving
Uses planning and problem solving strategies to achieve goals

$\ggg$ $\ggg$

Flexible Thinking
Demonstrates flexibility in thinking and behavior

$\ggg$

(t) Hybrid Images/Cultura RF/Image Source; (b) Samuel Borges Photography/Shutterstock

Throughout the grades, students continue to progress in each aspect of their social emotional growth.

GRADE 2 ⟫⟫⟫ GRADE 3 ⟫⟫⟫ GRADE 4 ⟫⟫⟫ GRADE 5

During class discussions, the child can wait until called upon to provide a response, without shouting out.

When responding to a text, the child can identify text evidence from notes previously recorded.

The child willingly works with any other child in the class on partner or group activities that are assigned.

When working on a project in a small group, the child negotiates roles and cooperates with others to complete the task.

In class discussion, the child is not fearful of sharing a unique perspective while respecting the opinions of others.

The child finds a creative way to gather information needed for a writing assignment.

When assigned to read a difficult text, the child applies routines or strategies learned to complete the reading.

Through logic and reasoning, the child is able to figure out how the author's choices of words and structures affect the communication of ideas.

When working on a long-term research project, the child can think through how to complete the different parts of the assignment over a period of time.

As the child struggles with an activity, the child can determine a different way to complete the activity successfully.

Text Complexity Rubric

In *Wonders*, students are asked to read or listen to a range of texts within a text set to build knowledge. The various texts include:

- Interactive Read Alouds
- Shared Reads
- Anchor Texts
- Paired Selections
- Leveled Readers
- Differentiated Genre Passages

Understanding the various factors that contribute to the complexity of a text, as well as considering what each student brings to the text, will help you determine the appropriate levels of scaffolds for students. Quantitative measures, such as Lexile scores, are only one element of text complexity. Understanding qualitative factors and reader and task considerations is also important to fully evaluate the complexity of a text.

At the beginning of each text set in the *Wonders* Teacher's Edition, information on the three components of text complexity for the texts is provided.

Qualitative		
The qualitative features of a text relate to its content or meaning. They include meaning/purpose, structure, language, and knowledge demands.		
Low Complexity	**Moderate Complexity**	**High Complexity**
Meaning/Purpose The text has a single layer of meaning explicitly stated. The author's purpose or central idea of the text is immediately obvious and clear.	**Meaning/Purpose** The text has a blend of explicit and implicit details, few uses of multiple meanings, and isolated instances of metaphor. The author's purpose may not be explicitly stated but is readily inferred from a reading of the text.	**Meaning/Purpose** The text has multiple layers of meaning and there may be intentional ambiguity. The author's purpose may not be clear and/or is subject to interpretation.
Structure The text is organized in a straightforward manner, with explicit transitions to guide the reader.	**Structure** The text is largely organized in a straightforward manner, but may contain isolated incidences of shifts in time/place, focus, or pacing.	**Structure** The text is organized in a way that initially obscures meaning and has the reader build to an understanding.
Language The language of the text is literal, although there may be some rhetorical devices.	**Language** Figurative language is used to build on what has already been stated plainly in the text.	**Language** Figurative language is used throughout the text; multiple interpretations may be possible.
Knowledge Demands The text does not require extensive knowledge of the topic.	**Knowledge Demands** The text requires some knowledge of the topic.	**Knowledge Demands** The text requires siginifcant knowledge of the topic.

Quantitative

Wonders provides the Lexile score for each text in the text set.

Low Complexity	Moderate Complexity	High Complexity
Lexile Score Text is below or at the lower end of the grade-level band according to a quantitative reading measure.	**Lexile Score** Text is in the midrange of the grade-level band according to a quantitative reading measure.	**Lexile Score** Text is at the higher end of or above the grade-level band according to a quantitative reading measure.

Reader and Task Considerations

This component of text complexity considers the motivation, knowledge, and experiences a student brings to the text. Task considerations take into account the complexity generated by the tasks students are asked to complete and the questions they are expected to answer.

In *Wonders*, students are asked to interact with the texts in many different ways. Texts such as the Shared Reads and Anchor Texts are read over multiple days and include tasks that increase in difficulty. The complexity level provided for each text considers the highest-level tasks students are asked to complete.

Low Complexity	Moderate Complexity	High Complexity
Reader The text is well within the student's developmental level of understanding and does not require extensive background knowledge.	**Reader** The text is within the student's developmental level of understanding, but some levels of meaning may be impeded by lack of prior exposure.	**Reader** The text is at the upper boundary of the student's developmental level of understanding and will require that the student has background knowledge of the topic.

Task

The questions and tasks provided for all texts are at various levels of complexity, ensuring that all students can interact with the text in meaningful ways.

Index

A

Key 1 = Unit 1

Key 1 = Unit 1

Key 1 = Unit 1

Key 1 = Unit 1

M

N

figurative language, **2:** T198, **4:** T167, T168, **6:** T191, T192, T252

imagery, **2:** T198

line breaks, **2:** T198–T199, **6:** T266

metaphor, **4:** T167, T168, T188

meter, **4:** T169, T172–T173, T174, T175, T188, T190, T191

personification, **2:** T196

precise language, **6:** T267

repetition, **2:** T192, T194, T195, T196, T198

rhyme/rhyme schemes, **4:** T174, T175

rhythm, **2:** T178, T180, **6:** T191, T212, T246

simile, **4:** T167, T168, T188

stanzas, **2:** T191, **4:** T167, T169, T172–T173, T174, T175, T188

theme, **2:** T180, **6:** T267

Possessives, 2: T276–T277, **4:** T272–T273, T274–T275. *See also* **Grammar: possessives**

Predictions, 1: T70, T76, T90, T123, T140, T150, T156, T171, T204, T214, T220, **2:** T16, T43, T60, T70, T76, T88, T91, T93, T96, T97, T115, T120, T123, T140, T150, T156, T204, T214, T220, **3:** T9, T39, T54, T64, T70, T85, T134, T144, T150, T198, T208, T214, **4:** T9, T15, T43, T60, T70, T76, T119, T136, T146, T152, T166, T200, T210, T216, **5:** T8, T43, T58, T68, T74, T86, T89, T94–T95, T110, T111, T119, T138, T148, T154, T168, T202, T212, T218, **6:** T8, T41, T58, T74, T123, T150, T156, T170, T204, T214, T220

confirm and revise, **1:** T93, T171, **2:** T9, T88, T89, T96, T97, T113, T114, T119, T173, **3:** T216, **4:** T60, T70, T76, T169, **5:** T11, T68, T74, T86, T91, T94–T95, T110, T113, T118, T138–T139, T147, T148–T149, T153, T154–T155, T159, T171, **6:** T58, T68, T74, T89, T140, T150, T156, T173

make, **1:** T60

and purposes, return to, **1:** T43

Prefixes. *See* **Spelling; Vocabulary**

Prepositional phrases. *See* **Grammar: prepositions and prepositional phrases**

Prereading strategies. *See* **Predictions,** make; **Previewing literature**

Presentation Options, 1: T308–T313, **3:** T302–T307, **4:** T304–T309, **5:** T304–T309, **6:** T306–T311

Previewing literature, 1: T6, T60, T70, T76, T88, T140, T150, T156, T168, T204, T214, T220, **2:** T6, T60, T70, T76, T88, T140, T150, T156, T168, T204, T214, T220, **3:** T6, T54, T64, T70, T82, T134, T144, T150, T162, T198, T208, T214, **4:** T6, T60, T70, T76, T88, T136, T146, T152, T164, T200, T210, T216, **5:** T6, T58, T68, T74, T86, T138, T148, T154, T166, T202, T212, T218, **6:** T6, T58, T68, T74, T86, T140, T150, T156, T168, T204, T214, T220

Primary sources, 1: T10, T16, T17, T49, T52, T62, T72, T78, **2:** T39

Problem and solution. *See* **Comprehension: text structure**

Project-based learning. *See* **Inquiry Space; Research and inquiry**

Pronouns. *See* **Grammar: pronouns**

Publishing Celebrations, 1: T308, **3:** T302, **4:** T304, **5:** T304, **6:** T306

Punctuation. *See* **Grammar: punctuation**

Q

Questions. *See* **Comprehension strategies: ask and answer questions; Monitor and adjust comprehension**

Quotation marks, 1: T42, T102, T245, **2:** T178, **4:** T269

R

Read Aloud. *See* **Interactive Read Aloud**

Reader's Theater, 1: T296–T297, T308, **2:** T296–T297, T308, **3:** T290–T291, T302, **4:** T292–T293, T304, **5:** T292–T293, T304, **6:** T294–T295, T306

Readers to Writers, 1: T17, T53, T133, T143, T159, T199, T207, T217, T295, **2:** T17, T53, T63, T73, T79, T105, T133, T143, T153, T159, T179, T199, T207, T223, T295, **3:** T17, T57, T67, T73, T127, T137, T147, T153, T193, T201, T211, T217, **4:** T17, T53, T63, T73, T79, T99, T129, T139, T149, T155, T175, T195, T203, T213, T219, T291, **5:** T17, T51, T61, T71, T77, T97, T131, T141, T151, T157, T177, T197, T205, T215, T221, T291, **6:** T51, T61, T71, T77, T133, T143, T153, T159, T179, T199, T207, T217, T223, T293

print and graphic features, **1:** T63, T73, T79

Reading and responding. *See* **Literary response**

Reading digitally, 1: T294–T295, **2:** T294–T295, **3:** T288–T289, **4:** T290–T291, **5:** T290–T291, **6:** T292–T293

Reading independently, 1: T11, T14, T47, T69, T75, T81, T127, T149, T155, T161, T213, T219, T225, T317, **2:** T11, T14, T69, T75, T81, T149, T155, T161, T195, T213, T219, T225, T317, **3:** T11, T14, T63, T69, T75, T143, T149, T155, T189, T207, T213, T219, T311, **4:** T11, T14, T47, T69, T75, T81, T123, T145, T151, T157, T191, T209, T215, T221, T313, **5:** T11, T14, T47, T67, T73, T79, T125, T147, T153, T159, T193, T211, T217, T223, T313, **6:** T11, T14, T45, T67, T73, T79, T149, T155, T161, T195, T213, T219, T225, T315

Reading Literature

central idea and relevant details, **1:** T100–T101, T113, T114, T116, T118, T122, T123, T149, T155, T161, **3:** T18, T30, T290, **4:** T9, T31, T35, T36, T40, T88, T98, T100, T112, T113, T114, T116, T122, T125, T126, T136, T138, T144, T145, **5:** T98–T99, T112, T116, T118, T120, T124, **6:** T6, T9, T14, T18, T22, T30, T31, T34, T37, T39, T60, T61, T66, T67, T68, T70, T73, T75, T76, T77, T79, T130, T294, T295

compare and contrast

characters, **3:** T56, T75, T96, **5:** T98–T99, T112, T116, T118, T120

events, **3:** T56, T71, **5:** T98–T99, T112, T116, T118, T120, T124

genre, **5:** T69

poems, **2:** T207, T217, T223, **4:** T192, **6:** T182–T183, T196, T207, T217, T223

point of view, **4:** T192, **5:** T100–T101, **6:** T207, T217, T223

setting, **5:** T98–T99, T112, T116, T118, T120

stories, **3:** T57, T67, T70, T73, T75

theme, **6:** T207, T217, T223

craft and structure

cast of characters, **1:** T296, **2:** T296, **3:** T290, **4:** T98–T99, T292, **5:** T292, **6:** T294

dialogue, **3:** T16–T17, **4:** T98–T99, T115

scene, **4:** T91, T98–T99, T115

setting, **1:** T296, **2:** T296, **3:** T290, **4:** T91, T92, T98–T99, T115, T292, **5:** T292, **6:** T294

stage directions, **4:** T91, T98–T99, T111, T115

structural elements of drama, **1:** T296, **2:** T296, **3:** T290, **4:** T91, T98–T99, T111, T115, T292, **5:** T292, **6:** T294

cultures, reading about diverse, **2:** T98, T142, T152, T158, **3:** T6–T7, T8–T11, T28–T43, T44–T45, T50–T51, T54–T57, T64–T67, T70–T73, T164–T167, T208–T209, **4:** T186–T187, **6:** T28–T45, T68–T69

drawing inferences, **2:** T103, T116, T123, **3:** T33, T34, **4:** T35, T37, T50, **5:** T117, **6:** T21, T31, T35, T38, T40

events, **1:** T100–T101, T113, T114, T116, T118, T120, T122, T123, **5:** T124, **6:** T73, T129

genre

drama, **1:** T296–T297, **2:** T296–T297, **3:** T290–T291, **4:** T90–T93, T98–T99, T110–T121, T292–T293, **5:** T292–T293, **6:** T294–T295

folktales, **2:** T90–T93, T110–T127

poetry, **2:** T190–T191, T192–T193, T196–T197, **4:** T166–T169, T186–T187, T192–T193, T200–T203, T212–T213, T218–T219, **6:** T190–T193, T192–T193

realistic fiction, **4:** T200–T201, T210–T211, T216–T217

main idea. *See* **Reading Literature: central idea and relevant details**

make inferences, **1:** T119, T121

plot, **1:** T100–T101, T113, T114, T116, T118, T120, T122, T123

S

Key 1 = Unit 1

T

Key 1 = Unit 1

W

Key 1 = Unit 1